T0318484

THE PROFESSIONAL PRACTICE SERIES

The Professional Practice Series is sponsored by the Society for Industrial and Organizational Psychology (SIOP). The series was launched in 1988 to provide industrial/organizational psychologists, organizational scientists and practitioners, human resource professionals, managers, executives, and those interested in organizational behavior and performance with volumes that are insightful, current, informative, and relevant to organizational practice. The volumes in the Professional Practice Series are guided by five tenets designed to enhance future organizational practice:

1. Focus on practice, but grounded in science
2. Translate organizational science into practice by generating guidelines, principles, and lessons learned that can shape and guide practice
3. Showcase the application of industrial/organizational psychology to solve problems
4. Document and demonstrate best industrial and organizational-based practices
5. Stimulate research needed to guide future organizational practice

The volumes seek to inform those interested in practice with guidance, insights, and advice on how to apply the concepts, findings, methods, and tools derived from industrial/organizational psychology to solve human-related organizational problems.

Previous Professional Practice Series volumes include:

Published by Jossey-Bass

Improving Learning Transfer in Organizations
Elwood F. Holton III, Timothy T. Baldwin, Editors

Resizing the Organization
Kenneth P. De Meuse, Mitchell Lee Marks, Editors

Implementing Organizational Interventions
Jerry W. Hedge, Elaine D. Pulakos, Editors

Organization Development
Janine Waclawski, Allan H. Church, Editors

Creating, Implementing, and Managing Effective Training and Development
Kurt Kraiger, Editor

The 21st Century Executive
Rob Silzer, Editor

Managing Selection in Changing Organizations
Jerard F. Kehoe, Editor

Evolving Practices in Human Resource Management
Allen I. Kraut, Abraham K. Korman, Editors

Individual Psychological Assessment
Richard Jeanneret, Rob Silzer, Editors

Performance Appraisal
James W. Smither, Editor

Organizational Surveys
Allen I. Kraut, Editor

Employees, Careers, and Job Creation
Manuel London, Editor

Published by Guilford Press

Diagnosis for Organizational Change
Ann Howard and Associates

Human Dilemmas in Work Organizations
Abraham K. Korman and Associates

Diversity in the Workplace
Susan E. Jackson and Associates

Working with Organizations and Their People
Douglas W. Bray and Associates

Employment Discrimination Litigation

Employment Discrimination Litigation

Behavioral, Quantitative, and Legal Perspectives

Frank J. Landy

Editor

Foreword by Eduardo Salas

 JOSSEY-BASS
A Wiley Imprint
www.josseybass.com

Published by Jossey-Bass
A Wiley Imprint
989 Market Street, San Francisco, CA 94103-1741 www.josseybass.com

Jossey-Bass books and products are available through most bookstores. To contact Jossey-Bass directly call our Customer Care Department within the U.S. at 800-956-7739, outside the U.S. at 317-572-3986 or fax 317-572-4002.

Jossey-Bass also publishes its books in a variety of electronic formats. Some content that appears in print may not be available in electronic books.

Library of Congress Cataloging-in-Publication Data

Employment discrimination litigation: behavioral, quantitative, and legal perspectives / edited by Frank J. Landy; foreword by Eduardo Salas.
 p. cm.
"A Wiley imprint."
Includes bibliographical references and index.
 ISBN 13: 978-0-470-59825-2
 1. Discrimination in employment—Law and legislation—United States. I. Landy, Frank J.
 KF3464.E446 2005
 344.7301'133—dc22

2004017027

FIRST EDITION
HB Printing 10 9 8 7 6 5 4 3 2 1

The Professional Practice Series

Contents

Foreword

This book is a first of its kind in our field. No other book collects all the relevant issues for our field—law, statistics, case law, the litigation process. No other book brings together lawyers, scientists, and judges to discuss employment discrimination litigation. No other book offers the kinds of insights, facts, lessons learned, and trends assembled here in this volume. It is a one-of-a-kind gem for our field, a remarkable collection of chapters that is bound to inspire and guide those practitioners (and scientists) immersed in employment discrimination issues. I hope all the readers agree.

Frank Landy and colleagues have done a wonderful job in orchestrating all the pieces needed to produce this outstanding collection. Each chapter and topic has been painstakingly reviewed, edited, and crafted to deliver a crisp and focused message. Even those who are not involved in employment discrimination litigation will learn something. Again, a wonderful piece of work by Frank and his associate authors. Our field owes you.

The Professional Practice Series Editorial Board continues to promote excellence in the practice of our science. We hope that this volume, and future ones, continues to illustrate the potential impact that I-O psychologists can have in the workplace and in society. We do this one brick at a time. This volume is just one more brick in building a reputation that our science matters. Enjoy!

University of Central Florida   Eduardo Salas
October 2004   *Editor*

Preface

This nation has now experienced more than thirty years of litigation related to employment discrimination. This litigation involves a complex interaction of disciplines (such as psychology, statistics, economics, and sociology) in many different arenas (legal, scientific, public policy), and the rules and authorities for proceeding with such litigation (for example, the APA Standards, the SIOP Principles, case law) are changing regularly. Another source of change is the science and practice of personnel selection. We learn more every day from empirical research and sophisticated analyses of that research (for example, meta-analyses). This makes it even more difficult for an employer or a consultant to navigate his or her way through the tangle of employment law, trying to serve two masters. On the one hand the employer wants to do what is good for the organization—to hire the most promising workers. On the other hand, the employer wants to avoid the damaging effects of a lawsuit alleging discrimination or unfairness in some selection or employment practice.

There are few comprehensive treatments of the deep and broad topic of employment discrimination litigation. To be sure, some texts offer a narrow focus on one or another aspect of the litigation forest. For example, Gutman (2000) has an insightful and encyclopedic volume on case law and statutes or laws that shape employment discrimination. Another text that provides an excellent view of the entire litigation process is Lindemann and Grossman (1996), and Brodsky (1999) presents material on the art of expert witness testimony. The APA publishes a journal titled *Psychology, Public Policy and Law*, which deals with, among other topics, employment litigation. Finally, there are many law journals and bulletins published by law schools around the country. So if one wanted to become knowledgeable about employment litigation, there are many sources that one might turn to.

The current volume attempts to bring many of these knowledge bases together under one cover. There is no intention to be encyclopedic in this effort. Instead, knowledgeable and experienced psychologists, lawyers, judges, and statisticians have been asked to present the fundamental issues of employment discrimination litigation in these early years of the twenty-first century. Much of what is presented represents recent history, to show how we arrived at the point where we find ourselves today. These views of the past and present set the stage for some speculation about the future. This speculation is done by individual authors in the context of their chapters and also in the concluding chapter.

There is a conceptual theme to many of the chapters. That theme is adverse impact. *Adverse impact* is a construct that defines a particular theory of discrimination. This theory of discrimination (known variously as adverse impact, disparate treatment, unintentional discrimination, or statistical discrimination) accepts that any discrimination that did occur was unintentional and is observed through statistical patterns (such as more men or whites getting job offers than women or African Americans do). This is in contrast to an *adverse treatment* theory (variously known as adverse treatment, disparate treatment, or intentional discrimination), which proposes that any discriminatory actions were not inadvertent but were intended. Adverse impact cases tend to be more complex, often involve larger numbers of plaintiffs, often involve psychologists and statisticians as expert witnesses, and when coupled with class action status, represent substantial economic exposure for employers, as well as enhanced economic leverage for plaintiff's counsel in settlement discussions. There are of course certain protections provided to employees that do not require the calculation or demonstration of statistical evidence of adverse impact. These include protections for older applicants or employees and for disabled applicants or employees. Nevertheless, in the chapters dealing with the statutes (Gutman), race (Outtz), gender (Gutek and Stockdale), statistics (Siskin and Trippi), management practices (Malos), and cut scores (Kehoe and Olson), the discussion will often assume an adverse impact scenario.

In other areas the role of adverse impact, at least for the present, is a less relevant issue, but because these areas of litigation are well within the domain of I-O psychology, we have included treatments of them as well. These discussions are found in the chapters on age (Sterns, Doverspike, and Lax), disability (Papin-chock), and the Fair Labor Standards Act (Banks and Cohen).

Audience

We have particular audiences in mind for this volume. The primary audiences are the graduate students and professional psychologists who are interested but possibly not well informed in the area of employment discrimination litigation. Most of the critical topics that need to be reviewed by these persons will be found in one or more of the chapters. Additional audiences are law students and lawyers interested in employment litigation. Much of what is presented in the book will serve to demystify the psychological content in discrimination suits. A final audience consists of the members of human resource and legal departments in institutions, those departments typically on the front line of the employment litigation battleground.

Overview of the Contents

This volume is divided into several sections. Part One is largely procedural and descriptive. The first chapter, by Frank J. Landy, presents a temporal description of a typical employment discrimination case from start to finish. This is followed by Arthur Gutman's description of the relevant statutes and case law that frame discrimination litigation in Chapter Two. In Chapter Three, Richard Jeanneret presents a description of the three major sets of guidelines, or authorities, that are often invoked in employment litigation—the APA Standards (American Educational Research Association, American Psychological Association, & National Council on Measurement in Education, 1999), the SIOP Principles (Society for Industrial and Organizational Psychology, 2003), and the Uniform Guidelines (1978). Donald L. Zink and Arthur Gutman provide descriptive statistics that identify trends in employment discrimination litigation in Chapter Four. Bernard R. Siskin and Joseph Trippi describe common statistical issues in employment litigation in Chapter Five. Increasingly important issues in employment litigation are who may testify as an expert and what are experts permitted to testify about? In Chapter Six, George C. Thornton III and Peter H. Wingate deal with these issues.

In Part Two, knowledgeable I-O psychologists describe the various lines of attack and defense in employment litigation. James L. Outtz describes cases that focus on race in Chapter Seven. In Chapter Eight, Barbara A. Gutek and Margaret S. Stockdale outline the critical characteristics of gender cases. Harvey L. Sterns, Dennis Doverspike, and Greta A. Lax deal with the issue of age in Chapter Nine. Jone McFadden Papinchock reviews disability cases in Chapter Ten. Finally, Cristina Banks and Lisa Cohen address litigation related to the Fair Labor Standards Act in Chapter Eleven.

Part Three addresses special topics. In Chapter Twelve, Stan Malos reviews various trends in litigation and, more important, in written judicial opinions that relate to the activities and devices most often employed by industrial and organizational psychologists. In Chapter Thirteen, Jerard F. Kehoe and Angela Olson deal with the complexity and increasing importance of cut scores in employment discrimination litigation. In Chapter Fourteen, three employment lawyers—David Copus, Richard S. Ugelow, and Joshua Sohn—present their views of the contribution of I-O psychology to the employment litigation arena. In Chapter Fifteen, six federal judges present their views on a wide variety of topics related to the interface of I-O psychology and the law in the courtroom, most notably their opinions regarding expert witnesses.

In Part Four, Outtz and Landy pull all of this information together, summarizing and integrating the key points of the earlier chapters and also anticipating the future of employment discrimination litigation.

Acknowledgments

I am grateful that so many high-quality experts in the area of employment discrimination agreed to participate in this project. All are heavily involved in professional or academic pursuits, or both, and this was a sacrifice for them. Nevertheless, they are leaders in their respective areas, and the reader benefits from their willingness to participate. I owe special thanks to David Copus for helping me express some complicated statutory and procedural concepts in Chapter One. In addition, Arthur Gutman was kind enough to join me in reviewing some of the more arcane legal issues and interpretations as expressed by fellow authors. I am also gratified that six federal judges were willing to sit for interviews on topics central to this text. If anything, their schedules are even more crowded and hectic than those of the authors. In addition they had to take a chance that the text would be a fair and evenhanded treatment of important issues in employment litigation. I hope they feel their confidence has been well placed. Several colleagues at SHL were also of substantial assistance, both for research and production purposes. Bonnie Beverly transcribed many hours of interviews as well as assisted in other manuscript production chores. Barbara Nett created the figure of litigation phases that appears in Chapter One and also assisted in other research tasks. Heather Grab, Geoff Burcaw, and Will Lambe also provided invaluable research assistance. Finally, I would like to thank Ed Salas, Wayne Cascio, and other members of the Society for Industrial and Organizational Psychology Professional Practice Series Board of Directors and the editorial staff of Jossey-Bass for supporting this volume.

Breckenridge, Colorado   Frank J. Landy
October 2004

References

American Educational Research Association, American Psychological Association, & National Council on Measurement in Education. (1999). *Standards for educational and psychological testing.* Washington, DC: American Educational Research Association.

Brodsky, S. L. (1999). *The expert witness: More maxims and guidelines for testifying in court.* Washington, DC: American Psychological Association.

Gutman, A. (2000). *EEO law and personnel practices* (2nd ed.). Thousand Oaks, CA: Sage Publications.

Lindemann, B., & Grossman, P. (1996). *Employment discrimination law* (3rd ed., Vol. II). Washington, DC: Bureau of National Affairs.

Society for Industrial and Organizational Psychology. (2003). *Principles for the validation and use of personnel selection techniques* (4th ed.). Bowling Green, OH: Author.

Uniform Guidelines on Employee Selection Procedures, 29 C.F.R. § 1607 (1978).

The Authors

Frank J. Landy received his PhD degree with Bob Guion at Bowling Green State University in 1969. He was on the faculty of the Psychology Department at Penn State for twenty-six years and still holds the rank of professor emeritus there. In 1994, he moved to full-time consulting with Landy, Jacobs and Associates, a company he founded with Rick Jacobs in 1984. In 1998, LJA was acquired by SHL, an international testing firm, and Landy has directed the Litigation Support Division of that company from its Boulder office since then. Landy is frequently called on as an expert witness in both employment discrimination and human factors cases. He has authored or coauthored eleven books, twenty chapters and monographs, and over seventy refereed articles in scholarly journals. His most recent book is the introductory I-O text *Work in the 21st Century: An Introduction to Industrial and Organizational Psychology* (with Jeff Conte) (McGraw Hill, 2004).

Cristina Banks is a senior vice president of the Empower Group. She has consulted on and testified as an expert in over thirty job misclassification lawsuits and on ADA and discrimination cases. She has over thirty years' experience in organizational and management consulting, and created the wage and hour litigation support practice at Empower. She has published articles and chapters on several topics and most recently on wage and hour litigation issues. She has worked extensively with a wide range of federal and private sector clients on a variety of topics such as human resource strategy, organizational functioning and restructuring, organization and culture change, and assessment. Banks holds a PhD degree (1979) in industrial and organizational psychology from the University of Minnesota. She is also a senior lecturer at the Haas Business School, University of California, Berkeley.

Lisa Cohen is a principal consultant at the Empower Group and the leader of Empower's Litigation Support Practice. She has helped design and execute job analyses for over twenty-five organizations facing wage and hour litigation. She has developed systems and approaches to prevent and assess wage and hour risk and to improve overall organizational performance. She has presented at conferences and published on job design and misclassification, wage and hour issues, and related topics. Cohen holds an MBA degree from the Fuqua School of Business at Duke University and a PhD degree in organizational behavior and industrial relations from the Haas School of Business at the University of California, Berkeley, where she taught organizational behavior.

David Copus is a veteran employment discrimination lawyer. He is an honors graduate of both Northwestern University (1963) and Harvard Law School (1966). The *National Law Journal* has named him as "among the nation's best litigators in employment law." He is a member of the advisory board of the National Employment Law Institute and of the American Bar Association's Litigation and Labor and Employment Law sections and a former board member of the National Organization for Women's Legal Defense and Education Fund. He has written numerous books and articles related to the law (and one book on coaching youth soccer). He began his legal career in 1969 at the Equal Employment Opportunity Commission (EEOC), where for many years he directed the National Programs Division. Since 1977, he has been in private practice representing employers. He has been interested in gender stereotyping since 1971, when, as an EEOC lawyer in his very first trial, he hired Sandra Bem, Daryl Bem, and Judith Long Laws to present their expert opinions on the operation of alleged gender stereotypes at AT&T. He can be reached at alive1now@aol.com.

Dennis Doverspike is full professor of psychology at the University of Akron, Fellow of the Institute for Life-Span Development and Gerontology, and director of the Center for Organizational Research. He is an American Board of Professional Psychology diplomate in industrial and organizational psychology and a licensed psychologist in the state of Ohio. In addition to his academic experience, Doverspike has over twenty years of experience working with consulting firms and with public and private organizations. His areas of research and applied specialization include legal issues, the training of older workers, Internet-based testing, and employee selection. He is the author of two books and over one hundred articles. He received his PhD degree in psychology in 1983 from the University of Akron and his BS degree in 1976 from John Carroll University. He is currently serving as a member of the board of the International Public Management Association's Assessment Council.

Barbara A. Gutek, who received her PhD degree in psychology from the University of Michigan in 1975, holds the chair of Women and Leadership Professor, Department of Management and Policy, Eller College of Business and Public Administration, University of Arizona. Formerly director of the Institute for Research on Women and Gender and professor of psychology and women's studies at the University of Michigan and McClelland Professor and department head in the Department of Management and Policy, University of Arizona, she has also been on the faculties of the University of California at Los Angeles and the Claremont Graduate School. She is the author of over one hundred books and articles and is best known for her research on sexual harassment. In 1994, Gutek received the Division 35 Heritage Award for a "substantial and outstanding body of research on women and gender" and the Committee on Women in Psychology Award as a "Distinguished Leader for Women in Psychology" from the American Psychological Association and the Sage Scholarship Award from the Women in Management Division of the Academy of Management. Over the last fifteen years or so, Gutek has served as an expert witness, mostly in cases of sexual harassment.

Arthur Gutman is professor of psychology and past chair of the I-O graduate program at Florida Institute of Technology. He received his PhD degree in psychology from Syracuse University in 1975. He did his undergraduate work (class of '70) at Lehman College of the City University of New York, also in psychology. He spent two years at the University of Colorado as an NIMH Postdoctoral Fellow and two years on the faculty at Georgia State University. He has been at Florida Tech since 1979. Gutman is author of *EEO Law and Personnel Practices* (Sage, 2000, 2nd ed.) and the originator of "On the Legal Front," a column on workplace discrimination issues that appears quarterly in *The Industrial-Organizational Psychologist.* He has consulted with public and private employers—creating and validating tests, doing program evaluations, and working on legal issues relating to workplace discrimination, including functioning as an expert witness. His main teaching interests are personnel law, personnel selection, and statistics and research design.

Richard Jeanneret received his BA degree from the University of Virginia, his master's degree from the University of Florida, and his PhD degree from Purdue University. He has practiced for over thirty years as a management consultant. He is an adjunct faculty member of the University of Houston and Rice University Psychology Departments. In 1981, he founded Jeanneret & Associates. Jeanneret is a Fellow and past officer of the Society for Industrial and Organizational Psychology (SIOP) and was the chair of the SIOP committee responsible for the 2003 revision of *Principles for the Validation and Use of Personnel Selection Procedures.* In 1990, he received the SIOP Distinguished Professional Contributions Award, in recognition of his substantial and long-term contributions to the practice of I-O psychology. Jeanneret's experience in employment litigation dates back to 1974. He has served as a consulting expert or testifying expert in more than two hundred lawsuits, has provided testimony on more than one hundred occasions, and has been qualified as an expert in almost all the U.S. federal circuits.

Jerard F. Kehoe received his doctorate in quantitative psychology in 1975 from the University of Southern California. After serving on the Virginia Polytechnic Institute's psychology faculty, he joined AT&T in 1982. At AT&T, he was responsible, in various positions, for the design, implementation, validation, and maintenance of selection programs for manufacturing, customer service, sales, technical, management, and leadership jobs. From 1997 to 2003, he provided overall leadership and direction for AT&T's selection program. In 2003, he founded Selection & Assessment Consulting and currently serves as its president. Kehoe publishes and makes conference presentations on employment selection topics, including computerized testing, fairness, and test validity. He is the editor of the Society for Industrial and Organizational Psychology (SIOP) Professional Practice Series volume *Managing Selection in Changing Organizations: Human Resource Strategies* (2000) and an associate editor of the *Journal of Applied Psychology*. He also has served on numerous professional committees, including the SIOP subcommittee that revised *Principles for the Validation and Use of Employment Selection Procedures* in 2003. In 2002, SIOP awarded him Fellow membership status.

Greta A. Lax received her bachelor's degree in psychology from St. Norbert College, De Pere, Wisconsin, in 1995. She holds an MS degree in industrial and organizational psychology from the University of Wisconsin, Oshkosh, and is pursuing a doctorate in I-O psychology, with a specialty in industrial gerontological psychology, at the University of Akron. She has made presentations on occupational stress, aging, career management, and retirement at conferences of the Society for Industrial and Organizational Psychology and the Gerontological Society of America. Her additional research interests include understanding individual social responsibility at work and applying I-O psychology in nonprofit organizations.

Stan Malos is a former practicing trial attorney who earned his law degree from the University of California at Los Angeles, his MBA degree from the University of Washington, and his PhD degree in organizational behavior and human resource management from Purdue University. A professor of management and human resources in the San Jose State University College of Business, Malos conducts research on such topics as professional career mobility, affirmative action, performance appraisals, professional service firms, legal issues in technology management, and legal issues in human resource management (HRM). He currently serves as a consulting editor for the *Journal of Applied Behavioral Science* and has published in such outlets as *Academy of Management Journal*, *Academy of Management Review*, *Journal of Applied Psychology*, *Employee Responsibilities and Rights Journal*, and *The Industrial-Organizational Psychologist*. He has also presented numerous papers at professional conferences and has lectured on comparative international issues in strategic HRM and employment law in Canada, New Zealand, and Singapore.

Angela Olson currently works in the Litigation Support Division of SHL USA. She performs research for race, gender, and age employment discrimination litigation and for human factors litigation. She received her BA degree from Creighton University and her PhD degree in industrial and organizational psychology from Texas A&M University. She has worked as an associate research scientist at the Institute of Behavioral Research at Texas Christian University, where she project managed a five-year, $2.2 million grant, funded by the National Institute of Drug Abuse, to study the prevalence and impact of drugs in municipal workplaces. She also has industry experience, having worked as a corporate psychologist for US West Communications (subsequently Qwest), where she developed, validated, and implemented selection systems for 55,000 employees in a fourteen-state region and provided technical consultation to staffing, human resource operations, and business entities on testing and staffing issues.

James L. Outtz received his PhD degree in industrial and organizational psychology from the University of Maryland in 1976. As president and founder of Outtz and Associates, he has been involved in the development and validation of personnel selection procedures for over a quarter century. He is a Fellow of the Society for Industrial and Organizational Psychology and of the American Psychological Association. He has served as a consulting editor to the *Journal of Applied Psychology* and has authored numerous articles and chapters on a variety of topics, including the effect of the testing medium on validity and subgroup performance, implementation of fair selection strategies, and the use of test score banding as a referral method. Outtz has advised both public and private sector employers on the legal defensibility of specific employment practices, including interviewing, hiring, promotion, and performance appraisal. He has testified as an expert witness for plaintiffs and defendants in court cases involving a wide range of employment practices.

Jone McFadden Papinchock received her PhD degree in industrial and organizational psychology from the University of South Florida. She has seventeen years of internal and external consulting experience, primarily in job analysis, selection, compensation, downsizing, union negotiations, and equal employment opportunity (EEO) and Office of Federal Contract Compliance Programs (OFCCP) reporting and compliance. For the last six years she has served as managing director of SHL's Litigation Support Group. In this capacity she has consulted on all phases of employment discrimination and human factors litigation. Her experience with the Americans with Disabilities Act (ADA), the subject of her chapter in this volume, began in 1990 when she served as the I-O psychologist on an interdisciplinary planning team formed to ensure that the City of Clearwater, Florida, was in compliance with the ADA. Since that time she has recommended test and job accommodations and contributed to cases brought under the ADA.

Bernard R. Siskin received his BS degree in mathematics from the University of Pittsburgh and a PhD degree in statistics from the University of Pennsylvania. For many years he taught statistics at Temple University and served as chairman of the Department of Statistics. Siskin has specialized in the application of statistics in law, particularly in the area of analyzing data for statistical evidence of discrimination. He has testified for plaintiffs and defendants in more than two hundred cases. He has frequently been appointed by federal judges as a neutral expert to aid the court with statistical issues, and he was the statistical consultant to the Third Circuit Court of Appeals Task Force on Equal Treatment in the Courts. Siskin is the author of many articles and textbooks on statistics and quantitative techniques, including *Elementary Business Statistics, The Encyclopedia of Management,* and *Quantitative Techniques for Business Decisions.* He has also written and lectured extensively on the use of statistics in litigation. He has served as a statistical consultant to the U.S. Department of Justice, the Equal Employment Opportunity Commission, the U.S. Department of Labor, the Federal Bureau of Investigation, the Central Intelligence Agency, the Environmental Protection Agency, the National Aeronautics and Space Administration, and Fannie Mae (the Federal National Mortgage Association) and Freddie Mac (the Federal Home Loan Mortgage Corporation), as well as numerous other federal, state, and city agencies and Fortune 500 corporations.

Joshua Sohn is an associate in the litigation department of the New York office of Piper Rudnick LLP. He is a commercial litigator whose practice focuses on the defense of broker and dealers, securities industry professionals, and public and private companies (as well as their employees, directors, and officers) in litigations and investigations concerning claims of breach of fiduciary duty, securities fraud, violations of the securities laws, and other commercial disputes. In addition to his commercial practice he has an active pro bono practice concentrating on racial discrimination cases. Sohn is a graduate of the University of Michigan and the Benjamin N. Cardozo School of Law.

Harvey L. Sterns is professor of psychology and director of the Institute for Life-Span Development and Gerontology at the University of Akron. He is also a research professor of gerontology at Northeastern Ohio Universities College of Medicine. He is a faculty member in both the applied cognitive aging and industrial and organizational psychology graduate programs and chairs the specialization Industrial Gerontological Psychology at the University of Akron. He has published extensively on work and retirement, career development, training and retraining, and maintaining professional competence. He served on the Institute of Medicine Study of Airline Pilot Age, Health, and Performance: Scientific and Medical Considerations, and was a consultant to the National Research Council Study on Ending Mandatory Retirement for Tenured Faculty. He has served as an expert witness for the Equal Employment Opportunity Commission. Sterns is a licensed psychologist in Ohio and a Fellow of the Gerontological Society of America, American Psychological Association (APA), American Psychological Society, Association for Gerontology in Higher Education (AGHE), and Ohio Academy of Science. He is a past president of the AGHE and of Sigma Phi Omega, the national academic honor and professional society in gerontology. He is immediate past president of Division 20, Adult Development and Aging, of the APA. He currently serves as a member of the board of trustees of the American Society on Aging. He received his PhD degree from West Virginia University in 1971.

Margaret S. "Peggy" Stockdale is professor of psychology at Southern Illinois University at Carbondale (SIUC). She received her PhD degree in industrial and organizational psychology from Kansas State University in 1990. She is the coauthor or editor of four books, and her research articles have appeared in *Psychology*,

Public Policy and the Law, Law and Human Behavior, Psychology of Women Quarterly, Journal of Vocational Behavior, and Basic and Applied Social Psychology, among other peer-reviewed journals. Her primary research concerns gender issues in the workplace, primarily sexual harassment. Stockdale is also an active applied psychology consultant, having conducted training programs, needs assessments, and program evaluations for major corporations, local agencies and businesses, and public agencies. She teaches graduate and undergraduate courses in workplace diversity, I-O, and applied social science research methods. She is director of the applied psychology PhD program at SIUC.

George C. Thornton III is professor of psychology at Colorado State University, an American Board of Professional Psychology diplomate in industrial and organization psychology, and a Fellow of the Society for Industrial and Organizational Psychology (SIOP). He received a PhD degree from Purdue University in 1966. In 2002 he received the Outstanding Professional Contributions Award from SIOP for his work on assessment centers and expert testimony in employment discrimination litigation. He teaches industrial psychology, consults in personnel assessment, studies the implications of employment discrimination law for personnel psychology, and provides litigation support for employment discrimination. Thornton is the author of fifty-five articles, four chapters, and three books. He has developed selection and promotional procedures for private and public organizations. In 1995, he was chosen by plaintiff and defendant groups to be the court-appointed, third-party monitor of police promotional examinations for the City of Denver, a role he filled for five years. Currently he is providing oversight services to the City of Dallas Civil Service Commission during the implementation of job analysis and assessment centers for Fire Department examinations. Thornton has provided litigation support services to plaintiffs and defendants in nearly fifty legal cases on such matters as race or ethnicity, sex, and age claims involving selection, promotion, pay, and layoffs; this work includes expert witness testimony in twelve depositions or court hearings.

Joseph Trippi received a BA degree in psychology from Mansfield State University and a PhD degree in education from Pennsylvania State University, with educational measurement and statistics as his area of specialization. He specializes in the application of statistical analysis to issues in litigation. His areas of expertise include research design, psychometrics, and test development and validation. Prior to joining LECG as a managing consultant, he served as senior consultant at the Center for Forensic Economic Studies.

Richard S. Ugelow is on the faculty of the Washington College of Law, American University, Washington, D.C. Prior to joining the law school faculty in June 2002, he was a deputy section chief of the Employment Litigation Section, Civil Rights Division, U.S. Department of Justice. There, he supervised investigations and litigation to enforce Title VII of the Civil Rights Act of 1964. During the course of his twenty-nine-year career at the Department of Justice, he tried several complex "pattern or practice" cases of employment discrimination filed against public sector and private employers pursuant to Title VII. He was also the government's lead trial attorney in defending challenges to the constitutionality of federally sponsored affirmative action programs, particularly statutes and programs designed to provide contracting opportunities to minority, disadvantaged, and women-owned businesses. Prior to joining the Department of Justice, he served in the Judge Advocate General's Corps of the U.S. Army for four years. He received a BA degree from Hobart College in 1965, a JD degree from the Washington College of Law in 1968, and an LLM degree from Georgetown University in 1973.

Peter H. Wingate conducts research and analysis, mediates employment disputes, and serves as a liaison to the public for the Colorado Division of Labor. He has provided expert witness services in federal employment discrimination litigation for over five years and has consulted extensively with public and private organizations on workplace issues. Wingate is an active member of numerous professional and scientific societies and is recognized for his publications in such outlets as *Human Performance, Law and Human Behavior,* and *Research in Personnel and Human Resources Management.* He received his PhD degree in industrial and organizational psychology from Colorado State University, holds a master's degree in clinical psychology from San Diego State University, and obtained his bachelor's degree in economics and psychology from Colby College.

Donald L. Zink has had two separate but related careers. The first was in the U.S. Air Force, working mostly as a research psychologist with the Air Force Personnel and Training Research Center and the Aerospace Medical Research Laboratory performing human factors research. He attended graduate school at the University of Michigan, under Air Force sponsorship, where he received his master's degree in experimental psychology, in the mathematical psychology program. After twenty years he retired with the rank of major. After retirement he began his second career as an I-O psychologist when he joined AT&T under the tutelage and guidance of Mary Tenopyr, primarily developing and validating selection procedures. He first became interested in employment law when he interacted with AT&T attorneys in the defense of challenged tests. After the breakup of the Bell System, he continued his I-O career, as a consultant. He later returned to school, this time at the University of Denver College of Law, where he received his JD degree, emphasizing the areas of employment law and civil rights. Although he is a licensed attorney, he does not practice but prefers to continue his professional participation within the I-O community.

Employment Discrimination Litigation

PART 1

Foundations
of Litigation

CHAPTER 1

Phases of Employment Litigation

Frank J. Landy

A typical employment discrimination case can be bewildering in its complexity. From start to finish it may last for five or more years. Various stages (for example, discovery) may be postponed or extended. The trial itself may be delayed for various reasons, including requests by one or both of the parties or a scheduling problem experienced by the judge. What will be presented in this chapter is a common, though not universal, series of stages in an employment discrimination trial from its inception to its ultimate conclusion. Because the most complex and encompassing lawsuits tend to be class actions, the description will follow the course of a class action employment discrimination lawsuit. Further, I will present a disparate impact (unintentional discrimination) rather than a disparate treatment (intentional discrimination) scenario. Figure 1.1 presents a simplified version of the flow of a discrimination case. It may be helpful to return to this figure as the various stages are introduced. A more elaborate view of the process can be found in Lindemann and Grossman (1996).

Investigation and Conciliation

When an applicant, employee, or former employee feels that he or she has been treated unjustly, the first step is most often contacting a federal, state, or local governmental agency (the Equal

3

Figure 1.1. Phases of Employment Litigation.

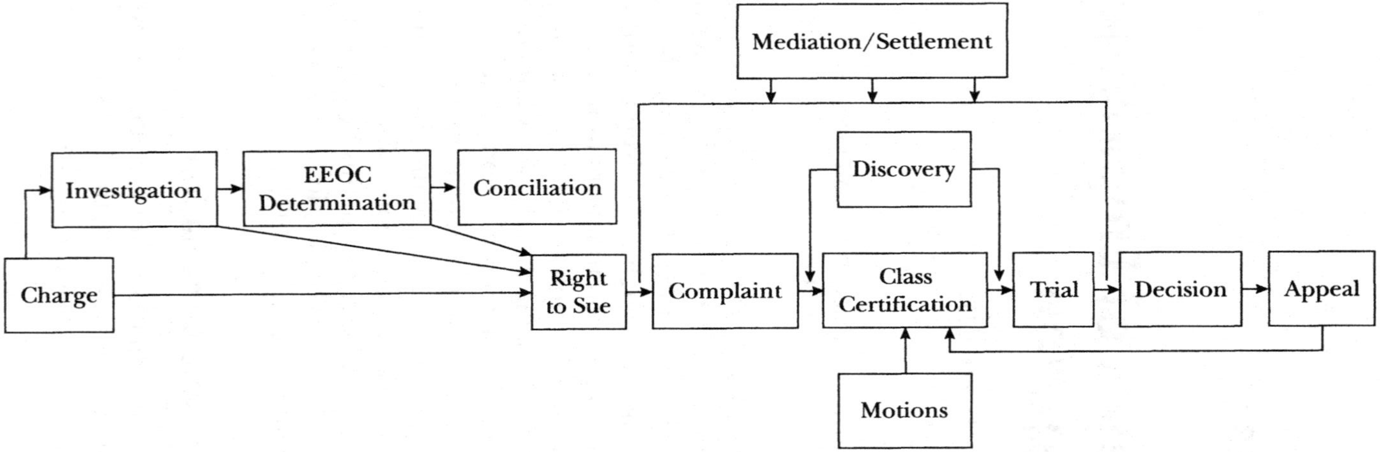

Employment Opportunity Commission [EEOC], a state or local human relations commission, and so forth) to register that protest formally. That agency will then contact the employer and request some basic information about the charge of discrimination. This phase of the process is often known as an *investigation*. Using the information gathered in the investigation, the agency will render a determination on the merits of the charge. If the agency finds that the charge has merit, the agency will then attempt to achieve an amicable resolution through a process known as *conciliation*. The agency may suggest a remedy, the employer may counter with an alternative resolution, and the dispute may be settled at this stage. Or the employer and the agency may fail to reach an agreement, and the dispute may enter the more formal arena of litigation. Alternatively, following an investigation the agency may find the charge to be without merit.

The Right to Sue

When an individual or group believes that an employment practice is illegal, the first step in challenging that practice is the filing of a formal charge of discrimination with an administrative agency, as I have just described. The individual filing a charge is known as the *charging party*. In order to file a formal lawsuit in federal court under Title VII of the 1964 Civil Rights Act, the administrative charge needs to be processed by an agency (for example, the EEOC). The individual or group must go through this regulatory agency before filing a suit. By requiring such processing, it is hoped that the more frivolous claims by charging parties may be abandoned after a negative regulatory review. Nevertheless, a charging party has an absolute right to file a lawsuit regardless of the findings of a regulatory agency such as the EEOC. This means in practice that anyone who is upset about an employer's decision can file a federal lawsuit, thus increasing the case load in the civil court system. (The interviews with federal judges presented in Chapter Fifteen show that this is exactly what some judges believe is happening.) A charging party may receive a *right to sue* notification in three ways: (1) the charging party may simply ask for it after a fixed time period has passed, and the EEOC is required to comply; (2) it will be automatically issued if the EEOC finds the charge without merit; and (3) it will be automatically issued if the EEOC finds the charge to have merit but is not able to resolve the charge with the employer.

Note that if the defendant is a public employer, such as a state personnel department or municipal police department, the case may be taken over by the Department of Justice. If the defendant is a private employer such as Home Depot or the Ford Motor Company, the case may be litigated by the EEOC. The Department of Justice and the EEOC do not get involved in very many cases in which a right-to-sue letter has been issued. Like the Supreme Court these agencies pick and choose cases which they choose to litigate. Thus, even though the EEOC may be the agency that permits a suit to be filed, this does not make it an "EEOC" case. Typically a charge to the EEOC must be filed within 300 days of the practice that gives rise to the claim of discrimination. If a right-to-sue letter has been issued by the EEOC, the complainant (whom we will call the *plaintiff*) may then retain a lawyer and pursue the charge against the employer in federal court. The overwhelming majority of charging parties do not file lawsuits.

The Complaint

For those charging parties who choose to file a lawsuit, the next step in an employment case is the filing of a formal complaint with the court. The complaint will identify the plaintiff or plaintiffs; the reason for the complaint; the right that the plaintiff has to file the charge, including things such as protected status (for example, race or gender); the practice purported to be discriminatory; and the remedy sought by the plaintiff.

Class Certification

A plaintiff can sue an employer individually, as part of a group of other plaintiffs, or on behalf of a class of *similarly situated* individuals. For example, a rejected African American applicant for a job with a manufacturing company might attempt to file a suit in which he or she represents not only himself or herself but also all African Americans who were rejected by that company in the three previous years. This larger group of applicants would be proposed by plaintiff's counsel to be a *class* (this designation having produced in turn the term *class action suit*). If the plaintiff wins the case, then all members of the class may be entitled to share in the award, although the actual plaintiffs who file the suit (called *named plaintiffs*) will usually be awarded a larger amount because of their continued involvement in the case. Surprisingly, very few lawsuits are filed by rejected job applicants.

A judge decides whether or not the lawsuit may proceed on behalf of a class (that is, the judge determines whether class certification is warranted). A number of criteria must be met for class certification; the most important are (1) that the plaintiffs are all members of a protected class (for example, women or African Americans), (2) that the named plaintiff does actually have a claim that is common to a large group of people (for example, failure to hire), (3) that the number of plaintiffs is so large as to make consolidation of complaints more efficient (for example, 500 or more potential plaintiffs), and (4) that there is a common basis for the complaints of class members (for example, the same hiring process was used to reject all the plaintiffs). The advantages to the lawyers representing the plaintiffs of gaining class certification are substantial. If a lawyer represents a single individual in a discrimination case, a win and an award of $400,000 may result in a fee of $100,000 to the lawyer. If, instead, a class is certified and that class includes 500 plaintiffs, the award may be in the multimillion-dollar range and the fee for the lawyer may be in the millions of dollars. A winning plaintiff in a Title VII lawsuit is normally awarded back pay and often is awarded front pay as well. Title VII imposes no limit on the amount of those awards, but they must bear a direct relation to the actual monetary losses of income suffered by the plaintiff. In addition to these actual damages, which are not capped, Title VII provides for punitive damages and damages for emotional distress. The range for such extra damages to each plaintiff has a ceiling that runs between $50,000 and $300,000 for each award, depending on the size of the company—the larger the company, the higher the ceiling. For companies with less than 100 employees, the ceiling for the extra damages is set at $50,000. For companies with more than 500 employees, the ceiling is $300,000.

In the class certification stage, an I-O psychologist is often called on to determine whether the members of the class were all subject to the same practice. For example, the challenged practice may be a hiring system that used several different standardized tests or procedures over a period of three years—a different practice each year. The practice in year 1 might have included a written test of intelligence and an interview. In year 2 the organization might have changed to a series of work sample tests. And in year 3 the company might have used a situational interview. The I-O psychologist would examine the practices in question. In this case it is likely that the psychologist would offer the opinion that each of the devices was conceptually and psychometrically different, making the applicants within each year similar, but across the three years dissimilar. And, basing the decision on the opinion of the psychologist, the judge might certify three separate subclasses of plaintiffs, one class for each of the three years. In contrast, if instead of three distinct practices, the company had used three tests (one each year), tests that were simply parallel forms of the same basic test, then the psychologist might agree that the tests represent a common practice, and a single class might be certified by the court.

The process by which classes are certified may take different forms. It is within the discretion of the judge to simply examine reports submitted by both sides in favor of or opposing class certification. Alternatively the judge may request both sides to submit reports, then hold an actual hearing or mini-trial with oral testimony from expert and nonexpert witnesses as a way of making a decision. In either case the judge will issue a written opinion identifying which, if any, classes have been certified. This opinion is subject to appeal and may be questioned by either party in a U.S. court of appeals.

A word of explanation might be in order here for the reader new to the judicial process. The lowest of the three levels of the federal judicial system consists of the U.S. district (trial) courts. The actual employment discrimination suit is heard by a district court judge (and possibly a jury). The trial judge or jury renders an opinion at the conclusion of the trial, declaring a judgment in favor of the plaintiff or the defendant. Either party may claim that the judge has made legal errors during the trial and may appeal the decision to the next level, which consists of the U.S. courts of appeals (also referred to as *circuit courts,* in reference to the eleven geographical areas in which they have jurisdiction, or by circuit number, for example, *ninth circuit*). For example, a losing party might complain that the trial judge made a legal error by excluding the testimony of the losing party's expert witness. The court of appeals will review the written record of the trial as well as the motions supporting and attacking the appeal and render a decision regarding the legitimacy of the appeal. But the court addresses only legal issues, not factual issues. The losing party at trial has an automatic right of appeal to the court of appeals, and the court of appeals must accept the appeal and rule on its merits.

The third and highest level of the federal judiciary is the U.S. Supreme Court. The losing party at the court of appeals does not have an automatic right to appeal to the Supreme Court. The losing party at the court of appeals must file a special *petition* that explains why the Supreme Court should accept an appeal in this particular case. The Supreme Court hears only a small fraction of the appeals it receives. The Supreme Court has no written standards for determining which appeals to accept, although a few trends have appeared over time. For example, the Supreme Court is more likely to accept an appeal when important constitutional issues are at stake or when there is conflict between the legal rulings of two or more circuit courts of appeal.

Discovery

In television dramas and movies depicting high-profile civil and criminal trials there is often a moment of high suspense when a witness blurts out an admission or explanation that comes as a complete surprise to the examining lawyer, resulting in a radical shift in the course of the trial. This virtually never happens in real-life civil trials because of a process called *discovery*. Through the discovery process, lawyers are given access to witnesses who will be called by the other side and to any documents relevant to the allegations of discrimination. Lawyers may send a series of *interrogatories* to the opposing party asking for specific written answers to specific questions. A plaintiff may contend, for example, that he or she was passed over for a position in favor of a less qualified applicant. The plaintiff will be asked to identify explicitly who that less qualified person was and to state why the plaintiff believes that this person was less qualified. In addition the lawyers may ask for documents such as the past employment record of the plaintiff or the company policy covering promotions or discipline. Finally, the lawyers may request to take the depositions of any persons who may testify at trial. A *deposition* is a formal interview under oath conducted by an opposing attorney. If the lawyers are good at what they do, by the time a trial actually occurs there are few secrets or uncharted areas of testimony. Lawyers use the information gathered through the discovery process to plan their trial strategy.

The role of the I-O psychologist in the discovery process is varied. The most obvious role is as an expert. The I-O psychologist will be deposed by the opposing attorney. Prior to deposition the expert submits a report containing any and all opinions the expert expects to offer at trial and the foundation for each opinion. This represents a valuable document for the opposing attorney and forms the foundation for the deposition of the expert. Occasions often arise when the initial report may be supplemented. These occasions may involve additional data that are uncovered or the presentation of an opposing expert report that warrants rebuttal in the form of a supplemental report. Procedures for submission of expert reports vary. Often reports by opposing experts are filed simultaneously, at the court's direction. In these cases supplemental reports are more common. Alternatively the plaintiff expert may be required to file a report first, and then the defendant expert will be required to file a responding report within some time period, often thirty to forty-five days, with a rebuttal report by the plaintiff's expert after that. Supplemental reports are somewhat less common when the initial reports are not filed simultaneously. Experts may be subsequently redeposed on supplemental reports after the deposition based on their initial report. If reports are filed by experts for class certification requests, the experts will likely be deposed on those reports as well. Thus it is conceivable that a given expert might be deposed on at least three separate occasions in a large complex case—after a class certification report, after an initial report on the substance of the case (often called a *merits report*), and after any supplemental reports have been submitted.

The I-O psychologist can also be of help in other parts of the discovery process. He or she can advise the lawyers about the technical or procedural documents to request from either the plaintiff or defendant. In our example, defendant documents might include the tests themselves and their technical manual and backup information, as well as company policy statements, procedural memos, and the like. Plaintiff documents might include training records, correspondence with the employer, and so forth. Because the I-O psychologist is very familiar with human resource (HR) procedures and test information, he or she can help the lawyers understand the meaning and relevance of these documents. The psychologist may also be involved in helping the lawyers prepare for the deposition of witnesses on the other side, both fact witnesses and other expert witnesses. In some cases the psychologist may attend the deposition of the opposing expert and assist his or her lawyer in understanding technical answers or in framing technical follow-up questions.

Discovery may also involve data sets that will provide the foundation for statistical analyses carried out by the I-O psychologist or by a retained statistician. There is often lengthy discussion of the appropriate data set and of the interpretation and management of the data set, because the data are seldom in a form amenable to easy or immediate analysis. On some occasions a court (judge or magistrate) may rule on what data set will used by each side (often referred to as a *stipulated database*). Once an expert does a particular analysis on a data set and that analysis becomes the foundation for an expert opinion, then the specific analysis and underlying data must be provided to an opposing expert for verification.

Although I discuss discovery as if it followed the class certification process, discovery will also precede a class certification hearing or motion. Either side may request information that would assist in the determination of who does and does not belong in a particular proposed class.

Motions

Throughout the course of the litigation, lawyers will file various motions with the judge asking for a wide range of actions. As an example, in the course of discovery, lawyers for the plaintiffs may request information from the defendant company and the company may decline to provide that information, claiming that it is irrelevant as well as expensive to produce. The opposing lawyers will then file a motion asking the judge to compel or require the defendant to provide the information.

In Limine Motions

As will be seen in later chapters (especially Chapters Six, Fourteen, and Fifteen), motions to exclude the testimony of an expert are often made by opposing attorneys. These motions are usually referred to as *in limine* motions, meaning that the judge is being asked to either exclude or limit the testimony of the expert. It is not unusual for *in limine* motions to be filed before a motion for class certification. As will be discussed in Chapter Six, *Daubert* motions are attempts to exclude the testimony of an expert on the argument that the expert testimony is not sufficiently scientific and would mislead the judge or the jury. A motion may also be made to exclude an expert because he or she does not possess the relevant credentials (for example, education, training, or experience) to be qualified as an expert. Daubert motions are usually made before a trial begins. Often there will be a Daubert hearing preceding the trial, conducted by the judge to determine what testimony will be permitted at trial. At the Daubert hearing the I-O psychologist may be expected to defend his or her opinions as scientifically sound. In defending these opinions as based on science the psychologist is expected to present relevant literature showing that the theory on which his or her opinion is based is accepted in the I-O literature, can be tested, and so forth.

Challenges to expert credentials are commonly made at trial, immediately preceding the expert's testimony. First, the lawyer representing the side that retained the expert questions the expert regarding his or her credentials. Following that questioning the lawyer requests that the judge *qualify* the witness as an expert in some area (for example, testing, psychometrics, or HR). The judge then permits the opposing attorney to cross-examine the expert in an attempt to demonstrate that the witness is *not* qualified to testify as an expert. After the direct and cross-examination testimony the judge rules that the witness is or is not qualified to testify as an expert.

Summary Judgment Motions

A motion for *summary judgment* asks the judge either to rule on behalf of the plaintiff (if filed by the lawyers for the plaintiffs) or to dismiss the complaint (if filed by lawyers for the defendants) before going to trial. Summary judgment motions are often filed after discovery has been completed. They may be filed earlier when a clear legal issue is present. Plaintiffs might argue that the evidence uncovered to that point shows a clear violation of the law by the defendant company. Defendants might argue that the discovery process has demonstrated that there was no factual foundation for the charges in the first place. Whichever side makes the motion for summary judgment is claiming that the material facts are not subject to dispute, that there is no need for a trial to determine the factual issues. There may be legal issues to be decided, but the judge alone always decides those issues. A trial is needed only to resolve factual issues. If a judge grants a summary judgment motion, then the litigation is over and there is no trial. As evidenced in the interviews with judges (Chapter Fifteen), motions for summary judgment are considered seriously by judges and often granted.

Mediation and Settlement

Because trials are costly and risky for both sides, the parties often conduct settlement discussions in an attempt to reach a mutually satisfying resolution of the complaint before proceeding with all the other steps that lead to a trial. Such discussions are often facilitated (and sometimes required) by the judge assigned to the trial or possibly by a federal magistrate associated with the court to which the case has been assigned. Because the case load of federal judges is so high, it is to the advantage of the judge to use any means possible to eliminate the need for a trial. Most cases do settle before trial, and settlement discussions can start at any time from the filing of an initial complaint to the moment before the jury is about to announce its verdict. In fact most settlement discussions begin well in advance of any trial. Of course, in the early discussions the parties are often far apart. As the trial date approaches, settlement discussions become more serious, and the gap between the parties often narrows.

Settlement agreements may involve money (for example, back pay) as well as changes in procedures (for example, an agreement by a company to stop using a particular hiring procedure). Serious settlement discussions usually occur after discovery has been completed and each side is aware of the relative strengths and weaknesses of its respective case. In addition, if the plaintiffs prevail at trial, their lawyers may be awarded substantial fees. Winning defendants almost never are awarded fees. A winning plaintiff gets attorney's fees automatically. This is an additional driving force in settlement discussions.

I-O psychologists are not directly involved in settlement discussions. The actual discussions include lawyers, plaintiffs, and possibly the judge. Nevertheless, to the extent that the discussions revolve around HR practices, the I-O psychologist may be asked to assist the lawyer, defendant, or plaintiff in understanding the implications of any changes in that practice. As an example, the plaintiffs might demand that a particular test or testing technique be dropped from the hiring sequence. The I-O psychologist helps both sides understand the implications for validity of dropping that test and may suggest alternative techniques or tests acceptable to both parties.

Trial

When an actual trial is held, it may last anywhere from a week to a month or more, depending on the complexity of the case. The trial may take place in front of a jury or in front of a judge, although most Title VII cases involve jury trials. If it is a jury trial, it will typically take longer, because juries are typically less familiar than a judge is with the technical issues and more time must be taken to educate the jury on issues such as statistics, HR policy, and scientific literature. The role of the judge in a jury trial is to rule on objections and motions that occur in the course of the trial and to deal with all legal issues. It is the responsibility of the jury to deal with all fact issues. In addition the judge may ask questions of witnesses in order to provide the jury with additional relevant information or to clear up any confusion in the testimony. Finally, after both sides rest, the judge issues a *charge* to the jury, instructing its members with respect to the law and what they are to consider in their deliberations. Ultimately, however, in a jury trial it is the jury that decides the outcome of the case, not the judge. In a bench trial the judge rules on both legal and factual issues.

In the trial itself the plaintiffs present their case first. This is followed by the defendants' case, which is expected to respond to and rebut the case presented by the plaintiffs. After both sides have presented their respective cases, there may be additional rebuttal testimony permitted for both sides. Occasionally the judge will further refine the presentation of evidence, asking the plaintiffs to first present evidence of adverse impact (the prima facie burden of the plaintiffs) to be rebutted by the defendants and then asking the plaintiffs to present their evidence on the substantive issues (a *merits* or job-relatedness defense, assuming adverse impact has been shown) to be rebutted by the defendants. There is often a third phase of the trial as well—the consideration of *alternatives*. If the plaintiffs demonstrate adverse impact for a device or procedure and the defendants demonstrate the job-relatedness of that device or procedure, the plaintiffs still have the opportunity to demonstrate that there was an alternative device or procedure available to the defendants for making the personnel decision, an alternative that had equal validity and less adverse impact. The defendants typically attempt to rebut that showing of an alternative by demonstrating that it was not a "real" alternative (that is, had never been shown to reduce adverse impact while leaving validity intact) or that it was not a "feasible" alternative (for example, it would have been impossible to administer fairly and effectively or would have been prohibitively expensive). I-O psychologists and statisticians are commonly involved in testifying about alternatives. For an individual expert there are often several phases of testimony. First, the expert is questioned by his or her lawyer regarding opinions. This is known as *direct testimony*. Then the opposing lawyer cross-examines the expert on his or her direct testimony. This may be followed by *redirect testimony* in which the lawyer for the side that retained the expert may follow up on the cross-examination questions and answers. Finally, the opposing counsel may have an opportunity to re-cross-examine the expert on testimony elicited during redirect. Expert testimony may last as little as an hour or may extend over several days, depending on the complexity of the case. It is also not uncommon for each side to have more than one expert (for example, an I-O psychologist, an economist, and a statistician), extending the period of expert testimony even longer.

In the trial phase an I-O psychologist may play a central role. Because much of what will be discussed is technical and unfamiliar to both the judge and the jury, it is the psychologist's role to help the judge and jury understand the intricacies of things such as validity designs, test reliability, and validity generalization theory. Because the psychologist testifies as an expert, his or her credibility and expertise may be pivotal to the outcome of the case. In nonjury trials the judge will often cite the testimony of the I-O psychologist in the written opinion.

Witnesses

There are two types of witnesses in employment discrimination trials. *Fact witnesses* provide information about the factual issues in the case. For example, plaintiffs may testify as fact witnesses with respect to what happened to them when they applied for a job or a promotion and what the consequences of the company action were for them in terms of lost income or physical or psychological distress. Managers may testify about how they gathered and analyzed information about applicants or about discussions with individual plaintiffs.

Another type of fact witness (called a *30(b)6 witness* in reference to the section of the Federal Rules of Procedure that define this person) may testify as an official spokesperson for the company about a policy or procedure. This person is knowledgeable about the history and implementation of one or more parts of company policy. Although other fact witnesses may have things to say about the policy and its implementation, their statements reflect personal experiences with the policy. Because the 30(b)6 witness speaks for the company, that testimony carries substantial weight in the case.

The second type of witness is the *expert witness,* and I have discussed the role of that person earlier in this chapter. The expert witness is qualified by training, education, or experience to offer opinions about issues in the case, such as the effectiveness of an assessment device or a staffing strategy. In employment discrimination cases the typical expert witnesses include statisticians who consider issues related to adverse impact determination, economists who consider issues of monetary damages, social psychologists who discuss issues of stereotyping, and I-O psychologists who consider HR and psychometric issues. These issues may be as detailed as the specific method for setting a cut score or as broad as "best practices" in implementing a downsizing. Because I-O psychologists are likely to be retained by both the plaintiffs and the defendant, it is also necessary for the I-O psychologist to understand what an opposing expert is saying and to explain to the judge or jury why he or she disagrees with the other expert.

Decision

When all of the evidence has been presented, a decision is rendered by the judge or the jury. If it is a jury trial, the decision may come in hours or days, depending on the extent of the jury deliberations. In a nonjury trial (also called a *bench trial*), the ruling or verdict may not come for a year or more. A jury trial results in a verdict without any written explanation by the jurors. A bench trial usually results in a lengthy written opinion from the judge, describing what he or she sees to be the facts of the case, the relevant law and previous court decisions on similar topics, and the conclusion about which side prevailed. Thus reviews of the factors that may influence the outcome of an employment discrimination trial (for example, persuasive expert testimony, prior court decisions) are limited to bench trials for which a written opinion is available. Very little is known, at least in any formal way, about the factors that influence jury members in rendering a decision.

When the decision is in favor of the plaintiffs, there is usually a monetary award of some amount. In addition to a monetary award a judge may also order changes in procedures or practices. When the defendants win, the judge may order the plaintiffs to pay some portion of the costs incurred by the defendants in defending against the charge, but these costs are usually minimal and cover only administrative expenses such as copying, fees for court reporters, and limited travel costs. The cost award may represent less than 1 percent of the total costs incurred by the company. When the decision requires a change in a practice (for example, the performance appraisal process), the judge may direct the company to install a new practice with the assistance of a trained I-O psychologist.

Appeals

It is common for the losing party in a case to be dissatisfied with the outcome. This often results in an appeal, because a losing party has the automatic right to appeal an unfavorable decision and when an appeal is filed the court of appeals must hear that appeal. Whether a trial is a bench trial or a jury trial, decisions on factual issues are final and may not be appealed. Only legal issues may be appealed. The appeal is heard by a panel of judges in the judicial circuit in which the case was tried. These judges do not reconsider the factual issues of the case, but look only at the record to make sure that correct procedures or processes were used. For example, the trial judge may have decided to exclude the testimony of a particular witness. The losing party may argue that the judge made an incorrect decision and that this testimony would have changed the verdict.

An appeal to the court of appeals can result in one of three actions. The appeals court will either affirm (that is, agree with), reverse (come to a conclusion different from the trial judge's), or remand (send the case back to the trial judge with a requirement to reconsider a particular issue). Remands usually result in a new trial, although the second trial may be much narrower than the first, simply requiring the judge to consider points raised by the appeals court judges. In some cases the losing party on appeal may request the entire roster of circuit judges to consider the appeal (known as a request for an *en banc* hearing). This request may be granted or denied.

The highest level of appeal is to the U.S. Supreme Court. The nine justices of the Supreme Court will consider appeals related to any legal issues. They will often decide to hear an appeal to resolve inconsistencies in decisions between circuits. The Supreme Court agrees to consider a very small fraction of the cases sent to it. Unlike the court of appeals, the Supreme Court can simply decline to become involved or can affirm a decision, reverse a decision, or remand a case to a lower court for rehearing. Various appeals will often add years to the length of a litigation action.

Because appeals are based on procedural arguments and legal issues and not factual issues, the I-O psychologist will not have an active role. If the appeal is successful, and the case is remanded for a rehearing, the I-O psychologist may be involved as an expert witness once again in the rehearing.

Reference

Lindemann, B., & Grossman, P. (1996). *Employment discrimination law* (3rd ed., Vol. II). Washington, DC: Bureau of National Affairs.

CHAPTER 2

Adverse Impact
Judicial, Regulatory, and Statutory Authority
Arthur Gutman

Adverse (or *disparate*) *impact* implicates any facially neutral trigger negatively affecting some more than others. For example, a street curb adversely impacts people in wheelchairs, physical requirements adversely impact females, cognitive tests adversely impact minorities, and so on. Adverse impact differs from *facial discrimination,* where entire groups are openly excluded (for example, "women need not apply"). It also differs from *disparate treatment,* where a cause for exclusion is selectively applied (for example, terminating blacks for rules violations, but not whites). Critically, facial discrimination and disparate treatment imply illegal motives to discriminate. In comparison, adverse impact may occur by design, but there is no requirement to prove an illegal motive. For example, in *Griggs* v. *Duke Power* (1971), to be discussed shortly, Duke Power likely knew more blacks than whites would be excluded by the company's newly established selection procedures, but the U.S. Supreme Court did not evaluate the motives Duke Power had for implementing these selection procedures and, instead, focused only on the procedures' statistical impact.

More generally, I associate four unique features with adverse impact: (1) it has a unique judicial scenario, (2) that was born in case law, (3) is unique to Title VII, and (4) applies best to selection procedures.

Regarding feature 1, the adverse impact judicial scenario was established by the Supreme Court in *Griggs* v. *Duke Power* (1971) and *Albemarle* v. *Moody* (1975). The Uniform Guidelines on Employee Selection Procedures (1978) (Guidelines) were then written to interpret *Griggs* and *Albemarle*, and adverse impact was then codified for Title VII by Congress in the Civil Rights Act of 1991 (CRA-91) to overturn the Supreme Court's ruling in *Wards Cove* v. *Atonio* (1989). The adverse impact judicial scenario is described in the first main section that follows.

Regarding feature 2, the adverse impact judicial scenario does not apply to Executive Order 11246 (EO 11246) on voluntary affirmative action because EO 11246 affords no private right to sue. It was deemed inapplicable to constitutional claims in *Washington* v. *Davis* (1976) and, practically speaking, to age discrimination claims in *Hazen* v. *Biggens* (1993). The Equal Pay Act has a unique scenario wherein adverse impact is irrelevant. Lastly, even though it is codified within the Americans with Disabilities Act (ADA), adverse impact is facially apparent in such claims (for example, a written test is an obvious barrier for people with dyslexia), and job relatedness, the traditional Title VII defense, is merely a prelude to the larger issue of reasonable accommodation.

Regarding feature 3, Section 1607C of the Guidelines applies to "selection procedures" for "employment decisions." To protect EO 11246 from adverse impact claims, the Guidelines state, "recruitment practices" are not "selection procedures." For example, in *Spaulding* v. *University of Washington* (1984), a comparable-worth case, market forces were alleged to adversely impact "female" jobs. The U.S. Court of Appeals for the Ninth Circuit ruled that "market prices" do not represent a "specific employment practice." As we will witness in the final topical section of this chapter, the Supreme Court could have applied analogous reasoning in *Wards Cove* (1989), where the alleged causes of adverse impact amounted to recruitment procedures, not selection procedures as defined in the Guidelines.

The sections that follow focus on (1) the adverse impact judicial scenario, (2) comparisons to other key judicial scenarios, (3) early case law on standardized tests, from *Griggs* v. *Duke Power*

(1971) through *Connecticut* v. *Teal* (1982), (4) other causes of adverse impact beside standardized tests, (5) critical challenges to these earlier traditions in *Watson* v. *Fort Worth Bank* (1988) and *Wards Cove* v. *Atonio* (1989), (6) CRA-91, and (7) the general disconnect between case law, regulatory law, and scientific principles. Many of the key background issues relating to these topics are discussed in greater detail by Gutman (2000, chaps. 2 and 3; 2004).

The Adverse Impact Judicial Scenario

Equal employment opportunity (EEO) civil trials have shifting burdens across three phases, and the trial can end in any phase. Phase 1 is for prima facie evidence of a violation, phase 2 is for defense, and phase 3 is for proving the defense used is a pretext for discrimination. The scenario has a burden of proof (or persuasion) in each phase. Phase 1 requires statistical proof of adverse impact, and phase 2 requires proof that the cause (or causes) of adverse impact is job related and consistent with business necessity. Phase 3 entitles plaintiffs to offer alternative, job-related selection procedures that produce less or no adverse impact. The following scenario represents the latest version, as codified in CRA-91.

Phase 1: Proving Adverse Impact

Plaintiffs must identify the cause(s) of adverse impact and prove disproportionate exclusion. For example, in *Griggs*, cognitive tests resulted in a 58 percent pass rate for actual white applicants and a 6 percent pass rate for actual black applicants. Also, a requirement to possess a high school diploma implied adverse impact for potential applicants, because the high school graduation rate in North Carolina at the time was 34 percent for whites and 12 percent for blacks. A similar analysis was used in *Dothard* v. *Rawlinson* (1977) to conclude that height and weight requirements disproportionately exclude more females than males. Critically, if more than one possible cause exists and if adverse impact occurs for the total selection process (that is, at the *bottom line*), plaintiffs must identify the specific cause(s). However, if individual selection procedures cannot be disaggregated, the employer must defend the entire process.

Phase 2: Employer Defense

The defense to adverse impact for standardized tests amounts to test validity as specified in the Guidelines. However, other causes imply other proofs. For example, in *New York City* v. *Beazer* (1979), an articulation (verbalization) of the dangers of hiring methadone users as transit authority officers sufficed. In contrast, in *Dothard* v. *Rawlinson* (1977) it was easier to facially exclude all women as prison guards than to exclude anyone, male or female, based on height and weight criteria. As we will witness in the later discussion of early case law, biographical factors (for example, high school diplomas and college degrees) are easier to defend and physical factors (for example, height and weight criteria or a no-beard policy) are harder to defend than standardized tests.

Phase 3: Less Discriminatory Alternatives

In *Albemarle* v. *Moody* (1975), the Supreme Court ruled plaintiffs can prove pretext by "showing that less discriminatory alternatives to the achievement of the employer's goal were available." I know of no successes in this domain, but there are near misses. For example, in *Bridgeport Guardians* v. *Bridgeport* (1991), an expert witness proposed intensive scrutiny of individual applicants using, among other things, videotaping. However, the second circuit ruled that extra expenses for implementing alternatives are not required. Analogously, Barrett (1997) implemented a course in the 1970s on content valid issues (for example, on laws and procedures), and there was no adverse impact among police recruits who passed this course. However, as Barrett relates, the City of Akron, Ohio, discontinued the course for economic reasons. In short there is no reasonable accommodation requirement for alternative procedures as there is in the ADA. Nevertheless, the issue of alternatives to adverse impact is evolving and is likely to garner increased attention as case law evolves.

Other Relevant Judicial Scenarios

The disconnects between case law, regulatory law, and science featured later in this chapter are, by and large, products of confusion of portions of the adverse impact scenario with portions of other judicial scenarios. Some courts, including the Supreme Court, have incorporated key aspects of other scenarios into the adverse impact scenario. These other scenarios include McDonnell-Burdine in relation to individual disparate treatment claims, statistical disparities in pattern or practice claims, and the business necessity proof in bona fide occupational qualification claims.

McDonnell-Burdine

This scenario derives its name from two major disparate treatment cases: *McDonnell Douglas* v. *Green* (1973), in which it was introduced, and *Texas Department of Community Affairs* v. *Burdine* (1981), in which it was confirmed. In *McDonnell Douglas* v. *Green* the fact was that Green was laid off and then later excluded from reemployment. The key issue was whether he was intentionally excluded owing to racial motives or whether he was excluded for legitimate reasons, most notably for committing illegal acts against the company during the layoff (a *stall-in* to prevent employees from entering the plant and a *lock-in* to prevent them from exiting). In general the McDonnell-Burdine scenario may be used anytime one party claims intentional exclusion based on class membership and the other party claims a legitimate motive for exclusion (for example, poor performance) that would result in the exclusion of any member of any protected class.

To set a framework for such cases, the Supreme Court established a presumptive burden for phase 1 (that Green applied, was qualified, was passed over, and the search continued) and a burden of production in phase 2 (to articulate [without proving] a legal reason for exclusion). The company stated Green was excluded due to his illegal acts during the layoff, leaving Green the phase 3 burden to prove with direct or indirect evidence that the company's articulation was a pretext for racial discrimination.

In short, compared to the adverse impact scenario, with its burdens to persuade in each of the three phases, McDonnell-Burdine has lighter and equally matched burdens in phases 1 and 2, leaving the only burden of persuasion on the plaintiff in phase 3. For present purposes the key factor to note is that in *Wards Cove*, a five-to-four majority voted to replace the business necessity defense in phase 2 of the adverse impact scenario with the burden of production from phase 2 of the McDonnell-Burdine scenario, thus making a lighter burden for the defense and asymmetrical burdens across phases 1 and 2 in the adverse impact scenario.

Pattern or Practice

The McDonnell-Burdine scenario is for disparate treatment on a case-by-case basis, which is often termed *individuous* disparate treatment. When disparate treatment becomes a companywide habit and many members of a protected class are mistreated simultaneously, it is termed *pattern* or *practice*. Unlike adverse impact or McDonnell-Burdine, pattern or practice is outlawed in plain statutory Title VII language. In *International Teamsters* v. *U.S.* (1977), a case featured later in this chapter, Justice Stewart defined pattern or practice as a companywide "standard operating procedure." Because pattern or practice features statistical disparities, it is easy to confuse it with adverse impact. However, as we will witness later, the statistical disparities in adverse impact and pattern or practice are not the same, and neither is the defense.

The landmark pattern or practice cases are *International Teamsters* v. *U.S.* (1977) and *Hazelwood School District* v. *U.S.* (1977). In *Teamsters* there was a statistical anomaly termed the *inexorable zero*. Minority bus drivers were employed on local (lower-paying) routes, but not a single one drove the longer (higher-paying) routes. In *Hazelwood* there was an alleged statistical disparity between minority teachers in the workforce and qualified and available minority teachers in the relevant labor pool. Ultimately, the Teamsters lost because they could not explain the inexorable zero, and the Hazelwood defendants won because the relevant statistical disparity was not statistically significant. More specifically, there was a significant difference when the Hazelwood workforce was compared to the surrounding county but not when it was compared to the local area, which was the relevant comparison. The Supreme Court also concluded the school district had a reasonable articulation, but the Teamsters did not.

A key aspect of both rulings was that statistical disparities across jobs (*Teamsters*) or in the composition of a workforce and a labor pool (*Hazelwood*) did not force a job-relatedness defense as did the applicant flow disparities in *Griggs* and *Albemarle*. Rather, significant cross-job or composition disparities implied the same burden of production as in McDonnell-Burdine. Lost in the controversy surrounding *Wards Cove* was that in *Teamsters,* the defendant had no reasonable legal articulation for the inexorable zero. However, there was a reasonable articulation in *Hazelwood* (that is, competition for minority teachers, from the city of St. Louis). As we will witness later, prior to the Supreme Court's review in *Wards Cove,* an en banc panel of the ninth circuit treated what should have been *Teamsters* revisited as an adverse impact case in the mold of *Griggs* and *Albemarle.*

Bona Fide Occupational Qualification

Pattern or practice violations are generally characterized by illegal facial discrimination. For example, in *Teamsters* minority bus drivers were openly excluded from the higher-paying job, and that is how the inexorable zero occurred. However, there are conditions under which facial discrimination is legal, and the defense for legal facial discrimination is termed *bona fide occupational qualification* (BFOQ). It is a statutory defense in Title VII that has been used primarily for facial exclusion based on sex. It may also apply to religion and national origin, but never to race or color. It is also a statutory defense in the Age Discrimination in Employment Act (ADEA).

To succeed in the BFOQ defense, the defendant must prove it is reasonably necessary to exclude all or most members of a given class. For example, in *Dothard* v. *Rawlinson* (1977), the State of Alabama argued, successfully, that there would be an extra and unnecessary threat to prison safety if women were prison guards in an all-male, maximum-security prison where 20 percent of the men were sex offenders. Similarly, using Federal Aviation Administration regulations, airlines have proven it is reasonably necessary to exclude all or most airline captains at age sixty (*Keating* v. *FAA,* 1979; *Touhy* v. *Ford,* 1982; *Gathercole* v. *Global,* 1984).

The key point for present purposes is that BFOQ implies a threat to business survival, a far heavier burden than implied for adverse impact in the Guidelines. To put it in perspective, a statistically significant correlation between a standardized test and job performance suffices in most adverse impact cases. However, it does not, by itself, prove the business will fail without the test. As we will witness in discussing the Civil Rights Act, there was some confusion between the adverse impact and BFOQ defenses in the debates on the aborted Civil Rights Restoration Act of 1990 (CRRA-90). In the final section we will witness that at least one court has misinterpreted the meaning of *business necessity* in the phrase "job relatedness and consistent with business necessity," creating a major disconnect relative to adverse impact case law as it existed prior to the *Wards Cove* ruling.

Early Case Law on Standardized Tests

There are eight major Supreme Court rulings on adverse impact. Four of them featured standardized cognitive tests: *Griggs* v. *Duke Power* (1971), *Albemarle* v. *Moody* (1975), *Washington* v. *Davis* (1976), and *Connecticut* v. *Teal* (1982). There are critical messages in each ruling.

Griggs v. *Duke Power* (1971)

The Fifteenth Amendment entitled former slaves to vote, but some states used property ownership, poll taxes, and other facially neutral arbitrary barriers to limit that right, a practice that was outlawed in the Twenty-Sixth Amendment in 1964. The facts in *Griggs* were analogous. Before July 2, 1965, the effective date of Title VII, blacks at Duke Power were limited to lower-level labor department jobs. They were facially excluded from upper-level jobs in the coal handling, operations, maintenance, and laboratory and test departments. On July 2, 1965, Duke Power announced that anyone seeking entry into any of the four higher levels or promotion to the upper three levels had to meet diploma and testing requirements. The diploma requirement was not new. It was instituted in 1955 for white workers seeking promotion to upper-level jobs. Interestingly there was no evidence that upper-level whites with diplomas performed any better than upper-level whites without diplomas. Thus there was reason to believe the new requirements were as arbitrary to job performance as owning property and paying poll taxes were to voting one hundred years earlier.

Duke Power relied on statutory Title VII language making it legal to use "professionally developed ability tests" provided they are "not designed, intended or used to discriminate based on race, color, religion, sex or national origin." The lower courts ruled there was insufficient evidence of a motive to discriminate (that is, disparate treatment). However, a unanimous Supreme Court deferred to the definition of "professionally developed ability tests" in the 1966 EEOC Guidelines: such a test is one which measures "the knowledge or skills required by the particular job or class of jobs which the applicant seeks, or which fairly affords the employer a chance to measure the applicant's ability to perform a particular job or class of jobs." The message from the Court, given by Justice Burger, was that Title VII covers the "consequences of employment practices, not simply the motivation" of employers, and that a "manifest relationship" between the challenged practice and the "employment in question" must be proven if adverse impact is shown.

Albemarle Paper Company v. Moody (1975)

Aware of the *Griggs* ruling, the Albemarle Paper Company attempted to validate its cognitive tests four months prior to trial. It also used a high school diploma requirement and two cognitive tests, one of which was the same as a test that was featured in *Griggs* (Bennett Mechanical Comprehension Test). Albemarle hired a consultant who, in a half-day visit, developed a criterion validation strategy but did not supervise the actual work. The company won in district court for the same reasons given by the lower courts in *Griggs*. But it lost at the second circuit and at the Supreme Court. The Supreme Court ruling borrowed heavily from the then applicable EEOC guidelines and the 1974 edition of the American Educational Research Association, American Psychological Association, and National Council on Measurement in Education's *Standards for Educational and Psychological Testing* (Standards), which in 1974 was titled *Standards for Educational and Psychological Tests*. Ironically, Justice Burger, so eloquent in his *Griggs* ruling, dissented in *Albemarle*.

The message in *Albemarle* was that the validation study was unacceptable in light of the EEOC guidelines and the Standards. Justice Stewart cited four major defects. First, there were significant correlations for only three of ten job classifications and no evidence of any basis for generalizing to the other seven because none of them were job analyzed. Second, Stewart rejected the supervisory rankings used in the study because "there was no way of knowing precisely what criteria for job performance the supervisors were considering." Third, the study used upper-level jobs without evidence of an orderly progression from the lower-level jobs from which applicants were excluded. Fourth, the study used "job-experienced white workers," and it was questionable whether the results were valid for "new job applicants, who are younger, largely inexperienced, and in many instances, nonwhite."

Washington v. Davis (1976)

Washington v. Davis featured a Fifth Amendment challenge to a Civil Service Commission verbal test known as Test 21. Test 21 was routinely used by federal agencies but was challenged for its adverse impact when used by the Washington, D.C., Police Department. One message, delivered by Justice White, was that the due process clause of the Fifth Amendment and the equal protection clause of the Fourteenth Amendment do not apply to "racially disproportionate impact." Therefore it is necessary to prove illegal motive in constitutional claims. However, Justice White delivered a message on adverse impact anyway, ruling that a positive correlation between test scores and performance in the police training program was sufficient to validate the test "wholly aside from its possible relationship to actual performance as a police officer," a ruling that benefits police and fire departments and other organizations with safety-sensitive jobs where content-valid training programs serve as a prerequisite for entry into the job.

Connecticut v. Teal (1982)

Section 1607.4C of the Guidelines states the EEOC will not take "enforcement action" against individual components of a selection system when there is no adverse impact for the "total selection process" (that is, at the bottom line). One message in Connecticut v. Teal (1982) was that no regulation is foolproof. Speaking for a slim, five-to-four majority, Justice Brennan noted that failure to take "enforcement action" does not render an at-issue selection procedure legal. He then ruled that adverse impact in any component of a selection system must be defended, regardless of the bottom-line outcome.

In *Teal* provisional promotions to welfare eligibility supervisor were rescinded based on failing grades on a written test, which served as the first step of a multiple hurdle. Some affected employees had already served nearly two years in the new position. The test pass rate for blacks was 68 percent of the pass rate for whites. However, when all hurdles were completed, the promotion rate for blacks (22.9 percent) was higher than the promotion rate for whites (13.5 percent). A second message in Brennan's ruling was that Title VII protects individuals as well as groups, and good treatment of the group is not insulation for discrimination against individuals. A similar ruling had previously been rendered in *Furnco* v. *Waters* (1978), a disparate treatment case in which a supervisor mistakenly believed he could legally exclude minority applicants for construction jobs after the percentage goals of the company's affirmative action plan were achieved.

In summary, *Griggs* and *Albemarle* read like a two-act play in which the three-phase scenario for standardized tests was clearly established. Then additional messages regarding training programs and bottom-line statistics were sent in *Davis* and *Teal*. Of course the Guidelines were then codified in 1978 to incorporate and enlarge upon this *Griggs-Albemarle* play.

Other Causes of Adverse Impact

I have elsewhere used the labels *adverse impact light* for biographical causes of adverse impact and *adverse impact heavy* for physical causes (see Gutman, 2000, chap. 2). Lighter defenses are seen in *NYC* v. *Beazer* (1979) and like cases, and heavier defenses are seen in *Dothard* v. *Rawlinson* (1977) and like cases.

Adverse Impact Light

In some cases there is an obvious threat to public safety, and a simple articulation suffices as a defense to adverse impact. For example, in *Beazer* it was obvious to the Supreme Court that methadone users should not be transit authority cops. In *Hyland* v. *Fukada* (1978), it was obvious to the ninth circuit that a felon convicted of armed robbery should not hold a security job. In *Davis* v. *Dallas* (1985), the Dallas Police Department successfully defended a policy of excluding recent drug users by articulating that drug use shows a disregard for the law.

The high school diploma was featured in both *Griggs* and *Albemarle*, but neither case featured a defense. In other cases involving educational requirements, the defense has featured outside research and expert opinions. In *U.S.* v. *Buffalo* (1978), federal task force reports from 1967 and 1968 sufficed to prove "a high school education is a bare minimum requirement for successful performance of the policeman's responsibilities." In *Davis* v. *Dallas* these same task force reports supported the requirement of forty-five hours of college credit with C or better grades. The Dallas Police Department also defended exclusion based on "poor driving," citing research that past driving habits predict future driving habits. Lastly, in *Spurlock* v. *United Airlines* (1972) the airline defended a four-year degree to become a commercial pilot based on expert testimony that a college degree is necessary to "cope" with classroom training requirements.

Adverse Impact Heavy

At the other end of the spectrum the defendants in *Dothard* found it was easier to defend facial exclusion of all women than to defend exclusion of anyone below a certain height and weight. In *Dothard* the height and weight criteria were surrogates for another ability (strength), prompting Justice Rehnquist to rule "if the job-related quality that the appellants identify is bona fide, their purpose could be achieved by adopting and validating a test for applicants that measures strength directly." In a related case (*Horace* v. *Pontiac*, 1980), the defendant asserted that being tall helps police officers fend off criminals and gain their respect. The sixth circuit, taking its cue from *Dothard*, ruled there were superior and more direct methods of assessing these capabilities. There are, however, rare instances in which a pure physical attribute is a legitimate target attribute. For example, in *Boyd* v. *Ozark* (1977) an airline proved that pilots shorter than five foot seven could not safely operate all the cockpit instruments.

Two other cases are worth noting, both involving a no-beards policy. Such a policy adversely impacts black males due to greater incidence of PFB, a skin condition that makes it difficult to shave closely. In *Bradley* v. *Pizzaco* (1993) the defendant presented survey data indicating customer preference for cleanly shaven counter and delivery staff, but the eighth circuit ruled that beards do not "affect in any manner Domino's ability to make or deliver pizzas to their customers." In contrast, a no-beards policy was upheld in *Fitzpatrick* v. *Atlanta* (1993) because of its relationship to proper functioning of facial safety equipment on firefighters. Clearly, this policy made sense because danger to one firefighter means danger to others. However, it made no sense to credit customer preference in *Bradley* because preference could easily serve as a basis for exclusion for any purpose (for example, housing as well as jobs).

In summary, prior to *Wards Cove* ample case law indicated there were heterogeneous causes and flexible defenses in the adverse impact scenario. However, as we will witness shortly, a five-to-four majority of the justices in *Wards Cove* nevertheless voted to lighten the burden of defense to adverse impact for any cause.

Critical Challenges to Earlier Traditions

As with *Griggs* and *Albemarle*, *Watson* and *Wards Cove* were consecutive acts in the same play. The difference is that when the curtain fell after *Wards Cove*, traditions were altered, not strengthened. These two cases had little in common. *Watson* featured subjective causes of applicant flow disparities, and *Wards Cove* featured recruitment policies in relation to cross-job disparities. They will be forever linked only because a plurality opinion in *Watson* was turned into a majority ruling in *Wards Cove*.

Watson v. *Fort Worth Bank* (1988)

Clara Watson, a black woman, was passed over for promotion four times, each time in favor of a white applicant and each time based on subjective ratings by white supervisors. There was adverse impact for the "total selection process," thus satisfying the *Teal* requirement. The problem was in disaggregating three selection procedures, including job performance ratings, interview performance, and ratings of past experience. Any or all could have produced adverse impact at the bottom line, but it was unclear how or if these procedures were scored or combined. Under similar circumstances lower courts used the *Teal* precedent to pressure defendants to disaggregate and defend their selection procedures (for example, *Gilbert* v. *Little Rock*, 1983; *Griffen* v. *Carlin*, 1985; *Green* v. *USX*, 1988). However, Justice O'Connor offered a different solution.

Only eight justices heard this case, as Justice Kennedy was not yet seated on the Court. All eight of them agreed that subjective causation of adverse impact is a legitimate claim. However, speaking separately for three other justices, Justice O'Connor proposed major alterations in the adverse impact scenario. First, she proposed a prima facie burden to identify the cause(s) of adverse impact and prove causality. The causality part was nothing new and merely reflected the statistical proofs from prior cases. However, the identification part was problematic, particularly when applied to cases where it is unclear how selection decisions are made, as in *Watson*. As noted earlier, other courts in similar scenarios used the *Teal* precedent as a basis for pressuring the defendant. However, O'Connor used *Teal* as the basis for pressuring the plaintiff, unless the plaintiff can produce evidence the selection process with multiple components cannot be disaggregated. In this scenario the employer would have to defend the entire process.

Although ultimately objectionable to some members of Congress, O'Connor's identification provision was not a make-or-break issue. Indeed it lives and breathes in CRA-91. It was her next proposal that fanned the flames. O'Connor opined that the defense consist of "producing evidence that [the] employment practices are based on legitimate business reasons," a literal transplant of the McDonnell-Burdine defense into the adverse impact scenario. The pretext requirement was untouched. Thus O'Connor's adverse impact scenario was (1) identifying the cause(s) of adverse impact and proving causality, (2) articulating a legitimate business reason for a targeted selection procedure(s), and (3) showing proof of job-related alternatives with less or no adverse impact.

Justice Blackmun, speaking for two others, raised two objections. First, citing *Beazer* and other rulings on adverse impact light, he saw no need to change anything because case law already reflected a variety of defenses, including "nationwide studies and reports," "expert testimony," and "psychologist's testimony explaining job-relatedness." Second, he suggested the McDonnell-Burdine defense made sense for disparate treatment because the burdens in the initial two phases are light and equally matched. However, because the plaintiff "has already proved that the employment practice has an improper effect" in the adverse impact scenario, he argued the defendant should "prove that the discriminatory effect is justified." In other words, two burdens of persuasion on the plaintiff matched against a single burden of production on the defendant is unfair. Also, it should be noted that the Supreme Court had ruled in other cases that direct proof of a violation must be answered in kind (see, for example, *TWA* v. *Thurston*, 1985).

Wards Cove v. Atonio (1989)

In *Wards Cove,* cross-job disparities served as the basis for both pattern or practice and adverse impact charges. Two Pacific Northwest salmon-packing companies had a hiring-hall arrangement for selecting unskilled salmon packers but used different procedures to select skilled workers. The skilled workers had higher pay, better food, and better housing. Minorities (Eskimos and Filipinos) were congregated in the unskilled jobs, and nonminorities were congregated in the skilled jobs. The plaintiffs charged that the skilled positions were filled using discriminatory practices, including nepotism, word-of-mouth recruitment, and "vague, subjective hiring criteria." Therefore on its face this was *Teamsters* revisited. Specifically, skilled jobs in *Wards Cove* paralleled higher-paying bus routes in *Teamsters,* and unskilled jobs in *Wards Cove* paralleled lower-paying bus routes in *Teamsters.* However, the minority and nonminority workers were equally qualified in *Teamsters,* whereas this was the arguable issue in *Wards Cove.*

The ninth circuit tried a similar case in *Domingo* v. *New England Fish* (1984) and found a pattern or practice violation. However, this court saw no need for an adverse impact analysis because it viewed the cross-job disparities as merely demonstrating "the consequences of Nefco's discriminatory hiring practices." This raised no eyebrows at the time because the defendants had already lost on the pattern or practice (or motive) charges. Indeed, aside from the ninth circuit ruling in *Wards Cove,* I am unaware of even a single case where plaintiffs won on adverse impact after losing on motive charges when both charges were fueled by the same statistical disparities, be they cross-job disparities (as in *Teamsters*) or composition disparities (as in *Hazelwood*). This is true of both pre–*Wards Cove* cases (for example, *EEOC* v. *Federal Reserve Bank of Richmond,* 1983) and post–*Wards Cove* cases (for example, *EEOC* v. *Chicago Miniature Lamp,* 1991; *EEOC* v. *Consolidated,* 1993).

In *Wards Cove* the district court favored the defendants on the motive charges and the ninth circuit agreed. However, the district court also ruled that "subjective employment practices" are not actionable under adverse impact theory and an en banc panel of the ninth circuit (prior to *Watson*) examined this issue and disagreed. The three-judge panel of the ninth circuit assigned to this case then ruled that "comparative statistics" provided by the plaintiffs "supported [the] inference of discrimination," and directed the district court to "evaluate business necessity of identified practices which allegedly caused disparate impact." This ruling triggered the Supreme Court review in which the O'Connor plurality from *Watson,* joined by the newly seated Justice Kennedy, formed a slim, five-to-four majority that turned the O'Connor plurality opinion in *Watson* into case law.

Justice White spoke for the majority and ruled that "racial imbalance in one segment of an employer's workforce does not, without more, establish a prima facie case of disparate impact with respect to the selection of workers for the employer's other positions" unless there are "barriers or practices deterring qualified nonwhites from applying for non-cannery positions." This ruling is consistent with *Teamsters* and *Hazelwood.* Indeed, there might have been peace in the valley if the next part was that "subjective employment practices" can cause adverse impact, but the prima facie case requires applicant flow–type disparities, and pattern or practice rules are invoked for cross-job and composition disparities. But that did not happen.

Instead, citing a "similar mistaken analysis" in *Hazelwood,* Justice White ruled that the "the proper basis for the initial inquiry in a disparate impact case" is the comparison between "the racial composition of the qualified persons in the labor market and persons holding the at-issue jobs." That was the mistaken analysis in *Hazelwood*, but for pattern or practice, not adverse impact. There was no basis in prior Supreme Court precedents, particularly in the *Griggs-Albemarle* tradition, to broadly apply the burden of production to all adverse impact cases.

In summary, a plurality opinion in *Watson* became case law in *Wards Cove*, at least until CRA-91. Based on *Teamsters* and *Hazelwood*, the McDonnell-Burdine burden of production is appropriate for statistically significant cross-job and composition disparities but not for cases such as *Griggs* or *Albemarle* involving standardized tests, or even *Watson*, where the selection process could have been standardized by the defendant but was not.

Civil Rights Act of 1991

CRAA-90 addressed several Supreme Court rulings: *Lorrance* v. *AT&T*, *Martin* v. *Wilks*, *Patterson* v. *McLean*, *Price Waterhouse* v. *Hopkins*, and *Wards Cove*. However, disagreement on *Wards Cove* was alone sufficient to elicit the veto. In a nutshell, the Democrats favored the *Dothard* v. *Rawlinson* (1977) defense that challenged practices are "essential for job performance." In contrast, the Republicans viewed *Wards Cove* as the correct interpretation of *Griggs*. Thus, despite the variety of causes and the flexible defenses in prior case law, Democrats were stuck on adverse impact heavy and Republicans were stuck on adverse impact light. Even after the Civil Rights Act of 1991 was finalized, Robert Dole, the Republican Senate minority leader, stated that the Act "has codified the 'business necessity' test in *Beazer* and reiterated in *Wards Cove*" (see *Congressional Record*, 136, p. S16570, 1990). Nevertheless most observers believe that CRA-91 compromised on *Wards Cove* by maintaining the identification and causation provisions and overturning on the burden of production. However, critically, Congress limited the legislative history on *Wards Cove* to an "interpretive memorandum" from the *Congressional Record* (127, p. S15276, 1991). In substance, the memorandum contains two paragraphs, one on identification and causation and one on the burden of defense.

Identification and Causation

A critical issue here is that as in *Watson*, components of a selection process may not be easily separated. In pre-*Watson* cases, defendants were pressured to explain such ambiguities. For example, in *Gilbert* v. *Little Rock* (1983), an objective written test was Step 1 for promotion, and pass rates for blacks and whites were about equal. Adverse impact then occurred after Step 2, which featured subjective oral tests. The results of the two tests were combined into a rank, and promotions were made in strict rank order. Blacks routinely made the cutoff for eligibility but were never promoted. The eighth circuit viewed this as a scam in which high oral scores were assigned to blacks with lower written scores and low oral scores were assigned to blacks with high written scores, an interpretation deemed provable if the correlation between the two tests was negative for blacks and either zero or positive for whites.

However, the memorandum does nothing to benefit plaintiffs in cases like *Watson* and *Gilbert*. It states that if "a decision-making process includes particular, functionally-integrated practices which are components of the same criterion," as in the "height and weight requirements designed to measure strength in *Dothard* v. *Rawlinson*," then "the particular, functionally-integrated practices may be analyzed as one practice." Obviously, a psychometric surgeon is not needed to separate the components in *Dothard* or to prove causality. Therefore plaintiffs in scenarios like *Watson* or *Gilbert* have to rely on CRA-91 statutory language stating that if the plaintiff can "demonstrate" that "the elements of a respondent's decision making processes are not capable of separation for analysis, the decision making process may be analyzed as one employment practice."

Burden of Defense

The memorandum states that "the terms 'business necessity' and 'job-related' are intended to reflect the concepts enunciated by the Supreme Court in . . . [*Griggs*] . . . and in other Supreme Court decisions prior to *Wards Cove*." Of course this includes *Beazer*, which provided the fuel for the statement made by Senator Dole. Nevertheless, statutory CRA-91 language states adverse impact is unlawful if the defendant "fails to demonstrate that the challenged practice is job related and consistent with business necessity."

Although some have argued this language is ambiguous (for example, Varca & Pattison, 1993; Bloch, 1994), key Republicans (other than Senator Dole) acknowledged it as a reversal of the *Wards Cove* burden of defense. For example, Senator Hatch stated, "this compromise does overturn *Wards Cove* on the burden of persuasion issue" (*Congressional Record*, 137, p. S15237, 1991). Also, upon signing the bill, President Bush himself stated that CRA-91 contains "a compromise provision that overturns *Wards Cove* by shifting to the employer the burden of persuasion on the 'business necessity' defense."

In summary, entering the debates on CRRA-90, the Democrats and Republicans voiced polar opposite views. Neither view squared with prior case law indicating the adverse impact scenario was already sufficiently flexible to handle these extremes. At least as far as *Wards Cove* was concerned, CRA-91 did compromise by adding a burden of production for plaintiffs trying to decipher the components of ambiguous selection processes, but in return the burden of persuasion was recovered, albeit with language that still remains to be fully interpreted.

Case Law, Regulatory Law, and Science

One of major goals of this chapter has been to demonstrate the authority of case law in the adverse impact scenario. Critical to this authority are regulations such as the Guidelines and congressional responses to key decisions, most notably *Wards Cove*. However, this survey of case law reveals gaps among court rulings, between regulations and case law, and between case law and the state of the art in the psychological profession. The following discussion samples, though hardly exhausts, the nature of these gaps.

Gaps in Case Law

In my opinion the most glaring gap in case law is the failure of the *Wards Cove* majority to recognize that flexible assessment of heterogeneous causes of adverse impact was already featured in prior

Supreme Court rulings. There was no need to change anything, and it should have been clear that any winner-take-all policy contradicted eighteen years of good case law, at least temporarily. The *Wards Cove* majority also abandoned the pattern or practice scenario, which already contained a burden of production for cross-job and composition disparities apart from the burden of persuasion for applicant flow disparities. Ironically, the *Wards Cove* majority recognized that the facts in *Wards Cove* resembled the facts in *Teamsters* and *Hazelwood* more closely than the facts in *Griggs* and *Albemarle*, and still broadly applied pattern or practice rules to adverse impact.

Interestingly, on remand, the *Wards Cove* plaintiffs pushed for bottom-line applicant flow disparities for the higher-level noncannery jobs (as in *Teal*). In *Atonio* v. *Wards Cove* (1993) the ninth circuit rejected this argument because there was nothing to distinguish "among those applying for at-issue and other jobs" and "no way of knowing how many of those persons were qualified for those jobs." Using the identification provision in CRA-91, the ninth circuit also found no link between the statistics cited and "one or more specific practices," and no link to "subjective hiring criteria." The ninth circuit then ruled that "word-of-mouth recruiting by predominantly white superintendents" and "recruiting among native villagers only for cannery jobs" was sufficient to remand on pattern or practice, a view it had previously rejected. Had the ninth circuit so ruled in its first pass, *Wards Cove* would have mirrored the court's prior ruling in *Domingo* v. *New England Fish* (1984). *Wards Cove* would then be a footnote in case law history consistent with other faulty attempts to claim both pattern or practice and adverse impact using a single set of cross-job disparities, and the Supreme Court would have required another venue to settle the issue of "subjective or discretionary" causes of adverse impact.

Case Law and Regulatory Law

The most glaring illustration of disconnect in this domain is a statement in Section 1607C(1) of the Guidelines that "a selection procedure based on inferences about mental processes cannot be supported solely or primarily on the basis of content validity." This guidance was struck down shortly thereafter in *Contreras* v. *Los Angeles* (1980). In *Contreras* a 100-item exam for the job of auditor was devised through a "job analysis phase," in which one set of subject matter experts (SMEs) constructed test items based on job analysis data, and an "examination review phase," in which only those items agreed on by five or more (out of seven) members of a second SME panel were kept. The ninth circuit ruled that the test was valid because "the examination-review phase demonstrated that the auditor examination was significantly correlated with those elements of work behavior identified in the job-analysis phase."

Similar rulings were then rendered in *Guardians* v. *Civil Service* (1980) and *Williams* v. *Vukovich* (1983), where the second and sixth circuits ruled that "if a test is content valid, it may be reasonable to infer that the test scores make some useful gross distinctions between candidates." In *Gillespie* v. *Wisconsin* (1985), the plaintiffs claimed the Guidelines "prefer" criterion to content validity, prompting the seventh circuit to rule that "neither the Uniform Guidelines nor the psychological literature express a blanket preference for criterion-related validity." Then in *Police Officers* v. *City of Columbus* (1990) the sixth circuit accepted a content validity study to support strict rank ordering based on the 1987 Principles of the Society for Industrial and Organizational Psychology (SIOP).

It should be noted, however, that courts have rejected poorly conducted content validity studies (for example, *U.S.* v. *State of New York*, 1990; *Green* v. *Washington State*, 1997). For example, in *Green* v. *Washington State* the court ruled that many test items were unrepresentative of critical knowledge, skills, and abilities (KSAs), they measured abstract concepts, they did not measure intended KSAs, some items had no clear-cut answers, and some of the target KSAs required on-the-job training. Each of these would be a major violation of recommendations contained in the Guidelines and the Principles.

However, when content validity study is properly established, it can overshadow criterion validity. For example, in *Brunet* v. *City of Columbus* (1995), job analysis data targeted both physical and cognitive abilities for firefighters. With input from its consultant the city weighted these data 70 to 30 in favor of the data from the Physical Capability Test (PCT), even though criterion validity data revealed the Cognitive Ability Test (CAT) was slightly more predictive of job performance. The plaintiffs argued that the tests were equally valid and there would be less adverse impact in a 50-50 weighting. However, the consultant convinced the trial court that content validity data revealed that physical abilities distinguish superior firefighters from average ones, whereas cognitive abilities do not. The case law surveyed in this chapter is consistent with the opening statement in the 1987 SIOP Principles that any evidence of what a test measures contributes to its validity, without a priority ranking. From the professional literature and consultation, we know criterion studies for valid predictors can fail due to technical problems. After reading the cases discussed here, I believe an employer with content validity but not criterion validity faces an easier challenge than an employer with criterion validity who cannot explain why a predictive relationship exists.

Case Law and Science

The resolution on content validity proves a disconnect can be connected, but there are other disconnects still waiting for service. In my opinion the most important of these is Justice O'Connor's treatment of the terms *subjective* and *discretionary* as synonyms in *Watson*.

Historically, courts have treated different types of subjective causes as cut from the same cloth. To illustrate, in *Harris* v. *Ford* (1981), Harris was fired for poor performance and asserted that "Ford's subjective decisions" for termination "impact disproportionately on women." In *Talley* v. *U.S. Postal* (1983), a postal worker fired for losing mailbox keys (twice) asserted "subjective decision-making by the primarily white supervisory force has disproportionately affected blacks and females." No applicant flow disparity existed in either case. However, the Harris court offered a totally unnecessary statement that "subjective decision-making" is "outlawed under *Griggs*," the party line in many of these cases.

Consider also culprits in *Watson* and *Wards Cove*. Clara Watson identified causes of adverse impact that the 1987 SIOP Principles view as amenable to psychometric scrutiny (interviews, experience requirements, and appraisals of job performance). In contrast, the *Wards Cove* plaintiffs identified causes that defy psychometric scrutiny (word-of-mouth recruitment, walk-in hiring, nepotism, and "vague subjective selection procedures"). They are also objectionable in relation to the Guidelines because they imply recruitment violations for affirmative action purposes, not selection procedures.

In *Watson* Justice O'Connor surveyed the early case law on subjective causes of adverse impact and referred to them as "subjective or discretionary" causes of adverse impact, thus treating the terms "subjective" and "discretionary" as synonyms. The ninth circuit did likewise in its review of *Wards Cove*. *Black's Law Dictionary* (1990) defines discretionary acts as having "no hard and fast rule as to the course of conduct that one must take or not take," meaning legal scholars also view discretionary and arbitrary acts as one and the same. The Principles have no place for validating arbitrary decisions, but they do articulate how subjective judgments are as readily standardized and validated as objective scores.

Furthermore, in a brief expressing the APA's view in *Watson*, Bersoff (1988) pointed out that subjective tests (or "devices") use the same psychometric procedures for validation as objective tests. The Blackmun plurality accepted this argument, but Justice O'Connor did not, stating that "[s]tandardized tests" can be justified through formal "validation studies" but that "validating" subjective criteria in this way is impracticable." In a nutshell the critical difference between our view and the legal view is that we see that we can standardize and validate any subjective judgments based on evidence of some sort (for example, current and past behaviors), but not discretionary or arbitrary decisions, which require no justification.

Other Disconnects

There are many other disconnects. For example, in *Lanning* v. *Southeastern Pennsylvania Transportation Authority (SEPTA)* (1999) the third circuit took a literal interpretation of *business necessity* when it ruled a test must measure the "minimal qualifications necessary for successful job performance." This contradicts plain statutory language in CRA-91 stating the terms "business necessity" and "job-related" should "reflect the concepts enunciated by the Supreme Court in *Griggs* . . . and in other Supreme Court decisions prior to *Wards Cove*." In essence, it advocates the adverse impact heavy rules from *Dothard*, because that would require a showing that all or most applicants below a cutoff cannot succeed on the job (see also Sharf, 1999). In my opinion the third circuit misconstrued the meaning of "job related and consistent with business necessity," particularly the idea of "consistent with."

Consider also *Bernard* v. *Gulf Oil* (1989), where criterion validity studies emerged with significant correlations with job performance for only two of five jobs. In keeping with the traditions discussed here, the fifth circuit noted that job analysis data revealed "sufficient similarity in the skills required for the various crafts" to support generalization across all five jobs. However, this statement preceded CRA-91, and some (for example, the American Civil Liberties Union) viewed it as an example of the lax standards in *Wards Cove*. More than a decade later this issue is more ambiguous, owing to the emergence in the validity generalization literature of meta-analytic techniques that are controversial in their own right. (Issues relating to validity generalization are discussed by Stan Malos in Chapter Twelve in this volume.)

In summary, connections among case law, regulations, and the state of the art in our field may be viewed as a vibrant but youthful wireless network. Some areas have strong connections (for example, content validity), some have dead spots (for example, subjectivity and discretion and the *Lanning* ruling), and the signals in other places are sometimes weak and sometimes strong (for example, validity generalization).

Conclusion

The most difficult thing in writing about the law is realizing that no sooner is the ink dry than the chapter must be rewritten. Some changes in adverse impact case law have been slow and gradual, as in the series of cases from *Griggs* (1971) through *Connecticut* v. *Teal* (1982) and the surrounding lower court rulings up to *Watson* (1988). Other changes have been relatively rapid, as in the events from *Watson* through CRA-91. The Supreme Court has not ruled on adverse impact since *Wards Cove*, yet we have seen the dawning of a fourth edition of the Principles. Furthermore, even though there is evidence above that some of the Guidelines have grown old and are in need of repair, there is a statement in the Guidelines that "new strategies for showing the validity of selection procedures will be evaluated as they become accepted by the psychological profession."

This book speaks to that statement. However, the fact that this volume's editor traveled far and wide to seek input from lawyers and judges illustrates that science is important but there must also be effective communication with other authorities.

References

Books, Articles, and Government Documents

Barrett, G. V. (1997). An historical perspective on the Nassau County Police entrance examination. *The Industrial-Organizational Psychologist, 35*(2), 42–50.

Bersoff, D. N. (1988). Should subjective employment devices be scrutinized? *American Psychologist, 43,* 1016–1018.

Black, H. C. (1990). *Black's law dictionary* (6th ed.). St. Paul, MN: West.

Bloch, F. (1994). *Antidiscrimination law and minority employment: Recruitment practices and regulatory constraints.* Chicago: University of Chicago Press.

Gutman, A. (2000). *EEO law and personnel practices* (2nd ed.). Thousand Oaks, CA: Sage.

Gutman, A. (2004). Groundrules for adverse impact. *The Industrial-Organizational Psychologist, 41*(3), 109–119.

Sharf, J. (1999). Third circuit's *Lanning* v. *SEPTA* decision: "Business necessity" requires setting minimum standards. *The Industrial-Organizational Psychologist, 37*(2), 138–149.

Society for Industrial and Organizational Psychology. (1987). *Principles for the validation and use of personnel selection procedures* (3rd ed.). College Park, MD: Author.

Uniform Guidelines on Employee Selection Procedures, 29 C.F.R. § 1607 *et seq.* (1978).

Varca, P. E., & Pattison, P. (1993). Evidentiary standards in employment discrimination: A view toward the future. *Personnel Psychology, 46,* 239–258.

Cases

Albemarle Paper Co. v. Moody, 422 U.S. 405 (1975).

Atonio v. Wards Cove Packing Company, 768 F.2d 1120 (1993).

Bernard v. Gulf Oil, 890 F.2d 735 (5th Cir. 1989).

Boyd v. Ozark Airlines, 568 F.2d 50 (8th Cir. 1977).

Bradley v. Pizzaco of Nebraska Inc., 7 F.3d 795 (8th Cir. 1993).

Bridgeport Guardians, Inc. v. City of Bridgeport, 933 F.2d 1140 (2d Cir. 1991).

Brunet v. City of Columbus, 58 F.2d 251 (6th Cir. 1995).

Connecticut v. Teal, 457 U.S. 440 (1982).

Contreras v. Los Angeles, 656 F.2d 1267 (1980).

Davis v. Dallas, 777 F.2d 205 (No. 97-843) (5th Cir. 1985).

Domingo v. New England Fish, 727 F.2d 1429 (9th Cir. 1984).

Dothard v. Rawlinson, 433 U.S. 321 (1977).

EEOC v. Chicago Miniature Lamp Works, 947 F.2d 292 (7th Cir. 1991).

EEOC v. Consolidated Services Systems, 989 F.2d 233 (7th Cir. 1993).

EEOC v. Federal Reserve Bank of Richmond, 732 F. Supp. 72 (4th Cir. 1983).

Fitzpatrick v. City of Atlanta, 2 F.3d 1112 (11th Cir. 1993).

Furnco Construction Corp. v. Waters, 438 U.S. 567 (1978).

Gathercole v. Global, 727 F.2d 485 (9th Cir. 1984).

Gilbert v. City of Little Rock, 722 F.2d 1390 (8th Cir. 1983).

Gillespie v. State of Wisconsin, 771 F.2d 1035 (7th Cir. 1985).

Green v. USX, 843 F.2d 1511 (3d Cir. 1988).

Green v. Washington State, WL 17802 (1997).

Griffen v. Carlin, 755 F.2d 1516 (11th Cir. 1985).

Griggs v. Duke Power Co., 401 U.S. 424 (1971).

Guardians of New York v. Civil Service Commission, 630 F.2d 79 (2d Cir. 1980).

Harris v. Ford Motor Company, 651 F.2d 609 (4th Cir. 1981).

Hazelwood School District v. United States, 433 U.S. 299 (1977).

Hazen v. Biggens, 507 U.S. 604 (1993).

Horace v. Pontiac, 624 F.2d 765 (6th Cir. 1980).

Hyland v. Fukada, 580 F.2d 977 (9th Cir. 1978).

International Brotherhood of Teamsters v. United States, 431 U.S. 324 (1977).

Keating v. FAA, 610 F.2d 611 (9th Cir. 1979).

Lanning v. Southeastern Pennsylvania Transportation Authority, 181 F.3d 478 (3d Cir. 1999).

Lorrance v. AT&T, 109 S. Ct. 2261 (1989).

Martin v. Wilks, 490 U.S. 755 (1989).

McDonnell Douglas Corp. v. Green, 411 U.S. 792 (1973).

New York City v. Beazer, 440 U.S. 568 (1979).

Patterson v. McLean Credit Union, 491 U.S. 164 (1989).

Police Officers for Equal Rights v. City of Columbus, 916 F.2d 1092 (6th Cir. 1990).

Price Waterhouse v. Hopkins, 490 U.S. 228 (1989).

Spaulding v. University of Washington, 740 F.2d 686 (9th Cir. 1984).

Spurlock v. United Airlines, Inc., 475 F.2d 216 (10th Cir. 1972).

Talley v. United States Postal Service, 720 F.2d 505 (8th Cir. 1983).

Texas Department of Community Affairs v. Burdine, 450 U.S. 248 (1981).

Touhy v. Ford, 675 F.2d 842 (6th Cir. 1982).

TWA v. Thurston, 469 U.S. 111 (1985).

United States v. City of Buffalo, 457 F. Supp. 612 (W.D. N.Y. 1978).

United States v. State of New York, 475 F. Supp. 1103 (N.D. N.Y. 1990).

Wards Cove Packing Company v. Atonio, 490 U.S. 642 (1989).

Washington (Mayor, DC) v. Davis, 426 U.S. 229 (1976).

Watson v. Fort Worth Bank and Trust, 487 U.S. 977 (1988).

Williams v. Vukovich, 720 F.2d 909 (6th Cir. 1983).

CHAPTER 3

Professional and Technical Authorities and Guidelines

Richard Jeanneret

There are three sources of authoritative information and guidance that can be relied upon in matters of employment litigation that involve a selection procedure. These sources are the *Standards for Educational and Psychological Testing* (American Educational Research Association, American Psychological Association, & National Council on Measurement in Education, 1999) (*Standards*), the *Principles for the Validation and Use of Personnel Selection Procedures* (Society for Industrial and Organizational Psychology, 2003) (*Principles*), and the *Uniform Guidelines on Employee Selection Procedures* (1978) (*Uniform Guidelines*). The term *selection procedure* in this instance should be interpreted broadly to be inclusive of any process used in personnel decision making. Selection procedures include (but are not limited to) all forms and types of tests (for example, cognitive, personality, work sample, assessment center), job performance appraisals, and estimates of potential. These procedures may be paper-and-pencil or computer-based instruments and may be administered, scored, and interpreted by individuals internal or external to the organization. This broad view is consistent with the interpretations expressed by the authoritative sources. Oftentimes the term *test* is used in one of the sources, and for the purposes of this chapter *test* is synonymous with *selection procedure*.

Purpose, Design, and Application

The purpose of this chapter is to describe the history and substance of each of the three authoritative sources, compare and contrast their technical content, and provide some guidance as to how they might be particularly useful to those directly associated with employment litigation. It is recognized that this chapter is placed early in the book and may provide valuable background information to subsequent and more focused chapters on race, gender, disability, age, and pay discrimination and perhaps those chapters that otherwise address psychometric[1] issues.

Each of the three authoritative sources is discussed separately, in chronological order defined by the date of initial publication. Each discussion begins with the purpose and brief history of the document. Then its content relevant to employment decision making is described. Of course much of this content is technical by necessity, but every attempt is made to describe the material in nontechnical terms. Finally, the three sources are compared in order to examine inconsistencies among them and how these inconsistencies might be resolved.

The *Standards* in particular and the *Principles* perhaps to a lesser extent have potential relevance to settings outside employment litigation, such as forensic, academic, counseling, program evaluation, and publishing venues that involve psychological instruments and measurements. However, these applications are not addressed here, and the focus of this chapter is strictly on organizational settings and employment-related litigation.

Importance of the Authorities

For the most part these authorities are retrospective rather than prospective. By necessity they must rely on the state of knowledge in the fields of measurement and applied psychology. Reality of course is that knowledge changes as research in the field develops more information about the psychometrics of employment selection procedures. Therefore the authoritative sources become outdated and either offer guidance no longer relevant to current times or fail to offer guidance important in current times. Nevertheless there are several reasons why these three authoritative sources are valuable resources that can be relied on by individuals associated with employment litigation:

1. The study of the psychometrics (and particularly the validity) of selection procedures has been taking place for over ninety years. Accordingly, there is a body of knowledge that is stable, well researched, and directly relevant to understanding the measurement properties of a selection procedure. Much of this knowledge is embedded in all three authorities with little, if any, contradiction. Consequently, the authoritative sources are able to provide accurate information about the state of the science that can support the proper development and use of an employment selection procedure.

2. The three documents describe and discuss a number of specific concepts and terms associated with the psychometric qualities of a selection procedure. Although not intended as teaching documents per se, they do frequently summarize bodies of research that are otherwise buried in textbooks and research journal articles.

3. Two of the documents (the *Standards* and the *Principles*) have undergone extensive professional peer review. Although their initial preparation was accomplished by committees of experts in the field, both documents were open for comment by the membership of the American Psychological Association (APA) and, especially in the case of the *Principles*, the document was subject to review by the entire membership of the Society for Industrial and Organizational Psychology (SIOP), a division of the APA. Whereas the *Standards* was authored jointly by three professional organizations, the *Principles* was authored by a committee of SIOP members. Both the *Standards* and the *Principles* were adopted as policy by the APA and hence have formal professional status. Accordingly, there was a much greater level of scrutiny and approval of the scientific content of both the *Standards* and *Principles* than typically occurs for a textbook or journal article.

The *Uniform Guidelines* was authored by the Equal Employment Opportunity Commission (EEOC), the Civil Service Commission (CSC), the Department of Labor (DOL), and the Department of Justice (DOJ). The preparation of the *Uniform Guidelines* also relied on input from a number of individuals with expertise in psychological measurement, but others (for example, attorneys) were also influential in creating the document. Given this complement of authors it is understandable that the document has less psychometric content and more emphasis on the documentation of validity evidence that would be satisfactory in a judicial proceeding. Interestingly, when the *Uniform Guidelines* was under development and when the U.S. House of Representatives was holding hearings on revisions to the *Uniform Guidelines,* both the APA and SIOP submitted information that was for the most part not incorporated into the final document. In 1985, an APA representative gave congressional testimony that there were four technical issues psychologists disagreed about as these topics were addressed in the *Uniform Guidelines:* (1) validity generalization, (2) utility analysis, (3) differential prediction, and (4) validity requirements and their documentation. Similarly, SIOP believed the *Uniform Guidelines* was incorrect with respect to requiring fairness studies, its definition of construct validity, and its consideration of validity generalization and utility analyses (Camara, 1996). Both the EEOC and the DOL Office of Federal Contact Compliance Programs (OFCCP) currently rely on the *Uniform Guidelines* to determine whether or not a selection procedure is discriminatory.

4. For those who are involved in the judicial process (particularly judges and lawyers) the authoritative sources are reference sources additional to case law and other judicial writings. Unfortunately, the actual citation of and apparent use of the three sources is limited, as indicated by the judicial interviews in Chapter Fifteen of this volume and by the frequency analysis of employment cases that cite the authoritative sources presented later in this chapter (Table 3.1).

5. These sources have been relied on by experts in the fields of industrial, organizational, and measurement psychology when formulating opinions about selection procedures. In such instances the authoritative sources have become benchmarks that help define sound professional practice in the employment setting. Concepts such as "equally valid alternative selection procedure" and the "four-fifths" rule have been taken from these authorities and are discussed later in this chapter. In particular the *Uniform Guidelines* provides a specific framework for the validation and use of

selection procedures, and per the issuing federal agencies, requires a user to conduct a validation study if a selection procedure has adverse impact.[2]

Standards for Education and Psychological Testing

Brief History

The *Standards* has a history dating back fifty years. The first edition was titled *Technical Recommendations for Psychological Tests and Diagnostic Techniques* and was authored by a committee of APA members and published in 1954. A sister publication was prepared by a committee comprising members of the American Educational Research Association (AERA) and the National Council on Measurement Used in Education (NCMUE). This document was titled *Technical Recommendations for Achievement Tests* and was published in 1955 by the National Education Association.

In 1966, these two separate documents were revised and combined into a single document, the *Standards for Educational and Psychological Tests and Manuals,* authored by a committee representing APA, AERA, and the National Council on Measurement in Education (NCME). These three organizations have continued to jointly publish various revisions ever since. A revision completed by another joint committee comprising AERA, APA, and NCME members was published in 1974, and the document title was changed to *Standards for Educational and Psychological Tests.* The 1966 document delineated about 160 standards, and this number was increased to over 225 standards in 1974. However, the number of standards declined to about 180 after the 1985 revision. The 1985 document was titled *Standards for Educational and Psychological Testing,* a title retained for the 1999 revision.

In 1991, the APA began an initiative to revise the 1985 *Standards.* In 1993, a joint AERA, APA, and NCME committee was formed, and after six years of effort a final document was published. It incorporates 264 standards and has been adopted as APA policy. The *Standards* is intended to be proscriptive but does not have any associated enforcement mechanisms. More so than with past versions, the 1999 *Standards* devotes considerable attention to fairness; testing individuals with disabilities; scales, norms, and score comparability; reliability; and the responsibilities of test users.

Application

The 1999 *Standards* is applicable to the entire domain of educational and psychological measurement. In fact one chapter is devoted completely to educational testing and assessment. Because the *Standards* provides a comprehensive wealth of information on psychological measurement, it is not possible to adequately discuss this document in its entirety. Consequently, this review will focus on those components of the *Standards* most applicable to psychometric issues in employment settings.

Purpose of the *Standards*

As stated in the document introduction, "The intent of the *Standards* is to promote the sound and ethical use of tests and to provide a basis for evaluating the quality of testing practices" (p. 1). It is further emphasized that the evaluation of a test or its application should rely heavily on professional judgment and that the *Standards* provides a set of references or benchmarks to support the evaluation process. Finally, the *Standards* is not intended to respond to public policy questions that are raised about testing; rather the psychometric information embedded in the *Standards* may be very useful for informing those involved in debates and decisions about testing from a public policy perspective.

This said, it is also reasonable for the *Standards* to have some role in the judicial processes concerned with the use of selection procedures and associated matters of employment discrimination. This is so because the *Standards* preceded and was the foundation for both the *Uniform Guidelines* and the *Principles*.

Validity Defined

Key terms that will be appearing throughout both this chapter and other chapters are *validity* and its derivatives (for example, *validation process*). It is appropriate to introduce the basic term now because the *Standards* has established the most current thinking regarding validity and provides the definition that should be accepted by all professionals concerned with the psychometrics of a selection procedure.

According to the *Standards:* "Validity refers to the degree to which evidence and theory support the interpretations of test scores entailed by proposed uses of tests. Validity is, therefore, the most fundamental consideration in developing and evaluating tests. The process of validation involves accumulating evidence to provide a sound scientific basis for the proposed score interpretation of test scores required by proposed uses that are evaluated, not the test itself. When test scores are used or interpreted in more than one way, each intended interpretation must be validated" (p. 9).

Validity is a unitary concept and can be considered an argument based on scientific evidence that supports the intended interpretation of a selection procedure score (Binning & Barrett, 1989; Cronbach & Meehl, 1955; McDonald, 1999; Messick, 1980, 1989; Wainer & Braun, 1988). Twenty-four specific standards regarding validity are incorporated in the 1999 document.

Generally speaking, if a test does not have validity for a particular purpose, it will also not have utility. *Utility* is an estimate of the gain in productivity or other practical value that might be achieved by use of a selection procedure. Several measures are used to estimate utility, including reduced accidents, savings in employee costs, reduction in time to complete a task, reduction in turnover, training success, and increases in job proficiency (Cascio, 2000; Cronbach & Gleser, 1965; Hunter & Hunter, 1984; Naylor & Shine, 1965; Schmidt, Hunter, McKenzie, & Muldrow, 1979). Consequently, it would be unusual for an organization to want to use a test that lacks both validity and utility. Furthermore, if a test lacks validity it is possible that some unintended consequence might result from its use. Thus reliance on test scores that are not valid will not yield results intended by the selection process and may in fact yield outcomes detrimental to the organization.

Application to Litigation

Of the three authoritative sources, the *Standards* offers the greatest amount of detail regarding the psychometric properties and use of selection procedures. Terms are clearly defined; all standards are not necessarily equally important in a given situation, but no attempt is made to categorize some standards as "primary" and others as "secondary," as occurred in earlier versions; an entire chapter that incorporates twelve standards is focused on fairness; another chapter devotes thirteen standards to the rights and responsibilities of test takers; and still another chapter is focused on testing individuals with diverse linguistic backgrounds (eleven standards). The level of description is oftentimes less precise in the *Principles* and *Uniform Guidelines*.

The differences in the scientific rigor and level of detail reflected in the three authoritative sources do not, however, influence their frequency of use in employment litigation. A search of Lexis-Nexis U.S. district court civil cases involving employment actions filed under labor law statutes over a ten-year period revealed the data presented in Table 3.1.

Table 3.1. Frequency of Civil Rights Cases Commenced and of Citations to the Uniform Guidelines, Principles, and Standards, 1994–2004.

Civil Rights Cases		Uniform Guidelines	Principles	Standards
2004	NA	2	—	—
2003	NA	33	2	1
2002	NA	34	—	—
2001	21,121	40	—	2
2000	21,404	52	2	2
1999	22,948	63	—	2
1998	23,804	65	1	—
1997	23,707	92	1	1
1996	22,150	53	1	1
1995	18,225	45	1	1
1994	15,256	43	—	—

Source: Data from Lexis-Nexis. The number of cases for the years 2002–2004 was not reported at the time of the search.

First, it is obvious that the large majority of cases do not cite any one of the three sources. (It is noted in Frank Landy's interviews with Judges Baer and Graham in Chapter Fifteen of this book that if the attorneys do not introduce one or more of the authoritative sources, the judges do not rely on those sources.)

Second, the *Uniform Guidelines* received the largest number of citations by a considerable amount. In fact it is rare for either the *Principles* or *Standards* to be cited. Consequently, it seems that the role that any of the three sources and particularly the *Principles* and *Standards* has played in case law is minimal.

Cautions Offered by the *Standards*

The *Standards* sets forth five cautions intended to prevent misinterpretations:

1. Evaluation of a selection procedure is not just a matter of checking off (or not) one standard after another to determine compliance. Rather the evaluation process must consider (1) professional judgment, (2) satisfaction of the intent of a relevant standard, (3) alternate selection procedures that are readily available, and (4) the feasibility of complying with the standard given past experience and research knowledge.
2. The *Standards* offers guidance to the expert in a legal proceeding but professional judgment determines the relevance of a standard to the situation.
3. Blanket statements about conformance with the *Standards* should not be made without supporting evidence, and care should be exercised in any other assertions about compliance with the *Standards.*
4. Research is ongoing and knowledge in the field will continue to change. The *Standards* will need to be revised in time.
5. The *Standards* is not intended to mandate use of specific methodologies. The alternative use of a "generally accepted equivalent" is always understood with regard to any method provided in the *Standards.*

Sources of Validity Evidence

There are multiple ways in which validity evidence might be assembled for a selection procedure, and no one method is necessarily superior to another. Rather the validation strategy should be consistent with the nature and intended use of the selection procedure.

Here, briefly described, are the five validation strategies or sources of validity evidence set forth in the *Standards:*

1. *Content.* This evidence is based on an analysis of the relationship between the content of a selection procedure and the construct it is intended to measure. This construct is typically an important job requirement (knowledge, skill, ability, other characteristic), job behavior, or job performance (for example, task or duty). Often reference is made in employment settings to the job content domain. The analysis can be completed using either empirical findings or logical judgments made by subject matter experts (SMEs). The analysis should be appropriate to the intended purpose and to the inference to be drawn from the selection procedure.

2. *Internal structure.* Empirical analysis (for example, factor analysis, differential item functioning) of the internal structure of a selection procedure can provide evidence about the extent to which the relationships between test items conform to the construct that is the foundation for test score interpretations (McDonald, 1999). For example, a test may be expected to measure a single construct (such as numerical ability) or several constructs (such as five different dimensions of personality). The extent to which the test item relationships conform to the hypothesized dimensionality is evidence of validity. Another aspect of internal structure is the extent to which test items function differently for different subgroups of applicants (differential item functioning). Typically, the expectation is that there will be no differential item functioning (Sackett, Schmitt, Ellingson, & Kabin, 2001).

3. *Response processes.* Studying the processes followed by individuals in responding to a selection procedure can provide validity evidence about the fit between the construct being measured and the behavior actually engaged in by respondents. For

example, if a work sample test is given to select applicants for an electronics technician job, the examiner may want to know not only whether the candidate ultimately identified the correct solution but also what analytical processes he or she used to find the solution.

4. *Consequences of testing.* This is probably the most recent source of validity evidence to be addressed in the literature on selection procedures. The question being asked is whether or not the specific benefits expected from the use of a selection procedure are being realized and whether there are other consequences that are not expected or desired. In the employment context an unintended consequence might be differential pass rates for various subgroups of job candidates. This alone does not detract from the validity of test score interpretations. Only if the subgroup differences can be linked to a specific source of bias or contamination in the selection procedure will the negative consequences detract from the validity of score interpretations. Said differently, if the selection procedure is assessing an important skill underlying job performance, and any subgroup differences are attributed to unequal distributions of that skill in the applicant pool, then the observation of those differences does not undermine the validity of the inferences drawn from the selection procedure. The *Standards* is very clear on this point and explicitly states that there is a difference between issues of psychometric validity and issues of social policy and that the *Standards* is addressing only validity. (Messick, 1980, 1989).

5. *Relations to other variables.* This source of evidence has typically been labeled *criterion-related validity.* However, it also includes what was once called *construct validity.* It is based on the empirical relationship(s) between scores on a selection procedure and some external variable(s). The relationship between a test and a measure of job performance is called *criterion-related validity evidence.* The relationship between a selection procedure and some other measure(s) of the same or different construct(s) has been labeled construct validity in the past. The essential point is that one or more empirical relationships are established between a selection procedure of interest and one or more external variables, a hypothesis is set forth as to the

nature of the relationship, and this hypothesis is tested using appropriate statistical methods. Criterion-related validity evidence can be collected in two ways: concurrently and predictively. In a *concurrent* study both the selection procedure scores and the measurement(s) of the criterion (or criteria) are obtained at the same time (concurrently) for an incumbent group. The data are then analyzed to determine the accuracy with which the selection procedure scores predict criterion performance. In a *predictive* criterion-related validity study, selection procedure scores are obtained but not used in decision making for an applicant group. Some portion of the applicants is hired, and at some later point (usually at least six months later) the criterion measure is obtained and the accuracy of the selection procedure is evaluated. Generally, concurrent and predictive studies reach the same conclusions about the validity of inferences from selection procedure scores, at least for cognitive ability measures (Barrett, Phillips, & Alexander, 1981; Bemis, 1968; Pearlman, Schmidt, & Hunter, 1980).

The *Standards* sets forth five sources of validity evidence, as just discussed; however, the evidence based on relations to other variables is further explained in terms of two strategies that can be used to understand those relationships: convergent and discriminant validity and validity generalization. These two strategies are briefly discussed next:

Convergent and discriminant validity. When selection scores and other measures of the same or similar constructs are correlated, this is *convergent* validity evidence. When selection procedure scores are not correlated to measures of different constructs, this is evidence of *discriminant* validity (Campbell & Fiske, 1959; McDonald, 1999). Although both types of evidence are useful, studies more frequently examine convergent validity. In the typical criterion-related validity study, for example, the relationship between a cognitive selection procedure and a measure of job performance (such as decision making) is purportedly concerned with the same or very similar constructs (that is, convergent validity). However, if a selection procedure comprised a cognitive measure and a test of interpersonal skills and there were two job performance indices (decision making and teamwork), the lack of relationship (or low relationship) between the cognitive measure and teamwork (or the low correlation between the interpersonal skills test and decision making) would provide discriminant evidence. Both convergent and discriminant evidence can be equally valuable.

Validity generalization. The issue at hand here is whether or not validity evidence obtained in one situation can be generalized to a new situation without further study of the validity of the procedure in the new setting. When criterion-related validity evidence has been accumulated for a selection procedure, meta-analysis has been a statistical method useful for studying the validity generalization question. There are numerous methodological and statistical issues associated with meta-analytic studies, and these matters are too lengthy to be addressed here. The interested reader is referred to Hunter and Schmidt (1990) or Rosenthal (1991).

Integrating Validity Evidence

A comprehensive and sound validity argument is made by assembling the available evidence indicating that interpretations of scores from a well-developed selection procedure can accurately predict the criterion of interest. Although the various sources of validity evidence discussed above are directly relevant, there are many other valuable information sources, including prior research; reliability indices; information on scoring, scaling, norming, and equating data; standard settings (for example, cut scores); and fairness information. All of these information sources, when available, contribute to the final validity argument and decision on the use of a selection procedure.

Validity Standards

There are twenty-four specific standards presented in the validity chapter of the *Standards.* Although all twenty-four are important, certain themes are particularly relevant in the context of employment litigation. A brief summary of these themes follows:

• The rationale for and intended interpretation for selection procedure scores should be set forth at the outset of a validity study. When new interpretations or intended uses are contemplated, they should be supported by new validity evidence.

- Descriptions of individuals participating in validation studies should be as detailed as is practical. When subject matter experts are used, their qualifications should be documented, as should the procedures they followed in developing validation evidence.
- When criterion-related validity studies are completed, information about the quality and relevance of the criterion should be reported.
- When several variables are predicting a criterion, multiple regression should be used to evaluate increments in the predictive accuracy achieved by each variable. Results from the analyses of multiple variables should be verified by cross-validation whenever feasible.
- When statistical adjustments (such as the correction of correlations for restriction in range) are made, the unadjusted and adjusted correlations and the procedures followed in making the adjustments should be documented.
- When meta-analyses are relied on as criterion-related validity evidence, the comparability between the meta-analytic variables (predictors and criteria) and the specific situation of interest should be determined to support the applicability of the meta-analytic findings to the local setting. All assumptions and procedures for conducting the meta-analytic study should be reported and clearly described.

Reliability and Measurement Errors

Chapter Two of the *Standards* describes reliability and errors of measurement and sets forth twenty standards on this topic. The chapter is concerned with understanding the degree to which a selection procedure score is free from error. To the degree to which a score is contaminated, it is due to errors of measurement that are usually assumed to be unpredictable and random in occurrence. There are two sources of error: (1) within individuals subject to the selection procedure and (2) in the conditions external to the individuals, such as problems in the testing environment or mistakes in scoring the selection procedure.

Reliability is an index indicating the degree to which selection procedure scores are measured consistently across one or more sources of error such as time, test forms, or administrative settings.

Reliability has an impact on validity in that to the extent the selection procedure is not reliable, it will be more difficult to make accurate predictions from the selection procedure scores. Excellent treatments of reliability may be found in McDonald (1999), Nunnally and Bernstein (1994), Pedhazur and Schmelkin (1991), and Traub (1994).

The reliability chapter of the *Standards* develops many of the basic concepts embedded in reliability theory. It is important to note that no single index of reliability exists that measures all the variables that influence the accuracy of measurement. The two major theoretical positions regarding the meaning of reliability are classical reliability theory and generalizability theory. Under classical reliability theory a test score is made up of two components: a true score and error. Hypothetically, a true score can be obtained through numerous repeated applications of the same test and a calculation of the average score. The comparable concept under generalizability theory is a universe score. The hypothetical difference between an observed score and a universe score is measurement error, which is random and unpredictable. A generalizability coefficient is similar to a reliability coefficient in that both are defined as the ratio of true (or universe) score variance to observed score variance. The major difference is that using analysis of variance techniques, generalizability theory provides for the partitioning of variance as universe score variance, error variance, and observed score variance.

What is important is that the method used to determine reliability be appropriate to the data and setting at hand and that all procedures be clearly reported. Furthermore, various reliability indices (for example, test-retest, internal consistency) are not equivalent and should not be interpreted as being interchangeable. Finally, the reliability of selection procedure scoring by examiners does not imply high candidate consistency in responding to one item versus the next item that is embedded in a selection procedure. In other words, the finding that the scoring of a test is reliable does not mean that the test itself is reliable.

Standards in Employment and Credentialing

Chapter Fourteen of the *Standards* is devoted to testing used in employment, licensure, and certification. In the employment setting, tests are most frequently used for selection, placement, and promotion.

There are seventeen standards set forth in Chapter Fourteen. They address the collection and interpretation of validity evidence, the use of selection procedure scores, and the importance of reliability information regarding selection procedure scores. The chapter's introduction emphasizes that the contents of many other chapters in the *Standards* are also relevant to employment testing. One point of emphasis in Chapter Fourteen is the influence of context on the use of a selection procedure. Nine contextual features are identified (pp. 151–153); their labels are self-explanatory:

- Internal versus external candidate pool
- Untrained versus specialized jobs
- Short-term versus long-term focus
- Screen-in versus screen-out
- Mechanical versus judgmental decision making
- Ongoing versus one-time test use
- Fixed applicant pool versus continuous flow
- Small versus large sample size
- Size of applicant pool, relative to number of job openings

The *Standards* emphasizes that the validation process in employment settings is usually grounded in only two of the five sources of validity evidence: relations to other variables and content. One or both types of evidence can be used to evaluate how well a selection procedure (predictor-measure or -construct domain) predicts a relevant outcome (criterion-measure or -construct domain). However, there is no methodological preference or more correct method of establishing validity; rather the selection situation and professional judgment should be the determiners of the appropriate source(s) of evidence.

Evaluating Validity Evidence

Perfect prediction does not occur, and the evaluation of validity evidence is often completed on a comparative basis (for example, how an observed validity coefficient compares to coefficients reported in the literature for the same or similar constructs). Consideration may be given to available and valid alternative selection procedures, utility, concerns about applicant reactions, social issues, and organizational values. Any or all of these considerations could influence the final conclusions drawn about the validity evidence as well as the implementation of the selection procedure.

Professional and Occupational Credentialing

The *Standards* also addresses in Chapter Fourteen the specific instance of credentialing or licensing procedures that are intended to confirm that individuals (for example, medical doctors, nuclear power plant operators) possess the relevant knowledge or skills to the degree that they can safely and effectively perform certain important occupational activities. The credentialing or licensing procedures are intended to be strict in order to provide the public as well as governmental and regulatory agencies with sound information regarding the capabilities of practitioners. The procedures are designed to have a gatekeeping role and often include a written examination as well as other specific qualifications (for example, education, supervised experience). Content validity evidence is usually obtained to support the use of the credentialing procedures, because criterion information is generally not available. Establishing a cut score is a critical component of the validation process, and the cut score is usually determined by subject matter experts. Arbitrary passing scores (such as 70 percent correct) typically are not very useful and may not be related to the level of credentialing procedure success equivalent to acceptable job performance and the assurance that there will be no resultant harm to the public.

Review of the Seventeen Standards in Chapter Fourteen

The present chapter will not discuss all seventeen standards in detail; however, certain standards deserve some emphasis because they bear directly on issues that have emerged in employment-related litigation. A brief discussion of these standards follows:

- The objective of the employment selection procedure should be set forth, and an indication of how well that objective has been met should be determined.

- Decisions regarding the conduct of validation studies should take into consideration prior relevant research, technical feasibility, and the conditions that could influence prior and contemplated validation efforts.
- The representativeness of any criterion used (such as important work behaviors, work output, or job-relevant training) should be documented.
- Inference about the content validity of a selection procedure for use in a new situation is only appropriate when "critical job content factors are substantially the same (as is determined by a job analysis), the reading level of the test material does not exceed that appropriate for the new job, and there are no discernable features of the new situation that would substantially change the original meaning of the test material" (p. 160).
- When multiple items of information about an employment process are available to decision makers, the use of each informational component should be supported by validity evidence. Furthermore the role played by each component as it is integrated into a final decision should be clearly explained. In credentialing situations, the rules and procedures followed when combining scores from multiple information sources should be available to candidates.
- Cut scores for credentialing tests should be determined on the basis of the skill or knowledge level necessary for acceptable job performance and not on the basis of the number or proportion of candidates passing.

Fairness

For the first time an entire chapter in the *Standards* has been devoted to fairness. The 1985 edition offered no standards related to fairness; the 1999 edition presents considerable background information plus twelve standards devoted to the topic. *Fairness* is defined in the *Standards* as "the principle that every test taker should be assessed in an equitable way" (p. 175). There are a number of viewpoints as to exactly what fairness means, and several of these perspectives are addressed in this chapter, as follows:

- The requirement that the overall passing rates be comparable or equal across groups is not a definition that is accepted in the professional literature.
- There is agreement that equality of treatment for all candidates is mandatory and one acceptable definition of fairness.
- The absence of bias in the test instrument itself or in how it is used is also an acceptable definition of fairness.
- The fourth definition discussed in the *Standards* gives consideration to the opportunity to learn the material assessed by a test and is specific to educational achievement testing.

In employment testing the issue of fairness is typically addressed by a statistical examination of test results for evidence of bias. It is not simply a matter of whether or not test score averages differ by majority and minority groups but of whether or not there are differences in test score predictions by subgroup. If the predictions are equivalent (that is, finding no difference in the slopes or intercepts), then there is no bias. Another statistical perspective is that of *differential item functioning* (DIF). In this instance, if there is bias, candidates of equal ability differ in their responses to a specific item according to their group membership. Unfortunately, the underlying reason for DIF, when it has been observed, has not been detected; oftentimes items work in the favor of one group relative to another for no explainable reason such as item content. Use of sensitivity review panels comprising individuals representative of the subgroups of interest has been one mechanism intended to prevent item content from being relevant for one group but not another. Thus members of the review panel would be expected to flag items potentially unfair to a subgroup. However, there has not been research evidence indicating that sensitivity review panels find a great deal to alter in test item content.

Selection Procedure Development and Administration

Chapters Three, Four, Five, and Six in the *Standards* are concerned with the development, implementation, and documentation of selection procedures. For the most part the discussions and standards are very technical and will not be reviewed in this text.

However, a couple of topics especially relevant to employment litigation will be mentioned:

- A cut score is used to partition candidates into two groups; one passing or successful and the other not passing or not successful. There is no single or best method for setting a cut score. Further, because selection procedures are not perfect, there will be errors—some candidates will pass who do not have adequate skills (false positives), and some will fail when they do have adequate skills (false negatives). Changing a cut score to correct for one concern will increase the occurrence of the other. Thus professional judgment always must be considered in setting a cut score.
- Normative data should be clearly documented in terms of demographics, sampling procedures, descriptive statistics, and the precision of the norms.
- The psychometric characteristics of different forms of the same test should be clearly documented, and the rationale for any claim of equivalency in using test scores from different test forms must be reported.
- Standardization in the administration procedures is extremely important, and all instructions should be clear.
- Selection procedures and results (including individual scores) should be treated as confidential and kept in a secure manner.
- Documentation for a selection procedure typically includes information about intended purpose, prior research evidence, and the development process and technical information about validity, reliability, fairness, score interpretation, scaling or norming, if appropriate, administration, and use of the results (for example, pass-fail).

Rights and Responsibilities

Four chapters in the *Standards* discuss such matters as test-user and test-taker rights and responsibilities, testing individuals with diverse linguistic backgrounds, and assessing individuals with disabilities. The standards set forth in these chapters are concerned with policy and administrative issues for the most part. Generally, these matters become more relevant in specialized circumstances (for example, when an applicant with a verified disability needs an accommodation to a selection procedure). Professional judgment is often required because of the individualized conditions.

Summary

The 1999 *Standards* reflects the state of the science and the most current professional knowledge available regarding psychological testing. Revised in the past, the *Standards* will need to be revised again in the future. Nevertheless, the *Standards* is extremely informative about the requirements associated with the development and application of a selection procedure in an employment setting. The document has been published in order to promote the professionally sound and ethical use of selection procedures and to provide a set of standards that can be the basis for evaluating the quality of a selection procedure and practice. The *Standards* sets forth a frame of reference for use in employment litigation but makes no attempt to answer public policy questions regarding the use of selection procedures.

Principles for the Validation and Use of Personnel Selection Procedures

Brief History

The first edition of the *Principles* was published in 1975 in response to a growing concern about the need for professional standards for validation research identified by the leadership of Division 14 of the American Psychological Association. Furthermore, because early versions of what became the *Uniform Guidelines* were being prepared by various governmental organizations, Division 14 representatives wanted to set forth the perspective of industrial and organizational psychology, particularly with regard to validation studies. The second edition was published five years later and for the first and only time cited specific references regarding equal employment opportunity and associated litigation. Because of continuing changes in employment case law, subsequent editions have not attempted to stay current with them. Further, it has not been the purpose of the *Principles* to interpret these cases in terms of the science of industrial and organizational psychology.

In 1987, the third edition of the *Principles* was published by the Society for Industrial and Organizational Psychology (SIOP).[3] This edition consisted of thirty-six pages of text and sixty-four citations to published research to support the various principles contained in the document. An appended glossary defined seventy-six terms used in the *Principles*.

The fourth edition of the *Principles* was published by SIOP and adopted as policy by the APA in 2003. This edition consists of forty-five pages of text and a glossary of 126 terms. There are sixty-five research literature citations that support the scientific findings and professional practices that underlie the principles for conducting validation research and using selection procedures in the employment setting. The increase in glossary terms reflects some of the more recent scientific findings or thinking related to such topics as generalized evidence of validity, work analysis, internal structure validity evidence, models of reliability and fairness, and test development and implementation.

Purpose of the *Principles*

The *Principles* was revised in 2003 to maintain consistency with the 1999 *Standards,* especially with respect to the concept of validity and the understanding of fairness and bias. The *Principles* does not attempt to interpret federal, state, or local statutes, regulations, or case law related to matters of employment discrimination. However, the *Principles* expects to inform decision making in employment litigation and offers both technical and professional guidance that can help others (judges, lawyers, experts) understand and reach conclusions about the validation and use of employment selection processes.

The *Principles* establishes ideals and sets forth expectations for both the validation process and the professional administration of selection procedures. The document also can inform those responsible for authorizing the implementation of a validation study or selection procedure program. Finally, the *Principles* is a valuable resource for those who assess the adequacy and appropriateness of an employee selection process, including those who might be involved in resolving matters of litigation. Given these various capabilities, the *Principles* gives both technical and informative guidance to a diverse audience.

The *Principles* Versus the *Standards*

The *Principles* was revised in 2003 with the full understanding that the document would be consistent with the *Standards*. This is especially true with regard to the psychometric topics of validity, reliability, and bias. Both documents are grounded in research and express a consensus of professional opinion regarding knowledge and practice in personnel selection. However, there are also some important differences between the two documents.

First, unlike the *Standards*, the *Principles* does not enumerate a list of specific principles in the same manner as the *Standards* sets forth 264 standards. Consequently, the *Principles* is more aspirational and facilitative in content, and the *Standards* is more authoritative.

Second, the *Standards* is much broader than the *Principles* with respect to psychological measurement. For example, although many of the concepts expressed in the *Principles* could be relevant to the field of educational testing, the *Standards* directly addresses that topic. The same is true for such topics as testing in program evaluation and public policy.

Third, the *Standards* gives somewhat more attention to the rights and responsibilities of test takers, whereas the *Principles* focuses more on the responsibilities of selection procedure users. This is no doubt at least partially due to the fact that the *Principles* places most of the responsibility for proper selection processes on the employer rather than the candidate, whereas the *Standards* considers a much wider group of test takers, including students, patients, and counselors as well as applicants. These test takers oftentimes have reason (and the right) to know more about the nature of a test, the intended use of the test score, and the confidentiality of results in order to determine whether or not they should even take a test and to evaluate the consequences of not taking a test. Reporting of test score information is also an important issue in the *Standards;* individuals should be labeled in the least stigmatizing way, which is of particular concern in educational and clinical settings.

Finally, the *Principles* provides more guidance on how to plan a validation effort and collect validity evidence within the context of an employment setting. Consequently, it offers more discussion of such topics as feasibility of a validation study; strategies for collecting information about the work and work requirements (for example, work analysis) and about job applicants or incumbents and their capabilities; the analysis of data, including such topics as multiple hurdles versus compensatory models, cutoff scores, rank orders, and banding; and information to be included in an administrative guide for selection procedure users.

Application to Litigation

The *Principles* offers the most up-to-date and relevant information and guidance regarding personnel selection procedures that might be the subject of litigation. Although the document is not written in absolute terms, it provides a wealth of information that defines best practices in both the validation and implementation processes required to properly use a selection procedure. When examining the qualities of a validation study or the implementation of a selection procedure, a decision maker in litigation proceedings might find that one or more expectations set forth in the *Principles* were not met and ask why. Sound and logical explanations might be forthcoming; if not, then the unexplained issues could be strong indicators that the processes being scrutinized were not established in accord with accepted professional expectations.

The Analysis of Work

Given that the *Principles* is focused on selection procedures in the employment setting, there is a particular emphasis on the analysis of work. Such an analysis establishes the foundation for collecting validity evidence. More specifically, information from the analysis of work defines relevant worker requirements and determines the knowledge, skills, abilities, and other characteristics (KSAOs) needed by a worker to successfully perform in a work setting. Second, the work analysis defines the criterion measures that, when appropriate for the validation strategy being used, indicate when employees have successfully accomplished relevant work objectives and organizational goals.

Historically, the analysis of work was labeled *job analysis,* and that term is still frequently used. The *Principles* expanded the term to the analysis of work to give clear recognition to the realization that the concept of a traditional job is changing. Furthermore, the "analysis" should incorporate the collection of data about the workers, the organization, and the work environment as well as about the specific job or some future job if that is relevant to the study. As implied by the variety of permutations that might be appropriate, there is no one preferred method or universal approach that is appropriate for completing an analysis of work.

The *Principles* encourages the development of a strategy and a sampling plan to guide an analysis of work. Further, the work analysis should be conducted at a level of detail consistent with the intended use and availability of the work information. Any method used and outcomes obtained should be well documented in a written report.

Validation

The *Principles* adopts the same definition of validity as given in the *Standards*. Validity is a unitary construct, and different sources of evidence can contribute to the degree to which there is scientific support for the interpretation of selection procedure scores for their proposed purpose. If a selection procedure is found to yield interpretations that are valid, it can be said to be job related. The *Principles* recognizes the five sources of evidence discussed in the *Standards*. However, the *Principles* also recognizes that two sources of evidence—criterion-related and content—are most frequently relied on in the employment context.

The *Principles* emphasizes several issues related to obtaining criterion-related validity evidence:

- *Feasibility:* Is it technically feasible to conduct the study in terms of measures, sample sizes, and other factors that might unduly influence the outcomes?
- *Design:* Is a concurrent or predictive design most appropriate?
- *Criterion:* Is the criterion relevant, sufficient, uncontaminated, and reliable?
- *Construct equivalence:* Is the predictor measuring the construct that underlies the criterion?
- *Predictor:* Is the selection procedure theoretically sound, uncontaminated, and reliable?

- *Participants:* Is the sample of individuals in the study representative, and will it support the generalization of results?
- *Analyses:* Are analytical methods appropriate for the data collected?
- *Strength of relationships:* What effect size and statistical significance or confidence intervals were hypothesized and observed?
- *Adjustments:* What adjustments are necessary given that uncorrected observed validity relationships typically underestimate the predictor-criterion relationship? It may be appropriate to adjust for restriction in range and unreliability in the criterion.
- *Combining predictors and criteria:* How are predictor and criteria scores weighted if combined?
- *Cross-validation:* Should the estimates of validity be cross-validated in order to avoid capitalization on chance? Typically, when regression analyses are used and the sample is small, adjustments should be made using a shrinkage formula or a cross-validation design.
- *Interpretation:* Are the results observed consistent with theory and past research findings?

Similarly, the *Principles* emphasizes several issues related to obtaining content validity evidence:

- *Feasibility:* Are job-determinant conditions (for example, whether or not work is stable or constantly changing), worker-related variables (for example, whether or not past experiences are still relevant for the current work), or contextual matters (for example, whether or not work conditions are extremely different from the testing environment) that might influence the outcome of the validity study under sufficient control so as not to contaminate the study?
- *Design:* Has an adequate sample of important work behaviors or worker KSAOs been obtained and analyzed?
- *Content domain:* Has the work content domain been accurately and thoroughly defined and linked to the selection procedure?
- *Selection procedure:* Does the selection procedure adequately represent the work content domain? The fidelity of this relationship is the basis for the validity inference.

- *Sampling:* Is there a sound rationale for the sampling of the work content domain?
- *Specificity:* Has the level of specificity necessary in the work analysis and selection procedure been described in advance?
- *Administrative procedures:* Have adequate guidelines been established for administering and scoring the selection procedure?

In addition there is the issue of internal structure validity evidence. The *Principles* points out that evidence based on the structure of a selection procedure is not sufficient alone to establish the validity of the procedure for predicting future work performance or other work-related behaviors (for example, attendance or turnover). However, consideration of the internal structure can be very helpful during the design of a selection procedure.

Generalizing Validity Evidence

In comparison to the *Standards,* the *Principles* provides considerably more detail about the generalization of validity evidence. There are at least three strategies for generalizing evidence, known as transportability, synthetic validity/job component validity, and meta-analysis. The *Standards* discusses meta-analysis in some detail but not the other two strategies.

Transportability. This line of evidence refers to relying on existing validity evidence to support the use of a selection procedure in a very similar but new situation. The important considerations underlying the transport argument are work or job comparability in terms of content and requirements. Similarity in work context and candidate groups may also be relevant.

Synthetic/job component validity. This type of generalization relies on the demonstrated validity of selection procedure scores for one or more domains or components of work. The work domains or components may be within a job or across different jobs. If a sound relationship between a selection procedure and a work component has been established for one or more jobs, then the validity of the procedure can be generalized to another job that has a comparable component. As in the transportability argument, establishing the comparability of work content on the basis of comprehensive information is essential to the synthetic/job component validity process.

Meta-analysis. The information on meta-analysis in the *Standards* and in the *Principles* is very similar. Both documents point out that meta-analytic findings may be useful but not sufficient to reach a conclusion about the use of a selection procedure in a specific situation. Instead, a local validation study may be more appropriate. Both sources also emphasize that professional judgment is necessary to evaluate the quality of the meta-analytic findings and their relevance to the specific situation of interest. The general conclusion in the *Principles* is that meta-analytic findings for cognitive tests indicate that much of the difference in validity coefficients found from one study to the next can be attributed to statistical artifacts and sampling error (Callender & Osburn, 1981; Hartigan & Wigdor, 1989; Hunter & Hunter, 1984), and similar but not conclusive evidence is occurring for noncognitive measures (Barrick & Mount, 1991; Barrick, Mount, & Judge, 2001).

Fairness and Bias

As presented in the *Standards,* the topics of fairness and bias are also prominent in the *Principles.* The *Principles* endorses the definitions and positions taken by the *Standards.* Further, the *Principles* is somewhat more precise than the *Standards* in defining predictive bias versus measurement bias.

Predictive bias. An alternative term for predictive bias is *differential prediction,* but in any case, bias has occurred if consistent, nonzero errors of prediction are made for individuals in a particular subgroup. Multiple regression is the typical method used to assess predictive bias, which is indicated when slope or intercept differences are observed in the model. Research on cognitive ability measures has typically supported the conclusion that there is no predictive bias for African American or Hispanic groups relative to whites and that when predictive differences are observed they indicate overprediction of the performance of the minority group. It is also important to note that there can be mean score differences on a selection procedure for minority versus majority subgroups but no predictive bias.

Measurement bias. This form of bias is associated with one or more irrelevant sources of variance contaminating either a predictor or criterion measure. There are no well-established approaches to assessing measurement bias, as is the case for predictive bias. However, differential item functioning (DIF) and item sensitivity analyses are suggested as options in the *Principles*, although exercising considerable caution about the value of such analyses is also mentioned. As noted by Sackett, Schmitt, Ellingson, and Kabin (2001), the research results indicate that item effect is often very small and there is no consistent pattern of items that favors one group of individuals relative to another group.

Operational Considerations

Almost one-half of the *Principles* is devoted to operational considerations. The issues discussed are related to initiating and designing a validation effort; work analysis; selecting predictors, a validation strategy, and criterion measures; collecting data and performing analyses; implementing; preparing recommendations and reports (technical and administrative); and recognizing other circumstances that may influence the validation effort (for example, organizational changes, candidates with disabilities, and responsibilities of selection procedure developers, researchers, and users).

A few of the topics discussed in the operational considerations section of the *Principles* could be critical issues in employment litigation:

Combining selection procedures. When selection procedure scores are combined in some manner, the validity of the inferences derived from the composite is most important. In other words, it is not sufficient to simply report the validity index for each procedure as a stand-alone predictor; rather an index of validity should be reported for the combined selection procedure score that is used for decision making.

Multiple hurdle versus compensatory models. There is no definitive guidance as to which model is most appropriate; rather, each situation must be evaluated on its own merits. It is important to realize that combining scores into a compensatory sum may affect the overall reliability and validity of the process. When multiple predictors (with different reliabilities and validities) are combined into a single weighted composite score, the result produces a single-stage selection decision. The psychometric characteristics of the compensatory selection procedure score will reflect how each predictor has been weighted, and the final reliability and validity indices may be lower than if used in their individual capacities in a multistage selection process (Sackett & Roth, 1996).

Cutoff scores versus rank orders. A cutoff score may be set as high or low as needed relative to the requirements of the using organization, given that a selection procedure demonstrates linearity or monotonicity across the range of predictions (that is, it is valid). For cognitive predictors the linear relationship is typically found using a criterion-related validity model and is assumed with a content validity process. Under these circumstances using a rank order (top-down) process will maximize expected performance on the criterion. Whether this same premise holds true for noncognitive measures has not been determined.

In a rank order model the score of the last person selected is the lower-bound cutoff score. A cutoff score set otherwise usually defines the selection procedure score below which applicants are rejected. Professional judgment that considers KSAOs required, expectancy of success versus failure, the cost-benefit ratio, consequences of failure, the number of openings and the selection ratio, and organizational diversity objectives is important to setting a cutoff score. In the case of organizational diversity objectives, using lower cutoff scores could result in higher proportions of minority candidates passing some valid initial hurdle, with the expectation that subsequent hurdles might have less adverse impact. In such instances cutoff scores are set low, with the realization there will be a corresponding reduction in job performance and selection procedure utility but that the trade-offs regarding minority hiring are sufficient to overcome such reductions. (Chapter Thirteen in this book is devoted entirely to cutoff scores. Chapter Five also addresses cutoff scores.)

Utility. Gains in productivity, reductions in outcomes (for example, accidents, manufacturing rejects, absenteeism), and comparisons among alternate selection procedures can be estimated by utility computations. Typically, a number of assumptions must be made with considerable uncertainty in order to satisfy the computational requirements of the utility models. Thus caution should be observed in relying on such utility estimates.

Bands. When a range of selection procedure scores is established that considers all candidates within the range to be alike, a band results. Bands may be established for a variety of reasons and require sound professional judgment. There are many banding procedures, and no one process is necessarily correct. It is fully recognized that band scores are less precise in the prediction of criterion outcomes than are individual selection procedure scores.

Technical validation report requirements. Every validation study should be documented with a technical report that contains sufficient information to allow an independent researcher to replicate the study. Such a report should accurately present all findings, conclusions, and recommendations. In particular the technical report should give clear information about the research sample and the statistical analyses conducted, as well as recommendations on implementation and the interpretation of the selection procedure scores.

Summary

The *Principles* offers a current and comprehensive resource for use by decision makers in the context of employment litigation. Because the *Principles* is focused specifically on the employment setting, it frequently offers more guidance on matters that arise in employment litigation than will be found in the *Standards*. Nevertheless the two documents are very compatible and not at all contradictory. The *Principles* has undergone substantial professional peer review and represents the official policy of both SIOP and the APA. Consequently, given that the *Principles* has relevance to a matter undergoing litigation, one might easily wonder why this authoritative source would not have value for the decision maker. It is my speculation that the *Principles* is not well known in the judicial community, and this notion has some support from the interviews with judges reported in Chapter Fifteen of this volume. Another speculation is that even when experts testify who are aware of the *Principles* they do not rely on it to support their opinions.

Uniform Guidelines on Employee Selection Procedures

Brief History

When the U.S. Congress passed the Equal Employment Opportunity (EEO) Act of 1972, it created the Equal Opportunity Coordinating Council, which comprised the directors and secretaries of the Equal Employment Opportunity Commission (EEOC), the Civil Service Commission (CSC), the Civil Rights Commission (CRC), the Department of Justice (DOJ), and the Department of Labor (DOL). The council was given the mandate to develop and implement policies, practices, and agreements that would be consistent across the agencies responsible for enforcing EEO legislation. In 1977, the council began developing the *Uniform Guidelines* document, and it was adopted on August 25, 1978, by the EEOC, the CSC, the DOJ, and the DOL Office of Federal Contract Compliance Programs (OFCCP), with an effective date of September 25, 1978. (Also see Chapter Two in this volume.) On March 2, 1979, the EEOC, Office of Personnel Management (OPM), DOJ, DOL, and Department of the Treasury adopted the "Questions and Answers to Clarify and Provide a Common Interpretation of the Uniform Guidelines On Employee Selection Procedures" (Q&A's). (The differences between the agencies adopting the *Uniform Guidelines* and those adopting the Q&A's are due to the fact that the CSC had been succeeded by the OPM and to some degree by the Office of Revenue Sharing in the Treasury Department.)

Although some psychologists participated in the development of the *Uniform Guidelines,* there was no consensus from the professional associations (for example, SIOP and APA) that the document reflected the state of the scientific knowledge regarding the validation and use of employee selection procedures. Ad hoc committees of psychologists from both SIOP and APA reviewed draft versions of the *Uniform Guidelines* and offered considerable input, but most of the suggestions were not incorporated (Camara, 1996). When Congress considered revising the *Uniform Guidelines* in 1985, the APA offered testimony that the document was deficient with respect to differential prediction, validity generalization, utility analysis, and validity requirements and documentation. SIOP concurred with the APA's concerns and further argued that the *Uniform Guidelines* was in error in defining construct validity and in determining the acceptable types of validity evidence

Purpose

The guidelines in the *Uniform Guidelines* are intended to ". . . incorporate a single set of principles which are designed to assist employers, labor organizations, employment agencies, and licensing and certification boards to comply with requirements of federal law prohibiting employment practices which discriminate on grounds of race, color, religion, sex, and national origin. They are designed to provide a framework for determining the proper use of tests and other selection procedures. These guidelines do not require a user to conduct validity studies of selection procedures where no adverse impact results. However, all users are encouraged to use selection procedures which are valid, especially users operating under merit principles" (§ 1607.1B).

The Q&A's were prepared ". . . to interpret and clarify, but not to modify, the provisions of the *Uniform Guidelines*" ("Questions and answers . . .," 1979, Introduction).

All subsequent references in this chapter to the *Uniform Guidelines* should be considered to be inclusive of the Q&A's.

Application and Limitations

The *Uniform Guidelines* applies to Title VII of the Civil Rights Act, Executive Order 11246, and equal employment opportunity laws regarding race, color, religion, sex, and national origin. It does not apply to the Age Discrimination in Employment Act of 1967 or to Sections 501, 503, and 504 of the Rehabilitation Act of 1973, which prohibit discrimination on the basis of disability. Because the Americans with Disabilities Act (ADA) was not enacted until 1991, the *Uniform Guidelines* was not able to address this legislation and the protection it affords people with disabilities. Generally, the *Uniform Guidelines* applies to most public and private sector employers.

Selection Procedures and Employment Decisions

In general the *Uniform Guidelines* defines selection procedures and employment decisions in a manner similar to that of the *Standards* and the *Principles*. Thus processes related to hiring, promotion, retention, and certification are covered. These processes include tests, assessment centers, interview protocols, scored applications, physical ability measures, work samples, and performance evaluations. Further, the *Uniform Guidelines* applies to any intermediate process (for example, having to complete a certification program to be eligible for a promotion) that leads to a covered employment decision. Two practices are exempt or are not considered selection procedures: recruitment (excluded to protect the affirmative recruitment of minorities and women) and bona fide seniority systems.

Discrimination and Adverse Impact

The *Uniform Guidelines* explicitly defines discrimination and introduces the term adverse impact. In essence, *discrimination* occurs when a selection procedure results in unjustifiable adverse impact. *Adverse impact* occurs when the selection rate for a potential group is less than four-fifths (80 percent) of the rate for the group with the highest rate (typically the nonprotected group). This rule of thumb is not intended as a legal definition and for good reason, because it is problematic from a couple of perspectives. First and foremost, it is highly influenced by sample size. For example, if there are fifty male and fifty female applicants and twenty open positions, the only way a selection process will not violate the 80 percent rule is to hire at least nine females. If eleven males are hired (22 percent of the male applicants), then 8.8 females must be hired (that is, four-fifths of the 22 percent is 17.6 percent, and 17.6 percent of the fifty female applicants equals 8.8). Stated in terms of the procedures set forth in the Q&A's, the 17.6 percent selection rate for females is divided by the 22 percent rate for males and the result is 80 percent, in compliance with the four-fifths rule. In this instance, in order to hire 8.8 females the employer must actually select nine of the female candidates. If only eight females were hired (16 percent of the female applicants), then 16 percent divided by 22 percent equals 73 percent, a violation of the four-fifths rule.

Second, and perhaps more important, the 80 percent rule of thumb is not a statistical test. The null hypothesis is not stated, and there is no estimate of the likelihood that any difference observed will be due to chance. Such hypothesis testing is accomplished using either binomial or hypergeometric probability models. Typically, the .05 level of statistical significance under a two-tailed test (for example, 1.96 standard deviation units) is considered the threshold of significance. Although the 80 percent value has no standing in the scientific literature, the .05 level of significance is well accepted in social science research as indicating statistical significance.

Fairness

The concept of fairness is introduced in the discussion of criterion-related validity (*Uniform Guidelines*, 1978, §§ 7B-3, 14B-8). The *Uniform Guidelines* requires that a fairness investigation of a selection procedure be conducted if technically feasible before applying validity evidence from one situation to a new situation. Further, if adverse impact is observed during a criterion-related validation study, the user is expected to conduct a fairness analysis. Unfairness occurs when lower minority scores on a selection procedure are not reflected in lower scores on the criterion or index of job performance. The *Standards* and *Principles* consider this a matter of predictive bias, and it is found when consistent nonzero errors of prediction occur for a protected subgroup. Moderated multiple regression is the accepted statistical method for examining predictive bias, which occurs when there are slope or intercept differences between subgroups. As previously mentioned, there is no consistent research evidence supporting predictive bias on cognitive tests for African Americans or Hispanics relative to whites. Research studies of noncognitive test results by subgroups have not yet been conducted in sufficient numbers to draw any definitive conclusions.

Cutoff Scores

Cutoff scores are discussed first in the *Uniform Guidelines* as part of the general standards for validity studies (§ 5H) and then in the technical standards section (§ 14B-6). According to the *Uniform Guidelines*, "Where cutoff scores are used, they should normally be set so as to be reasonable and consistent with normal expectations of acceptable proficiency within the work force" (§ 5H). This definition seems to imply the need for professional judgment in setting a cutoff score, and such a stance is consistent with the *Standards* and the *Principles*.

The Bottom Line

Another concept introduced by the *Uniform Guidelines* is use of the bottom-line approach when trying to assess adverse impact or discrimination. When a selection procedure has multiple components, the final decision point is evaluated for adverse impact. According to the *Uniform Guidelines*, only when the adverse impact occurs at the bottom line must the individual components of a selection procedure be evaluated. However, this concept was struck down by the U.S. Supreme Court in *Connecticut* v. *Teal* (1982). Hence today it is typical that all components of a selection procedure are evaluated in terms of adverse impact if they can be examined individually.

Alternative Selection Procedure

The *Uniform Guidelines* introduced the concept that if two or more selection procedures are available and have substantially equal validity, then the procedure demonstrating the lesser amount of adverse impact should be used. Furthermore, with the passage of the Civil Rights Act of 1991, if an employer demonstrates validity for a selection procedure that has adverse impact and a plaintiff can then offer a procedure with approximate equal validity but less adverse impact, then the burden is on the employer to show why the less impactful alternative was not used.

Although conceptually the alternative selection procedure is understandable, it is difficult to contend with in practice. There is no clear definition for "substantially equal valid." Although there are many alternatives, the ones that might have a lesser adverse impact in a given situation are not easily discerned. Oftentimes the degree of adverse impact observed is specific to the numbers and qualifications of applicants at a particular point in time. And then there is the question as to what constitutes "lesser adverse impact."

Finally, many selection procedures are available "which serve the user's legitimate interest in efficient and trustworthy workmanship" but which still may not be feasible alternatives (§ 3B). Examples of concerns include faking or response distortions of personality and bio data inventories, costs of development and implementation, and the ability to assess very large numbers of applicants at the same time.

Job-Relatedness and Business Necessity

An employment selection procedure that has adverse impact may be justified in two ways: (1) by a showing that the procedure is job related or (2) by a showing that the procedure is justified by business necessity. Job-relatedness is demonstrated by the validation process. Business necessity is demonstrated when a selection procedure is necessary for the safe and efficient operation of the business entity. Oftentimes relevant statutes and regulations (such as legislation regarding public safety job requirements) define the business necessity argument; at other times information from the analysis of work will demonstrate the business necessity of a selection procedure.

Validity

The *Uniform Guidelines* sets forth what are considered acceptable types of validity studies and identifies these types: criterion-related, content, and construct. The document also notes that new validation strategies "will be evaluated as they become accepted by the psychological profession" (§ 5A). The *Uniform Guidelines* also states that the validation provisions "are intended to be consistent with generally accepted professional standards . . . such as those described in the *Standards for Educational and Psychological Tests . . .* and standard textbooks and journals in the field of personnel selection" (§ 5C). Of course the *Standards* referred to here are those published in 1974, and major revisions were published in 1985 and 1999. The *Uniform Guidelines* makes no specific reference to the *Principles* even though the first edition of the *Principles* was published in 1975. Consequently, it is easy to understand why the treatment of validity by the *Uniform Guidelines* is not more consistent with the state of the scientific knowledge as set forth in the current editions of the *Standards* and the *Principles*.

In introducing validity the *Uniform Guidelines* offers several warnings or conditions:

- Do not select on the basis of KSAs that can be learned on the job during orientation.
- The degree of adverse impact should influence how a selection procedure is implemented, and evidence sufficient to justify a pass-fail strategy may be insufficient for rank order.
- A selection procedure can be designed for higher-level jobs when a majority of employees can be expected to progress to those jobs in about five years.
- An employer can use a selection procedure when there is substantial validity evidence from other applications and when the employer has in progress, if technically feasible, a validity study that will be completed in a reasonable period of time.
- Validity studies should be reviewed for currency, particularly if alternative procedures with equal validity but less adverse impact may be available.
- There are no substitutes for validity evidence and no assumptions of validity based on general representation, promotional material, testimony, and the like.
- Employment agencies are subject to the guidelines in the same manner as employees.

Criterion-related validity. The *Uniform Guidelines'* position on criterion-related validity is consistent with the information set forth in the *Standards* and *Principles.* Job analysis is important for decisions about grouping jobs together and for selecting and developing criterion measures. An overall measure of job performance may be used as a criterion if justified by the job analysis (the *Principles* and *Standards* emphasize the need for construct equivalence for predictor and criterion measures and typically there is a greater degree of construct specificity than "overall performance" developed from the job analysis); success in training also may be used as a criterion. Both concurrent and predictive designs are recognized, and emphasis is placed on the representativeness of the sample of individuals participating in the validity study, regardless of its design.

Criterion-related validity evidence should be examined using acceptable statistical procedures, and the *Uniform Guidelines* establishes the .05 level of statistical significance as the threshold for concluding that there is a relationship between a predictor and a criterion. Usually the relationship is expressed as a correlation coefficient, which must be assessed in the particular situation: "... there are no minimum correlation coefficients applicable to all employment situations" (§ 14B-6). Additionally, care must be taken to not overstate validity findings.

Content validity. The technical standards for content validity studies begin by focusing on the appropriateness of such a study. A selection procedure must be a representative sample of the job content or purport to measure KSAs that are required for successful job performance. Selection procedures based on inferences about mental abilities or that purport to measure traits such as intelligence, common sense, or leadership cannot be supported on the basis of content validity alone.

Solid job analysis information that is representative of the jobs and, when necessary, operationally defined is critical to a content validity argument.

The *Uniform Guidelines* provides for the ranking of candidates assessed by a content valid selection procedure, given that the procedure is measuring one or more capabilities that differentiate between levels of job performance. This is generally compatible with the guidance offered by the *Principles,* although the Q&A's to the *Uniform Guidelines* gives more examples as to when it is, or is not, appropriate to use rank ordering.

Construct validity. This form of validity is defined in Section 14D-1 of the *Uniform Guidelines* as "a series of research studies, which include criterion related and which may include content validity studies." In Sections 14D-1 and 14D-3 it is stated that a *construct* is the intermediary between the selection procedure on the one hand and job performance on the other. A job analysis is required, and one or more constructs that are expected to influence successful performance of important work behaviors should be identified and defined. To accomplish a construct validity study, it should be empirically demonstrated "... that the selection procedure is validity related to the construct and that the construct is validity related to the performance of critical or important work behaviors" (§ 14D-3).

(This is the definition that drew the objections of the APA and SIOP.) In turn, a selection procedure is developed that will measure the constructs of interest.

Documentation required. The *Uniform Guidelines* sets forth a large number of documentation requirements for a validity study, and many of these requirements are labeled "essential." Generally speaking, the information expected as part of the documentation effort is consistent with the material presented in each of the various sections of the *Uniform Guidelines*.

Utility. There is one term that does not have a definition in the *Uniform Guidelines* that could have many interpretations; that term is *utility*. It is found in the sections dealing with the uses and applications of a selection procedure that has been evaluated by a criterion-related validity study. Specifically, documentation of the methods considered for using a procedure "should include the rationale for choosing the method of operational use, and the evidence of validity and utility of the procedure as it is to be used (essential)" (§ 15B-10). Identical sentences appear in the uses and applications sections for content and construct validity. Furthermore, in Section 5G the *Uniform Guidelines* states that "if a user decide to use a selection procedure on a ranking basis, and that method of use has a greater adverse impact than use of an appropriate pass/fail basis . . . the user should have sufficient evidence of validity and utility to support the use on a ranking basis."

Comparisons Among the Three Authorities

Given their different authors and different purposes, it is useful to make comparisons among the three authorities to identify areas of agreement and disagreement. Such information might be particularly valuable to a user who is deciding whether to rely on one or more of the authorities or who has relied on one of the authorities and not realized what one or both of the other two authorities had to say on the topic of interest.

The common themes across the three authorities are matters of validation and psychometric measurement. Exhibit 3.1 facilitates the present discussion by comparing the three authorities on the ways they define or explain a number of concepts or terms. As the exhibit makes clear, the *Uniform Guidelines* does not define or explain many

Exhibit 3.1. Validation and Psychometric Terminology Comparison.

	Standards	Principles	Uniform Guidelines
Validity (unitary concept)	The degree to which accumulated evidence and theory support specific interpretations of test scores.	The degree to which accumulated evidence and theory support specific interpretations of scores from a selection procedure entailed by the proposed uses of that selection procedure.	[Not defined.]
Sources of validity evidence			
1. Content	The linkage between a predictor and one or more aspects of a criterion construct domain.	The extent to which content of a selection procedure is a representative sample of work-related personal characteristics, work performance, or other work activities or outcomes.	Data showing that the content of a selection procedure is representative of important aspects of performance on the job.
2. Internal structure	The extent to which the relationships between test items conform to the construct that is the foundation for test score interpretation.	The degree to which psychometric and statistical relationships among items, scales, or other components within a selection procedure are consistent with the intended meanings of scores on the selection procedure.	[Not defined.]

Exhibit 3.1. Validation and Psychometric Terminology Comparison, Cont'd.

	Standards	Principles	Uniform Guidelines
3. Response process	The study of the cognitive account of some behavior, such as making a selection procedure item response.	The study of the cognitive account of some behavior, such as making a selection procedure item response.	[Not defined.]
4. Consequences of testing	Whether or not the specific benefits expected from the use of a selection procedure are being realized.	Evidence that consequences of selection procedure use are consistent with the intended meaning or interpretation of the selection procedure.	[Not defined.]
5. Relations to other variables/ criterion-related	The relationship of test scores to variables external to the test, such as measures of some criteria that the test is expected to predict.	The statistical relationship between scores on a predictor and scores on a criterion measure.	Empirical data showing that the selection procedure is predictive of or significantly correlated with important elements of work behavior.
Construct validity	An indication that test scores are to be interpreted as indicating the test taker's standing on the psychological construct measured by the test. The term construct is redundant with validity. The validity argument establishes the construct validity of a test.	Evidence that scores on two or more selection procedures are highly related and consistent with the underlying construct can provide convergent evidence in support of the proposed interpretation of test scores as representing a candidate's standing on the construct of interest.	Data showing that the selection procedure measures the degree to which candidates have identifiable characteristics which have been determined to be important for successful job performance.

Term			
Convergent validity	Evidence based on the relationship between test scores and other measures of the same constructs.	Evidence of a relationship between measures intended to represent the same construct.	[Not defined.]
Discriminant validity	Evidence based on the relationship between test scores and measures of different constructs.	Evidence of a lack of a relationship between measures intended to represent different constructs.	[Not defined.]
Validity generalization	Apply validity evidence obtained in one or more situations to other similar situations on the basis of simultaneous estimations, meta-analysis, or synthetic validation arguments.	Evidence of validity that generalizes to setting(s) other than the setting(s) in which the original validation evidence was documented. Generalized evidence is accumulated through such strategies as transportability, synthetic/job component validity, and meta-analysis.	[Not defined.]
Transport of validity	Reliance on a previous study of the predictor-criterion relationship done under favorable conditions (that is, large sample size and a relevant criterion) and the current local situation corresponds	A strategy for generalizing evidence of validity in which demonstration of important similarities between different work settings is used to infer that validation evidence for a selection procedure accumu-	Using evidence from another study when the job incumbents from both situations perform substantially the same major work behaviors as shown by appropriate job analyses;

Exhibit 3.1. Validation and Psychometric Terminology Comparison, Cont'd.

	Standards	Principles	Uniform Guidelines
	closely to the previous situation (that is, the job requirements or underlying psychological constructs are substantially the same) as determined by a job analysis, and the predictor is substantially the same.	lated in one work setting generalizes to another work setting.	the study should also include an evaluation of test fairness for each race, sex, and ethnic group that constitutes a significant factor in the labor market for the job(s) in question within the labor force of the organization desiring to rely on the transported evidence.
Synthetic/job component validity	[Not defined.]	Generalized evidence of validity based on previous demonstration of the validity of inferences from scores on the selection procedure or battery with respect to one or more domains of work (job components).	[Not defined.]
Meta-analysis	A statistical method of research in which the results from several independent, comparable studies are combined to determine the size	A statistical method of research in which results from several independent studies of comparable phenomena are combined to estimate a	[Not defined.]

	of an overall effect on the degree of relationship between two variables.	parameter or the degree of relationship between variables.	
Reliability	The degree to which test scores for a group of test takers are consistent over repeated applications of a measurement procedure and hence are inferred to be dependable; the degree to which scores are free of errors of measurement for a given group.	The degree to which scores for a group of assesses are consistent over one or more potential sources of error (for example, time, raters, items, conditions of measurement, and so forth) in the application of a measurement procedure.	The term is not defined but the reliability of selection procedures, particularly those used in a content viability study, should be of concern to the user.
Fairness and unfairness	The principle that every test taker should be assessed in an equitable way. There is no single technical meaning; in the employment setting fairness can be defined as an absence of bias and all persons being treated equally in the testing process.	There are multiple perspectives on fairness. There is agreement that issues of equitable treatment, predictive bias, and scrutiny for possible bias when subgroup differences are observed are important concerns in personal selection; there is not, however, agreement that the term *fairness* can be uniquely defined in terms of any of these issues.	When members of one race, sex, or ethnic group characteristically obtain lower scores on a selection procedure than members of another group, and the differences in scores are not reflected in differences in a measure of job performance.

Exhibit 3.1. Validation and Psychometric Terminology Comparison, Cont'd.

	Standards	Principles	Uniform Guidelines
Predictive bias	The systematic under- or overprediction of criterion performance for people belonging to groups differentiated by characteristics not relevant to criterion performance.	The systematic under- or overprediction of criterion performance for people belonging to groups differentiated by characteristics not relevant to criterion performance.	[Not defined, but see *unfairness*.]
Cut score or cutoff score	The specific point on a score scale above which scores are interpreted or acted on differently from scores below that point.	The score at or above which applicants are selected for further consideration in the selection procedure. The cutoff score may be established on the basis of a number of considerations (for example, labor market, organizational constraints, normative information). Cutoff scores are not necessarily criterion referenced, and different organizations may establish different cutoff scores on the same selection procedure, based on their needs.	Cutoff scores should normally be set so as to be reasonable and consistent with normal expectations of acceptable proficiency within the workforce.

Note: These definitions and explanations were taken verbatim from the glossaries or definition sections of the authoritative sources whenever possible. When that was not possible, they were extracted from document text on the subject.

of the terms at issue. There are no doubt several reasons for this situation; two explanations follow:

- The *Uniform Guidelines* is some twenty years older than the *Standards* and twenty-five years older than the *Principles*. The latter two documents have undergone one and two revisions, respectively, since the *Uniform Guidelines* was published, but the *Uniform Guidelines* has never been revised or brought up to date.
- The *Uniform Guidelines* was written to guide the enforcement of civil rights legislation. The *Standards* and the *Principles* were written to guide research and professional practice and to inform decision making in applicable areas of litigation. Hence the latter two documents have a more scientific focus and rely heavily on the current research literature; the *Uniform Guidelines* was intended to be consistent with generally accepted professional standards set forth in the 1974 version of the *Standards* but was not necessarily research based at the time of its preparation.

Standards Versus *Principles*

There are no areas of disagreement between the *Standards* and the *Principles*. In some areas the *Standards* offers more information and guidance than the *Principles*. Examples include (1) discussions of validity evidence based on response processes, internal structure, and the consequences of testing; (2) discussions of reliability and errors of measurement; (3) the test development and revision process; (4) scales, norms, and score comparability; and (5) the rights and responsibilities of test takers. There also are a few topics that are more broadly considered in the *Principles* than in the *Standards*. Examples include (1) the concept of the analysis of work (to incorporate the work context and organizational setting) rather than job analysis; (2) the clarification that the generalization of validity evidence can be accomplished by several methods, including transportability and synthetic/job component validity as well as meta-analysis; and (3) certain operational considerations associated with the conduct of a validation study in an organizational setting (for example, communications, organizational needs and constraints, quality control and security, implementation models, and utility).

Standards and Principles Versus Uniform Guidelines

The comparisons set forth in Exhibit 3.1 delineate many of the typical areas where the first two authoritative sources do not agree with the third. In several instances the term or concept is simply not defined or considered by the *Uniform Guidelines;* in other instances there is disagreement regarding the meaning or methods to be followed to satisfy a term or concept. A discussion of each of these points, in the order they appear in Exhibit 3.1, follows:

Validity. Both the *Standards* and the *Principles* view validity as a unitary concept, whereas the *Uniform Guidelines* partitions validity into three types: criterion-related, content, and construct. This partitioning of validity was the thinking thirty years ago but is clearly out of date now.

Sources of validity evidence:

- *Relations to other variables/criterion-related.* The *Uniform Guidelines'* focus on work behavior as a criterion excludes potential studies of the relationships between a selection procedure of interest and other tests hypothesized to measure the same or different constructs (that is, other external variables).
- *Content.* All three authorities agree that content validity is dependent on a sound determination that the selection procedure is a representative sample of work-related behavior. The analysis of work (or the job) is fundamental to establishing the predictor-criterion linkage. The *Uniform Guidelines* confines job analysis to a study of KSAs; the *Standards* and *Principles* call for the study of KSAOs and would include *o* variables in a selection procedure subject to a content validity study. *O* stands for *other* variables and would include measures of personality, biographic information, and characteristics of individuals "other" than knowledge(K), skills(S), or abilities(A). The *Uniform Guidelines* precludes use of a content strategy to study the validity of traits or constructs such as spatial ability, common sense, judgment, and leadership. Although it is important to describe the relevant work behavior or KSAO at a level of specificity that ensures no misunderstanding about what is being measured, it is not wise to reject content validity evidence simply because it is concerned with

linking an ability or characteristic (such as leadership) to the domain of job performance. Many constructs can be defined in terms of specific work behaviors even though they have broad labels. Further, there are many situations where content validity may be the only option. If leadership capabilities are critical to job performance, a content validity study may be the only alternative. There may not be adequate numbers of candidates or incumbents to conduct a criterion-related study. There may not be a sufficient and reliable criterion to measure. Consequently, a content validity study may be the only viable approach to evaluating the validity of a construct of interest or of importance to job performance.

- *Internal structure, response processes, and consequences of testing.* These three lines of evidence for a validity argument were not known or pursued at the time the *Uniform Guidelines* was written and hence are not discussed.
- *Construct validity.* The *Uniform Guidelines* treats construct validity as a separate type of validity. In the *Standards* and *Principles* all selection procedure scores or outcomes are viewed as measures of some construct. Consequently, any evaluation of validity is a *construct validity* study.
- *Convergent validity and discriminant validity.* Although these terms and their implications were well established at the time the *Uniform Guidelines* was prepared, there is no discussion about the value of these types of evidence in the document.
- *Validity generalization.* This concept was known at the time the *Uniform Guidelines* was prepared but is not specifically used in the document. Many have interpreted Section 7B of the *Uniform Guidelines* as providing for validity generalization arguments. The provisions of that section are described in Exhibit 3.1, under transport of validity evidence.
- *Transport of validity.* The three authoritative sources agree that a work or job analysis is necessary to support the transport of validity. The *Uniform Guidelines* goes further, however, and requires that there be an existing study of fairness for relevant protected subgroups. There is no guidance, however, as to the acceptability of transporting the validity of a selection procedure that has some demonstrated unfairness; furthermore, in many if not most situations sample sizes preclude fairness analyses.

- *Synthetic/job component validity.* This form of validity generalization has been known for more than thirty years but has not received much attention in validation research conducted outside the employment arena or in litigation. Consequently, neither the *Standards* nor the *Uniform Guidelines* has defined this form of validity generalization.

- *Meta-analysis.* Again, given the document date, the authors of the *Uniform Guidelines* did not have knowledge of the research findings that have emerged from meta-analytic research. This, unfortunately, is another void, and a significant amount of research is available today that might not be considered within the scope of validation strategies acceptable under the *Uniform Guidelines.*

- *Reliability.* This term is not defined in the *Uniform Guidelines* as it is in the other two authoritative sources but is considered to be important for selection procedures that have been supported with a content validity strategy. Both the *Standards* and *Principles* emphasize that the reliability of any measurement be considered whenever it is technically feasible to do so.

- *Fairness and unfairness and bias.* The *Standards* and the *Principles* consider fairness a broad concept with many facets. Alternatively, the two sources consider bias a specific term concerned with under- or overprediction of performance for a subgroup. This is basically the same interpretation that the *Uniform Guidelines* gives to the term *unfairness* while relying on the 1974 version of the *Standards.*

- *Cut score or cutoff score.* The *Principles* gives more attention than the other two authoritative sources to developing in detail many of the issues underlying the setting of a cutoff score. However, there does not seem to be any significant disagreement across the three documents about how a cutoff score will function or about the intent for a cutoff score to screen out those who will not achieve acceptable levels of job performance.

Summary

In summary there are some levels of consistency or agreement across the three authoritative sources but also consequential areas of disagreement. It is likely that the advances in selection procedure research and scholarly thinking regarding validity that have occurred over the last twenty-five years account for these differences. Sometime in the future it would be desirable for the *Uniform Guidelines* to be revised to reflect the current state of the science. Until that time the decision maker in employment litigation should look to the *Standards* and *Principles* for guidance on many issues that are now either incorrect or not addressed in the *Uniform Guidelines.*

Final Thoughts

The *Standards, Principles,* and *Uniform Guidelines* have been in place for a major portion of the time the investigation and litigation of civil rights issues in employment settings have been the responsibility of the EEOC and the Department of Justice. Further, numerous trials have taken place in which the validity of selection procedure outcomes and the subsequent use of those outcomes have played a major role in the allegations and final decisions. (See Chapter Two in this volume.) Although the three authoritative sources may not have contained the answers to all the questions raised in past litigation, they certainly would have offered some guidance in many instances. Furthermore, their use in the future is essential if the justice system is going to consider and recognize the importance of information from the scientific community.

As indicated by Thornton and Wingate in Chapter Six, currently the judiciary does not have a great deal of knowledge about industrial and organizational psychology. It is also recognized that some significant inconsistencies exist at this time between information provided by the *Standards* and *Principles* on the one hand and the *Uniform Guidelines* on the other. However, these differences can be resolved. Unfortunately, until a revision of the *Uniform Guidelines* is forthcoming, to the extent that more than one authority is introduced in a trial setting—that is, offered as support to only one side of an argument—resolution of differences that appear in print will need to be part of the judicial decision-making process. In this regard it is incumbent on those who do rely on any of the authoritative sources during the course of litigation to be clear about both the relevance and currency of the source(s) providing guidance to their opinions.

Notes

1. *Psychometric* is defined as pertaining to the measurement of psychological variables or characteristics such as knowledge, skills, abilities, or other personal traits.
2. *Adverse impact* is defined by the *Uniform Guidelines* (§ 16B) as "a substantially different rate of selection in hiring, promotion or other employment decision which works to the disadvantage of members of a race, sex, or ethnic group."
3. Division 14 of the American Psychological Association incorporated as the Society for Industrial and Organizational Psychology in 1982.

References

American Educational Research Association, American Psychological Association, & National Council on Measurement in Education. (1999). *Standards for educational and psychological testing.* Washington, DC: American Educational Research Association.

Barrett, G. V., Phillips, J. S., & Alexander, R. A. (1981). Concurrent and predictive validity designs: A critical reanalysis. *Journal of Applied Psychology, 66,* 1–6.

Barrick, M. R., & Mount, M. K. (1991). The big five personality dimensions and job performance: A meta-analysis. *Personnel Psychology, 44,* 1–26.

Barrick, M. R., Mount, M. K., & Judge, T. A. (2001). The FFM personality dimensions and jobs: Meta-analysis of meta-analysis. *International Journal of Selection and Assessment, 9,* 9–30.

Bemis, S. E. (1968). Occupational validity of the General Aptitude Test Battery. *Journal of Applied Psychology, 52,* 240–249.

Binning, J. F., & Barrett, G. V. (1989). Validity of personnel decisions: A conceptual analysis of the inferential evidential bases. *Journal of Applied Psychology, 74,* 478–494.

Callender, J. C., & Osburn, H. G. (1981). Testing the constancy of validity with computer-generated sampling distributions of the multiplicative model variance method estimate: Results for petroleum industry validation research. *Journal of Applied Psychology, 66,* 274–281.

Camara, W. J. (1996). Fairness and public policy in employment testing: Influences from a professional association. In Richard S. Barrett (Ed.), *Fair employment strategies in human resource management* (pp. 3–11). Westport, CT: Quorum Books.

Campbell, D. T., & Fiske, D. W. (1959). Convergent and discriminant validity by the multitrait-multimethod motive. *Psychological Bulletin, 56,* 81–105.

Cascio, W. F. (2000). *Costing human resources: The financial impact of behavior in organizations* (4th ed.). Cincinnati, OH: Southwestern.

Connecticut v. Teal, 457 U.S. 440 (1982).

Cronbach, L. J., & Gleser, G. C. (1965). *Psychological tests and personnel decisions* (2nd ed.). Urbana, IL: University of Illinois Press.

Cronbach, L. J., & Meehl, P. E. (1955). Construct validity in psychological tests. *Psychological Bulletin, 52,* 281–302.

Hartigan, J. A., & Wigdor, A. K. (Eds.). (1989). *Fairness in employment testing.* Washington, DC: National Academy Press.

Hunter, J. E., & Hunter, R. F. (1984). Validity and utility of alternative predictors of job performance. *Psychological Bulletin, 96,* 72–88.

Hunter, J. E., & Schmidt, F. L. (1990). *Methods of meta-analysis.* Thousand Oaks, CA: Sage.

McDonald, R. P. (1999). *Test theory: Unified treatment.* Mahwah, NJ: Erlbaum.

Messick, S. (1980). Test validity and the ethics of assessment. *American Psychologist, 35,* 1012–1027.

Messick, S. (1989). Validity. In R. L. Linn (Ed.), *Educational measurement* (3rd ed., pp. 13–104). New York: Macmillan.

Naylor, J. C., & Shine, L. C. (1965). A table for determining the increase in mean criterion scores obtained by using a selection device. *Journal of Industrial Psychology, 3,* 33–42.

Nunnally, J. C., & Bernstein, I. H. (1994). *Psychometric theory* (3rd ed.). New York: McGraw-Hill.

Pearlman, K., Schmidt, F. L., & Hunter, J. E. (1980). Validity generalization results for tests used to predict job proficiency and training success in clerical occupations. *Journal of Applied Psychology, 65,* 373–406.

Pedhazur, E. J., & Schmelkin, L. P. (1991). *Measurement, design, and analysis: An integrated approach.* Mahwah, NJ: Erlbaum.

Questions and Answers to Clarify and Provide a Common Interpretation of the Uniform Guidelines on Employee Selection Procedures, 44 Fed. Reg. 43 (March 2, 1979).

Rosenthal, R. (1991). *Meta-analytic procedures for social research.* Thousand Oaks, CA: Sage.

Sackett, P. R., & Roth, L. (1996). Multi-stage selection strategies: A Monte Carlo investigation of effects on performance and minority hiring. *Personnel Psychology, 49,* 549–572.

Sackett, P. R., Schmitt, N., Ellingson, J. E., & Kabin, M. B. (2001). High stakes testing in employment, credentialing, and higher education. *American Psychologist, 56,* 302–318.

Schmidt, F. L., Hunter, J. E., McKenzie, R. C., & Muldrow, T. W. (1979). Impact of valid selection procedures on work-force productivity. *Journal of Applied Psychology, 64,* 609–626.

Society for Industrial and Organizational Psychology. (2003). *Principles for the validation and use of personnel selection procedures* (4th ed.). Bowling Green, OH: Author.

Traub, R. E. (1994). *Reliability for the social sciences: Theory and applications.* Thousand Oaks, CA: Sage.

Uniform Guidelines on Employee Selection Procedures. 29 C.F.R. § 1607 *et seq.* (1978).

Wainer, H., & Braun, H. I. (Eds.). (1988). *Test validity.* Mahwah, NJ: Erlbaum.

CHAPTER 4

Statistical Trends in Private Sector Employment Discrimination Suits

Donald L. Zink
Arthur Gutman

The Equal Employment Opportunity Commission (EEOC) was created through statutory authority in Title VII of the Civil Rights Act of 1964 (CRA-64). Originally, its duties were limited to technical assistance, outreach and education, and conciliation in private sector claims. Title VII was amended by the Equal Employment Opportunity Act of 1972 (EEO-72), which authorized the EEOC to litigate private sector claims. EEO-72 also provided first-time Title VII coverage of federal, state, and local governments. Enforcement duties for the Equal Pay Act (EPA) and Age Discrimination in Employment Act (ADEA) were then inherited from the Department of Labor (DOL) in President Carter's Reorganization Plan No. 1 of 1978, and enforcement duties for the Americans with Disabilities Act (ADA) were written in plain statutory language with the passage of the ADA in 1990.

The purpose of this chapter is to summarize and organize statistical facts and analyze trends in relation to Title VII, the ADA, ADEA, and EPA in accordance with four major topics: (1) charges filed, (2) resolution of charges short of litigation, (3) litigation statistics, and (4) emerging trends identified in recent news releases. The data reported are from the EEOC official Web site (www. eeoc.gov)[1] and cover only private sector lawsuits.

Most of the data presented in this chapter relate to Title VII, which has the largest number of protected groups (or classes) (race and color, religion, national origin, and sex) and covered entities (private, state, local, and federal). Title VII also applies to all terms and conditions of employment (hiring, training, promotion, benefits, discharge, and so forth). In contrast the EPA is the narrowest statute, with one protected class (sex) and one covered practice (equal pay for equal work). The ADEA covers terms and conditions for people over forty years of age, and the ADA covers terms and conditions for individuals with current or past physical or mental impairments that substantially limit at least one major life function or who are perceived as being physically or mentally impaired and who are qualified (with or without reasonable accommodations) to perform all essential job functions (for the latter, see Chapter Ten in this volume).

Four additional points are worth noting. First, there are other EEO laws in addition to those just cited. Executive Order 11246 (EO 11246) imposes affirmative action and nondiscrimination requirements on contractors who do business with the federal government and on the federal agencies that oversee those contracts. Sections 501, 503, and 504 of the Rehabilitation Act of 1973 (Rehab 73) apply to federal (§§ 501, 503) and nonfederal (§ 504) entities and are critical precursors to the ADA. There are also constitutional amendments with overlapping and independent coverage of some of the same protected classes, covered entities, and covered practices as Title VII. These include the Fifth Amendment (federal entities), the Fourteenth Amendment (state and local entities), and the Thirteenth Amendment (private entities). Supporting legislation for the Thirteenth Amendment is codified in 42 U.S. Code as Section 1981, and for the Fourteenth Amendment as Section 1983. It should be noted that in addition to the major enforcement duties covered in this chapter, the EEOC has enforcement duties for affirmative action (or, as the EEOC calls it, *affirmative employment*) for federal agencies and Sections 501 and 503 of Rehab 73. The independent and overlapping coverage of the various EEO laws cited here is discussed in greater detail by Gutman (2000a).

Second, by virtue of two close (five to four) Supreme Court rulings, the ADEA (*Kimel* v. *Florida Board of Regents*, 2000) and ADA

(*Board of Trustees of Alabama* v. *Garrett,* 2001) no longer apply to state entities, although they apply to municipal entities. The Supreme Court ruled that Congress overstepped its Fourteenth Amendment powers to override Eleventh Amendment sovereign state immunity in both statutes. The applicable principle is known as *congruence and proportionality,* where *congruence* means having a basis for overriding immunity (for example, evidence of past discrimination) and *proportionality* means statutory provisions reasonably related to the congruent factors. Expanded coverage of the Kimel and Garrett cases is provided by Gutman (2000c, 2001b).

Third, the ADA does not apply to federal entities. Federal employees are, however, protected by Sections 501 and 503 of Rehab 73. Prior to the ADA, nonfederal entities were protected in Section 504 of the Rehabilitation Act, but this statute proved to be weaker than Sections 501 and 503. Indeed, Gutman (2000a) suggests the whole point of the ADA was to provide the same depth of coverage for nonfederal employees that had already existed for federal employees in Sections 501 and 503. It should be noted that Rehab 73 is still relevant law, and by ADA statutory authority, it must be interpreted in harmony with the ADA. Therefore there is no longer any major difference in how federal and nonfederal employees are protected, other than the fact that state employees are no longer among the nonfederal entities protected by the ADA.

Fourth, each statute cited previously and other EEO laws proscribe retaliation against employees who assert their rights. Retaliation provisions generally protect employees who engage in *participation* (for example, filing a claim) and *opposition* (for example, good faith questioning of employer policies). In a recent case (*Robinson* v. *Shell Oil,* 1997) the Supreme Court unanimously ruled that the participation provision extends to retaliatory references made against *former* employees.

In summary, one cannot in a single chapter exhaust all possible permutations relating to EEO laws and how they are administered. The information presented in this chapter should therefore be viewed only as a snapshot of some of the more important decisions that are made when plaintiffs claim workplace discrimination based on race or color, religion, sex, national origin, age, and disability.

Charges

The majority of the EEOC reports span the most recent twelve-year period, from fiscal year 1992 (FY92) through fiscal year 2003 (FY03). Occasionally, the EEOC releases a report spanning a twenty- to twenty-five-year interval on a major category of discrimination (for example, sexual harassment) or a five-year study on a specific function (for example, litigation). The discussion that follows is based on the twelve-year tables, with an emphasis on the more recent years. The early years from FY92 to FY96 are particularly difficult to interpret, primarily because of two major considerations. First, there is influence from the Civil Rights Act of 1991 (CRA-91), which among other things introduced compensatory and punitive damages and jury trials into Title VII and grandfathered both of these features into the ADA. Second, the ADA itself did not take effect until the third quarter of 1992. Even then, it applied to entities with twenty-five or more employees until 1994, when the magic number was reduced to fifteen or more employees (as in Title VII). Of course, the recent years are also characterized by special events, including major Supreme Court rulings; the September 11, 2001, tragedies at the World Trade Center and the Pentagon; and the recent economic downturn. Therefore we will point out, when appropriate, special events that may have influenced the statistics under review.

A Seven-Year Snapshot

Table 4.1 contains a snapshot of the most recent seven-year period, from FY97 to FY03. These are simple means and percentages from the twelve-year table rounded to the nearest integer. Charges are broken out separately for the Title VII classes in rows 1 to 4; for ADEA, ADA, and EPA, respectively, in rows 5 to 7; and for retaliation in row 8. The retaliation charges are nonspecific and may come from any of the four statutes. The percentages in rows 1 through 7 sum to greater than 100 percent, as individual claims often involve concurrent charges invoking more than one statute and, within Title VII, concurrent charges based on two or more protected classes. Indeed, closer inspection of Table 4.1 (that is, summing the percentage column) reveals that approximately half of all charges filed with the EEOC invoked more than one cause of action.

Table 4.1. Means and Percentages of Charges by Causes of Discrimination, FY97–FY03.

Charge	Mean	Percentage
1. Race or color	29,019	36%
2. Sex	24,760	31
3. National origin	7,701	10
4. Religion	2,068	3
5. ADEA	16,796	21
6. ADA	16,657	21
7. EPA	1,170	1
8. Retaliation	20,904	26

Inspection of Table 4.1 reveals that on average, about 80 percent of all charges are for or include alleged Title VII violations. Furthermore, over 65 percent of the Title VII charges can be attributed to race or sex. In comparison, the ADA and ADEA charges, though substantial in their own right, are less by percentage than either the Title VII race or sex charges, and there are fewer EPA charges than any other cause has. The retaliation charges are also substantial by percentage and are within the same range as the ADA and ADEA charges. According to data from the twelve-year reports (see Tables 4.2 and 4.3), retaliation charges related to Title VII have a seven-year average equal to 19,016, which represents about 91 percent of the total for retaliation charges in Table 4.1. Closer inspection of Table 4.1 (that is, the sum of percentages) indicates that approximately half of all charges filed with EEOC over the last seven years invoked more than one cause of action.

Twelve-Year Trends

For purposes of exposition the twelve-year tables are examined separately for the Title VII classes (Table 4.2) and for the ADEA, ADA, and EPA statutes (Table 4.3). The total charges, which apply to all four statutes, are presented in the top row of Table 4.2. On average, the EEOC receives approximately 81,700 charges each year. As in Table 4.1, percentages do not add up to 100 percent because

Table 4.2. Breakout of Title VII Charges Per Year, FY92–FY03.

	FY92	FY93	FY94	FY95	FY96	FY97	FY98	FY99	FY00	FY01	FY02	FY03
Total charges	72,302	87,942	91,189	87,529	77,990	80,680	79,591	77,444	79,896	80,840	84,442	81,293
Race or color	29,548	31,695	31,656	29,986	26,287	29,199	28,820	28,819	28,945	28,912	29,910	28,526
	40.9%	36.0%	34.8%	34.3%	33.8%	36.2%	36.2%	37.3%	36.2%	35.8%	35.4%	35.1%
Sex	21,796	23,919	25,860	26,181	23,813	24,728	24,454	23,907	25,194	25,140	25,536	24,362
	30.1%	27.2%	28.4%	29.9%	30.6%	30.7%	30.7%	30.9%	31.5%	31.1%	30.2%	30.0%
National origin	7,434	7,454	7,414	7,035	6,687	6,712	6,778	7,108	7,792	8,025	9,046	8,450
	10.3%	8.5%	8.1%	8.0%	8.6%	8.3%	8.5%	9.2%	9.8%	9.9%	10.7%	10.4%
Religion	1,388	1,449	1,546	1,581	1,564	1,709	1,786	1,811	1,939	2,127	2,572	2,532
	1.9%	1.6%	1.7%	1.8%	2.0%	2.1%	2.2%	2.3%	2.4%	2.6%	3.0%	3.1%
Retaliation	10,499	12,644	14,415	15,342	14,412	16,394	17,246	17,883	19,753	20,407	20,814	20,615
	14.5%	14.4%	15.8%	17.5%	18.5%	20.3%	21.7%	23.1%	24.7%	25.2%	24.6%	25.4%

of concurrent claims. Also, the retaliation charges in Table 4.2 are associated with Title VII, whereas the retaliation charges in Table 4.3 include all four statutes enforced by the EEOC.

Inspection of Table 4.2 reveals a sharp rise in total charges from FY92 to FY93. The initial rise is maintained through FY94 and FY95 before declining sharply in FY96 and leveling off at an average of roughly 81,000 in FY97 through FY03. The initial rise coincides with the passage of CRA-91, with expanded remedies and jury trials. A common perception, held by many lawyers among others, is that jury trials are more plaintiff-friendly than bench trials (before only a judge). However, the expanded remedies are what likely stimulated the increase in Title VII charges, by making for larger awards and thereby attracting more plaintiff attorneys. The newer remedies include compensatory damages for pain and suffering and punitive damages against employers who willfully violate the law or who should have known a violation was committed (that is, who had a reckless disregard for the law). These damages are, however, capped, ranging from $50,000 to $300,000, depending on the size of the entity. As a result there is an inducement for concurrent Title VII and Section 1981 (Thirteenth Amendment) charges because the damages in constitutional claims are not capped.

The twelve-year trend for total charges is representative for race and sex but *not* for the other three categories. For example, the charges and percentages are relatively flat for race and sex from FY97 through FY03, the years represented by the snapshot in Table 4.1. In comparison, for national origin and religion, they are relatively flat from FY97 to FY99 and rise thereafter, particularly in FY02 and FY03. This latter interval coincides with an increase in so-called backlash charges by Arab and Muslim groups after the September 11, 2001, tragedies. Backlash charges are discussed again later in this chapter. The charges and percentages for retaliation appear to increase steadily from FY97 to FY00 and then to have reached a plateau. The increase is possibly due to greater awareness by employees who in the past might have withheld a claim for fear of retaliation. Now they are more likely to recognize that retaliation is itself actionable, even if the original charges lack merit.

Table 4.3 focuses on the ADEA, ADA, EPA, and retaliation charges, the latter aggregated across all statutes (including Title VII). Inspection of Table 4.3 reveals a pattern for retaliation similar to that in Table 4.2, which is expected because, as previously noted,

Table 4.3. Charges for ADEA, ADA, EPA, and Retaliation (All Statutes), FY92–FY03.

	FY92	FY93	FY94	FY95	FY96	FY97	FY98	FY99	FY00	FY01	FY02	FY03
Retaliation	11,096	13,814	15,853	17,070	16,080	18,198	19,114	19,694	21,613	22,257	22,768	22,690
	15.3%	15.7%	17.4%	19.5%	20.6%	22.6%	24.0%	25.4%	27.1%	27.5%	27.0%	27.9%
ADEA	19,573	19,809	19,618	17,416	15,719	15,785	15,191	14,141	16,008	17,405	19,921	19,124
	27.1%	22.5%	21.5%	19.9%	20.2%	19.6%	19.1%	18.3%	20.0%	21.5%	23.6%	23.5%
ADA	1,048*	15,274	18,859	19,798	18,046	18,108	17,806	17,007	15,864	16,470	15,964	15,377
	1.4%	17.4%	20.7%	22.6%	23.1%	22.4%	22.4%	22.0%	19.9%	20.4%	18.9%	18.9%
EPA	1,294	1,328	1,381	1,275	969	1,134	1,071	1,044	1,270	1,251	1,256	1,167
	1.8%	1.5%	1.5%	1.5%	1.2%	1.4%	1.3%	1.3%	1.6%	1.5%	1.5%	1.4%

*EEOC began enforcing the ADA on July 26, 1992.

the retaliation data for Title VII account for about 91 percent of all retaliation charges across the seven-year snapshot period. The trends for the ADEA, ADA, and EPA are different from each other, and different from trends observed for the Title VII classes in Table 4.2.

The charges and percentages for the EPA are relatively flat for the entire twelve-year period, ranging between 1,134 and 1,294 for nine of the twelve years, and are sporadically lower in some years (FY96, FY98, and FY99). There is no noticeable pattern corresponding to CRA-91, which is expected because CRA-91 did not alter any EPA remedies, and jury trials have always been available in this statute.

The charges and percentages for the ADEA are noticeably larger in the first three and last two fiscal years, and decline during the seven years between FY95 and FY01. The absence of a coincident trend with CRA-91 is as much expected for the ADEA as for the EPA, because CRA-91 did not alter any ADEA remedies, and jury trials have always been available under this statute as well. However, the noticeable increase in charges and percentages for FY02 and FY03 relative to the preceding seven-year period may be related to the most recent two-year interval in which the economy was in deep recession and there was considerable loss of jobs. As noted by Gutman (2000a, chap. 6), there are two major age-based scenarios that are likely heightened in reduction-in-force (RIF) conditions. In the first scenario older workers charge that they are discriminated against during the RIF or in reassignment to other jobs within the company after the RIF. The second type of charge features induced retirement, sometimes by coercion (for example, threatened loss or devaluation of severance or retirement benefits). (See Chapter Nine in this volume.)

Finally, Table 4.3 reveals that once the ADA took hold, there was a steady stream of charges from FY94 through FY99, followed by a decrease in FY00 through FY03. For example, the average number and percentage of ADA charges from FY96 through FY99 is 17,742 and 22.5 percent, in comparison to 15,919 and 19.5 percent for FY00 to FY03. This latter trend is coincident with three 1999 Supreme Court ADA rulings (*Albertsons* v. *Kirkingburg, Murphy* v. *United Parcel Service,* and *Sutton* v. *United Airlines*) that are widely believed to have limited in scope the definition of being disabled in accordance with the ADA (although an alternative account of these cases is provided by Gutman, 2000b).

In summary, Title VII elicits nearly four times as many claims from the private sector as the ADEA or the ADA, and the vast majority of these claims are for race or sex-related charges. Not surprisingly, the EPA, the narrowest of the four statutes, elicits only 1 to 2 percent of the claims. About 25 percent of all claims have additional retaliation charges, which are treated as separate actions. Trends across recent years suggest an increase in ADEA claims, possibly due to RIF-related actions by employers during the recent economic downturn, and a decrease in ADA claims, possibly due to three major Supreme Court rulings in 1999.

Resolutions

The EEOC must formally resolve in some way every charge it receives. Tables provided by the EEOC report the number and manner of resolution of charges filed under each cause of action, over a twelve-year period. For purposes of exposition, these resolution data will be presented as three subsets. The first subset shows the determination by EEOC of charges that have and that lack merit. The other two subsets show how meritorious claims are resolved. As in the prior section the tables cover the twelve-year period from FY92 to FY03. Tables 4.4 through 4.6 depict the three subsets for total charges summed over the four major statutes. Table 4.7 contains a snapshot breakdown of the four statutes, including the four Title VII classes, for FY03.

Subset 1: Administrative Closures, No Reasonable Cause, and Merit Resolutions

All charge resolutions fall into one of three categories: administrative closures, no reasonable cause, and merit resolutions. The data for subset 1 are depicted in Table 4.4. The reader will note that on a year-to-year basis, total charges (Table 4.2) do not match total resolutions. Simply stated, charges filed in a given year are not necessarily resolved in that year. Therefore, comparing Table 4.2 to Table 4.4, in some years there are more charges than resolutions; in other years more resolutions than charges. More important, because many factors enter into whether charges are resolved quickly or slowly, the twelve-year trend for total resolutions is neither very meaningful nor necessarily important.

Table 4.4. Administrative Closures, No Reasonable Cause, and Merit Resolutions for All EEOC Statutes, FY92–FY03.

	FY92	FY93	FY94	FY95	FY96	FY97	FY98	FY99	FY00	FY01	FY02	FY03
Total resolutions	68,366	71,716	71,563	91,774	103,467	106,312	101,470	97,846	93,672	90,106	95,222	87,755
Administrative closures	16,003 23.4%	20,285 28.3%	26,012 36.3%	34,153 37.2%	30,821 29.8%	30,077 28.3%	27,118 26.7%	23,570 24.1%	19,156 20.5%	18,636 20.7%	19,633 20.6%	15,262 17.4%
No reasonable cause	41,736 61.0%	40,183 56.0%	34,451 48.1%	46,700 50.9%	63,216 61.1%	64,567 60.7%	61,794 60.9%	58,174 59.5%	54,578 58.3%	51,562 57.2%	56,514 59.3%	55,359 63.1%
Merit resolutions	10,627 15.5%	11,248 15.7%	11,100 15.5%	10,921 11.9%	9,430 9.1%	11,668 11.0%	12,558 12.4%	16,102 16.5%	19,938 21.3%	19,908 22.1%	19,075 20.0%	17,134 19.5%

What is important is the relative breakdown of the no-merit and merit categories. Rounding error aside, the three categories shown in Table 4.4 sum to 100 percent of the total resolutions. There are two no-merit categories. The first category is *administrative closures*. These closures most often occur when the charging party cannot be located or has not responded to EEOC communications. There are also other possibilities. The charging party may request withdrawal of charges without resolution or benefits or may already have accepted full relief. In some instances, related litigation may render further processing futile, or the EEOC may determine it has no statutory jurisdiction. A right-to-sue letter is *not* issued for administrative closures. Inspection of Table 4.4 reveals that administrative closures have decreased from a high of about 37 percent in FY95 to the 20 percent range over the last four years.

The other no-merit category is the finding of *no reasonable cause,* which means the EEOC has investigated the charges and concluded there is no reason to believe discrimination has occurred. The charging party still has a right to go to court, and a right-to-sue letter *is* issued. Inspection of Table 4.4 reveals that the finding of no reasonable cause has consistently averaged in the 60 percent range across the last eight years. Thus a large majority of charges are resolved on the basis of being without merit. Using FY03 as an example, the two no-merit categories sum to 80.5 percent of the total resolutions. The final category, *merit resolutions,* consists of those charges that are resolved on the basis of the merit of the charge.

Subset 2: Breakdown of Merit Resolutions

Table 4.5 breaks the merit resolutions down into three categories. *Negotiated settlements* are charges that are settled with benefits to the charging party, as warranted by the evidence found during an investigation. These settlements may include the full range of remedies available (for example, back pay, reinstatement, and damages). *Withdrawals with benefits* are charges that have been withdrawn by the charging party after he or she has received the desired benefits. This may occur after an appropriate benefit is granted to the charging party by the respondent or after a non-negotiated settlement is reached. *Reasonable cause* findings result

Table 4.5. Breakdown of Merit Resolutions for All EEOC Statutes, FY92–FY03.

	FY92	FY93	FY94	FY95	FY96	FY97	FY98	FY99	FY00	FY01	FY02	FY03
Total merit resolutions	10,627 15.5%	11,248 15.7%	11,100 15.5%	10,921 11.9%	9,430 9.1%	11,668 11.0%	12,558 12.4%	16,102 16.5%	19,938 21.3%	19,908 22.1%	19,075 20.0%	17,134 19.5%
Negotiated settlements	4,348 6.4%	4,138 5.8%	3,938 5.5%	3,811 4.2%	3,163 3.1%	3,992 3.8%	4,646 4.6%	6,094 6.2%	7,937 8.5%	7,330 8.1%	8,425 8.8%	8,401 9.6%
Withdrawals with benefits	4,673 6.8%	5,145 7.2%	5,236 7.3%	5,035 5.5%	4,009 3.9%	3,635 3.4%	3,219 3.2%	3,593 3.7%	3,753 4.0%	3,654 4.1%	3,772 4.0%	3,700 4.2%
Reasonable cause	1,606 2.3%	1,965 2.7%	1,926 2.7%	2,075 2.3%	2,258 2.2%	4,041 3.8%	4,693 4.6%	6,415 6.6%	8,248 8.8%	8,924 9.9%	6,878 7.2%	5,033 5.7%

from the EEOC's determination of a reasonable basis for believing, based on evidence obtained during an investigation, that discrimination actually occurred.

The percentages reported in Table 4.5 are the percentages of *all* resolutions (not just merit resolutions) for a given fiscal year that fall into each category. Inspection of Table 4.5 reveals that over the last four years, about 42 percent of the total merit resolutions have been negotiated settlements, about 20 percent withdrawals with benefits, and about 38 percent reasonable cause determinations. Furthermore, in comparison to most of the years preceding FY96, in the years following FY96 negotiated settlements and reasonable cause determinations are up and withdrawals with benefits are down, a trend the EEOC attributes to its introduction of a national enforcement plan that prioritizes processing of charges at the time of intake and puts a greater emphasis on mediation and conciliation as methods of resolution (as discussed later in this chapter).

Subset 3: Breakdown of Reasonable Cause Determinations

Reasonable cause determinations are generally followed by efforts at conciliation to resolve the issues, giving rise to the charge of discrimination without litigation. Such efforts may result in *successful conciliations* or *unsuccessful conciliations*. Charges categorized as having reasonable cause that are subsequently resolved through negotiated settlements or withdrawals with benefits are *not* categorized as successful conciliations. Table 4.6 summarizes the breakdown for successful and unsuccessful conciliations. As in Table 4.5 the percentages shown are relative to all resolutions. Also shown are the percentages of reasonable cause findings that resulted in successful conciliations (that is, the *hit rate*). Inspection of Table 4.6 reveals that over the last seven years, the hit rate has been stable in the 25 to 28 percent range. However, the fact that most conciliations are not successful is misleading because favorable outcomes for the charging parties also accrue through settlements and withdrawals with benefits. When these categories are included (see Table 4.5), the favorable outcome rate is much higher. For example, in FY03 about 79 percent of the merit resolutions resulted in outcomes favorable to the charging parties.

Table 4.6. Breakdown of Reasonable Cause Determinations for All EEOC Statutes, FY92–FY03.

	FY92	FY93	FY94	FY95	FY96	FY97	FY98	FY99	FY00	FY01	FY02	FY03
Total reasonable cause	1,606 2.3%	1,965 2.7%	1,926 2.7%	2,075 2.3%	2,258 2.2%	4,041 3.8%	4,693 4.6%	6,415 6.6%	8,248 8.8%	8,924 9.9%	6,878 7.2%	5,033 5.7%
Successful conciliations	545 0.8%	589 0.8%	607 0.8%	500 0.5%	749 0.7%	1,041 1.0%	1,343 1.3%	1,578 1.6%	2,040 2.2%	2,365 2.6%	1,940 2.0%	1,432 1.6%
Unsuccessful conciliations	1,061 1.6%	1,376 1.9%	1,319 1.8%	1,575 1.7%	1,509 1.5%	3,000 2.8%	3,350 3.3%	4,837 4.9%	6,208 6.6%	6,559 7.3%	4,938 5.2%	3,601 4.1%
Hit rate	33.9%	30.0%	31.5%	24.1%	33.2%	25.8%	28.6%	24.6%	24.7%	26.5%	28.2%	28.5%

Snapshot of Statutes and Title VII Classes for FY03

The EEOC reports resolution data disaggregated for the major statutes and the Title VII protected classes as well as for major types of discrimination within the statutes (for example, harassment). For purposes of exposition, Table 4.7 provides a snapshot of resolutions for FY03 for the four statutes (and the Title VII protected classes) for the three subsets defined earlier. Also presented is a snapshot of monetary benefits for settlements and conciliations. Owing to concurrent charges, the raw totals for resolutions of all charges combined (87,555) is less than the sum for the four major statutes; the same is true for the Title VII sum (52,227) relative to the sum of its four classes.

FY03 was chosen for convenience, in that the data for FY03 are representative of the last three to five years and generally are consistent with the subset data in Tables 4.4, 4.5, and 4.6. More specifically, relative to the percentages in the first column (total resolutions), the relationships among administrative closures, no reasonable cause, and merit resolutions (subset 1, Table 4.4) are similar among the various statutes and classes, with the exception of those for the EPA, which appear somewhat higher than the others in terms of merit resolutions. However, the number and percentage of EPA charges are extremely low in any year, thus making it easier to obtain larger variations in percentages. The same generalization holds for subset 2 as well, which addresses the merit resolution data (Table 4.5). The percentage of reasonable cause findings for EPA is relatively greater than that for other causes. The reasonable cause data for Subset 3 (Table 4.6) show the same pattern. The EPA exhibits a higher percentage of unsuccessful conciliations. Table 4.7 also shows the hit rates for each cause of action. These are generally in the same range, with the exception of the ADA, where the hit rate is notably higher than it is for the other statutes and classes.

Table 4.7 also shows the monetary benefits gained through favorable outcomes other than litigation. These outcomes are negotiated settlements, withdrawals with benefits, and successful conciliations. An estimate of monetary benefits per favorable outcome may be obtained by dividing the monetary benefit by the total number of resolutions in these three categories. Of course, it is unknown what

Table 4.7. Breakout of Resolutions for Individual Statutes and Title VII Classes, Including Monetary Benefits, FY03.

	Total	Title VII	Race	Sex	N.O.	Rel.	ADEA	ADA	EPA
Total resolutions	87,555	52,227	30,702	27,146	9,172	2,690	17,352	16,915	1,071
Administrative closures	17.4%	17.7%	15.5%	20.2%	14.8%	16.1%	16.3%	17.7%	16.6%
No reasonable cause	63.1%	62.1%	66.8%	57.1%	66.7%	64.8%	69.0%	60.6%	57.2%
Merit resolutions	19.5%	20.3%	17.7%	22.7%	18.6%	19.0%	14.7%	21.7%	26.1%
Settlements	9.6%	10.0%	9.4%	10.6%	9.1%	8.2%	7.4%	10.3%	11.6%
Withdrawals with benefits	4.2%	4.2%	3.7%	4.9%	3.6%	3.2%	4.1%	4.4%	4.1%
Reasonable cause	5.7%	6.1%	4.6%	7.2%	5.8%	7.6%	3.2%	6.9%	10.5%
Successful conciliations	1.6%	1.4%	1.3%	1.9%	1.2%	2.5%	1.0%	2.9%	2.7%
Unsuccessful conciliations	4.1%	4.7%	3.4%	5.3%	4.6%	5.1%	2.3%	4.0%	7.7%
Hit rate	28.5%	23.5%	27.6%	26.7%	21.1%	32.7%	29.8%	41.6%	25.9%
Monetary benefits (in millions)*	$236.2	$138.7	$69.6	$98.4	$21.3	$6.6	$48.9	$45.3	$3.4
Per favorable outcome (in thousands)**	$17.5	$17.0	$15.8	$20.8	$16.6	$17.6	$22.6	$15.2	$17.6

*Does not include monetary benefits obtained through litigation.

**Favorable outcomes = settlements + withdrawals with benefits + successful conciliations.

percentage of these outcomes is associated with class actions, which normally garner awards that are bigger overall but potentially smaller for individual claimants. Also, because concurrent charges are considered, there is some double (or more) counting, particularly in and among the Title VII classes. With this in mind, it would appear that on a per statute (and protected class) basis, there are only minor variations in the award per favorable outcome, except for the relatively higher values for sex and ADEA claims.

The EEOC also reports (not shown in Table 4.7) that approximately 56 percent of all sex-based charges involve an allegation of sexual harassment, and that 23 percent of these charges are resolved through means other than litigation, compared to 17 percent of all sex-based charges. Therefore nonlitigated sexual harassment charges account for 73 percent of nonlitigated resolution of all sex-based charges. Yet the monetary award per favorable outcome averages $14,600 for sexual harassment resolutions, compared to $20,800 for all sex-based resolutions. A suggested explanation for this result is that following the Supreme Court's 1998 rulings in *Burlington* v. *Ellerth* and *Faragher* v. *Boca Raton* (discussed in greater detail later in this chapter), more complainants are agreeable to accepting a change in employer policy and practices, without a monetary award for damages. Alternatively, nonharassment charges are likely to have implications for promotions and pay increases and therefore greater monetary implications. As for ADEA, the observed difference seems most likely attributable to increases in buyout or retirement provisions associated with organizational downsizings.

In summary, in FY03 about 80 percent of all resolutions were in the nonmerit category, leaving 20 percent as merit resolutions. About 71 percent of the merit resolutions were settlements and withdrawals with benefits, and the remaining 29 percent were findings of reasonable cause for which conciliation by the EEOC is attempted. Of the conciliations, about 28 percent were successful, leaving 72 percent that the EEOC considered for possible litigation. As discussed in the following section, very few charges were actually litigated.

Litigation

Although the EEOC must resolve all charges it receives, it has a choice regarding the charges it litigates. The EEOC reports data for the number of lawsuits it files, how lawsuits are resolved, and monetary benefits. The EEOC also released a five-year study of its litigation statistics covering FY97 to FY01, and facts not available in its traditional twelve-year tables are presented in its *Annual Report for FY 2002*. Data from these reports are presented in Tables 4.8 to 4.11. Therefore, for exposition purposes, the emphasis will be on the fiscal years covered in these tables.

Lawsuits Filed

Tables 4.8, 4.9, and 4.10 detail the span from FY92 through FY03. Table 4.8 depicts lawsuits filed. The first row (*all suits filed*) is a combination of *direct suits,* filed by EEOC against an employer with allegations of discrimination, and *subpoena enforcement actions,* which may be filed during investigations if employers refuse to provide information relevant to a charge. For example, in FY03, there were 393 suits filed, of which 361 (91.8 percent) were direct suits and 32 (8.2) percent were subpoena actions. The percentages in Table 4.8 sum to 100 percent of the direct suits in any given year (except for rounding errors) for the four statutes and concurrent charges. The focus of the following tables is on direct suits, because subpoena actions have no direct bearing on eventual resolution, and monetary awards. The EEOC reports actual numbers in these breakdowns, but these have been converted to percentages in Table 4.8 for purposes of exposition.

Inspection of Table 4.8 reveals that since FY92, the EEOC has filed between 167 (FY96) and 437 (FY99) direct suits, a number that has varied in a narrower band (between 290 and 361) over the past four years. Coinciding with the breakdowns for charges in Table 4.1, Title VII lawsuits are most frequent, EPA lawsuits are rare events, and ADA and ADEA lawsuits are somewhere in between (see, for example, the percentages for FY03, the most recent year reported).

More important, Table 4.8 also reveals how few lawsuits the EEOC actually files in any given year. The data first show that the number of unsuccessful conciliations dramatically increased beginning in FY97, with an average of 4,639 per year, compared to an average of 1,368 per year for the five-year prior period. At the same time, the number of direct suits filed by EEOC remained approximately the same (with only a slight increase to an average of 354 per year for the seven-year period, compared to an earlier average

Table 4.8. Lawsuits and Subpoena Actions, FY92–FY03.

	FY92	FY93	FY94	FY95	FY96	FY97	FY98	FY99	FY00	FY01	FY02	FY03
All suits filed	447	481	425	373	193	330	411	464	328	430	364	393
Subpoena actions	100	83	68	45	26	31	40	27	38	45	32	32
Direct suits	**347**	**398**	**357**	**328**	**167**	**299**	**371**	**437**	**290**	**385**	**332**	**361**
Title VII	69.7%	65.3%	65.8%	58.8%	64.1%	58.2%	63.3%	74.4%	76.6%	69.9%	74.1%	76.7%
ADA*	0.0%	0.8%	9.5%	24.7%	22.8%	26.4%	21.3%	11.7%	7.9%	16.1%	12.3%	12.7%
ADEA	24.2%	28.9%	20.7%	12.5%	7.8%	12.0%	9.7%	9.4%	9.3%	8.3%	8.7%	5.8%
EPA	0.6%	0.5%	0.0%	0.3%	0.6%	0.0%	0.5%	0.7%	1.0%	1.3%	0.6%	0.0%
Concurrent	5.5%	4.5%	3.9%	3.7%	5.4%	3.3%	5.1%	3.9%	5.2%	4.4%	4.2%	4.7%
Unsuccessful conciliations (UCs)	1,061	1,376	1,319	1,575	1,509	3,000	3,350	4,837	6,208	6,559	4,938	3,601
Percentage UCs filed as direct suits	32.7%	28.9%	27.1%	20.8%	11.1%	10.0%	11.1%	9.0%	4.7%	5.9%	6.7%	10.0%

*The ADA did not come into effect until the fourth quarter of FY92.

of 319), with a resulting decrease in the percentage of direct suits resulting from unsuccessful conciliation. Over the past seven-year span, EEOC has filed suit for 7.6 percent of unsuccessful conciliations, compared to an earlier average of 23.3 percent.

In its five-year study of litigation by its Office of General Counsel, covering FY97 to FY01, the EEOC reported that 570 suits (31.9 percent) were filed on behalf of individuals and 1,212 suits (68.1 percent) were class actions. Interestingly, only 87 out of the 1,782 direct suits filed during that period went to trial (less than 5 percent).

Resolutions

Table 4.9 depicts the data for resolutions. As in Table 4.8, the top row (all resolutions) is a combination of the number of direct suits and subpoena enforcement actions. However, in this table the direct suits also include interventions (that is, cases in which the EEOC joins a lawsuit filed by a private plaintiff) and, beginning in FY02, lawsuits to enforce administrative settlements. The percentages for the statutes and concurrent cases sum to 100 percent (except for occasional rounding errors) of the direct suits and interventions, and numbers were converted to percentages for purposes of exposition.

Inspection of Table 4.9 reveals that since FY92, the EEOC has resolved between 214 (FY97) and 532 (FY92) direct suits and interventions, a number that has varied in a narrower band (between 319 and 405) over the past five years. Resolutions have averaged 320.6 per year for FY97 through FY03, compared to an average of 378.9 for the five-year prior period. The percentages for resolutions in Table 4.9 virtually mirror the percentages for filings in Table 4.8 for the statutes and concurrent filings. More important, as the EEOC reported in its litigation study for FY97 to FY01, over 90 percent of the 1,552 lawsuits resolved were successful resolutions, where successful resolution equates to a consent decree, settlement agreement, or favorable court order resulting in monetary relief, job placement, changes in discriminatory policies and practices, accommodation for disability or religious beliefs, or training for employees. The EEOC also reports that over 60 percent of the eighty-seven trials between FY97 and FY01 resulted in a favorable outcome, compared to a 26.8 percent victory rate for suits filed by private plaintiffs.

Table 4.9. Resolutions of Lawsuits and Subpoena Actions, FY92–FY03.

	FY92	FY93	FY94	FY95	FY96	FY97	FY98	FY99	FY00	FY01	FY02	FY03
All resolutions	626	427	469	338	296	245	331	349	438	360	373	378
Subpoena actions	94	65	61	19	18	31	36	30	33	41	28	31
Direct suits and interventions	**532**	**362**	**408**	**319**	**278**	**214**	**295**	**319**	**405**	**319**	**345**	**347**
Title VII	67.7%	64.9%	65.2%	67.7%	62.9%	57.0%	61.4%	60.2%	75.3%	68.7%	71.6%	73.8%
ADA*	0.0%	0.3%	2.2%	7.8%	18.7%	21.0%	23.4%	20.4%	12.8%	13.2%	17.7%	13.8%
ADEA	24.4%	27.3%	26.7%	19.1%	12.6%	16.4%	11.9%	12.9%	8.6%	10.7%	5.8%	8.1%
EPA	2.1%	0.6%	0.7%	0.6%	0.0%	0.0%	0.3%	0.0%	1.0%	1.9%	0.9%	0.6%
Concurrent	5.8%	6.9%	5.1%	4.7%	5.8%	5.6%	3.1%	6.6%	2.2%	5.6%	4.1%	3.7%

*The ADA did not come into effect until the fourth quarter of FY92.

Monetary Benefits

Table 4.10 depicts the monetary benefits (in millions of dollars) obtained from resolutions. Raw numbers again were converted to percentages for the statutes and concurrent cases. Inspection of Table 4.10 reveals considerable year-to-year variability in total monetary benefits, with no obvious pattern for any length of time. Furthermore, with the exception of the EPA, where the monetary benefits were low in each year, the relationships among the remaining three statutes do not show the same proportions as the relationships in Table 4.8 (suits filed) or Table 4.9 (resolutions). Most notably, Title VII is not as dominant in monetary awards, particularly in recent years. Also, the relationship between the ADA and ADEA varies depending on the year examined.

A clearer picture for monetary benefits is provided by the EEOC in the *Annual Report for FY 2002*, a year in which there were 345 resolutions (see Table 4.9) resulting in monetary benefits of $52.8 million (see Table 4.10). These data are presented in Table 4.11. The relief per suit column reveals that the monetary benefits are significantly higher per suit for concurrent charges than for any of the statutes. Among the statutes, the ADA gets close to 1.7 times the amount per suit relative to Title VII, about 2.8 times relative to the ADEA, and about 4.5 times relative to the EPA.

What is unknown in is how the monetary distribution is affected by the ratio of class actions, which likely garner more money per resolution than individual claims. Although the *Annual Report for FY 2002* explains that of the 345 resolutions, 113 were filed as class actions (with a total relief of $38,991,862 and an average of $345,060) and 232 as individual filings (for a total relief of $13,853,637 and an average of $59,714), it is not clear how relief was distributed over causes of action or individual plaintiffs. For example, the concurrent claims data in Table 4.11 are derived from only fourteen resolutions. Thus two or three extremely large class action settlements could easily distort the picture relative to what happens in most of the cases. Another unknown is how indicative or anomalous the FY02 data are, because the EEOC litigation study also reports that for the period from FY97 to FY01, the average monetary benefit for 1,552 resolved claims was $263,945. Even when adjusted for total number of claims (1,782), the monetary average is still $255,206 per suit, which is about $100,000 per suit higher relative to the average for FY02.

Table 4.10. Monetary Benefits, FY92–FY03.

	FY92	FY93	FY94	FY95	FY96	FY97	FY98	FY99	FY00	FY01	FY02	FY03
Monetary benefits (in millions)	71.1	36.4	39.6	18.9	50.8	114.7	95.5	98.4	49.8	51.2	52.8	148.7
Title VII	20.7%	19.2%	59.6%	47.6%	37.0%	82.8%	64.9%	50.0%	70.5%	58.2%	54.8%	58.6%
ADA*	0.0%	0.5%	1.0%	7.4%	4.9%	1.0%	2.5%	2.9%	6.0%	4.3%	22.8%	1.7%
ADEA	78.1%	73.1%	37.9%	42.3%	20.7%	15.7%	30.9%	43.2%	22.5%	6.1%	2.6%	38.9%
EPA	0.3%	0.3%	0.1%	1.1%	0.0%	0.3%	0.7%	0.3%	0.4%	0.6%	0.3%	0.0%
Concurrent	1.0%	6.9%	1.3%	1.6%	37.4%	0.3%	0.9%	3.6%	0.6%	30.9%	19.5%	0.8%

*The ADA did not come into effect until the fourth quarter of FY92.

Table 4.11. Snapshot of Monetary Benefits, FY02.

	Relief (in millions)	Relief (percentage)	Relief (per suit)
Title VII	$28.95	54.8%	$117,206
ADA	12.03	22.8	197,213
ADEA	1.39	2.6	69,500
EPA	0.17	0.3	56,666
Concurrent	10.30	19.5	735,714
Total	$52.84	100%	$153,175

A final point is that the EEOC's *Annual Report for FY 2002* provides additional detail about resolutions for types of discrimination. Recognizing that the percentages do not sum to 100 percent (owing to concurrent claims), 40.6 percent of all resolutions involved harassment charges (24.9 percent involved sexual harassment), 34.2 percent involved discharge (18.0 percent involved constructive discharge), 14.8 percent involved hiring, 7.8 percent involved reasonable accommodation (disability), 7.5 percent involved promotion, 5.8 percent involved wages, 4.6 percent involved reasonable accommodation (religion), and 0.6 percent involved language (for example, rules requiring that employees speak only English).

What stands out in the litigation data is how few cases, both in absolute terms and percentages, actually go to trial. According to the five-year report data for FY97 to FY02, the average is seventeen or eighteen cases a year. Additionally, given the FY02 annual report data, it would appear that harassment and discharge are the two dominant causes for resolution. Within the discharge category more than half the resolutions are for constructive discharge and are likely, therefore, to be concurrent to a large extent with harassment or other charges, such as age discrimination during a reduction in force. The monetary data should be interpreted with caution. They do indicate that the EEOC wins a lot of money per resolution, but it is not clear what this means for individual statutes (or for individual plaintiffs) and concurrent claims because the breakdown for class action versus individual suits, though given overall (class action = 31.9 percent versus individual = 68.1 percent) is not provided for the statutes or the concurrent cases.

Monthly Reports and News Releases

In addition to statistics on charges, resolutions, and litigation, the EEOC releases news as it occurs, and files it on a monthly basis. There are two particularly interesting types of releases related to the topics discussed in this chapter. The first is monthly reports titled "EEOC Litigation Settlements." These are settlements short of court rulings on cases the EEOC chose to litigate. The second includes general press releases on any topic the EEOC finds important, including some of the settlements cited in the "EEOC Litigation Settlements" reports. The discussions that follow sample material from both types of releases from December 2002 through February 2004.

EEOC Litigation Settlements

Between December 2002 and February 2004, the EEOC cites 113 settlements of cases that started out in the filings-for-litigation column (see Table 4.8). For the most part these settlements are dispersed in proportions similar to those seen in the charge tables (see Table 4.1). As in the charge tables, many of the cases have concurrent charges, both within Title VII and across statutes. Otherwise, about 75 percent of the cases involve or include Title VII and less than 1 percent involve or include the EPA. The remaining 20 percent or so are divided nearly equally between the ADEA ($n = 11$) and the ADA ($n = 13$), and about 12 percent of all cases have associated retaliation charges (most of which are associated with Title VII).

Within the Title VII settlements, nearly 70 percent involve harassment charges, and about 24 percent involve other traditional topics such as discrimination in hiring and promotion (the remaining 5 to 6 percent are concurrent claims). Among the harassment cases, about 60 percent involve or include sex, 30 percent involve or include race, and the remaining 10 percent or so combine race with religion or national origin, or both, and there are occasional cases in which racial or sexual harassment is combined with another Title VII class or another statute.

Among the remaining settlements, most of the ADEA cases address traditional age-related issues, including hiring ($n = 3$) and RIF-related charges (involving, for example, reassignment or benefits) ($n = 6$). Two of them involve harassment. Among the ADA cases, only one disability (deafness) is represented twice. Ten of the remaining eleven settlements involve a different disability, with a seven-to-three distribution between physical and mental disabilities. Broken down another way, eleven of the thirteen settlements involve failure to reasonably accommodate, and two involve general policies for refusal to hire or retain.

A final point is that the majority of the cases, particularly those involving sexual or racial harassment charges, focused on small- to medium-sized businesses. In many cases these businesses were franchises of larger chains, including fast-food restaurants such as Pizza Hut, Taco Bell, and Church's Chicken; major hotel chains such as Holiday Inn; retail outlet stores such as Home Depot, Target, Wal-Mart, and Victoria's Secret; car dealerships for such major car brands as Ford, Nissan, Honda, and the like; and banks such as Wells Fargo and First National Bank.

News Releases

The value of examining these news releases is that they feature, among other things, three emerging issues that are difficult to learn about elsewhere on the EEOC Web site or, for that matter, any Web site. The first of these is a much-anticipated announcement by the EEOC on clarification of the definition of "Job Applicant" for "Internet and Related Technologies" (See Harris, 2003). According to the EEOC, there are three key considerations, including that (1) the employer has acted to fill a particular position, (2) the individual has followed the employer's standard procedures for submitting an application, and (3) the individual has indicated an interest in the particular position.

The second emerging issue concerns the EEOC's announcement on March 24, 2003, about its intent to use alternative dispute resolution (ADR) as a method for resolving charges of discrimination short of court action. The EEOC cites four major advantages of ADR: (1) quicker resolutions, (2) less litigation and lower related costs, (3) creative solutions that are more satisfactory to all parties, and (4) fewer future complaints (as a result of ADR's fostering better communication among employees and employers). Under the EEOC's ADR plan, the employee agrees to suspend his or her claim for sixty days to give the employer a chance to resolve the dispute though internal mechanisms. The internal mechanisms must satisfy six criteria. There must be (1) voluntary participation and (2) the existence of an established program with (3) clearly written procedures that are (4) free to the employee. Additionally, (5) the program must address all claims and relief under EEOC-enforced statutes, and (6) settlements must be in writing and enforceable in court. At the latest count, twenty-nine of the Fortune 500 companies have satisfied these criteria, as have 500 other companies. The technical name for this mediation program is National Universal Agreement to Mediate (NUAM).

The third emerging issue concerns the backlash suits alluded to earlier in this chapter. These relate to alleged acts of discrimination against Arabs or Muslims after the 9/11 World Trade Center and Pentagon tragedies. At latest count there were eight such claims. The employers alleged to have committed such violations include a hospital, a seafood restaurant, an airline, and a hotel, suggesting that the EEOC is trying to sample broadly among potential industries in prosecuting such claims.

Conclusion

Everything presented in this chapter was obtained from the EEOC Web site (www.eeoc.gov). The Web site facilitates two major EEOC goals. The first and more obvious goal is to enforce EEO laws through such activities as processing and resolving claims of discrimination, writing guidelines and regulations to interpret laws, and writing policy guidance in response to major court rulings. All of this information is available on the Web site. The second and less obvious goal involves public relations and is served by making available statistics and news releases such as those sampled in this chapter.

The public relations goal also reflects on two major objectives. The more obvious objective is to show potential violators and victims how good the EEOC is at investigating and remedying claims of discrimination it deems to have merit. The less obvious objective relates to policies and procedures the EEOC believes may prevent discrimination from occurring or, if it occurs, may streamline and improve the process of complaint resolution. An example of prevention is the way the EEOC responded to the recent series of backlash suits by preparing a forum for Arab, Sikh, and South Asian employers and employees designed to provide information about rights and responsibilities under federal law (July 7, 2003). The ADR program illustrates how the EEOC proposes to streamline and improve the complaint resolution process.

The processing and resolution data reveal how selective the EEOC is with respect to claims it labels meritorious. About 80 percent of all claims are administratively closed for procedural reasons or are found to have no basis for reasonable cause. However, even among the remaining 20 percent, only 25 percent on average pass the EEOC criteria for believing discrimination has occurred. The EEOC resolves nearly 80 percent of those claims through settlements, withdrawals with benefits, and successful attempts at conciliation. Of the charges for which conciliation has been unsuccessful, less than 10 percent (about 350 per year) are selected for filing of a direct suit for possible litigation, and only a very select few (an average of seventeen or eighteen cases a year) actually go to trial. Therefore it is not surprising that the EEOC wins about 60 percent of its trials in comparison to about 27 percent for private claims. Assuming a large percentage of these private claims are no-reasonable-cause cases, and assuming the EEOC is good at judging which cases have merit and which lack merit, it follows that the EEOC tries the stronger cases.

The processing and resolution data also reveal Title VII dominance, although the ADA and ADEA do get significant numbers (especially relative to the EPA). Furthermore, most Title VII claims are for race and sex charges, and both the EEOC data and the EEOC news releases show that most of these charges involve harassment. Harassment also occurs as a charge in ADEA, religion, and national origin cases, and perhaps more so for religion and national origin in the wake of the September 11, 2001, tragedies. Gutman (2001a) has previously noted the dominance of sexual and racial harassment cases, even before the events of September 11, 2001, in a sample of EEOC settlements surveyed for the six-month period covering January 2001 through July 2001.

The focus on harassment is consistent with the focus on ADR. In the two 1998 sexual harassment rulings cited earlier (*Burlington* v. *Ellerth* and *Faragher* v. *Boca Raton*), the Supreme Court ruled employers are vicariously liable for actions by supervisors who commit hostile environment harassment. However, the Supreme Court also ruled employers may invoke an affirmative defense if (1) they take *reasonable care* to prevent and correct such actions and (2) the victim shows an *unreasonable failure* to take advantage of such policies. Inspection of the six criteria companies must meet to qualify as having a NUAM program reveals these criteria are consistent and overlap with establishing reasonable care policies. Because it is in the interest of employers to qualify for ADR, it is in their further interest to coordinate ADR plans with written policies and protections designed to prevent and correct any form of harassment or other form of employment discrimination, not just sexual harassment.

Note that there are major differences between ADR, which the EEOC strongly endorses, and binding arbitration as a condition of employment, which the EEOC strongly opposes (see Gutman, 2002). In *Gilmer* v. *Interstate* (1991) the Supreme Court denied a sixty-two-year-old terminated securities dealer's private right to sue under the ADEA because he had signed a binding arbitration agreement years earlier when he was initially employed. The EEOC responded with policy guidance opposing such binding agreements (see Policy Order 915.002, 1997), and subsequently took the fight to the Supreme Court, in *EEOC* v. *Waffle House* (2002). In *Circuit City* v. *Adams* (2001), a related case, the Supreme Court ruled the EEOC has independent authority to litigate even when the private right to sue is lost, as in *Gilmer*. In *Waffle House* the EEOC was permitted to sue for monetary remedies in such cases. Critically, unlike the binding arbitration agreement, the ADR program is voluntary, and the EEOC controls the criteria for qualification.

Finally, in his prior review of the EEOC Web site, Gutman (2001a) noted the EEOC's penchant for suing Wal-Mart in the 1990s (easily in the double digits) but treated it as nothing more than an interesting fact. Our review in this chapter of the settlements and news releases since December 2002 suggests it is more than merely human interest. Rather, it reads like a larger plan to pressure all franchise companies (such as the large fast-food chains) on the issue of lack of control over what happens at individual outlets. In this context, Wal-Mart is just another franchise with as many outlets as a McDonald's, Burger King, or Wendy's. The larger implication, therefore, is that stronger central authority over what happens at franchise outlets is required, and the EEOC will continue to sue such outlets until that central authority is strengthened to properly deal with complaints of workplace discrimination by employees.

Note

1. On the Web site www.eeoc.gov home page, for the twelve-year tables, see both "Enforcement Statistics" under the heading "Statistics" and "Statistics" under the heading "Litigation"; for the five-year study, see "A Study of the Litigation Program: 1995–2001" under the heading "Litigation"; for the annual reports see "Annual Reports" under the heading "About the EEOC." The material in this chapter was accessed in 2004.

References

Books and Articles

Gutman, A. (2000a). *EEO law and personnel practices* (2nd ed.). Thousand Oaks, CA: Sage.

Gutman, A. (2000b). Recent Supreme Court ADA rulings: Mixed messages from the Court. *The Industrial-Organizational Psychologist, 37*(3), 31–41.

Gutman, A. (2000c). The Supreme Court curtails the 14th Amendment powers of Congress. *The Industrial-Organizational Psychologist, 38*(1), 99–104.

Gutman, A. (2001a). So what's new at eeoc.gov? *The Industrial-Organizational Psychologist, 39*(2), 78–84.

Gutman, A. (2001b). Tightening the reins of justice? *The Industrial-Organizational Psychologist, 39*(1), 105–112.

Gutman, A. (2002). Two January 2002 Supreme Court rulings: Toyota v. Williams and EEOC v. Waffle House. *The Industrial-Organizational Psychologist, 39*(4), 58-66.

Harris, M. (2003). Speeding down the information highway: Internet recruitment and testing. *The Industrial-Organizational Psychologist, 41*(2), 103–106.

Cases

Albertsons v. Kirkingburg, 527 U.S. 555 (1999).
Board of Trustees of Alabama v. Garrett, 531 U.S. 356 (2001).
Burlington Industries, Inc. v. Ellerth, 524 U.S. 742 (1998).
Circuit City v. Adams, 532 U.S. 105 (2001).
EEOC v. Waffle House, 534 U.S. 279 (2002).
Faragher v. City of Boca Raton, 524 U.S. 775 (1998).
Gilmer v. Interstate, 500 U.S. 20 (1991).
Kimel v. Florida Board of Regents, 528 U.S. 62 (2000).
Murphy v. United Parcel Service, 527 U.S. 516 (1999).
Robinson v. Shell Oil Co., 519 U.S. 337 (1997).
Sutton v. United Airlines, 527 U.S. 471 (1999).

CHAPTER 5

Statistical Issues in Litigation

Bernard R. Siskin
Joseph Trippi

The nature and the importance of statistical evidence in a discrimination context vary depending on the legal theory of the case (that is, disparate impact versus disparate treatment) and the type of action (that is, individual versus class or pattern and practice). Any statistical analysis looks at only the pattern of results. Therefore, if the issue is one of classwide discrimination, statistical analysis may be dispositive. However, if the issue concerns an individual allegation of discrimination, the role of statistics is limited, by definition. In the case of individual allegations, fact testimony is much more likely to shed light on the individual circumstances and allegations and be dispositive. An overall pattern adverse to the protected class may be probative in assessing the context of the individual arguments (it may also be sufficient to allow a prima facie inference of discrimination if not rebutted; however, the rebuttal may deal only with the circumstances of the individual claim and need not rebut the finding of a statistical pattern of discrimination), but such a pattern is of limited value in assessing whether a specific individual experienced discrimination. For an illustration, consider a scenario in which you play a supposedly fair game of chance in which the probability that you will win or lose is supposed to be 50 percent. You play the game twenty times, and you lose twenty times. In studying the pattern of outcomes you can be reasonably certain that the game was not fair overall and you have been cheated. However, the overall pattern of results cannot specify any specific game in which you have been cheated, because you should have lost ten games and won ten games, and your chance of losing any specific game was 50 percent. Hence, if compelling fact evidence is presented that a specific game was fair, the statistical pattern is irrelevant.

There are two legal theories that address how discrimination can affect an individual in an employment context: disparate impact and disparate treatment.

Disparate *impact* claims involve an allegation that a specific, neutrally applied objective or subjective *test* has caused the disproportionate exclusion of protected class members. The terms *objective* and *subjective* are used in a purely statistical sense. An *objective test* is one in which the resulting score can be replicated by any individual scorer (excluding measurement error), whereas a *subjective test* is one in which the resulting score cannot necessarily be replicated by any individual because the scoring requires judgment on the part of the scorer. Here a *test* refers to any specific employment practice, ranging from a paper-and-pencil test to a requirement that one have a certain level of education to a subjective interview process as to who to retain. Because disparate impact claims concern a challenge to a policy or practice that although applied facially neutrally has the *unintended* effect of disproportionately harming or disadvantaging a protected class, intent to discriminate is not at issue. The basic question under disparate impact theory centers on group-level differences in the consequences of an employer action rather than on the administration of the actions themselves. Hence, although disparate impact claims can involve an individual, they are by nature class actions. Moreover the role of statistical evidence is more fundamental in establishing liability in allegations of disparate impact than it is in allegations of disparate treatment.

The Civil Rights Act of 1991 confirmed the courts' view of what constitutes prima facie disparate impact (outlined initially in the case of *Watson v. Fort Worth Bank and Trust*, 1988). That is, the plaintiff must (1) identify the specific practice being challenged (a cognitive written test, an education requirement, an interview practice, and so forth) and (2) offer statistical evidence to show that the questioned practice significantly disadvantages the protected group.

It is the plaintiff's burden to isolate and measure each specific practice of interest in the selection process being challenged. However, in some cases it is impossible to isolate and measure the practices of interest because data to do so do not exist. In such cases one can look only at the bottom line: that is, at the result of the total process (or subset of practices). An example of a practice that engenders discrimination by means of disparate impact is the use in a selection process of an education requirement (that cannot be shown to be job related) that results in the disqualification of a larger proportion of minority than majority candidates.

If statistical evidence demonstrating the disparate impact of the test is offered by the plaintiff, the burden shifts to the employer to demonstrate the *business necessity* of the test (that is, that the outcome of the test bears some impact on the job or predicts job performance). If the defendant can meet that burden, the burden shifts back to the plaintiff, who must then establish that the employer had available but failed to use a feasible alternative test having less disparate impact but equal or greater validity in satisfying the employer's business necessity.

In contrast, disparate *treatment* claims in the employment arena involve allegations of *intentional* discrimination against employees or potential employees *because of* their age, race, national origin, religion, or gender. Accordingly, intent is the deciding issue. Disparate treatment claims can be individual or classwide. In addition to anecdotal testimony the plaintiff may proffer statistical evidence showing significant differences in employment outcomes between protected and nonprotected employees who are argued to be *similarly situated*. Even in the absence of other evidence, statistical evidence based on a showing of a statistically significant difference between reasonably similarly situated protected and nonprotected class members alone may lead the decision maker to an inference of intentional discrimination and disparate treatment.

The critical aspect of the statistical evidence in disparate treatment claims concerns the notion of similarly situated employees and the likelihood that discrimination (as opposed to other factors not considered) might be the cause of the disparity. Similarly situated employees are those who share a number of relevant characteristics (for example, they work in a given department or have a given level of education). It is important to note that the plaintiff *need not account for all relevant factors* to make a statistical case. The Supreme Court in 1986, reviewing a 1984 circuit court decision in *Bazemore* v. *Friday*, stated that "a plaintiff in a Title VII suit need not prove discrimination with scientific certainty." As noted by the U.S. Court of Appeals for the Ninth Circuit in *EEOC* v. *General Telephone Company of Northwest* (1989): "Since *Bazemore*, several circuits have applied the principles articulated in that decision when addressing the use of regression analyses to prove discrimination. The majority of those courts have concluded that *Bazemore* requires that the defendant do more than simply point out possible flaws in the proponent's statistical analyses in order to rebut the inference of discrimination raised by the statistical evidence . . ."

In *Palmer* v. *Shultz* (1987), the District of Columbia circuit court found that "[i]mplicit in the *Bazemore* holding is the principle that a mere conjecture or assertion on the defendant's part that some missing factor would explain the existing disparities between men and women generally cannot defeat the inference of discrimination created by plaintiffs' statistics . . . [I]n most cases a defendant cannot rebut statistical evidence . . . without introducing evidence to support the contention that the missing factor can explain the disparities as a product" of a legitimate, nondiscriminatory selection criterion.

Unless the statistical comparisons are *obviously* inappropriate or misleading, the plaintiff's statistical presentation will serve to shift the burden to the employer (see *Sheehan* v. *Purolator,* 1998). The burden is on the employer to show that such omitted factors would eliminate the disparity. Thus, if employee age (for example) is significantly correlated to layoff decisions, the employer must present evidence that omitted measurable factors (extent and type of experience, educational attainment, performance, and so forth) would eliminate the statistical discrepancy (see *Palmer* v. *Schultz,* 1987; *Sobel* v. *Yeshiva,* 1988; *Catlett* v. *Missouri Highway,* 1987; *EEOC* v. *General Telephone,* 1989).

The prima facie evidence in disparate impact claims is *always statistical.* The statistical presentation for a prima facie disparate impact claim is typically fairly straightforward and dispositive in that the plaintiff need only demonstrate that the test adversely impacts the protected class. A prima facie finding of disparate impact requires the employer to demonstrate the business necessity of the test. Conversely, the statistical presentation for a disparate treatment claim tends to be more complicated, due to the necessity of defining and measuring the relevant characteristics of similarly situated employees and assessing the likelihood that discrimination, rather than factors not studied, is the cause of the disparity. In addition the role of nonstatistical evidence will be more central in disparate treatment claims than in disparate impact claims because intent is at issue. Moreover, in individual allegations of disparate treatment, the role of statistics is limited and seldom dispositive.

In the rest of this chapter we focus on issues involved in using statistics in allegations of disparate impact.

Assessing Disparate Impact

Statistical Significance

A practice (a test) is deemed to have a disparate impact when the disparity between groups taking the test is statistically significant and the impact is large enough to be of practical significance. In discussing the need for statistical significance and the level at which a disparity reaches statistical significance, the *Uniform Guidelines on Employee Selection Procedures* (1978, § 1607.4D) does not specifically state what level of significance to use. However, in discussing validity, the Uniform Guidelines suggest using a .05 level of significance, the standard commonly used by statisticians and psychometricians. The Uniform Guidelines do not state whether one should conduct a one-tailed or two-tailed test. In addressing the standard the Supreme Court chose to discuss the magnitude of the disparity in equivalent units of a standard normal variate rather than the probability of occurrence by chance, which is the standard more commonly used by statisticians and psychometricians. In the case of *Hazelwood School District* v. *United States* (1977) the Supreme Court suggested the statistical standard to use in employment discrimination cases, stating that "a fluctuation of more than two or three units of standard deviation would undercut the hypothesis that decisions were being made randomly with respect to race." With respect to disparate impact, particularly when the practice being challenged is a paper-and-pencil test or a scored interview, the minimum standard that most courts have relied on is a disparity of at least two units of standard deviation. The two units of standard deviation level, of course, corresponds to approximately a .05 level of probability for a two-tailed test and a .025 level of probability for a one-tailed test. A .05 level of significance corresponds to a disparity of at least 1.65 units of standard deviation of a standard normal variate when a one-tailed test is considered and a disparity of at least 1.96 units of standard deviation of a standard normal variate when a two-tailed test is considered. In *Palmer v. Schultz* (1987), relying on *Hazelwood,* the D.C. circuit stated that the appropriate standard is a .05 level of probability to define statistical significance if one uses a two-tailed test or a .025 level if one uses a one-tailed test. That is, the court suggested the equivalent of a disparity of at least 1.96 units of standard deviation of a standard normal variate as the minimum standard for statistical significance.

Disparate impact cases typically make two major claims. One is that the test disproportionately excludes the protected class from further consideration. In essence the issue is whether the pass rate of the protected class (that is, the proportion of the class deemed qualified by the test to proceed further in an employment process) is statistically and practically lower than that of the nonprotected class. The concept of passing can be defined by a *formal* passing score (for example, 70 or above on a paper-and-pencil test) or by an *effective* passing score, the actual lowest score a candidate may obtain and still possibly be selected. Often, if there are many candidates for few positions and the test (alone or in combination with other decision criteria) is used to rank order the candidates, the effective passing score may be well above any formal passing score. If the test is the only device being used to rank order candidates, the effective passing score is simply the lowest score obtained by anyone selected (assuming the list is not exhausted; if it is, the formal pass-fail score is the effective passing score). If other criteria are factored into the process, ascertaining the effective passing score becomes more complex, because one must determine what the minimum qualifying score on the challenged component would be if the candidate had achieved the best possible scores on the other components.

In cases in which two categorical variables (for example, pass-fail and protected–nonprotected class) are being analyzed, two tests are available to the statistician. When the number of those who pass and fail overall is considered fixed (that is, *fixed marginal[s]* exist), Fisher's exact test is the proper test. This test result can be approximated by a chi-squared test. If one does not consider the marginals fixed (that is, if the number of those who pass and fail overall is not fixed), the proper test is the binomial test for the difference in two populations. Although there is debate as to which test is appropriate (and the choice of test may depend on the specifics of the case), there is no simple exact test for the two-sample binomial. It can be approximated based on the normal distribution and the results are identical to the chi-squared approximation for Fisher's exact test. For moderate and large samples the chi-squared test will be a very good approximation to both Fisher's and the two-sample binomial. The chi-squared approximation is often adjusted by use of Yates's correction factor. However, this correction tends to overadjust. In practice, if the results are close to the level of significance, one should use the exact test to obtain the precise answer.

For an illustration of the difference between a fixed marginal and nonfixed marginal situation, consider the case where employees are rated as either acceptable performers or unacceptable performers. Frequently in such a case the decision rule is that a given (fixed) percentage of the employees must be rated as unacceptable. Here the process has fixed marginals. Conversely, when there is no such fixed decision rule so that any (or all) employee(s) could be rated unacceptable, the process does not have fixed marginals. That is, a test for which the number of passers is fixed at some given percentage has fixed marginals, whereas a test that all test takers may pass or fail does not.

Of course one could ask the question, "Assuming that x percent of test takers pass the test, what is the likelihood that protected class status and passing are independent?" This question creates a fixed marginal situation, and the exact answer is obtained by Fisher's exact test. Generally, the courts have adopted the fixed marginal theory and hence consider Fisher's exact test as the proper test.

The second major claim in disparate impact cases is that use of the test results in rank order has a disparate impact on protected class members. This is a separate claim and implies that even among those who pass the test, protected class members are disproportionately affected because they rank lower and therefore (1) are less likely to be selected or (2) must wait longer to be hired. If one uses an effective passing score to conduct one's pass-fail analysis, then the only issue of ranking is that of possibly having to wait longer for selection.

The most definitive statistical test available to conduct an analysis of disparate impact as a result of rank ordering is the Mann-Whitney rank sum test. This test compares the rankings of nonprotected and protected class members. It is the most definitive test because it specifically isolates the practice at issue. If the Mann-Whitney rank sum test result is significant, plaintiffs will have clearly established the disparate impact of the ranking process. However, if the result is adverse to protected class members (but not to the level of statistical significance), one can run a Mann-Whitney rank sum test using the sample of both *test passers* and *test failers*. The statistical rationale is that one is considering a single test and ranking process and by studying the rankings of all test takers one obtains greater statistical power to determine whether the differences in rankings found in the effective passer sample are real or are simply the result of chance. Assuming that the test scores of each class follow the same monotonic distribution but with different means, this statistical rationale is correct.

Practical Significance

Statistical significance is a necessary condition for practical significance and disparate impact to exist, but it is not a sufficient condition by itself. To establish that a test has a disparate impact, not only must the resulting disparity between groups be statistically significant but also the impact must be large enough to constitute sufficient practical importance to warrant further investigation (that is, will the test pass the business necessity requirement?). Practical significance is ultimately a judgment that must be made by the trier of the facts; it is not a statistical test.

Many laypersons believe incorrectly that the greater the units of standard deviation, the greater the practical significance. This does not necessarily follow. Statistical significance depends not only on the size of the disparity (which would correlate with practical significance) but also on the size of the sample being studied. Hence a disparity that represents a larger number of units of standard deviation may be the result of a larger sample rather than a larger disparity. Consider the example in Table 5.1.: Test A has a greater disparity in pass rates than Test B, but the disparity for Test A is based on fewer test takers than the disparity for Test B, and thus represents fewer units of standard deviation.

140 EMPLOYMENT DISCRIMINATION LITIGATION

Table 5.1. Statistical Significance in Relation to Sample Size.

	Test A	Test B
Number of test takers	50	500
Protected	10	100
Nonprotected	40	400
Pass rate		
Protected	20%	30%
Nonprotected	80%	70%
Disparity in units of standard deviation	3.64	7.37

Two measures of practical significance are usually considered: (1) the measure referred to as the 80 percent rule and (2) the shortfall in selections experienced by the protected class. A third measure of practical significance, the standardized mean score difference by protected class status, is also presented to allow for the comparison of different tests (that is, the test at issue versus alternatives). The 80 percent rule is the measure of practical significance suggested by the Uniform Guidelines. The 80 percent rule compares the ratio of the selection rate (for example, pass rate) of the protected group (for example, African Americans or Hispanics) to that of the nonprotected group (for example, whites) in order to quantify the disparity and determine whether it is numerically large enough to constitute practical importance. This rule provides that a selection rate for any age, race, national origin, religion, or gender group that is less than four-fifths, or 80 percent, of the rate of the group with the highest selection rate will generally be regarded as evidence that the test has adverse impact.

Although widely used in practice and relied on frequently by enforcement agencies, the 80 percent rule has often been rejected by the courts. It is arbitrary and used simply as a rule of thumb. It cannot offer insight into many of the myriad factors the court must consider when determining whether the extent of injury to the protected class is sufficient to warrant an employer's having to validate its test.

The shortfall measure is more useful to the courts because it specifies the number of protected class members who would have been expected to pass the test if their pass rate had equaled that of the nonprotected class members (that is, it finds the shortfall in passers); it can also estimate the additional number of protected class members who would have been ultimately selected (for example, the shortfall in hires or promotions or the surplus in terminations). Thus the court has information about the actual magnitude of the impact on the protected class. Shortfall numbers allow the decision maker to consider the benefits of altering the practice versus the costs of proceeding further. In assessing practical significance courts will often consider factors such as the net impact of the shortfall on the profile of the company. The 80 percent rule, although easy to calculate and to apply, fails to capture most of the relevant factors one should consider in evaluating the practical implications of the observed, real disparate impact.

Some parties in litigation offer an adjusted shortfall number: the shortfall (or change) in protected-class test passers necessary for the disparity to become nonstatistically significant. Such an approach assumes that if the court found discrimination, it would remedy the process only to the point of eliminating statistical or practical significance. However, once a court has found a test to be discriminatory, the remedy is to bring about parity. Some parties in litigation may offer the shortfall numbers necessary to pass the 80 percent rule. This approach has the same problem: that is, it allows for the continuation of some disparity *after* the court has concluded discrimination exists.

Controlling for Confounding Factors

In conducting a disparate impact analysis it is necessary to restrict the sample being studied to those who have the *minimum qualifications* necessary to take the test. This is normally an automatic function because usually only those who meet the minimum qualifications are permitted to undergo the testing procedure. However, in some situations this is not necessarily the case. For example, some applicants may take the test by mistake (inadvertently or by false representation). Alternatively, when screening for certain qualifications (such as lack of a criminal record or ability to pass a physical) is more costly than administering the test, employers may screen for those minimum qualifications only after the test and only for test passers. In the first case there is little dispute that the persons not minimally qualified should be removed from the analysis. In the second case it is not clear. First, removing all those not minimally qualified may be impossible, because such minimum qualifications are determined only for test passers. Second, one can view the determination of such minimum qualifications as the second step in the process. The first step is the test in question. Meeting the minimum qualifications is the second step and, although necessary for selection, is not necessary for taking the test. The latter approach was adopted by the Court in *United States* v. *State of Delaware* (2004).

Employers occasionally attempt to control statistically for other factors (such as education or prior experience) to explain a disparate impact. Statistically controlling for such factors to explain the disparate impact of a test is improper. The legal issue is not *why* the test has a disparate impact but rather *whether* it has a disparate impact. There is, however, one confounding factor that may be considered in adjusting the analysis. The Uniform Guidelines recognize as a possibility that special affirmative recruitment may affect the observed disparity: "Greater differences in selection rates may not constitute adverse impact . . . where special recruiting or other programs cause the pool of minority or female candidates to be *atypical* of the normal pool of applicants from that group" [emphasis added]. Simply affirmatively recruiting would not require any adjustment to the statistical tests for disparate impact. In contrast to the case of affirmative recruitment, a particular group could be discouraged from applying for the position, and hence the availability may underestimate the true percentage of that group interested in the job. In the situation where the issue is whether a particular test disproportionately impacts a group, the implication of such a situation is relevant only if discouragement is directly correlated with the likelihood of passing the test. For example, if a posting or advertisement for a position includes a height requirement, only persons who meet that requirement may apply, and among these applicants the height test will appear to have no impact. Yet, if applied to those who would be interested absent such a requirement, the height test may in fact have an impact. The real issue under the Uniform Guidelines is whether the test-taker pool is *atypical* of what would be expected without recruitment. If affirmative recruitment occurs *and those recruited tend to be protected class members who are less qualified,* then and only then would recruitment result in artificially increasing the disparate impact of a test. The appropriate analysis would be to attempt to identify and remove from the analysis those candidates who would not normally have applied or those candidates whose qualifications would not normally have led them to apply.

Aggregating Data

Frequently, a test is administered multiple times. For example, a department might have posted an opening for team leader ten times over a period of a year. Suppose that one of the selection practices (tests) consisted of giving certain candidates an interview. From a statistical viewpoint one should aggregate the data over all administrations of the interview because the larger the sample, the more powerful (that is, reliable) the statistical analysis, provided (1) the test remains the same and (2) the test takers are drawn from the same theoretical population across the administrations. Whether a test is the same (that is, either is identical or is a psychometrically alternative form) is a nonstatistical question to be answered by a testing or personnel expert. The *same theoretical population* is one for which the eligibility requirements do not change significantly, so the disparity of the test would not be significantly affected. For example, a certain test may have a disparate impact upon African Americans if (1) no experience is required, (2) the results are correlated with experience, and (3) African Americans in the population have less experience. But the same test would have no disparate impact if a given level of experience were to become a requirement. In the latter case it would be incorrect to aggregate the results because it is improper to aggregate across administrations in which the eligibility requirements are different.

Whether to aggregate results is not a decision based on statistics. How to aggregate results is a statistical decision that depends on whether the overall success rates differ by administration and whether such a difference occurs by chance. If the results differ by administration, then the data cannot simply be combined and treated as a single data set. Doing so can create biased and misleading results. In such a case one must control or stratify the data for each administration and combine the individual results via statistical techniques such as the Mantel Haenszel or aggregated binomial tests. Consider, for example, the hypothetical data in Table 5.2. Two interviews take place, and the overall selection rate (and race mix) vary by interview but each interview is perfectly race neutral. Proper aggregation shows no disparate impact, whereas simply combining the data without controlling for interview date leads to biased, misleading results.

Special issues in combining, or aggregating, data occur when some of the test takers in the various administrations are repeat test takers. If these multiple test takers number only a few individuals, one can simply keep the first test observation and delete the rest. (Keeping the first test minimizes the effect of practice and learning because, in general, most, if not all, of the other test takers will be first-time takers of this test.) However, consider the case described earlier where a department posted an opening for team leader ten times over a period of a year and used an interview process to make its selections. Now, assume that the same unsuccessful candidates bid for and were interviewed for each of the ten promotional opportunities. In such a case the use of the Mantel Haenszel or aggregated binomial tests may be invalid because these procedures assume independence of selection between administrations.

To further understand the conceptual issue, consider the following hypothetical example. We have a bowl with ten tickets: Nine are red and one is green, representing a population of white and Hispanic customer service representatives. From this bowl we select one red ticket and one green ticket and place them in a second bowl that represents the pool of eligible applications for the team leader position. From this eligible applications bowl we randomly make a selection, picking the red ticket. We replace the selected red ticket in the eligible applications bowl with another red ticket from the population bowl and select again. We repeat this procedure nine more times. Imagine that the first nine selections are red and the last and remaining selection is the green ticket. If we assume that the red and green tickets are the same in all respects but color and have been selected randomly, then we should have been equally likely to have selected a red or green ticket on each

Table 5.2. Aggregation of Results With and Without Controls.

	Interviews		Hires		Expected	
	African American	Non–African American	African American	Non–African American	African American	Shortfall
Date						
1/95	100	900	10	90	10[a]	0
1/96	100	400	4	16	4[b]	0
Overall						
Controlled for date	—		14	106	14	0
No controls	200	1,300	14	106	16[c]	2

[a] [100 / (100 + 900)] × 100.
[b] [100 / (100 + 400)] × 20.
[c] [200 / (200 + 1,300)] × 120.

draw. If we then focus on each selection and compute the likelihood of choosing a red ticket the first nine times and the green ticket last, the computation would be $(\_)^9 = 0.002$. This means that the chance of passing over the green ticket until the final selection was only two in one thousand. In this example, because the chance of selecting a red or green ticket was the *same* in each selection, the analysis focused on *applications* for each position and who was selected.

Consider, however, a case in which the tickets are *different sizes* (a metaphor for the applicants' characteristics as measured by the test) *and the largest tickets are always drawn*. In this case we assume the largest ticket equates to the most qualified applicant according to the test. But we further assume that ticket size is independent of color (hence the test should not have an adverse impact). In this case the likelihood that the green ticket would be picked last by chance is also the likelihood that the smallest ticket would be green. Because we have ten tickets and one of them is a green ticket, the chance probability that the smallest ticket would be green is 0.10. That is, the chance that the green ticket would be passed over until the last selection is one in ten, because the chances of selection are determined by the relationship (size) of each individual ticket to the others. Following this example, the analysis should focus on *unique tickets*, rather than on the number of applications in which a single ticket may have participated.

To the extent that repeat observations for the same subjects (individuals) are correlated, the standard errors in the Mantel Haenszel are biased. Generally, the result of the bias is to favor a finding of significance in between-group analyses (for example, comparisons by race and gender) by underestimating the standard error. The problem is that effects due to individuals have the potential of being confounded with effects due to protected class status.

In such cases one can use a logistic regression, where the dependent variable is the selection, the independent variable(s) are protected class status and administration, and one controls for multiple test takers within a generalized estimating equation. Generalized estimating equation analysis allows for the modeling of within-subject effects (that is, repeat observations) using unbalanced data (that is, some subjects have one or a few observation points and others have many observation points) for a binary response variable (for example, hires, promotions, inclusions in a reduction in force) (Stokes, Davis, & Koch, 1997). The independent variables or factors may be categorical (for example, stratification dimensions that may define similarly situated groups or pools) or continuous (for example, seniority).

Setting Cutoff Scores in the Aftermath of *Lanning* v. *SEPTA*

The *Lanning* Decision and the Criterion of Minimum Qualification

Title VII holds that it is the employer's burden to prove business necessity in disparate impact cases. The standard by which the employer's burden may be met has been interpreted variously over time and in different judicial decisions. However stringent the standard of proof imposed by the courts, the employer's burden has typically been to demonstrate that the *selection procedure* (defined in the Principles of the Society for Industrial and Organizational Psychology [2003] as "any procedure used to make a personnel decision" [p. 3]) having a disparate impact is job related (that is, is related to job performance, is valid). Less often the employer's burden has concerned various possible placements of the cutoff score, or cut score, as constituting alternative valid procedures with lesser or greater disparate impact (Cascio, Alexander, & Barrett, 1988). That view of the employer's burden held until the third circuit's ruling in *Lanning* v. *Southeastern Pennsylvania Transportation Authority (SEPTA)* in 1999.

In *Lanning* v. *SEPTA* (1999) the third circuit placed the strictest standard for the employer burden ever directed at the placement of cutoff scores for a test that was used on a pass-fail basis, with other selection devices being used to select from among the passers. The third circuit ruled that the selection procedure must "measure the minimum qualifications necessary for the successful performance of the job in question" (p. 490). For a comparison, consider the language in the Uniform Guidelines that states that cutoff scores should "be normally set so as to be reasonable and consistent with normal expectations of acceptable proficiency within the workforce" (§ 5H). Also consider the statement in the SIOP Principles that "[i]f based on valid predictors demonstrating linearity or monotonicity throughout the range of prediction, cutoff scores may be set as high or as low as needed to meet the requirements of the organization" (p. 46).

In another case, *United States* v. *Delaware State Police* (2004), which was held in a district court in the third circuit prior to the Bush administration's announcement that it would no longer join with plaintiffs in cases brought under the "*Lanning* decision," evidence heard during the trial explicitly concerned methods and procedures in setting a cutoff score on a cognitive ability (that is, prose literacy) test. The judge decided for the plaintiffs in finding that the disputed cutoff score of 75 percent of items correct was unlawfully high. Moreover, evidence presented during the trial regarding statistical and psychometric issues in setting cutoff scores was considered and relied on by the judge in defining a range of alternative cutoff scores satisfying the standard for business necessity established in *Lanning* v. *SEPTA* (1999, 2002).

Methods for Setting Cutoff Scores After *Lanning*

The SIOP Principles draw a distinction between cutoff and critical scores. *Critical* scores represent the point in the distribution of test scores above which candidates and applicants are considered successful, and *cutoff* scores refer to the point in the distribution of test scores below which candidates and applicants are rejected. Assuming a linear or at least monotonic relationship between test scores and performance, the use of cutoff scores generally defines accepted and rejected groups that differ, on average, in expected job performance, regardless of the specific point selected as the cutoff. However, the likelihood that a rejected applicant would have otherwise gone on to be a successful employee (false negative decision) need not be an explicit consideration, and other factors, including administrative expediency and costs of advancing a larger applicant pool to additional components of a selection system, may be the overriding criteria when choosing a cutoff score. In contrast a critical score is defined in terms of its discrimination between successful and unsuccessful applicants and is therefore more consistent with a minimum qualifications standard for the employer's defense of business necessity when using selection procedures having a disparate impact.

In the *Lanning* situation the effort was to define the critical score. If we believe that there is a true critical score (that is, a value on the test below which one cannot perform the job), then empirical statistical analysis will generally be useless in determining that value. For example, if one must be able to lift fifty pounds to do a certain job, no one in the job will *not* be able to lift fifty pounds. By definition, the critical score must be below the score of the lowest-scoring person on the job. Moreover, because the critical score point reflects a cliff function (below that score the performance curve falls to zero), the point at which it falls (that is, the cliff point) cannot be estimated from the incumbent data. In such a case that level must be established through statistical experimentation or by nonstatistical methods. It is interesting to note that in *Lanning* the minimum was justified primarily through nonstatistical evidence. The *Lanning* standard, however, is applicable for the more common situation where a true critical score simply does not exist. Persons with lower scores are more likely to fail, but some percentage of persons with lower scores can minimally do the job because either (1) the test is not a perfect measure of the relevant characteristics or (2) the relevant characteristics are not absolutely necessary to do the job.

In a review of the legal context for setting cutoff scores and of the methods and procedures used in setting cutoff scores, done prior to the *Lanning* v. *SEPTA* (1999, 2002) decisions, Cascio, Alexander, and Barrett (1988) concluded that in most testing situations a true pass score or critical score simply cannot be found. Nevertheless, these authors considered criterion-related validity approaches preferable and potentially more defensible than methods they classify as either norm referenced or content related: norm-referenced methods lack any direct linkage to job performance and content-related methods rely on subjective judgment and agreement between judges.

Among the criterion-related procedures discussed by Cascio, Alexander, and Barrett (1988) are two formulations of a regression approach to the problem of selecting a cutoff score consistent with the notion of minimum qualifications and a critical score. These formulations differ in the direction of the prediction (Figure 5.1).

The first approach is to regress performance onto test scores (that is, direct or forward regression):

$$P = A + BT$$

where p = performance and, t = test score.

Figure 5.1. Two Formulations of a Regression Approach.

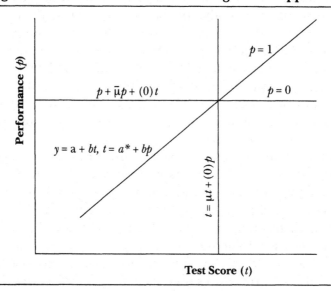

The second approach is to regress test scores onto performance (that is, reverse regression):

$$T = A + BP.$$

When the correlation between test scores and performance is less than 1, the two regression results will diverge. The lower the correlation, the more diverse the regression lines. This is so, of course, because the regressions are asking two distinctly different questions. The direct regression asks what the employee's performance would be predicted to be if the employee's test scores were known, and the other asks what the employee's test scores would be predicted to be if the employee's performance were known.

Which is the proper question to ask, and how should the alternative regressions be used? Under *Lanning*, the court seemed concerned that the cutoff score not be set so high as to eliminate many persons who could actually do the job. Although the *Lanning* court stressed the public safety role of SEPTA officers in its discussion of acceptable risks of false positives (suggesting that the cost of accepting unqualified candidates would be higher in a public safety context than in other job situations), the court ultimately allowed a high degree of risk of accepting unqualified candidates to proceed in the screening process:

> Plaintiffs argued, however, that within the group that failed the run test, significant numbers of individuals would still be able to perform at least certain critical job tasks. They argued that as long as some of those failing the run test can do the job, the standard cannot be classified as a "minimum." In essence, plaintiffs proposed that the phrase "minimum qualifications necessary" means "some chance of being able to do the job." Under this logic, even if those failing the test had a 1% chance of successfully completing critical job tasks, the test would be too stringent.
>
> We are not saying, as our distinguished brother in dissent suggests we are saying, that "more is better." While, of course, a higher aerobic capacity will translate into better field performance—at least as to many job tasks which entail physical capability—to set an unnecessarily high cutoff score would contravene *Griggs*. It would clearly be unreasonable to require SEPTA applicants to score so highly on the run test that their predicted rate of success be 100%. *It is perfectly reasonable, however, to demand a chance of success that is better than 5% to 20%* [Lanning v. SEPTA, 2002, emphasis added].

Thus the implication of the *Lanning* court is that a cutoff of p (perform minimally in job/cut score) ≥ 0.20 is reasonable for a pass-fail test that allows candidates to continue in the screening process.

From a reverse regression view, clearly the court was concerned with the Type 1 error of rejecting candidates who could perform on the job. Mathematically, the *Lanning* court was concerned that α be low where p (fail test/perform at minimally acceptable standard) $= \alpha$.

If one interprets this as the *Lanning* reverse regression standard, then the appropriate statistical methodology is to run a proper reverse regression and, at the point where performance equals minimum performance, construct a (1 − α) percent lower confidence level on all test scores. That is:

$$\text{Cutoff score} = (a + bp_{min}) - Z_{(1-\alpha)} \sqrt{s^2_{t \cdot p_{min}}}$$

where $a + bp_{min}$ is the average or predicted test score associated with the minimum performance standard p_{min}, $Z_{(1-\alpha)}$ is the maximum acceptable probability of rejecting an acceptably performing candidate (for example, 20 percent), and $s^2_{t \cdot p_{min}}$ is the conditional variance of test scores conditioned on p_{min} from the regression.

Under the *Lanning* standard, it would be improper to set the cutoff score at the test score predicted to be obtained by those who can minimally do the job. To do so would, by definition, eliminate from further consideration 50 percent of the population of persons who could minimally do the job: the cutoff score would be equally as likely to eliminate from further consideration as to include for further consideration those who could minimally do the job.

Reverse regression has two problems. The first problem is that if the selection of incumbents is based on the test scores, the test scores among the incumbents are truncated, because there will be no data on the dependent variable (that is, test scores) below the cutoff test scores that have been used. In such a case the regression of test scores onto performance yields a biased result that will *overestimate* the predicted test scores associated with minimum performance. As shown in Figures 5.2, 5.3, and 5.4, the higher the cutoff score, the more one overestimates the predicted test scores associated with minimum performance. No solution to this estimation problem exists without making assumptions about the values of the truncated data. Even when incumbent samples used in concurrent validation studies were selected by using a different selection procedure, their test score distributions were likely truncated. This is the logical inference from the expectation of higher correlations between different measures of the same construct (for example, two tests of cognitive ability) than between measures of different constructs, as in the correlation between test scores and performance (Guion, 1998; Nunnally, 1978).

Figure 5.2. Illustration of Limited Dependent Variable Truncation Bias of OLS Regression.

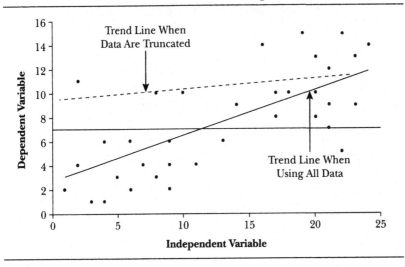

Figure 5.3. Illustration of Limited Dependent Bias of OLS Regression in Predicting Test Score from Performance: Only Test Scores Above 70 Percent Are Considered.

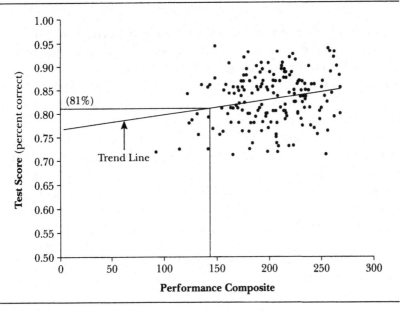

Figure 5.4. Illustration of Limited Dependent Bias of OLS Regression in Predicting Test Score from Performance: Only Test Scores Above 80 Percent Are Considered.

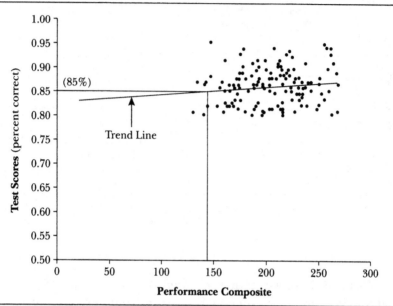

In *U.S.* v. *Delaware State Police* the incumbent participants in the validation sample were selected using the same test of cognitive ability. In his ruling the judge explicitly recognized the issue of truncation in setting aside the results of the defendant expert's use of reverse regression in justifying the cutoff score at or higher than the contested 75 percent of items correct.

One may be tempted to get around the truncation problem by using the inverse estimation process. Such a technique does not work well unless R is extremely high. Hence inverse regression should not be considered. Inverse regression uses the algebraic transformation of the regression equation for predicting performance from test scores in setting a cutoff score, has the effect of compounding error, and is not advised. In the statistical literature this is referred to as the calibration problem (Snedecor & Cochran, 1980; Seber, 1977; Williams, 1969). Consider the following:

1. Response generating
   model: $y' = b_0 + b_1 x_1 + e_1$

2. Inverse estimation: $x' = [(y' - b_0)/b_1] + e_2$

   $x' = \{[(b_0 + b_1 x_1 + e_1) - b_0]/b_1\} + e_2$

The problem is due to double estimation in using predicted scores made with error (y') to compute another point estimate (x') also made with error. Also note that the criterion (y, not its estimate y') drops out of the equation, resulting in the final estimate of cutoff score x' on the test made without direct reference to performance, y.

The second problem with reverse regression, explained in detail in the next section, is that the less valid the test, the higher the cut score and greater the disparate impact of cut scores. Therefore the protected class is asked to pay the price of the employer's inability to develop a better test.

Conceptually, the problem with the *Lanning* court's approach is that it is concerned only with the error of rejecting candidates who could minimally do the job. An alternative approach would be to consider the employer's actual dilemma in setting cutoff scores: that is, the trade-off between rejecting applicants who can do the job and accepting applicants who cannot do the job, because the higher the cut score, the lower the risk of accepting persons who cannot do the job but the higher the risk of rejecting persons who can do the job. The trade-off can be measured by

p (performance < acceptable/test score $\geq t^*$)

versus

p (performance > acceptable/test score < t^*)

where t^* = cut score on test.

In order to measure these risks, the appropriate regression would be the direct regression (performance = $a + b$ test score). Considering these risks, along with judgment as to the relative costs and benefits associated with the trade-off, would lead to the appropriate cut score that maximizes utility.

One may be tempted to use the direct regression and set the cut score at the value that predicts that on average an employee will be able to perform at a minimum level. However, at that value, there will be a 50 percent chance of selecting someone who cannot do the job. Using direct regression (for example, 80 percent), one could first decide the level at which one is sufficiently comfortable that someone proceeding further in the process could, at least minimally, do the job. Then one would set the cut score at that value in the direct regression at which that level of confidence (for example, 80 percent) is achieved: that is, that point at which one is comfortable that the performance of individuals will equal or exceed minimum performance.

Clearly, there is no "best" cut score. The issue simply concerns the definition of a reasonable trade-off. When the test is pass-fail and is only one in a series of selection hurdles, the *Lanning* decision clearly places a much greater cost on not further considering candidates who could do the job than on further considering candidates who could not. The acceptable trade-offs and the concomitant cut score should depend on the specific circumstances and the costs associated with the trade-offs inherent in setting a cut score.

Issues in Analyses Relative to Different Definitions of Test Fairness

The minimum qualification standard of expected job performance for setting cutoff scores may well lead to judicial examination of statistical evidence in keeping with various alternative definitions of *test bias*. The two major definitions of test bias, alternatively stated as *test fairness*, come from Cleary (1968) and Thorndike (1971). Guion (1998) referred to Cleary's definition as the regression model and labeled the definitions of Thorndike (1971) and Cole (1973) as the group parity models of test fairness. Guion noted widespread, though less than universal, support for Cleary's notion of test bias and suggested consideration of opposing argument and empirical evidence presented in Wigdor and Sackett (1993).

The SIOP Principles (1987, 2003) have long favored the regression model of test bias credited to Cleary (1968). To Cleary, "[a] test is biased for members of a subgroup of the population if, in the prediction of the criterion for which the test was designed, consistent non-zero errors of prediction are made for members of the subgroup. In other words, the test is biased if the criterion score predicted from the common regression line is consistently too high or too low for members of the subgroup" (p. 115).

Evidence of test bias consistent with this definition includes findings of significant slope or intercept differences for protected and nonprotected subgroups. Significant slope differences denote interaction effects in the rate or pattern of change in job performance in response to increases in test scores for different subgroups. Significant intercept differences refer to main effect differences in average job performance for protected and nonprotected subgroups.

The Cleary definition and the methods of testing for bias do not concern the placement of cutoff scores directly. If applied to questions regarding the appropriateness of the cutoff score selected, the finding of nonsignificant intercept and slope differences would justify the selection of any test score as the cutoff. A finding of significant slope differences would make questionable the appropriateness of the use of the selection procedure for certain subgroups, regardless of the cutoff score selected. A finding of nonsignificant slope but significant intercept differences would indicate the use of different cutoff scores for subgroups.

In contrast, Thorndike (1971) defined test bias with explicit reference to the placement of test scores for different subgroups relative to a consistent performance standard: "the qualifying scores on a test should be set at levels that will qualify applicants in the two groups in proportion to the fraction of the two groups reaching a specified level of criterion performance" (p. 63). Adding specificity to the definition, Cole (1973) described the conditional probability model of test bias, saying, "for both minority and majority groups whose members can achieve a satisfactory criterion score there should be the same probability of selection regardless of group membership" (p. 240).

As suggested by the label *group parity*, the Thorndike (1971) and Cole (1973) definitions include language that implies strict equality in rates of selection for qualified applicants of different protected class groups. However, as these models are applied in the course of litigation, it is unlikely that the courts will establish a different standard for statistical evidence. Under the standard for statistical evidence established in *Hazelwood* v. *U.S.* (1977), deviations from strict parity of less than two units of standard deviation would be attributed to chance. Therefore a finding of nonsignificant differences in the rate of selection for protected and nonprotected class members meeting the minimum qualifications criteria would likely be accepted as statistical evidence supporting the fairness of the test under the group parity model.

Research findings on the relative differences between African Americans and whites in test scores and measures of job performance indicate that the group parity standard for test fairness often goes unmet. The magnitude of the difference for African Americans and whites in measures of job performance is typically less than one-half of their difference in test scores (Wigdor & Sackett, 1993; Ford, Kraiger, & Schechtman, 1986; Thorndike, 1971). This means that at any given performance point used in defining minimum qualifications, African Americans are likely to have test scores approximately one-half standard deviation below those of whites having the same job performance scores. Assuming adequate power to detect differences of this magnitude in incumbent samples used in concurrent validation studies, the expected statistical conclusion is that African Americans meeting minimum qualifications will have statistically lower rates of selection at almost any test score point used as the cutoff score. The finding of significantly lower rates of selection for protected class members meeting the minimum qualification standard of performance implies that the selection procedure fails the group parity model of test fairness and that a different cutoff score may have served as a less discriminatory alternative.

In reference to diagrams depicting different patterns of effects from subgroup regressions, Guion (1998) observed that the Cleary (1968) and group parity models are incompatible in that fairness under one model is unfairness under the other. Nevertheless, in logic and intent, the group parity model is well matched to the standard of minimum qualifications for an employer's defense to a finding of disparate impact based on business necessity, as articulated by the third circuit in *Lanning* v. *SEPTA* (1999). For that reason, as further cases are brought under the *Lanning* standard, courts will be asked to consider evidence under both models and may not be amenable to motions to censure evidence merely because "the Cleary model has generally been accepted as perhaps the best of a poor set of choices" (Guion, 1998, p. 442).

As a means of examining the implications of these two different models of test fairness, Monte Carlo simulations were conducted for several populations defined as follows: Population 1: protected class members represented as 10 percent of the total population, with equal means and standard deviations of test and performance scores; Population 2: equal representation of protected and nonprotected class members and the same between protected class equality of mean and standard deviations of test and performance scores; Population 3: protected class members represented as 10 percent of the total population, with protected class members having average test scores one standard deviation and average performance scores one-half standard deviation below nonprotected class members; and Population 4: equal representation of protected and nonprotected class members and the same one standard deviation and one-half standard deviation below protected class members in average test and performance scores, respectively. For protected and nonprotected class members in each population, the correlation between test and performance scores was set to .40. Two million observations were produced to conform to each of four population definitions and to generate 10,000 random samples of 200. The sample size of 200 was taken to represent the typical size of an incumbent sample used in concurrent validation studies.

Populations 1 and 2 represent fair tests whereas Populations 3 and 4 represent unfair tests.

The results, presented in Table 5.3, show the expected findings in the test of the Cleary model of test fairness in the various populations. The Cleary model denotes a hierarchical two-step analysis of first assessing significant slope differences, followed by the test of intercepts. The response-generating model for the test of significant slope differences for subgroups is $y' = b_0 + b_1 x_1 + b_2 x_2 + b_3 (x_1 x_2)$ + e, where x_1 = test scores, x_2 = protected class status, and the quantity $(x_1 x_2)$ = the interaction of test scores and protected class status. Following a finding of nonsignificant slope differences based on the estimate of the regression parameter b_3 in the interaction model, the test of significant intercept differences can be assessed by a test of the model without the cross-product interaction term,

Table 5.3. Cleary Model of Test Fairness: Effects in Ten Thousand Random Samples in Four Populations.

	Slope Differences in Percent (1)	Intercept Differences in Percent (2)
[a]*Population 1*		
Overall rate of significance	4.88	4.17
Rate of significance adverse to protected class members	(2.52)	(1.98)
[b]*Population 2*		
Overall rate of significance	4.87	4.66
Rate of significance adverse to protected class members	(2.26)	(2.30)
[c]*Population 3*		
Overall rate of significance	4.88	6.45
Rate of significance adverse to protected class members	(2.52)	(5.76)
[d]*Population 4*		
Overall rate of significance	4.87	11.53
Rate of significance adverse to protected class members	(2.26)	(11.33)

[a]Population 1: 10 percent protected class representation, equal means and standard deviations on test scores and performance measure.

[b]Population 2: 50 percent protected class representation, equal means and standard deviations on test scores and performance measure.

[c]Population 3: 10 percent protected class representation, equal standard deviations, protected class test scores one full standard deviation and performance measure one-half standard deviation below nonprotected class members.

[d]Population 4: 50 percent protected class representation, equal standard deviations, protected class test scores one full standard deviation and performance measure one-half standard deviation below nonprotected class members.

as in $y' = B_0 + b_1x_1 + b_2x_2 + e$. The finding of significance for the regression weight b_2, representing the effect of protected class status, is evidence of subgroup differences in intercepts under the Cleary model of test fairness.

As a result of this two-step approach the investigator runs a one-in-ten risk of falsely concluding that the selection procedure fails the Cleary standard of test fairness, instead of the one-in-twenty chance implied by the two units of standard deviation criterion for statistical evidence. A correction for this problem is to set the criterion for declaring the parameter estimates significant at 2.24 units of standard deviation in the test of each of the two models (Ryan, 1959). This would set the overall risk of failing the Cleary model of test fairness at the two units of standard deviation standard acceptable to the Courts.

The result, presented in Table 5.4 for Populations 3 and 4, refers to the expected consequences in the test of the Cleary model of the typical relative differences in test scores and performance measures for African Americans and whites. Both the rate of finding significant intercept differences and the negative direction of the effect for African Americans increase in both populations having average African American test scores one full standard deviation and average performance scores just one-half standard deviation below those for whites. The higher rates of significance in Population 4 reflect the consequences of low statistical power from the 10 percent sample representation of African Americans in Population 3.

Considered together, the simulations conducted indicate that the tests of the Cleary model are relatively insensitive to the differential relative disparity in test and performance scores for African Americans and whites. Under circumstances in which selection will result in the disqualification of a greater proportion of African Americans than whites meeting the same performance threshold, the test of the Cleary model yields results that support the incorrect conclusion of test fairness in at least 85 percent of cases. The correction for Type I error attributed to Ryan (1959) would result in a rate greater than 85 percent of failing to detect differences in the selection of whites and African Americans having similar performance scores by application of the Cleary model.

The test of the group parity model requires the specification of a cutoff score. For the simulations reported in Table 5.4 , cutoff scores were defined based on a regression between performance and test scores conducted for each sample in the simulation. Using the regression, the cutoff on the test was set at the point at which one could be certain with 80 percent confidence that the person's performance would be greater than one standard deviation below the mean of the sample's performance. Choosing a higher level of confidence would result in a lower cut score being used.

The group parity model was tested using Fisher's exact test. This test of significance was applied to differences in the rates of selection for protected and nonprotected class members exceeding the performance standard of minus one standard deviation below the incumbent mean performance score. For Populations 1 and 2, where the test is fair, the results indicate incorrectly significant differences in rates of selection for those meeting the

Table 5.4. Group Parity Model of Test Fairness: Effects in Ten Thousand Random Samples in Four Populations.

	Overall	Adverse to Protected Class Members
	(1)	(2)
[a]Population 1	3.63%	2.50%
[b]Population 2	3.68	1.80
[c]Population 3	81.72	81.72
[d]Population 4	99.77	99.77

[a]Population 1: 10 percent protected class representation, equal means and standard deviations on test scores and performance measure.

[b]Population 2: 50 percent protected class representation, equal means and standard deviations on test scores and performance measure.

[c]Population 3: 10 percent protected class representation, equal standard deviations, protected class test scores one full standard deviation and performance measure one-half standard deviation below nonprotected class members.

[d]Population 4: 50 percent protected class representation, equal standard deviations, protected class test scores one full standard deviation and performance measure one-half standard deviation below nonprotected class members.

minimal performance standards (that is, they indicate the test is unfair) in approximately 3.5 percent of cases.

When examined for Populations 3 and 4 (where significant differences should be found), the expected rates of correctly concluding significant differences (that is, that the test is unfair) are very high (81.72 to 99.77 percent) and the direction of the effect in Populations 3 and 4 is appropriately consistently negative for protected class members. This reflects the power of the group parity statistical test to detect differences of one-half standard deviation in test scores for protected and nonprotected class members with equal performance scores. The comparable power of the Cleary model in the same population is 11 to 16 percent.

It is interesting to note that when the group parity model in Population 1 incorrectly rejects the fairness hypothesis, it tends to do so more frequently (to a statistically significant level) for the smaller population (here, the protected class). The overall Type 1 error rate for the protected class, however, is in line with the benchmark .025 level. The overall lower Type 1 error rate (3 percent versus 5 percent) is due to almost never incorrectly concluding bias against the majority group.

In sum, the results of the simulations indicate that the Cleary model of test fairness has low power to detect unfairness in subgroup differences in test and performance scores of the order typically found for African Americans and whites in practice, whereas the group parity model has the power to detect such test unfairness.

Reverse Versus Direct Regression in Setting Cut Scores

In setting a cut score, should one use reverse or direct regression? Putting aside the problem of truncation, which biases the reverse regression results, we studied the issue of setting cut scores by simulations: (1) using a reverse regression, which meant setting the cut score at that value in the sample data that we are 80 percent confident the minimally performing candidates (estimated at one unit of standard deviation below the mean in performance in the population) will score higher than, and (2) using a direct regression, which meant setting the cut score at that point in the sample data at which we are 80 percent confident that the performance of the test taker will exceed the minimum.

The reverse regression places the burden on *not rejecting* qualified candidates, whereas the direct regression places the burden on *not accepting* candidates who cannot do the job. It follows logically (and the simulation shows) that the cut score is on average considerably higher for the direct regression. These results are not that interesting, because the cut score using either approach will vary depending on the level of confidence one chooses, reflecting what risks one is willing to take.

However, the analysis does yield an interesting result when focusing on the effect of a higher correlation between test and performance on the cut score when the selection risk is held constant. Using direct regression to set the cut score we find a +.41 correlation between cut score and test validity. That is, the better the test, the higher the cut score. Hence a test with greater disparate impact can be justified only if it is a better test.

However, using reverse regression we find the correlation between cut score and test validity to be –.28. That is, the worse the test, the higher the cut score and the greater the disparate impact. Hence, when using reverse regression to set cut scores, one is faced with a situation in which the worse the test, the greater the disparate impact. Thus a test with greater validity will have less adverse impact. In this case the employer bears the burden of having to justify to the court why the cost of the employer's failure to develop a better test should be born disproportionately by the protected class.

The same observation can be made in reference to the values lists presented by Kehoe and Olson in Table 13.2 in Chapter Thirteen. The point estimates Kehoe and Olson report for various minimal competence levels denote the same trend of higher cutoff scores at lower validity levels when using the reverse regression approach.

Setting Cutoff Scores as a Matter of Judicial Ruling

In arriving at the cutoff score interval (that is, 66 to 70 percent of items correct) defined as satisfying the *Lanning* (1999, 2002) standard in his ruling, the judge in *U.S.* v. *Delaware State Police* considered both the truncation problem of reverse regression and the need to define a band around the mean estimate of the test scores of minimally performing officers such that there would be a high probability that a minimum performer would pass. In setting the 66 percent of items correct cutoff score, the court applied the plaintiff expert's calculation of the *standard error of the regression* for the reverse regression analysis but did not apply it to the reverse regression estimate of the mean test score of the minimally performing officers. Instead the court applied that error estimate in defining a confidence band around the original cutoff score of 75 percent of items correct. The original cutoff score of 75 percent of items correct had been defined by another of the defendant's experts using a hybrid content-related and norm-referenced approach.

The use of the original 75 percent of items correct to construct a confidence interval having 66 percent of items correct as the lower bound was the result of the court's stated concerns that (1) both defendant and plaintiff experts had not used a direct measure of minimum qualifications in their criterion-related regression analyses and (2) the expected value from the reverse regression was biased as a result of truncation stemming from its use in the selection of incumbents who served as validation study participants.

References

Books, Articles, and Government Documents

Cascio, W. F., Alexander, R. A., & Barrett, G. V. (1988). Setting cutoff scores: Legal, psychometric, and professional issues and guidelines. *Personnel Psychology, 41,* 1–24.

Cleary, T. A. (1968). Test bias: Prediction of grades of Negro and white students in integrated colleges. *Journal of Educational Measurement, 5,* 115–124.

Cole, N. S. (1973). Bias in selection. *Journal of Educational Measurement, 10,* 237–255.

Ford, J. K., Kraiger, K., & Schechtman, S. L. (1986). Study of race effects in objective indices and subjective evaluation of performance: A meta-analysis of performance criteria. *Psychological Bulletin, 99,* 330–337.

Guion, R. M. (1998). *Assessment, measurement, and prediction for personnel decisions.* Mahwah, NJ: Erlbaum.

Nunnally, J. C. (1978). *Psychometric theory.* New York: McGraw-Hill.

Ryan, T. A. (1959). Multiple comparisons in psychological research. *Psychological Bulletin, 56,* 26–47.

Seber, G.A.F. (1977). *Linear regression analysis.* New York: Wiley.

Snedecor, G. W., & Cochran, W. G. (1980). *Statistical methods* (7th ed.). Ames: Iowa State University Press.

Society for Industrial and Organizational Psychology. (1987). Principles for the validation and use of personnel selection systems (3rd ed.). College Park, MD: Author.

Society for Industrial and Organizational Psychology. (2003). *Principles for the validation and use of personnel selection systems* (4th ed.). Bowling Green, OH: Author.

Stokes, M. E., Davis, C. S., & Koch, G. G. (1997). *Categorical data analysis using the SAS system.* Cary, NC: SAS Institute.

Thorndike, R. L. (1971). *Concepts of culture fairness. Journal of Educational Measurement, 8,* 63–70.

Uniform Guidelines on Employee Selection Procedures, 29 C.F.R. § 1607 *et seq.* (1978).

Wigdor, A. K., & Sackett, P. R. (1993). Employment testing and public policy: The case of the general aptitude test battery. In H. Schuler, J. L. Farr, & M. Smith (Eds.), *Personnel selection and assessment: Individual and organizational perspectives* (pp. 183–204). Mahwah, NJ: Erlbaum.

Williams, E. J. (1969). A note on regression methods in calibration. *Technometrics, 11,* 189–192.

Cases

Bazemore v. Friday, 751 F.2d 622, 667 (4th Cir. 1984), 478 U.S. 385 (1986).

Catlett v. Missouri Highway, 828 F.2d 1260 (8th Cir. 1987).

EEOC v. General Telephone Company of Northwest (9th Cir. 1989).

Hazelwood School District v. United States, 433 U.S. 299.31 n. 17 (1977).

Lanning v. Southeastern Pennsylvania Transportation Authority, 181 F.3d 478 (3d Cir. 1999).

Lanning v. Southeastern Pennsylvania Transportation Authority, 308 F.3d 286 (3d Cir. 2002).

Palmer v. Schultz, 815 F.2d 84 (D.C. Cir. 1987).

Sheehan v. Purolator Inc., 39 F. 2d 99 (2d Cir. 1998).

Sobel v. Yeshiva, 839 F.2d 18 (2d Cir. 1988).

United States of America v. Delaware State Police, No. 01-070-RRM (D. Del. 3d Cir. 2004).

United States of America v. State of Delaware, No. 01-020-KAJ (D. Del. 2004).

Watson v. Fort Worth Bank and Trust, 487 U.S. 977 (1988).

CHAPTER 6

Industrial and Organizational Psychologists as Expert Witnesses

Affecting Employment Discrimination Litigation Post *Daubert*

George C. Thornton III
Peter H. Wingate

There are two inextricably intertwined issues in employment discrimination litigation: who is qualified to speak as an expert, and what qualifies as admissible testimony. These two issues are addressed in the Federal Rules of Evidence and a growing body of case law and opinion related to the *Daubert* Supreme Court decision and its progeny. This chapter first explores the prescribed standards and guidelines by which courts are to decide on the qualifications of experts and the admissibility of scientific and expert evidence, and then discusses empirical research into the application of these standards to the admissibility of social science and industrial and organizational psychology testimony. The chapter continues with an analysis of how the methods and knowledge of industrial and organizational (I-O) psychology conform to the standards for expert testimony and the roles of I-O psychologists in providing such testimony. It concludes with a discussion of issues faced by I-O psychologists in offering expert testimony in employment discrimination litigation and suggestions for practice.

The methods by which a court determines whether evidence is admissible are determined by formal rules of evidence and relevant case law. In the United States, federal courts must adhere to the Federal Rules of Evidence and U.S. Supreme Court rulings, whereas state courts generally follow state rules of evidence, imposed by state legislatures, and are directed by applicable rulings in state courts. This chapter explores the issues of assessment of expert testimony and the admissibility of evidence primarily at the federal level. Although many state courts have adopted the Federal Rules of Evidence, it should be noted that some states have unique standards for the admissibility and use of evidence in litigation (Groscup, Penrod, Studebaker, Huss, & O'Neil, 2002).

Judicial Guidance on Admissibility of Expert Testimony: Seminal Supreme Court Cases

For approximately seventy years the *Frye* standard governed the admissibility of expert testimony in federal courts. According to *Frye* v. *United States* (1923), expert testimony was admissible if it was generally accepted by members in the relevant field of expertise or the relevant scientific community. Rapid advances and growth in science and technology, combined with confusion on how to apply the austere *Frye* general acceptance standard to the presentation of novel evidence, generated a pressing need for modern guidance on how to sort through the varying types of physical, behavioral, and social science evidence presented to the courts. Three recent Supreme Court cases have supplanted the *Frye* general acceptance standard and provide greater clarification on the admissibility and assessment of proposed expert testimony in federal litigation (Berger, 2000).

The influential *Daubert* decision (*Daubert* v. *Merrell Dow Pharmaceuticals,* 1993) emerged from a patchwork of contradictory state and federal court decisions that applied different standards, with different rigor, to evidence tendered by scientific experts hailing from different fields of expertise (Shuman & Sales, 1999). *Daubert* involved the conflicting testimony of experts concerning the use of a prescription drug, Bendectin, and its potential to cause birth defects. In *Daubert,* the Supreme Court determined that the district court and court of appeals had relied almost exclusively upon general acceptance, as gauged primarily by publication of scientific studies and the decisions of other courts, in their assessment of the expert evidence on the possibility of a link between Bendectin and birth defects. The *Daubert* court held that the Federal Rules of Evidence superseded the simplistic *Frye* general acceptance standard for admitting expert scientific testimony. It decided that the Federal Rules of Evidence place a gatekeeping obligation on trial judges to screen proffered scientific evidence to ensure both adequate relevance and reliability. According to *Daubert*, trial judges must assess whether an expert's underlying reasoning or methodology is scientifically valid and can be applied to the facts at issue.

The Supreme Court delineated in *Daubert* four independent factors that a trial judge may use to assess the reliability of proposed expert scientific testimony: whether the expert's theory or technique (1) can be or has been tested, (2) has been subjected to peer review or publication, (3) has a known or potential error rate, and (4) has gained general acceptance in a relevant scientific community. The Supreme Court envisioned such an inquiry to be flexible: the four factors are nonexhaustive, and the focus on testimony must be primarily on the expert's principles and methodology and not necessarily on the conclusions that the principles and methodology generate. The I-O expert providing scientific testimony is advised to explain how the methods employed satisfy the four guidelines regarding reliability of the evidence.

A word of clarification on terminology may be useful at this point: the concept of *reliability* in this context is closely related to what most I-O psychologists mean when they use the term *validity* in reference to a study. Cook and Campbell (1979) described the features of research that demonstrate internal and external validity. *Internal validity* involves such features as random assignment to control and experimental treatments, sound measurement of dependent variables, and elimination of alternative explanations for the effect of the independent variable of interest. *External validity* is present when the conditions of a particular study, for example, subjects, situations, and times, are representative of the conditions to which one wishes to generalize. These features specify more definitively what I-O psychologists would say are the characteristics of a study that provides *good*, that is, *reliable*, evidence.

In *General Electric Co. v. Joiner* (1997), the Supreme Court added to the *Daubert* decision by clarifying that abuse of discretion is the correct standard for an appellate court to use when reviewing a district court *Daubert* ruling to admit or exclude expert scientific evidence. This liberal standard grants wide latitude to district court judges in evidentiary admissibility decisions; a district court's decision will be overturned only when it is manifestly erroneous (Sanders, Diamond, & Vidmar, 2002). Thus *Joiner* reaffirmed the importance of trial judges as gatekeepers, as any given decision to admit or exclude expert evidence may be difficult to challenge at the appellate level. Moreover, the *Joiner* case was notable for conceding that conclusions and methodology may oftentimes be intertwined, thereby resolving confusion over the *Daubert* notion of a stark distinction between the methodology an expert employs and concomitant conclusions drawn from data. This ruling alerts the I-O expert to (1) the importance of presenting a description of the methods in initial proceedings (for example, depositions, pretrial hearings, the district court trial) because the decision by a district judge will hold great weight on appeal, and (2) the need to thoroughly describe methods and not anticipate the luxury of having a judge just accept the expert's conclusions.

In *Kumho Tire Co. v. Carmichael* (1999), the Supreme Court extended the gatekeeping obligation of trial judges to all expert testimony, not only scientific testimony as expressed in *Daubert*. Therefore the four *Daubert* factors may be applied to nonscientific expert testimony; as the Supreme Court noted, there is not necessarily a clear dividing line between scientific, technical, and other specialized knowledge. I-O psychologists may be in a position of offering expert testimony in areas where a body of scientific evidence is not available or definitive. Their expertise coming from education, training, and experience may be scrutinized, and testimony may be excluded from trial.

Rules on the Admissibility of Expert Testimony: Federal Rules of Evidence

The *Daubert* decision and its progeny affirmed the standards for admitting expert testimony that were promulgated by the Federal Rules of Evidence (U.S. House of Representatives, Committee on the Judiciary, 2002). Originally enacted in 1975, and most recently amended in 2002, the Federal Rules of Evidence govern proceedings in the courts of the United States and before U.S. bankruptcy judges and magistrate judges. The *Daubert* trilogy revolved around the essential importance of Rule 702, which places limits on the admissibility of expert evidence. An amendment to Rule 702 in December 2000 codified and clarified the principles originally outlined in *Daubert* (Dixon & Gill, 2002).

Rule 702 provides the core foundation for I-O psychologists and other experts to participate in federal litigation as expert witnesses. Rule 702, entitled "testimony by experts," states: "If scientific, technical, or other specialized knowledge will assist the trier of fact to understand the evidence or to determine a fact in issue, a witness qualified as an expert by knowledge, skill, experience, training, or education, may testify thereto in the form of an opinion or otherwise, if (1) the testimony is based upon sufficient facts or data, (2) the testimony is the product of reliable principles and methods, and (3) the witness has applied the principles and methods reliably to the facts of the case."

On first glance the text of Rule 702 appears to provide significant latitude regarding expert witness qualifications and associated testimony; a witness may be qualified as an expert based on either knowledge, skill, experience, training, or education. However, embedded in Rule 702 is the two-pronged test that requires an expert's testimony to be both relevant and reliable in accordance with *Daubert* and its progeny. Experts seeking to offer testimony in employment discrimination litigation are strongly advised to familiarize themselves with the relevancy and reliability requirements for expert testimony that are mandated by the *Daubert* trilogy of cases and the Federal Rules of Evidence; testimony that fails to meet either standard may be excluded from trial.

Relevance of Expert Testimony

The locus of the relevancy requirement for expert testimony is Federal Rules of Evidence 401, 402, 403, and 702. Rule 401 defines relevant evidence as "evidence having any tendency to make the existence of any fact that is of consequence to the determination of the action more probable or less probable than it would be without the evidence." This definition of relevance must be viewed in conjunction with the statement in Rule 702 that the evidence or testimony must "assist the trier of fact to understand the evidence or to determine a fact in issue." In other words, to surmount the relevancy hurdle, the expert testimony must be sufficiently tied to the facts of a case and aid a judge or jury in resolving a factual dispute (*Daubert* v. *Merrell Dow Pharmaceuticals,* 1993). However, it should be noted that relevance alone does not guarantee that expert testimony will be admitted; Rule 403 provides that "[a]lthough relevant, evidence may be excluded if its probative value is substantially outweighed by the danger of unfair prejudice, confusion of the issues, or misleading the jury, or by considerations of undue delay, waste of time, or needless presentation of cumulative evidence."

Reliability of Expert Testimony

Daubert provided that an expert's opinion must have a reliable basis in the knowledge and experience of his or her discipline and that many factors (such as the four listed in *Daubert*) may bear on the reliability inquiry. The 2000 amendment to Rule 702 has incorporated the ideas posited in *Daubert,* and now explicitly requires expert testimony to (1) be based upon sufficient facts or data, (2) be the product of reliable principles and methods, and (3) apply the principles and methods reliably to the facts of the case.

Empirical Research on Admissibility of Expert Witness Testimony

The drastic changes to the standards for scrutinizing expert testimony instituted by the *Daubert* trilogy have generated significant scholarship and debate. Researchers, academics, and legal practitioners have remained divided on whether *Daubert* has loosened or tightened the standards for admissibility of expert testimony, whether judges are qualified to act as gatekeepers of complex scientific evidence, and what the long-term outcomes of *Daubert* may bode for expert witnesses and litigation. Only recently has empirical research addressed the actual use of *Daubert* and its associated consequences. Our review of the limited extant research first examines the role of *Daubert* and its effects on expert testimony generally and then shifts to the impact of *Daubert* on expert witness testimony in the realm of the social sciences and employment discrimination litigation.

Overall Effect of *Daubert:*
Surveys of Judges and Attorneys

A series of recent surveys conducted by the Federal Judicial Center (Krafka, Dunn, Johnson, Cecil, & Miletich, 2002) provides the most current and comprehensive information from active federal judges on expert testimony in federal civil trials. To examine changes in the handling of expert testimony pre- and post-*Daubert,* Krafka et al. (2002) administered surveys in 1991 and 1998 to all active federal district judges, and subsequently in 1999 administered a survey to attorneys. The two surveys of federal district judges gathered information regarding their most recently completed civil trial that included expert testimony, and the 1999 survey of attorneys collected information from the lead attorneys for the plaintiffs and defendants in the cases presided over by judges in the 1998 survey.

In the study by Krafka et al. (2002), the distribution of case types involving expert testimony that went to trial in 1998 were categorized into tort cases (45 percent), civil rights cases (23 percent), contract cases (11 percent), intellectual property cases (10 percent), labor cases (2 percent), prisoner cases (2 percent), and other civil cases (8 percent). The numbers total more than 100 percent due to rounding. The trial characteristics were observed to be very similar across the 1991 and 1998 surveys of judges. In 1998, 92 percent of the surveyed trials included expert testimony by plaintiffs, and 79 percent of the trials included testimony by defendants. Seventy-three percent of the trials included experts testifying for both parties. Twenty-three percent of the civil trials in 1998 were bench trials, while 77 percent were conducted in front of juries; these numbers also mimic the rates observed in 1991. As 64 percent of all civil trials in 1998 involved a jury, the fact that 77 percent of the civil trials involving experts were jury trials in 1998 leads to the conclusion that experts may be disproportionately represented in jury trials.

The testifying experts' areas of expertise were also consistent across the 1991 and 1998 surveys. Medical and mental health specialists accounted for more than 40 percent of the experts presented overall in 1998, followed by experts from business, law, and financial areas (25 percent); engineering and other safety and process specialists (22 percent); and scientific specialties such as chemistry, ballistics, toxicology, and metallurgy (8 percent). Economists provided testimony with the greatest frequency of any one profession, accounting for 12 percent of all testifying experts.

One of the most notable findings from the Krafka et al. (2002) study was that judges were more likely to scrutinize evidence and then subsequently limit or exclude testimony in federal civil trials post-*Daubert* in 1998 (when judges limited or excluded some testimony in 41 percent of the referenced cases) than were judges pre-*Daubert* in 1991 (when judges limited or excluded some testimony in 25 percent of the referenced cases). These figures suggest that judges may be exerting significantly more gatekeeping activity over evidence in civil trials as a result of *Daubert*.

Pretrial hearings on the admissibility of expert testimony, also known as *Daubert* hearings, significantly increased post-*Daubert*, as 77 percent of judges indicated that they used these procedures in 1998 versus only 51 percent in 1991. Moreover, judges frequently encountered admissibility issues in the context of objections to expert evidence or motions *in limine*. (A motion *in limine* is a pretrial motion to exclude evidence that may be irrelevant, inadmissible, or prejudicial.) In 1991, judges reported that they ruled on a motion *in limine* in only 32 percent of the cases, whereas in 1998, when admissibility was raised as an issue, 72 percent of the cases contained a motion *in limine* pertaining to admissibility issues.

The data gathered from attorneys surveyed in 1999 also support the contention that greater scrutiny of expert testimony is being exercised post-*Daubert*. Forty-eight percent of attorneys stated that they examine the credentials of their own potential expert witnesses more closely post-*Daubert*. In addition, 40 percent of attorneys indicated that they are more involved in the preparation of expert testimony, and 22 percent related that they retain experts earlier in a case due to *Daubert*. In regard to opposing experts, 41 percent of attorneys professed to making more objections to the admissibility of expert testimony at trial, and 24 percent stated that they make more summary judgment motions in the instance where the opposing party's testimony has been limited or excluded. Attorneys' responses also were in accord with the perceptions of judges on motions *in limine;* 54 percent of attorneys reported using such motions to a greater degree post-*Daubert.* Only 35 percent of attorneys maintained that their approaches to expert testimony did not change post-*Daubert.*

Overall Effect of *Daubert:* Written District Court Opinions in Civil Cases

A study that systematically examined a sample of 399 written federal district court opinions issued from civil trials between 1980 and 1999, conducted by Dixon and Gill (2002), provides additional evidence that judges may have become more watchful gatekeepers of expert evidence since *Daubert.* The results from Dixon and Gill's study have important implications for the effect of *Daubert* on (1) evidentiary reliability standards, (2) the judicial gatekeeping function, and (3) federal civil case processes and outcomes.

Dixon and Gill concluded from their analyses that post-*Daubert* the reliability of expert evidence has been examined more closely by judges and that a higher proportion of evidence has been determined to be unreliable. All of the *Daubert* factors were addressed by judges more frequently at some point in the years following *Daubert* than in preceding years. Moreover, directly following *Daubert,* from 1993 to 1997, judges appeared to initially increase their scrutiny of the *Daubert* factors when evaluating reliability but then shifted their attention in the period from 1997 to 1999 to additional facets and indicators of reliability. For example, the clarity and coherence of an expert's explanation of his or her theory, methods, and procedures, which is not one of the factors explicitly described in *Daubert,* appears to have more recently gained significant scrutiny from judges. Dixon and Gill's explanation for this phenomenon is that immediately after *Daubert,* judges needed to learn more about the evaluation of reliability and their latitude as gatekeepers and used the *Daubert* factors as a crutch. In later years, after appellate courts reinforced the authority of their decisions, district judges may have felt more autonomy and ability to incorporate other useful indicators of reliability into their admissibility decisions.

This analysis of opinions reveals gatekeeping trends that extend past the issue of reliability; Dixon and Gill (2002) avow that judges also started evaluating evidence more critically post-*Daubert* in relation to both relevance of the testimony and the expert's qualifications. Success rates for challenges based on relevance, qualifications, and other criteria rose post-*Daubert*, although those increases were not all statistically significant. Lastly, Dixon and Gill found that the proportion of challenges to expert evidence that actually resulted in summary judgment rose post-*Daubert* and that it was likely that the challenges to the plaintiffs' evidence led to increases in case dismissals.

The findings by Krafka et al. (2002) and Dixon and Gill on the effects of *Daubert* must be qualified by noting that it is extremely difficult to empirically assess changes in judicial decision making and isolate cause-and-effect relationships involving the law. For example, the published district court opinions examined by Dixon and Gill and the surveys administered by Krafka et al. attempted to examine changes pre- and post-*Daubert*, yet in each study it was unknown if results were affected by judges who may have been sampled multiple times (for example, in multiple opinions or in both the 1991 and 1998 surveys). Many other difficulties exist in isolating the effect of *Daubert* as various factors evolve over time, including changes to Federal Rules of Civil Procedure and alterations to the composition of the bench due to presidential appointments (Dixon & Gill, 2002).

Judicial Understanding and Application of *Daubert*

Although the studies described previously provide useful information on certain trends that appear to have occurred post-*Daubert* on the admissibility of expert testimony, they fail to answer the questions of whether judges are able to actually differentiate between reliable and unreliable evidence and whether the gatekeeping role envisioned by *Daubert* is attainable by judges who are frequently untrained in the scientific method. The following studies have begun to address these crucial questions.

Kovera and McAuliff (2000) provided Florida circuit court judges with descriptions of an expert's research in which the internal validity and peer review status of the evidence were manipulated. Judges were asked to role-play presiding over a hypothetical civil case where the plaintiff alleged that she was the victim of sexual harassment in a hostile workplace environment. The proposed expert witness testimony on behalf of the plaintiff relied on gender stereotyping research and, more specifically, the results of a study (based on an actual award-winning study on gender stereotyping) that was conducted for the trial. Within the study, peer review status and internal validity (for example, presence of a control group, amount of experimental confounds, and so forth) were varied to correspond with classic threats to internal validity as described by Cook and Campbell (1979).

Overall, regardless of the version presented, only 17 percent of the judges believed that the expert's testimony should be admitted. Furthermore, judges were no more likely to admit testimony based on the internally valid study (which Kovera and McAuliff profess would meet both the *Frye* and *Daubert* criteria) than testimony based on a study that contained a serious threat to internal validity, such as experimenter bias, lack of a control group, or other confounds. The peer review manipulations also failed to appreciably alter the judges' admissibility decisions. These findings may point to negative views of psychology by judges, an inability by judges to identify flawed research, or both. Judges were most likely to cite legal justifications for their admissibility decisions; when judges did object to the study, this objection was frequently based on the laboratory setting of the research and not the methodological flaws inherent in the research. Most indicative of the limited scientific sophistication of the judges is the fact that only 12 percent of the judges presented with the flawed experiment version mentioned the flaws present in the research in their justification.

In a recent survey of 400 state court judges, Gatowski, Dobbin, Richardson, Ginsburg, Merlino, and Dahir (2001) provided additional evidence that judges may encounter difficulties with the notion of reliability and *Daubert*. Gatowski et al. found that only 5 percent of the judges could demonstrate a clear understanding of the notion of falsifiability, and only 4 percent could demonstrate a clear understanding of the notion of error rate. Approximately 71 percent of the judges demonstrated a satisfactory understanding of the scientific peer review process, and 82 percent of the judges provided convincing understanding of the general acceptance standard. Moreover, few significant differences were found to exist in judicial treatment and beliefs regarding admissibility of expert evidence among judges located in states with different admissibility standards (*Daubert* versus non-*Daubert*). Ninety-one percent of the judges claimed that a gatekeeper role for the judge is an acceptable one, irrespective of their states' admissibility guidelines.

The results from their study led Gatowski et al. (2001) to conclude that although the judges surveyed were extremely supportive of *Daubert* guidelines and the gatekeeping role, their confidence may be unwarranted; the judges' "bench philosophy of science" appeared to reproduce the rhetoric, rather than the substance, of *Daubert*.

I-O Psychology Expert Witness Testimony and Employment Discrimination: Survey of Federal Judges

A survey with responses from 150 active federal district and magistrate judges, conducted by Wingate and Thornton (2004), extended the nascent empirical literature on the admissibility of expert witness testimony by examining judicial perceptions of I-O psychology expert witness testimony in age discrimination litigation. In a mail survey, judges were presented with one of four prototypical descriptions of expert witness testimony: an I-O psychologist proposed to testify for the defense regarding an organization's actions during a layoff, and the plaintiff moved to exclude the expert's testimony. In the first scenario the proposed expert witness testimony was based solely on the expert's education, expertise, training, and interactions with the organization. Each of the other three scenarios added one of the following as a basis for the testimony: (1) reference to a relevant unpublished empirical study, (2) reference to a relevant published empirical study, or (3) reference to a relevant published meta-analysis.

Wingate and Thornton (2004) found that the judges surveyed were relatively unacquainted with the field of I-O psychology; only 21 percent had ever heard or read the testimony of an I-O psychologist. Moreover, a mere 8 percent of the judges rated themselves as at least "familiar" with the field of I-O psychology. Notwithstanding their lack of familiarity with I-O psychology, the majority of the judges rated themselves as at least moderately likely to admit the expert's testimony, regardless of the scenario presented. Only 19 percent of the judges rated themselves as not at all likely to admit the evidence. These findings appear to clash with Kovera and McAuliff's results (2000), where only 17 percent of the judges in their study decided to admit valid and relevant psychological expert testimony in a sexual harassment civil case. The fact that the expert witness in the study by Wingate and Thornton (2004) had actual contact and experience with the organization may account for this discrepancy; the expert testimony in Kovera and McAuliff's (2000) study relied on scientific research on stereotyping that was not tailored to the specific workplace in litigation.

The basis for the expert testimony in Wingate and Thornton's study did not noticeably affect admissibility decisions; it appears that the information contained in the first scenario was typically sufficient to persuade judges that the testimony was adequately reliable and relevant. This result may point to the essential importance of an expert's credentials, background, and experience or to the possibility that judges are not swayed by empirical research conducted in another workplace setting. Furthermore, regardless of the scenario presented, judges did not claim to place much overt emphasis on the *Daubert* factors in their assessment of evidentiary reliability, although judges did ascribe somewhat greater importance to the general acceptance factor in their assessment of evidentiary reliability. This may lend credence to the notion that judges may have difficulty in operationalizing *Daubert* for social science evidence and instead are more comfortable with relying on witness credentials, qualifications, and interactions with an organization in their admissibility decisions. This possibility is given additional support by the fact that both judicial familiarity with I-O psychology and previous exposure to I-O psychology courtroom testimony were discovered to be positively related to the admissibility decision. Judges previously exposed to I-O psychology may have subsequently possessed more confidence in its scientific basis and methods than did judges who were unfamiliar with the field.

In addition to such analyses of written court decisions and responses of judges to survey questionnaires, judges' conversations with Landy (in Chapter Fifteen of this volume) provide unique insight into judicial decision making about I-O psychologists and their testimony. The interviews reveal a wide range of familiarity with I-O psychology, and idiosyncratic interpretation of whether I-O testimony can meet *Daubert* standards.

Testimony by I-O Psychologists

We opened this chapter with a statement of two issues: who is qualified to speak as an expert and what qualifies as admissible expert testimony. We now explore how I-O psychologists become qualified as experts and whether the testimony they may have to offer is admissible. Many issues that arise in employment discrimination litigation involve questions that can be addressed with the methods I-O psychologists use to study employment discrimination and with results from scientific studies in I-O psychology. This section ends with a discussion of some of the ethical, professional, and personal challenges I-O psychologists face when involved with employment discrimination litigation.

Roles of I-O Psychologists as Experts

A framework for considering the place of I-O psychology in employment discrimination litigation can be provided by considering the roles I-O psychologists may play in the litigation process. Industrial and organizational psychologists may be called on by attorneys for the plaintiff or the defendant to carry out one or more of the following roles when providing expert testimony about the methods and findings in the field: (1) conduct original scientific research and present evidence, (2) summarize findings from past scientific studies, (3) provide expert testimony based on past education and experience, (4) critique testimony offered by an expert for the opposing party, or (5) conduct research but not testify as an expert. In addition, I-O psychologists may be appointed to serve as third-party advisers to the court or may be allowed to submit amicus curiae briefs. From the point of view of Judges Graham and Sifton (see Chapter Fifteen of this volume), the core role of the expert is to educate the trier of fact (that is, the judge or jury). This includes doing several things: do not assume the judge is familiar with I-O psychology; do not assume the judge has read or understood all expert reports; recognize that judges deal with cases involving a wide variety of technical matters other than employment; clearly explain the data to support a conclusion; provide a complete "tutorial"; show how to use the evidence to apply common sense. In all of these roles, the I-O psychologist will be called on to provide information that is relevant and reliable, that satisfies the guidelines for expert testimony as set forth by *Daubert* and its progeny.

Qualifications of I-O Psychologists

Research summarized earlier in this chapter showed that credentials offered by the expert may affect judicial admissions decisions. Many I-O psychologists have the qualifications to contribute to employment discrimination litigation as a result of their education and experience. This education typically includes considerable preparation in research methods as they apply to the study of work behavior and human resource management. At the level of master's and doctoral degree study it typically includes courses in data management, statistics, research design, measurement theory, and test construction. Content courses typically cover topics referred to as "personnel psychology" (including such areas as job analysis, recruiting and selection, performance appraisal, and training) and "organizational psychology" (including such areas as work attitudes, leadership, motivation, and teams).

I-O psychologists typically have experience relevant to issues raised in employment discrimination litigation. Many work in public and private organizations as internal consultants, human resource managers, and trainers. In conjunction with operational and human resource managers they develop, implement, and evaluate programs in areas such as personnel selection, training, performance management, and organizational development. Other I-O psychologists work in consulting firms and serve as external consultants to a variety of organizations. Such experience gives breadth of exposure to state-of-the-art practices in diverse organizations. Still other I-O psychologists teach and do research in departments of psychology and management and often consult part-time with organizations. Work in academic settings often gives the expert an independent view of issues related to employment discrimination. Judge Posner (Chapter Fifteen of this volume) presents a somewhat contradictory point of view by pointing out that academicians may be coopted by the hiring attorney and may feel little accountability for their testimony.

Specific qualifications and credentials for an expert are not specified, and the courts defer to the Federal Rules of Evidence and *Daubert*. In practice, to qualify as an expert witness a person will typically be asked to show evidence of relevant education, knowledge, skill, training, experience, and credentials. Although a doctoral degree is not required to qualify as an I-O expert and offer scientific testimony in employment discrimination litigation, an expert typically has earned a PhD (or PsyD) degree, has conducted research on topics relevant to the case, and has some relevant experience. Although having published research is not a requirement, it helps if the expert can state that he or she has published relevant studies in peer-reviewed journals. Possessing a state license to practice psychology is seldom an issue either. Whether holding a license to practice psychology has any weight may depend on a judge's perspective and may vary by state, depending on state-specific requirements for licensure. In a state requiring licensure for I-O psychologists, an opposing attorney may try to discredit an I-O psychologist for failing to hold a license. (More information about licensing for I-O psychologists can be found at the Web site of the Society for Industrial and Organizational Psychology [www.siop.org].)

Even though the decision to admit evidence should be based on the methodological soundness of that evidence, admission decisions may be based on the credentials of the expert. The presence of any single credential is neither a necessary nor a sufficient condition to determine qualification. Absence of any of the standard credentials may cause scrutiny from the opposing attorney and disqualification by some judges. For contrary points of view, see Landy's interviews with Judges Sifton and Baer (Chapter Fifteen in this volume), in which these judges assert that credentials are less important than the expert's ability to explain technical matters to the jury.

Other Professionals as Expert Witnesses

Professionals in areas other than I-O psychology may be qualified as experts in employment discrimination litigation due to the relevance of research and experience in their specialty fields. Examples include social psychologists, sociologists, statisticians, economists, and human resource management professionals. Each discipline may provide a unique perspective and diverse understanding of complex employment matters, but I-O psychologists bring a unique perspective and set of skills to the role of expert witness in employment discrimination litigation. I-O psychologists are trained to conduct strong empirical research on behavior at work.

Methods Used by I-O Psychology

I-O psychology has a long history of using scientific methods to study behavior in work settings. Expertise in these methods allows the I-O psychologist to fulfill the roles of conducting original research and critiquing research carried out by opposing experts. I-O research methods employ principles of empirical research and incorporate procedures that satisfy the *Daubert* admissibility factors. Many I-O techniques (1) have been extensively tested, (2) have been published in peer-reviewed journals, (3) have a known error rate, and (4) have gained general acceptance. The last point is not meant to claim there is universal acceptance; there are healthy debates in the literature around the adequacy of most research techniques. The *Handbook of Research Methods in Industrial and Organizational Psychology* (Rogelberg, 2002) provides detailed explorations of many issues in research, ranging from the foundations of quantitative and qualitative research methods to procedures for data collection and data investigation.

Table 6.1 summarizes some of the established methods in the field of industrial and organizational psychology. Job analysis methods include reading source documents, observing incumbents on the job, and interviewing and administering questionnaires to various subject matter experts. Established methods exist for building reliable and valid measurement tools such as paper-and-pencil tests, interviews, simulation techniques, and assessment centers. Established authorities exist to guide methods of validating selection procedures (see Chapter Three in this volume). A wide array of methods for evaluating worker performance exist, including objective measurement systems, supervisory ratings, and ratings from multiple sources such as peers, subordinates, and customers (these methods are often referred to as *360-degree feedback* or *multisource rating* systems). Methods for setting pay scales include job evaluation to establish internal equity and to match market rates. Methods for analyzing training needs and developing specific skills and abilities have been built on principles of learning and adult education. Methods of program evaluation are applied to study the various impacts of broader human resource management systems.

Table 6.1. Methods of Research
in Industrial and Organizational Psychology.

Area of Expertise	Method	Authoritative Sources
Analyzing work duties and responsibilities	Job analysis Task analysis	Brannick & Levine (2002)
Developing measuring techniques	Construction of achievement and aptitude tests	AERA et al. (1999) Guion (1998)
	Design of interviews	Eder & Harris (1999)
	Building simulation techniques	Thornton & Mueller-Hanson (2004)
	Assessment centers	International Task Force (2000)
Validating predictors	Validation procedures	AERA et al. (1999) SIOP (2003) *Uniform Guidelines* (1978)
Evaluating worker performance	Performance appraisal	Smither (1998)
	Multisource feedback system	Bracken, Timmreck, & Church (2001)
Training and developing employees	Needs analysis	Brannick, Salas, & Prince (1997)
	Skill development	Goldstein & Ford (2002)
Creating and managing human resource systems	Program evaluation	Edwards, Scott, & Raju (2003)
Analyzing statistical data	Descriptive and inferential statistical tests	Cohen & Cohen (1983) Siskin & Trippi (Chapter Five, this volume) Wingate & Thornton (2000)

With all of these methods, I-O psychologists use statistical techniques to analyze data gathered in both laboratory and field research settings. Descriptive statistics provide summaries (such as the mean and standard deviation) of samples of data, whereas inferential statistics provide methods to generalize from samples to populations and to make statements about the "statistical significance" of findings in samples under study (that is, to infer the probability that the findings occurred by chance alone). Statistical methods enable the I-O psychologist to make statements about the level of confidence one can have in research findings, and thus they address the *Daubert* guideline of estimating the error rate in one's method. Various issues related to statistical analyses in employment discrimination litigation are discussed by Wingate and Thornton (2000) and Siskin and Trippi (in Chapter Five of this volume).

The *Daubert* standards for expert testimony place great emphasis on the quality of the methods used to generate evidence. Judges are charged with the responsibility of determining if the testimony is based on methods that are reliable and accurate. Therefore an I-O psychologist will be expected to demonstrate that his or her methods are acceptable in the profession. Many sources provide guidance for the accepted methods for gathering evidence about the effectiveness of I-O practices, and Table 6.1 provides only a partial list of these sources for selected methods. I-O psychologists serving as expert witnesses will want to be able to refer to the sources they consider authoritative in their areas of work.

Bodies of Knowledge in I-O Psychology

Table 6.2 summarizes some of the areas where I-O psychologists have accumulated substantial knowledge relevant to employment practices. Mastery of these bodies of knowledge enables I-O experts to fulfill the role of summarizing findings and forming conclusions from past research relevant to the issue being adjudicated. I-O psychologists have used scientific methods to study the nature of work (including duties, responsibilities, tasks, and worker attributes); taxonomies of the knowledge, skills, abilities, and other characteristics relevant to effectiveness; descriptions of the dimensions of work performance (including completion of formal and informal job requirements); procedures to attract and screen applicants; techniques to socialize and train newcomers into the organization; and procedures to evaluate performance effectiveness. In each of these areas, and many more, substantial bodies of empirical evidence have been amassed (Anderson, Ones, Sinangil, Viswesvaran, 2001; Borman, Ilgen, & Klimoski, 2002; Dunnette & Hough, 1990). Such accumulated bodies of research evidence are relevant to many types of employment discrimination cases involving such employment status issues as recruitment, selection, promotion, layoffs, and pay and benefits.

Table 6.2. Areas of Accumulated Knowledge in Industrial and Organizational Psychology.

Topic	Sources
Nature of work	Howard (1995)
	Landy & Conte (2004)
Taxonomies of worker attributes	Fleishman, Quaintance, & Broeding (1989)
O*NET	Dye & Silver (1999)
Taxonomies of performance	Campbell, McCloy, Oppler, & Sager (1993)
Recruiting and selection procedures	Kehoe (2000)
	Thomas (2003)
Learning principles and training techniques	Goldstein & Ford (2002)
Performance evaluation	Murphy & Cleveland (1995)
Teamwork	Brannick et al. (1997)

The potential expert witness will want to carefully study each body of scientific evidence to determine its relevance to the specific employment discrimination case in each organizational setting under review. All scientific evidence may not be relevant. For example, after carefully examining the conflicting research findings on gender stereotyping, David Copus (in Chapter Fourteen in this volume) concludes that whereas laboratory studies using stranger-to-stranger designs with little interaction and motivation sometimes show the negative effects of gender stereotypes, no prior research captures the reality of organizational decision making. Thus, according to Copus, testimony on gender stereotypes does not meet the standards of relevance required to meet *Daubert* standards.

Moreover, the dynamic nature of scientific research in a field like I-O psychology must be recognized. What may appear to be confusion or conflict in scientific evidence may really be the result of an evolutionary process. Early studies done with rudimentary methods may be improved on or refuted by recent studies using more sophisticated methods. For example, early studies of race differences in test validity that relied on evidence of "valid in one group but not in a second group" suggested black-white differences, only to be supplanted by the appropriate tests of statistical significance of differences in validities that have typically failed to reveal minority and gender group differences in test validity. Gutman (Chapter Two of this volume) points out a number of disconnects between legal rulings and current science in areas such as test validation, subjective causes of adverse impact, and business necessity.

Rejection of evidence may also result from the healthy skepticism and debate that permeate the field of I-O psychology. Such debates lead to scientific advances but may appear to the court to reflect lack of general acceptance on many topics.

Stages of Litigation in Which I-O Psychologists Can Contribute

The complex stages of an employment discrimination case are described by Landy in Chapter One of this volume. I-O psychologists can make contributions to many of these stages for plaintiffs, defendants, and the courts.

Contributions can come before a trial when the expert partici-
pates in conferences to craft litigation strategy, conducts research,
helps to craft interrogatories during discovery, prepares the attorney to conduct depositions of opposing witnesses, gives depositions,
prepares the attorney to question himself or herself, and prepares
the attorney to cross-examine opposing witnesses including experts.
Expert testimony can be challenged at several points in the proceedings of employment litigation. In some instances the judge may
hold a hearing to examine the evidence and its foundation in order
to rule whether the testimony meets the *Daubert* standards and thus
can be presented in court as "scientific" testimony.

The first step after an expert is sworn in is the process of qualifying the person as an expert. The parties may stipulate on qualification or the attorney may ask the person to describe his or her
education, relevant background and experience, current job, and
so forth. The attorney then asks that the court accept the person as
an "expert." The judge then asks if the opposing attorney has any
objections. Typically, this step proceeds quickly as a result of earlier
acceptance by the opposing attorney. During the trial the expert
can contribute by providing direct testimony and helping to craft
settlement agreements. Normally, the expert witness will not be
allowed to attend the trial, but the expert can meet with the attorneys and clients after hours to confer on progress. After the trial
the expert can help implement consent agreements.

One of the more controversial roles for I-O psychologists
comes when an I-O psychologist serves as a *privileged* trial expert
(Lindemann & Grossman, 1996), that is, conducts research but
does not testify. This role is occasionally described as a *consulting*
expert as opposed to a *testifying* expert. In this role the expert can
explore alternative strategies for investigating the validity and
adverse impact of a challenged test or practice. The results of such
investigation may be privileged from discovery by the opposing
party so long as the expert is not used as a trial witness. Although
the I-O psychologist may have some ethical concern about being
on the "dirty team," the one that knows all the supportive and nonsupportive findings (as opposed to the "clean team," the one that
conducts research and testifies only on selected topics), provision
for such a role is written in the Federal Rules of Civil Procedure,
Rule 26(b)(4)(B). Judge Posner (Chapter Fifteen of this volume)
acknowledges the contributions of consulting experts but sees a

serious problem in that the attorney may allow only the experts with supporting evidence to testify.

Scrutiny of Various Types of Expert Testimony

Whereas the *Daubert* guidelines applied originally only to the admissibility of scientific testimony, *Kumho Tire Co.* v. *Carmichael* (1999) extended judges' responsibility to the scrutiny of all forms of expert testimony. Although the *Daubert* factors are to be applied by judges when scrutinizing all expert testimony, the application of these guidelines may be more complex when examining evidence that is not strictly scientific. Thus, when reviewing different forms of expert testimony, judges may use a variety of standards for admission ("Note . . . ," 2003). I-O testimony commonly falls into one of three categories: (1) scientific evidence based on a local scientific study that the expert has conducted—here the *Daubert* factors provide relatively clear guidance for the judge to evaluate the expert's method; (2) scientific evidence based on a summary of a series of studies done in various locations by various researchers—here the judge may not have such clear guidance on how to evaluate an expert's conclusions that summarize a variety of evidence; (3) expert testimony with respect to accepted practices in comparable situations, in which case the expert will be basing conclusions on training and experience—here the education, experience, and other qualifications of the witness may guide the judge ("Note . . . ," 2003). Thus the relevance of the expert's credentials may be a function of the type of testimony offered: whereas credentials may not be so important in the first and second situations, they may be controlling in the third situation. For example, if the expert is offering testimony about standard practices in personnel selection or performance appraisal, the expert's experience in related organizations may determine whether the judge will allow testimony.

Judicial Methods of Reviewing Expert (But Not Scientific) Testimony

When engaging in original scientific research, whether basic or applied, I-O psychologists have a well-defined set of methods in many areas of practice, and the expert is well served to be intimately familiar with and to follow standard methods if the testimony about such research is to be offered in court. In contrast, when expert testimony based on knowledge generated in prior studies or testimony based on the expert's experience is being offered, there are fewer specific, commonly accepted methods of forming conclusions. Rather the judge will scrutinize the general reasoning used by the expert. The judge will rely on his or her evaluation of how the expert gathered information, used the data, and formed conclusions. An analysis in the *Harvard Law Review* ("Note . . . ," 2003) summarized the process of evaluating reliability and admissibility of this sort of evidence as a process of "deconstructing an argument: assessing the logic of argument, the validity of its premises, the rigor with which the witness applied the technique, the faithfulness of the witness's application of the methodology to her description of it, the magnitude of the inference drawn by the witness in forming her opinion, and the sufficiency of the facts to support the inference" (p. 2150). This situation suggests that the I-O expert will need to carefully explain all steps in the process of gathering, integrating, and evaluating information used to form an expert (but not scientific) opinion. Because judges may not be familiar with the field of I-O psychology, the I-O expert may need to educate the judge in the field of expertise and methods used to form opinions (Kovera & McAuliff, 2000; Gatowski et al., 2001).

Challenges I-O Psychologists Face as Expert Witnesses

I-O psychologists providing expert testimony in employment discrimination litigation face a number of challenges they may not have encountered in other aspects of their professional life. These pressures may come from a lack of familiarity with the rules of evidence and rules for courtroom proceedings, lack of knowledge of the full range of relevant evidence, the contentious and adversarial nature of legal proceedings, failure to appreciate the approach taken initially by the retaining attorney and later by opposing council, the oath witnesses take in court, and the ethical principles of psychologists.

I-O psychologists may face pressures that come from retaining and opposing attorneys. To respond appropriately, the I-O psychologist should be thoroughly familiar with the methods used to set up, implement, and evaluate the procedure in question. Of course this assumes the methods themselves are professionally sound. Pressures on the expert from the retaining attorney can come in various forms. This attorney may ask the expert to provide only testimony that is most beneficial to his or her client. Judge Smith (Chapter Fifteen of this volume) voices her concern that experts may not be impervious to becoming advocates, and thus she has a healthy skepticism for their neutrality. In this situation the expert will need to hold firmly to professional principles and the obligations to the research evidence and court rules. These take precedence over any responsibility to the attorney or client. In the purposefully adversarial setting of litigation the impartial expert may need to resist the temptation to get drawn into the competitive climate. The expert should avoid becoming overly zealous and trying to win. Rather the expert should stick to the evidence revealed by the methods used (Brodsky, 1999). The retaining attorney may also pressure the expert to criticize the expert testimony of opposing witnesses. In this situation the expert should focus on the methodology used by the opposing expert and not make disparaging remarks about the other expert's position, experience, credentials, or personal character. In all cases, avoid ad hominem attacks. Personal attacks on colleagues in employment discrimination litigation are never appropriate.

In addition experts are often asked to make simple, summary, categorical statements. For example, the attorney may seek a yes or no answer to questions such as: "Is the test valid?" "Are supervisory ratings biased?" *Valid* is a generic concept, and relevant evidence may include supportive and nonsupportive evidence. *Bias* has many meanings and may be present for some groups and types of comparisons but not others. In these and other matters, it is often impossible to generalize with one-word answers (Brodsky, 1999). Nevertheless, judges often grow impatient if a witness refuses to answer a yes or no question. It is often best to agree to answer but to say that after answering the question you would like to qualify or explain your answer. If the attorney refuses to permit you to explain, your attorney can follow up the answer on redirect. Or the judge may ask you to elaborate even if the attorney will not.

Additional pressures may come from opposing attorneys in depositions and cross-examination. Opposing attorneys may try to discredit the expert and the testimony. Experts face challenges in maintaining a balanced perspective regarding the strength of scientific evidence. Research methods are never perfect or totally flawless, and research evidence is seldom unequivocal or totally supportive of one position (Brodsky, 1999). The expert must guard against overstating conclusions from research studies. Experts will be more credible if they acknowledge the limitations in a research study.

A number of sources provide sound advice for any psychologist serving as an expert witness in court (Baute, 2001; Brodsky, 1991, 1999; Harris, 2000). This advice ranges from obvious suggestions on matters of dress and speech to advice on how to deal with the often subtle actions opposing attorneys take to discredit and befuddle the expert (Brodsky, 1991). Brodsky (1999) advises that when faced with a *Daubert* hearing, the expert should be fully prepared to describe support for the methodology used to arrive at conclusions more than the results themselves. In areas of I-O psychology this often means the expert will want to demonstrate how the evidence was gathered in conformance with the standard authority documents covering personnel selection, such as *Standards for educational and psychological testing* (American Educational Research Association, American Psychological Association, & National Council on Measurement in Education, 1999), *Principles for the validation and use of personnel selection procedures* (Society for Industrial and Organizational Psychology, 2003), and *Uniform Guidelines on employee selection procedures* (1978).

Ethical Issues

I-O psychologists confront many ethical issues when serving as expert witnesses in employment discrimination litigation (Bersoff, 2003; Thornton & Benson, 1980). The impartiality of expert witnesses may be challenged if the expert appears to have a pro-plaintiff prejudice (*James* v. *Stockham Valves,* 1975) or prodefendant prejudice (Lindemann & Grossman, 1996). Some experts attempt to dispel the perception of bias for either party by balancing their service as an expert between employment discrimination litigation plaintiffs and defendants. Nevertheless, once retained by one side, experts may still have difficulty being impartial during the sometimes heated and emotional proceedings.

At times I-O psychologists confront conflicts between their ethical principles of professional behavior as scientists (American Psychological Association, 1992) and the canon of ethics guiding those in the profession of attorney (Thornton & Benson, 1980). Whereas attorneys' canons of ethics call for zealous defense of the client within the bounds of legal proceedings, psychologists' ethical principles call for full disclosure, conservative statements, and impartial reliance on the empirical data resulting from systematic research methods.

One place where these ethical conflicts come to the fore is the oath one takes before testifying in court. Each witness is asked: "Do you promise to tell the truth, the whole truth, and nothing but the truth?" The first phrase ("tell the truth") is relatively easy to comply with: state only true facts as you know them. Although the last phrase ("nothing but the truth") is ostensibly easy to comply with, in the heat of a courtroom exchange, experts may make claims that are unsubstantiated. The middle phrase ("the whole truth") can be the most difficult to comply with, especially when a body of research evidence is complex and may include data injurious to the case of the party who has retained the expert. In Judge Sifton's interview (Chapter Fifteen of this volume) he voices the concern that the very title of *industrial* psychologist begins to raise questions of bias in his mind. In addition the expert seldom has time to relate *all* the facts or relevant information and thus faces the challenge of faithfully presenting a representative sample of the population of information available. Sifton also comments that when an expert is offering an expert *opinion,* it make little sense to ask him or her to "swear to the truth" of that opinion.

Another challenge is how to deal with evidence that may or may not meet *Daubert* standards. In some areas of I-O psychology a body of empirical literature will demonstrate a consistent pattern of support or nonsupport for some commonly used human resource practice. Similarly, an I-O psychologist may have conducted in the defendant organization a systematic study that provides persuasive arguments for or against a practice. In such cases the scientific evidence may meet *Daubert* standards. In other areas of I-O psychology no body of evidence is available that consistently or persuasively supports or refutes a practice. For example, in the third phase of a Title VII hearing (that is, when the plaintiff can propose an *alternative* that is supposedly just as valid as the job-related device or process at issue but has lesser impact), there is often a great deal of speculation based on single studies, anecdotes, or just pure speculation. Moreover, a local research study, one done by a psychologist for a plaintiff or defendant, will almost certainly not be flawless. In these cases it may be controversial whether or not the study meets *Daubert* standards (Thornton & Webb, 1988). The I-O psychologist must use professional judgment to assess the balance between supportive and nonsupportive evidence before forming a conclusion and testifying.

Summary, Conclusions, and Implications

The effects of *Daubert* and its progeny on expert testimony in employment discrimination litigation are substantial and still unfolding. Judges are given and are using great autonomy in admissibility decisions, and decisions at the district level are not likely to be overturned on appeal. The factors judges rely on may vary widely, based on the court (state or federal), the type of case (criminal or civil), the type of evidence (as it falls, for example, on a continuum from scientific to nonscientific or from generic to case specific), the judge's ability and familiarity with the field, and the expert's qualifications, among other factors.

An expert may be qualified as such by *any one* of the following: knowledge, skills, experience, or training. Although an I-O psychologist will typically be expected to have a doctoral degree in order to be qualified as an expert, persons with lesser degrees may qualify if they show other relevant qualifications. When confronted with complex or contradictory evidence, judges may use the credentials of the expert as a proxy for the reliability of the evidence itself.

Relevance is relevant. Expert testimony should be tied to the facts of the case and not be overly prejudicial, confusing, or biased. Concrete interactions or experience with an organization or workplace issue may be more persuasive than abstract studies (however scientific and well designed they may be) that are not tied specifically to the facts of the present case in a particular organization.

Demonstration that evidence is reliable and appears to meet the *Daubert* factors may or may not lead the judge to admit the testimony. The *Daubert* factors are merely guidelines; they do not constitute a definitive checklist. Judges do not appear to be using these factors methodically in admissibility decisions. Other indicators of reliability are frequently being used. Experts are advised to address the issue of reliability in a manner that judges can understand, without speaking down to judges, who are typically highly intelligent and self-confident individuals. Although judges are increasingly becoming more knowledgeable about scientific matters, experts should be aware that judges are typically not scientists and may have difficulty understanding the scientific method, error rate, and falsifiability.

Industrial and organizational psychologists serving as expert witnesses in employment discrimination litigation need to recognize that judges may not be familiar with the methods and content of industrial and organizational psychology. When taking the role of expert witness, I-O psychologists will need to explain clearly how their methods and expertise are relevant to the issues being litigated.

Above all, industrial and organizational psychologists should do good work, which in this context means following standard, state-of-the-art methods that satisfy the *Daubert* guidelines. I-O psychologists should recognize the inherently adversarial nature of legal proceedings and maintain professional integrity and impartiality as they contribute scientific knowledge and other forms of expertise in the often contentious climate of legal proceedings. They may need to resist understandable tendencies to react emotionally, become defensive, or strive to "win" for one side. Coping mechanisms include a continuous recognition that expert testimony should focus on reliable methods and associated conclusions relevant to the case at hand.

References

Books, Articles, and Government Documents

American Educational Research Association, American Psychological Association, & National Council on Measurement in Education. (1999). *Standards for educational and psychological testing.* Washington, DC: American Educational Research Association.

American Psychological Association. (1992). Ethical principles of psychologists and code of conduct. *American Psychologist, 47,* 1597–1611.

Anderson, N., Ones, D. S., Sinangil, H. K., & Viswesvaran, C. (Eds.). (2001). *Handbook of industrial, work, and organizational psychology: Vol. 1. Personnel psychology.* Thousand Oaks, CA: Sage.

Baute, P. (2001). Further guidelines for the organizational psychologist preparing for expert witness. *The Industrial-Organizational Psychologist, 38*(3), 128–130.

Berger, M. A. (2000). The Supreme Court's trilogy on the admissibility of expert testimony. In Federal Judicial Center, *Reference manual on scientific evidence* (2nd ed., pp. 9–38). Retrieved in 2000 from http://www.fjc.gov.

Bersoff, D. N. (2003). *Ethical conflicts in psychology* (3rd ed.). Washington, DC: American Psychological Association.

Borman, W. C., Ilgen, D. R., & Klimoski, R. (Eds.). (2002). *Handbook of psychology: Vol. 12. Industrial and organizational psychology.* New York: John Wiley & Sons.

Bracken, D. W., Timmreck, C. W., & Church, A. (2001). *The handbook of multisource feedback.* San Francisco: Jossey-Bass.

Brannick, M. T., & Levine, E. L. (2002). *Job analysis.* Thousand Oaks, CA: Sage.

Brannick, M. T., Salas, E., & Prince, C. (1997). *Team performance, assessment, and measurement: Theory, methods, and applications.* Mahwah, NJ: Erlbaum.

Brodsky, S. L. (1991). *Testifying in court: Guidelines and maxims for the expert witness.* Washington, DC: American Psychological Association.

Brodsky, S. L. (1999). *The expert expert witness: More maxims and guidelines for testifying in court.* Washington, DC: American Psychological Association.

Campbell, J. P., McCloy, R. A., Oppler, S. H., & Sager, C. E. (1993). A theory of performance. In N. Schmitt & W. C. Borman (Eds.), *Personnel selection in organizations* (pp. 35–70). San Francisco: Jossey-Bass.

Cohen, J., & Cohen, P. (1983). *Applied multiple regression/correlation analysis for the behavioral sciences* (2nd ed.). Mahwah, NJ: Erlbaum.

Cook, T. D., & Campbell, D. T. (1979). *Quasi-experimentation: Design and analysis issues for field settings.* Boston: Houghton Mifflin.

Dixon, L., & Gill, B. (2002). Changes in the standards for admitting expert evidence in federal civil cases since the *Daubert* decision. *Psychology, Public Policy, and Law, 8*(3), 251–308.

Dunnette, M., & Hough, L. (Eds.). (1990). *Handbook of industrial and organizational psychology* (2nd ed.). Palo Alto, CA: Consulting Psychologists Press.

Dye, D., & Silver, M. (1999). The origins of ONET. In N. B. Peterson, M. D. Mumford, W. C. Borman, P. R. Jeanneret, & E. A. Fleishman (Eds.), *An occupational information system for the 21st century* (pp. 9–20). Washington, DC: American Psychological Association.

Eder, R. W., & Harris, M. M. (1999). *The employment interview.* Thousand Oaks, CA: Sage.

Edwards, J. E., Scott, J. S., & Raju, N. S. (Eds.). (2003). *The human resources program-evaluation handbook.* Thousand Oaks, CA: Sage.

Fleishman, E. A., Quaintance, M. K., & Broeding, L. A. (1984). *Taxonomies of human performance: The description of human tasks.* San Diego, CA: Academic Press.

Gatowski, S. I., Dobbin, S. A., Richardson, J. T., Ginsburg, G. P., Merlino, M. L., & Dahir, V. (2001). Asking the gatekeepers: A national survey of judges on judging expert evidence in a post-*Daubert* world. *Law and Human Behavior, 25,* 433-458.

Goldstein, I. L., & Ford, J. K. (2002). *Training in organizations: Needs assessment, development, and evaluation* (4th ed.). Belmont, CA: Wadsworth.

Groscup, J. L., Penrod, S. D., Studebaker, C. A., Huss, M. T., & O'Neil, K. M. (2002). The effects of *Daubert* on the admissibility of expert testimony in state and federal cases. *Psychology, Public Policy, and Law, 8,* 339-372.

Guion, R. M. (1998). *Assessment, measurement, and prediction for personnel decisions.* Mahwah, NJ: Erlbaum.

Harris, M. M. (2000). I-O psychology in the courtroom: Implications of the *Daubert* standard. *The Industrial-Organizational Psychologist, 38*(2), 42-46.

Howard, A. (Ed.). (1995). *The changing nature of work.* San Francisco: Jossey-Bass.

International Task Force on Assessment Center Guidelines. (2000). Guidelines and ethical considerations for assessment center operations. *Public Personnel Management, 29,* 315-331.

Kehoe, J. F. (2000). *Managing selection in changing organizations.* San Francisco: Jossey-Bass.

Kovera, M. B., & McAuliff, B. D. (2000). The effects of peer review and evidence quality on judge evaluations of psychological science: Are judges effective gatekeepers? *Journal of Applied Psychology, 85*(4), 574-586.

Krafka, C., Dunn, M. A., Johnson, M. T., Cecil, J. S., & Miletich, D. (2002). Judge and attorney experiences, practices, and concerns regarding expert testimony in federal civil trials. *Psychology, Public Policy, and Law, 8,* 251-308.

Landy, F. J., & Conte, J. M. (2004). *Work in the 21st century.* New York: McGraw-Hill.

Lindemann, B., & Grossman, P. (1996). *Employment discrimination law* (3rd ed., Vol. I). Washington, DC: Bureau of National Affairs.

Murphy, K. R., & Cleveland, J. N. (1995). *Understanding performance appraisal: Social, organizational, and goal-based perspectives.* Thousand Oaks, CA: Sage.

Note. Reliable evaluation of expert testimony. (2003). *Harvard Law Review, 116,* 2142-2163.

Rogelberg, S. G. (Ed.). (2002). *Handbook of research methods in industrial and organizational psychology.* Malden, MA: Blackwell.

Sanders, J., Diamond, S. S., & Vidmar, N. (2002). Legal perceptions of science and expert knowledge. *Psychology, Public Policy, and Law, 8*(2), 139–153.

Shuman, D. W., & Sales, B. D. (1999). The impact of *Daubert* and its progeny on the admissibility of behavioral and social science evidence. *Psychology, Public Policy, and Law, 5,* 3–15.

Smither, J. W. (1998). *Performance appraisal.* San Francisco: Jossey-Bass.

Society for Industrial and Organizational Psychology. (2003). *Principles for the validation and use of personnel selection procedures* (4th ed). Bowling Green, OH: Author.

Thomas, J. (Ed.). (2003). *Comprehensive handbook of psychological assessment: Vol. 4. Industrial/organizational assessment.* New York: Wiley.

Thornton, G. C., III & Benson, P. G. (1980). Industrial psychologists as expert witnesses: Role conflicts in fair employment litigation. *Labor Law Review, 31,* 417–429.

Thornton, G. C., III & Mueller-Hanson, R. A. (2004). *Developing organizational simulations: A practical guide for practitioners and students.* Mahwah, NJ: Erlbaum.

Thornton, G. C., III, & Webb, J. R. (1988). Can evidence about employment testing meet the *Daubert* standards? *Employment Testing: Law and Policy Reporter, 7,* 161–165, 176.

Uniform Guidelines on Employee Selection Procedures, 29 C.F.R. § 1607 *et seq.* (1978).

U.S. House of Representatives, Committee on the Judiciary. (2002). *Federal rules of evidence.* Washington, DC: U.S. Government Printing Office.

Wingate, P. H., & Thornton, G. C., III. (2000). Statistics and employment discrimination law: An interdisciplinary review. *Research in Personnel and Human Resources Management, 19,* 295–337.

Wingate, P. H., & Thornton, G. C., III. (2004). Industrial/organizational psychology and the federal judiciary: Expert witness testimony and the *Daubert* standard. *Law and Human Behavior: Special Issue on Psychology, Law, and the Workplace, 28,* 97–114.

Cases

Daubert v. Merrell Dow Pharmaceuticals, Inc., 509 U.S. 579 (1993).

Frye v. United States, 293 F. 1013 (D.C. Cir. 1923).

General Electric Co. v. Joiner, 522 U.S. 136 (1997).

James v. Stockham Valve, 394 F. Supp. 434 (D. Ala. 1975).

Kumho Tire Co. v. Carmichael, 526 U.S. 137 (1999).

PART 2

Case Law, Case Strategy, and Protected Groups

CHAPTER 7

Race Discrimination Cases
Common Themes
James L. Outtz

There are common themes in employment discrimination cases that arise from claims that race was a factor in employment decisions. These themes involve the old-boy network of recruiting and decision making, the role of stereotypes in personnel decisions, the funneling or channeling of certain successful applicants into job ladders with built-in ceilings, and so on. Similarly, there are common strategies for both making and defending against these and other claims. This chapter will examine these themes and the related strategies.

Title VII of the 1964 Civil Rights Act prohibits employment discrimination based on race, color, religion, sex, or national origin. This chapter will focus on cases based on claims of racial discrimination. Race cases differ little from sex, religion, and national origin cases in terms of the legal elements involved. However, the primary intent of the 1964 Civil Rights Act was to address *institutionalized* discrimination. Historically, institutionalized discrimination has been most prevalent against African Americans and other racial groups. Thus race cases have a unique historical perspective and context. Race cases differ from age discrimination cases in that the regulations and standards used to assess the existence of age discrimination are not as clear-cut as those for cases based on race claims. As an example, the *Uniform Guidelines on Employee Selection Procedures* (1978) is a document adopted in 1978 by federal enforcement agencies to provide employers with guidance about compliance with Title VII. Courts have deferred to these guidelines in several landmark class action race discrimination cases (*Griggs* v. *Duke Power Co.*, 1971; *Albemarle Paper Co.* v. *Moody*, 1975; *Washington* v. *Davis*, 1976; *Guardians Association of N.Y. City Police Department* v. *Civil Service Commission*, 1980). The guidelines state clearly that the provisions therein do not apply to age discrimination cases.

Race discrimination cases differ significantly from disability cases (see Chapter Ten in this volume for a detailed consideration of disability litigation). Because the Americans with Disabilities Act (ADA) was passed quite recently (in 1990), there is less case law in this area than in the race discrimination arena. In addition race is a relatively straightforward self-categorization on which a plaintiff can bring race-based claims. In contrast, under ADA a disability is defined as a physical or mental impairment that substantially limits a major life activity (Heneman & Judge, 2003). This means that a determination must be made as to whether a person has a disability before that person can bring a discrimination claim under the Act. Unlike race-based claims, discrimination claims based on a disability inevitably involve the issue of whether the claimant is in fact disabled and the relevance of his or her disability to the employment practice at issue.

The trend in race discrimination cases has not changed very much over the past five to seven years. Approximately 77,600 discrimination charges of all kinds were filed with the Equal Employment Opportunity Commission (EEOC) in 1997 (Kline, 2001). That figure rose to approximately 80,000 in fiscal year 2000. During the period from 1992 through 2003, the percentage of discrimination charges based specifically on race fluctuated very little, ranging from 41 percent in 1992 to 35 percent in 2003. The recent years have seen a notable increase in race cases dealing with retaliation. In fiscal year 2000, for example, 27 percent of all charges filed included a claim of retaliation (see Chapters Eight and Twelve in this volume for additional coverage of retaliation charges), whereas only 15 percent of the charges in 1992 involved such claims (Kline, 2001). The increase in retaliation cases may be due to the fact that the retaliation provisions of Title VII provide broad protection for persons who file charges with the EEOC, and the EEOC has a policy of expediting the investigation of retaliation charges and seeking injunctive relief (EEOC, 1995). A..other important reason for this increase may be that a claimant does not have to prove that the employer behavior that the claimant opposed (thus, according to the claimant, bringing about the retaliation) was in fact illegal. If the employer did not discriminate against the claimant but did retaliate against him or her for making the charge of discrimination, the employer can be found to have violated Title VII. Plaintiffs may have come to the conclusion in recent years that it is possibly in their best interest to make a retaliation claim in response to any adverse employment action that occurs subsequent to an initial charge of discrimination.

Title VII prohibits racial discrimination in hiring, firing, layoffs, promotion, compensation, job assignments, and other terms and conditions of employment. The Act covers employers with fifteen or more employees as well as federal, state, and local government employees. Remedies for racial discrimination in employment include

- Injunctive relief. A court order that the employer is not to discriminate in the future. Injunctive relief may also enjoin the employer from using a particular selection device or engaging in a specific employment practice.
- Reinstatement. Giving the claimant the job that he or she would have had if no discrimination had occurred.
- Back pay with interest. Wages that accrue from the date on which the discrimination first occurred, but no more than two years prior to the date of the filing of an EEOC charge.
- Front pay. Compensation awarded to a complainant who was denied a job or terminated and cannot be immediately reinstated because no vacancy currently exists. The complainant is awarded front pay until a vacancy becomes available.
- Attorney's fees.
- Compensatory damages. Compensation for harm suffered as a result of the discrimination.
- Punitive damages. Compensation as punishment for discrimination based on malice or reckless indifference to the complainant's rights.

Two Forms of Racial Discrimination

There are two major categories of discrimination under the 1964 Civil Rights Act, intentional discrimination and neutral conduct that has an adverse impact on protected groups (EEOC, 1995).

Disparate Treatment

The most common complaint of racial discrimination concerns intentional discrimination. This form of discrimination is known as *disparate treatment*. Under a disparate treatment claim the plaintiff must prove not only that he or she was treated unfairly but also that the unfair treatment was due to his or her race. If, for example, an African American employee and a white employee apply for a promotion and the white employee gets it, the African American may feel that the employer's action was unfair and may be tempted to file a discrimination charge. But even if the action was unfair, it may not have been discriminatory. As pointed out by the judges that Landy interviewed (see Chapter Fifteen in this volume), many employees who feel unjustly treated want their day in court and alleging discrimination based on a protected characteristic such as race gets them that day. The key issue is whether the African American employee was treated differently *because* of his or her race. If, for example, this employee has overheard the selecting manager say that he or she would never promote an African American employee if a qualified white employee were available, this would constitute direct evidence of discrimination. However, it is rare that a manager would make such a statement. Therefore disparate treatment claims are typically proven on the basis of circumstantial evidence. Defense against such claims must also rest on circumstantial evidence. That is, it is unlikely that the selecting manager would be able to provide *direct* evidence that the African American employee could not have performed the job as well as the person who was promoted but instead, would present indirect or circumstantial evidence as an explanation for the promotion decision. In a disparate treatment case the plaintiff must persuade the court that the employer's explanation for the employment practice at issue is not credible and that the true reason is discrimination. In other words, the plaintiff attempts to show that the employer's explanation for its actions is simply a pretext for discrimination. Methods of proving intentional discrimination or disparate treatment include showing that the information on which the employer bases its explanation is false. The complainant can also prove his or her case by showing that an individual of a different race but otherwise similarly situated was treated differently. A *similarly situated* person is one whose qualifications or job-related circumstances are similar to those of the complainant. Statistical evidence may be used to bolster charges of disparate treatment. For example, the complainant may be able to show that the employer seldom hires or promotes a person of the complainant's race.

Some disparate treatment claims are categorized as *mixed-motive* cases. In a mixed-motive case the complainant attempts to show that at least one of the motives for an employer's actions was discrimination. If the complainant is successful, then he or she is entitled at a minimum to injunctive relief and attorney's fees.

Disparate Impact

The second category of cases covered under Title VII arises when an employer carries out an employment practice that is not intended to be discriminatory but has the effect of excluding or otherwise adversely affecting members of protected groups. This form of discrimination is known as *disparate impact,* or *adverse impact.*

In a disparate impact case based on race, the plaintiff attempts to demonstrate that a particular employment practice excludes members of a protected racial group (for example, African Americans) at a rate higher than that for a majority group (for example, whites). This is usually accomplished through the use of statistics that compare the success rate of the protected group or groups with the success rate of nongroup members.

In addition to using statistics to demonstrate adverse impact, plaintiffs can also use an administrative rule of thumb known as the *four-fifths rule.* Simply put, the four-fifths rule is based on the concept that the minority group should experience a success rate that is no less than four-fifths, or 80 percent, of the success rate of the majority group. The important point to remember about the four-fifths rule and the statistical approaches used in disparate impact cases is that they examine group effects or outcomes rather than the treatment of a single individual. (See a detailed discussion of both the four-fifths rule and statistical rules for adverse impact in Chapter Two of this volume.)

If a plaintiff demonstrates that the employment practice at issue does in fact have adverse impact, the burden shifts to the employer to prove that the practice is job related and consistent with business necessity. If the employment practice involves a test or similar scored selection device, the Uniform Guidelines require that the device be validated. The criteria for demonstrating validity are spelled out in the Uniform Guidelines and other documents that describe accepted professional practice in this area. One such document is the *Principles for the Validation and Use of Personnel Selection Procedures* (Society for Industrial and Organizational Psychology, 2003). The Principles establish scientific findings and generally accepted professional practice with regard to personnel selection procedures. (See Chapter Three of this volume for a detailed discussion of the various authorities cited in reviewing the adequacy of professional and scientific practice.)

Even if the employer is able to demonstrate the job relatedness of the employment practice at issue, this may not be sufficient for the defendant to prevail. The plaintiff may still prevail if it can be shown that there is a less discriminatory, equally valid, and practicable alternative selection device or an alternative method of using the employer's selection device that is less discriminatory yet equally valid and practicable.

Thus far a general overview of the two categories of discrimination cases has been presented. What follows is a discussion of common themes in both categories of cases from the standpoint of typical complaints as well as defendants' typical responses.

Common Charges of Applicants

A common race-based complaint with regard to an employer's hiring practices is that the employer (1) failed to recruit in locations where there are protected racial groups or (2) recruited through a medium (for example, newspaper and magazine ads or Web-based search engines) that is less accessible to members of protected racial groups. These claims are common with regard to high-level management positions. If members of protected racial groups are not represented in high-level positions in an organization and those positions are typically filled from outside the company, failure to recruit protected racial groups is likely to be one claim made by plaintiffs. The mere absence of some racial groups from high-level positions in a company can trigger claims of racial discrimination. Members of protected racial groups tend to perceive such situations as unfair from the standpoint of distributive justice. They perceive a lack of equity in the distribution of high-level jobs (Anderson, Born, & Cunningham-Snell, 2001). But perceptions do not always mirror reality. Often the conclusion of unfair discrimination is made without consideration of the nature of the job(s) at issue or the qualifications required for those jobs. This can sometimes result in weak lawsuits. For example, suppose there are no African Americans in senior management positions in the finance department of a company. The conclusion that this fact in and of itself shows racial discrimination is unwarranted if the employer can show, for example, that (1) successful incumbents have a master's degree in finance and at least five years' experience in finance and (2) no African Americans with these qualifications have applied.

A critical issue when assessing recruitment is what constitutes a *qualified applicant*. Employers typically take the position that equal opportunity in recruitment can be assessed only on the basis of qualified applicants who seek employment. The employer typically defines a qualified applicant as a person who meets at least the minimum qualifications for the position. Plaintiffs question this approach, claiming that it allows employers to establish screening criteria that are unnecessarily high and thus screen out members of underrepresented racial groups when in fact they are qualified to seek the position. The employer typically counters by claiming that defining an applicant as anyone who happens to file an application is tantamount to ignoring qualifications. The EEOC has published a clarification of the Uniform Guidelines that is intended to provide additional guidance to employers regarding the definition of *applicant* in the context of the Internet and related electronic data processing technology ("Adoption of Additional Questions and Answers . . . ," 2004). Under the EEOC's clarification, the following conditions must be met for an individual to be considered an applicant in the context of the Internet and related electronic data processing technologies:

1. The employer has acted to fill a position.
2. The individual has followed the employer's standard procedures for submitting an application.
3. The individual has indicated an interest in the particular position.

This clarification indicates that it is not sufficient for an individual to post resumes in third-party resume banks or on personal Web sites for all employers who search such sites. The individual must indicate an interest in a particular position with a particular employer. Also, all search criteria that an employer uses to screen a database of applicants are subject to disparate impact analysis. That is, the search criteria can be analyzed for adverse impact based on workforce or census data. The employer's search criteria become, in essence, hiring standards. Thus, based on the traditional definition of *applicant* and the clarification provided by the EEOC for use in the context of the Internet, the employer will have to establish through job analysis or other means that minimum qualifications or Internet search criteria (for example, a driver's license, professional training and experience, college coursework, or a college degree) are necessary to perform the job if such criteria are used to define qualified applicants. If an employer cannot demonstrate the validity or legitimacy of the minimum qualifications or search criteria, plaintiffs should question why a broader definition of *applicant* cannot be used.

Hiring Practices

Turner, Fix, and Struyk (1991) conducted a study in which they sought to measure differential treatment of white and black job seekers applying for entry-level positions. They used audit methodology that has been used for over twenty years in housing discrimination studies. In housing audits, *testers,* or *auditors,* from two different racial groups are paired on the basis of income, work history, marital status, and other factors known to be used in the real estate industry to determine whether an applicant qualifies to rent an apartment or purchase a home. Each tester is then sent to a specific landlord or lending institution to apply for an apartment or purchase a house. The testers record the treatment received during the application process and the ultimate outcome. Given that each pair of testers is matched to control for relevant factors, the influence of race can be determined. Turner et al. (1991) used the same paradigm to study hiring. In their study, black and white male testers were matched on age, physical size, education, and experience. They were given identical job qualifications and trained so that other attributes (for example, demeanor, openness, energy level) were as similar as possible. The testers were between the ages of nineteen and twenty-four and recruited from major universities in Washington, D.C., and Chicago, the cities where the audits took place. The jobs sampled were drawn randomly from newspaper advertisements. The researchers were able to schedule a total of 486 audits. The occupational categories audited included hotel services, restaurant work, sales, office work, general labor, technical, and management. Twenty young men (ten white and ten black) served as testers, applying for an average of fifty jobs each. The testers reported their treatment at every stage of the hiring process. The twenty young men were grouped into ten pairs of two each—one black and one white. Each pair applied for entry-level jobs advertised in the newspaper in Washington, D.C., and Chicago. The hiring process was divided into three stages: (1) submission of an employment application, (2) obtaining an interview with someone in authority at the company, and (3) receiving a job offer. Turner et al. reported finding evidence of differential treatment at each stage of the hiring process. At the application stage, black and white testers were found to have an equal possibility of success in filing an application. However, in Washington, D.C., black testers experienced more incidents of discouraging treatment than their white counterparts when attempting to obtain an application. Specifically, black applicants in Washington, D.C., were more likely to be questioned about their qualifications before being given an application form, whereas white applicants were routinely just handed the form. Favorable comments were made to white applicants about their chances of being hired. Such comments were not made to black applicants. If typical applicants (rather than testers) were subjected to such treatment, it might well discourage them from applying and thus reduce their opportunity for employment. Turner et al. concluded that given the more negative treatment of the black testers in Washington, D.C., these testers had greater difficulty in the application stage of the hiring process than their white counterparts. This did not occur in Chicago, however. In that city the researchers found no difference between black and white testers in the manner in which they were treated in the application stage of the hiring process.

Differential treatment during the interview phase of the hiring process was measured on five factors—length of waiting time, length of the interview, number of interviewers (more than one interviewer increases the reliability of the interview process), positive comments during the interview, and negative comments during the interview. The results for both cities showed that after arriving at the interview site, black testers had to wait longer for their interview than their white counterparts did. In Washington, D.C., black testers were more likely to receive shorter interviews and less likely to receive encouraging comments during the interview. In the subsequent job offer stage, Turner et al. found that whites were more likely than blacks to receive a job offer in both Chicago and Washington, D.C.

In assessing all three phases of the hiring process, Turner et al. (1991) concluded that even though whites were matched with blacks on qualifications and other characteristics that could affect the hiring decision, whites (1) were more likely to advance to the hiring decision phase of the process and (2) were more likely to be hired. This research is instructive primarily because it illuminates some of the factors that could lead applicants who are members of protected racial groups to perceive an employer's hiring process as racially discriminatory and to be more likely to challenge the practice because of that perception. At a minimum, negative treatment such as that found by Turner et al. could discourage members of protected racial groups from applying. One of the strategies often used by plaintiffs in hiring cases is to show that members of protected racial groups are less likely to apply, either (1) because they are not recruited as heavily as nongroup members or (2) because the hiring process is so negative that it has a chilling effect.

Applicant Screening

A screening practice frequently challenged in both the public and private sectors in the '70s, '80s, and early '90s was the use of employment tests (particularly cognitive tests) to hire employees. Challenges to employment tests have decreased since the mid '90s, particularly in the private sector. However, challenges to employment tests in the public sector, particularly in the areas of public safety (for example, police officer and firefighter selection), are not uncommon. The falloff in these cases in the private sector may be due to several factors. Employers may be less willing to use paper-and-pencil tests as the primary determinant in selecting employees. Also, when such tests are used as a key selection component, it may be that employers are better able to produce validity evidence to justify them. When these tests are challenged and the employer cannot produce validity evidence, the case is usually settled prior to a trial. When employment tests are challenged, plaintiffs are likely to raise the issue of consideration of less discriminatory but equally valid alternatives in addition to challenging the validity of the test. Consideration of alternatives should take place at two different phases of a selection process. Initially, an employer should consider alternative screening devices prior to choosing or developing a given device for actual use. In challenging the employer's selection procedure, the plaintiff can claim that the chosen selection device is not valid. But even if the employer is successful in showing that the selection device is valid, the plaintiff can claim that there were alternative selection devices available to the employer that were equally valid, would have had less adverse impact, and were practicable (that is, not unduly expensive or cumbersome). The employer's burden does not end there, however. After the selection device has been administered and selection decisions made, plaintiffs can attempt to show that there were alternative methods of using the selection device (banding as opposed to strict rank ordering, or differential weighting of subtests, and so forth) that would have been substantially equal in validity, would have had less adverse impact, and would have been practicable.

Race discrimination cases concerning initial screening devices increasingly involve disputes concerning the search for alternatives.

The employer cannot use *ignorance* as a defense at any stage of the selection process where alternatives should be considered. That is, the employer can be held accountable for failing to use an alternative if the plaintiff can show that the alternative could have been identified via a reasonable search. Expanded access to research via the Internet has made it even more difficult for employers to use the ignorance defense. It should be noted that the plaintiff must demonstrate that a reasonable search by the employer would have produced evidence that the proposed alternative is substantially equal in validity *and* has less adverse impact. The research literature in this area is at best evolving, therefore the plaintiff's burden is a difficult one.

Common Charges of Employees: Promotion, Employee Development, and Compensation

Even though claims of racial discrimination by employees are varied, some central or common issues emerge. Some of the common race-based claims are described in this section.

Failure to Post Job Vacancies

When there is a claim that members of protected racial groups are not promoted at the same rate as nongroup members, the employer's method of making job vacancies known to employees will invariably become an issue. The plaintiff will attempt to show that information regarding job vacancies is conveyed by word of mouth and that members of the plaintiff's racial group are systematically denied access to this information, that is, that an *old-boy network* is operating.

Another form of the old-boy network that is claimed in race discrimination cases is *tailoring.* Tailoring occurs when a manager or supervisor determines the qualifications required for promotion by identifying the characteristics of a particular individual (or individuals) from a nonprotected group (for example, whites) whom the manager or supervisor wishes to promote. Thus the promotion process appears to be based on legitimate job requirements but is in fact rigged to result in the promotion of nonprotected employees. If the tailoring is based on factors other than race (for example, the manager simply prefers one employee over another), the manager's decision is not actionable. Tailoring is much more subtle than the typical old-boy network and therefore more difficult to prove.

Excessive Subjectivity

Race discrimination claims involving promotion and compensation often focus on the subjectivity of the employer's personnel practices. A common theme in such cases is the claim by plaintiffs that the employer's personnel practices are *excessively subjective*. The implication is that excessive subjectivity allows racism to influence personnel practices such as promotions, job assignments, compensation, and other terms and conditions of employment.

Performance appraisal systems are common targets of the excessive subjectivity claim. Plaintiffs argue that the performance appraisal process allows supervisors too much discretion in evaluating subordinates. One of the difficulties with the excessive subjectivity claim is that there is no clear-cut standard for what constitutes *excessive*. It is generally accepted in human resource management that performance appraisals have to involve human judgment and therefore must be based on some level of subjectivity. The central issue is when does human judgment become excessive subjectivity?

The excessive subjectivity claim takes on added significance when compensation decisions are tied to performance appraisals. Pay raises, bonuses, and stock options are often tied to the employee's annual performance appraisal, with the highest-rated employees receiving the highest compensation. The notion of tying pay to performance is considered a good business practice (Gerhart, 2000). However, if the performance appraisal process is flawed (and plaintiffs will argue that it is flawed if there is excessive subjectivity), this will lead to a domino effect in terms of the scope of plaintiff's case. Not only will the performance appraisal and compensation practices be called into question, any personnel practice that relies on or is in any way influenced by the performance appraisal system (for example, promotions or layoffs) will also be questioned. It is easy to see why the excessive subjectivity claim can take on tremendous significance in race discrimination cases.

A key step in establishing a claim that racial discrimination exists in performance appraisals is to show that the company's performance appraisal system has adverse impact. Plaintiffs must show that members of their racial group receive significantly lower (in a statistical sense) performance appraisal ratings than nonmembers. This is often not difficult to show with regard to African American employees, given that a number of meta-analyses of black-white differences in performance appraisal ratings have shown a difference in favor of whites on the order of a tenth to one-half of a standard deviation (McKay & McDaniel, 2003; Sackett & DuBois, 1991; Kraiger & Ford, 1985). Thus comparisons of performance ratings between African Americans and whites are likely to show statistically significant differences adverse to African Americans. The question is whether these differences are attributable to race. Most courts now permit the defendant to control for various relevant factors. These relevant factors might include pay grade, tenure, experience, and job title. Thus the plaintiff will need to show that even when relevant controls are exercised, differences in performance appraisals remain.

Failure to Monitor Personnel Practices

A racial discrimination claim that is closely related to the excessive subjectivity argument is the claim that the employer failed to properly monitor personnel practices and procedures. This perhaps is the area where an employer is likely to be most vulnerable. In essence the failure-to-monitor claim is that even if the employer has properly designed its personnel practices (for example, its performance appraisal system), the employer has failed to monitor those practices to ensure that they were implemented as designed. If plaintiff can show, for example, that a company's performance evaluations are not conducted in the manner called for in the official policies and procedures of the organization, the claim will be that this constitutes a critical if not fatal flaw that allows racial discrimination to flourish.

The Glass Ceiling

In some corporations in America few members of protected racial groups occupy top positions. The obstacles they face in reaching such positions are known as the *glass ceiling* (Morrison, White, Van

Velsor, & Center for Creative Leadership, 1992; U.S. Senate, Committee on Governmental Affairs, 1991; U.S. House of Representatives, Committee on Government Reform, 2002). A glass ceiling is said to exist when members of protected groups face barriers to top management positions because of their race, gender, or other protected characteristics. The glass ceiling phenomenon is often an element of plaintiffs' claims in race discrimination cases when statistics show that members of protected racial groups are significantly underrepresented in upper-management positions compared to their numbers in lower-level positions in a company. Glass ceiling claims are prevalent in race discrimination cases because most companies in America have greater racial diversity in low- and middle-level positions than in top-level positions. For example, Powell and Butterfield (2002) studied the influence of the selecting official's race and gender on promotions to top management positions in a U.S. federal agency from January 1987 to November 1999. The promotion process had two stages. In the first stage a review panel decided which applicants to refer for the position. During the second stage, the selecting official chose one of the referred applicants for the position. The review panels for each promotion varied in racial composition and gender. The same was true of the selecting officials. Overall the results of the study showed that the promotion process favored female applicants but worked to the disadvantage of African American and Hispanic men. The Powell and Butterfield study illustrates that the concept of a glass ceiling need not be limited to gender. Employers are being held accountable for artificial barriers to the upward mobility of any group protected under Title VII.

Glass Walls

Barriers to upward mobility can come from sources other than the glass ceiling. Sometimes employees are channeled into dead-end careers, those outside a business's mainstream (Morrison et al., 1992). Women were the first to call attention to this phenomenon. Today members of protected racial groups are calling attention to the fact that they too are often the victims of *glass walls*. Placed in staff roles and tolerated as specialists in what they see as dead-end pockets of the company, protected racial group members are challenging what they see as the glass wall with increasing frequency.

For example, in a large class action case filed against Texaco, plaintiffs alleged that the employer "relegated African Americans to jobs with less visibility, prestige, responsibility and prospects for promotion than those held by equally qualified Caucasians" (*Roberts* v. *Texaco*, 1994). This case was eventually settled prior to trial.

Failure to Mentor

One of the less obvious processes that takes place in organizations is mentoring of subordinates by managers. So-called high-potential employees are identified and groomed for promotion to high-level executive positions. This may be done formally as part of a succession-planning process or informally as part of the normal interaction between managers and their subordinates. In either case this activity might be called *mentoring*. The benefits of being accepted into the mentoring process may include specialized training, plum job assignments designed to accelerate development of special skills, and rapid advancement within the company. Members of protected racial groups are increasingly calling into question the fairness of mentoring programs (particularly informal programs) if steps are not taken by the organization to ensure that all qualified employees are allowed to participate. One difficulty with plaintiffs' position on mentoring is that the utility of mentoring, in terms of accelerating advancement within an organization, is sometimes assumed without sufficient supporting data. If plaintiffs perceive that mentoring results in accelerated advancement when actually it does not, this could lead to a weak or unsuccessful lawsuit. Plaintiffs should be prepared to show that there is a link between mentoring and some organizational benefit such as promotion in order to prevail on this issue.

Discriminatory Discipline

Disciplining some small number of employees is inevitable in any organization. Strict adherence to rules and regulations is an integral part of the personnel policies of certain organizations, particularly paramilitary organizations such as police and fire departments and federal law enforcement agencies (for example, the Federal Bureau of Investigation, the Secret Service, and the Bureau of Alcohol,

Tobacco, and Firearms). In organizations of this type, members of protected racial groups often believe that the disciplinary process is applied according to a double standard. A typical complaint has two elements. First, members of protected groups charge that they are disciplined more often than nonmembers for the same offenses. Second, these groups charge that the punishment their members are given for violating a rule or regulation is far more severe than that given to majority group members who violate the same rule.

Retaliation

Title VII prohibits retaliation against an individual because the individual (1) opposed an employer's unlawful employment practice, (2) made a charge of discrimination, or (3) plans to testify or did testify in an investigation, proceeding, or hearing responding to the initial complaint (EEOC, 1995). This provision of Title VII is designed to prevent employers from taking adverse employment actions against employees for actions in opposition to the employer that are protected under Title VII.

Protected forms of opposition include the following (EEOC, 1995, p. A-19):

- Threatening to file or assisting in filing a charge, complaint, grievance, or lawsuit alleging discrimination
- Complaining about discrimination (for example, to high management, union officials, other employees, or newspapers)
- Organizing or participating in a group that opposes unlawful discrimination
- Refusing to obey an order that one believes constitutes unlawful employment discrimination

Statistics show that retaliation charges filed with the EEOC have almost doubled in the past ten years (Kline, 2001).

Class Action Cases: Class Certification

The first step for plaintiff in a discrimination case based on a race claim is to establish prima facie evidence that he or she (or his or her racial group) has been adversely affected by a given personnel practice. In a class action a group, or class, of plaintiffs sues an employer. (See Chapter One in this volume for an additional discussion of issues related to the class certification process.) Before plaintiffs can do this, however, a court must determine whether they meet the legal criteria for certification as a class. Plaintiffs' argument for class certification must satisfy the following criteria:

- The case poses substantial questions of law and fact that are common to the class and affect the rights of all members of the class.
- The claims of the named plaintiffs are typical of and not adverse to the class.
- Final injunctive relief with respect to the class as a whole is appropriate.
- The questions of law and fact common to the members of the class predominate over questions affecting the individual members.

The purpose of a motion for class certification is not to obtain a ruling on the relative merits of plaintiffs' claims but rather to determine if a common question of law or fact exists among the potential class members and makes class litigation appropriate. In theory the certification of a class makes the process of litigation more efficient. Instead of many individual cases that present the same basic evidentiary foundation, cases can be consolidated and heard as a class.

Making a case against class certification requires the employer to defeat the plaintiffs' petition for class certification on any of the parameters just cited. If on the one hand the case involves the use of a paper-and-pencil test, it may be relatively simple for plaintiffs to demonstrate that all applicants in a protected group who failed the test constitute a class. If on the other hand the employment practice at issue is a performance appraisal process, the employer may be able to show that differences in performance appraisals are a function of factors unique to each employee (for example, tenure with the company, tenure in current position, work location, or pay grade), and thus class certification is unwarranted.

An example of the factors a court may consider in determining whether to grant plaintiff's motion for class certification can be found in the case of *Murray et al.* v. *Rent-A-Center* (2001). In this case four plaintiffs filed a class action against Rent-A-Center, Inc. on behalf of themselves and other similarly situated individuals. These plaintiffs were current and former African American employees. They claimed they were discriminated against with regard to compensation, promotion, and discipline. They also claimed they were subjected to job requirements different from those imposed on similarly situated or less qualified Caucasian employees. Finally, they charged that they were subjected to a racially hostile work environment and suffered retaliation when they complained of the company's racially discriminatory practices.

In making such a wide range of charges, the plaintiffs took on the burden of having to demonstrate that the grievances they suffered had common elements, were typical of the class, and raised questions of law common to the class that predominated over questions affecting only the individual members.

The plaintiffs presented a variety of evidence in support of their motion for class certification. Statistical evidence was presented to show that there were significant disparities between African American and Caucasian employees with regard to pay and promotion. The plaintiffs attempted to support their claim of a hostile work environment by presenting evidence of allegedly racist comments, actions, and attitudes expressed by the defendant's president and management. The plaintiffs identified approximately 5 of 600 market managers, 9 of approximately 5,600 store managers, and 5 of 15 regional directors as having made allegedly racist comments or having expressed racist attitudes.

In examining the plaintiffs' evidence regarding disparities in pay, the court found that a number of important factors were excluded from the analysis. Specifically, the court found that factors such as time in position, time with the company, age, and whether the employee was newly hired in the last year were not considered. The defendant presented evidence through an expert showing that when these factors were taken into account, there was no evidence that African Americans were paid systematically less than whites. The court concluded that without clearly defined statistical results to support the plaintiffs' claim of pay disparity, determining the appropriateness of class certification was influenced by the fact that there were many variables that would likely require individual analysis of pay disparity.

The plaintiffs' evidence regarding promotion was found to be similarly flawed. In analyzing disparities in promotions the court determined that plaintiffs found statistically significant results in less than half of the positions analyzed. The court further determined that even if statistically significant findings had been more prevalent, the plaintiffs had conducted their analysis with the assumption that all employees are equally promotable. That is, the analysis failed to take into account important factors such as job performance, absenteeism, education, prior experience, and training that could influence promotion decisions.

The court found the plaintiffs' evidence regarding hostile work environment unconvincing because few instances of racial comments and attitudes were found. The number of instances that were presented constituted, in the court's opinion, a few isolated incidents that were not sufficient to exhibit a corporate culture hostile to African Americans.

Murray et al. v. *Rent-A-Center* is indicative of the kinds of issues raised in connection with a motion for class certification. This case shows that obtaining class certification can be a difficult task. The plaintiffs' evidence must be targeted at specific employment practices and include analyses that rule out alternative explanations of racial group disparities.

General Defense Strategies

Obviously an employer charged with racial discrimination has the right to present a defense. What follows is a brief discussion of strategies employers use to mount a defense against some race-based claims.

Whenever a personnel practice is challenged by either applicants or employees as racially discriminatory, a question arises as to whether the practice meets the standards of accepted professional practice. A useful defense strategy in general is to show that the personnel practice meets or exceeds the applicable standards for accepted professional practice. Although this strategy may seem trivial at first, it can be effective as the starting point for a solid defense. If the employer's personnel practices meet or exceed the industry standard, the plaintiff's claims as to what the employer should be doing may seem unreasonable. If, for example, the average performance appraisal rating of blacks in an organization is lower than that of whites, does this constitute racial discrimination, given that black-white mean differences reported in the psychological literature range from one-fifth to one-half of a standard deviation in favor of whites? The point is that assessing black-white differences in performance appraisal ratings based on the hypothesis that such differences are zero in the population may be inappropriate. The more relevant question may be whether the black-white differences in performance ratings in a given organization are significantly greater than the one-fifth to one-half standard deviation difference reported in the meta-analytic literature.

A second effective strategy for an employer is to show that its personnel practices are based on accurate information about the job or jobs at issue. Accepted professional practice dictates that personnel decisions be based on accurate job information. If the employer can produce documentation such as job descriptions, or better yet job analysis reports, that show how personnel practices are linked to the job, the legitimacy of those personnel practices is enhanced.

A third strategy that is frequently helpful to an employer's defense is to demonstrate the professional competence of the human resource personnel and other employees in the organization who are directly responsible for implementation of the personnel practices and procedures at issue. Similarly, if an employer can show (perhaps via training records) that managers and supervisors are routinely provided training in personnel practices and procedures, it gives credibility to the employer's claim that those practices are being implemented properly throughout the organization.

Specific Defense Strategies: Applicants

Recruitment

The best defense against race discrimination claims involving recruitment is to be able to demonstrate that recruitment extends to all of the relevant applicant subgroups. This can be accomplished by using multiple recruitment media (newspapers, radio, visits to college campuses, referrals from current employees, and so forth). It is also helpful to maintain documentation showing the elements of the recruitment process, the personnel responsible for recruitment, and the number of contacts made within each of the relevant applicant subgroups.

Hiring Practices

When an employer's hiring practices are challenged, the employer should show the relationship between hiring requirements and specific job requirements. This is particularly important for upper-management and executive positions, because these are the levels at which the greatest underrepresentation of protected racial groups is most likely to occur. Often hiring decisions can be justified simply by showing that (1) specific qualifications and experience are required and (2) the qualifications and experience of applicants from protected racial groups are not equal to those of the person or persons hired. The employer's case is strengthened if it can be shown that hiring less qualified or unqualified persons would lead to serious negative consequences (such as increased accidents or lower individual or group performance). In making this showing the employer is demonstrating business necessity. *Business necessity* means simply that there is a clear relationship between hiring or selection criteria and job performance. Title VII requires that an employer demonstrate the business necessity of a selection procedure if that procedure has adverse impact on a protected group.

If there is validation evidence that supports the employer's hiring practices, it should be presented. This evidence does not have to be limited to validation studies conducted by the company. A substantial body of psychological literature demonstrates the validity of a variety of selection devices, including paper-and-pencil tests, job interviews, work samples, and personality and interest measures (Schmidt & Hunter, 1998).

Failure to Search for Alternatives

In some instances the plaintiff's claims will be based on the argument that the employer failed to search for an equally valid alternative with less adverse impact. The employer may be able to rebut this argument by showing that (1) there were no alternatives with equal or substantially equal validity, (2) an equally valid alternative would not have had less adverse impact, or (3) the alternative proposed is not practicable (meaning it is administratively impossible or horrendously expensive). Sackett and Ellingson (1997), for example, have shown that simply combining selection device A with another selection device, B, that has less adverse impact than device A will not necessarily result in adverse impact below the level produced by device A.

If the plaintiff claims there is an equally valid method of using the employer's selection device or procedure that would have less adverse impact, the employer may be able to rebut such claims by showing that the proposed alternative method of use is not feasible. Also, the employer may be able to show that applicants are in fact allowed to use different methods to demonstrate that they are qualified for hire or promotion, that is, that alternatives are *already* built into the system.

Specific Defense Strategies: Employees

Job Posting

Defending against claims of improper job posting is relatively straightforward. Either the organization has a documented policy regarding job posting or it does not. If the policy is to post for only certain positions, the employer should be able to articulate a legitimate reason for that policy. Plaintiffs will typically argue that all vacancies should be posted companywide. A legitimate reason for not posting vacancies companywide might be that there are sufficient qualified applicants within a given department or operating unit. It is also possible that the vacant position requires specialized skills unique to employees in particular jobs. In manufacturing environments, safety is also often an issue because the actual work processes are so different from department to department. The point is that the employer's defense should show that there is an articulated policy (preferably written) and a legitimate rationale for that policy. The employer should be able to demonstrate how employees are made aware of job vacancies and how job-posting policies are tied to legitimate business interests.

Excessive Subjectivity in Performance Appraisals

The issue of excessive subjectivity has come to be a favorite refrain of plaintiffs, particularly in cases involving promotion. The fact, however, that a personnel practice such as performance appraisal is based on judgment does not automatically support an inference that the practice is excessively subjective. Even if, for example, a supervisor errs in making performance ratings, the plaintiff's claim of discrimination may be discredited if it can be shown that the errors were not related to race. The most important issue with regard to the excessive subjectivity in performance appraisals is that one cannot establish an employee's "true" performance level. Therefore the absolute accuracy of performance appraisals is almost impossible to determine. It seems reasonable to conclude, however, that subjectivity is minimized to the extent that (1) performance ratings are linked to important job behaviors or performance objectives, (2) there are written policies governing the manner in which performance ratings are to be made, (3) there is second-level review of the ratings, and (4) there is a procedure in place for resolving ratings disputes between employees and supervisors. These would seem to be appropriate goals for any employer laying the foundation for a defensible performance appraisal system. Research on court decisions in employment discrimination cases involving performance appraisals indicates that the decisions are influenced by four factors: use of job analysis, provision of written instructions, employee review of results, and agreement among raters (Werner & Bolino, 1997; see also Chapter Twelve in this volume).

Failure to Monitor Personnel Practices

An employer should have in place a method of determining whether personnel practices are implemented in the manner intended. If the issue is, for example, a challenge with regard to promotions, the employer should have in place a mechanism for documenting the basis for any given promotion. The mechanism can be as simple as identifying a number of *core competencies* that are important to achieving the organization's business objectives, and ensuring that promotion decisions are linked to those core competencies. Similarly, if the personnel practice at issue is job assignments or access to training, a mechanism should be in place for documenting the manner in which these decisions are made.

The Glass Ceiling

Claims that members of protected racial groups are prevented from reaching the highest positions in a company due to race can usually be rebutted by identifying the qualifications and experience needed to perform the jobs at issue, then comparing plaintiffs with the employees in those positions. At a minimum this will reduce the scope of the case to those plaintiffs who are actually qualified. Obviously, the employer must be able to show how the necessary qualifications were established. Accurate job descriptions will be indispensable in this regard.

Glass Walls

The claim that members of protected racial groups are funneled into dead-end jobs or units in an organization can be difficult to defend against. Plaintiffs will attempt to show the existence of glass walls by tracing the career paths leading to the most coveted positions in the company. For example, if the career paths of prominent senior managers can be traced back only to particular departments and those departments have historically not had minority employees, plaintiffs will assert that other departments that employ significant numbers of such groups are basically occupational ghettos. The employer will need to identify the factors that dictate job placement (for example, self-selection, qualifications and experience, frequency of vacancies, turnover, and job location). A relationship between specific employee skills and job placement should be discernible.

Conclusion

Race discrimination cases have contributed significantly to case law resulting from Title VII of the 1964 Civil Rights Act. The issue of race and equality of opportunity remains hotly debated in almost every facet of American society, from housing and education to employment. There seems little doubt therefore that these cases will remain a part of the legal landscape for some time to come. It appears, however, that some forms of race cases, such as large class actions, have decreased in frequency in recent years, whereas others, such as race-based claims of retaliation, have almost doubled. From the employer's perspective, there has been a trend toward viewing workforce diversity not as a legal requirement but more as a matter of strategic organizational planning. The changing demographics of American society (including greater and greater diversity) are causing American employers to focus on acquiring, properly managing, and retaining a talented and diverse workforce. The most immediate results of these efforts seem to have been (1) placing high priority on eliminating employment practices that could be perceived as racially discriminatory and (2) avoiding litigation of discrimination cases based on race whenever feasible.

References

Books, Articles, and Government Documents

Adoption of Additional Questions and Answers to Clarify and Provide a Common Interpretation of the Uniform Guidelines on Employee Selection Procedures as They Relate to the Internet and Related Technologies, 69 Fed. Reg. 43 (2004).

Anderson, N., Born, M., & Cunningham-Snell, N. (2001). Recruitment and selection: Applicant perspectives and outcomes. In N. Anderson, D. S. Ones, H. K. Sinangil, & C. Viswesvaran (Eds.), *Handbook of industrial, work, and organizational psychology: Vol. 1. Personnel psychology* (pp. 200-218). Thousand Oaks, CA: Sage.

Equal Employment Opportunity Commission, Technical Assistance Program. (1995). *Theories of discrimination: Intentional and unintentional employment discrimination.* Washington, DC: Equal Employment Opportunity Commission.

Gerhart, B. (2000). Compensation strategy and organizational performance. In S. Rynes & B. Gerhart (Eds.), *Compensation in organizations: Current research and practice* (pp. 151–194). San Francisco: Jossey-Bass.

Heneman, H., & Judge, T. (2003). *Staffing organizations.* New York: McGraw-Hill.

Kline, S. (2001). Employment law: Survey of employment law developments for Indiana practitioners. *Indiana Law Review, 34,* 675–717.

Kraiger, K., & Ford, J. (1985). A meta-analysis of ratee race effects in performance ratings. *Journal of Applied Psychology, 70*(11), 56–65.

McKay, P., & McDaniel, M. (2003, April). *A re-examination of black-white differences in work performance: The moderating effects of criterion content, job complexity, level of measurement, measurement method, source of data, and criterion cognitive load.* Paper presented at the 18th annual conference of the Society for Industrial and Organizational Psychology, Orlando.

Morrison, A., White, R., Van Velsor, E., & Center for Creative Leadership. (1992). *Breaking the glass ceiling.* Reading, MA: Addison-Wesley.

Powell, G., & Butterfield, D. (2002). Exploring the influence of decision makers' race and gender on actual promotions to top management. *Personnel Psychology, 55*(2), 397–428.

Sackett, P., & DuBois, C. (1991). Rater-ratee race effects on performance evaluation: Challenging meta-analytic conclusions. *Journal of Applied Psychology, 76*(6), 873–877.

Sackett, P., & Ellingson, J. (1997). The effects of forming multi-predictor composites on group differences and adverse impact. *Personnel Psychology, 50*(3), 707–721.

Schmidt, F., & Hunter, J. (1998). The validity and utility of selection methods in personnel psychology: Practical and theoretical implications of 85 years of research findings. *Psychological Bulletin, 124*(2), 262–274.

Society for Industrial and Organizational Psychology. (2003). *Principles for the validation and use of personnel selection procedures* (4th ed.). Bowling Green, OH: Author.

Turner, M., Fix, M., & Struyk, R. (1991). *Opportunities denied, opportunities diminished: Racial discrimination in hiring.* Washington, DC: Urban Institute Press.

Uniform Guidelines on Employee Selection Procedures, 29 C.F.R. § 1607 *et seq.* (1978).

U.S. House of Representatives, Committee on Government Reform. (2002). *Women in management: Are they breaking the glass ceiling?* 107th Cong., Serial No. 107–170. Washington, DC: U.S. Government Printing Office.

U.S. Senate, Committee on Governmental Affairs. (1991). *The glass ceiling in federal agencies: A GAO survey on women and minorities in federal agencies.* Washington, DC: U.S. Government Printing Office.

Werner, J., & Bolino, M. (1997). Explaining U.S. courts of appeals decisions involving performance appraisal: Accuracy, fairness, and validation. *Personnel Psychology, 50*(1), 1–24.

Cases

Albemarle Paper Co. v. Moody, 422 U.S. 405 (1975).

Griggs v. Duke Power Co., 401 U.S. 424 (1971).

Guardians Association of N.Y. City Police Department v. Civil Service Commission, 539 F. Supp. 627, 32 (2nd Cir. 1980).

Murray et al. v. Rent-A-Center, Inc., No. 00-0573-CV-W-4-ECF (W.D. Mo. 2001).

Roberts v. Texaco, 94 CIV. 2015 (CLB) first amended complaint (S.D. N.Y. 1994).

Washington v. Davis, 96 U.S. 2574 (1976).

CHAPTER 8

Sex Discrimination in Employment

Barbara A. Gutek
Margaret S. Stockdale

Title VII of the 1964 Civil Rights Act, as amended, is the major federal law prohibiting sex-based discrimination in employment. Title VII case law relating to any protected classification can be applied to cases of other protected groups defined in Section 703a of Title VII. For example, case law that developed on the basis of a race discrimination case is likely to apply to sex discrimination as well. Therefore cases such as *Griggs* v. *Duke Power Co.* (1972), which inaugurated the disparate impact theory of employment discrimination, apply as well to sex discrimination cases.

Initially, this chapter discusses several important sex discrimination cases, referencing other critical Title VII discrimination cases dealing with other protected classifications when necessary. Subsequently, we focus on the ways psychological and other social and management science research is used in sex discrimination cases, as well as on issues arising from the application of research findings to these cases. We pay special attention to sexual harassment as one kind of sex discrimination, both because it is an area of expertise for both of us and because the issues it raises are likely to be different from issues raised by other forms of discrimination involving protected classes.

We would like to thank Layne Paddock for providing very helpful feedback on an early draft of this chapter.

Summary of Legal Issues

Generally speaking, there are two classifications of sex discrimination theories: disparate treatment and disparate impact. *Disparate treatment* concerns cases in which employers treat some people less favorably because of their sex but deny this central fact. In such cases the employer may proffer an explanation that its practices are not discriminatory. Then the burden shifts to the complainant to show that the employer's explanation is pretext for discrimination. In *disparate impact* cases, discriminatory intent (either on its face or through pretext) is not necessary to prove discrimination. Impact alone is sufficient. This doctrine was diluted through various Supreme Court cases (notably *Wards Cove Packing Co. v. Atonio*, 1989), but was reinstated in the 1991 Civil Rights Act. We will briefly review these two forms of discrimination and their permutations and then discuss the role of the expert testimony and the psychological research that inform decisions in these types of cases.

Disparate Treatment

Facial Discrimination Claims

One type of disparate treatment is *facial* discrimination, which refers to discriminatory employment practices that are explicitly directed toward some protected characteristic, such as sex. To the contemporary reader, many of the early facial discrimination cases appear blatantly sexist. For example, in *Diaz v. Pan American World Airways* (1971), a male claimant sued for sex discrimination because he was denied employment as a flight attendant. Pan Am argued that being female was a bona fide occupational qualification (BFOQ) for the flight attendant job because only women could impart the pleasant and nurturing atmosphere that Pan Am wished for its passengers. Similarly, in *Sprogis v. United Airlines* (1971) a female complainant took issue with the company's no-marriage rule for female flight attendants—a rule that applied to no male employees or to any female employees in other jobs. Again the defense argued, among other things, that flight attendants were to impart a pleasant travel environment for United's customers, apparently a job that only an unmarried, young woman could perform. One wonders what it was that these airlines really wanted from their flight attendants.

The BFOQ defense has been raised in many facial discrimination cases, and the courts have developed specific standards for its application (see *Phillips* v. *Martin Marietta Corp.*, 1971). For example, in *Weeks* v. *Southern Bell Telephone & Telegraph* (1969) the employer invoked the BFOQ defense against hiring female switchmen, on the assumption that many (if not most) women could not meet the difficult lifting requirements and would be uncomfortable taking unaccompanied late-night service calls. The court, however, reasoned that gender stereotypes, even if statistically true of a group of individuals (for example, women), cannot be used to disqualify an individual member of that group. When valid tests exist to measure the skill or ability, then an individual who passes the test, regardless of gender, should be deemed qualified for the position. In addition, the job requirement in question must entail a major, central component of the job, not a peripheral requirement. This component of the standard has been put to the test in cases of discrimination against female prison guard applicants (for example, *Torres* v. *Wisconsin Department of Health and Social Servs.*, 1989), because the guard job may entail exposure to nude prisoners. Because the circumstance of being exposed to nude prisoners was not thought to be central to the job, it was not considered a strong enough defense to invoke a BFOQ ruling. However, in *Dothard* v. *Rawlinson* (1977), an earlier female prison guard case, the Court was persuaded by the employer's argument that the complainant's "very womanhood" rendered her unable to perform the essential functions of the job.

Pregnancy discrimination cases have also been argued as facial discrimination cases (for example, *Cleveland Board of Education* v. *La Fleur*, 1974). So compelling were plaintiffs' arguments that they not only should not be discriminated against because of their pregnant status but should also be entitled to the same disability benefits afforded male employees (for example, extended sick leave) that Congress passed the Pregnancy Discrimination Act of 1978 and eventually the Family and Medical Leave Act of 1993 to protect both women's and men's family leave–related rights. However, *UAW* v. *Johnson Controls* (1991) highlighted an interesting confluence of both BFOQ and pregnancy discrimination issues. This class action case concerned women of reproductive age who (unless sterile) were barred from employment in certain occupations in a battery-producing company where they would have had exposure to lead, under the argument that lead exposure is damaging to fetuses. The company felt it was its moral and benevolent duty to protect the unborn. Men were not barred from such employment, even though evidence existed that lead exposure put men at risk of infertility. The U.S. Supreme Court, however, did not accept the employer's argument that "male sex" was a BFOQ. Applying the *Phillips* and related standards, the Court argued that BFOQs could be raised only where the performance is central to the enterprise. A fetus is neither a customer nor a third party whose safety is essential to the business of battery manufacturing. Thus moral and ethical concerns do not suffice to establish a BFOQ. The fact that the employer did not feel a moral duty to protect male fertility was also damning to its "morality" defense.

Customer Preferences. Although the U.S. Supreme Court in *Dothard v. Rawlinson* (1977) ruled that coworkers' preferences for male colleagues cannot serve as a basis for a BFOQ, can customer preferences to interact with employees of one gender over another compel a BFOQ defense? In the same case the Court also accepted the premise that a woman could not be rejected as a prison guard because the prisoners (the "customers" in the *Dothard* case) preferred male guards. Similarly, patrons of the popular restaurant chain Hooters may prefer female waitresses to male waiters, or firms that conduct international business in certain countries may send male representatives rather than female representatives under the assumption that the international customer may prefer to do business with the former. However, the appellate court in *Diaz v. Pan American* (1971) tightened the BFOQ standards to denounce all but the most essential arguments for the BFOQ. Specifically, the employer must show that using sex as a basis for employment decisions must address a business necessity, not merely a business convenience. Only when the essential functions of the job cannot be performed by any member of one sex or when the cost or effort of assessing applicants of the dispreferred gender is prohibitive can a BFOQ defense stand. In the case of Hooters, however, where the

EEOC conducted an investigation on the part of four men who were denied employment as waiters, the popular restaurant chain argued that it was "in the business of providing vicarious sexual recreation and [that] female sexuality is a bona fide occupational qualification" (Hampshire, 1999). The EEOC dropped its investigation. If Hooters claims to be in the business of selling sex rather than burgers and chicken, perhaps a criminal charge of prostitution would stand a better chance of succeeding than a civil suit against sex discrimination.

The Role of Gender Stereotypes in Facial Discrimination. Although it seems obvious that many of the early cases that raised the BFOQ defense were based on stereotypical assumptions about men's and women's capacities—for example, that men by their nature cannot be nurturing flight attendants or sexy waiters and that women by their nature cannot be strong maintenance workers or prison guards—another class of cases has raised more nuanced issues (certainly more nuanced than the Hooters case) about the role of stereotypes in employment decision making. In *Price Waterhouse* v. *Hopkins* (1989) the Supreme Court held that if gender stereotypes play a substantial role (but perhaps not the only role) in an adverse employment decision, then Title VII is violated. The case raised many issues about *mixed-motive* employment decisions, where legitimate reasons for the disputed employment decision may exist in addition to the unlawful use of gender stereotypes. But for the purpose of this discussion, we focus on the role of gender stereotypes as a form of facial discrimination.

Ann Hopkins was a senior manager at Price Waterhouse, a national professional accounting firm. She was proposed for partnership in the firm. Partners in the office where she worked were divided in their support for her. She was noted for having the most successful record of any of the candidates for partnership at that time. However, many of her detractors believed that she had a particularly rough, masculine style. They felt that she did not conform to traditionally female stereotypes. She was even advised to walk, talk, and dress femininely and to wear more makeup. She failed in her initial quest for partner status. When she wasn't reproposed for partnership the next year, she resigned and filed a sexual discrimination suit. Hopkins argued that reliance on sex stereotypes about how a woman is expected to look and behave affected how she was treated and thus constituted sex discrimination. After Hopkins won an initial judgment at the district court level, the appeals court overturned that ruling on the opinion that she had not proven that "but for" her sex she would have been promoted. The Supreme Court reversed the appellate court's ruling and remanded the case back to the district court, where she subsequently won. This case subsequently fueled an industry of expert testimony on the substantive role that sex stereotyping can have on employment decisions, despite the fact that the Civil Rights Act of 1991 somewhat softened the U.S. Supreme Court's ruling in *Price Waterhouse*. The Court determined that if the employer demonstrates that it would have taken the same action even absent the impermissible motivating factor (stereotyping), the Court may grant the plaintiff declaratory relief (for example, partial attorney's fees), *but* it may not award damages. (See also David Copus's discussion in Chapter Fourteen in this volume of a defense-based argument on the role of stereotyping in sex discrimination.)

Sexual Harassment. Sexual harassment is a special case of facial discrimination. After feminist consciousness raising in the 1970s and a particularly convincing legal argument by Catherine MacKinnon (1979), the Equal Employment Opportunity Commission ("Guidelines on Discrimination Because of Sex," 1980) issued guidelines for dealing with sexual harassment under Title VII. The EEOC delineated two types of prohibited sexual harassment: *quid pro quo* harassment, in which favorable employment decisions depend on sexual cooperation, and *hostile work environment* harassment, in which a person is subjected because of his or her sex to severe or pervasive unwanted sexual behavior. When the guidelines were adopted, even though no new law was passed, quid pro quo harassment cases were successfully litigated. Since 1998, the Supreme Court has heard five sexual harassment cases (two were joined) and in that process helped to resolve the definition of sexual harassment. (See O'Connor and Vallabhajosula, 2004), for a more detailed review of the legal and psychological issues in each of these cases.)

The first cases won by plaintiffs fit the EEOC's definition of quid pro quo harassment involving tangible job loss. It was not until 1986 that the Supreme Court (*Meritor Savings Bank* v. *Vinson*, 1986) recognized that even without a tangible job loss a hostile work environment constituted sex discrimination. In *Meritor* the Court rejected the employer's argument that Title VII is only concerned with tangible economic loss (or benefit), for example, being passed over for advancement. Instead it argued that Title VII addresses the terms, conditions, or privileges of employment, not just tangible economic loss, and is thus intended to strike at the entire spectrum of disparate treatment of men and women in employment. Essentially, *Meritor* solidified the "hostile work environment" component of the EEOC's definition. Furthermore, this case distinguished between voluntary behavior and unwelcomeness. Vinson submitted to and maintained a sexual relationship with her employer, but under duress. She did not welcome it and feared losing her job if she did not comply.

Harris v. *Forklift Systems* (1993) addressed the definition of severity in hostile work environment sexual harassment claims and the level of proof necessary to prove that the harassment created an offensive or abusive work environment. Teresa Harris was a manager at an equipment rental company, Forklift Systems, Inc. Charles Hardy, the company president, often made her the target of unwanted sexual innuendos and insulted her because of her sex. When confronted by Harris, he promised to change his behavior, but his offensive behavior continued. In one instance, after Harris had arranged a customer deal, Hardy asked her in front of other employees, "What did you do, promise the guy . . . some [sex] Saturday night?" Harris quit her job and filed a suit for sexual harassment. The federal district court agreed that she was subjected to offensive treatment but felt that it was not so severe as to cause psychological damage; therefore the court ruled that her treatment did not meet the severity or pervasiveness standard set forth in *Meritor*. The Supreme Court disagreed. Justice O'Connor, writing for the unanimous majority, noted that although the facts of *Meritor* were so egregious that Mechelle Vinson suffered emotional and psychological injury, this did not set the boundary for what is considered actionable. The Court unanimously affirmed *Meritor*'s standard that articulated a middle-ground severity standard, noting that "when a workplace is permeated by discriminatory intimidation, ridicule, and insult that is sufficiently severe or pervasive as to alter the conditions of a victim's employment and to create an abusive working environment" (*Harris* v. *Forklift*, 1993, p. 21), Title VII is violated. A mere offensive epithet is not sufficient to be actionable, but neither is evidence of psychological injury necessary to be actionable. Instead the severity of a case is judged by both an objective standard (would a reasonable person perceive the situation to be hostile or abusive?) and a subjective standard (does the victim perceive the situation to be hostile or abusive?).

Whereas *Meritor* and *Harris* maintained the distinction between quid pro quo harassment and hostile work environment harassment, two cases in the late 1990s blurred this distinction. In *Burlington Industries* v. *Ellerth* (1998), Ted Slowik, a midlevel manager, made repeated boorish and offensive remarks and gestures toward Kimberly Ellerth, a salesperson. On three occasions these remarks were construed as threats to deny her tangible job benefits, but the threats were never carried out. The court of appeals reversed the district court's grant of summary judgment for Burlington. At issue was whether the case constituted a hostile work environment (which does not require the plaintiff to demonstrate that she suffered a tangible job loss) or quid pro quo harassment (which does entail such a requirement). In *Faragher* v. *City of Boca Raton* (1998) male lifeguard supervisors created a sexually hostile atmosphere for petitioner Beth Ann Faragher, a lifeguard, by repeatedly subjecting her and other female lifeguards to uninvited and offensive touching, by making lewd remarks, and by speaking of women in offensive terms. In this case, the court of appeals and the district court disagreed over whether the employer, City of Boca Raton, should be held liable. The district court held in favor of Faragher, but the court of appeals reversed this judgment, opining that the supervisors acted outside their scope of employment and had not been assisted by their agency relationship with the city and that the city lacked actual or constructive knowledge of the harassment.

The Supreme Court stated with regard to the *Burlington* case that the quid pro quo and hostile work environment labels do not control employer liability, and in both the *Burlington* and *Faragher* cases it distinguished between treatment that leads to tangible employment consequences and that which does not. In the latter the employer can raise an *affirmative defense*, meaning the burden of proof is on the employer. An affirmative defense is composed of two elements: the employer shows (1) that it took reasonable care to promptly prevent or correct any sexually harassing behavior and (2) that the employee unreasonably failed to take advantage of corrective or preventative opportunities or otherwise failed to avoid harm. If this affirmative defense is satisfied, the employer can avoid liability or damages. As will be discussed later in the chapter, this option of raising an affirmative defense has led to detailed examination of companies' sexual harassment policies as indicators that an employer either did or did not take reasonable care to prevent sexual harassment.

Finally, in *Oncale* v. *Sundowner Offshore Serv.* (1998) the Court further grappled with definitional issues. This was a case of same-sex sexual harassment. The petitioner, Joseph Oncale, had been subjected to humiliating sex-related actions, including physical sexual assault and threat of rape by male coworkers. There had been considerable disagreement in different circuits among judicial levels (for example, district versus appeals courts) with this and similar cases over whether same-sex sexual harassment constituted discrimination because of sex (see Franke, 1997, for a review of these cases). In the view of some jurists, same-sex sexual harassment constitutes sexual discrimination only if the harasser(s) was homosexual, that is, the harasser directs his or her sexual attention toward members of the same sex and therefore is discriminating against these targets because of their sex. The Supreme Court noted that sexual harassment need not be motivated by sexual desire to be actionable as sex discrimination; however, the plaintiff must prove that the conduct constituted discrimination because of sex. The Court reasoned that it is possible for a victim to show that he or she was subjected to sex-specific derogatory behavior by a member of the same sex. However, the conduct must go beyond mere offensive sexual connotations; it must be based on sex, and it must be severe or pervasive enough to affect the victim's conditions of employment. The social context should be taken into consideration when judging how the target experienced the behavior.

The Reasonable Woman Standard. As noted earlier, in *Harris* v. *Forklift* (1993) the U.S. Supreme Court said the severity of a sexual harassment case is to be judged on both an *objective* and a *subjective* standard. In a hostile work environment case, the Court of Appeals for the Ninth Circuit overturned earlier decisions and adopted a new standard for the *objective* prong for such cases. Instead of using the standard of a reasonable person, the court wrote: "A complete understanding of the victim's view requires, among other things, an analysis of the different perspectives of men and women" (*Ellison* v. *Brady*, 1991, p. 878). The new standard—the reasonable woman standard, based on "the notion that a reasonable person standard often allows male bias to creep in" (Goodman-Delahunty, 1999, p. 527)—requires that a reasonable *woman* would find the work environment hostile or abusive.

Although other circuits have not adopted this new standard and the U.S. Supreme Court has not evaluated it, it has been a topic of research by psychologists. Research comparing the reasonable woman standard with the reasonable person standard suggests that both standards result in generally similar decisions about whether or not the plaintiff was sexually harassed (Gutek, O'Connor, Melançon, Stockdale, Geer, & Done, 1999; Perry, Kulik, & Bourhis, 2004; Wiener, Hurt, Russell, Mannen, & Gasper, 1997), suggesting that perhaps the particular standard may have relatively little effect on decisions.

Disparate Treatment Claims

For one type of disparate treatment claim, called a *pattern-and-practice* claim, the plaintiff produces statistical evidence that members of her or his class (for example, she and other women in the potential promotion pool) receive disproportionately unfavorable employment decisions (for example, promotions) compared to the other class. If the court accepts this finding, suggesting a pattern and practice of discriminatory treatment, the burden shifts to the employer to demonstrate that its actions are not based on discrimination. If such an explanation is proffered, then the fact finder decides whether this reason is legitimate or is pretext for sex discrimination. The plaintiff, for example, a woman passed over for promotion, can counter the defendant's explanation, and thus support a conclusion of pretext, by showing that (1) the articulated reason is false or irrelevant, (2) the reason is not applied equally to men but only to her, (3) she fares better on the relevant criteria than the favored party at each stage of the selection process, (4) an examination of the beliefs and actions of the supervisors making the decisions at each stage indicates that they are motivated by conscious or unconscious bias toward women, or (5) statistics indicate that the particular refusal to promote conformed to a general pattern of discrimination against women (Babcock et al., 1996; see also *McDonnell Douglas* v. *Green*, 1973; *Texas Department of Community Affairs* v. *Burdine*, 1981).

One of the critical factors in charges of disparate treatment in hiring concerns how the *hiring pool* is defined. If very few women apply for a job, the plaintiff may have a hard time arguing that women applicants are subject to discriminatory treatment. In *EEOC* v. *Sears* (1988), Sears argued via an expert witness that lack of women in the hiring pool meant that men and women have different values and job preferences and thus it is not the employer's responsibility to change the job to be more appealing to women. The EEOC countered with an expert witness who stated that employers make all sorts of attempts to communicate a preferred gender for a job without outright advertising that the job is for men only, such as using masculine adjectives in the job descriptions (for example, suggesting that a successful job candidate should have "considerable physical vigor" and "has a liking for tools"). Women get the message that they are not wanted and therefore do not apply (see also *EEOC* v. *Joe's Stone Crab Restaurant*, 2000). In this case Sears won, perhaps because of its strategy of highlighting beliefs about women's special nature, which the court found compelling (Babcock et al., 1996). Nonetheless the case sparked considerable commentary by feminist legal scholars (annotated in Babcock et al.), arguing that conservative judges appear to be blind to social forces, such as gendered hiring practices, that shape women's career options.

Disparate Impact

The final class of discrimination cases concerns facially neutral employment policies that have a discriminatory impact on a protected class of individuals. In such cases it is not necessary to prove that the employer had discriminatory intent. *Griggs* v. *Duke Power Co.* (1972), a race-based discrimination claim, was the seminal case and is reviewed in Chapter Seven in this volume. In brief the complainant must demonstrate, typically through statistical evidence, that an employment practice causes adverse or disparate impact. If this burden is met, then the burden of proof shifts to the employer to show that the employment practice (for example, a test) is job related and addresses a business necessity. The standard for demonstrating job relatedness is that the practice has a manifest relationship to the employment in question. Validation studies are the preferred method for demonstrating that the employment practice has a manifest relationship with job performance.

Sex-based disparate impact cases have often been fought on height and weight requirements or on physical ability tests. In a series of cases involving *Berkman et al.* v. *City of New York* (1982, 1983, 1987), a class action suit was filed against New York City for sex discrimination in firefighter positions (for more background, see the interview with Judge Charles Sifton, the trial judge in the Berkman case, in Chapter Fifteen of this volume). At issue was a physical fitness exam that appeared to have face validity (for example, one of the subtests measured the time it took an applicant to run one mile). More extensive construct validity testing revealed, however, that in aggregate the tests did not measure the very important job-related construct of aerobic endurance but instead measured a different construct, anaerobic endurance (more commonly known as speed). Therefore the tests were ruled invalid. Similarly, in *Lanning* v. *Southeastern Pennsylvania Transportation Authority* (1999), female applicants for transit police officer positions filed a disparate impact claim arguing that a fitness cutoff score (running 1.5 miles in twelve minutes) had an adverse impact on female applicants because it measured speed, not endurance. At issue was whether there was a business justification for this cutoff score and whether it was empirically valid. The employer could show that "more is better"—that is, that the faster an applicant could run, the better he or she would presumably be as a police officer—but the employer could not garner validity evidence for its cutoff score. Moreover, it could not garner evidence that the physical ability test was substantially related to a major portion of the job as police officer. The appellate court reversed the previous ruling, which was in favor of the employer, and remanded the case back to the district court for further proceedings. Nevertheless the plaintiffs did not win their second trial nor their appeal.

The Role of Experts in Sex Discrimination and Sexual Harassment Cases

In this section we focus on the role and experiences of experts engaged by plaintiffs and defendants in cases alleging sex discrimination and sexual harassment. The role of the expert here, as in other areas, is to assist the finder of fact (judge or jury) by providing technical or scientific information that would not otherwise be known. In this section we rely heavily on our own experiences as expert witnesses.

Differences Between Plaintiff and Defense Experts in the Use of Social Science Evidence

There appear to be major differences between plaintiffs and defendants in their use of social science evidence in discrimination and harassment claims. We begin by describing some of those differences.

Plaintiffs' experts typically borrow liberally from the literature, citing broad-based findings. They typically assume that research findings will generalize to the particular case at issue. Their view is shared by many academics. Why engage in research at all if the findings cannot be generalized beyond the particular study or survey? But plaintiffs' experts also often make a slightly different assumption: they assume that the facts of the current case are similar enough to the facts underlying the majority of research findings to make those findings applicable to the current case. This is not always true. For example, the first author was hired as an expert in a case (unpublished) in which a company owning fast-food restaurants located in over a dozen states in the East and Midwest was involved in a class action charge of sexual harassment. Class members argued that a permissive environment fostered sexually harassing behavior and that such behavior permeated the organization. Yet in this case "the organization" consisted of hundreds of different fast-food restaurants in more than a dozen states. The plaintiff did not identify any mechanism to explain how a hostile environment could be created across several hundred separately situated fast-food restaurants when most employees never had contact with employees at other restaurants (except perhaps occasionally as customers). Identifying such a mechanism was especially important given that the defendant organization prominently posted its sexual harassment policy and provided some consistent training across sites. In addition the average employee worked part-time and stayed with the company for less than six months, providing a very narrow window of opportunity for communicating the characteristics of such a hostile environment from store to store across eleven states.

In the same case a plaintiff's expert asserted that the amount of sexual harassment discovered through questionnaires sent to current and former employees demonstrated that sexual harassment was underreported. She opined that the amount of sexual harassment reported in response to a solicitation by the EEOC represented "the tip of the iceberg," and that the real amount of harassment was much larger. This opinion was an extrapolation from research suggesting that some people who are harassed (using a broad definition of sexual harassment) do not report the harassment—for any number of reasons, such as thinking that the behavior is not serious enough to report or that nothing will be done or that they will experience retaliation for complaining. Yet the research findings from which she drew her conclusions came from studies of current employees. In the case at hand, about nine out of ten of the people surveyed by the EEOC were former, not current, employees. It is hard to see how a fast-food restaurant where one worked previously (for example, for a summer during one's high school or college years) could elicit the same kind of fear of retaliation as could a current employer.

If plaintiffs' experts err on the side of assuming research findings are relevant to the case at hand, defendants' experts err on the side of assuming that few or none of the research findings are applicable. Defendants' experts frequently try to exclude as much of the social science research base as possible, arguing that the research is too limited to apply to the facts of a particular case. In so doing they may try to exclude whole bodies of research that regularly appear in top-ranked, peer-reviewed journals. Laboratory research is often particularly suspect in their view or they place such stringent requirements on the research that it cannot be done. (Also see David Copus's section of Chapter Fourteen in this volume.)

Defense experts may argue that in order to be useful in court, research on stereotyping or a hostile work environment would have to be done in the defendant organization and that research done elsewhere is not sufficiently relevant. Furthermore, such research would have to be conducted using accepted probability sampling and would have to be analyzed using state-of-the-art social science methods. Placing any such restrictions on research certainly makes it much harder to use data to argue that discrimination or harassment has occurred and places a tremendous financial burden on the plaintiff (or in some cases, the defendant). The plaintiff may have a difficult time gaining access to the employees. However, if the court requires the defendant to cooperate, then the cost burden is shifted to the defense. Furthermore, one can argue that doing research in a defendant organization under such circumstances may yield responses biased by the respondents' views about the lawsuit. Finally, such a restriction differentiates social science research from other areas of expertise. For example, in the case of medical claims the expert does not have to perform surgery on the plaintiff in order to opine about the quality of care that person received or the risk associated with the surgical procedure at issue.

Although defendants' attorneys may argue that the only research applicable is research conducted in the relevant organization, they may also argue against the admissibility of any data collected. In fact the first author has served as defendant's expert in a case where she objected to data obtained *in* the organization being sued. In that particular case, as is so often true of other cases as well, the devil is in the details. This is what happened: attorneys for the plaintiffs in a class action case had sent a questionnaire to members of the class saying that the employer was being sued for sexual harassment and that there might be a financial settlement depending on the court's ruling. Defendants then argued that respondents were biased in favor of reporting discrimination in part because they thought they might gain financially if they reported that they were harassed. In a different legal proceeding (*EEOC v. Dial Corp.*, 2002), the plaintiff's expert also sent questionnaires to current and former employees. The defense expert, the first author, found that this questionnaire contained almost no opportunity to say anything positive about the (former) employer. In spite of that obstacle, some employees wrote positive comments in the margins or sent the questionnaire back with notes suggesting that the questionnaire was not impartial and was focused on finding evidence to support the plaintiff's position.

The bottom line is that the defense may object to the research whether it is conducted in the defendant organization or elsewhere, whereas plaintiffs are more likely to embrace research findings that support their claims, regardless of how applicable that research is to the case at hand.

Plaintiff's experts need to make sure that the published research is indeed applicable to the legal proceedings at hand. We believe that on the whole, published research findings are much less suspect than a survey conducted by the expert for one side or the other, although that does not preclude the possibility that an expert might conduct an impartial survey. A survey conducted for a particular legal case is, however, not subject to peer review, making it more vulnerable to challenge by the opposing party (see also *Daubert* v. *Merrell Dow Pharmaceuticals,* 1993). In addition, an expert may not have the time (or take the time) to consider plausible alternative explanations for his or her findings. For these reasons, conducting such a survey will not, in and of itself, lead to fewer challenges by the other side.

Social Framework Analysis in Sex Discrimination Litigation

Building on the fact that it has become commonplace for courts and commentators to distinguish uses of social science in law, Monahan and Walker (1986; Walker & Monahan, 1987) identified a "new use" of social science in law. In two law review articles in the 1980s, they introduced the concept of *social frameworks:*

> Social science is said either to prove "legislative facts" that concern general questions of law and policy, or to prove "adjudicative facts" that pertain only to the case at hand. . . . We identify a new generic use of social science in law that . . . incorporates aspects of both of the traditional uses: general research results are used to construct a frame of reference or background context for deciding factual issues crucial to the resolution of a specific case. We call this new use of social science in the law the creation of social frameworks [Walker & Monahan, 1987, p. 559].

Social framework analysis differs from other forms of expert testimony in that it does not attempt to conclude that a disputed fact or claim is or is not supported by research. Instead, it uses research to help jurors understand social phenomena that may be misunderstood by laypersons, such as why sexual harassment targets tend not to file formal complaints. Walker and Monahan (1987) provide examples of social frameworks involving information that is not commonly known by lay fact finders. They cite areas such as victims' responses to rape and the accuracy of eyewitness testimony, where juries' "common knowledge" may be incorrect or where jurors' logic drawn from their own experiences may lead to an incorrect conclusion. They conclude that "a growing number of courts have held that the use of social frameworks to correct beliefs that are erroneous does indeed 'assist the trier of fact'" (p. 580).

Social frameworks have been used by experts in matters having to do with sex discrimination and harassment (for example, *Robinson v. Jacksonville Shipyards*, 1991). Consider the research finding that targets of sexual harassment frequently do not complain about the harassment (for example, Gutek, 1985; Stockdale, 1998; see also Fitzgerald, Swan, & Fischer, 1995). Some put up with it for years before complaining, and others never complain until they do so in an attorney's office or to the EEOC. A defense attorney may argue that common sense suggests that if a person was really harassed, he or she would have complained. In that case common sense may be wrong, so the plaintiff may hire an expert to discuss the research literature on the topic. The goal of the plaintiff's expert is to educate the judge or jury about reasons why the plaintiff might not complain, other than that he or she was not harassed.

It is important to point out that a social framework analysis does not demonstrate that discrimination or harassment either did or did not occur but provides information to help the jury determine whether or not discrimination or harassment occurred. For example, it is possible that a woman who did not complain about sexual harassment while she was employed never was sexually harassed but was angry with her employer or was encouraged by well-meaning friends to file a lawsuit. But it is also possible that she was afraid to complain or thought that complaining would be a waste of time.

Walker and Monahan (1987, p. 560) argue that although social frameworks are "typically offered by one of the parties through the oral testimony of expert witnesses for evaluation and application by a jury," frameworks should be evaluated by the judge according to accepted common law principles and only then should the information be conveyed to a jury.

How Experts' Opinions Contribute to Determining Whether a Company Tried to Prevent Sexual Harassment

Another area that occasions expert testimony is the extent to which a company could have prevented sexual harassment through appropriate policies or practices. As noted earlier in this chapter, as a result of the *Burlington* and *Faragher* decisions, the quality of a company's sexual harassment policy is a major factor in showing whether the company has taken reasonable care to prevent sexual harassment. Plaintiffs' experts often closely scrutinize it. Indeed, the first author has seen numerous critiques of companies' sexual harassment policies, some substantially longer than the policy itself. A company that fails to have an acceptable policy might be charged with being remiss in its responsibility to prevent sexual harassment.

Employers have fought back by tinkering with the wording of their policies. One popular approach is to create a *zero tolerance* policy. In effect the employer changes the wording of the sexual harassment policy to say that the employer has zero tolerance for sexual harassment. One might question whether such close scrutiny of the wording of sexual harassment policies makes either legal or psychological sense. How many people starting a new job expect that they may need to refer to the sexual harassment policy someday? How carefully do people read a sexual harassment policy when it is first given to them? And if at some time they think they may have been sexually harassed, how carefully will they examine the written policy to try to determine whether they will be treated fairly or appropriately if they do make a complaint? And will it make any difference whether the policy says the company has zero tolerance for harassment or whether it has some other wording indicating that the company will take action if sexual harassment is found to have occurred? We know of no evidence that having a zero tolerance policy is an effective strategy for avoiding litigation or that the absence of such a policy is associated with more sexual harassment or more complaints of sexual harassment (see Stock-dale, Bisom-Rapp, O'Connor, & Gutek, 2004).

In light of unpublished research findings (Gutek & Done, 2003) and common sense, we are inclined to think that in most cases the wording of the policy plays a minor role in a person's decision to file a formal complaint of sexual harassment or file a complaint with the EEOC or seek the help of a private attorney. Moreover, even well-crafted policies may be variously interpreted as supporting the plaintiff's or defendant's position.

Results Interpreted to Support Both Plaintiff and Defense

Sometimes a particular finding is used to support both sides of an argument. Let's take an example from charges of sexual harassment. Are complaints an indication of no harassment or a lot of harassment? In fact, both positions have been argued.

Let's say that an employer is genuinely concerned about sexual harassment and wants to eradicate it and make the work environment comfortable and conducive to productive work for everyone. So the employer talks to an employment attorney who advises that having a sexual harassment policy is crucial. In order to ensure that no illegal behavior occurs, the policy may be more stringent than the law requires. For example, both authors have seen policies telling employees that they should not touch other employees. Next, the employment attorney advises having training in order to ensure that employees will be aware of the policy. The policy may be given to all employees, who also may be expected to sign a statement saying they received and read the policy. The employees also need to be told where to go if they have a complaint. They may also be told to report any behavior they see that looks like sexual harassment. Now employees know the policy and know where to go if they wish to lodge a complaint because they experienced or saw something that fits the definition of sexual harassment they heard in training or read in the policy. In fact, let us assume that several people go to their company's human resource department and complain about sexual harassment. After an investigation the organization finds that one person was engaging in behavior that violated the policy and was probably illegal. It terminates that employee. Now another employee comes forward and lodges a complaint. This time the employer finds no basis for the claim. So the employee, a woman, sues the company for sexual harassment. Now what?

The defendant can demonstrate that it has a sexual harassment policy and that it has taken action when it found the policy had been violated. Nevertheless the plaintiff hires an expert who examines the situation at her workplace and finds that most of the employees are male, the language is rough or crude, and the organization has already fired at least one person for sexual harassment. The expert concludes that the work environment fosters sexual harassment and that the plaintiff was harassed.

Now let's change one fact in this hypothetical case. This time, the employer finds no evidence that either employee was harassed and does nothing to punish the alleged harasser in either case. Again the second complainant sues the company for sexual harassment. Now what?

Once again the defense argues that it has a policy and has investigated complaints but did not apply any sanctions because it found no evidence that the policy had been violated. Once again the plaintiff hires an expert who examines the situation at work and finds the same set of contributory factors—mostly male employees who engage in rough or crude language. But the employer has never fired anyone for sexual harassment. The expert concludes that the employer tolerated sexual harassment, by virtue of the fact that no employee has been sanctioned for harassment despite contributory factors and two complaints.

The first author has seen both of these arguments in expert reports. She has also seen similar arguments made with respect to the number of complaints. If the company has a record of complaints, that is taken as evidence for the presence of sexual harassment. If the company has no complaints, the plaintiff's expert infers that the company's policy is ineffective, under the assumption that if the policy were effective, some number of people should have come forward to complain. Obviously, the mere fact of complaints and the mere fact of disciplinary action cannot be used to prove or disprove whether the company's sexual harassment policy is effective or whether the organization tolerated sexual harassment.

Measuring Sexual Harassment

Often there are no outside observers of sexual harassment and the perpetrator may deny the alleged behavior. Furthermore, there are typically no tangible job indicators, such as differences in pay or probability of being promoted. In the 1980s and early 1990s, some courts expected plaintiffs to show physical or psychological effects in order to bring forward a charge of sexual harassment. In 1993, in *Harris* v. *Forklift*, the U.S. Supreme Court struck down that requirement.

In a charge of hostile work environment sexual harassment, rather than focusing on tangible job loss the plaintiff must show that unwelcome harassment based on sex was severe or pervasive enough to create an intimidating or hostile work environment. (For a more detailed discussion, see O'Connor and Vallabhajosula, 2004.) In class action lawsuits and some individual lawsuits, one tool that has been employed by plaintiffs is survey research. In conducting a survey of the class and nonclass members (in a class action charge) or of employees (in an individual action), the plaintiff seeks information about the extent to which a hostile work environment exists.

In a number of charges of illegal sexual harassment, plaintiffs have distributed the Sexual Experiences Questionnaire (SEQ) (see Fitzgerald et al., 1988; Fitzgerald, Gelfand, & Drasgow, 1995) and other survey instruments to a group of employees or former employees, or both, as a way to determine the extent of harassment in the work environment. The SEQ is a self-report inventory containing a varying number of items that asks respondents to indicate the frequency of the described behaviors. Its authors assert that the SEQ measures "psychological sexual harassment" (Fitzgerald, Swan, & Magley, 1997). In addition, Fitzgerald, Gelfand, and Drasgow (1995) propose that their operationalization of sexual harassment (the items of the SEQ) links their psychological definition to the legal concept. They conclude that their ". . . model provides a parsimonious yet comprehensive answer to the question, 'What is sexual harassment?'" (p. 430). (A more complete discussion of the SEQ is contained in Fitzgerald, Gelfand, and Drasgow, 1995.)

The SEQ is described as measuring ". . . offensive, sex-related behavior that is unwanted, unwelcome, and unreciprocated" (Fitzgerald et al., 1997). There is, however, no evidence in the material provided about the SEQ that all of the items are worded to assess only behavior that is unwanted, unwelcome, or unreciprocated. None of the items in the material provided in published articles on the SEQ through 1997 assess reciprocation and only some include words that explicitly assess or imply unwelcomeness (for example, made offensive remarks, unwanted sexual attention). Furthermore, some items, such as the one abbreviated as ". . . told suggestive stories," do not necessarily imply behavior that is unwanted, unwelcome, or unreciprocated, although it certainly could be.

Various versions of the SEQ have also been given to employees and former employees as part of plaintiffs' (and in at least one case, defendant's) experts' research to determine the level of sexual harassment in a particular work environment. However, evidence garnered from the EEOC's use of the SEQ was rejected in a civil suit filed by the EEOC against Dial Corporation (*EEOC* v. *Dial Corp.*, 2002), based in part on concerns about its lack of standardization and construct validity. Gutek, Murphy, and Douma (2004) comprehensively critique the SEQ as a forensic measure of sexual harassment. With regard to the Dial case, the concerns focused on the SEQ's inability to measure the amount of sexual harassment that has been or is occurring in an organization, or because the SEQ lacks normative data, whether the harassment measured by the SEQ corresponds to an "illegal" level. Specifically, there are no norms that might inform managers, attorneys, or judges whether any particular firm, workgroup, occupational setting, and so forth, is above or below average on social-sexual behavior. In addition the SEQ measures a definition of sexual harassment that is much broader than the EEOC definition used as a standard in litigation. Such an assessment may be useful for research or clinical purposes in order to document the associations between any amount of exposure to social-sexual behavior in the workplace and various outcomes such as job dissatisfaction or health complaints, but as a measure of sexual harassment per se it is likely to overestimate both harassment's prevalence and the amount of underreporting.

Conclusions

Industrial and organizational psychologists and scholars in related disciplines have had much to offer to the legal system in helping fact finders make informed judgments and in some cases helping to shape the law. Similarly, the legal arena provides a rich source of ideas for socially important research. In the case of sexual harassment, research on individual differences in perceptions of sexual harassment has helped develop interesting if controversial conventions such as the reasonable woman standard. I-O scholarship has also helped jurists better understand the various motives underlying acts of same-sex harassment.

Almost ten years ago Burns (1995, p. 194) wrote that "a legal claim of unlawful workplace sexual harassment is in large part a factual claim at the heart of which is the contest of credibility." This understanding suggests a need for research to address how a plaintiff's character affects her believability. Is only a "ladylike" plaintiff able to garner sufficient sympathy to sway triers of fact in her direction? What about male plaintiffs? Are there double standards? In other arenas psychological research on stereotyping has helped to keep the BFOQ defense appropriately narrow. No longer can companies claim that only unmarried, attractive women can do the job of a flight attendant. The airlines are not in the business of selling sex. Future research could address whether this defense can be substantiated in any claim (Hooters—watch out!).

Despite the positive contributions of research to an understanding of sex discrimination and sexual harassment, we see some problems with the way it might be used in court. Most notably, many of the behaviors that might be illegal under some circumstances are nevertheless very common and do not rise to the level of illegal behavior most of the time. How can experts know what amount of stereotyping is sufficient to interfere with decision making to an extent that leads to illegal discrimination? Because stereotyping is ubiquitous and very likely influences many decisions to some extent, are not many if not all organizations guilty, with only some unlucky enough to be sued? (In Ann Hopkins's case [*Price Waterhouse* v. *Hopkins*, 1989], there was evidence that her colleagues judged her behavior by relying on a stereotype of women rather than, or in addition to, her record of productivity.) How can the defense protect a company against behavior that occurs whether or not illegal behavior has occurred? So far, it appears to us that the main tack has been to denigrate the scientific integrity of the research base.

In the area of sexual harassment, how can experts know what amount of social-sexual behavior at work it takes to produce a hostile, intimidating work environment—except to appeal to common sense? It is not surprising that plaintiffs' attorneys would find an instrument like the SEQ appealing if they thought it would successfully quantify the amount of hostile environment sexual harassment in an organization. The many different versions of the SEQ, however, do not do that. Some SEQ behaviors are, like stereotyping, common to many if not most organizations. Even if a standardized instrument existed to measure social-sexual behavior, how much sexually harassing behavior is too much? Over time, researchers and the courts may come to some consensus on how to determine whether the development of a standardized instrument to measure illegal hostile environment sexual harassment would simplify the court's task.

We do find several areas of research to be extremely helpful to the court. Just as it is helpful to the jury to know that eyewitness testimony can be wrong, it is also useful to the jury to know that women who are sexually harassed do not always complain. In both of these areas the expert can sometimes testify about the research that has been done without even knowing many of the details of the case at hand. Neither of these areas, furthermore, addresses the ultimate decision of guilt or innocence and thus does not invade the province of the jury.

It may be useful to the jury to know that stereotyping can influence decisions and that more sexual harassment occurs in a male-dominated work environment than a female-dominated one, but it is also useful to know that the presence of either of these does not mean that illegal behavior has occurred. It may also be useful to know when an expert's opinion is not based on research. As discussed earlier, we know of no research showing the elements of an effective sexual harassment policy or even any concurrence about what effectiveness means in this context. Should an effective policy yield more or fewer complaints than no policy or an ineffective policy? Or is there no relationship between the effectiveness of a policy and complaints: that is, can it be assumed that the wording of a written policy generally has little or no effect on the filing of complaints of harassment?

Although research conducted solely for the purpose of gathering information for litigation is likely to be challenged by the other side, it can also help plaintiffs or defendants meet their respective burdens. Research may be conducted in a number of areas, such as to help establish a prima facie case of harassment, to argue that a defendant's explanation for questionable employment practices is pretext for discrimination, to establish that an employer's employment practices are valid and justifiable, or to document the fact that employees knew about the company's sexual harassment policy.

Plaintiffs and defendants have long used clinical psychologists as experts in charges of sex discrimination, but employing experts to talk about relevant research findings is a newer phenomenon. We do not see any reason why that trend will not continue.

References

Books, Articles, and Government Documents

Babcock, B. A., Freedman, A. E., Ross, S. D., Williams, W. W., Copelon, R., Rhode, D., et al. (1996). *Sex discrimination and the law: History, practice, and theory* (2nd. ed.). Boston: Little, Brown.

Burns, S. E. (1995). Issues in workplace sexual harassment law and related social science research. *Journal of Social Issues, 51,* 193–207.

Fitzgerald, L. F., Gelfand, M. J., & Drasgow, F. (1995). Measuring sexual harassment: Theoretical and psychometric advances. *Basic and Applied Social Psychology, 17*(4), 425–445.

Fitzgerald, L. F., Shullman, S. L., Bailey, N., Richards, M., Swecker, J., Gold, Y., et al. (1988). The incidence and dimensions of sexual harassment in academia and the workplace. *Journal of Vocational Behavior, 32,* 152–175.

Fitzgerald, L. F., Swan, S., & Fischer, C. (1995). Why didn't she just report him? The psychological and legal implications of women's responses to sexual harassment. *Journal of Social Issues, 51,* 117–138.

Fitzgerald, L. F., Swan, S., & Magley, V. J. (1997). But was it really sexual harassment? Legal, behavioral, and psychological definitions of the workplace victimization of women. In W. O'Donohue (Ed.), *Sexual harassment: Theory, research, treatment* (pp. 5–28). Boston: Allyn & Bacon.

Franke, K. M. (1997). What's wrong with sexual harassment? *Stanford Law Review, 49,* 691–772.

Goodman-Delahunty, J. (1999). Pragmatic support for the reasonable victim standard in hostile workplace sexual harassment cases. *Psychology, Public Policy, and Law, 5*(3), 519–555.

Guidelines on Discrimination Because of Sex, 45 Fed. Reg. 1604.11, 74676–74677 (1980).

Gutek, B. A. (1985). *Sex and the workplace.* San Francisco: Jossey-Bass.

Gutek, B. A., & Done, R. (2003). *What influences evaluations of sexual harassment policy effectiveness?* Unpublished manuscript, University of Arizona, Tucson.

Gutek, B. A., Murphy, R. O., & Douma, B. (2004). A review and critique of the Sexual Experiences Questionnaire (SEQ). Law and Human Behavior, 28(4), 457-482.

Gutek, B. A., O'Connor, M., Melançon, R., Stockdale, M. S., Geer, T., & Done, R. (1999). The utility of the reasonable woman legal standard in hostile environment sexual harassment cases: A multimethod, multistudy examination. *Psychology, Public Policy, and Law, 5*(3), 596–629.

Hampshire, C. (1999, August 23). Hooters restaurant to open downtown by January. *Alligator Online.* Retrieved March 16, 2004, from http://www.alligator.org

MacKinnon, C. (1979). Sexual harassment of working women: A case of sex discrimination. New Haven, CT: Yale University Press.

Monahan, J., & Walker, L. (1986). Social authority: Obtaining, evaluating, and establishing social science in law. *University of Pennsylvania Law Review, 134,* 477–517.

O'Connor, M., & Vallabhajosula, B. (2004). Sexual harassment in the workplace: A legal and psychological framework. In B. J. Cling (Ed.), *Sex, violence & women: A psychology & law perspective* (pp. 115–147). New York: Guilford Press.

Perry, E. L., Kulik, C. T., & Bourhis, A. C. (2004). The reasonable woman standard: Effects on sexual harassment court decisions. *Law and Human Behavior, 28*(1), 9–27.

Stockdale, M. S. (1998). The direct and moderating influences of sexual harassment pervasiveness, coping strategies, and gender on work-related outcomes. *Psychology of Women Quarterly, 22,* 521–535.

Stockdale, M. S., Bisom-Rapp, S., O'Connor, M., & Gutek, B. A. (2004). Coming to terms with zero-tolerance sexual harassment policies. *Journal of Forensic Psychology Practice, 4,* 65–78.

Walker, L., & Monahan, J. (1987). Social frameworks: A new use of social science in law. *Virginia Law Review, 73,* 559–598.

Wiener, R. L., Hurt, L., Russell, B., Mannen, K., & Gasper, C. (1997). Perceptions of sexual harassment: The effects of gender, legal standard, and ambivalent sexism. *Law and Human Behavior, 21,* 71–93.

Cases

Berkman et al. v. City of New York, 536 F. Supp. 177 (E.D. N.Y. 1982).

Berkman et al. v. City of New York, 705 F.2d 584 (2d Cir. 1983).

Berkman et al. v. City of New York, 812 F.2d 52 (2d Cir. 1987).

Burlington Industries, Inc. v. Ellerth, 118 S. Ct. 2257 (1998).

Cleveland Board of Education v. La Fleur, 414 U.S. 632 (1974).

Daubert v. Merrell Dow Pharmaceuticals, 113 S. Ct. 2786 (1993).

Diaz v. Pan American World Airways, Inc. 442 F.2d 385 (5th Cir.), cert. denied, 404 U.S. 950 (1971).

Dothard v. Rawlinson, 433 U.S. 321 (1977).

EEOC v. Dial Corp., No. 99 C 3356 (N.D. Ill. 2002).

EEOC v. Joe's Stone Crab Restaurant, 220 F.3d 1263 (11th Cir. 2000).

EEOC v. Sears, Roebuck & Co., 839 F.2d 302 (7th Cir. 1988).

Ellison v. Brady, 924 F.2d 872 (9th Cir. 1991).

Faragher v. City of Boca Raton, 118 S. Ct. 2275 (1998).

Griggs v. Duke Power Co., 401 U.S. 424 (1972).

Harris v. Forklift Systems, Inc., 114 S. Ct. 367, 510 U.S. 17 (1993).

Lanning v. Southeastern Pennsylvania Transportation Authority, 181 F.3d 478 (3d Cir. 1999).

McDonnell Douglas v. Green, 411 U.S. 792 (1973).

Meritor Savings Bank v. Vinson, 477 U.S. 57 (1986).

Oncale v. Sundowner Offshore Serv., Inc., 118 S. Ct. 998 (1998).

Phillips v. Martin Marietta Corp., 400 U.S. 542 (1971).

Price Waterhouse v. Hopkins, 490 U.S. 228 (1989).

Robinson v. Jacksonville Shipyards, Inc., 760 F. Supp. 1486 (M.D. Fl. 1991).

Sprogis v. United Airlines, Inc., 444 F.2d 1194 (7th Cir.), cert. denied, 404 U.S. 991 (1971).

Texas Department of Community Affairs v. Burdine, 450 U.S., 248, 256 (1981).

Torres. v. Wisconsin Department of Health and Social Servs., 838 F.2d 944 (7th Cir.), rev'd in part en banc, 859 F.2d 1523 (7th Cir. 1988), cert. denied, 489 U.S. 1017 and 489 U.S. 1082 (1989).

UAW v. Johnson Controls, Inc., 499 U.S. 187 (1991).

Wards Cove Packing Co., Inc. v. Atonio, 490 U.S. 642 (1989).

Weeks v. Southern Bell Telephone & Telegraph, 408 F.2d 228 (5th Cir. 1969).

CHAPTER 9

The Age Discrimination in Employment Act

Harvey L. Sterns
Dennis Doverspike
Greta A. Lax

Hundreds of thousands not yet old, not yet voluntarily retired find themselves jobless because of arbitrary age discrimination. . . . Today, more than three-quarters of a billion dollars in unemployment insurance is paid each year to workers who are 45 or over. . . . In 1965, the Secretary of Labor reported to Congress and the President that approximately half of all private job openings were barred to applicants over 55; a quarter were closed to applicants over 45. In economic terms, this is a serious—and senseless—loss to a nation on the move. But the greater loss is the cruel sacrifice in happiness and well-being which joblessness imposes on these citizens and their families [Edelman & Siegler, 1978, p. 73; Lyndon B. Johnson presented these remarks on January 23, 1967, as part of his Special Message to the Congress Proposing Programs for Older Americans].

On December 15, 1967, President Johnson signed into law the Age Discrimination in Employment Act (ADEA), which became effective on June 12, 1968. Every state and the District of Columbia, Puerto Rico, the Virgin Islands, and Guam have statutes prohibiting age discrimination in employment, with Colorado having enacted the first state statute related to age in employment in 1903 (AARP, 2001a; Edelman & Siegler, 1978; Rosen & Jerdee, 1985).

Until 2000, ADEA was considered applicable across public and private sectors. With the Supreme Court decision in *Kimel* v. *Florida Board of Regents* (2000), however, states are allowed to use age as a proxy for other qualities, abilities, and characteristics relevant to the state's interests, and state employees may therefore seek remedy only through their state statutes. In addition, state statutes are of import to all older workers, as they may provide remedies superior to those available under ADEA. Despite the obvious importance of state laws, it would be impossible to cover all the legal developments at the state level in this review. Therefore, we have concentrated on the ADEA and developments at the federal level. Nevertheless, for the practitioner or lawyer, it is essential to be familiar with the laws and provisions of the state(s) in which one practices as well as with the federal laws (AARP, 2001a).

Provisions of the ADEA

Age discrimination is an important area of equal employment opportunity (EEO) law. In 2003, age accounted for 23.5 percent of the total EEO charges, ranking it behind only race, sex, and retaliation (Equal Employment Opportunity Commission, 2004a). Although there are many similarities between litigation under the ADEA and litigation under Title VII, there are also important differences. These differences include the types of human resource issues involved, the role of disparate impact evidence, and the importance of benefits issues. There is also an interesting psychological difference in that it can be argued that Title VII was intended to prevent discrimination based on membership in the protected class whereas the ADEA was intended to prevent discrimination based on stereotypes or beliefs about members of the protected class (Gutman, 2000; *Hazen* v. *Biggins,* 1993). Further, the ADEA is unique in that discrimination can occur within the protected class. That is, discrimination can occur even when an older worker is replaced by another worker over forty, if the age difference is great enough, so long as the decision has been based on age (*O'Connor* v. *Consolidated Coin,* 1996; *Showalter* v. *University of Pittsburgh Medical Center,* 1999).

The Age Discrimination in Employment Act was enacted in order to promote the employment of older persons based on their ability rather than their age, to prohibit arbitrary age discrimination in employment, and to help employers and workers find ways of meeting problems arising from the impact of age on workforce participation. The original ADEA covered employers with twenty-five or more employees. In 1974, coverage was extended to include federal, state, and local governments and employers with at least twenty workers. The current definition of *employer* for the purposes of ADEA is "a person engaged in an industry affecting commerce who has twenty or more employees for each working day in each of twenty or more calendar weeks in the current or preceding calendar year" (ADEA, 2004). The ADEA provides that it is unlawful for an employer (1) to fail or refuse to hire or to discharge any individual or otherwise discriminate against any individual with regard to his or her compensation, terms, conditions or privileges of employment or (2) to limit, segregate, or classify employees in any way that would tend to deprive any individual of employment opportunities or otherwise adversely affect his or her status as an employee because of that individual's age. (For a complete and concise review of the ADEA and its practical application and implications, see Edelman and Siegler, 1978; Gutman, 2002; Levine, 1998.)

The ADEA is enforced by the Equal Employment Opportunity Commission (EEOC) and originally was intended to cover individuals forty through sixty-five years of age. A 1978 amendment to the ADEA raised the maximum age to seventy and eliminated the upper age limitation for government employees. Another amendment, in 1986, ensured coverage for all individuals forty and over, with a number of exemptions.

Exemptions

The first exemption is that the law allows the mandatory retirement at age sixty-five of *bona fide executives* or *high policymaking employees*. *Bona fide executives* refers to individuals who have executive authority. This area would seem to be an important one for future litigation, although only a few cases to date have dealt with this exception. To be covered under this exemption, the employee must also be entitled to retirement benefits of at least $44,000 annually, and thus the exemption requires financial compensation (*Morrisey* v. *Boston Bank*, 1995). It has been applied to college presidents (*EEOC* v. *Wayne Community College*, 1983) and division heads (*Passer* v. *American Chemical Society*, 1990). In *Whittlesly* v. *Union Carbide* (1984) the plaintiff was able to counter the employer's claim of an exemption by demonstrating that he was primarily an attorney and had minimal supervisory duties; this argument was successful despite the fact that he was chief labor counsel in charge of the labor section of the company's law department.

A second exemption allows for the retirement of safety officers (firefighters and law enforcement officers) in accordance with state and local laws, although this exemption does not apply to local decisions based on the adoption or application of federal rules (*Johnson* v. *Mayor and City Council of Baltimore*, 1985). This exemption was to remain in effect until the results of a joint study by the Department of Labor and the EEOC determined whether physical or mental testing was a valid, effective measure of ability and competency. A technical report by Landy (1992) recommended removal of age as a *bona fide occupational qualification* (BFOQ), citing individual differences, relative effectiveness of physical ability testing, and the ability to modify age-related decline. Inaction by Congress allowed this exemption to expire December 31, 1993. Further action by Congress in 1996 reinstated the exemption and repealed the expiration date. It would seem that the *Kimel* v. *Florida Board of Regents* (2000) decision would be relevant to the continued debate over the meaning and reach of this exemption (for example, what does the term *bona fide* in the exemption mean), as it effectively eliminated the question at least at the state level.

A third exemption covered tenured faculty. However, this exemption also expired December 31, 1993, as recommended by the National Research Council Committee on Mandatory Retirement in Higher Education (Hammond & Morgan, 1991).

The law also specifies that *bona fide apprenticeship programs* accepting only individuals under a specific maximum age are exempt from the ADEA's requirements. However, the court in *Quinn* v. *New York State Electric and Gas* (1983) ruled that unless an employer could establish that age upon entry into the training program was a BFOQ, the policy would be found to be discriminatory.

There is also an exemption for certain types of elected or appointed officials. In *Gregory* v. *Ashcroft* (1991), the Supreme Court ruled that appointed state judges were not covered by the ADEA.

Thus a state retains the right, under the Tenth Amendment and the Guarantee Clause of Article IV, to determine such qualifications, as long as such decisions can be deemed *rational* and in the legitimate interest of the state.

The current Age 60 Rule (14 C.F.R. § 121.383) for commercial airline pilots is an example of a BFOQ exemption under the ADEA. The rule states that no commercial airline may use any pilot or copilot after he or she reaches his or her sixtieth birthday. These pilots do have the option of downbidding to the position of flight engineer (as discussed later in this chapter, *Western Airlines* v. *Criswell,* 1985). Exemptions to the ADEA similarly exist for air traffic controllers. Individuals past thirty years of age may not be initially hired for the position, with the exception of retired military air traffic controllers. In addition, these individuals may remain in the position only until the last day of the month that they turn fifty-six (ADEA, 2004).

ADEA and ADA Coordination and Overlap

The Americans with Disabilities Act (ADA, 1990) can be viewed as providing additional protections to older workers, beyond those provided by the ADEA (Doverspike & Hollis, 1995; Hollis-Sawyer & Doverspike, 2000; Sterns, Sterns, & Hollis, 1996). The ADA requires that employers make reasonable accommodations for individuals with disabling impairments, so long as the accommodations do not impose undue hardship on the employer. Although the decrements in physical functioning associated with normal aging are not a disability, age does appear to interact with various physical conditions leading to increases in disabilities with age, including impairments in vision and hearing and a range of diseases including diabetes and arthritis. The ADA should provide a range of protections to the older individual returning to the workplace following age-related illnesses including heart attacks and strokes (Sterns et al., 1996). These individuals have already demonstrated their competence in performing the job, and they must be allowed to return to work, so long as they can still perform the essential functions of the job. It should be noted that in *Board of Trustees of the University of Alabama* v. *Patricia Garrett* (2001), the Supreme Court ruled that states may not be sued by employees for violations of the ADA.

Areas and Activities Covered

The ADEA covers a wide range of human resource decisions. In a later section we discuss specific legal issues related to various human resource issues. Among the human resource decisions covered by the ADEA are those that address retirement, hiring, wages, discharges, reductions in force, promotions, hours worked, overtime, benefits, access to training programs, access to career development programs, vacations, and sick leave.

Legal Issues and Approaches

In this section we begin by discussing the establishment of a prima facie case under the ADEA. Although there are many parallels to similar arguments under Title VII, at the present time it appears that a claim of age discrimination cannot be made at the federal level under a disparate impact theory. We then discuss the various legal defenses under the ADEA. This is followed by a discussion of the role of the expert witness. Finally, we discuss damages and other legal issues.

Establishing a Prima Facie Case

The ADEA parallels Title VII (Civil Rights Act, 1964) in many respects, and most courts apply Title VII–type standards to age discrimination cases. These standards previously allowed plaintiffs to develop their claims under one of two distinct theories, *disparate treatment* and *disparate impact*. However, the future of disparate impact rules was darkened in a major Supreme Court ruling (*Hazen v. Biggins,* 1993), where the court raised questions as to the appropriateness of this approach under the ADEA because of the differences in the legislative histories of the ADEA and the Civil Rights Act and the nature of age as a protected class.

There are three major approaches to establishing a prima facie case of age discrimination under the disparate treatment theory. The plaintiff may show intentional discrimination on the part of the employer through the use of direct evidence, such as an employer's admission that age was the reason for his or her action. A second approach is to demonstrate intentional discrimination through circumstantial evidence, such as an employer's decision to discharge an employee before benefits are vested. In the case of the circumstantial approach, a logical relationship must be demonstrated between the plaintiff's age and the discriminatory act. A third approach relies on statistical evidence. One use of such data is to demonstrate a pattern of differential treatment. A second use is to support disparate impact cases; however, the acceptability of an age-related disparate impact case under federal law is currently questionable, as will be discussed later.

Direct proof of discrimination, a so-called *smoking gun,* is difficult to demonstrate (one is unlikely to receive a memo from a supervisor proclaiming, "You're too old to do the job"). Of course even a smoking gun is insufficient if the age comments are not accompanied by clear evidence of disparate treatment (*DeLoach* v. *Infinity Broadcasting,* 1999).

As a result of the difficulties involved in finding direct proof, circumstantial evidence is most often presented. Cases involving indirect evidence follow the guidelines of the *McDonnell-Burdine* scenario, as set forth in Supreme Court decisions involving Title VII cases (*McDonnell Douglas* v. *Green,* 1973; *Texas Department of Community Affairs* v. *Burdine,* 1981). To establish a case using indirect evidence, the plaintiff must present facts from which it can be inferred that the employer intentionally discriminated against the older employee. To establish a prima facie case the employee (plaintiff) must meet the burden of proof with *presumptive* evidence that (1) the plaintiff is a member of the protected class (forty years old or older); (2) the plaintiff has the necessary job qualifications or, in many ADEA cases, the necessary level of satisfactory job performance; (3) the plaintiff received an adverse personnel decision; and (4) the personnel decision favored someone younger with similar qualifications (*Reeves* v. *Sanderson Plumbing Products,* 2000).

Once the plaintiff has established a prima facie case, the burden of going forward shifts to the defendant (employer), who must provide *articulation* of a nondiscriminatory reason for the personnel action. If the defendant articulates a legitimate, nondiscriminatory reason for the employment action, then the burden shifts back to the plaintiff to prove that the employer's reason was a *pretext* for intentional discrimination. The burden of proof always rests with the plaintiff.

In Snyder and Barrett's (1988) and Lee, Havighurst, and Rassel's (2004) analyses of decisions, the defendants had been successful in a majority of the court cases, but a number of legal refinements have occurred in recent years that may change employers' success rate. For example, there has been a debate as to how far the plaintiff must go to establish a prima facie case. At issue in particular is whether age must be the sole factor in a personnel action or whether it is enough to show that age was one of several factors (*Golomb* v. *Prudential Insurance*, 1982; *Hagelthorn* v. *Kennecott*, 1983; *Kelly* v. *American Standard*, 1981; *Mastie* v. *Great Lakes Steel*, 1976; *Pena* v. *Brattleboro Retreat*, 1983; *Tribble* v. *Westinghouse Electric*, 1982). This issue has largely been settled in the plaintiff's favor. As long as the employee can show that age made a difference in the personnel decision (that is, that it was the determining or "but for" factor), then a prima facie case has been established. This greatly eases the plaintiff's burden of proof in establishing age discrimination.

Another development easing the plaintiff's burden in establishing a prima facie case involves the age of the person replacing the older worker. A few courts had required proof that the person replacing the older worker was outside the protected class (*Houser* v. *Sears, Roebuck*, 1980; *Pace* v. *Southern Railway System*, 1983; *Price* v. *Maryland Casualty*, 1977). Other courts had felt this requirement defeated the purpose of the Act (*Douglas* v. *Anderson*, 1981; *Loeb* v. *Textron*, 1979; *Moore* v. *Sears, Roebuck*, 1982; *Williamson* v. *Owens-Illinois*, 1984). In a 1996 decision, the Supreme Court clarified that an employee suing for age discrimination did not need to prove that he or she was replaced by someone under forty, as long as there was a sufficient age range between the two individuals (*O'Connor* v. *Consolidated Coin Caterers*, 1996; *Showalter* v. *University of Pittsburgh Medical Center*, 1999).

In a very recent case, *General Dynamics Land Systems* v. *Dennis Cline et al.* (2004), the U.S. Supreme Court ruled that *younger* older workers cannot sue under the ADEA over alleged favorable treatment of *older* older workers. This is often viewed as a type of reverse discrimination case in that the younger workers were arguing the older workers received better outcomes in terms of benefits. In this case General Dynamics Land Systems entered into a collective bargaining agreement to limit health benefits in retirement to those over the age of fifty. Those workers under the age of fifty but over the age of forty argued that they had been discriminated against under the ADEA. Although the EEOC and the Sixth Circuit Court of Appeals agreed, the Supreme Court reversed that decision and found that the ADEA did not prohibit employers from treating older workers in a more favorable manner.

In the past when disparate impact arguments have been allowed, they followed the same basic logic as they do in Title VII cases. However, there has also been heated debate whether it is appropriate to use the disparate impact theory with age discrimination cases. This argument centers around the fact that chronological age, unlike race, is not an immutable characteristic of the individual (*Kimel* v. *Florida Board of Regents,* 2000). In the 1993 case of *Hazen* v. *Biggins* the Supreme Court noted that it had never explicitly approved disparate impact cases under the ADEA, and since then that theory has been under a cloud of doubt (Henkle, 1997). In addition to the not-an-immutable-characteristic argument, this decision was based on the idea that at one time or another everyone is at risk of being discriminated against on the basis of age and that there is no history of purposeful unequal treatment surrounding age (*Kimel* v. *Florida Board of Regents,* 2000; *Massachusetts Board of Retirement* v. *Murgia,* 1976). Thus, according to this legal argument, one can fire all the most expensive employees using a cost-savings approach, even if most of those employees are older (*Mastie* v. *Great Lakes Steel,* 1976); note that we do not mean to endorse this approach, only to present its logic. It was hoped that the case of *Adams* v. *Florida Power* (2002) would further clarify the Supreme Court's view of the disparate impact argument in ADEA cases. However, this case was dismissed by the Court without a decision being rendered. A reading of the questioning before the Court suggests that (1) disparate impact evidence may be used in making a disparate treatment argument; (2) however, the Court continues to be skeptical of the value of disparate impact arguments in ADEA cases, at least those involving a reduction in force.

Legal Defenses

There are four legitimate defenses the employer is afforded (ADEA, 2004). The first states that it is not unlawful to take any action otherwise prohibited where age is a bona fide occupational qualification reasonably necessary to the normal operations of a particular business. The second defense allows employers to differentiate based on *reasonable factors other than age* (RFOA). The third defense allows an employer to observe the terms of a bona fide seniority system or benefit plan, if it is not a subterfuge to evade the purposes of the Act. The fourth defense states that it is not unlawful to discharge or discipline an employee for good cause.

Any of these defenses may be used to justify a personnel action, and most cases do not involve an explicit assertion of a particular defense. Instead, the employer merely denies discriminating against the employee.

Bona Fide Occupational Qualifications

A BFOQ is an affirmative defense. In the last few years very few BFOQ cases have reached the decision stage, apparently because BFOQ defenses receive strict scrutiny and because the evolving gerontological literature suggests the age-related changes need to be evaluated on an individual basis and in relation to the demands of a specific job situation (Sterns & Alexander, 1987). However, historically, the BFOQ has been an important and controversial defense.

In a BFOQ case the employer admits that age was used in making an employment decision but argues that age was a necessary consideration in that decision. As with gender cases under Title VII, most BFOQ defenses have involved issues of public safety (concerning, for example, bus drivers, airline pilots, police officers, and firefighters). In these cases the employer must demonstrate, based on a fairly stringent standard (*Western Airlines* v. *Criswell*, 1985), that the age restriction serves a public safety objective and that an alternative procedure does not exist for achieving this important social goal. This standard usually involves the presentation of convincing empirical evidence (*Campbell* v. *Connelie*, 1982; *Hahn* v. *City of Buffalo*, 1985; *Johnson* v. *Mayor and City Council of Baltimore*, 1985) linking age to declines in functioning or competency or to threats to the public safety (*EEOC* v. *City of East Providence*, 1986; *EEOC* v. *City of St. Paul*, 1982; *EEOC* v. *Missouri State Highway Patrol*, 1984; *EEOC* v. *State of New Jersey*, 1986; *EEOC* v. *University of Texas Health Science Center*, 1983). Further, this must be demonstrated for a particular employer and a specific narrow occupation or job (*EEOC* v. *Trabucco*, 1986; *EEOC* v. *City of Janesville,* 1980; *EEOC* v. *City of Minneapolis,* 1982; *EEOC* v. *City of St. Paul,* 1982; *EEOC* v. *Commonwealth of Pennsylvania,* 1986; *Mahoney* v. *Trabucco,* 1984; *Popkins* v. *Zagel,* 1985).

Of course the plaintiff's attorney and expert will try to counter the claims regarding the relationship between age and either declines or public safety. The plaintiff may present evidence from experts that argues that there is no relationship between age and physical decline or age and public safety. The expert might also argue that there are substantial individual differences in the amount of physical decline accompanying aging. Or the plaintiff may argue that even if there is a relationship between age and physical decline, there is no relationship between age and job performance. In general the psychological literature does not support a link between age and job performance (Avolio, Barrett, & Sterns, 1984; Davies & Sparrow, 1985; Doering, Rhodes, & Schuster, 1983; McEvoy & Cascio, 1989; Meier & Kerr, 1976; Rhodes, 1983; Sterns & McDaniel, 1994; Waldman & Avolio, 1986; Welford, 1977).

In alternative approaches the plaintiff may try to show that there are ways to compensate for any declines (*EEOC* v. *Missouri State Highway Patrol,* 1984; *Johnson* v. *Mayor and City Council of Baltimore,* 1985; *Marshall* v. *Goodyear Tire,* 1979; *Orzel* v. *City of Wauwatosa Fire Department,* 1983) or may argue the employer should test for declining ability or performance (*EEOC* v. *City of Minneapolis,* 1982; *EEOC* v. *City of St. Paul,* 1982). Snyder and Barrett (1988) point out that if it is possible to show the link between ability and performance, then it should also be possible to develop valid tests of those abilities and test for the requisite abilities. They also point out that the same diminished ability argument that is often applied to older individuals does not seem to apply to female job candidates.

BFOQ cases fall into two categories: those involving selection and those involving mandatory retirement. In a selection situation the employer establishes a maximum age for entry-level purposes—such as arguing that police officers must be under the age of forty when initially hired. This type of initial hire case is extremely rare today. In a mandatory retirement situation the employer argues that all individuals must retire at a certain age—for example, all police officers must retire at the age of sixty. In either case the general approach taken by the employer would be to show a relationship, usually empirical, between age and increased risk to public safety; age and physical ability, agility, or decline; or age and risk of personal injury or trauma (*Campbell* v. *Connelie*, 1982; *Hahn* v. *City of Buffalo*, 1985; *Johnson* v. *Mayor and City Council of Baltimore*, 1985; *Western Airlines* v. *Criswell*, 1985; *EEOC* v. *City of East Providence*, 1986; *EEOC* v. *Commonwealth of Pennsylvania*, 1986; *EEOC* v. *State of New Jersey*, 1986). In doing so, the employer must demonstrate that the age cutoff is reasonably necessary and that a failure to set the age cutoff will lead to an increased risk to the public (*Hodgson* v. *Greyhound Lines*, 1984; *Usery* v. *Tamiami Trail Tours*, 1976). The employer must also demonstrate that age is an effective proxy for job-related knowledge, skills, and abilities (*Western Airlines* v. *Criswell*, 1985).

Mandatory retirement has been involved in a large number of BFOQ cases (Snyder and Barrett, 1988). As noted earlier in the chapter, pilots and copilots are not allowed to fly commercially after age sixty, according to current Federal Aviation Administration (FAA) regulations. Most commercial airlines allow their pilots and copilots to continue beyond age sixty in the role of flight engineer. This is referred to as downbidding, and this process has lead to a number of significant court cases (*Stone* v. *Western Airlines*, 1982; *Transworld Airlines* v. *Thurston*, 1985; *Western Airlines* v. *Criswell*, 1985).

Reasonable Factors Other Than Age and Good Cause.

In the RFOA defense the employer argues that a valid job requirement led to the human resource decision. Thus it might be argued that it was the applicant's lack of adequate physical agility that led to the employer's failure to hire that older applicant for a police officer position. The RFOA is applied on an individual basis even if it affects a group of members of a protected class. In this situation the defendant need provide only a legitimate, nondiscriminatory reason for the decision-making outcome. The plaintiff would reply by asserting that the reason was a pretext for discriminatory intent.

The good cause defense is very similar to the RFOA defense, except it seems to be specifically intended for cases of layoffs and discipline. This does bring in a number of human resource issues, such as the role of performance, productivity, education, and experience in such decisions. Due to the importance of human resource issues to this type of case, an expert such as an industrial psychologist can play a critical role in framing the issues and evaluating the adequacy of the procedures or tests used in reaching a personnel decision.

Bona fide Seniority Systems and Employee Benefit Plans

A seniority system may be qualified by such factors as merit, capacity, or ability, but to qualify as a *bona fide seniority system*, it must use length of service as the primary criterion for the equitable allocation of available opportunities or prerogatives among workers. Because seniority systems should not only distinguish between employees on the basis of their length of service but give greater rights to those with longer service, the adoption of a purported seniority system that gives those with longer service fewer rights and results in discharge or less favored treatment depending on the situation may be a subterfuge to evade the purposes of the ADEA (Edelman & Siegler, 1978).

The benefits area is one of the more complex areas of the law and one that is currently evolving to take into account shifts in health care policy and economics (EEOC, 2000; *Erie County Retirees Ass'n. v. County of Erie,* 2000). Further, although there have been a number of cases under the ADEA involving benefits, some of the legal issues related to the cost of benefits and employees' waivers of rights in exchange for benefits were changed in 1990 when Congress passed the Older Workers Benefit Protection Act (OWBPA). The EEOC has recently issued a new rule providing guidance on this issue. The ruling creates a narrow exemption from the prohibitions of the ADEA for changing health benefits provided to retirees once they become eligible for Medicare or comparable State programs (ADEA, 2004; EEOC, 2004b).

The Role of the Expert

In this section we consider the role of the expert. The expert in an age discrimination case could represent any of a number of disciplines, such as economics, statistics, human resources, or sociology, or an area of psychology, such as social psychology, gerontological psychology, cognitive aging psychology, or industrial psychology. However, regardless of his or her field, an expert involved in an age discrimination case should be familiar with the unique research methods often required in studies of older workers. This would include familiarity with life-span developmental and gerontological methodologies such as cross-sectional, longitudinal, and time lag approaches and sequential approaches (Baltes, 1968; Schaie, 1965).

In addition, in recent years it has become more common to challenge either experts or their testimony under either *Daubert* (*Daubert* v. *Merrell Dow Pharmaceuticals,* 1993) or *Frye* (*Frye* v. *United States,* 1923) standards (see Chapter Six in this volume). Thus experts need to be prepared to show (1) that they are relying on science or technology and (2) that the results of that science or technology are relevant to the case. They should also be prepared for personal challenges on the limits of their expertise. One of the best ways to demonstrate expertise is to have had direct involvement in research or practices relevant to the case. In addition, as discussed by Snyder and Barrett (1988), the courts look at the adequacy of the data presented by the expert and consider issues such as sample sizes and the accuracy of the data analysis (*Fink* v. *Western Electric,* 1983; *Miller* v. *General Electric,* 1983; *Parker* v. *Federal National Mortgage Ass'n.,* 1984). Experts in ADEA cases, or in cases held under a state law, may have the added burden of explaining their data effectively to a jury. This brings into play skills beyond mere technical or statistical expertise.

An expert may be retained by either the plaintiff, usually an older worker claiming discrimination, or the defendant, usually an employer. Regardless, there seem to be three main types of testimony that might be offered by the expert, especially where that expert is a psychologist (our view of the expert's role is obviously shaped by our focus on industrial and gerontological psychology): (1) social psychological evidence, (2) evidence on psychological changes or physical changes, or both, and (3) statistical evidence.

Social Psychological Evidence

Given the unique emphasis of the ADEA on the role of stereotypes and beliefs about older workers, social psychological evidence would appear to be a particularly appropriate area of testimony (Gutman, 2000; *Hazen* v. *Biggins,* 1993). Many legal theorists (Gutman, 2000; *Hazen* v. *Biggens,* 1993) today argue that it was the intent of Congress, and now of the courts, that the ADEA be a tool for eliminating discrimination based on false beliefs or stereotypes of older workers.

In this regard an expert could offer testimony on either the prevalence of negative and damaging stereotypes of older workers or, conversely, on the possibility of positive stereotypes regarding older workers. In either case there is a substantial body of research on age stereotypes and their effects on older workers. Of course it is not sufficient to just posit the existence of such stereotypes. The expert must also show their relevance to the case, and this is often accomplished through a process referred to as a *social framework analysis* (Fiske & Borgida, 2000). (For a critical treatment of this approach, see David Copus's section of Chapter Fourteen in this volume.) In this analysis the expert will usually review relevant data, documents, and business records, along with the professional literature. In addition the expert will take into consideration technical and professional standards associated with the human resource practice in question in the case. The expert will then come to conclusions concerning whether discrimination did or did not occur. This decision will be based on the review and on whether there is evidence that the decision was based on stereotypes and whether the human resource practices employed provided adequate safeguards against the expression of such stereotypes.

An interesting question in ADEA cases is whether the use of stereotypes can be automatic. In Title VII cases the argument that the use of stereotypes was automatic can lead to an inference that this use was not illegal because it was not intentional. Without getting into a debate over this issue in Title VII situations, it would seem that there would be a difference under the ADEA, in that the intent is to eliminate employment decisions based on age stereotypes. We do not know whether this legal question has been considered by any courts.

Evidence of Physical or Psychological Changes

An expert could be called on by the defendant to present data or evidence of age-related changes that indicate that an individual cannot perform the job in an effective manner given assumed biological and psychological changes. The plaintiff could then counter with an expert who would argue the relevance of the defendant's expert's testimony, questioning the appropriateness of the research sample the testimony is based on to current populations. Oftentimes the data used to justify treating capacity as a function of age are derived from long-term longitudinal studies. Even though these studies use an effective research design, this design may also mean the data are thirty to forty years old. Such data may not accurately reflect the current level of functioning of today's older adult. The plaintiff's expert could also argue that the defendant's expert had placed inappropriate emphasis on mean differences without taking into account individual differences. The experts could also debate the potential presence of confounds related to performance, which can influence assessments and the adequacy of any measures used. Another area of challenge is the adequacy of the job analysis and whether age-related changes have any real meaning in performing a job.

It is also within this area that human factors and industrial gerontological psychology experts might be called on to testify and where the ADEA and the ADA might intersect. These experts could determine whether the workplace could be redesigned in order to improve older worker performance (Sterns, Sterns, & Hollis, 1996).

Statistical Evidence

One of the main roles of an expert in a Title VII case is and has been the presentation, interpretation, and explanation of statistical evidence. Snyder and Barrett (1988) found this was especially true in mass termination or layoff cases where a disparate impact argument was made. However, the statistical evidence remains critical and relevant even when disparate impact approaches are not allowed (see Chapters Two and Five in this volume). Adverse impact information can still be used and is used in many disparate treatment cases to support other arguments and to build a case based on circumstantial evidence.

The computation of statistical evidence in an ADEA case is very similar to that encountered in a Title VII case. This is especially true when age is dichotomized and treated as older versus younger. In this case older becomes the minority group and younger the majority group, and the adverse impact analysis is exactly the same as that encountered in sex or race discrimination cases. Thus one may conduct z tests looking for statistically significant differences indicating the presence of adverse impact (*Hazelwood School District* v. *U.S.*, 1977). Or one may create a crosstabs or contingency table to show a correlation between age and the decision-making process.

One difference between age and other minority statuses is that age can also be treated as a continuous variable. This allows the use of t tests to demonstrate significant mean differences in the age of those laid off versus the age of those retained or the age of those hired versus the age of those rejected. Another method is to calculate the average age of those in the workforce both before and then after some personnel action. When analyzing age, it is also possible to calculate correlations between age and other variables, such as test scores or salary.

Damages and Other Issues

As with Title VII cases, after-acquired evidence (that is, evidence of previous wrongdoing that was not known at the time of the original personnel action but that suggests the plaintiff would have been fired for some other reason anyway) cannot be used to escape liability for discrimination based on age. However, it may limit the amount and type of damages (*McKennon* v. *Nashville Banner*, 1995).

In *Julian* v. *City of Houston, Texas, et al.* (2002), the Fifth Circuit Court of Appeals ruled in an ADEA case that a firefighter, a candidate for promotion, did not need a notice of right to sue from the EEOC and that the damages could include front pay.

Major Human Resource Issues

Previously, we listed various human resource actions covered by the ADEA. Although the implications of the ADEA should be considered in any HR decision, in this section we have decided to concentrate our review on those HR areas where most of the litigation activity has taken place. Snyder and Barrett's (1988) content analysis led them to develop a framework with eight personnel action areas: reduction in workforce, termination, mandatory retirement, selection, promotion, constructive discharge, benefits, and demotion. We have adopted their framework with some changes and combinations. Our six areas are reduction in force (including arguments based on cost), performance management, changes in employment status (including termination, discharge, and demotion), selection (including promotion), mandatory retirement, and benefits.

Reductions in Force

Reductions in force are a common source of ADEA court cases (Snyder and Barrett, 1988). They also lead to cases, discussed later, that address actions involving termination, demotion, mandatory retirement, and performance management. In cases where one firm takes over another firm, they may involve selection decisions. Although they do then overlap with other types of human resource activity, reductions in force usually involve an explicit economic argument. That is, the employer usually argues a large-scale reduction in force was required due to economic considerations. As a result of the business environment or changes in technology, the employer argues that a reduction in force was a business necessity. As a result of this business necessity, the employer argues, it was forced to lay off or reclassify incumbents in order to reduce the size of the workforce. Therefore the employer makes a two-part argument. First, economic factors forced a reduction in the size of the workforce. Second, those incumbents affected by the reduction were chosen based on some factor other than age.

According to the review by Snyder and Barrett (1988), claims of business necessity leading to reductions in force have been rarely challenged by the courts (*Ackerman* v. *Diamond Shamrock*, 1982; *Parcinski* v. *Outlet Co.*, 1982). However, the plaintiff may counter by arguing that the reduction in force was simply a cost-cutting move designed to eliminate older and more expensive incumbents (*Robb* v. *Chemetron*, 1978). In order to demonstrate this argument the plaintiff may argue that those individuals eliminated were actually replaced by younger workers, thereby questioning the reduction-in-force argument (*Fugate* v. *Allied*, 1984).

Regardless of the justified need for the reduction in force, the associated personnel actions must be made based on factors other than age. In the next section we will take up the situation of decisions made based on performance appraisals. Decisions can also be made based on seniority or costs. In general, making decisions based on seniority not only is looked on favorably by the courts but should also benefit older workers.

A recent noteworthy case was *Cerutti v. BASF Corporation* (2003). This case involved a reduction in force. The company used assessments of competencies developed by a national firm. The Seventh Circuit Court of Appeals affirmed the lower court's decision that the ADEA was not enacted to immunize older workers from being terminated for legitimate reasons. The seventh circuit also ruled that a company may change the core qualifications for a position so long as that change is made in a nondiscriminatory fashion. This latter finding is important because it ties into an argument often made by organizations that such decisions are made for the purpose of improving the workforce.

Performance Management

Legal defenses and arguments in both RFOA cases and good cause cases often come down to the adequacy or perceived adequacy of an older employee's job performance. The defendant will argue that the older individual was laid off not because of his or her age but because of either poor performance or declining performance as revealed through formal or informal performance appraisals. The plaintiff will argue that his or her performance was acceptable or had not declined and that the performance arguments were a cover for age discrimination. These arguments usually occur in reduction-in-force cases or termination cases but may arise in selection cases as well, especially those involving promotion or access to training. Although performance may be documented through formal performance appraisals, information may come from other sources as well, including objective data such as sales performance (*Reeves v. Sanderson Plumbing Products*, 2000). The more common argument by the employer is not that performance declined but that the skill mix that might have been salient some years ago was no longer salient or that downsizing required outstanding performers to be retained, not simply average or acceptable performers.

As in Title VII cases, performance appraisals will be subject to appropriate scrutiny (Barrett & Kernan, 1987). Issues to be considered include appraisal reliability, validity, and construction and rater training. When properly constructed, performance appraisals can be found to be a valid source of performance data for use in human resource decision making (*Allison v. Western Union Telegraph*,

1982; *EEOC* v. *Transworld Airlines,* 1982; *Grubb* v. *Foote Memorial Hospital,* 1984; *Woodfield* v. *Heckler,* 1984). In addition to considering appraisals' psychometric properties (Sterns & Alexander, 1988), the courts are more likely to look favorably on decisions based on performance appraisals when the employee has had previous warning concerning poor performance (*Harpring* v. *Continental Oil,* 1980; *Reich* v. *New York Hospital,* 1981) and has had the opportunity to correct that poor performance (Woodfield v. *Heckler,* 1984). (See Chapter Twelve in this volume).

The A-B-C grading method of performance appraisal has been the subject of a great deal of controversy. In this method, also called the *forced ranking method,* employees are graded on a curve, which requires a certain number of employees to receive each rating. Cynics refer to this as the *rank and yank* method (Landy & Conte, 2004). An employee who receives C's two years in a row faces termination. The problem is that this method has the potential to result in both disparate impact on older workers and disparate treatment of older workers. This policy as implemented at the Ford Motor Company forced a 10 percent A, 80 percent B, and 10 percent C distribution. Anger over this policy led to lawsuits over gender and race discrimination and reverse discrimination. In 2002, this resulted in a $10.6 million settlement between Ford and a group of its older managers and the elimination of the forced distribution system (AARP, 2001b, 2002; Landy & Conte, 2004). Similar problems with forced ranking have resulted in court cases involving Goodyear (Associated Press, 2002; Lowery, 2003).

Performance appraisal data will be met with more doubt when there is a sudden shift in the performance ratings. This is especially true when the sudden shift occurs right before or in conjunction with layoff or reorganization decisions (*Reeves* v. *Sanderson Plumbing Products,* 2000). It is especially important to review employment records to be sure that they support the layoff or reorganization decision. (It is common to have rating methods developed specifically for the layoff decisions so there are no "former" ratings).

A recent review of court cases by Lee, Havighurst, and Rassel (2004) looked at decisions involving performance cases at the appellate level. They found that a large percentage of performance cases were decided in favor of the defendant. An intriguing aspect of their argument is that they categorized decisions based on whether the emphasis was on the fairness of the outcome or the validity of the process. In age cases, there appeared to be an approximately equal emphasis on the validity of the process and the fairness of the outcome.

Termination and Demotion

Termination cases have often involved the specific replacement of an older worker with a younger worker. In many cases discriminatory statements have been made by company officials (*Blackwell* v. *Sun Electric*, 1983; *Hagelthorn* v. *Kennecott*, 1983; *Koyen* v. *Consolidated Edison*, 1983; *Wildman* v. *Lerner Stores*, 1985; *Wilhelm* v. *Blue Bell*, 1985).

The company's defense may be performance or cost based, as with reduction in force cases. In addition, as pointed out by Snyder and Barrett (1988), a number of termination cases involve some type of violation of a company policy by the older worker (*Bohrer* v. *Hanes*, 1983; *Houser* v. *Sears, Roebuck*, 1980; *Jackson* v. *Sears, Roebuck*, 1981; *Needham* v. *Beecham*, 1981).

Constructive discharge cases are similar to termination cases except that the worker argues that he or she has been forced to resign in order to avoid termination. In some cases the employer may admit this was true but claim it was due to poor performance.

These cases often ultimately revolve around the employee's performance in relation to that of other workers or to some performance standard enforced by management. For example, in *Woodfield* v. *Heckler* (1984) the plaintiff was demoted because his performance fell below the company's 86 to 88 percent accuracy requirements. The evidence presented in demotion cases may address such things as performance evaluation, inability to carry out responsibilities, or attitude problems.

Mandatory Retirement

The ADEA has basically eliminated the idea of mandatory retirement except in special circumstances. When mandatory retirement does arise as an issue, it usually is connected to a reduction in force or a kind of forced retirement. That is, as an alternative to a layoff, the older worker is offered the possibility of retirement. However, forcing an employee into retirement in this situation violates the ADEA (*EEOC* v. *City of Altoona*, 1983; *Wilson* v. *Sealtest Foods*, 1974). The OWBPA makes it illegal for employers conducting layoffs to pressure older workers to waive their rights to sue for age discrimination in exchange for additional benefits such as severance or early retirement.

Selection and Promotion

Pure selection cases are rare under the ADEA (Gutman, 2000; Snyder & Barrett, 1988). Most of those that do occur involve either promotion or failure to rehire after a reduction in force or a layoff. This type of case often follows the classic disparate treatment argument. That is, the older worker, who is qualified in that he or she previously performed the job, is not rehired and a younger worker is hired in the older worker's place. In some cases the individual may not be rehired because of his or her cost or experience (*Geller* v. *Markham*, 1980; *Keval* v. *Block*, 1981; *Leftwich* v. *Harris-Stowe State College*, 1983; *Bunch* v. *U.S.*, 1982; *Marshall* v. *Board of Education of Salt Lake City*, 1977). If the employee can show that experience or time to retirement was used as a proxy for age, the employer may be charged with discrimination.

In a promotion case the older worker argues that he or she was qualified for a higher-level job but was passed up for promotion in favor of a younger worker. For example, in *Dorsey Jr. et al.* v. *Pinnacle Automation* (2002), the plaintiffs argued that they had been consistently passed over for promotions that went to younger workers; the promotions also involved a slight pay raise. The plaintiffs did establish their prima facie case; however, they failed to show (1) that the reasons offered by the company for the promotions were a pretext and (2) that the company intended to discriminate. Although it was not clear that the older workers were better qualified for the jobs, they did not offer any proof that the reasons offered by the company for the promotions, such as education, were a pretext for discrimination. It did not matter to the court whether the reasons for the promotions were valid or fair or whether the decisions were correct, only that the reasons offered were true. Of course we would urge companies to use valid tools in making promotion decisions. However, making inappropriate decisions does not constitute discrimination (*Dorsey Jr. et al. v. Pinnacle Automation*, 2002).

Benefits

Although there were a number of early cases involving benefits, pensions, and severance pay, the impact of some of these decisions has been altered in part by various amendments to the ADEA, including the Older Workers Benefit Protection Act. The OWBPA amended the ADEA by enumerating a number of conditions that must be met before an older employee can waive his or her protections under the ADEA. Benefits are also protected by the Employee Retirement Income and Security Act (ERISA, 1974). Under the OWBPA, older workers must receive benefits equal to those provided to younger workers unless the employer can prove that the cost of providing an equal benefit is greater for an older worker than for a younger worker. During a reduction in force an employer cannot offer benefits as a way of forcing older workers to waive their rights. The implications of the OWBPA still appear to be open to various interpretations, and the EEOC (1998) has attempted to issue clarifying regulations. In *Oubre v. Entergy Operations* (1998) the Supreme Court held that a waiver agreement must comply with all OWBPA requirements.

In a recent major settlement between the EEOC and the California Public Employees' Retirement System (*Arnett and EEOC v. California Public Employees' Retirement System*, 2003), more than 1,700 retired state and local public safety officers were to receive benefits of approximately $250 million. The settlement related to the disability practices of the retirement system, in which disability benefits had been reduced based on the age of the person at hire.

Another complex area is the coordination of benefits and Social Security. The EEOC (2000) had instructed employers that they could alter health benefits to retired employees in light of their receipt of Medicare or other government benefits. However, in *Erie County Retirees Ass'n. v. County of Erie* (2000), the court ruled that the coordination of benefits with Medicare violated the ADEA.

Prevention Issues

In this section, techniques for identifying and correcting problems involving employment decisions related to age are discussed. We are not lawyers and do not pretend to give legal advice, nor is that our intent in this section. A lawyer might give very different advice on preventing problems, and we will not try to speculate on those methods. Rather, our approach is based on the premise that it is better to (1) increase the diversity of the workforce and (2) improve the treatment of older workers through the identification and correction of possible problems before they lead to expensive litigation. Thus organizations should perform audits of their human resource practices and should take a proactive approach in terms of being aware of applicable federal, state, and local civil rights legislation. This should include the identification of HR practices that may lead to adverse impact or bias against older workers (Arthur & Doverspike, in press; Robinson, Franklin, & Wayland, 2002), even if adverse impact is not technically a violation of the ADEA. It should also include proactive efforts aimed at increasing the age-based diversity of the workforce.

Performance Appraisal

Organizations should regularly audit their performance management systems to ensure that they are fair to all workers. This includes making sure that performance appraisal scales are not biased against older workers and that evaluations are conducted in a fair manner. In addition organizations should make sure they follow their own internal procedures or policies as spelled out in personnel manuals or other company memorandums. This includes establishing policies for the review and appeal of personnel decisions. It is also important that organizations document both the procedures used and the steps taken in reaching decisions. Supervisory personnel should be trained in making ratings in a nondiscriminatory fashion. Although the literature has indicated that age may have an effect on performance evaluations, age effects become much smaller when ratings are based on observable behaviors and are made using behaviorally based performance appraisal forms and when training is provided to raters (Latham & Wexley, 1994; Sterns & Alexander, 1987). In summarizing this area Landy and Conte (2004) state that when scales are well developed, performance evaluations do not systematically discriminate against protected subgroups (age, gender, race, disability).

Gutman (2000, based on Hartman and Schnadig, 1990) offers suggestions for conducting a reduction in force, including documenting the layoff process, documenting the consideration of alternatives, and using length of service to determine layoffs. Gutman also offers the suggestion that layoff decisions be made by individuals other than the individual department heads. We would add that when companies are performing large-scale reductions in force, it is essential for them to develop a rational approach to the rank ordering of employees according to performance-related factors.

Training and Career Development

Organizations may be less willing to train older workers in that they may believe training for older workers is more expensive, older workers are harder to train, and it is less likely they will see a return on their investment. As a result, older workers face a number of obstacles in pursuing full access to training programs (Sterns & Doverspike, 1989; Sterns, Junkins, & Bayer, 2001). These obstacles often relate to stereotypes concerning the inability of older workers to learn or the likely relative tenures of older and younger workers. Organizations should audit their training programs to make sure older employees have equal access to training and development programs and that such programs are designed so as to be appropriate for the older worker (Sterns & Doverspike, 1988, 1989; Sterns et al., 2001).

Recruitment and Selection

Not only should organizations be more proactive in recruiting older workers, we predict that in the future they will have to be (Cober, Brown, Blumenthal, Doverspike, & Levy, 2000; Doverspike, 2004; Doverspike, Taylor, Shultz, & McKay, 2000; Taylor, Shultz, & Doverspike, in press). In order to recruit older workers, organizations need to analyze and adapt their current recruiting practices. The job search behavior of older workers is often shaped by their health, finances, and education. The older worker is likely to be attracted by work options and the availability of retirement programs (Sterns & Miklos, 1995). Thus organizations should (1) emphasize health and retirement benefits, (2) monitor the content and placement of advertising, and (3) emphasize social aspects of the job.

The selection process should be audited to ensure that adverse impact does not occur against older workers. If adverse impact does occur, then the tests should be demonstrated to be valid predictors of performance. It may also be possible to modify tests and selection tests by considering reducing the importance of speed in testing (Sterns, Sterns, & Hollis, 1996), using large fonts, and ensuring adequate lighting (Sterns et al., 1996). One particular problem area may be the interview. As with performance appraisal, in designing an interview to select and attract older adults make sure that questions and rating scales are not oriented toward younger workers or traits associated with youth (Sterns & Alexander, 1988). Organizations should also engage in training and development efforts with interviewers in order to address any negative beliefs about the capabilities of older workers and in order to encourage positive attitudes toward older adults (*Mathis v. Phillips Chevrolet,* 2001).

Benefits and Compensation

Industrial and organizational psychologists usually have minimal influence over benefits decisions. However, this is clearly one of the most controversial and litigated areas of age discrimination law. Thus it seems critical to develop an understanding of the benefits process and to audit benefits in order to ensure they comply with the ADEA.

Pay discrimination is difficult to study in that older workers will usually have higher pay levels than younger workers. In fact it is those higher pay levels that often lead to the argument that older workers are more costly and thus should be eliminated. However, a compensation factor that can negatively affect older workers is salary compression. Salary compression occurs when entry-level salaries rise quickly (Griffeth & Hom, 2001), so that newer employees are hired at salary levels equal to or higher than those earned by experienced, older employees. It will be interesting to see if salary compression emerges as an area for future pay litigation involving age.

Affirmative Action

Affirmative action is a controversial legal and applied topic (Dover-spike, Taylor, & Arthur, 2000), and we do not have space to do the topic justice here. Both affirmative action and diversity initiatives attempt to increase the number of underrepresented group members in the workforce. The issue of affirmative action based on age is debated by Sterns and Sterns (1997a, 1997b) and Longman (1997a, 1997b). Longman argues that older workers do not fit the traditional definition of discrimination, have suffered no history of discrimination, and receive entitlements that younger workers do not receive. On this reasoning Longman concludes that affirmative action is not an appropriate approach for use with older workers. Sterns and Sterns, on the other hand, argue that as with other minority groups, older workers are victims of discrimination and therefore should be entitled to benefit from affirmative action. A major position paper on affirmative action issues by Kravitz et al. (1997) is available from the Society for Industrial and Organizational Psychology. One can see parallels between the affirmative action debate and the basic debate over the applicability of disparate impact arguments. Regardless of the legal foundation, we believe that diversity initiatives should include older workers in order to increase perceptions of justice and provide a working environment that is proactive for those of all ages.

Future Issues

In this section we summarize what appear to be the key legal issues for the future. We then discuss areas where research may inform the debate about age issues. Finally, we speculate on what role changes in the demographics of the workforce and in technology will play in the debate over age discrimination.

Future Court Cases

Prediction is always difficult. This is especially true in the legal arena, where an amendment to current laws or a Supreme Court decision can rapidly and totally reshape the debate. However, given the present laws, there appear to be several key issues still requiring further clarification. In our opinion, these include the following:

The feasibility of disparate impact approaches in ADEA cases. Despite the recent Supreme Court rulings, this appears to remain an issue. As mentioned earlier, there was hope that the Supreme Court would reach a relevant decision in *Adams* v. *Florida Power* (2002). However, this case was decertified, further clouding the issue. The Civil Rights Act of 2004, introduced by Senator Ted Kennedy and Representative John Lewis, would specifically allow disparate impact cases under the ADEA. The Supreme Court has now agreed to hear another case, *Smith* v. *Jackson* (2003), that involves the issue of disparate impact. However, it is different from many other cases in that it involves a pay system. This pay system resulted in greater increases for younger workers than for older workers. Thus the issues in this case are likely to be quite different from those addressed in a reduction-in-force case. One can see the Supreme Court allowing a disparate impact approach in this case but arguing that it was allowed because it involved a single neutral device. This could then be seen as still precluding the use of a disparate impact approach in reduction-in-force cases, most of which involve employment decisions made on an individual basis.

The use of cost and other factors closely associated with age as a defense. Recent court cases suggest that it is easier to defend an ADEA case with a cost argument than with a performance argument. However, the close linking of cost and age in many cases would appear to make this an area in need of further clarification.

The relationship between ADEA and ADA. The major challenge here would appear to be in areas related to the return to work and the appropriate accommodation of the older worker. This area is further complicated when there are changes in capability due to illness. From the standpoint of the human resource practitioner, there is a need to give the individual the full opportunity to return to his or her previous position or, if that is not possible, to provide reasonable alternatives, including exploring the option of placing the individual on disability.

The immunity of states to ADEA lawsuits brought by state employees. This is a controversial area and a bill, S. 928, has already been introduced in Congress that would require states to waive their immunity from ADEA suits.

Research Needed

Research on Stereotypes and Beliefs About Age

There have been a large number of studies of stereotypes and beliefs about age and their impact on human resource decisions (Rosen & Jerdee, 1985). However, many of these studies have been conducted in highly artificial situations (See Copus's section of Chapter Fourteen in this volume). This has led to criticisms that current knowledge in this area is based on paper people. More research on the influence of age on human resource decisions needs to be conducted in situations involving higher fidelity to reality.

Another problem with any measure of age stereotypes is demand effects. Recent years have seen the emergence of implicit measures of stereotyping, including age stereotyping. Interesting research programs could be developed around implicit measures of stereotypes, including investigations of the effects of implicit stereotypes on human resource decision making. Another topic related to age stereotyping is the effect of generational differences. As baby boomers age, the question can be asked whether their opinions of the aging process will be different from those of previous generations (Blumental, Cober, & Doverspike, 2000; Zemke, Raines, & Filipczak, 2000).

Research on What Constitutes a Meaningful Age Difference

Recent court cases suggest that age discrimination can occur within the protected class of older workers when the age difference is large enough. This leads to what could be an interesting research area: defining the size of the age difference that makes a practical difference. It would seem that what constitutes a large age difference may vary as a function of the type of job and the age typing of that job. On one hand, for example, among college faculty members the difference between a forty-year-old and a sixty-year-old may be seen as relatively small. On the other hand, among firefighters the difference between a forty-year-old and a sixty-year-old may be perceived as much greater. It would seem that psychologists could contribute to the understanding of what constitutes a meaningful age difference and how that number varies as a function of a job's age type.

Change

The demographics of the workforce have changed drastically since the 1960s. Today we often find ourselves called on to write articles on the topic of recruiting and retaining older workers. There is a demand from both public sector agencies and private companies for psychological research and human resource practices dealing with methods for training and retraining older workers, and also for techniques for attracting older applicants or convincing them to stay in the workforce (Cober et al., 2000; Doverspike, 2004; Doverspike, Taylor, Shultz, & McKay, 2000; Taylor et al., in press). Much of this is driven by changing demographics. Around 2008, large numbers of older workers will be deciding whether to retire or to remain in the workforce. Unless there is some dramatic shift elsewhere in the demographics of the workforce, organizations will need to engage in human resource planning that increases their recruitment, selection, and retention of older workers.

At the same time, technology is changing the way employees are recruited and selected for jobs and also the way in which companies are organized. On the one hand, in general, older workers appear to have adapted well to increased reliance on computer and Web-based testing. Still, as we discussed earlier, this would appear to be an area where further research is needed. On the other hand, many of the "hot" employment areas, such as information technology or IT jobs, often seemed to be stereotyped as younger jobs. This means that older workers may be especially likely to be discriminated against in these areas. The congressional debates surrounding the ADEA suggest that one reason for its passage was a fear that technology was having a negative impact on older workers and served to displace older workers (Proceedings and Debates of the 88th Congress, 1964). It would be interesting to see research on the effects of recent technology changes on the employment of older workers and on the appropriateness of older workers for newly created technology jobs.

Conclusions

In writing this chapter we have attempted to take a balanced view, presenting the arguments from the points of view of the plaintiff and the defendant as well as from the point of view of the court system. However, this nation now finds itself at a point in history where there are new challenges presented by people wanting to work longer either from desire or from need. The ADEA was a uniquely U.S. piece of legislation whose tenets are now being adopted slowly throughout the world. The intention of ADEA was that every individual should be able to work as long as he or she was capable and able. Age should not be the critical factor in the decision whether an individual should be entitled to the psychological and financial well-being offered by continuing employment. Industrial psychologists have an obligation to promote the well-being of all individuals in their roles as workers. Therefore organizations should be encouraged to take proactive steps to promote a diversified workplace where older workers are valued through opportunities for continued training and growth and are given equitable treatment in all personnel decisions, including decisions about leaving the workforce when they can no longer perform in a satisfactory manner.

References

Books, Articles, and Government Documents

AARP. (2001a). *Age discrimination in employment: Survey of state laws—2000* [Brochure]. Washington, DC: Author.

AARP. (2001b). Litigation: Siegel et al. v. Ford Motor Company. Retrieved March 2004 from http://www.aarp.org/research/litigation/show_case?case_id=525

AARP. (2002). Court OKs $10.6 million settlement of Ford age bias case. Retrieved March 2004 from http://www.aarp.org/research/press/presscurrentnews/cn-2002/Articles/a2003–06–02-nr031402ford.html

Age Discrimination in Employment Act of 1967, 29 U.S.C. § 621 *et seq.* (2004).

Age Discrimination in Employment Act; Retiree Health Benefits, 68 Fed. Reg. 134 (July 14, 2003). Retrieved January 2004 from http://edocket.access.gpo.gov/2003/03–17738.htm

Americans with Disabilities Act, 42 U.S.C. § 12101 *et seq.* (1990).

Arthur, W. Jr., & Doverspike, D. (in press). Achieving diversity and reducing discrimination in the workplace through human resource management practices: Implications of research and theory for staffing, training, and rewarding performance. In R. L. Dipboye & A. Colella (Eds.), *Discrimination at work: The psychological and organizational bases.* San Francisco: Jossey-Bass. Associated Press. (2002). Goodyear workers file age discrimination lawsuit. Retrieved March 2004 from http://www.freep.com/news/latestnews/pm10936_20020912.htm

Avolio, B. J., Barrett, G. V., & Sterns, H. L. (1984). Alternatives to age for assessing occupational performance capacity. *Experimental Aging Research, 10*(2), 101–105.

Baltes, P. B. (1968). Longitudinal and cross-sectional sequences in the study of age and generation effects. *Human Development, 11*(3), 145–171.

Barrett, G. V., & Kernan, M. C. (1987). Performance appraisal and terminations: A review of court decisions since *Brito* v. *Zia* with implications for personnel practices. *Personnel Psychology, 40*(3), 489–503.

Blumental, A. J., Cober, R. T., & Doverspike, D. (2000). Appreciating differences in work ethic: Comparing techno-savvy Generation Xers to baby boomers. *Journal of e.Commerce and Psychology, 1,* 60–77.

Civil Rights Act of 1964, Title VII, 42 U.S.C. § 2000e *et seq.* (2003).

Cober, R. T., Brown, D. J., Blumenthal, A., Doverspike, D., & Levy, P. L. (2000). The quest for the qualified job surfer: It's time the public sector catches the wave. *Public Personnel Management, 29,* 479–496.

Davies, D. R., & Sparrow, P. R. (1985). Age and work behaviour. In N. Charness (Ed.), *Aging and human performance* (pp. 293–326). Chichester: Wiley.

Doering, N., Rhodes, S. R., & Schuster, N. (1983). *The aging worker.* Thousand Oaks, CA: Sage.

Doverspike, D. (2004, February). Recruiting, selecting and retaining the older worker. *International Public Management Association for Human Resources News,* pp. 14–15.

Doverspike, D., & Hollis, L. (1995, May). Diversity issues in testing: Assessing older adults. *IPMA Assessment Council News, 5,* 10–12.

Doverspike, D., Taylor, M. A., & Arthur, W., Jr. (2000). *Affirmative action: A psychological perspective.* Commack, NY: Nova Scientific.

Doverspike, D., Taylor, M. A., Shultz, K. S., & McKay, P. F. (2000). Responding to the challenge of a changing workforce: Recruiting nontraditional demographic groups. *Public Personnel Management, 29,* 445–460.

Edelman, C. D., & Siegler, I. C. (1978). *Federal age discrimination in employment law: Slowing down the gold watch.* Charlottesville, VA: Michie.

Employee Retirement Income and Security Act, 29 U.S.C. § 1001 *et seq.* (1974).

Equal Employment Opportunity Commission. (1998). Questions and answers: Final regulation on "tender back" and related issues concerning ADEA waivers. Retrieved March 2004 from http://www.eeoc.gov/policy/regs/tenderback-qanda.html

Equal Employment Opportunity Commission. (2000). The 2000s: Charting a Course for the 21st Century. Retrieved September 2003 from http://www.eeoc.gov/35th/2000s/.

Equal Employment Opportunity Commission. (2004a, March 8). EEOC issues fiscal year 2003 enforcement data. Retrieved March 2004 from http://eeoc.gov/press/3-8-04.html.

Equal Employment Opportunity Commission. (2004b, April 22). Equal Employment Opportunity Commission: 29 CFR Parts 1625 and 1627, RIN 3046-AA72, Age Discrimination in Employment Act; Retiree Health Benefits. Retrieved August 2004 from http://www.eeoc.gov/policy/regs/retiree_benefits/retiree_benefits.html.

Fairness and Individual Rights Necessary to Ensure a Stronger Society: Civil Rights Act of 2004, H.R. 3809, 108th Cong. (2004).

Fairness and Individual Rights Necessary to Ensure a Stronger Society: Civil Rights Act of 2004, S. 2088, 108th Cong. (2004).

Fiske, S. T., and Borgida, E. (2000). Social framework analysis as expert testimony in sexual harassment suits. In S. Estreicher (Ed.), *Sexual harassment in the workplace: New York University 51st annual conference on labor* (pp. 575–583). New York: NYU Press.

Griffeth, R. W., & Hom, P. N. (2001). *Retaining valued employees.* Thousand Oaks, CA: Sage.

Gutman, A. (2000). Recent Supreme Court ADA rulings: Mixed messages from the Court. *The Industrial-Organizational Psychologist, 35,* 75–81.

Gutman, A. (2002). *EEO law and personnel practices* (2nd ed.). Thousand Oaks, CA: Sage.

Hammond, P. B., & Morgan, H. P. (Eds.). (1991). *Ending mandatory retirement for tenured faculty: The consequences for higher education.* Washington, DC: National Academy Press.

Hartman, G. S., & Schnadig, R. H. (1990). *Personnel law handbook.* Winston-Salem, NC: University of Wake Forest Law School.

Henkle, J. (1997). The Age Discrimination in Employment Act: Disparate impact analysis and the availability of liquidated damages after Hazen Paper Co. v. Biggins [Electronic version]. *Syracuse Law Review, 47,* 1183. Retrieved March 2003 from http://lexis-nexis.com.

Hollis-Sawyer, L., & Doverspike, D. (2000). Reasonable accommodation in the workplace: Implications of the ADEA and ADA for older workers. *Ethics, Law, and Aging Review, 6,* 207–222.

Kravitz, D. A., Harrison, D. A., Turner, M. E., Levine, E. L., Chaves, W., Brannick, M. T., et al. (1997). Affirmative action: A review of psychological and behavioral research (Monograph). Bowling Green, OH: Society for Industrial and Organization Psychology.

Landy, F. J. (1992). *Alternatives to chronological age in determining standards of suitability for public safety jobs: Executive summary.* State College: Pennsylvania State University, Center for Applied Behavioral Sciences.

Landy, F., & Conte, J. (2004) *Work in the 21st century: An introduction to industrial and organization psychology.* New York: McGraw-Hill.

Latham, G. P., & Wexley, K. N. (1994). *Increasing productivity through performance appraisal* (2nd ed.). Reading, MA: Addison-Wesley.

Lee, J. A., Havighurst, L. C., & Rassel, G. (2004). Factors related to court references to performance appraisal fairness and validity. *Public Personnel Management, 33,* 61–77.

Levine, M. L. (1998). Age discrimination: The law and its underlying policy. In H. Dennis (Ed.), *Fourteen steps in managing an aging work force* (pp. 25–35). San Francisco: New Lexington Press.

Longman, P. (1997a). Should there be an affirmative action program for hiring older persons? No. In A. E. Scharloch & L. W. Kaye (Eds.), *Controversial issues in aging* (pp. 40–43). Needham Heights, MA: Allyn & Bacon.

Longman, P. (1997b). Should there be an affirmative action program for hiring older persons? Rejoinder to Professor Sterns and Mr. Sterns. In A. E. Scharloch & L. W. Kaye (Eds.), *Controversial issues in aging* (p. 39). Needham Heights, MA: Allyn & Bacon.

Lowery, M. (2003, October 16). Forcing the performance ranking issue. *Human Resource Management Executive.* Retrieved February 2003 from http://www.workindex.com/editorial/hre/hre0312-16.asp

McEvoy, G. W., & Cascio, W. F. (1989). Cumulative evidence of the relationship between employee age and job performance. *Journal of Applied Psychology, 74,* 11–17.

Meier, E. L., & Kerr, E. A. (1976). Capabilities of middle-aged and older workers. *Industrial Gerontology, 3,* 147–156.

Older Workers Benefit Protection Act, 29 U.S.C. § 623 *et seq.* (1990).

Proceedings and Debates of the 88th Congress, 110 Cong. Rec. 2597 (February 8, 1964).

Rhodes, S. R. (1983). Age-related differences in work attitudes and behavior: A review and conceptual analysis. *Psychological Bulletin, 93*(2), 328–367.

Robinson, R. K., Franklin, G. M., & Wayland, R. (2002). *The regulatory environment of human resource management.* New York: Harcourt.

Rosen, B., and Jerdee, T. H. (1985). *Older employees: New roles for valued resources.* Burr Ridge, IL: Irwin.

Schaie, K. W. (1965). A general model for the study of developmental change. *Psychological Bulletin, 64,* 92–107.

Snyder, C. J., & Barrett, G. V. (1988). The Age Discrimination and Employment Act: A review of court decisions. *Experimental Aging Research, 14,* 3–47.

Sterns, A. A., & Sterns, H. L. (1997a). Should there be an affirmative action program for hiring older persons? Rejoinder to Mr. Longman. In A. E. Scharloch & L. W. Kaye (Eds.), *Controversial issues in aging* (pp. 43–44). Needham Heights, MA: Allyn & Bacon.

Sterns, A. A., & Sterns, H. L. (1997b). Should there be an affirmative action program for hiring older persons? Yes. In A. E. Scharloch & L. W. Kaye (Eds.), *Controversial issues in aging* (pp. 35–39). Needham Heights, MA: Allyn & Bacon.

Sterns, A. A., Sterns, H. L., & Hollis, L. A. (1996). The productivity and functional limitations of older adult workers. In W. H. Crown (Ed.), *Handbook on employment and the elderly* (pp. 276–303). Westport, CT: Greenwood Press.

Sterns, H. L., & Alexander, R. A. (1987). Industrial gerontology. In G. Maddox (Ed.), *The encyclopedia of aging* (pp. 349–351). New York: Springer.

Sterns, H. L., & Alexander, R. A. (1988). Performance appraisal of the older worker. In H. Dennis (Ed.), *Fourteen steps in managing an aging work force* (pp. 97–112). San Francisco: New Lexington Press.

Sterns, H. L., & Doverspike, D. (1988). Training and developing the older worker: Implications for human resource management. In H. Dennis (Ed.), *Fourteen steps in managing an aging work force* (pp. 85–96). San Francisco: New Lexington Press.

Sterns, H. L., & Doverspike, D. (1989). Aging and the training and learning process in organizations. In I. Goldstein & R. Katzell (Eds.), *Training and development in work organizations* (pp. 299–332). San Francisco: Jossey-Bass.

Sterns, H. L., Junkins, M. P., & Bayer, J. (2001). Work and retirement. In B. R. Bonder & M. B. Wagner (Eds.), *Functional performance in older adults* (2nd ed., pp. 179–195). Philadelphia: Davis.

Sterns, H. L., & McDaniel, M. A. (1994). Job performance and the older worker. In S. E. Rix (Ed.), *Older workers: How do they measure up? An overview of age differences in employee costs and performances* (pp. 27–51). Washington, DC: Public Policy Institute, American Association of Retired Persons.

Sterns, H. L., & Miklos, S. M. (1995). The aging worker in a changing environment: Organizational and individual issues. *Journal of Vocational Behavior, 47,* 248–268.

Taylor, M. A., Shultz, K. S., & Doverspike, D. (in press). Recruiting and retaining talented older workers. In P. T. Beatty & R. Visser (Eds.), *Managing an aging workforce.* Melbourne, FL: Krieger.

Waldman, D. A., & Avolio, B. J. (1986). A meta-analysis of age differences in job performance. *Journal of Applied Psychology, 71*(1), 33–38.

Welford, A. T. (1977). Motor performance. In J. Birren & K. W. Schaie (Eds.), *Handbook of the psychology of aging* (pp. 450–496). New York: Van Nostrand Reinhold.

Zemke, R., Raines, C., & Filipczak, B. (2000). *Generations at work: Managing the clash of veterans, boomers, xers, and nexters in your workplace.* New York: American Management Association.

Cases

Ackerman v. Diamond Shamrock Corp., 670 F.2d 66 (6th Cir. 1982).

Adams v. Florida Power, 535 U.S. 228 (2002).

Allison v. Western Union Telegraph Co., 680 F.2d 1318 (11th Cir. 1982).

Arnett and EEOC v. California Public Employees' Retirement System, No. 95-03022 CRB (N.D. Cal. 2003).

Blackwell v. Sun Electric Corp., 696 F.2d 1176 (6th Cir. 1983).

Board of Trustees of the University of Alabama v. Patricia Garrett, 531 U.S. 356 (2001).

Bohrer v. Hanes Corp., 715 F.2d 213, 218 (5th Cir. 1983).

Bunch v. United States, 680 F.2d 1271 (9th Cir. 1982).

Campbell v. Connelie, 542 F. Supp. 275 (N.D. N.Y. 1982).

Cerutti v. BASF Corporation, 349 F.3d 1055 (7th Cir. 2003).

Daubert v. Merrell Dow Pharmaceuticals, 509 U.S. 579 (1993).

DeLoach v. Infinity Broadcasting, 164 F.3d 398 (7th Cir. 1999).

Dorsey Jr. et al. v. Pinnacle Automation Company, d/b/a Alvey, Inc., 278 F. 3d 830 (8th Cir. 2002).

Douglas v. Anderson, 656 F.2d 528 (9th Cir. 1981).

EEOC v. City of Altoona, Pennsylvania, 723 F.2d 4 (3rd Cir. 1983).

EEOC v. City of East Providence, 798 F.2d 524 (1st Cir. 1986).

EEOC v. City of Janesville, 630 F.2d 1254 (7th Cir. 1980).

EEOC v. City of Minneapolis, 537 F. Supp. 750, 756 (D. Minn. 1982).

EEOC v. City of St. Paul, 671 F.2d 1162 (8th Cir. 1982).

EEOC v. Commonwealth of Pennsylvania, 645 F. Supp. 1545 (M.D. Pa. 1986).

EEOC v. Missouri State Highway Patrol, 748 F.2d 447 (8th Cir. 1984).

EEOC v. State of New Jersey, 631 F. Supp. 1506 (D. N.J. 1986).

EEOC v. Trabucco, 791 F.2d 1 (1st Cir. 1986).

EEOC v. Transworld Airlines, Inc., 544 F. Supp. 1187 (S.D. N.Y. 1982).

EEOC v. University of Texas Health Science Center at San Antonio, 710 F.2d 1091 (5th Cir. 1983).

EEOC v. Wayne Community College, 723 F.2d 509 (6th Cir. 1983).

Erie County Retirees Ass'n. v. County of Erie, 220 F.3d 193 (3rd Cir. 2000).

Fink v. Western Electric Co., 32 EPD 33, 619 (4th Cir. 1983).

Frye v. United States, 293 F. 1013 (DC Cir. 1923).

Fugate v. Allied Corp., 582 F. Supp. 780 (N.D. Ill. 1984).

Geller v. Markham, 635 F.2d 1027 (2nd Cir. 1980).

General Dynamics Land Systems Inc. v. Dennis Cline et al., 124 S. Ct. 1236 (2004).

Golomb v. Prudential Insurance Co. of America, 688 F.2d 547 (7th Cir. 1982).

Gregory v. Ashcroft, 501 U.S. 452 (1991).

Grubb v. Foote Memorial Hospital, Inc., 741 F.2d 1486 (6th Cir. 1984).

Hagelthorn v. Kennecott, 710 F.2d 76 (2nd Cir. 1983).

Hahn v. City of Buffalo, 770 F.2d 12 (2nd Cir. 1985).

Harpring v. Continental Oil Co., 628 F.2d 406 (5th Cir. 1980).

Hazelwood School District v. United States, 433 U.S. 299 (1977).

Hazen v. Biggins, 507 U.S. 604 (1993).

Hodgson v. Greyhound Lines, Inc., 499 F.2d 859 (7th Cir. 1984).

Houser v. Sears, Roebuck & Co., 627 F.2d 756 (5th Cir. 1980).

Jackson v. Sears, Roebuck & Co., 648 F.2d 225 (5th Cir. 1981).

Johnson v. Mayor and City Council of Baltimore, 53 U.S.L.W. 4766 (1985).

Julian v. City of Houston, Texas, et al., No. 01–20541 (5th Cir. 2002).

Kelly v. American Standard, 640 F.2d 974 (9th Cir. 1981).

Keval v. Block, 33 FEP Cases 774 (D. D.C. 1981).

Kimel v. Florida Board of Regents, 528 U.S.U.S. 62 (2000).

Koyen v. Consolidated Edison Co., 560 F. Supp. 1161 (S.D. N.Y. 1983).

Leftwich v. Harris-Stowe State College, 702 F.2d 686 (8th Cir. 1983).

Loeb v. Textron, 600 F.2d 1003 (1st Cir. 1979).

Mahoney v. Trabucco, 738 F.2d 35 (1st Cir. 1984).

Marshall v. Board of Education of Salt Lake City, 15 FEP Cases 368 (D. Utah 1977).

Marshall v. Goodyear Tire, 22 FEP Cases 775 (W.D. Tenn. 1979).

Massachusetts Board of Retirement v. Murgia, 427 U.S. 307 (1976).

Mastie v. Great Lakes Steel Corp., 424 F. Supp. 1299 (E.D. Mich. 1976).

Mathis v. Phillips Chevrolet, Inc., No. 00–1892 (7th Cir. October 15, 2001).

McDonnell Douglas v. Green, 411 U.S. 792 (1973).

McKennon v. Nashville Banner Publishing Co., 115 S. Ct. 879 (1995).

Miller v. General Electric Corp., 562 F. Supp. 610 (E.D. Pa. 1983).

Moore v. Sears, Roebuck & Co., 683 F.2d 1321 (11th Cir. 1982).

Morrissey v. Boston Bank, 54 F.3d 27 (1st Cir. 1995).

Needham v. Beecham, Inc., 515 F. Supp. 460 (D. Me. 1981).

O'Connor v. Consolidated Coin Caterers Corp., 116 S. Ct. 1307 (1996).

Orzel v. City of Wauwatosa Fire Department, 697 F.2d 743 (7th Cir. 1983).

Oubre v. Entergy Operations, 118 S. Ct. 838 (1998).

Pace v. Southern Railway System, 701 F.2d 1383 (11th Cir. 1983).

Parcinski v. Outlet Co., 673 F.2d 34 (2nd Cir. 1982).

Parker v. Federal National Mortgage Association., 741 F.2d 975 (7th Cir. 1984).

Passer v. American Chemical Society, 53 FEP Cases 1442 (D D.C. 1990).

Pena v. Brattleboro Retreat, 702 F.2d 322 (2nd Cir. 1983).

Popkins v. Zagel, 611 F. Supp. 809 (C.D. Ill. 1985).

Price v. Maryland Casualty Co., 561 F.2d 609 (5th Cir. 1977).

Quinn v. New York State Electric and Gas Corp., 569 F. Supp. 655 (N.D. N.Y. 1983).

Reeves v. Sanderson Plumbing Products, Inc., 120 S. Ct. 2097 (2000).

Reich v. New York Hospital, 513 F. Supp. 854 (S.D. N.Y. 1981).

Robb v. Chemetron Corp., 17 FEP Cases 1535, 1545 (S.D. Tex. 1978).

Showalter v. University of Pittsburgh Medical Center, 190 F. 3d 231, 234 (3d Cir. 1999).

Smith v. Jackson, 351 F. 3d. 183 (5th Cir. 2003).

Stone v. Western Airlines, Inc., 544 F. Supp. 33 (S.D. Cal. 1982).

Texas Department of Community Affairs v. Burdine, 450 U.S. 248 (1981).

Transworld Airlines v. Thurston, 105 S. Ct. 613 (1985).

Tribble v. Westinghouse Electric Corp., 669 F.2d 1193 (8th Cir. 1982).

Usery v. Tamiami Trail Tours, Inc., 531 F.2d 224 (5th Cir. 1976).

Western Airlines v. Criswell, 53 U.S.L.W. 4766 (1985).

Whittlesly v. Union Carbide Corp., 35 FEP Cases 1089 (2nd Cir. 1984).

Wildman v. Lerner Stores Corp., 771 F.2d 605 (1st Cir. 1985).

Wilhelm v. Blue Bell, Inc., 773 F.2d 1429 (4th Cir. 1985).

Williamson v. Owens-Illinois Inc., 589 F. Supp. 1051 (N.D. Ohio 1984).

Wilson v. Sealtest Foods, 501 F.2d 84 (5th Cir. 1974).

Woodfield v. Heckler, 591 F. Supp. 1390 (E.D. Pa. 1984).

CHAPTER 10

Title I of the Americans with Disabilities Act
The Short but Active History of ADA Enforcement and Litigation
Jone McFadden Papinchock

An alternate title for this chapter might be "The ADA: A Search for the Forty-Three Million." When Congress wrote the Americans with Disabilities Act (1990), it indicated that the ADA was intended to protect the "some 43,000,000 Americans [who] have one or more physical or mental disabilities" (§ 12101a-1). Since Title I of the ADA became effective, there has been a constant search for an understanding of whom Congress intended to protect by its reference to the forty-three million. It is unclear whether Congress intended this estimate to define the total population covered by the ADA. Regardless, this estimate of forty-three million has taken on a definitional role in district, circuit, and U.S. Supreme Court rulings.

The Act included some information about who was covered and the Equal Employment Opportunity Commission (EEOC) developed regulations ("Regulations to Implement the Equal Employment Provisions of the Americans with Disabilities Act," 1997) and guidance. Nevertheless, a significant portion of the ADA litigation still focuses on whether a specific plaintiff or a type of plaintiff is within the scope of the protected class. Congress increased the complexity of the search for the forty-three million with two other facets of the Act. The ADA protects additional groups: those with a record of a disability and those who are perceived as having a disability. It is not obvious whether these individuals were included in the forty-three million estimate. However, it is unlikely because they would not have counted traditionally among those with disabilities.

Yet the forty-three million number continues to be given deference, as will be described, in several Supreme Court ADA rulings. In fact, the Supreme Court explicitly considered the origin and intent of the "forty-three million" in *Sutton* v. *United Airlines* (1999) (at 2147–2149). The *Sutton* decision, like some later decisions of the Supreme Court (for example, *Murphy* v. *United Parcel Service*, 1999; *Albertsons, Inc.* v. *Kirkingburg*, 1999), has been interpreted by some as "narrowing" the focus of the ADA. Numerous articles have been written on the concept of narrowing the focus and the appropriateness of using the forty-three million estimate (Anfang, 2003; Coyle, 1999; Locke, 1997; National Council on Disability, 2002, 2003; Petrila, 2002; Toner & Arnold, 1999; Tucker, 2000). To make a determination of narrowing, one would have to know Congress's original intent for the ADA and the forty-three million estimate, but unless Congress amends the Act this will not be known.

Given these issues, one cannot escape the irony of the first line of the Act: "To establish a clear and comprehensive prohibition of discrimination on the basis of disability." To begin to understand these issues, one must start with a basic understanding of the myriad definitions in the ADA. This chapter attempts to provide information relevant to understanding the Act and the related definitions. Only a cursory treatment of lower court rulings is presented, given the volume and inconsistency of these rulings. Emphasis will instead be placed on the rulings of the U.S. Supreme Court.

History of the Law

The ADA (1990) is a federal civil rights law enacted to prevent discrimination and to ensure that individuals with disabilities can participate in all aspects of society. The law has five parts: Title I (employment), Title II (public services), Title III (public accommodations and services provided by private entities), Title IV (telecommunications), and Title V (miscellaneous provisions).

This chapter addresses only Title I. The purpose of Title I of the Act is

(1) to provide a clear and comprehensive national mandate for the elimination of discrimination against individuals with disabilities;

(2) to provide clear, strong, consistent, enforceable standards addressing discrimination against individuals with disabilities;

(3) to ensure that the Federal Government plays a central role in enforcing the standards . . . and

(4) to invoke the sweep of congressional authority, including the power to enforce the fourteenth amendment and to regulate commerce, . . . to address the major areas of discrimination faced . . . by people with disabilities [§ 12101].

Title I was originally intended to apply to private employers, state and local governments, employment agencies, and labor unions. A U.S. Supreme Court decision in 2001 (*Board of Trustees of University of Alabama* v. *Garrett*) ruled that ADA suits could not be brought in federal courts by state employees to recover money damages. These cases are barred by the Eleventh Amendment.

Title I took effect on July 26, 1992, for employers with twenty-five or more employees, with coverage extended to employers with fifteen or more employees on July 26, 1994. The ADA also covers the legislative branch of the federal government. The executive branch remains under Title V of the Rehabilitation Act of 1973. Title I is enforced by the EEOC, and to this end the EEOC developed regulations for implementing the ADA, which were originally published in 1997 ("Regulations to Implement . . . ,").

To gain insight into the level of enforcement and litigation activity arising from the ADA, one need only review the tables presented in Chapter Four in this volume and the statistics on the EEOC's Web site (EEOC, 2004b). For a law that has been enforced for less than twelve years, there are significant levels of activity. This is not surprising given that in the first year of enforcement (starting July 26), there were 1,048 EEOC charges filed. In 1993, the number had risen to 15,274, or 17.4 percent of all charges received by the EEOC.

A significant indicator of the active litigation history of the ADA is the number of ADA cases heard by the U.S. Supreme Court. As will be discussed in this chapter, eleven Title I cases have been heard by the Supreme Court, in addition to *Board of Trustees of University of Alabama* v. *Garrett*. An understanding of these decisions is essential because they provide significant insight into how ADA terms (considered by many to be vague; see Locke, 1997, for example) are being interpreted. These cases provide an understanding of whom the Court views as the forty-three million.

Important Definitions

The ADA introduced new terminology with which employers, industrial and organizational psychologists, and human resource managers must be familiar. Many of the definitions provided in this section may seem straightforward, yet their meaning is often the crux of litigation. Sample cases related to the definitions are presented after each definition to provide initial consideration of how the terms have been litigated. As will be described in greater detail later in this chapter, interpretation of these terms is still being decided in the courts.

Disability

- "The term 'disability' means (A) a physical or mental impairment that substantially limits one or more of the major life activities of such individual; (B) a record of such an impairment; or (C) being regarded as having such an impairment" (§ 12102-2). As stated, physical or mental impairment does not directly imply a disability. For a physical or mental impairment to be categorized as a disability there must be substantial limitations in one or more major life activities.
- *Lusk* v. *Christ Hospital* (2000). The district court ruled there was insufficient evidence to link the plaintiff's depression and breast cancer to substantially limiting any major life activity. For this reason the depression and breast cancer did not meet the definition of a disability. The plaintiff was discharged for

poor performance but had made only a weak link between her reduced performance and the physical and mental impairment.

Major Life Activity

- "Major Life Activities means functions such as caring for oneself, performing manual tasks, walking, seeing, hearing, speaking, breathing, learning, and working" ("Regulations to Implement . . . ," [2004], § 1630.2-i). The EEOC has provided specific guidance on the major life activity of work, indicating that the claimant must "significantly be restricted in the ability to perform either a class of jobs or a broad range of jobs in various classes as compared to the average person having comparable training, skills and abilities. The inability to perform a single, particular job does not constitute a substantial limitation." . . . Factors that may be considered include ("Regulations to Implement . . . ," 2004 § 1630.2-j.3):
  - "[The] geographical area to which the individual has reasonable access"
  - "The job from which the individual has been disqualified because of an impairment, and the number and types of jobs utilizing similar training, knowledge, skills or abilities, within that geographical area, from which the individual is also disqualified because of the impairment (class of jobs)"
  - "The job from which the individual has been disqualified because of an impairment, and the number and types of other jobs not utilizing similar training, knowledge, skills or abilities, within that geographical area, from which the individual is also disqualified because of the impairment (broad range of jobs in various classes)"
- *Fraser* v. *Goodale* (2003). The ninth circuit remanded the case to the trial court after asserting that eating can be a major life activity. In this case the court considered the case of an employee with diabetes who was instructed not to eat at her desk. The circuit indicated that there was a triable question as to whether the employee's diabetes substantially limited the major life activity of eating because of her regimented diet.

Substantially Limiting

- An impairment is *substantially limiting* if the individual is "unable to perform a major life activity that the average person in the general population can perform; or [is] significantly restricted as to the condition, manner, or duration under which an individual can perform a particular major life activity" ("Regulations to Implement . . . ," 2004, § 1630.2-j.1.i) . . .
- *Skomsky* v. *Speedway SuperAmerica* (2003). "The [Minnesota Federal] Court holds that the activity of commercial truck driving is distinct from other kinds of driving jobs and a sufficiently broad category of jobs to constitute the activity of working, as contemplated by the ADA."

Qualified

- "The term 'qualified individual with a disability' means an individual with a disability who, with or without reasonable accommodation, can perform the essential functions of the employment position that such individual holds or desires" (ADA, 1990, § 1211-8).
- *Murphy* v. *UPS* (1999). The U.S. Supreme Court affirmed the tenth circuit's summary judgment. The Court found that the plaintiff, a mechanic, was dismissed from his position due to hypertension. He was deemed "not qualified" because he was unable to obtain DOT health certification.

Essential Functions

- ". . . A job function may be considered essential for any of several reasons, including but not limited to the following" ("Regulations to Implement . . . ," 2004§ 1630.2-n):
  - . . . "The position exists . . . to perform that function."
  - . . . There are a "limited number of employees available among whom the performance of that job function can be distributed."
  - "The function may be highly specialized so that the incumbent in the position is hired for his or her expertise or ability to perform the particular function."

- Some of the information that may be used to establish an essential function includes job descriptions, the percentage of time spent performing the function, the impact if the function is not performed, collective bargaining agreements, and the work experience of current and former incumbents in the job (§ 1630.2).
- *Shannon* v. *New York City Transit Authority* (2003). The second circuit found that a bus driver with color blindness that made him unable to distinguish a traffic signal was not a qualified individual with a disability because distinguishing traffic signals was an essential function of the job. In this case the court relied on a state standard requiring that all bus drivers pass a color vision test as evidence that this was an essential function.
- *Ray* v. *Kroger Co.* (2003). The trial court found that an employee with Tourette's syndrome was substantially limited in the major life activity of communicating. However, his termination for using racial epitaphs was not covered under ADA because he was not "otherwise qualified" due to the fact that interacting with customers and coworkers was an essential function of his job of clerk in the frozen food section of a grocery store.
- *Waggoner* v. *Olin Corp.* (1999). The seventh circuit found for the defendant saying . . . that "in most instances the ADA does not protect persons who have erratic, unexplained absences, even when such absences are a result of a disability." The plaintiff was terminated after attending work for fourteen of the twenty months employed. The court ruled that an implied essential function was attendance and that if the person did not work it was axiomatic that he or she could not perform the essential functions of the job.

Direct Threat

- By *direct threat*, the ADA means, "A direct threat to the health or safety of other individuals in the workplace" (§ 12113b). The EEOC extends this to *harm* to the *individual*, stating: "Direct Threat means a significant risk of substantial harm to the health or safety of the individual or others that cannot be eliminated or reduced by reasonable accommodation. . . . In determining . . . a direct threat, the factors . . . include the duration of the risk; the nature and severity of the potential harm; the likelihood that the potential harm will occur; the imminence of the potential harm" ("Regulations to Implement . . . ," 2004, § 1630.2-r).

- *Mauro* v. *Borgess Medical Center* (1998). The sixth circuit affirmed summary judgment on the basis of direct threat. A surgical technician with HIV was moved to a semiskilled position due to the risk of transmission of HIV to surgical patients. The U.S. Supreme Court denied the petition for review.

Reasonable Accommodation

- The term *reasonable accommodation* means "modifications . . . to a job application process that enable a qualified applicant with a disability to be considered for the position . . . ; or modifications or adjustments to the work environment, or to the manner or circumstances under which the position . . . is customarily performed, that enable a qualified individual with a disability to perform the essential functions of that position; or modifications . . . that enable . . . [an] employee with a disability to enjoy equal benefits and privileges of employment as are enjoyed by [an organization's] other similarly situated employees without disabilities" ("Regulations to Implement . . . ," 2004, § 1630.2-o). "To determine the appropriate reasonable accommodation it may be necessary for the covered entity to initiate an informal, interactive process with the qualified individual with a disability in need of the accommodation. This process should identify the precise limitations resulting from the disability and potential reasonable accommodations that could overcome those limitations" (§ 1630.2-o).
- *Keever* v. *City of Middletown* (1998). A city police officer was offered a desk officer job in response to his request for a lower-stress job. The sixth circuit found this was a reasonable accommodation even though the officer had specifically requested assignment to a detective job on the night shift.

Undue Hardship

- "In general. Undue hardship means . . . significant difficulty or expense incurred . . . when considered in light of
the factors set forth in paragraph (p)(2) of this section."
These factors are ("Regulations to Implement . . . ," 2004,
§ 1630.2-p) . . .
  - "The nature and net cost of the accommodation . . .
  taking into consideration the availability of tax credits
  and deductions, and/or outside funding"
  - "The overall financial resources of the facility or facilities . . . , the number of persons employed at such
  facility, and the effect on expenses and resources"
  - "The overall financial resources of the covered entity,
  the overall size of the business . . . with respect to the
  number of its employees, and the number, type and
  location of its facilities"
  - "The type of operation or operations of the covered
  entity, including the composition, structure and functions of the workforce of such entity, and the geographic
  separateness and administrative or fiscal relationship of
  the facility or facilities in question to the covered entity"
  - "The impact of the accommodation upon the operation
  of the facility, including the impact on the ability of other
  employees to perform their duties and the impact on the
  facility's ability to conduct business"
- *US Airways* v. *Barnett* (2002). The U.S. Supreme Court determined that an accommodation that required disregarding a
seniority system may impose an undue hardship on the business (unless special circumstances can be demonstrated).

Employment Activities Covered By ADA

The ADA has application to a broad range of employment conditions including "job application procedures, the hiring, advancement, or discharge of employees, employee compensation, job
training, and other terms, conditions, and privileges of employment" (§ 12112). The EEOC (1997a) has advised that the ADA also
specifically covers recruitment, advertising, tenure, layoff, leave,

and fringe benefits. Further, the EEOC regulations expressly state that an entity is not allowed

- ". . . to limit, segregate, or classify a job applicant or employee in a way that adversely affects his or her employment opportunities or status on the basis of disability" ("Regulations to Implement . . . ," 2004, § 1630.5) . . .
- . . . "[T]o participate in a contractual or other arrangement . . . that has the effect of subjecting the covered entity's own qualified applicant or employee with a disability to the discrimination prohibited by this part" (§ 1630.6). . .
- . . . "[T]o . . . use standards, criteria, or methods of administration, which are not job-related and consistent with business necessity, and: (a) That have the effect of discriminating on the basis of disability" (§ 1630.7) . . .
- . . . "[T]o exclude or deny equal jobs or benefits to, or otherwise discriminate against, a qualified individual because of the known disability of an individual with whom the qualified individual is known to have a family, business, social or other relationship or association" (§ 1630.8) . . ."
- . . . "[Not] to make reasonable accommodation . . . [unless] the accommodation would impose an undue hardship on the operation of its business. . . . A qualified individual with a disability is not required to accept an accommodation. . . . However, if such individual rejects a reasonable accommodation . . . that is necessary to enable the individual to perform the essential functions . . . and cannot, as a result of that rejection, perform the essential functions of the position, the individual will not be considered a qualified individual with a disability" (§ 1630.9) . . .
- . . . "[T]o use qualification standards, employment tests or other selection criteria that screen out or tend to screen out an individual with a disability or a class of individuals with disabilities, on the basis of disability, unless the standard, test or other selection criteria . . . is shown to be job-related for the position in question and is consistent with business necessity" (§ 1630.10) . . .
- . . . "[T]o ensure that, when a test is administered to a job applicant or employee who has a disability that impairs

sensory, manual or speaking skills, the test results accurately reflect the skills, aptitude, or whatever other factor of the applicant or employee that the test purports to measure, rather than reflecting the impaired sensory, manual, or speaking skills of such employee or applicant (except where such skills are the factors that the test purports to measure)" (§ 1630.11) . . .

• . . . "[T]o discriminate against any individual because that individual has opposed any act or practice . . . or because that individual made a charge, testified, assisted, or participated in any manner in an investigation, proceeding, or hearing to enforce any provision contained in this part" (§ 1630.12).

• . . . "[T]o conduct a medical examination (or require a medical examination) of an applicant or to make inquiries as to whether an applicant is an individual with a disability or as to the nature or severity of such disability" . . . except as allowed by Section 1630.14 (§ 1630.13).

Comparison of the ADA and Title VII

As many chapters in this volume are dedicated to discussion of issues related to Title VII of the Civil Rights Act of 1964, it should be useful to describe some general similarities and differences of the two statutes. The ADA relies on the Title VII process of investigation, definition of statutory limits for filing, and role of the EEOC in issuing a right-to-sue letter. However, there are several differences between the two laws:

• The ADA does not require affirmative action.
• Class membership is not automatic (as ADA plaintiffs have to establish both a disability and qualifications).
• Protection under the ADA can be extended beyond the person with the disability. "The ADA prohibits discrimination based on relationship or association in order to protect individuals from actions based on unfounded assumptions that their relationship to a person with a disability would affect their job performance" (EEOC, 1997a). The EEOC resolved 303 claims that were based on "relationship-association" in the period from July 1992 to September 2003 (EEOC, 2004a).

- Title VII does not require reasonable accommodations (Congressional Research Service, 2001).
- Establishing the job-relatedness of an employment decision is not sufficient to prevail in an ADA case. The employer must respond as to whether there were reasonable accommodations that could have been made.

U.S. Supreme Court Rulings: Defining the Forty-three Million

As stated in the introduction to this chapter, understanding the ADA can be conceptualized as a search for the forty-three million Americans with "physical or mental disabilities." As will be described in this section, most of the Supreme Court's Title I cases have focused on defining the protected class.

1998 Rulings

The U.S. Supreme Court heard one ADA Title I case in 1998, *Wright* v. *Universal Maritime Service*. The Court ruled that the arbitration clause in the collective bargaining agreement at issue in the case was not sufficiently explicit to inform the parties that it applied to employee claims under federal employment discrimination statutes. The Court also indicated that it was not ruling on whether such a waiver could be enforceable if written more explicitly.

1999 Rulings

In 1999, the U.S. Supreme Court heard four ADA Title I cases with significant impacts on the interpretation of ADA. The two major outcomes of these rulings were that

1. Claiming total disability for a Social Security Disability Insurance (SSDI) determination does not automatically mean the individual is not a qualified disabled person under ADA, but the apparent inconsistency must be explained (*Cleveland* v. *Policy Management Systems*, 1999).
2. Mitigating measures should be considered when determining whether an individual has a disability (*Sutton* v. *United Airlines*, 1999; *Murphy* v. *UPS*, 1999; *Albertsons* v. *Kirkingburg*, 1999).

In *Cleveland* v. *Policy Management Systems* (1999) the Supreme Court considered the role of SSDI claims in relationship to determining qualified status. The plaintiff had received SSDI benefits after claiming a stroke had left her unable to work. She also filed an ADA suit against her employer indicating that she was terminated because a stroke affected her speech, concentration, and memory. She alleged she had requested accommodations (computer training, permission to work at home, and a transfer) that she did not receive.

There was a history of lower court summary judgments against plaintiffs, which were sometimes upheld on appeal, in cases in which the plaintiff had filed both an SSDI claim and an ADA suit (Gutman, 2000b). The premise of these summary judgments was generally that a person could not be both completely unable to work by SSDI standards and qualified under ADA standards. In ruling summary judgment the courts often referred to judicial estoppel. *Judicial estoppel* is "estoppel that prevents a party from contradicting previous declarations made during the same or a later proceeding if the change in position would adversely affect the proceeding or constitute a fraud on the court" (Garner, 2001). "The doctrine is designed to prevent parties from making a mockery of justice by changing positions as it suits their needs" (Barth, 2000, p. 1323).

The Supreme Court unanimously decided that SSDI claims should not result in automatic judicial estoppel of an ADA claim. Justice Breyer wrote:

> . . . Despite the appearance of conflict that arises from the language of the two statutes, the two claims do not inherently conflict to the point where courts should apply a special negative presumption like the one applied by the Court of Appeals here. . . . For one thing, as we have noted, the ADA defines a "qualified individual" to include a disabled person "who . . . can perform the essential functions" of her job "with reasonable accommodation." . . . By way of contrast, when the SSA determines whether an individual is disabled for SSDI purposes, it does not take the possibility of "reasonable accommodation" into account [at 1602]. . . .

The Court cautioned that although the two claims were not *necessarily* contradictory, the claimant should present an explanation in the ADA case. "To defeat summary judgment, that explanation must be sufficient to warrant a reasonable juror's concluding that, assuming the truth of, or the plaintiff's good faith belief in, the earlier statement [on an SSDI claim], the plaintiff could nonetheless 'perform the essential functions' of her job, with or without 'reasonable accommodation'" (at 1604).

In 1999, the Supreme Court also had a major impact on the interpretation of the term *disability* in the *Sutton* v. *United Airlines* (1999) case, which was echoed in *Murphy* and in *Albertsons*. Prior to the *Sutton* ruling the EEOC had advised that the decision on whether or not an individual had a disability should be made without regard to mitigating measures. The EEOC's interpretive guidance stated, "the determination of whether an individual is substantially limited in a major life activity must be made on a case-by-case basis, without regard to mitigating measures such as medicines, or assistive or prosthetic devices" (Appendix to "Regulations to Implement the Equal Employment Provisions of the Americans with Disabilities Act," 1998, § 1630.2-jh). Contrary to that guidance, in *Sutton* the Supreme Court ruled that the mitigating circumstances should be considered. The Supreme Court considered the role of the forty-three million in the following way: "Because it is included in the ADA's text, the finding that 43 million individuals are disabled gives content to the ADA's terms, specifically in the term 'disability.' Had Congress intended to include all persons with corrected physical limitations among those covered by the Act, it undoubtedly would have cited a much higher number of disabled persons in the findings. That it did not is evidence that the ADA's coverage is restricted to only those whose impairments are not mitigated by corrective measures" (at 2149).

In *Sutton* twin sisters filed suit alleging that they were not hired as commercial airline pilots because of their disability. The sisters had uncorrected vision of 20/200 or worse and as such did not meet the visual acuity requirement (20/100 or better) set by United Airlines. Justice O'Connor indicated that the plaintiffs could not make a disability claim because their impairments were mitigated. Justice O'Connor wrote, "we hold that the determination of whether an individual is disabled should be made with reference to measures that mitigate the individual's impairment, including, in this instance, eyeglasses and contact lenses" (at 2143).

The opinion is also important because it confirmed the individual nature of a disability determination: "'The determination of whether an individual has a disability is not necessarily based on the name or diagnosis of the impairment the person has, but rather on the effect of that impairment on the life of the individual.' Thus, the guidelines approach would create a system in which persons often must be treated as members of a group of people with similar impairments, rather than individuals. This is contrary to both the letter and the spirit of the ADA" (at 2147).

The Court specifically did not consider whether the plaintiffs were "regarded due to their impairments as substantially limited in the major life activity of seeing" (at 2150) because the plaintiffs had proposed they were regarded as limited in a major life activity of working in a "class of employment." (In their initial complaint the plaintiffs included "seeing" and "working," but in their amended complaint they listed only "working.") The Court did not agree that global airline pilot was a class of jobs so the plaintiffs did not meet the standard of a limitation in the major life activity of working in a "class of employment."

Similarly, in *Murphy* the Supreme Court affirmed the tenth circuit finding that the plaintiff did not meet the definition of disability. Although his blood pressure exceeded the federal Department of Transportation (DOT) limits (for over-the-road truck drivers), it was controlled by medication. The Court found that the plaintiff was terminated from his job as a mechanic because of the DOT regulation, not because of a disability or because he was considered by United Parcel Service to have a disability. The *Murphy* court also indicated that the plaintiff (like those in *Sutton*) was not excluded from a class of jobs, only mechanic jobs that required a commercial driver's license. This did not meet the broad class standard because the plaintiff had worked for over twenty-two years at mechanic jobs that did not require DOT certification (at 2139). UPS was not required to make a reasonable accommodation because the termination decision was not related to a disability. Further, the Court accepted UPS's use of the DOT regulation as a qualification standard. Even if a disability had been established, the plaintiff would not meet the qualified standard. The Court also reiterated from *Sutton* that an individual assessment has to be made in determining whether an individual has a disability. It should be noted that the Court did not rule on whether the plaintiff was disabled when on medication (that is, whether "limitations . . . persist despite his medication or the negative side effects from the medication)" (at 2137).

In *Albertsons* v. *Kirkingburg* (1999), the Supreme Court considered *mitigation*. Unlike the plaintiffs in *Murphy* and *Sutton,* this plaintiff had mitigated his visual problems (20/200 vision in one eye that in effect resulted in monocular vision) through compensation. The Court stated that there was "no principled basis for distinguishing between measures undertaken with artificial aids, like medications and devices, and measures undertaken, whether consciously or not, with the body's own systems" (at 2169). The plaintiff alleged he was dismissed from his driving job because of a disability. The defendants countered that the plaintiff did not meet DOT standards (20/40 corrected distant vision in each eye and distant binocular vision of at least 20/40). The Court found the driver had compensated for his impairment and as a result was not substantially limited in the major life activity of seeing. The Supreme Court delineated three problems with the ninth circuit's ruling on the existence of a disability:

1. For a disability to "substantially limit" it should have a "significant restriction," not simply (as in this case) seeing differently (at 2168).
2. The plaintiff's ability to compensate should be considered. The condition of monocular vision alone is insufficient for establishing a disability (at 2168).
3. The determination of a substantial limitation in a major life activity has to be made on an individual analysis. "While some impairments may invariably cause a substantial limitation of a major life activity . . . we cannot say that monocularity does. . . . We simply hold that the Act requires monocular individuals, like others claiming the Act's protection, to prove a disability by offering evidence that the extent of the limitation in terms of their own experience, as in loss of depth perception and visual field, is substantial" (at 2169).

In terms of job qualifications, Justice Souter also wrote that it was not necessary for the employer to justify enforcement of a job qualification requiring an employee to meet federal safety regulations (at 2165). The plaintiff was not qualified because Albertsons had set the DOT's "standard as defining an 'essential job function' of the employment position" and the plaintiff could not meet that standard (at 2169).

2002 Rulings

There were no ADA cases heard by the Supreme Court in 2000. In 2001, the Court heard *University of Alabama* v. *Garrett*, as considered earlier. Four cases in 2002 established that

1. The EEOC can pursue a case in which the complainant had signed a binding arbitration agreement with the employer (*EEOC* v. *Waffle House*, 2002).
2. A strict definition should be applied when determining whether an impairment rises to the level of substantially limiting a major life activity (*Toyota Motor Manufacturing, Kentucky* v. *Williams*, 2002).
3. An employer can refuse to hire a person who would be harmed in the work environment due to a disability (thus extending the harm clause to self in addition to others) (*Chevron U.S.A.* v. *Echazabal*, 2002).
4. If an accommodation requires overriding provisions of a seniority system, ordinarily this will meet the definition of an undue hardship (*US Airways* v. *Barnett*, 2002).

In *EEOC* v. *Waffle House* (2002) the Supreme Court considered whether the EEOC was precluded from pursuing an ADA charge if the claimant had agreed to binding arbitration on an employment application. In this case the EEOC sought back pay, reinstatement, compensatory damages, and punitive damages. The fourth circuit had ruled that the arbitration agreement (as specified through the employment application) did not preclude the EEOC from pursuing injunctive relief (only, as opposed to victim-specific relief) in the case under its statutory authority. The Supreme Court reversed the fourth circuit's decision and remanded the case. The Supreme Court did not agree that the EEOC was able to seek only injunctive relief. The Court ruled that because the EEOC was not a party to the arbitration agreement, it could not be bound by it.

The *Toyota* decision has been considered a "narrowing" of the forty-three million (Petrila, 2002). Justice O'Connor's opinion addressed the definition of a major life activity. The plaintiff alleged she was disabled (by weakness and pain in her arms) in major life activities. She requested an accommodation, which was to perform two of the four tasks of a quality inspection job. In fact the plaintiff had been performing these two tasks prior to the company's decision that all four tasks needed to be performed. In district court, the plaintiff alleged disability in the major life activities (gardening and housework, playing with her children, lifting, performing manual tasks, and working). This court ruled that gardening, housework, and playing with children were not major life activities and that there was insufficient evidence related to lifting and working. The court indicated that the plaintiff's assertions that she could perform paint and paint inspection tasks were contradictory to a substantial limitation in the major life activity of performing manual tasks. The sixth circuit found that the plaintiff was substantially limited in manual tasks, thus finding her disabled. The Supreme Court considered what would constitute a substantial limitation in the major life activity of manual tasks. It ruled that "to be substantially limited in performing manual tasks, an individual must have an impairment that prevents or severely restricts the individual from doing activities that are of central importance to most people's daily lives . . . [and that this impairment] must also be permanent or long-term" (at 691). The Court stated that the interpretation of *disability* should be applied "strictly," based on Congress's "43,000,000 Americans" standard (at 691). It also indicated that the sixth circuit had erred by focusing on the manual tasks of the plaintiff's job as opposed to the plaintiff's ability to perform manual tasks in daily life, both in and out of the workplace.

What should also be noted in this ruling is the Supreme Court's clarification of its intent in *Sutton* related to the need to show a "broad range of jobs" to support "working." The Court indicated that it did not mean that a "class-based analysis should be applied to any major life activity other than working. . . . Nothing in the text of the Act, our previous opinions, or the regulations suggests that a class-based framework should apply outside the context of the major life activity of working" (at 693).

In *Chevron U.S.A. v. Echazabal* (2002) the Supreme Court ruled that the harm clause in ADA referred to self as well as to others. Chevron had withdrawn a hire offer because the plaintiff's hepatitis C would be aggravated by the toxins in the refinery. Chevron's defense was that the plaintiff could not perform the work without bringing harm to himself. The harm clause in the ADA statute indicates that a defense will be "a requirement that an individual shall not pose a direct threat to the health or safety of other individuals in the workplace" (§ 12113b). The ninth circuit ruled that the EEOC had inappropriately extended the wording of the Act from harm to others to harm to self and others. In his opinion on the case, Justice Souter indicated that the EEOC interpretation was correct. Chevron appropriately excluded the plaintiff based on a clear link between a direct threat to the applicant's health and the plant environment.

The Supreme Court also decided *US Airways* v. *Barnett* in 2002. In this case the Court determined that if an accommodation request conflicts with seniority rules (even if imposed by the employer and not as the result of a collective bargaining agreement), the request may not be deemed reasonable. However, the Court did not impose a hard-and-fast exclusion in the presence of a seniority rule. Justice Breyer wrote, "In our view, the seniority system will prevail in the run of cases. As we interpret the statute, to show that a requested accommodation conflicts with the rules of a seniority system is *ordinarily* to show that the accommodation is not 'reasonable'" (at 1519, emphasis added). The employer had accommodated a cargo handler by moving him to a mailroom position. However, the mailroom position was subject to seniority-based bidding, and the company refused the requested accommodation of not opening the position to seniority bid. The plaintiff was removed from the position when an employee with higher seniority bid on the position. The Court remanded the case with the guidance that the lower court should consider whether the plaintiff had evidence to show special circumstances (such as the employer's frequently not following the system) that would draw into question the employer's undue hardship defense.

2003 Rulings

The Supreme Court responded to two Title I cases in 2003. In *Raytheon* v. *Hernandez* (2003) the Court was asked to consider whether "ADA confers preferential rehire rights on disabled employees lawfully terminated for violating workplace conduct rules" (at 513). The plaintiff had been discharged (that is, to put it more correctly, he quit in lieu of discharge) for violation of company rules resulting from a positive drug test for cocaine. When the plaintiff reapplied to Raytheon, his company file was reviewed, and it was determined he was not eligible for rehire. The plaintiff alleged that he was eligible under ADA because he was in recovery. The Supreme Court vacated the ninth circuit's opinion and remanded the case. The Court, however, did not base this on answering the question of whether ADA confers preferential rights. Instead the decision was based on the finding that the ninth circuit had made its ruling based on disparate impact evidence for a disparate treatment claim. This was inappropriate because the plaintiff's disparate impact claim had been disallowed in the lower courts because it was not timely pleaded. As a result that claim was not to be considered. Yet the evidence that the ninth circuit considered in support of the disparate treatment claim was that the neutral, no-rehire policy had a negative impact on individuals recovering from drug abuse.

Clackamas Gastroenterology Associates v. *Wells* (2003) is noteworthy because, as with *Chevron*, in this case the Supreme Court specifically endorsed an EEOC interpretation of the ADA. The role of EEOC guidance came into question after the Supreme Court's disregard for the guidance on mitigating factors. This case demonstrated that the Supreme Court was not completely dismissing EEOC guidance. This case considered whether the employer was subject to the ADA. If the physician shareholders were considered to fit the *employee* definition, then there would be fifteen or more employees and the organization would be subject to ADA. If they were not considered employees, then the plaintiff could not bring an ADA suit. The Court endorsed standards in the EEOC Compliance Manual (EEOC, 2000a, § 605) related to the determination of whether a shareholder-director is an employee. The Court remanded the case to the ninth circuit for further consideration, noting that the record included information providing support for both a finding that the physicians were employees and a finding that they were not employees.

Case Strategies

Overview of Lower Court Outcomes

In general plaintiffs are not successful in ADA Title I cases (Colker, 1999). A 1998 study reported that plaintiffs lost in 86 percent of the ADA cases handled by the EEOC and 92 percent of the court cases (Barth, 2000). Similarly, according to a 2001 review of 429 Title I cases, employers prevailed in 314 cases, employees won in 14 cases, and 101 cases were not resolved (Allbright, 2002). In addition these findings may well be underestimates of the number of cases that plaintiffs lose, because unpublished decisions are more likely to be dismissals of plaintiff's cases (Lee, 2003) and unpublished cases are also more likely to be affirmations of defendant's arguments (Colker, 1999).

These statistics indicate that defendants are usually in a superior position in ADA cases. However, it would be foolhardy for employers to "play the odds" and abrogate their compliance responsibilities given this information. Besides the obvious ethical and moral issues surrounding ADA cases and the substantial costs involved in litigation for the losers and the winners, there is also a strong possibility that an organization's reputation would be negatively affected by EEOC investigations and litigation. Rulings against large employers are often widely publicized. There may also be direct financial impacts of varying degrees:

- In *EEOC* v. *CEC Entertainment, Inc., d/b/a Chuck E. Cheese's* (2000), a Wisconsin jury awarded $13 million in damages against the pizza chain. The judge reduced this to $230,000 (the maximum allowed under ADA) and upheld the jury's award of $70,000 in damages. The judge ordered reinstatement, and ADA training for managers.
- The EEOC entered a consent decree with Wal-Mart amounting to $6.8 million. The EEOC contended that Wal-Mart's pre-employment questionnaire (Matrix of Essential Job Functions) sought disability-related information prior to conditional offers.
- Browning-Ferris, Inc. settled a suit with the EEOC for termination of an employee with Crohn's disease for $194,000.
- A company was fined $150,000 and required to train employees about the ADA because a company supervisor was alleged to have told a temporary agency that the plaintiff was not to return because of his disability (*EEOC* v. *R. R. Donnelley & Sons*, 2002).

Prima Facie Case

For a plaintiff to prevail in a prima facie case he or she will have to provide extensive information about the impairment and its impacts on work and personal life. The plaintiff will also need to consider mitigating factors and whether the impairment persists beyond the mitigation. This is all information that although it might be considered highly private or sensitive by the plaintiff, is available to the plaintiff.

The plaintiff also has to describe how the essential work functions will be performed. Clearly, this is not an insignificant hurdle because it requires information that may not be readily available to the plaintiff. Particularly for external job applicants, understanding the essential functions and determining how they would be performed and what accommodations would allow their performance could present an insurmountable challenge. For comparison purposes, consider two simplified, hypothetical examples of employment discrimination cases, one based on gender and one based on disability:

Person A

- Was not hired for an engineering job after attending an interview.
- Was asked questions about her children and family during the interview.
- Decides to pursue charges of disparate treatment against the employer under Title VII on the basis of gender discrimination.
- Is qualified to pursue the charge because she is female.
- Pursues charge by providing details about the questions asked during the interview.

Person B

- Was not hired for an engineering job after attending an interview.
- Was asked questions about her medical condition during the interview.
- Decides to pursue charges of disparate treatment against the employer under ADA.
- Must establish that she has or is regarded as having an impairment. Describes the impairment in detail.
- May need to provide medical documentation.
- May need to describe mitigating factors and why the impairment persists.

- Describes the major life activity (or activities) affected.
- Demonstrates that there are substantial limitations in the major life activity resulting from the disability.
- If Person B cannot demonstrate a disability, she is not provided protection under ADA and the questions asked during the interview may go uninvestigated.

The prima facie case requires establishing the following elements:

- The plaintiff is disabled within the meaning of ADA.
- The plaintiff is qualified to perform the essential functions of the job, with or without accommodation.
- The defendant took adverse employment actions against the plaintiff on the basis of the disability.

As should be apparent at this point, each of these conditions requires an extensive amount of evidence. Summary judgment may be granted to the defendant if the plaintiff fails to meet any of these conditions. In addition the defendant has numerous defenses specified under the ADA. Given this complexity, the presentation of plaintiff and defendant case strategies is best made as a sequence of events.

1. *The plaintiff must establish that he or she has a physical or mental, or both, impairment that rises to level of disability.*
The plaintiff must describe the impairment, identify the major life activities that are affected, and show that there are substantial limitations on these major life activities.
The Supreme Court has stated that an impairment does not rise to the level of a disability simply through its diagnosis. It has been clear and consistent that the decision on whether an impairment can be considered a disability must be made on an individual basis (*Sutton, Murphy,* and *Albertsons*). Simply identifying oneself as a person with diabetes or a person with epilepsy, for example, is insufficient.
The plaintiff must identify the major life activity that is affected. Numerous major life activities have been identified, including sitting, standing, lifting (as in *Toyota*), reaching, thinking, concentrating, interacting with others, sleeping, and eating ("Regulations

to Implement . . . ," 2004, Appendix to § 1630.2-i; EEOC, 1997b, 1999b, 2000a, § 902.3-b).

Given the Supreme Court decision in *Sutton,* the major life activity of working might be approached by plaintiffs with caution. The Court questioned but did not decide whether working could be considered a major life activity. In fact, even prior to *Sutton* the major life activity of working was considered problematic for plaintiffs because it required them to obtain burdensome information (Locke, 1997). To establish that a disability places substantial limitation on working, a plaintiff must show that he or she is ineligible for a "class of jobs" (EEOC, 2000a, § 902.4), not just a particular job with a particular employer. The *Sutton* court commented that in determining the limitation, it would consider the jobs an individual can perform, not just those that cannot be performed. The Court specifically noted that the *Sutton* plaintiffs were able to work as regional pilots and pilot instructors. However, working has been used successfully as a major life activity since *Sutton* (*Davoll v. Webb,* 1999). If working is chosen as a major life activity of substantial limitation, the plaintiff might want to seek expert input for identification of the extent of the limitation in terms of number of jobs, types of jobs, his or her skills related to other jobs, and so forth (East, 2000).

The plaintiff must also demonstrate there is a substantial limitation. In *Toyota* a strict standard was set for defining a substantial limitation. The limitation should occur in work and nonwork life and should be related to activities of "central importance in most people's daily lives." As the Court said in *Albertsons,* there should be a "significant restriction," not just "seeing differently." It may be that to prevail in establishing a substantial limitation, the plaintiff has to emphasize the negative impact of an impairment by revealing "information that he or she would rather have kept private" (Petrila & Brink, 2001, p. 629).

Lawson v. CSX Transportation (2001) demonstrated a successful presentation of a substantial limitation. The seventh circuit was persuaded by the information that the plaintiff, even though taking insulin, had problems with erratic blood sugar levels and severe restrictions on eating (time of eating and availability, type, and quantity of food). The court specifically referenced *Sutton* in its consideration and indicated that there were negative outcomes associated with the mitigation.

Since the *Sutton* case, some believe that plaintiffs should consider more "record of disability" or "regarded as having a disability" strategies (Lee, 2003, p. 19). However, regarded-as claims have their own standards, which can be equally demanding. Some consider the major life activity of working as the only relevant factor for a regarded-as claim, because the argument is based on the employer's perception of the person's acceptability for the job (Locke, 1997).

Also, many courts have ruled in favor of defendants who could show simply that a plaintiff was not regarded as substantially limited in the major life activity of working because the employer had offered or given that person another job assignment or wanted him or her to return to work (*Thompson* v. *Holy Family Hospital*, 1997; *Miller* v. *City of Springfield*, 1998; *Foreman* v. *Babcock & Wilcox*, 1997). The EEOC's guidance says: "an employer that disqualifies an individual from a job on the basis of a criterion that pertains to a unique aspect of the job at issue does not regard the individual as substantially limited in the ability to work. Instead, the employer merely regards the individual as unsuitable for one particular job. The individual, therefore, does not meet the third, 'regarded as' part of the definition of the term 'disability' with respect to the major life activity of working" (EEOC, 2000a, § 902.8-f). Another exception to this defense would be cases in which the alternate job is not in the same class of occupations (*EEOC* v. *R. J. Gallagher Co.*, 1999).

For a plaintiff to establish that he or she is regarded as having a disability, evidence documenting the employer's perception must be presented:

- The plaintiff has an impairment but is not substantially limited in a major life activity although he or she is treated as if the impairment is substantially limiting.
- The plaintiff has an impairment that because of others' attitudes is substantially limiting.
- The plaintiff does not have an impairment but is treated as if he or she has an impairment that is substantially limiting.

The plaintiff must identify the impairment he or she is regarded as having and the major life activity the employer erroneously believes is affected. The plaintiff must also describe how the disability was related to the decision to take a specific employment action. Providing evidence only of the employer's awareness of information about the plaintiff (such as knowledge of physical therapy appointments) may be insufficient to establish that employer's erroneous perception (*Gorbitz* v. *Corvilla, Inc.*, 1999).

In *Katz* v. *City Metal* (1996) the court of appeals reversed summary judgment and remanded the case, finding that the plaintiff did establish a prima facie case that he was regarded as having a disability. The plaintiff established that the employer clearly knew of his heart attack, had been informed that he would return to work in a limited capacity, and had seen him unable to climb the stairs to the office. Further, the employer in its case did not directly respond to the plaintiff's allegation that he had been regarded as disabled.

Defendant positions that arise at this point in the case can be considered as "refuting class membership" (Gutman, 2000a, p. 320). The employer can pursue several approaches in seeking summary judgment on the issue of disability:

- Provide evidence that the plaintiff has not identified an impairment or does not have an impairment.
- Provide evidence that even though the plaintiff has an impairment it does not affect a major life activity or that the plaintiff did not identify a major life activity.
- Provide evidence that even though the plaintiff has an impairment that affects a major life activity that it does not place substantial limitations on that activity.
- If the plaintiff made a regarded-as claim, the defendant might provide evidence that the plaintiff's disability was not known to the defendant.
- If the impairment was known, the defendant might provide evidence that the defendant did not have the perception that it was a disability or did not make a decision on such knowledge or that the plaintiff was not regarded as unqualified in working a broad range of jobs. For example, in *Hamm* v. *Runyon* (1995) the court found for the defendant because of a lack of evidence that the supervisor making the termination decision was aware of the plaintiff's arthritis. There was also evidence that the employee had been performing his job.

2. *Since the Sutton ruling, when mitigating or corrective measures exist the plaintiff must describe in what way(s) the mitigation is not totally effective or has its own negative impact* (Colker, 1999).

The Supreme Court in *Murphy* specifically indicated that it had not considered whether the plaintiff had limitations despite the use of medication. Thus this is possibly a viable approach for a plaintiff whose condition is mitigated. Gutman (2000b) proposed that the Supreme Court opinions in *Sutton, Murphy,* and *Cleveland* included "'how to do it' instructions for crafting stronger ADA claims." The EEOC (1999b) has developed several questions to help field offices determine the extent to which a mitigating factor controls the limitations. These questions seek to identify the conditions that existed prior to the mitigation, and to determine what conditions exist after the mitigation, how effective the mitigation is (for example, is control consistent or variable), whether there has been a need to change mitigation because a prior form failed after a time, and whether the mitigation itself causes adverse effects.

It has been proposed that presenting conditions that exist beyond the mitigation may result in a "catch-22" for the plaintiff (Locke, 1997; Mayerson & Diller, 2000; National Council on Disability, 2003; Tucker, 2000). On one hand, if no negative conditions exist after mitigation, there is no disability. On the other hand, if the conditions that exist after mitigation are severe, it may be difficult to establish that the plaintiff is qualified. The plaintiff must be prepared to explain what conditions exist despite mitigation and to provide evidence that the essential functions can be performed with or without accommodations.

The defense at this point might consider the viability of moving for summary judgment, on the basis that the plaintiff is not substantially limited after consideration of mitigation and thus does not have a disability as defined by the Act.

3. *The plaintiff must demonstrate that he or she is qualified to perform essential functions of the job, with or without accommodations.*

The plaintiff should be prepared to demonstrate—from job postings, job descriptions, or other documents—that he or she meets the stated qualifications and requirements. In *Murphy* and *Albertsons* the Supreme Court accepted the company's reliance on DOT requirements as qualification standards. The EEOC regulations specifically indicate that "it may be a defense to a charge of discrimination under this part that a challenged action is required or necessitated by another federal law or regulation, or that another federal law or regulation prohibits an action (including the provision of a particular reasonable accommodation) that would otherwise be required by this part" ("Regulations to Implement . . . ," 2004, § 1630.15).

Presumably, for the plaintiff to prevail on such a standard he or she would need to show that the standard was not related to the essential functions. For example, the EEOC advised investigators to consider whether the regulatory requirement "absolutely" prohibits hiring the plaintiff or if the defendant "voluntarily" relied on the standard (EEOC, 1999b). In *Lawson* v. *CSX Transportation* (2001) the employer indicated that the plaintiff was not qualified (for conductor trainee) because he lacked a work history reflecting responsibility, safety, and dependability. The seventh circuit questioned whether those were actual requirements for the job because they were not listed on the job description and noted there were no company guidelines related to these qualifications and that the company had made exceptions to the qualifications.

The plaintiff must also provide evidence that he or she can perform the essential functions of the job, with or without accommodations. The plaintiff should identify accommodations linked to performing the essential functions and be prepared to establish that they are reasonable. To make the strongest argument in this regard the plaintiff may need an expert who can address the likelihood that the accommodation will address the individual's ability to perform the function (Blanck & Berven, 1999).

Another plaintiff approach might be a demonstration that the function at issue is marginal. The plaintiff might consider the EEOC's guidance in defining essential and marginal functions ("Regulations to Implement . . . ," 2004, § 1630.2-n).

The defendant should be prepared to provide documentation of the qualifications and essential functions of the job. The facts of a situation may form a rationale for summary judgment:

- If the plaintiff does not have the qualifications for the job, the employer should be prepared to support those qualifications. As in *Lawson,* it may be important to establish that those qualifications are consistently applied and are linked to essential functions.

- The defendant should be prepared to provide the information that demonstrates that functions said to be essential are in fact so. These functions should be clearly distinguishable from marginal functions as defined by the EEOC.
- Particularly when the defendant is not contesting the plaintiff's disability, it will be necessary to demonstrate that the plaintiff cannot perform the essential functions, with or without accommodations. More on this approach is presented in the next section.

4. The plaintiff must establish that a negative employment action occurred and provide evidence appropriate for the type of claim (disparate impact or disparate treatment) being made.

A plaintiff can pursue a disparate impact or a disparate treatment case. It is critical that the evidence be appropriate for the type of case, as demonstrated in *Raytheon*. In a disparate impact case the plaintiff must establish what employment action he or she believes resulted in a negative outcome.

In a disparate treatment case the plaintiff must identify the negative action *and* establish the organization's intent to discriminate (or proof that the action was taken because of his or her disability). The negative action may be any type of personnel decision, such as failure to hire or failure of the employer to provide a reasonable accommodation. If the negative action is a failure to accommodate, the plaintiff should provide evidence that accommodation was requested and refused. It is also possible for a plaintiff to prevail by establishing that although the employer provided an accommodation, it was not sufficient. Although the employer is not required to provide the *requested* accommodation, if an alternate accommodation is provided it should meet the plaintiff's needs. In *Vollmert* v. *Wisconsin Department of Transportation* (1999) an individual with learning disabilities required training on a new computer system. A letter from her doctor requested specialized training. The plaintiff alleged she was adversely affected because she was transferred to a new position (which did not have the same promotional opportunities) when she did not properly learn the new computer system. The seventh circuit found that the training provided by the department was not tailored to the plaintiff's needs.

The EEOC has promulgated a set of possible defenses to allegations of discrimination ("Regulations to Implement . . . ," 2004, § 1630.15) under disparate treatment and disparate impact motives and for allegations of denial of reasonable accommodation. For disparate treatment cases the EEOC regulations specifically state a defense may be that the challenged action was taken for a legitimate and nondiscriminatory reason and was not based on the alleged disability. An example of this defense is provided in *Dvorak* v. *Mostardi Platt Associates* (2002). In this case the employee alleged termination due to a disability. The court of appeals did not specifically question whether the plaintiff had a disability or whether he was qualified to perform the job. It upheld summary judgment finding that the plaintiff was terminated for reasons unrelated to the disability, relying on evidence from an insubordinate memo reflecting poor performance and misuse of a company computer.

In disparate impact cases the defendant must provide evidence of the job-relatedness and business necessity of a qualification standard or other selection criterion, uniformly applied standard, or policy alleged to discriminate against a protected class member. A defendant may provide evidence that a discriminatory action was in compliance with a federal law or regulation or that the action was specifically excluded from the Act. The defendant must also show that the criterion could not be met with a reasonable accommodation. Examples of such qualification standards are provided in *Sutton, Murphy,* and *Albertsons.*

The Act also recognizes that an acceptable qualification standard may be a requirement that the individual does not pose a direct threat to the health or safety of self or others. It should be noted that a direct threat is still subject to consideration of accommodations. For example, in *Mauro* v. *Borgess Medical Center* (1998), the sixth circuit accepted that there was no reasonable accommodation for reducing the direct threat posed by a surgical technician with the potential to transmit HIV to a patient. Yet in *EEOC* v. *Prevo's Family Market* (1998) the sixth circuit found that there was no direct threat of HIV transmission from a produce worker because the condition could be accommodated by the use of protective gloves, assigned knives, and hygiene.

When the plaintiff alleges denial of a reasonable accommodation, the defendant may consider several approaches:

- A primary consideration might be whether the employer knew about the disability or the need for an accommodation. In *Miller* v. *National Gas* (1995) the court determined that an employer's being told by the plaintiff's sister that the plaintiff was in a psychiatric facility was not notification of a disability.
- If the defendant is not rebutting that the plaintiff is a person with a disability and agrees that the plaintiff requested accommodations, the defendant should have a record of having attempted to pursue an interactive process. In *Beck* v. *University of Wisconsin* (1996) the decision was in favor of the employer because the plaintiff had cancelled a meeting to discuss her condition and had not signed medical releases for the employer's use.
- It may also be possible for the employer to show that no accommodation was necessary. In *Rauen* v. *U.S. Tobacco Manufacturing Limited Partnership* (2003) the court found that the plaintiff had a disability but did not need an accommodation. The plaintiff had been diagnosed and treated for cancer. Upon returning to work she requested the accommodation of working at home. Because she had been able to work without this accommodation from January 1999 through October 2001 (when the lower court ruled), the court found she did not need an accommodation.
- If the employer engaged in a process and offered an accommodation that was not accepted, this evidence should be produced. The employer is not required to provide the requested accommodation, only an efficacious accommodation (for example, *Schmidt* v. *Methodist Hospital of Indiana*, 1996).
- The employer may also be able to demonstrate that no reasonable accommodation exists that would enable the individual to perform the essential functions. In *Vande Zande* v. *State of Wisconsin Department of Administration* (1996), the seventh circuit ruled that accommodation was unreasonable if the costs were disproportionate to the benefit. The court ruled that regardless of financial standing, the employer "would not be required to bring about a trivial improvement in the life of a

disabled employee. If the nation's employers have potentially unlimited financial obligations to 43 million disabled persons, the . . . Act will have imposed an indirect tax potentially greater than the national debt" (*Vande Zande,* at 542). When relying on this defense, the defendant should not assume the cost of the accommodation. Rather, the defendant should perform research into making possible accommodations and be aware of the common direct and indirect costs associated with job accommodations.

- *Toyota* provides an example of an undue hardship defense. In this defense the defendant should have evidence of the "nature and cost of the accommodation needed, the overall financial resources of the business; the number of persons employed by the business; and the effect on expenses and resources of the business; and the impact of the accommodation on the business" (EEOC, 1999a).

5. *The plaintiff can rebut on the grounds of pretext.*
The plaintiff may respond to these defenses with evidence of pretext. The plaintiff may provide evidence that the employer's stated job-related reason was not the true reason for the employment decision. For example, in *Lawson* the employer indicated that it did not hire the plaintiff because of an inadequate work history, not because of his disability. The plaintiff provided evidence to rebut on the grounds of pretext. He established that the employer was aware of his diabetes and then provided information that the defendant had a record of hiring 98 percent of the people who completed the same training program he had attended, that everyone else in his class was hired, and that the defendant did not consistently use the work history standard.

ADA and the Role of the Industrial and Organizational Psychologist

The majority of industrial and organizational psychologists provide input into the development or administration of human resource (HR) systems (such as job analysis, job design, selection processes, performance appraisal, compensation and benefits, training, and layoffs). The decisions emanating from all these HR systems fall within the scope of the employment activities covered by the ADA. As a result, I-O psychologists can have a major impact on accomplishing the goals of the ADA. As organizations respond to the ADA, I-O psychologists may provide guidance to them on issues such as

- Developing test accommodations that consider the psychometric impacts of changes to test format or of presentations necessary to respond to a particular disability
- Defining minimum qualifications that tap only essential functions
- Determining appropriate job accommodations for a qualified individual with a disability
- Designing training that meets the needs of individuals with differing learning needs
- Responding to allegations of disability discrimination with internal investigations or expert testimony

One of the primary tools that the field of I-O psychology provides for ensuring compliance with the provisions of the ADA is job analysis. As has been discussed in various chapters in this book, job analysis is a process of gathering job information for developing selection systems, training programs, and other HR systems. Job analysis serves a critical role in responding to the ADA because it can identify essential job functions. Therefore a job analysis can ensure not only that selection systems, for example, are valid as required by Title VII and other statutes but also that selection decisions are based on the essential functions and do not tap nonessential functions. Once the essential functions have been differentiated from the nonessential functions through job analysis, the organization has the documentation necessary for making HR decisions that are in compliance with the ADA.

Just as I-O psychologists can affect the ADA, the ADA has affected the role of I-O psychologists (Bruyere, 2002; Cascio, 1994; Crewe, 1994; Pape & Tarvydas, 1994). I-O psychologists may need to acquire new knowledge, skills, and abilities responsive to the complexities of the ADA. Minimally, a substantial knowledge of the ADA, the case law that defines it, and EEOC guidance are imperative. In addition to understanding the ADA, I-O psychologists may need to seek assistance from clinical psychologists, human factors and ergonomic experts, specialists in learning and developmental disabilities, vocational rehabilitation specialists, occupational and physical therapists, specialists in developing accommodations (such as representatives from the Job Accommodation Network [JAN], a free service provided by the U.S. Department of Labor, Office of Disability Employment Policy), state and local agencies, and economists. The I-O psychologist cannot be a stand-alone professional in the face of the ADA. The I-O psychologist must become familiar with the missions and practices of these other fields in order to know whom to contact in given situations. Examples of these demands are presented in Table 10.1.

Table 10.1. Demands Placed by the ADA on I-O Psychologists.

Examples of Affected Activities	Additional Knowledge, Skills, and Abilities Required
Performing job analyses and writing job descriptions. ADA requires identification of "essential job functions." These must be identified through the job analysis or some other systematic approach and may need to be included on job descriptions and communicated to job applicants. Cascio (1994) recommends explaining "essential functions" to job experts and having them provide ratings that will identify essential or nonessential tasks.	Knowledge of the parameters identified by the EEOC for differentiating essential from marginal functions. Knowledge of EEOC guidance on the employment provisions of ADA (EEOC, 1992). Ability to identify and measure potential physical and environmental demands of jobs for the job analysis data gathering. Ability to identify experts in human factors, physiology, and other fields, as necessary, to gather input on physical, mental, and cognitive abilities required by a job.
Responding to requests for job accommodations. ADA requires that employers	Knowledge of EEOC guidance on common job accommodations (EEOC, 1999a).

Table 10.1. Demands Placed
by the ADA on I-O Psychologists, Cont'd.

Examples of Affected Activities	Additional Knowledge, Skills, and Abilities Required
consider job accommodations and provide them on an individualized basis unless employers can demonstrate that undue hardship would result. Because many accommodations are requested on the basis of mental, medical or physical, or learning or developmental disabilities with which the I-O psychologist lacks familiarity or expertise, I/O psychologists will need to seek input from other professionals. The employer should also be made aware of the common costs associated with job accommodations.	Ability to identify community resources for assisting with job accommodations.

Knowledge of federal and community programs that provide monetary assistance or tax incentives for making accommodations.

Familiarity with common costs. JAN (1999) reports cost information obtained from a random mail survey of employers who contacted JAN from 1992 though 1999. This survey (with 705 respondents) indicated that 71% of all accommodations cost $500 or less, with 20% costing nothing.

Blanck (2000) examined 600 workplace accommodations at Sears: more than 75% required no cost and less than 2% cost more than $1,000. On average the direct cost was $30.

Indirect costs are often referenced as unreasonable by employers. However, MacDonald-Wilson, Rogers, Massaro, Lyass, & Crean (2002) noted in their study of 322 accommodations for people with psychiatric disabilities that in 28% of the cases there were indirect costs such as extra supervisory hours but on average those amounted to 5 hours per month.

Ability to identify and collaborate with experts in other fields when necessary for assistance. |

**Table 10.1. Demands Placed
by the ADA on I-O Psychologists, Cont'd.**

Examples of Affected Activities	Additional Knowledge, Skills, and Abilities Required
Responding to requests for test accommodations, ensuring that no pre-employment tests include psychological or other factors protected by ADA, and making decisions on how to record scores from non-standard administrations. The purpose of the psychological test in a test battery should be considered. It may be acceptable if it is used to "predict necessary, job-related behavior rather than diagnose disability" Cascio, 1994, p. 200).	Knowledge of the psychometric impacts of changing test time, modality, or content. Knowledge of EEOC guidance on disability-related inquiries (EEOC, 2000b). Familiarity with the impact of learning and developmental disabilities on test taking. Ability to identify and collaborate with experts in other fields when necessary for assistance.
Developing and implementing performance appraisal and discipline systems (including terminations). Particular attention must be given to the role of attendance in rating performance or determining disciplinary actions. Consideration should be given to how absences arising under ADA will be handled.	Knowledge of case law related to absenteeism. Ability to distinguish essential functions from marginal functions when developing performance appraisal systems and when making decisions on termination for poor performance. Ability to identify and collaborate with experts as necessary, especially for assistance in determining the impact of mental illness on performance.

Conclusions

This chapter has considered two major issues:

• Who are the forty-three million protected by the ADA?
• How might I-O psychologists respond to the ADA?

On the first point, stated simply, case law is still being decided. On the second point it is fair to say that the field is in the process of responding but the role is still evolving.

Given the outcomes of district court cases, we know that most who pursue litigation under the ADA are not considered part of the forty-three million. Also, owing to Supreme Court rulings, we have more information about who is not likely to be counted among the forty-three million than we do about who is to be counted. Generally, the Supreme Court does not view as a part of the forty-three million those who have a disability that is mitigated, those who are excluded because of a job qualification based on federal standards, those who cannot establish a substantial limitation in a major life activity on a par with activities important to most people's daily lives, and those who posit a limitation in the major life activity of work but do not define a broad class of jobs.

The I-O psychologist can provide critical information to organizations that are responding to ADA issues. The tools of the field of I-O psychology, including job analysis, are essential to implementing the ADA within organizations. To respond effectively the I-O psychologist must have knowledge of the Act. Depending on the particular functions performed by the I-O psychologist, he or she may be called on to perform tasks such as

• Recommending job or test accommodations for an individual with physical or mental impairments with which the psychologist is not familiar, and doing so on an individual basis
• Integrating information on job redesign from human factors, medical, or occupational experts
• Coordinating with economists, building contractors or equipment suppliers, or individuals such as JAN representatives on determining the cost implications of an accommodation

In order to rise to these challenges and arrive at solutions, the I-O psychologist must demonstrate the knowledge, skills, and abilities that will support these activities as well as develop relationships with experts in related fields.

References

Books, Articles, and Government Documents

Allbright, A. L. (2002). 2001 employment decisions under ADA Title I: Survey update. *Mental and Physical Disability Law Reporter, 26,* 394–398.

Americans with Disabilities Act of 1990, 42 U.S.C. § 12101 *et seq.* 1993.

Anfang, S. A. (2003). *Toyota* v. *Williams:* Determining disability under the ADA. *Journal of the American Academy of Psychiatry and the Law, 31,* 97–100.

Barth, J. (2000). Disability benefits and the ADA after *Cleveland* v. *Policy Management Systems. Indiana Law Journal, 75,* 1317–1346.

Blanck, P. D. (2000). Studying disability, employment policy, and ADA. In L. P. Francis & A. Silvers (Eds.), *Americans with disabilities: Exploring implications of the law for individuals and* institutions (pp. 209–220). New York: Routledge.

Blanck, P. D., & Berven, H. M. (1999). Evidence of disability after *Daubert. Psychology, Public Policy, and Law, 5,* 16–40.

Bruyere, S. M. (2002). Disability nondiscrimination in the employment process: The role for testing professionals. In R. B. Ekstrom & D. K. Smith (Eds.), *Assessing individuals with disabilities in educational, employment, and counseling settings* (pp. 205–220). Washington, DC: American Psychological Association.

Cascio, W. F. (1994). The Americans with Disabilities Act of 1990 and the 1991 Civil Rights Act: Requirements for psychological practice in the workplace. In B. D. Sales & G. R. VandenBos (Eds.), *Psychology in litigation and legislation* (pp. 179–211). Washington, DC: American Psychological Association.

Colker, R. (1999). The Americans with Disabilities Act: A windfall for defendants. *Harvard Civil Rights–Civil Liberties Law Review, 34,* 99–162.

Congressional Research Service. (2001). *The Americans with Disabilities Act (ADA): Statutory language and recent issues.* Washington, DC: Library of Congress.

Coyle, M. (1999, July 5). ADA: Clarified or ruined? *National Law Journal,* p. A01.

Crewe, N. M. (1994). Implications of the Americans with Disabilities Act for the training of psychologists. In S. M. Bruyere & J. O'Keefe

(Eds.), *Implications of the Americans with Disabilities Act for psychology* (pp. 15–23). New York: Springer.

East, B. (2000). *The definition of disability after Sutton v. United Airlines.* Paper presented at the national AT conference. Retrieved February 2004 from http://www.nls.org/conf2000/brineast.htm

Equal Employment Opportunity Commission. (1992). *A technical assistance manual on the employment provisions of the Americans with Disabilities Act.* Washington, DC: Author.

Equal Employment Opportunity Commission. (1997a). *The ADA: Questions and answers.* Retrieved January 2004 from http://www.eeoc.gov/facts/adaqa1.html

Equal Employment Opportunity Commission. (1997b, March 25). *Enforcement guidance on the Americans with Disabilities Act and psychiatric disabilities.* EEOC Notice No. 915.002. Washington, DC: Author.

Equal Employment Opportunity Commission. (1999a). *Enforcement guidance: Reasonable accommodation and undue hardship under the Americans with Disabilities Act.* Washington, D.C.: Author.

Equal Employment Opportunity Commission. (1999b, July 26). *Instructions for field offices: Analyzing ADA charges after Supreme Court decisions addressing "disability" and "qualified."* Retrieved February 2004 from http://www.eeoc.gov/policy/docs/field-ada.html

Equal Employment Opportunity Commission. (2000a). *EEOC compliance manual.* Washington, DC: Author.

Equal Employment Opportunity Commission. (2000b). *Enforcement guidance on disability-related inquiries and medical examinations of employees under the Americans with Disabilities Act.* Washington, DC: Author.

Equal Employment Opportunity Commission. (2004a). ADA charge data by impairments/bases—Merit factor resolutions: July 26, 1992–September 30, 2003. Retrieved July 2004 from http://www.eeoc.gov/stats/ada-merit.html

Equal Employment Opportunity Commission. (2004b). *Charge statistics: FY 1992 through FY 2003.* Retrieved July 2004 from http://www.eeoc.gov/stats/charges.html

Garner, B. A. (Ed.). (2001). *Black's law dictionary* (2nd pocket ed.). St. Paul, MN: West.

Gutman, A. (2000a). *EEO law and personnel practices* (2nd ed.). Thousand Oaks, CA: Sage.

Gutman, A. (2000b). Recent Supreme Court ADA rulings: Mixed messages from the Court. *The Industrial-Organizational Psychologist, 37*(3), 31–41.

Job Accommodation Network. (1999). *Accommodation benefit/cost data.* Retrieved February 2004 from http://wwwjan.wvu.edu/media/Stats/BenCosts0799.html

Lee, B. A. (2003). A decade of the Americans with Disabilities Act: Judicial outcomes and unresolved problems. *Industrial Relations, 42,* 11–30.

Locke, S. S. (1997). Redefining the scope of disability. *University of Colorado Law Review, 68,* 107–146.

MacDonald-Wilson, K. L., Rogers, E. S., Massaro, J. M., Lyass, A., & Crean, T. (2002). An investigation of reasonable workplace accommodations for people with psychiatric disabilities: Quantitative findings from a multi-site study. *Community Mental Health Journal, 38,* 35–50.

Mayerson, A., & Diller, M. (2000). The Supreme Court's nearsighted view in ADA. In L. P. Francis & A. Silvers (Eds.), *Americans with disabilities: Exploring implications of the law for individuals and institutions* (pp. 124–125). New York: Routledge.

National Council on Disability. (2002, November 15). *The Americans with Disabilities Act policy brief series: Righting the ADA: No. 3. Significance of the ADA finding that some 43 million Americans have disabilities.* Retrieved February 2004 from http://www.ncd.gov/newsroom/ publications/43million.html

National Council on Disability. (2003, March 17). *The Americans with Disabilities Act policy brief series: Righting the ADA: No. 11. The role of mitigating measures on the narrowing of the ADA's coverage.* Retrieved September 2003 from http://www.ncd.gov/newsroom/publications/ mitigatingmeasures.html

Pape, D. A., & Tarvydas, V. M. (1994). Responsible and responsive rehabilitation consultation on the ADA: The importance of training for psychologists. In S. M. Bruyere & J. O'Keefe (Eds.), *Implications of the Americans with Disabilities Act for psychology* (pp. 169–186). New York: Springer.

Petrila, J. (2002). The U.S. Supreme Court narrows the definition of disability under the Americans with Disabilities Act. *Law and Psychiatry, 53,* 797–801.

Petrila, J., & Brink, T. (2001). Mental illness and changing definitions of disability under the Americans with Disabilities Act. *Psychiatric Services, 52,* 626–630.

Regulations to Implement the Equal Employment Provisions of the Americans with Disabilities Act, 29 C.F.R. § 1630 *et seq.* (1997, 1998, 2004).

Toner, M., & Arnold, D. W. (1999, October). U.S. Supreme Court clarifies definition of disability. *The Industrial-Organizational Psychologist,* pp. 132–133.

Tucker, B. P. (2000). The Supreme Court's definition of disability under the ADA: A return to the dark ages. *Alabama Law Review, 52.* Retrieved February 2004 from http://www.law.ua.edu/lawreview/ tucker521.htm

Cases

Albertsons, Inc. v. Kirkingburg, 527 U.S. 555; 119 S. Ct. 2162 (1999).

Beck v. University of Wisconsin, 75 F.3d 1130 (7th Cir. 1996).

Board of Trustees of University of Alabama v. Garrett, 121 S. Ct. 955 (2001).

Chevron U.S.A., Inc. v. Echazabal, 122 S. Ct. 2045 (2002).

Clackamas Gastroenterology Associates, P.C. v. Wells, 123 S. Ct. 1673 (2003).

Cleveland v. Policy Management Systems Corp., 119 S. Ct. 1597 (1999).

Davoll v. Webb, 194 F.3d 1116 (10th Cir. 1999).

Dvorak v. Mostardi Platt Associates, Inc., 289 F.3d 479 (7th Cir. 2002).

EEOC v. CEC Entertainment, Inc., d/b/a Chuck E. Cheese's, No. 98-C-698, verdict (W.D. Wis. Nov. 5, 1999). Retrieved February 2004 from http://www.wiwd.uscourts.gov/bcgi-bin/opinions/district_opinions/C/98/98-C-698-C-03-14-00.pdf

EEOC v. Prevo's Family Market, Inc., 135 F.3d 1089 (6th Cir. 1998).

EEOC v. R. J. Gallagher Co., 181 F.3d 645 (5th Cir. 1999).

EEOC v. R. R. Donnelley & Sons Co., No. 01 C 4218, consent decree (N.D. Ill., Dec. 13, 2002).

EEOC v. Waffle House, Inc., 534 U.S. 279 (2002).

Foreman v. Babcock & Wilcox, Co., 117 F.3d 800 (5th Cir. 1997).

Fraser v. Goodale, 342 F.3d 1032 (9th Cir. 2003).

Gorbitz v. Corvilla, Inc., 196 F.3d 879 (7th Cir. 1999).

Hamm v. Runyon, 51 F.3d 721 (7th Cir. 1995).

Katz v. City Metal Co., Inc., 87 F.3d 26 (1st Cir. 1996).

Keever v. City of Middletown, 145 F.3d 809 (6th Cir. 1998).

Lawson v. CSX Transportation, Inc., 245 F.3d 916 (7th Cir. 2001).

Lusk v. Christ Hospital, 2000 U.S. Dist. LEXIS 2691 (N.D. Ill. Feb. 29, 2000).

Mauro v. Borgess Medical Center, 137 F.3d 398 (6th Cir. 1998).

Miller v. City of Springfield, 146 F.3d 612 (8th Cir. 1998).

Miller v. National Gas Co., 61 F.3d 627 (8th Cir. 1995).

Murphy v. United Parcel Service, Inc., 119 S. Ct. 1331 (1999).

Rauen v. United States Tobacco Manufacturing Limited Partnership, 319 F.3d 891 (7th Cir. 2003). Retrieved from http://caselaw.lp.findlaw.com/data2/circs/7th/013973p.pdf

Ray v. Kroger Co., No. CV402-019, 2003 U.S. Dist LEXIS 9280 (S.D. Ga. May 27, 2003).

Raytheon Company v. Hernandez, 124 S. Ct. 513 (2003).

Schmidt v. Methodist Hospital of Indiana, Inc., 89 F.3d 342 (7th Cir. 1996).

Shannon v. New York City Transit Authority, 332 F.3d 95 (2nd Cir. 2003).

Skomsky v. Speedway SuperAmerica, 2003 WL 21382495 (D. Minn. 2003).

Sutton v. United Airlines, Inc., 527 U.S. 471; 119 S. Ct. 2139 (1999).

Thompson v. Holy Family Hospital, 121 F.3d 537 (9th Cir. 1997).

Toyota Motor Manufacturing, Kentucky, Inc. v. Williams, 534 U.S. 184; 122 S. Ct. 681 (2002).

US Airways v. Barnett, 535 U.S. 391; 122 S. Ct. 1516 (2002).

Vande Zande v. State of Wisconsin Department of Administration, 44 F.3d 538 (7th Cir. 1996).

Vollmert v. Wisconsin Department of Transportation, 197 F.3d 894 (7th Cir. 1999).

Waggoner v. Olin Corp., 169 F.3d 481 (7th Cir. 1999).

Wright v. Universal Maritime Service Corporation, 525 U.S. 70 (1998).

CHAPTER 11

Wage and Hour Litigation
I-O Psychology's New Frontier
Cristina Banks
Lisa Cohen

I-O psychologists are relatively new to the body of legislation under the Fair Labor Standards Act (FLSA), which was passed in the first half of the twentieth century and addresses work rules and pay. Although statisticians, labor economists, and compensation specialists have commonly testified as experts in these cases, it is only recently that I-O psychologists have joined their ranks. The U.S. Department of Labor (DOL) reports that the Employment Standards Administration Wage and Hour Division recovered $212 million in back wages from employers for FLSA violations in 2003, a 21 percent increase over record-setting collections in 2002 (Frank, 2003). A single case filed under California's wage and hour equivalent of the FLSA, *Bell* v. *Farmers Insurance* (2001), resulted in a judgment against Farmers of nearly $90 million in overtime payments. Few of these cases ever reach a jury. It is more likely that they will settle, and it is not uncommon for a class action wage and hour case to settle for up to $25 million (Flynn, 2001). The fact that they settle for such large dollar amounts is an indication of what the exposure would be at trial!

Exacerbated by the growing number of claims filed under the FLSA and state wage and hour regulations and the size of recent awards, human resource professionals and employers' legal counsel alike have been challenged to develop a strategy to avoid or, if necessary, successfully defend against wage and hour lawsuits (Joss & Rukin, 2002). Although the law is relatively straightforward in articulating worker protections and employer obligations, interpretations of terms such as *managerial work, primary duty, discretion and independent judgment,* and similar terms are far from straightforward and are a matter of considerable debate both in and out of courts. In this arena I-O psychologists are uniquely suited to join the debate and can add considerable clarity by applying state-of-the-art job analysis and work measurement methodologies and competencies to wage and hour issues. These methodologies and competencies include I-O psychologists' ability to understand work, techniques for describing tasks, and techniques for measuring aspects of work salient to wage and hour challenges, such as time spent in work activities and task criticality. This chapter elaborates on the links between I-O psychology and the interpretation of wage and hour laws, assessment of compliance with these laws, and collection of data relevant to wage and hour litigation.

The FLSA and State Wage and Hour Laws

The Fair Labor Standards Act (FLSA) was enacted by Congress in 1938 to help move the depression-ridden country to full employment and at the same time protect employees from exploitation. The Act governs issues related to compensation and establishes a minimum wage, maximum hours, overtime pay, pay equity, record-keeping requirements, and standards for meal and rest breaks as well as "off-the-clock" work. The FLSA provides the DOL with civil and criminal remedies and includes provisions for individuals to file private lawsuits. Civil financial penalties can also be levied for recurring minimum wage and overtime violations. Currently, workers covered by the FLSA are entitled to the minimum wage ($5.15 per hour) and to overtime pay at a rate of not less than one and one-half times their regular rate of pay after forty hours of work in a workweek. The Act applies in all states, although many states have enacted their own laws similar to the FLSA, usually in the form of wage and hour laws or wage orders.

Claimants can file a lawsuit as individuals or in a class action under either federal or state law, or under both. The choice depends on the circumstances of the case (for example, what the violation is, whether similar plaintiffs are found in other states, and whether the state requires potential class members to opt affirmatively into the class or opt out) and on the differences in requirements between state and federal laws (for example, what data are required for the defense and what damages can be collected). When an *opt in* requirement exists, potential members of the class need to indicate that they want to join the class in order to benefit from the lawsuit. When an *opt out* requirement exists, eligible people are automatically members of the class unless they indicate that they want to be excluded from the class. Consequently, the opt out requirement is considerably more favorable toward plaintiffs, as class members have to take action to be removed from the class. In contrast the opt in requirement builds the class by actively recruiting potential members to join the class.

In some states the differences between federal and state lawsuits can be considerable. Under California law, for example, to qualify for an exemption from overtime pay employees must spend at least 50 percent of all time worked in exempt activities, whereas under the federal standard, the employer must have evidence that employees' exempt work is a primary duty. Because the requirements for exemptions are more difficult for employers to meet in that state (for example, exceeding the threshold of 50 percent of time spent on exempt work), California leads the country in class action wage and hour lawsuits. Establishing a specific quantitative threshold gives plaintiff attorneys an advantage when employers do not have the relevant evidence or cannot demonstrate it empirically. Our discussions with labor and employment attorneys lead us to speculate that the wage and hour class action wave that started in California is likely to spread to the rest of the country as plaintiff lawyers learn to leverage FLSA wage and hour laws. Consistent with this speculation, the number of collective actions under the FLSA has increased by more than 70 percent since 2000 (Montwieler, 2004). Because so much of this litigation has taken place in California and because California case law is now well articulated, we will discuss both FLSA and California class action litigation and wage and hour requirements to illuminate wage and hour issues.

The Concept of an Exempt Job

The aspect of wage and hour law that has received the most attention is the classification of jobs. Under the FLSA and the California wage and hour equivalent, all employees are entitled to overtime pay unless they meet specific criteria for *exemptions.* This is where the action is—establishing whether a job is classified as *exempt* from the overtime pay or *nonexempt.* If a job has been improperly classified as exempt from overtime, employers may owe back pay and penalties.

The FLSA establishes four main exemptions: executive, administrative, professional, and outside sales jobs. In the years since the FLSA was enacted, the Department of Labor, which administers the law, has issued clarifications and revisions to these exemptions but generally the exemptions follow the criteria shown in Table 11.1.

Table 11.1. Criteria for Executive, Administrative, Professional, and Outside Sales Exemptions.

Exemption	Criteria
Executive	"[P]rimary duty consists of management of the enterprise in which he [or she] is employed or of a customarily recognized department or subdivision."
	"[C]ustomarily and regularly directs the work of two or more other employees."
	Hires or fires other employees or his or her recommendations on hiring, firing, or promotion are "given particular weight."
	"[C]ustomarily and regularly exercises discretionary powers."
Administrative	Primary duty is either
	"[P]erformance of office or nonmanual work directly related to management policies or general business operations of [the] employer or [the] employer's customers."
	or

**Table 11.1. Criteria for Executive, Administrative,
Professional, and Outside Sales Exemptions, Cont'd.**

Exemption	Criteria
	"[P]erformance of functions in the administration of a school system, or educational establishment or institution, or of a department or subdivision thereof, in work directly related to the academic instruction or training carried on therein."
	"[R]egularly and directly assists a proprietor, or an employee employed in a bona fide executive or administrative capacity."
	"[P]erforms under only general supervision work along specialized or technical lines requiring special training experience or knowledge."
	or
	"[E]xecutes under only general supervision special assignments and tasks."
	"[C]ustomarily and regularly exercises discretion and independent judgment."
Professional	Primary duty is
	"Work requiring knowledge of an advance type in a field of science or learning customarily acquired by a prolonged course of specialized intellectual instruction and study, as distinguished from a general academic education and from an apprenticeship, and from training in the performance of routine mental, manual, or physical processes."
	or
	"Work that is original and creative in character in a recognized field of artistic endeavor . . . and the result of which depends primarily on the invention, imagination, or talent of the employee."
	or
	"Teaching, tutoring, instructing, or lecturing in the activity of imparting knowledge and who is employed and engaged in this activity as a teacher in the school system or educational establishment or institution by which he [or she] is employed."
	or

Table 11.1. Criteria for Executive, Administrative, Professional, and Outside Sales Exemptions, Cont'd.

Exemption	Criteria
	"Work that requires theoretical and practical application of highly-specialized knowledge in computer systems analysis, programming, activities as a computer systems analyst, computer programmer, software engineer, or other similarly skilled worker in the computer software field."
	"Work is predominantly intellectual and varied in character and is of such character that the output produced or the result accomplished cannot be standardized in relation to a given period of time."
	"Consistent exercise of discretion and judgment in performance or work."
Outside sales	"[E]mployed for the purpose of and . . . customarily and regularly engaged away from his [or her] employer's place or places of business in:
	"Making sales"
	or
	"Obtaining orders or contracts for services or for the use of facilities for which a consideration will be paid by the client or customer."

Source: Information from the Fair Labor Standards Act, 29 U.S.C.§ 213; 29 C.F.R. § 541.

Despite these clarifications there is still considerable room for argument about which jobs fit into an exemption and which do not, and it is this room for argument that provides a role for I-O experts. As an illustration, it is far from obvious what would constitute work that is "directly related to management policies or general business operations." One argument has focused on whether resolving claims (for example, comparing insurance claims to eligibility criteria, reserving against claims, and collecting reimbursements from third parties) constitutes work directly related to the management policies or general business operations of an insurance company.

Issues in Class Certification

When a wage and hour lawsuit is filed as a class action, the first step in the process is to determine whether the plaintiffs *should* be certified as a class. In this step, common questions of law must predominate, and class representatives must be typical of the class and able to adequately represent the class. Typically, the plaintiff counsel argues that all employees within the period covered by the lawsuit perform basically the same work, and the defense counsel argues either that the named plaintiffs themselves are not similar enough to define a class or that regardless of their similarity they are not representative of *all* employees who held the job title, thus requiring that the duties and activities of employees with this title need to be examined on a case-by-case basis. To win this argument defense counsel needs to show that employees who hold the job in question perform the job so differently that they cannot be considered a class. Plaintiff counsel needs to show that all employees within the purported class perform essentially the same job. The question is, how do you determine the degree of variability in how employees perform the job? Or, alternatively, how do you show the lack of variability? In the *Fernandez & Scanlon* v. *Enterprise Rent-A-Car* (2002) case, the plaintiff lawyer obtained declarations from job incumbents, who stated that they spent over 90 percent of their time doing nonexempt work and thus counsel contended there was no variability in the responsibilities of plaintiffs who held the same job title. In response, defense counsel introduced a job study, conducted by an I-O psychologist, that showed job incumbents varied considerably in the amount of time spent on different aspects of the job. For example, the amount of time spent in the area of "customer service" ranged from 5 percent to 75 percent across job incumbents and for "fleet management," time spent ranged from 0 percent to 80 percent. In this particular case variability was analyzed and presented to the court in very different ways by the two sides. The plaintiffs presented fact witness evidence and the defense presented expert witness (I-O) evidence. The defense prevailed.

Across courts and cases this issue has been decided both *for* and *against* class certification, based on seemingly similar information about jobs. There does not appear to have been a definitive method or agreed-on type of data for determining the variability within a purported class nor has a single standard emerged for what information is needed to certify a class or deny certification. Judges appear to use very different levels of magnification, some focusing on the forest and others focusing on the trees. A few examples will illustrate this point.

In *Mynaf, Siddiqi, Merrick* v. *Taco Bell* (2001), defense counsel presented information on how restaurant general managers spent their time across various task areas constituting the job, and the judge, focusing on the forest, ruled that because a very high percentage of job incumbents spent 80 percent or more of their time performing exempt work, incumbents appeared to be performing the same job in the same way, and the class was certified. In another case, *O'Hara, et al.* v. *Factory 2-U* (2001), the judge focused on the trees, examining more detailed data describing how much time incumbents spent on different task areas constituting the job. Nevertheless, the judge concluded that the range of time spent on any one task area was small and thus employees were performing essentially the same job. Similarly, in *Metzler* v. *Food 4 Less* (2001), defense counsel presented evidence to show that assistant grocery managers differed in how much time they spent performing tasks across different task areas; however, the judge was not persuaded by this information and certified the class. Once classes were certified, all three cases moved to quick settlement. Often, class certification becomes the trigger for settlement.

Although these cases might appear discouraging with respect to using job analysis data to defeat class certification motions, several recent California cases provide more encouragement for the job analysis strategy. In *Rocher* v. *Sav-On Drug Stores* (2002), defense counsel interviewed job incumbents about their jobs and generated rich information about the tasks each incumbent performed and variations in the tasks performed by a single incumbent over time. Defense counsel then produced fifty-one declarations that emphasized differences in tasks performed across incumbents in general, across stores, and over time for the same incumbent. For instance, one manager declared that under one general manager he never prepared the store schedule but under another he often did, and other managers reported other levels of involvement with respect to scheduling. Similarly, declarants discussed their experience in hiring, supervising employees, and purchasing, which depended in part on such factors as the preferences or style of their general manager, the size of their management team, the skill and experience of the management team and associates, the size and location of their store, and the composition of their staff. The defendant submitted the declarations and a summary to the court to demonstrate that the job varied significantly from store to store and manager to manager. A class was initially certified, but the decision was reversed on appeal. The appeal decision is now being reviewed by the California Supreme Court. Depending on the outcome of the appeal, the *Sav-On* case has the potential to establish a standard for showing variability in the job. Although in the *Sav-On* case the job variability data were provided by nontechnical declarations, a case could be made even stronger by using more formal job analysis techniques such as questionnaires, observations, and incumbent interviews, among others, to capture detailed information regarding differences in work performed across incumbents.

In three other recent cases, *Fernandez & Scanlon v. Enterprise Rent-A-Car* (2002), *Reyna v. Anheuser-Busch* (2003), and *Perez v. LA Fitness* (2000), defense counsel defeated class certification, in part by using quantitative data collected from current incumbents by I-O psychologists. Defense counsel in these cases retained I-O psychologists to determine the amount of time each incumbent spent on different aspects of the job and the individual differences in tasks performed. In the *Enterprise* case the judge relied on the empirical evidence generated by job analysis in deciding in favor of the defense: "The Court finds that issues common to the proposed class and subclasses do not predominate over individual issues. It appears from the declaration and deposition testimony submitted by plaintiffs and defendants that factual issues relevant to a determination of the 'realistic requirements' of the Assistant Manager job vary significantly from branch to branch operated by defendants."

Similarly, the judge in the *Anheuser-Busch* case found that case-by-case analysis was necessary to determine which sales representatives spent more than 50 percent of their work time performing nonexempt duties and to assess damages due in the case:

> [Anheuser-Busch's] policy is not facially in violation of any law, it is instead the manner in which [Anheuser-Busch] applies that policy to each individual employee. Therefore, analysis of individual performance constitutes nothing more than a determination of

individual instances of compliant application or non-compliant application of a facially legal employment policy. The analysis of one claim will not further the determination of another. Therefore, this Court cannot conclude that the common question of interpreting and applying the Wage Order predominates over the highly individualized factual question of who performs what employment duties, when are they performed, and for what reasons.

Among the evidence examined by the judge in the Anheuser-Busch case were the results of an observation study of sales representatives. Trained job analysts observed these sales representatives for full days, recording all tasks they performed, the time spent on tasks, and reasons for performing nonexempt tasks.

In the third case, *Perez* v. *LA Fitness,* the judge made a tentative ruling (an initial judgment with the right to reconsider following additional argument) against class certification, a ruling based in part on data collected through observations of job incumbents' activities for varying shifts and for varying days within a workweek. As in the Anheuser-Busch case, trained observers tracked tasks performed and time spent on tasks during each shift.

In all three cases, traditional job analysis data helped the judges evaluate whether the job was performed similarly across members of the purported class. Because of the results of these studies, the cases did not go forward (*LA Fitness* settled before trial and in *Anheuser-Busch* and *Enterprise,* a class was not certified and individual actions were pursued), and thus employers were able to avoid a costly class action lawsuit. These latter cases illustrate the value of job analysis data: by providing detailed information regarding what job incumbents actually do on the job and how they spend their time, decisions and the basis for those decisions have greater clarity and better inform employers. When a case is not certified as a class action, the lawsuit converts to a series of individual actions that have much smaller payoffs and are much less attractive to plaintiff attorneys. These cases often settle quickly.

Issues in Establishing Exempt Status

The second step in a wage and hour class action lawsuit is to examine the merits of the case: is the job covered by one or more of the exemptions listed in Table 11.1? Although the specific requirements associated with each of these exemptions differ, there are several common themes. All the exemptions except the outside sales exemption require the following: (1) a minimum salary level, (2) a salary basis test, and (3) a duties test. Currently, the minimum salary level for the executive and administrative exemption is $155 per week and for the professional exemption, it is $170 per week. Note that at these salary levels, an employee can be classified as exempt even when he or she makes as little as $8,000 to $13,000 per year! The salary basis test simply requires that the employee is paid a fixed, predetermined salary that is not subject to reduction because of variations in quantity or quality of work.

The duties test requires that an employee perform particular job duties that are specified for each exemption. To meet this test, either a *long* test or *short* test is applied. As the names imply, the criteria one must meet to pass the long test are more extensive than those for the short test. The long duties test applies to lower-paid (currently up to $250 per week) positions, and the short duties test applies to higher-paid ("white-collar") positions with a salary of at least $250 per week. The duties test has not been updated since 1949, and salary levels were last updated in 1975. Because the salary levels are so low for the long test (below minimum wage), this test is seldom, if ever, used now. To meet the short duties test, an employee must (1) earn at least the minimum salary amount and (2) have the primary duty of performing duties specified for executive, administrative, or professional positions.

The concept of *primary duty* is key in establishing an exemption. Primary duty is determined from all the facts in a particular case, as there is no specific requirement for the amount of time that establishes a primary duty. Although 50 percent of an employee's time is suggested as a good rule of thumb for determining that an employee has management as a primary duty, it is not necessary for meeting the exemption requirement. An employee can still be considered exempt if other pertinent factors support such a conclusion ("Interpretations," Subpart B, 1993). For example, a manager will be considered exempt even though he spends more than 50 percent of his time in production or sales work (nonexempt work) if, while engaged in such work, he supervises other employees, directs the work of warehouse and delivery men, approves advertising, orders merchandise, handles customer complaints, authorizes payment of bills, or performs other management duties as the day-to-day operations require. The federal regulations allow considerable room for establishing a primary duty as long as the amount of time spent on nonexempt work is not significantly more than 50 percent.

Secretary of Labor Elaine Chao has proposed a revision of the FLSA's white-collar regulations that will change the criteria for determining who is excluded from the Act's overtime requirements. On April 20, 2004, the DOL issued the revised regulations—a slightly different version from the version proposed by the secretary of labor—which will go into effect 120 days after their official release (unless they are blocked by Congress). The major changes are (1) increasing the minimum salary level to $455 per week, or $23,660 per year; (2) allowing an automatic exemption for employees who earn a guaranteed total annual compensation of at least $100,000; (3) eliminating the long test; and (4) for the executive exemption, extending the short test to include evidence that an employee manages the entire enterprise or department or subdivision. The revised regulations also provide clearer and more modern examples of what are and are not exempt duties for all four exemption categories: executive, administrative, professional, and outside sales. These examples should make it easier for employers and employees to determine who may be exempt. It is also anticipated that these new criteria will enable employers to meet exemption requirements more easily. Despite these new regulations, there is still plenty of room for interpretation.

Exemptions are narrowly construed against the employer asserting them, so employers are advised to "closely check the exact terms and conditions of an exemption in light of the employee's actual duties before assuming that the exemption might apply to the employee" (U.S. Department of Labor, 2004a). The burden of proof is on the employer to support the actual application of an exemption. Employers must examine the actual duties (tasks) performed by individual employees and then determine the percentage of time spent on exempt versus nonexempt work.

The California Wage Orders, administered by the California Industrial Welfare Commission and interpreted by the California Division of Labor Standards Enforcement (DLSE), are considerably more protective of employees than the FLSA standards are.

Although modeled after the federal regulations, the California Wage Orders require employers to show that an employee is *primarily engaged* in exempt activities, meaning that an employee must spend *more than half* (> 50 percent) of his or her work time engaged in exempt activities, regardless of the number of hours worked (forty or more) in a workweek. California's quantitative standard was established in *Ramirez* v. *Yosemite Water* (1999), in which a route sales representative filed a complaint about unpaid overtime wages, claiming that he was improperly classified as an outside sales representative and that he spent little of his time engaged in solicitation of customers. The court applied the 50 percent time requirement and judged whether Ramirez was exempt on that basis. In the end Ramirez prevailed. This case also established that estimates of time spent must be calculated for each employee classified as exempt. Under the California standard, unlike the federal standard, an employee who does not meet the 50 percent threshold for exempt time is denied exempt status, regardless of other pertinent factors. This is why plaintiffs often choose to use a state statute rather than the federal statute as a basis for a complaint.

There is another important difference between federal and California exemption standards. Federal regulations allow time to be counted as exempt time when an employee is performing exempt work *while performing a nonexempt activity. Donovan* v. *Burger King* (1982) held that an exempt employee's managerial duties can be carried out at the same time as the employee performs nonexempt manual tasks. This case established that specific activities that are an essential part of and necessarily incident to an exempt activity can be considered exempt. For example, an employee writing a managerial report on a computer is performing exempt work even though the manual activity of typing would otherwise be considered nonexempt. Under the federal standard, employers can claim work as exempt if the activities performed are directly and closely related to exempt work.

In contrast, the California DLSE does *not* recognize work as exempt if in the course of performing that work an employee is engaged in nonexempt activities. For example, if a manager is observing and supervising employees in a fast-food restaurant but is also making tacos or ringing up charges at the cash register, the

DLSE regards all the time spent making tacos and ringing at the register as nonexempt time—regardless of what the manager may be doing with his or her eyes or thinking. California does not allow managers to count as exempt the time they spend performing managerial duties if they are also engaged in incidental activities. Therefore *dual tasking* does not exist, and time spent engaged in incidental activities is ascribed to nonexempt work. *Ramirez* held that an employee is engaged in either exempt or nonexempt work, not both at the same time, and time can be ascribed to exempt work only if the employee is primarily engaged in an exempt task. Once again, state law is more attractive to a prospective plaintiff than federal law.

Another case, *Bell* v. *Farmers Insurance* (2001), raised the bar for establishing the administrative exemption in California. In this case a class of claims representatives sued for nonpayment of overtime compensation, alleging that they were improperly classified as exempt employees under the administrative exemption. The court found that the claims representatives' work was primarily production work even though the job involved evaluating and determining payment of insurance claims. Despite the involvement of discretion and independent judgment in the work, the court found that claims representatives were not involved in work that was of importance to management policy or general business operations, stating that "there is no triable controversy and that claims adjusting is a product or service which FIE's [Farmers Insurance Exchange's] operation exists to provide. It is further found that the Personal Lines Claims Representatives devote their time to carrying out FIE's claims adjusting product/service as opposed to its 'administrative' functions. Therefore, as a matter of law, these Personal Lines Claims representatives . . . do not fall within the ambit of the 'administrative' exemption from overtime."

Discretion and independent judgment was insufficient for establishing this exemption. Unfortunately, no clear guidance was given for establishing the link between work activities and management policy or general business operations. *Bell* suggests that employers must show clearly how the tasks performed by administrative employees are explicitly linked to the "core" operations of the business; repetitive tasks, even when unique and even when involving discretion and independent judgment, constitute production work unless they directly support management policy or general business operations.

Establishing the exempt status of a job under either federal or state law requires an employer to show evidence that the characteristics of the job in question meet the terms described in the exemption guidelines. These terms are listed in Table 11.2 with their definitions (or illustrations).

Table 11.2. Definitions of Terms Describing Exempt Work.

Term	Definition and Illustration
Management	"[I]nterviewing, selecting, and training of employees; setting and adjusting their rates of pay and hours of work; directing their work; maintaining their production or sales records for use in supervision or control; appraising their productivity and efficiency for the purpose of recommending promotions or other changes in their status; handling their complaints and grievances and disciplining them when necessary; planning the work; determining the techniques to be used; apportioning the work among workers; determining the type of materials, supplies, machinery or tools to be used or merchandise to be bought, stocked and sold; controlling the flow and distribution of materials or merchandise and supplies; providing for the safety of the men and the property."
Primary duty	"[T]he major part, or over 50 percent, of the employee's time."
Two or more employees	"[T]wo full-time employees or the equivalent [who] must be employed in the department which the 'executive' is managing."
Authority to hire or fire	"[D]irectly concerned either with the hiring or the firing and other change of status of the employees under his [or her] supervision, whether by direct action or by recommendation to those

Table 11.2. Definitions of Terms Describing Exempt Work, Cont'd.

Term	Definition and Illustration
	to who the hiring and firing functions are delegated."
Discretionary powers	"A person whose work is so completely routinized that he [or she] has no discretion does not qualify for exemption."
Customarily and regularly	"[A] frequency which must be greater than occasional but which, of course, may be less than constant. The requirement will be met by the employee who normally and recurrently is called upon to exercise and does exercise discretionary powers in the day-to-day performance of his [or her] duties."
Work directly and closely related	"[A]ctivities which are closely associated with . . . supervisory functions or responsibilities. The supervision of employees and the management of a department include a great many directly and closely related tasks which are different from the work performed by subordinates and are commonly performed by supervisors because they are helpful in supervising the employees or contribute to the smooth functioning of the department for which they are responsible."
Occasional tasks	"In many establishments the proper management of a department requires the performance of a variety of occasional, infrequently recurring tasks which cannot practicably be performed by the production workers and are usually performed by the executive. These small tasks when viewed separately without regard to their relationship to the executive's overall functions might appear to constitute nonexempt work. In reality they are the means of properly carrying out the employee's management functions and responsibilities in connection with men, materials, and production."

Table 11.2. Definitions of Terms Describing Exempt Work, Cont'd.

Term	Definition and Illustration
Nonexempt work generally	"Nonexempt work is easily identifiable where, as in the usual case, it consists of work of the same nature as that performed by the nonexempt subordinates of the 'executive.' It is more difficult to identify in cases where supervisory employees spend a significant amount of time in activities not performed by any of their subordinates and not consisting of actual supervision and management."
Directly related to management policies or general business operations	"[T]hose types of activities relating to the administrative operations of a business as distinguished from 'production' or, in a retail or service establishment, 'sales' work. In addition to describing the types of activities, the phrase limits the exemption to persons who perform work of substantial importance to the management or operation of the business of his [or her] employer or his [or her] employer's customers."

Source: Information from U.S. Department of Labor, 2004b.

Although offering some guidance for employers, these definitions still require interpretation and a level of inference. It is this level of inference that provides the raw material for legal arguments made by opposing counsel. The legal arguments notwithstanding, it is the I-O psychologist who can add considerably more clarity to the legal arguments by applying I-O methodologies and techniques to create observable and verifiable standards.

Even more challenging than ambiguous criteria and terminology is the fact that in practice exempt status is attached to *both the employee* ("an exempt employee") *and to the job* ("an exempt job"). An employer must show that the job in general is exempt as well as each individual case *within* the job title. As a result, employers can find themselves in the position of having established that a *job* is exempt but that certain employees *within* the title perform the job in a nonexempt way and therefore are due overtime compensation. But, and this is an important "but," this is true only when these nonexempt employees are performing the job *satisfactorily*—employees cannot turn themselves into nonexempt employees and gain overtime pay by performing the job poorly! The message to employers is simple: to avoid a wage and hour lawsuit they should ensure that jobs are designed so that *all* incumbents in an exempt job can perform the job in an exempt way and so that *all* incumbents have all the necessary qualifications, training, and guidance to perform the job as directed.

The Relevance of I-O Psychology to the FLSA

I-O psychologists understand work: what people do, how they do it, how often they do it, what the work context is, and how to measure work. This knowledge is critical for correctly classifying jobs as exempt or nonexempt, for maintaining the exempt status of a job over time, and for auditing compliance with the law. The following is a brief discussion of ways in which I-O psychologists can contribute to this area of the law.

The Central Role of Job Analysis

Job analysis is the systematic study of the content of a job, and a variety of methods are used to collect reliable and valid job information (Gael, 1983; Harvey, 1991). Among the outcomes of most job analyses is the delineation of the important and frequently performed tasks and activities making up a specific job. Although job analyses also allow identification of the knowledge, skills, abilities, and other characteristics (KSAOs) central to performing these tasks and activities, KSAOs are less relevant to the FLSA than what work is actually performed. Nevertheless, KSAOs are relevant when one considers *how* an employee performs the job, and we discuss this later in this chapter. Job analysis often includes measures of time spent and other indicators of the relative importance or predominance of tasks and activities in the job (see Gael, 1988). As we have shown in the court cases described earlier, this type of data is often central to FLSA-based disputes about both class certification and exemptions. Tasks and activities must be described comprehensively and examined in the context of exemption criteria in order to properly classify a job as exempt or nonexempt. Therefore job analysis is directly relevant to determining a job's classification.

Tasks that are observable, repeatable or cyclical, predictable, logically connected, and stable over time are best suited for job analysis, whereas tasks that are unobservable, unpredictable, highly variable over time, and unique in their expression across incumbents are considerably more difficult to capture with traditional job analyses. Also, physical tasks are easiest to capture because they are easily observed and objectively described. Mental tasks, because they are unobservable and must be inferred or collected through verbal report, are more difficult to capture and describe comprehensively. Recent innovations in job analysis provide greater access to mental tasks. *Cognitive task analysis* (DuBois, Shalin, Levi, & Borman, 1998) captures mental content by applying the *think aloud protocol* technique (Ericsson & Simon, 1993) to track job incumbents' thought processes while these individuals are performing tasks. Through such methods these thought processes can be articulated as mental tasks, rendering the unobservable observable. Because a great deal of exempt work involves seemingly unobservable mental tasks like planning, strategizing, evaluating, monitoring, and observing, it is critical for a job analyst to capture job incumbents' thought processes and turn them into mental tasks so that *all* of the work performed can be comprehensively described. An experienced job analyst who becomes very familiar with the job at issue has the greatest likelihood of successfully applying job analysis techniques to identify all tasks for the purpose of properly classifying the job as either exempt or nonexempt.

The Communication of Job Responsibilities and Work Expectations

I-O psychologists have expertise in writing job descriptions, developing and communicating performance expectations, and measuring performance. This expertise is useful in understanding what employees believe is expected of them in the job and what tasks and activities they perceive to be important for meeting those expectations. I-O psychologists can assist in this understanding process by examining how an organization communicates job responsibilities and work expectations, in terms of the clarity, understandability, and consistency of those communications. This information can help employers to determine whether they can expect employees to perform the job as directed. For example, when employers clearly indicate to employees in all documents—job descriptions, performance evaluations, operations manuals for managers, and merit compensation criteria—that they should spend the majority of their time on managerial duties, employers have met their responsibility and have reason to expect job behavior consistent with those communications (assuming employees have the necessary resources for that behavior). To the extent the communications are unclear, ambiguous, internally inconsistent, or in conflict with other communications, employees may not fully understand the importance of managerial duties and may perform an exempt job in a nonexempt way. Moreover, employers may have a hard time claiming jobs are properly classified as exempt when their communications are not clear, regardless of their expectations.

Organizational Communication and the FLSA

Organizational communication is important for two reasons. First, the FLSA states that employers cannot classify a job as exempt solely on the basis of a written job description or other company documents. Classification must be based on what employees understand are their responsibilities and what they actually do on the job. Second, an employee cannot turn his or her exempt job into a nonexempt one by being a poor performer. If employees choose to spend the majority of their time on nonexempt activities, such as serving customers and preparing food, despite clearly stated expectations that they should be managing this work, their jobs may still be exempt. Therefore clearly written performance expectations and evaluation criteria that support the exempt aspects of the job help to support the employer's claim that a job is exempt and that claims of misclassification are inappropriate when a low-performing, exempt employee chooses to perform the job in a nonexempt way. Both of these reasons require employers to clearly and consistently communicate (reasonable) expectations to employees in order to establish and maintain the exempt status of a job.

Issues of Ability, Motivation, and Performance

I-O psychologists study issues related to employees' ability and motivation to perform tasks. This expertise is helpful in determining whether employees' poor performance of exempt job tasks and activities is a function of low ability or low motivation to perform a job in an exempt manner. If ability or motivation, or both, can be isolated and corrected, the exempt status of the job can be maintained.

Ability

On the ability side, I-O psychologists can examine the basis for selection into the exempt job to check for qualifications that enable an employee to perform the job as directed. For example, if selection criteria include the knowledge, skills, abilities, and other characteristics that underlie successful performance as a manager, administrator, or professional (or other exempt role), then it is reasonable to expect that people selected for the job will have the *ability* to perform the job in an exempt manner. If these KSAOs are missing, it may be unreasonable to expect that employees selected into the job could perform in the manner expected, regardless of their motivation. In addition, I-O psychologists can examine the tools and instruments used to evaluate the KSAOs of job candidates to determine whether these tools and instruments can identify employees who have the necessary KSAOs to perform the job effectively.

When employees are selected into the job without the necessary KSAOs, deficits can be addressed through training and development activities. To the extent selection criteria, KSAO assessments, or new-hire training activities are deficient, it is unlikely that employees will perform the job as required. This could result in an exempt job being reclassified as nonexempt because incumbents cannot, and therefore do not, perform the job in an exempt manner. Inadequate selection and training is not a defense against misclassification lawsuits.

Motivation

I-O psychologists can also examine employee motivation to determine factors that are associated with employees' decisions about *how* they will perform their job (Banks, 2004). For managerial jobs especially, employees make decisions about how restaurant, store, or department tasks get done: managers can attempt to do all the tasks themselves or to delegate and direct others to get them done. For jobs that fall within the executive exemption, the employee's managerial style may affect the classification of the job. Even though managers are ultimately responsible for completion of all tasks and all work outcomes, *how* managers get the work done can make the difference between whether their job is properly classified as exempt or is considered nonexempt. Managers who adopt a more participative, team-oriented, hands-on style run the risk of spending too much time performing nonexempt tasks. This style implicitly invites managers to do the same work as their staff and thus violates one of the requirements for establishing exempt status—a minimum of hands-on work. Alternatively, managers who adopt a more command-and-control style are likely to spend their time appropriately on managerial tasks, although they also run the risk of creating a disengaged staff that has difficulty working as a team. This latter style, although positive in terms of exempt status, may lead ultimately to performance problems among the staff. Note that the managerial style that produces the best-performing staff may be in direct conflict (if done in the extreme) with the criteria necessary for establishing the job's exempt status.

Employees' motivations apart from their typical managerial style may influence their decisions on how to deal with their workload and subsequently determine whether they perform their job in an exempt or nonexempt way. For example, when managers need to accomplish twenty tasks during a shift, they can choose to turn themselves into "extra pairs of hands" and do the work of nonexempt employees, or they can create a strategy for getting the work done and assign the work to others. They may choose one or the other approach in part by how they are rewarded or by what they find internally or externally rewarding. When managers are rewarded for ensuring that the tasks get done at a high level of quality and for getting results quickly, they may elect to do the work themselves when they are best at it (which is often the case). When they are rewarded for developing a skilled team, they may be more likely to spend their time training others and modeling the desired behaviors. In the former case the managers would be performing the work in a nonexempt manner; in the latter the work would be exempt. Therefore employee motivation provides clues regarding the choices employees are likely to make in determining *how* the work gets done, and this in turn will influence the classification of the job.

Performance

Task Versus Contextual Performance. As we will see in other sections of this chapter, there are places in this field of work where a chasm exists between I-O psychology practice and legal opinion. What is best for a well-functioning organization is sometimes at odds with legal requirements. The foregoing discussion illustrates one instance of this chasm. Another centers on the difference between *task performance* and *contextual performance* (Borman & Motowidlo, 1993). Whereas task performance focuses on an employee's accomplishment of tasks assigned, contextual performance includes extra-role behaviors, those elected by an employee to support the organizational, social, and psychological environment in which he or she works (Landy & Conte, 2004). Contextual performance, also described as *organizational citizenship behavior* (OCB) (Smith, Organ, & Near, 1983), may involve job behavior such as volunteering to complete tasks and activities assigned to others and helping others accomplish their work. This kind of behavior, if performed for a significant amount of the time spent on the job, will undermine that job's exempt status if the majority of that work is nonexempt. What is difficult about contextual performance is that it is tied to personality and is engaged in by some employees above and beyond their formal duties and responsibilities. I-O psychologists regard contextual performance an important component of success in any job; however, contextual performance is clearly undesirable from the point of view of compliance with the FLSA and wage and hour laws.

Performance Reviews. I-O psychologists understand that a job description rarely includes information about *how* the work gets done; basically, job descriptions communicate *what* needs to be done and at what level of quality. The performance review process identifies those areas of the job that are most important and outlines the level of effectiveness expected in those areas. Neither the job description nor the performance evaluation completely determines how an employee does his or her job. This leaves a great deal of room for managers to determine the tasks and activities they personally do.

There appears to be a moral here. A company that pays an employee to be a manager (or administrator or professional) is best served when that employee acts as a manager, and at the same time the employee's individual interest is also served. When the company rewards employees by paying them as managers but encourages them to do mostly hands-on work, it is opening itself to FLSA challenges. A carefully crafted job description that directs the employee to carry out his or her responsibilities in an exempt manner and a performance review process that clearly delineates the importance of exempt behavior will go a long way toward maintaining a job's exempt status *and* promoting overall business success.

Performance Expectations. Similarly, *how* an employee chooses to perform his or her job may be influenced by performance expectations set by his or her own manager. Beyond general performance criteria, specific expectations can be set by upper-level managers and consequently can drive the lower-level manager's behavior in one direction or another. The upper-level manager's leadership style or specific performance expectations for the lower-level manager can directly affect *how much time* that lower-level manager spends on tasks and activities within the domain of job responsibilities. For example, if an upper-level manager focuses on such specific issues as cleanliness, orderliness, merchandizing, and sales, the lower-level manager is likely to spend more time performing hands-on work than managerial work in order to respond to the upper-level manager's directives in a timely and effective manner. However, this lower-level manager also runs the risk of performing the job in a nonexempt way. In contrast, if the upper-level manager focuses on people issues such as recruiting, selecting, training, and coaching quality team members and evaluating the team, the lower-level manager is likely to spend more time performing managerial work in order to respond to the upper-level manager's directives. Thus the specific expectations set by an individual's manager or others in the organization (for example, the CEO, COO, or general manager), on top of the general responsibilities outlined in the job description, may cause lower-level managers to shift their focus in the job and spend more time on particular tasks, and this in turn may shift the job's classification from exempt to nonexempt, depending on how much the focus shifts and for how long. To the extent the performance management system can be customized to accommodate differences in individual upper-level managers' directives and emphasis, it may allow upper-level managers to undermine a lower-level job's exempt status.

I-O psychologists have ample opportunity to help companies understand the nature of the work performed and help those companies understand the contextual factors that can either support or challenge a job's exempt status. Whether through job analysis or through more conceptual analyses of the work setting and employee characteristics, I-O psychology can contribute to this developing area of the law. Detailed discussion of the specific ways I-O psychologists can contribute to the understanding of wage and hour compliance is presented in the following section.

Ways to Support FLSA Compliance

The Definition of a Class

Job analysis is a valuable analytical tool for collecting data in the class certification stage of a wage and hour lawsuit. Job analysis is used to identify the physical and mental tasks making up the job at issue. (In the next section we discuss how important—and difficult—it is to capture the mental content of work, in order to accumulate all the exempt time spent in the job.) Essentially the same steps are followed here as in classifying jobs, with two exceptions: (1) data collection may involve purported class members who may not have performed the job recently, and (2) the job may have changed from the way it was performed during the period covered by the lawsuit. There is another important difference: a judge is determining the exemption status, not management. These three differences need to be taken into account as data are collected and assembled for the purpose of making an argument for or against the exempt classification.

Job analysis identifies the physical and mental tasks making up the job through a variety of data collection methods and data sources, and once this information is collected, comparisons can be made across incumbents to determine the degrees of similarity and variability in work performed. Incumbents who are still employed (current employees) or who have only recently left the job (recent incumbents) can serve as subject matter experts (SMEs) for collecting preliminary job information. Various data collection methods (for example, observation, interviews, diary keeping) can be used to generate a list of tasks performed on the job. Next, an I-O expert (or legal expert) can categorize the tasks as either exempt or nonexempt, and then tasks can be sorted into exempt or nonexempt groups. Estimates of time spent in each exempt and nonexempt task group can be collected using various methodologies (for example, job analysis questionnaire, observation study) and aggregated into estimates of total time spent in exempt and nonexempt work for individual incumbents.

The Identification of Exempt Jobs

Job analysis is also a valuable analytical tool for classifying jobs. An I-O expert can assist in properly classifying jobs as either exempt or nonexempt, because an accurate classification would seem to require a comparison between information about the job and the exemption criteria. I-O psychologists can supply the kind of information needed to make these comparisons. As with the process of defining a class, a job analysis can be conducted to identify the physical and mental tasks comprising the job, and then these tasks can be classified as exempt or nonexempt for the purpose of determining the amount of time spent on each kind of work, exempt and nonexempt.

Identifying Tasks

Physical tasks can be easily identified through observation. They are also easily identified in interviews and questionnaires as they are relatively easy for employees to remember, particularly if they have been performed recently. Mental tasks, which are more difficult to observe and to recall, can be identified through cognitive task analysis in which the mental content of a job can be extracted through think-aloud protocol techniques, among others (as discussed earlier). These techniques capture information on the purpose and goals of the job as well as on how employees go about achieving desired outcomes. Interviewing and diary-keeping techniques also hold promise for gaining access to mental tasks by recording employees' thought processes while they are performing the job.

It is interesting that when employees are asked what they do in their jobs, they often report physical tasks and, with additional probing, may also report mental tasks. In contrast, if one shows employees a list of the mental and physical tasks identified in their job, they report mental tasks with higher frequency than they do when simply asked to describe what they do. It may be that mental tasks are more difficult for employees to access without probing because employees are both less aware of their mental operations and lacking in the relevant vocabulary for describing these operations. It has been our experience that if we can identify and describe a mental task in relatively simple terms, employees can more easily report it and ascribe time to it. In the wage and hour arena it is critical to capture all of the mental tasks involved in the job, as these are the building blocks for establishing exempt status. Therefore it is important to understand a job in enough depth to extract all of the tasks. In that way, employees can report all tasks they do, not just the tasks that are easily recalled. A job analysis that enables description of both physical and mental tasks will also enable correct classification of a job, taking account of *all* the tasks performed.

Classifying Tasks

Given knowledge of exemption criteria and information generated from the job analysis, the I-O expert can classify tasks as either exempt or nonexempt. For example, if an employee stocks shelves in a grocery store for an hour per day, the I-O expert would typically classify this task as nonexempt. However, if in the course of stocking shelves, the employee evaluates whether items have been correctly placed and labeled, that same task could be considered exempt. It becomes exempt when the task becomes evaluating hourly employees' merchandizing of items in the display rather than stocking. By understanding tasks in depth and in the context of how they are performed, the I-O expert can make correct inferences about the nature of the task (because the exemption guidelines require inference) and, using those inferences, allocate tasks to the exempt or nonexempt category. Correct categorization of tasks is important for determining how much of the job entails exempt versus nonexempt work.

Calculating Time Spent

After identifying the mental and physical tasks making up the job, the I-O psychologist can calculate the time spent performing exempt versus nonexempt work in order to determine whether the *primary duty* test, or 50 percent exempt time threshold, is met. The different amounts of time spent on exempt and nonexempt tasks can be estimated through various methods, including self-report job analysis questionnaires and observation studies. Self-report questionnaires can be designed to collect time-spent ratings on individual tasks performed and estimates of percentages of time spent on the various groupings of tasks, or task areas, that constitute the job. Observational studies consist of observers' detailed reports of tasks performed and time spent on tasks over a specified period of time (for example, one shift).

In both types of studies, time spent can be calculated for exempt and nonexempt work separately and then compared. The key to coming up with estimates of time spent on exempt versus nonexempt work is the *categorization* of tasks as either exempt or nonexempt and then the *aggregation* of time spent on all exempt tasks versus all nonexempt tasks. That is, tasks must be clustered into homogeneous groups (task areas), each group consisting of either exempt or nonexempt tasks. For example, tasks devoted to customer service can be sorted into two groups: tasks directly involved with delivering customer service (for example, helping customers with purchases and cashiering), which are nonexempt, and tasks involving oversight of customer service (for example, evaluating customer satisfaction and directing associates to help customers), which are exempt. Together, these two groups make up the customer service aspect of the job, and separately, they differentiate the hands-on (nonexempt) from the managerial (exempt) components of customer service. Similarly, food preparation tasks can be sorted into tasks involved in preparing food, which are nonexempt, and tasks involved in overseeing food preparation, which are exempt. Once tasks are categorized correctly, employees can ascribe time to these separate aspects of the job, and thus provide estimates of total time spent in exempt versus nonexempt work. Time estimates can be collected by individual, and each individual's time spent on exempt work can be compared to exemption criteria to determine whether criteria are met in each case.

Gathering Additional Information

Other information can be collected to further support the exempt versus nonexempt classification of the job. The exercise of discretion and independent judgment can be illuminated through job analysis. One way to collect this information is to obtain descriptions of decision-making authority. For example, employees can report how much authority they have in making a variety of decisions, hiring and firing decisions in particular. This authority might vary from making the final decision to not being involved at all in the decision. It can be argued that employees who make the final decision or give recommendations that are regularly or generally followed across a variety of decisions meet the exemption criterion of discretion and independent judgment.

In summary, job analysis generates a type of probative information needed in order to properly classify a job as exempt or nonexempt. By identifying the tasks and activities that make up the job, segregating those tasks into exempt and nonexempt categories, collecting estimates of time spent on aggregated groups of exempt and nonexempt tasks, and then aggregating time spent on exempt versus nonexempt work, employers with the aid of I-O experts can more confidently defend the classification of the job as either exempt or nonexempt. The reliability and defensibility of the classification depends heavily on the quality of data collected from employees as well as the correct allocation of tasks into exempt and nonexempt categories. Job analysis is the appropriate analytical tool for providing the quality data necessary for proper classification.

An Ancillary Issue: The Problem of Recall in Job Analysis

An interesting challenge is determining what to do about former employees who are covered by a lawsuit and how to deal with changes in the job over time. Employees who are no longer with the company may or may not be good subjects for the job analysis; the quality (reliability and validity) of the data they generate is suspect. Self-reports of tasks performed and the amount of time spent on tasks require accurate recall, and it can be argued that former employees are less likely to provide high-quality data due to significant memory decay. Former employees' reports of time spent on tasks may also be distorted by a variety of biases caused by memory decay. One bias, *availability bias,* is particularly relevant because it affects people's estimates of time or frequency. People make judgments of incidence or frequency based on the ease or speed of recall (Kahneman, Slovic, & Tversky, 1982). When former employees have a better memory for physical as opposed to mental tasks, availability bias may result in former employees' overreporting time spent on physical (nonexempt) tasks and underreporting time spent on mental (exempt) tasks, thus exaggerating time estimates in favor of plaintiffs. For these and other reasons, former employees are likely to be less reliable sources of job data than current employees and thus should be included in job studies cautiously.

When a job has not changed significantly over the years (for example, no major reorganizations have occurred), current employees serve as good proxies for all employees within the class period, including former employees. The best job analysis data are collected on current employees and on a recent period of time (for example, over the last year). When the job has changed over time, it is important to note the differences in tasks performed and shifts in time spent on tasks over the period covered by the lawsuit. A separate data collection may be necessary to cover the period prior to the significant changes in the job. For example, it may be useful to use questionnaires and interviews to collect information from employees who were in the job when it was performed differently. Current employees are likely to be the best subjects for these studies because they have performed a similar job recently and can use their present job as a reference point for recalling tasks performed and time spent on those tasks from an earlier period.

To reduce availability bias and to facilitate accurate recall of tasks performed and time spent on tasks, employees can be reminded of events occurring during the relevant period, both inside and outside the company, to trigger memories of that period. For example, asking employees whom they worked with, whom they reported to, who were their friends at work, what policies were in place, what things were called then, and the like, may increase the likelihood that memories from that period will be triggered, enabling the employee to remember more accurately what he or she did on the job and how much time was spent on tasks. It has been shown that priming and the eliciting of life history events have resulted in more accurate retrospective reports (Belli, 1998), and the application of these techniques to retrospective accounts of work performed may facilitate accurate recall in the employment context as well. If this can be done, then reports of tasks performed and time spent on exempt and nonexempt tasks from an earlier period could be an important addition to the data gathered on current employees and based on current practices.

It is important to present job analysis findings in ways that are easily understood by a naive audience. Care should be taken in packaging information for the purpose of presenting findings to the court. Put simply, pictures speak louder than words, and clarity and simplicity outdistance elegance. Graphs and charts that show how job incumbents spend time are effective. Complex statistical analyses are often lost in translation. Neither judges nor juries are I-O psychologists and they are unlikely to appreciate the finer points of job analysis or complex statistical arguments. (See Chapters Six and Fifteen of this volume.) Presentations should be developed to be simple and concise for maximum impact.

Job Design and Redesign

I-O psychologists can contribute job design elements that have the net effect of making a job *more exempt*. Although the classification is dichotomous, this approach is desirable for borderline exempt jobs, ones that barely exceed the exemption criteria. Jobs in which managers spend about half of their time engaged in exempt work are an example. The job may need a boost to clearly surpass the threshold for exemption. The employer may choose to change the job design or the selection or promotion criteria in order to change what employees do and how they spend their time. The following are specific ways in which I-O psychologists can assist.

1. *Redesigning the job.* A job analyst can identify tasks and activities that can be added or removed from the job so the employee can devote more time to exempt work. Nonexempt tasks can be delegated to staff and the employee's list of duties can include

more exempt tasks. A redesign of the work across members of a particular work process may enable exempt employees to focus more on exempt tasks and spend more time engaged in exempt work.

2. *Modifying performance expectations and evaluation criteria.* An I-O psychologist can examine the performance evaluation process and criteria to identify factors that drive day-to-day behavior. After identifying factors that encourage employees to focus on nonexempt work, the I-O psychologist can address these factors and in effect remove the incentive to do nonexempt work and at the same time help employees to focus on exempt tasks. A revised performance evaluation and management process can signal and reinforce desired work behavior to maintain the exempt status.

3. *Developing manager training to improve execution of managerial responsibilities.* Managers may not have the ability to perform the job in an exempt manner, so an I-O psychologist can develop and implement training that will develop the skills needed. Training might address delegating, evaluating performance, coaching, modeling, giving feedback, selecting and promoting, understanding financial information, and managing a store or a unit. An I-O psychologist can also identify training needs through a needs analysis, and this analysis can focus on those aspects of ability that enable the employee to perform exempt work effectively.

4. *Developing senior manager training to improve supervision and development of managers.* This training focuses on the employee's superior, who may have a significant impact on what the employee focuses on day to day and how much time is spent on exempt work. Again, a needs assessment can focus on those aspects of supervision that will enable the employee to perform exempt work more effectively.

5. *Modifying selection criteria and improving selection processes.* The organization may be selecting underqualified applicants into the job, resulting in new hires who are not capable of handling the job as intended. A change in selection criteria or selection processes may generate better qualified hires who have the ability to perform the job in an exempt manner. An I-O psychologist can examine the selection criteria in light of the job

description and performance criteria and suggest adjustments to make it more likely that applicants who have the skills and abilities to perform the job in an exempt way will be hired. The revised selection processes can be validated to ensure the best qualified applicants are hired.

6. *Modifying selection criteria and improving selection processes for employees' superiors.* Selection processes and criteria for employee's superiors can also be modified to ensure superiors are selected who have the skills and abilities to direct and supervise employees in exempt jobs. The revised selection processes can be validated to increase the likelihood that superiors will be successful managers of employees' time and focus.

7. *Designing performance management systems that track the amount of time spent in exempt and nonexempt work.* In addition to evaluating performance of managerial responsibilities, performance measurement and management systems can track how much time an employee spends on exempt versus nonexempt work. A measurement can be developed to obtain reasonably accurate time estimates. This evaluation might consist of self-reports of time spent on tasks or groups of tasks over a specific period of time. Accurate reporting is essential, and the company culture has to support honesty and accuracy over impression management. When well carried out, this measurement is an important tool for employees and their superiors, allowing them to recognize and then correct problems with each employee's focus and time spent.

8. *Designing compensation systems that are compatible with compliance requirements.* I-O psychologists can analyze the current compensation systems to determine whether exempt or nonexempt job behaviors are driven by such systems. If engagement in exempt work is not primary, then the existing compensation system needs to be modified or a new one developed and implemented that puts the focus on exempt work. For example, a compensation system that places a heavy emphasis on personal customer service or personal sales goals will encourage nonexempt job behavior. Alternatively, a compensation system that emphasizes development of staff, monitoring overall store performance, staff retention, and delivery of customer service by staff is more likely to reinforce exempt job behavior.

Conclusions

This chapter describes an area of the law that is relatively new to I-O psychologists and suggests several ways in which I-O psychologists can make a significant contribution to wage and hour litigation. Our experience leads us to believe that I-O psychologists have added value in this arena. Admittedly, our experience has been largely confined to litigation related to California statutes, but because California has been on the leading edge of wage and hour litigation, we believe that the emerging law, as articulated in California cases, provides a rich context for the consideration of potential contributions by I-O psychologists. In the last seven years we have studied over sixty jobs in the context of wage and hour regulations, and we can say without hesitation that methods and techniques developed and applied within the field of I-O psychology have been extremely helpful and well received in this context. We encourage I-O psychologists to play an active role in shaping future FLSA case law through expert testimony.

References

Books, Articles, and Government Documents

Banks, C. G. (2004). Keeping exempt jobs exempt: How to avoid wage and hour litigation. *HR Advisor, 10,* 21–27.

Belli, R. F. (1998). The structure of autobiographical memory and the Event History Calendar: Potential improvements in the quality of retrospective reports in surveys. *Memory, 6*(4), 383–406.

Borman, W. C., & Motowidlo, S. J. (1993). Task performance and contextual performance: The meaning for personnel selection research. *Human Performance, 10,* 91–109.

DuBois, D. A., Shalin, V. L., Levi, K. R., & Borman, W. C. (1998). A cognitively oriented approach to task analysis. *Training Research Journal, 3,* 103–142.

Ericsson, K. A., & Simon, H. A. (1993). *Protocol analysis: Verbal reports as data.* Cambridge, MA: MIT Press.

Flynn, G. (2001, October). Overtime lawsuits: Are you at risk? *Workforce,* pp. 36–42.

Frank, E. (2003). New data show record-breaking results from strong enforcement, compliance assistance (OPA news release). Retrieved Nov 18, 2003 from http://www.dol.gov/opa/media/press/opa/opa2003750.htm

Gael, S. (1983). *Job analysis: A guide to assessing work activities.* San Francisco: Jossey-Bass.

Gael, S. (Ed.). (1988). *The job analysis handbook for business, industry, and government.* New York: Wiley.

Harvey, J. (1991). Job analysis. In M. D. Dunnette & L. M. Hough (Eds.), *Handbook of industrial and organizational psychology* (Vol. 2, 71–163). Palo Alto, CA: Consulting Psychologists Press.

Interpretations, 29 C.F.R. § 541 *et seq.* (1993).

Joss, E. H., & Rukin, P. (2002). Awakening a sleeping giant: The resurgence of wage and hour litigation. *HR Advisor, 8*(4), 6–12.

Kahneman, D., Slovic, P., & Tversky, A. (Eds.). (1982). *Judgment under uncertainty: Heuristics and biases.* Cambridge, UK: Cambridge University Press.

Landy, F. J., & Conte, J. M. (2004). *Work in the 21st century: An introduction to industrial and organizational psychology.* New York: McGraw-Hill.

Montwieler, N. (2004, March 26). Wage hour collective actions jumped 70 percent since 2000, analysis shows. *Daily Labor Report,* p. C-2.

Smith, C. A., Organ, D. W., & Near, J. P. (1983). Organization citizenship behavior: Its nature and antecedents. *Journal of Applied Psychology, 68,* 653–663.

U.S. Department of Labor. (2004a). *Code of Federal Regulations pertaining to ESA: Title 29: Wage and Hour Division: Defining and delimiting the terms.* Retrieved from http://www.dol.gov/dol/allcfr/ESA/Title_29/Part_541/Subpart_B.htm

U.S. Department of Labor. (2004b). Exemptions. *Fair Labor Standards Act Advisor.* Retrieved from http://www.dol.gov/elaws

Cases

Bell v. Farmers Insurance, 87 Cal. App. 4th 805, 105 Cal. Rptr. 2nd 59 (2001).

Donovan v. Burger King, 675 F.2d 516 (2nd Cir. 1982).

Fernandez & Scanlon v. Enterprise Rent-A-Car, Superior Court of Cal., San Diego County Judicial Council No. 4223 (2002).

Metzler v. Food 4 Less, No. BC 206244 (Superior Court of Cal., L.A. County 2001).

Mynaf, Siddiqi, Merrick v. Taco Bell, No. CV 761193 (Superior Court of Cal., Santa Clara County 2001).

O'Hara, et al. v. Factory 2-U, No. 834123–5 (Superior Court of Cal., Alameda County 2001).

Perez v. LA Fitness, No. BC 199108(Superior Court of Cal., L.A. County, 2000).

Ramirez v. Yosemite Water Co., 20 Cal. App. 4th 785 (1999).

Reyna v. Anheuser-Busch, Inc., CV 02–9886-RGK (AJWx) (C.D. Cal. 2003).

Rocher v. Sav-On Drug Stores, Inc., 97 Cal. App. 4th 1070 (2002), rev. granted, decision pending in Cal. Supreme Court.

PART 3

Special Topics

CHAPTER 12

The Importance of Valid Selection and Performance Appraisal

Do Management Practices Figure in Case Law?

Stan Malos

It is beyond dispute that employment-related lawsuits have proliferated in recent years (Weisenfeld, 2003). Although some have argued that even high-profile class action litigation has done little to remediate past discrimination or to deter it in the future (Selmi, 2003), others continue to maintain that the quality of management practices can and should relate directly to the success or failure of discrimination claims against employers (see, for example, Schwartz & Moayed, 2001; Thrasher, 2003). It remains an open question, however, whether core personnel functions such as job analysis, validation, or performance appraisal have discernable relationships with the results of employment-related lawsuits.

When I last undertook a systematic review of the law in this area (Malos, 1998), I focused just on performance appraisals. Even then, I remarked on the daunting number of cases in which these and related management practices had become central to the outcome of employment litigation. This past experience and ongoing professional attention to the area should have prepared me for the enormity of the current round of research, but it did not; the exponential explosion in both number and magnitude of recent discrimination cases—not to mention some highly publicized multimillion-dollar settlements involving the likes of Coca-Cola, Home Depot, State Farm, Wal-Mart, and others—proved staggering. As a consequence, it was necessary to repeatedly refine my search criteria to avoid having to assimilate a truly unfathomable amount of potentially relevant case law. Ultimately, due to sheer volume and space constraints, I chose to focus on a noncomprehensive but (I hope) instructive sample of federal appellate court decisions published within the last five years. Such decisions tend to involve legal issues of greater general applicability and precedential value than the issues dealt with in the typically fact-intensive—and often fact-specific—opinions generated by lower court proceedings.

Having said that, and mindful of the dangers in attempting to capture policy from result-driven judicial opinions (Roehling, 1993), I believe I have been able to draw some conclusions that suggest not only that the case law informs practice but also that the converse may be true as well. Because validation processes—investigating the job-relatedness of and relationships among selection and evaluation criteria—remain central to both challenging and defending employment practices, I have organized this chapter around them. I begin by addressing the role of job analysis in validating selection processes, whose results may generate adverse impact against demographic classes protected under federal law. I continue by reexamining issues with the legal defensibility of performance appraisals, whose results may generate lawsuits when they are used to deny sought-after aspects of employment such as raises, promotions, or retention during reductions in force. I conclude by highlighting the potential for an integrating framework built around the notion of procedural justice that may hold promise for harmonizing judicial and practitioner perspectives on discrimination cases. In each of these sections, I review selected research and update the implications with a discussion of recent case law.

The Role of Job Analysis and Validation in Employment Discrimination Litigation

The validation of potentially discriminatory selection practices has figured prominently in employment litigation for at least three decades now, as has its cornerstone, job analysis. In this section I discuss the sources of an employer's obligation to present validation evidence in defense of adverse impact claims, and the courts' treatment of such evidence in their opinions when deciding such claims. I then review recent federal cases that deal more specifically with issues involving job analysis, minimum qualifications, validity generalization, and other validation processes, with a view toward identifying aspects of those that tend to survive judicial scrutiny.

Job Analysis and Validity: Prior Research on Their Role in Discrimination Claims

One of the earliest scholarly reviews of discrimination cases involving job analysis was done by Thompson and Thompson (1982). After noting that the need for job-relatedness (and thus by implication job analysis) was established by the U.S. Supreme Court in *Griggs* v. *Duke Power Co.* (1971) and reaffirmed in *Albemarle* v. *Moody* (1975), the authors reviewed selected federal court cases and extracted some common principles regarding legal standards for job analysis in test validation. Basing their conclusion in part on the *Albemarle* court's opinion that validation efforts in that case were deficient because "no analysis of the attributes of, or the particular skills needed in, the studied job groups" had been made, Thompson and Thompson suggested that a job analysis should be performed on the exact job for which selection is to be made; that it should include current information from individuals familiar with the job, relevant documents, and observed job performance; and that it should be conducted by an expert analyst using enough data that the sample is relevant for every job to which a particular selection device is meant to apply. Thompson and Thompson also recommended that minimum competency levels for all tasks, duties, and activities in the job be specified. They cautioned, however, that their conclusions were drawn largely from cases that involved content validation, and should thus, by implication, be applied beyond that context with due care.

Almost ten years later, Harvey (1991) reviewed some of the basic legal issues in collecting and using job analysis data. Harvey organized his review around two sets of sources: laws and court decisions and professional standards documents. In examining laws and court decisions, Harvey noted that job analysis data have proved useful in demonstrating the job-relatedness of selection tests under federal antidiscrimination laws (for example, Title VII of the Civil Rights Act of 1964, the Age Discrimination in Employment Act of 1967, and the Equal Pay Act of 1963) in that such data support the inference that selection decisions have been based on predictions of successful performance rather than discriminatory motives or effects. In examining professional standards documents, Harvey noted that various editions of the American Psychological Association's *Standards for Educational and Psychological Testing* (Standards) (for example, 1985; an earlier version was used by the Supreme Court in *Albemarle*), the Society for Industrial and Organizational Psychology's *Principles for the Validation and Use of Personnel Selection Procedures* (Principles) (1987, updated in 2003), and the Equal Employment Opportunity Commission's *Uniform Guidelines on Employee Selection Procedures* (Guidelines) (1978), in Title 29 of the Code of Federal Regulations, contain similar but not identical guidance that courts have continued to rely on to varying degrees in cases involving job analysis (see, for example, *Gulino et al.* v. *Board of Education,* 2003).

The SIOP Principles appear to be relatively liberal regarding the permissibility of validity generalization, whereas the APA Standards, the EEOC Guidelines, and a number of earlier judicial opinions have taken stricter views regarding the need for job-specific analyses directed toward the exact jobs and corresponding selection devices in question (Harvey, 1991; Thompson & Thompson, 1982). The Guidelines in particular have been criticized because of their apparent rigidity regarding job analysis and validation method specificity. Nonetheless, although not legally binding, they have often been given "great deference" by the courts, as is typical for regulations promulgated by administrative agencies within their area of expertise. Moreover, failure to comply with the Guidelines may be seen to have diminished the probative value of validation evidence in the eyes of some courts (see, for example, *Association of Mexican-American Educators et al.* v. *State of California,* 2000, citing *Albemarle* and *Clady* v. *County of Los Angeles,* 1985; for a recent case in which compliance with the Guidelines was required as part of a court-ordered consent decree, see *Reynolds et al.* v. *Alabama Department of Transportation,* 2003). The Guidelines, as well as other professional standards, are addressed more fully in Chapter Three of this book but will be summarized here as a baseline for further discussion about the evolving role of job analysis and validation in discrimination case law.

At the outset the Guidelines caution that the "use of any selection procedure which has an adverse impact on the hiring, promotion, or other employment . . . opportunities of members of any race, sex, or ethnic group will be considered discriminatory . . . unless the procedure has been validated in accordance with these guidelines" (§ 1607.3). The Guidelines' general standards provide that criterion-related, content, or construct validity studies are acceptable (§ 1607.5); whichever is used, the applicable technical standards require at minimum that "[a]ny validity study should be based upon a review of information about the job for which the selection procedure is to be used" (§ 1607.14). These standards do allow, however, that "[a]ny method of job analysis may be used if it provides the information required for the specific validation strategy used." Further flexibility is allowed in that "[u]sers may, under certain circumstances, support the use of selection procedures by validity studies conducted by other users" (§ 1607.7) where adequate evidence of job similarity and overall fairness is shown to exist.

Job Analysis and Validity: Recent Cases Illustrating Their Role in Discrimination Claims

Allen et al. v. *City of Chicago* (2003) offers a recent example of a case where the court relied heavily on the Guidelines in upholding dismissal of the plaintiffs' discrimination claims on summary judgment. In that case, the latest in a lengthy series involving the promotional practices of Chicago's police department, a panel of the U.S. Court of Appeals for the Seventh Circuit considered two class action challenges by minority officers, some of whom had failed a written qualifying test and were thus not eligible for further consideration, and others of whom had passed the qualifying exam but failed either the assessment component or the *merit* component that followed.

In response to the results of earlier litigation the City of Chicago had created the Promotion and Testing Task Force, which recommended adopting different types of tests to assess a broader range of relevant knowledge, skills, and abilities (KSAs) than had previously been the case. These tests included a qualifying test designed to evaluate the minimum levels of KSAs "needed by sergeants on their first day on the job." Those passing this test would be eligible for further consideration. The city hired outside consultants to design the promotional exam. Basing their suggestion on a job analysis, the consultants recommended a pass-fail qualifying exam, to be followed by a written assessment exercise; the results of this assessment exercise would be used to rank order successful candidates for promotion. The city then asked the consultants to add an additional merit component in accordance with task force recommendations. Noting that a "qualifying examination can test knowledge, skills and abilities, but it cannot identify police men and women who have exhibited exceptional leadership in the field," the recommendations called for a further process to "identify police officers who have demonstrated superior ability, responsibility, and dedication to police service." In response the consultants interviewed various subject matter experts and concluded that leadership, mentoring, decision making, and interpersonal relations should be considered. A nomination process was then put in place whereby command-level officers were permitted to identify up to five candidates in their chain of command whom they believed exhibited these traits. Such candidates would still have to pass the qualifying exam.

Both the written qualifying exam and assessment exercise, which involved a simulation to evaluate supervision and situational judgment skills, had been content validated in accordance with the Guidelines. In addition, command-level officers were required to attend training designed to minimize biases, stereotyping, and personal influences before nominating their subordinates for the alternative merit process. A committee of command personnel then reviewed these nominations and forwarded a select number to the police superintendent, who made a final decision regarding any such promotions. These promotions were limited to a maximum of 30 percent of total promotions and were separate from those based on the assessment exercise.

When the new qualifying test was first administered, African American candidates achieved a lower pass rate (about 73 percent) than white candidates (about 91 percent). However, although this difference was statistically significant, it was found acceptable by the court because it did not violate the Guidelines' four-fifths rule (see the ninth circuit's 2002 opinion in *Stout et al.* v. *Potter,* in which the court disregarded an apparent violation of the four-fifths rule due to small sample size in a U.S. Postal Service promotion case). Candidates who were successful with the qualifying test were then eligible for promotion based on either the assessment exercise or the merit selection process. On the subsequent assessment exercise, however, the success rates for both African Americans and Hispanics did in fact violate the four-fifths rule when compared to the success rate of white officers, thus showing adverse impact. In contrast, the merit process resulted in no adverse impact when comparing pass rates. However, African American and Hispanic officers who did *not* achieve promotion under this merit process challenged the allegedly arbitrary constraint on such promotions that limited their number to no more than 30 percent of promotions overall. Under this constraint, African American and Hispanic officers nominated under the merit process but not promoted did turn out to be excluded at a disproportionate rate.

After reviewing the burden-shifting process set forth by the Supreme Court in *Griggs* and *Albemarle* and incorporated into the Guidelines, the seventh circuit panel found that the district court had properly dismissed both sets of claims on summary judgment. Under that process, once adverse impact has been demonstrated, the burden shifts to the employer to show that any offending components of its selection practices are job related and consistent with business necessity. The court found job-relatedness due to the validation activities undertaken by the city's consultants. The burden then shifted back to the plaintiffs to show, in accordance with the Guidelines, the existence of an equally valid but less discriminatory alternative in order to negate the business necessity of the challenged practice, which they were unable to do.

In particular, with respect to the merit process, there was no showing that allowing more than the 30 percent relative cap on such promotions would be either equally valid or less discriminatory. The same was true for the proposed alternative practice suggested by the plaintiffs of allowing merit promotions without requiring a passing score on the qualifying exam. Although the opinion left open the possibility that such evidence might be developed with respect to future administrations of the promotional process, the court cautioned that it would consider "factors such as the cost or other burdens of proposed alternative selection devices" in determining whether they would be "equally as effective as the challenged practice in serving the employer's legitimate business goals" (quoting the U.S. Supreme Court's 1988 decision in *Watson* v. *Fort Worth Bank & Trust*, for a related case upholding the content validity of testing for promotion to lieutenant, see *Bryant* v. *City of Chicago*, 2000). Interestingly, another panel of the seventh circuit explicitly recognized the importance of racial balance in police selection procedures in *Petit et al.* v. *City of Chicago* (2003). Elsewhere along these lines, in a case also involving police promotions, the first circuit concluded in *Cotter et al.* v. *City of Boston et al.* (2003) that a violation of the four-fifths rule that *would have* occurred had the city used the results of its promotion exam in strict rank order justified preferential promotion of lower-scoring African American officers in order to remedy past discrimination.

Another instructive case in which the employer's validation efforts in accordance with the Guidelines were central to its successful defense of discrimination claims is *Williams et al.* v. *Ford Motor Co.* (1999). In that case the sixth circuit considered evidence of content validation, criterion-related validation, and validity generalization in upholding Ford's selection processes against the plaintiffs' adverse impact claims. Ford had begun using a preemployment test known as the Hourly Selection System Test Battery (HSSTB) as part of its process for screening applicants for unskilled labor positions. The test had been developed by Ford's human resource consultants to replace a state employment services test because Ford's workers were expected to rotate among assignments rather than to remain within one particular job classification and the state test was considered inadequate to assess workers' capacity to do so. The HSSTB was designed to measure abilities related to reading comprehension, arithmetic, parts assembly, visual speed and accuracy, and manual dexterity. The HR consultants conducted an extensive job analysis based on supervisory skill inventories and ratings of the relative importance of each skill set in each job category. Candidates scoring in the lowest 25th percentile on the HSSTB were excluded by Ford from further hiring consideration.

After several years Ford commissioned a criterion-related validation study of concurrent design that found a significant correlation of .30 between HSSTB scores and job performance in a sample of recently hired workers. Ford's consultants also conducted a meta-analytic validity generalization study using predictive validation data from other employers using similar tests. Ford then presented expert testimony that given the totality of the circumstances, the test appeared to have been professionally and validly developed. This conclusion was disputed by plaintiffs' expert, who felt that the underlying job analysis failed to demonstrate clear linkages between specific job requirements and actual duties performed on the job. The trial court found this latter contention unconvincing and summarily dismissed the case. The sixth circuit agreed.

The appellate court panel, after an extensive discussion of *Albemarle* and its progeny as well as the Guidelines, reviewed the burden-shifting process for adverse impact cases discussed earlier. Noting that "[n]either the case law nor the Uniform Guidelines purports to require that an employer must demonstrate validity using more than one method," the court went on to uphold the trial court's conclusion that both content- and criterion-related evidence and the meta-analytic validity generalization study (which looked at sixty-one previous studies of similar tests used to predict performance in similar jobs) were relevant to supporting the job-relatedness of the test. In particular the court commented on the adequacy of the employee sample used in the criterion study, noting that this sample was composed of employees of varying tenure, education, demography, and skill levels. Over the argument that this sample and Ford's concurrent design were unduly restricted (*compare Albemarle*) for failing to include a wider range of low scorers (as might be included, for example, in a predictive study), the court held: "The law does not require that an employer, simply in order that low scorers may be included in validation studies, hire individuals who do not pass a pre-employment test" (citing the ninth circuit's 1985 opinion in *Clady*). The court also noted that the Guidelines themselves provide that they "do not require a user to hire or promote persons for the purpose of making it possible to conduct a criterion-related study" (§ 1607.14).

It is worth observing that, although the *Williams* court did rely on compliance with the Guidelines to support the employer's defense, it is not clear that *failure* to comply with them would have been fatal to Ford's case. In reviewing Supreme Court precedent, including both *Griggs* and *Espinoza* v. *Farah Mfg.* (1973), the sixth circuit observed: "the Court has not ruled that every deviation from any of the Guidelines automatically results in a violation of Title VII." It went on to note that the Guidelines may well be more appropriately regarded as expert opinion than as binding legal precedent and, as such, should probably be applied with "the same combination of deference and wariness" that applies to the use of expert testimony overall.

In the final analysis, then, Ford's victory in *Williams* may be based on the court's belief that the employer did just about everything it could have done to validate its preemployment test, in a genuine effort to improve the performance of its workforce. Thus, notwithstanding the plaintiffs' examples of false-negative effects (anecdotal evidence about applicants who had scored poorly on the test but had performed well elsewhere for other companies), the court found insufficient reason to overturn the lower court's dismissal of the case.

Another case that involved the role of the Guidelines in discrimination issues surrounding the validation process is *Association of Mexican-American Educators et al.* v. *State of California* (2000). As mentioned earlier, the ninth circuit majority in that case reaffirmed the deference to which they felt the Guidelines were entitled. The case involves yet another class action brought by unsuccessful minority candidates, this time those excluded from pursuing the education profession because they had failed to pass the California Basic Education Skills Test (CBEST).

The CBEST, like some of the other qualifying exams considered here, is a pass-fail written test. It assesses reading, writing, and mathematical abilities with multiple-choice subtests. Candidates can pass the test by achieving minimum acceptable scores on each of the three subtests or a minimum overall score derived from compensatory averaging of the subtests. Historically, a disproportionate number of minority candidates had failed the test. In this action, such candidates attacked the use of the test based on the state's failure to adopt a less discriminatory process. Like the plaintiffs in *Allen,* they were unsuccessful with this argument at trial, where the district court found that the test was a valid measure of job-related skills, that the minimum passing score reflected reasonable professional judgment about the basic skill levels required for the jobs in question, and that the evidence adduced at trial was insufficient to demonstrate the existence of some other equally effective screening device. On appeal the plaintiffs challenged these findings, in part because of the court's reliance on advice from an expert who did not prepare a written report and was not subject to cross-examination at trial.

After concluding that Title VII, and thus the Guidelines' validation requirements, applied to the CBEST, the ninth circuit reaffirmed a three-step process for determining the job-relatedness of a selection device, a process previously set forth by the court in *Craig* v. *County of Los Angeles* (1980). That process requires that the employer (1) specify the particular trait or characteristic being measured, (2) determine that this trait or characteristic is an important element of work behavior, and (3) demonstrate by professionally acceptable methods that the selection device is predictive of or significantly correlated with the element of work behavior identified. Basing its conclusion on the expert's use of the "pooled judgments" of knowledgeable persons such as job incumbents about the relevance of the skills tested by the CBEST, the court found no error in determining that these criteria were satisfied based on the professional standards of the time. Although acknowledging that the district court had been somewhat critical of certain aspects of the validation process (for example, "matching" test questions to skills purportedly assessed on the CBEST based on the content of textbooks used in California schools), the ninth circuit took care to mention that validation studies "are by their nature difficult, expensive, time consuming and rarely, if ever, free from error." Thus the court found "evidence—even if not overwhelming evidence—that the development and evaluation of the CBEST were appropriate and that the test measures the types of skills that it was designed to measure." This comment would seem to support the notion that judges will be sympathetic to employers who appear to attempt in good faith to comply with validation requirements, even if the evidence they adduce in this regard is not as strong as it might be.

Finally, the court found no need for the CBEST's minimum passing score to be separately validated beyond the efforts already made with regard to the test overall. Rather the court relied on the Guidelines' provision that "where cutoff scores are used, they should normally be set so as to be reasonable and consistent with normal expectations of acceptable proficiency within the work force" (§ 1607.5). Thus, under the rather liberal "clearly erroneous" standard applicable to appellate review of trial court factual findings, the ninth circuit found the record adequate to support the district court's decision (for a similar outcome at the trial court level that relied in part on this analysis, see *Gulino et al.* v. *Board of Education*, 2002, 2003, in which the court ultimately upheld New York State teacher certification requirements as sufficiently job related despite the lack of "formal" evidence of their validity).

Like other appellate cases that have considered the propriety of minimum qualifications and cut scores, *Association of Mexican-American Educators et al.* generated multiple opinions dissenting at least in part from the majority's conclusions regarding the necessary level of performance that successful passage of a test should be designed to predict. Another example can be found in *Lanning et al.* v. *Southeastern Pennsylvania Transportation Authority* (SEPTA) (1999), a third circuit case that involved an aerobic capacity test, administered prior to the start of training for transit police positions, that was found to adversely impact women candidates. On remand to the district court following the third circuit's earlier 1999 decision (Lanning I), SEPTA prevailed when it was allowed to supplement the factual record with further evidence that its cut score, a maximum time of twelve minutes on a mile-and-a-half running test, had been "shown to measure the minimum qualifications necessary for successful performance of the job in question"—the legal standard for validating a discriminatory cut score adopted by the court in Lanning I (compare the Uniform Guidelines' standard in § 1607.5H, relied on by the ninth circuit in *Association of Mexican-American Educators et al.*, that cut scores "should normally be set so as to be reasonable and consistent with normal expectations of acceptable proficiency within the work force"). The original *Lanning* result, and the Lanning I legal standard underlying it, were thus upheld by the 2002 majority in Lanning II (an opinion joined only by a judge appointed to replace a member of the original three-judge panel who had died prior to the opinion's being rendered).

Although the majority opinion in Lanning II was highly deferential to the employer, both the definition of *minimum qualifications* and the validation methodologies used to justify them were hotly contested in the dissenting opinion, suggesting that the legal standard for proper validation remains at least partially unsettled. For example, the dissent noted that the aerobic capacity test was designed to screen for better physical fitness and thus argued for a more lenient standard of review that would allow a higher cut score in testing for jobs related to public safety. Nonetheless the results of these cases overall seem to suggest that some judges may reach a point where the economies of further validation efforts do not support requiring anything more of employers who appear to have "suffered" enough in justifying their selection devices. If so, then there may well be a trend away from the more specific job analysis and related validation requirements recommended by Thompson and Thompson (1982) and based on their review of the case law at the time.

A further example of this possible trend toward court acceptance of less rigorous but good faith validation efforts by the employer can be found in *Meeker et al. v. Merit Systems Protection Board* (2003). The case was brought by unsuccessful candidates for administrative law judge (ALJ) positions who challenged a decision by the director of the federal Office of Personnel Management (OPM) to deviate from strict adherence to the OPM's own applicable employment regulations. In that case the U.S. Court of Appeals for the Federal Circuit ultimately allowed a government employer to dispense with regulatory requirements for a professionally developed, job-specific job analysis that at least echo—and are perhaps even more exacting than—those in the Guidelines.

In order to alleviate unduly high failure rates the OPM had made a series of revisions to its applicant scoring system that made it easier for candidates to qualify. Whereas the previous system determined candidate eligibility based on a validly weighted combination of scores on relevant legal experience, panel interviews, written materials, and reference inquiries, the revised system made anyone who met a minimum experience requirement and merely *completed* the same four-part exam threshold qualified for consideration. At this stage the impact of performance on the four exam dimensions became compressed, statutory veteran preferences gained greater relative weight than had previously been the case, and Meeker and other nonveteran applicants were excluded from further consideration. Meeker challenged this result, citing government regulations applicable to the hiring process that required (1) a job analysis identifying the necessary duties, KSAs, and candidate qualifications for the position; (2) a professionally developed "employment practice" for the recruitment, measurement, ranking, and selection of individuals (so that a necessary relationship between the employment practice and job performance would thereby be demonstrated); and (3) nondiscrimination on the basis of race, color, religion, sex, age, national origin, partisan political affiliation, or "any other nonmerit factor" ("Employment Practices: Basic Requirements," 2004). In a class action appeal to the Merit Systems Protection Board, Meeker prevailed. On review, the federal circuit reversed.

Noting that the OPM's director is authorized to grant a variation from the strict letter of OPM regulations to avoid "practical difficulties and unnecessary hardships" so long as the variation is "within the spirit of the [OPM] regulations, and the efficiency of the Government and the integrity of the competitive service are protected" ("Civil Service Regulations," 2004), the court cited practical difficulties with revising the final ratings of more than 1,700 candidates who had already been named to the ALJ placement register. The court also found experience level to be a traditionally important threshold selection criterion, and the resulting scale compression and relative reweighting of the remaining criteria not inconsistent with the spirit of the regulations and integrity of the process. In short, despite the fact that the OPM admitted on the record that it did not have any of the job analysis data that would be required by its own regulations, it was permitted to use an unvalidated revised system in place of its prior, validated selection method. Admittedly, this case involves a specific fact situation and the fairly lenient "abuse of discretion" administrative standard of review. Nonetheless, it does seem anomalous that the "practical difficulties" and "hardships" of validating the revised system were used to justify deviation from regulatory requirements whose purposes undoubtedly include preserving the integrity of the hiring process.

Summary of Cases Involving Job Analysis and Validity

The results of *Meeker* and the other cases discussed earlier (summarized in Table 12.1) provide further arguable evidence of evolving judicial flexibility toward job analysis and validation requirements if and when fundamental fairness can be said to have remained intact. This issue will be revisited later (in the section discussing procedural justice as a possible integrating framework). However, a final point should be made before leaving this topic.

Table 12.1. Summary of Recent Federal Appellate Cases Involving Job Analysis and Validity.

Case	Issue	Outcome and Reasons
Allen et al. v. City of Chicago (7th Cir. 2003)	Defensibility of multipart police promotional process that adversely impacted minority candidates	Summary judgment for the employer upheld due to adequate job analysis and content validation in accordance with the Uniform Guidelines.
Williams et al. v. Ford Motor Co. (6th Cir. 1999)	Defensibility of multipart ability test for rotational production workers that adversely impacted minority candidates	Summary judgment for the employer upheld due to job analysis, content and criterion validation, and validity generalization in accordance with the Uniform Guidelines.
Ass'n of Mexican-American Educators et al. v. State of California (9th Cir. 2003)	Defensibility of basic skills test (reading, writing, and mathematics) for public school teaching eligibility that adversely impacted minority candidates	Trial judgment for the state upheld due to adequate—"if not overwhelming"—evidence of reasonable test development and cut scores in accordance with the Uniform Guidelines.
Lanning et al. v. SEPTA (3d Cir. 1999, 2002)	Defensibility of minimum aerobic capacity and maximum running time test for transit police officer trainees that adversely impacted women candidates	Trial judgment for the employer upheld due to adequate evidence that the test measured "minimum qualifications necessary for successful performance of the job in question."
Meeker et al. v. Merit Systems Protection Board (Fed. Cir. 2003)	Defensibility of unvalidated revised scoring system for administrative law judge positions that revalued veteran preferences and thus adversely impacted nonveteran candidates	Appeal in favor of plaintiffs overturned, thus upholding employer's decision to disregard its own specific regulations regarding job analysis and professional test development.

In several of the adverse impact cases discussed here, once the employer was able to successfully rebut a four-fifths rule violation with acceptable validation evidence, plaintiffs' arguments regarding possible alternative selection methods that might be equally effective with less adverse impact were given very short shrift by the courts. A likely explanation is that such plaintiffs were seldom able to present convincing evidence of *actual* methods that were equally effective and instead presented arguments or speculation about the possibility that such methods might exist (see, for example, *Gulino*, discussed earlier, in which the New York trial court rejected a teacher certification method used in Connecticut as insufficiently supported in this regard). Of course, given judges' willingness to factor in cost-benefit analyses in comparing the "effectiveness" of proposed alternatives, in light of the Supreme Court's ruling in *Watson* v. *Fort Worth Bank & Trust*, this is a tough standard to meet in actual practice. Indeed, it would be the rare plaintiff, even in a class action, who would be able to marshal the resources and access to necessary company data sufficient to conduct his or her own validation study of a different selection system within the time parameters of a typical lawsuit. Were plaintiffs to complain to the court that this sets up a playing field that is tilted against them, they might well be met with the ironic response that the very burden of obtaining such evidence shows the alternative procedure to be *not* equally effective. In any event, if future plaintiffs hope to achieve greater success in rebutting business necessity by proposing an alternative procedure, they will likely need to improve their showing in this regard.

The Role of Performance Appraisal in Employment Discrimination Litigation

Whereas selection has to do with predicting the performance of possible future hires, performance appraisal involves assessing both the actual performance of those hired and the efficacy of the prediction process. When either proves problematic or outdated or when economic conditions so require, appraisal results are typically relied on to modify or deny some desired benefit of the employment relationship. It is thus not surprising that appraisals generate disagreements with and challenges to their effects when an employee views the results as unfavorable. This has been particularly true in an environment of global competition, mergers and acquisitions, reorganizations, temporary layoffs, and permanent reductions in force (RIFs), in which performance is often asserted as the reason for adverse action (if indeed a reason is given) but discriminatory purposes are thereafter alleged (see, generally, Martin, Bartol, & Kehoe, 2000; Williams, Slonaker, & Wendt, 2003). In this section, I begin again with a discussion of selected prior research on the legal defensibility of performance appraisals, followed by a discussion of recent appellate case law.

Performance Appraisal: Prior Research on its Role in Discrimination Claims

Numerous reviews of the case law involving legal implications of performance appraisals have been written over the years. These date back at least as far as Lubben, Thompson, and Klasson (1980) and Klieman and Durham (1981) and continue forward to Martin et al. (2000), the latest update by Martin and his colleagues of several previous reviews. A fuller listing of these reviews can be found in my previous treatment of the topic (Malos, 1998, pp. 79–83). From this literature and analysis of the case law, I extracted some recommendations for improving the legal defensibility of performance appraisals. They include using specific, objective, behavioral, and job-related criteria, as well as ensuring procedural standardization, documentation, employee notification, opportunity to correct deficiencies, and other aspects of procedural justice. Along similar lines, Werner and Bolino (1997) found empirical support for the roles of job analysis, reviewability, and other aspects of due process in explaining appellate court decisions involving performance appraisals (this work will be revisited later).

Although reviews of the case law may be time-bound to the decisions on which they are based, at least two of the observations I made previously hold true today. First, the proliferation of cases involving performance appraisals seems to have continued virtually unabated; hundreds of such cases can be found at various levels in the reported federal court decisions alone in the five-year period since my last review. Second, unlike those involving validation processes, which tend to arise in the context of adverse impact claims, cases dealing with performance appraisals still arise most often in the disparate treatment context, which makes it more difficult to infer broadly applicable principles from them.

This latter point is particularly true in cases that use the burden-shifting process set forth by the Supreme Court in *McDonnell Douglas Corp.* v. *Green* (1973). Under that process, plaintiffs who allege discriminatory employment actions typically offer evidence of previous favorable appraisals as part of their prima facie case to show that they were qualified for the job in question. Employers then typically counter with evidence that performance was poorer than asserted or had deteriorated over time, that performance standards had changed due to increased competitive pressures, or that an individual who *was* selected or promoted instead of the plaintiff exhibited better likely performance, thus supporting the assertion that the plaintiff's treatment was based on a legitimate, nondiscriminatory reason. Because of the predominantly factual nature of such disputes, these cases usually entail extensive court discussion of lengthy records that can turn on the credibility of witnesses, the adequacy of evidence to support inferences drawn on summary judgment or by the jury at trial, the appropriate standard of appellate review, or some combination of all these factors. As a consequence, one can sort optimistically through numerous cases that appear to "involve" performance appraisals, only to find that many, if not most, reduce to subjective disputes about the quality or value of the plaintiff's work.

An apt example in the context of race-based, hostile environment allegations can be found in *Hawkins* v. *Pepsico* (2000), in which the African American plaintiff claimed that her termination for poor performance was in reality due to discriminatory animus that led to improper lowering of her appraisal results. A panel of the fourth circuit, after an exhaustive—and exhausting—review of the evidence, affirmed summary dismissal of the case, finding that the plaintiff "has shown nothing more than a routine difference of opinion and personality conflict with her supervisor . . . we refuse to transmute such ordinary workplace disagreements between individuals of different races into actionable race discrimination." (Further anecdotal support for this kind of sentiment— judicial impatience with court actions that center on the "fairness" of everyday management decisions that have no clear linkage to protected class status—can be found in Landy's interviews with judges in Chapter Fifteen of this volume.) For our present purposes, these cases, although interesting, provide little useful guidance about the overall propriety of performance appraisal *processes*. Thus, even though appraisals are theoretically considered *tests* subject to the Uniform Guidelines, it remains challenging to find opinions that explicitly address performance appraisal compliance with formal notions of job analysis, validation, and the like (see Malos, 1998, pp. 77–79, citing Barrett & Kernan, 1987).

Performance Appraisal: Recent Cases Illustrating Its Role in Discrimination Claims

Conversely, there are cases that stand for fairly straightforward propositions that are nonetheless important. For example, it is now widely understood in most jurisdictions that a negative appraisal, without additional consequences, will not constitute an adverse employment action giving rise to a civil rights claim (see, for example, the eighth circuit's 2000 opinion in *Spears* v. *Department of Corrections*, in which the court rejected the claim that reduction from a rating of "highly successful" to "successful" was sufficient to fend off summary judgment in favor of the employer where no further use of the evaluation to the plaintiff's detriment was ever made). However, where there is evidence that negative evaluations allegedly tinged with discriminatory animus resulted in a reduced bonus or other pay reduction, summary judgment dismissing the case clearly is not appropriate (for example, *Russell* v. *Principi*, 2001).

Another general principle involves the historically common fact pattern whereby previously favorable appraisals are suddenly replaced by one or more unfavorable assessments just prior to a layoff. Although such changes are now often defended as arising from the adoption of more stringent performance standards, showing such a pattern will often be sufficient for the plaintiff to avoid summary dismissal, thus putting the employer to the risk and expense of trial. In such cases it is not even a very strong showing that is always required. For example, in an opinion reversing the previous dismissal of a retaliation claim brought by a secretary at a large employment law firm against one of its partners, Chief Judge Posner of the seventh circuit noted that

It is common for supervisors to overrate their subordinates for purposes of building morale, avoiding conflict, and deflecting criticisms. . . . Not much weight can be given to [such] positive reviews. But not much does not equal zero. And by going out of his way to say nice things about the plaintiff [the defendant] made it possible for a reasonable trier of fact to infer that his later denigration of her performance was invented for purposes of the litigation . . .

. . . Of course we do not hold that this is the correct interpretation of the events, only that the matter is sufficiently in doubt to require a trial [*Pryor* v. *Seyfarth et al.*, 2000, at 979–980].

For a similar finding see *Shackelford* v. *Deloitte & Touche,* a 1999 case in which the fifth circuit reversed summary dismissal of Shackelford's retaliation and race claims, noting the "tight temporal proximity" between protected activity and adverse employment action: "After four years of positive reviews, Shackelford received her first negative performance appraisal [shortly] after the class action suit was filed against D & T." Shackelford also had been listed as a witness in the case prior to her termination for "poor performance."

Race and National Origin Cases

Other principles of general applicability arise in the context of particular types of cases. For example, in what was apparently a national origin case (the court repeatedly referred to plaintiff's "ethnicity" but, in applying New Jersey state antidiscrimination law, was unclear whether this was a national origin or race case), the third circuit reviewed allegations that the multicomponent performance scores of Cardenas, a Mexican American, had been systematically rounded downward by white supervisors, whereas those of nonminority employees had been rounded upward. The court found this sufficient to reverse the lower court's summary dismissal (*Cardenas* v. *Massey et al.,* 2001; also relevant in this hostile environment retaliation case were allegations that a supervisor referred to Cardenas as *mojado* ("wetback") and as the "boy from the barrio," regularly inquiring whether Cardenas intended to pull out a switchblade to settle professional disagreements).

However, as foreshadowed in *Hawkins* v. *Pepsico,* not every employment dispute involving performance appraisals will give rise to a cognizable civil rights violation. Thus in *Cullom* v. *Brown* (2000), a case involving alleged racial motivation in delaying the promotion of a fifty-five-year-old African American by the Veterans Administration, the seventh circuit rejected an allegation that the delay was attributable to unduly *favorable* performance appraisals because of his race, but for which Cullom would have qualified for a performance improvement plan, improved his performance sooner, and thus achieved an earlier promotion. The facts of the case suggest that Cullom had repeated and ongoing performance problems but that, in a misplaced effort to avoid his continuing complaints, the VA ordered that he be falsely overrated. In an opinion echoing Judge Posner's comments in *Pryor,* the court commented that Cullom's supervisors at the VA could hardly be seen to have "'retaliated' by giving him, an incompetent employee, undeserved *favorable* treatment and evaluations (and ultimately a promotion to GS-11) [when otherwise] he would have likely been demoted, placed on probation, and quite possibly terminated." In the final analysis the court ruled that the "undeniably poor policy" of "kicking someone upstairs (with more pay and a higher grade level) instead of kicking him down and possibly out" did not violate Title VII.

The foregoing case does illustrate, however, the dangers inherent in falsely evaluating someone favorably to avoid conflict in the short term, thereby creating a record that may make it difficult to discipline or terminate the employee when necessary later on. This fact pattern was illustrated some years earlier in *Vaughn* v. *Edel* (1990), a wrongful termination case in which Texaco took a hands-off approach to performance management with the plaintiff, a black attorney, out of fear of discrimination liability, but notified white employees in similar positions of performance deficiencies and afforded them the opportunity to improve. This well-meaning but misplaced conduct provided direct evidence of differential treatment, and thus discriminatory motive, based on race, thus supporting plaintiff's disparate treatment claims. A recent and highly similar fact pattern involving failure to offer a performance improvement plan (PIP) to an African American employee when such plans were offered to other, nonminority employees in similar jobs also led the sixth circuit to reverse summary dismissal in *Johnson* v. *Kroger* (2003).

Age and Other RIF Cases

Conversely, the eighth circuit in *Mayer* v. *Nextel* (2003), an age discrimination case, just as recently found no problem with an employer's failure to put sixty-year-old Mayer on a performance improvement plan prior to firing him for poor performance. Mayer, who had had a record of acceptable but not stellar performance as a sales manager, fared less favorably after Nextel adopted a more extensive, multifaceted appraisal mechanism with added levels of review. Mayer claimed that it showed discriminatory animus to have offered PIPs to younger sales managers but not to him. In finding this contention insufficient to fend off summary judgment in favor of the employer, the court accepted "Nextel's uncontroverted explanation [that] only managers who failed to meet quota were placed on PIPs. Because Mayer had met quota, he was not eligible for a PIP. Nextel can certainly choose how to run its business, including not offering at-will employees a PIP before termination, as long as it does not unlawfully discriminate in doing so. We refuse to sit as a super-personnel department who second-guesses Nextel's business decisions" (citing *Dorsey* v. *Pinnacle Automation*, 2002).

Another age case involving performance appraisals in which the employer prevailed, this time at trial, is *Sauzek and Koski* v. *Exxon Coal USA* (2000). In that case the age-protected plaintiffs alleged that Exxon had unfairly targeted them for inclusion in a RIF by evaluating their performance as extremely poor after twenty years of service with adequate appraisals. However, the seventh circuit found ample evidence on the record that employees both under and over forty years of age had experienced major fluctuations in their evaluations and that Exxon's rankings were not unusually harsh for older employees overall. The court thus concluded there was insufficient evidence to support an inference that the sudden drop in performance evaluation levels demonstrated underlying pretext in Exxon's assertedly performance-based termination.

Employers have met with mixed results in other cases alleging pretext in similar factual patterns, particularly those involving RIFs or other restructurings. For example, in *Thorn and Curran* v. *Sunderstrand Aerospace* (2000), the two age-protected plaintiffs were included in RIF layoffs for alleged low productivity. Thorn was able to adduce evidence that a previously favorable review was lowered by his supervisor to avoid application of a seniority tiebreaker under which Thorn would have been retained; not surprisingly, the seventh circuit found this evidence adequate to overturn the district court's summary dismissal of Thorn's claim (for another age case that found an employer's "conscious, unexplained departure" from its own RIF procedures problematic in the context of a pretext allegation, see *Tyler et al.* v. *Union Oil,* 2002; see also *Yates* v. *Rexton, Inc.,* 2001). Curran, however, unsuccessfully asserted that the employer had wrongfully retained lesser-performing younger employees because they might contribute more to the company in the long run. In rejecting the logic of this contention, and thus any basis for overturning the summary judgment against Curran, Chief Judge Posner reasoned that

> [I]n making RIF decisions an employer is free to decide which employees are likeliest to contribute most to the company over the long haul [citations from various circuits omitted]. It would be a foolish RIF that retained an employee who was likely to quit anyway in a few months while riffing one likely to perform well for the company over a period of years. High turnover of skilled workers can be very harmful to a company. The worker who leaves may take with him trade secrets valuable to a competitor or the benefits of specialized training that the employer had given him, at some expense, in the hope of recouping the expense in the worker's superior productivity now to be enjoyed by another employer. Since younger employees tend to be more mobile than older ones, there is no basis for an inference that employers interested in the long-term potential of an employee prefer young to old [at 389].

Another recent seventh circuit case that upheld an employer's discretion to make RIF decisions according to its own business judgment, particularly where its selection processes are carefully thought out, well documented, and reviewed by legal counsel, is *Cerutti et al.* v. *BASF et al.* (2003). In that case BASF had instituted a new business plan whose purpose was to reduce the personnel headcount and "repopulate" the organization with individuals who demonstrated specific behavioral skills and attributes considered necessary for the company's future success. These criteria included the ability to "do more with less."

After offering voluntary early retirement to certain long-term employees, the company and its consultants systematically developed new job families and corresponding key competencies within family. These competencies were in turn assessed via problem-solving exercises, role plays, and targeted interviewing, all of which were done by telephone to avoid disclosing age, race, or other demographic characteristics of individual candidates. The results of these processes were subject to review by panel discussion among assessment personnel and were then forwarded to BASF's in-house legal department, which reviewed them for possible problems. Finding no statistically significant adverse impact on any protected group, retention decisions were finalized but later challenged as discriminatory based on age and in some cases race and national origin. These challenges were dismissed by the district court, an outcome affirmed on appeal.

Plaintiffs had asserted that the new business plan was a pretext for discrimination in that it disregarded their prior positive performance reviews. The seventh circuit found it unnecessary even to address this contention, finding that the plaintiffs had not satisfied their burden of establishing they were qualified, a critical component of a prima facie case under *McDonnell Douglas* (the court had already disregarded as inconsequential "stray remarks" the use of colloquial phrases such as "out with the old, in with the new" that plaintiffs asserted were direct evidence of discriminatory motivation). Noting that the primary and well-documented purpose of the restructuring was to identify and apply new performance criteria to help the company become more competitive in the future, the court held that plaintiffs had not shown they were meeting the employer's "legitimate workplace expectations" (citing its 2002 decision in *Peele* v. *County Mutual Insurance Co.*), thus rendering prior positive reviews irrelevant either to show prima facie qualifications *or* to argue pretext. In so holding, the court also reaffirmed its prior decision in *Scott* v. *Parkview Memorial Hospital* (1999), in which it observed that employers are not legally required "to prefer paper-heavy evaluations over contextual assessments by knowledgeable reviewers, or to exalt an assessment of past conduct over a prediction of future performance" (for an analogous result in a similar context see *Haywood* v. *Lucent Technologies,* 2003).

A note of caution is in order, however, lest the foregoing discussion give an impression that past performance evaluations are unimportant during RIFs. In a case that should warn against use of potentially outdated and marginally relevant appraisals, the first circuit found problematic the resurrection of poor appraisal results that had not previously been used against a black customer service representative but were later used to justify her RIF layoff (*Thomas v. Eastman Kodak*, 1999). This conduct was found to extend by several years the usual six-month statute of limitations applicable to discrimination claims. In line with the principle discussed earlier that a poor evaluation, without more, would not be actionable, the first circuit upheld the district court's rationale that to decide otherwise would "require a given plaintiff to file EEOC charges successfully for each performance evaluation, informal feedback from a supervisor, or office rumor [suggesting poor performance], so long as these events—even if not harmful in themselves—might be informed by racial animus and could someday contribute to a later, harmful result. This requirement would surely disrupt the American workplace . . . [by] forcing employees to 'run to the EEOC' each time they disagree with a performance evaluation."

Retaliation Cases

A further point should be made about some of the cases already discussed (for example, *Cullom v. Brown; Cardenas v. Massey et al.; Sauzek and Koski v. Exxon*). These and other cases illustrate an apparent trend in recent years for litigants to routinely assert retaliation claims in what would otherwise seem to be fairly straightforward discrimination lawsuits. This trend is probably based on a desire to increase the likelihood of obtaining higher damage awards (compensatory and punitive damages for Title VII discrimination and harassment claims are capped under the Civil Rights Act of 1991 at $300,000 per plaintiff per incident for the largest employers, but are not capped for analogous cases brought under 42 U.S.C. § 1981 or for state law claims alleging retaliation for complaining about prohibited conduct). Whatever the reasons, these cases constitute a growing category in which close temporal proximity between complaints about prohibited conduct to the employer, the EEOC, or a state human rights agency and subsequent adverse consequences may require an employer to defend the efficacy of its appraisal practices in multiple contexts.

An example can be found in the ninth circuit's majority opinion in *Winarto* v. *Toshiba American Electronics* (2001). In that case the plaintiff was a woman of Indonesian ancestry who successfully sued Toshiba for discrimination and harassment on a variety of bases including race, sex, national origin, disability, and retaliation for complaining about these issues to Toshiba's HR department. The retaliation claims centered on her inclusion in a RIF after previously favorable performance ratings were lowered for allegedly improper reasons not long after some of her complaints. The district court granted a motion to set aside the jury's verdict for Winarto, but the ninth circuit reversed and reinstated most of the jury's conclusions, finding the trial record adequate to support Winarto's claims. The record contains a troubling factual history of coworker abuses, including ridicule of Winarto's ancestry and accent, as well as outright physical assault, followed by cursory management responses that if believed, probably offer a blueprint for how *not* to respond to discrimination and harassment claims. However, key to the ninth circuit's opinion was the fact that Winarto, who had degrees in fields relevant to her PC support analyst position and more programming experience than most other members of her management information systems workgroup, had made numerous complaints about wrongful conduct that were not adequately addressed other than by reduced performance evaluations that conclusorily discussed "declining performance." Of course, in a harassment case even *actual* declining performance may be used to prove hostile environment if that decline occurs as a result of severe and pervasive conduct involving a worker's protected status. In any event, the majority found ample evidence that Winarto had demonstrated a prima facie case of retaliation (causal linkage between protected activities and subsequent adverse employment actions) and that Toshiba's asserted performance-based reasons for including her in the RIF were pretextual (a partial dissenting opinion takes issue with whether Winarto was held to a high enough burden of proof in the lower court's jury instructions).

To be sure, the fact patterns in retaliation cases differ widely (see, for example, *Liu* v. *Amway Corp.*, 2003, in which it was alleged that the plaintiff's appraisal ratings were lowered in retaliation for failing to perform her duties while on extended leave under the terms of the Family and Medical Leave Act). The important point to keep in mind, however, is that an employer may successfully defend an underlying discrimination claim if its RIF criteria or other evaluation processes are upheld, only to face secondary liability for retaliation if complaints about the alleged discrimination appear causally linked with subsequent unfavorable actions (see, for example, *Fine* v. *Ryan International Airlines*, 2002; *O'Neal* v. *Ferguson Construction*, 2001; *Shannon* v. *Bell South Telecommunications*, 2002). Employers would thus be wise to scrutinize with particular care performance or other criteria used to terminate employees who have previously complained about improper conduct, whatever merit those complaints may be found to have held. The same is true for employees chosen for termination by supervisors who have been the subject of discrimination or harassment complaints in the past and whose decisions may thus more credibly be challenged based on similar allegations by other plaintiffs (see, generally, Malos, 1998, pp. 92–93, citing Cathcart, 1996).

Summary of Cases Involving Performance Appraisal

It may appear from the foregoing discussion that employers fared less well in recent cases involving performance appraisal than they did in those involving job analysis or validity (compare Table 12.1 with Tables 12.2 and 12.3, which summarize performance appraisal cases decided for and against the employer, respectively). In numerical terms this may well be so. However, most of the appraisal cases decided for employers generated substantial closure for the defense (for example, by upholding summary dismissal of plaintiffs' lawsuits), whereas those decided against employers often only reinstated plaintiffs' claims, leaving the outcome still to be determined at trial. Put another way, although the courts have allowed some plaintiffs to "keep the ball in the air" in factual disputes that arguably require a trial to resolve, they also seem to have had no trouble affirming summary dismissal of cases in which they are asked to second-guess the business judgment of employers but can find no convincing evidence of discrimination or other wrongful conduct that compels them to do so.

Table 12.2. Recent Federal Appellate Cases Involving Performance Appraisals: Results Favorable for the Employer.

Case	Issue	Outcome and Reasons
Hawkins v. Pepsico (4th Cir. 2000)	Defensibility of termination for poor performance where it is alleged that appraisal results were lowered due to racial discrimination motives	Summary judgment for the employer upheld due to lack of evidence that the case involved anything other than an "ordinary workplace disagreement" with a supervisor whose race differed from plaintiff's.
Spears v. Department of Corrections (8th Cir. 2000)	Defensibility of alleged race-based retaliation in reducing plaintiff's appraisal from "highly successful" to merely "successful" so as to have justified quitting in a constructive discharge case	Summary judgment for the employer upheld due to the well-accepted general rule that arguably negative performance appraisals, without tangible harm as a result, are not actionable.
Cullom v. Brown (7th Cir. 2000)	Defensibility of delay in black employee's promotion due to appraisal results allegedly too favorable, but for which employee would have known sooner that his performance had to improve	Summary judgment for the plaintiff overturned as improper due to lack of evidence of harm; retaliation not cognizable where arguably incompetent employee was promoted due to undeserved favorable rating, delayed or otherwise.

Case	Issue	Outcome
Mayer v. Nextel (8th Cir. 2003)	Defensibility of failure to put age-protected employee on a PIP prior to firing him for poor performance when younger employees were placed on such plans	Summary judgment for the employer upheld due to "uncontroverted explanation [that] only managers who failed to meet quota were placed on PIPs" when the plaintiff had in fact met quota.
Sauzek and Koski v. Exxon Coal USA (7th Cir. 2000)	Defensibility of appraisal scores markedly lower than previous ratings where pattern just prior to a RIF was alleged to suggest possible age-related pretext	Trial verdict for employer upheld due to evidence that appraisal scores for workers both over and under 40 years of age fluctuated to similar extents, thus belying pretext in the jury's view.
Thorn and Curran v. Sunderstrand Aerospace (7th Cir. 2000)*	Defensibility of RIF-based layoffs of age-protected plaintiffs for alleged low productivity	Summary judgment for the employer upheld—against Curran—based on apparent judicial notice that younger workers are more turnover-prone, thus belying claim that younger workers were retained due to greater long-term value.
Cerutti et al. v. BASF et al. (7th Cir. 2003)	Defensibility of RIF criteria developed pursuant to new business plan designed to "repopulate" the company with those who could "do more with less" but which disregarded prior favorable performance reviews, thus allegedly showing pretext	Summary judgment for the employer upheld due to well-developed, job-related layoff criteria and plaintiffs' inability to demonstrate threshold qualifications under the new criteria, thus rendering moot any pretext allegations for lack of a prima facie case.

*Mixed results.

Table 12.3. Recent Federal Appellate Cases Involving Performance Appraisals: Results Unfavorable for the Employer.

Case	Issue	Outcome and Reasons
Russell v. *Principi* (D.C. Cir. 2001)	Defensibility of alleged discrimination in elements of compensation or promotional processes based on lower appraisal ratings	Summary judgment for the employer over-turned as improper where evidence created triable issue as to whether a bonus was un-fairly low due to racial favoritism.
Pryor v. *Seyfarth et al.* (7th Cir. 2000)	Defensibility of appraisal scores markedly lower than previous ratings where pattern just prior to a layoff may suggest discriminatory pretext	Summary judgment for the employer over-turned as improper where evidence created triable issue as to whether such a pattern supported plaintiff's gender-based retaliation claim.
Shackelford v. *Deloitte & Touche* (5th Cir. 1999)	Defensibility of appraisal scores markedly lower than previous ratings where most recent ratings were used to justify termination for allegedly poor performance	Summary judgment for the employer over-turned as improper where "tight temporal proximity" between plaintiff's complaints and firing created triable issue as to whether pattern was retaliatory.
Cardenas v. *Massey et al.* (3d Cir. 2001)	Defensibility of rank and pay differentials due to alleged adjustment of appraisal scores in opposite directions based on ratees' race or national origin	Summary judgment for the employer over-turned as improper where evidence created triable issue regarding the plaintiff's claims amid allegations of epithets such as *mojado* ("wetback").

Thorn and Curran v. Sunderstrand Aerospace (7th Cir. 2000)*	Defensibility of RIF-based layoffs of age-protected plaintiffs for alleged low productivity	Summary judgment for the employer overturned as improper—against Thorn—where evidence created triable issue as to whether good review was reduced to avoid seniority tiebreaker under which Thorn would have been retained.
Thomas v. Eastman Kodak (1st Cir. 1999)	Defensibility of relying on unused but outdated prior poor appraisals to justify RIF-based layoff of minority employee	Lower court's rejection of employer's statute of limitations argument upheld because any complaint over negative appraisal results would not have been ripe until tangible harm occurred.
Winarto v. Toshiba American Electronics (9th Cir. 2001)	Defensibility of RIF-based layoff due to asserted poor performance when ratings were allegedly lowered in retaliation for complaining about discrimination	Lower court's order setting aside jury verdict for the plaintiff overturned as improper due to adequate evidence in the trial record to support plaintiff's claims.

*Mixed results.

Procedural Justice and Discrimination Litigation: Toward an Integrating Framework

Both procedural justice (a psychological construct) and procedural due process (a legal construct) have been discussed as possible frameworks for analyzing and improving the perceived fairness and corresponding defensibility of a variety of personnel practices (for the comparisons and contrasts among elements of these two constructs, as well as linkages among them, see Posthuma, 2003). These related concepts of procedural fairness are considered implicitly, if not explicitly, in many of the judicial opinions discussed earlier in this chapter.

They have also been addressed in various reviews and research articles, fewer of which deal with selection processes and more of which deal with performance appraisals or discrimination claims in general (for a broader recent treatment of this topic, see Landy & Conte, 2004).

For example, in a study of applicant reactions to selection practices, Bauer, Truxillo, Sanchez, Craig, Ferrara, and Campion (2001) investigated and supported the validity of an instrument designed to capture aspects of procedural justice developed in previous research (Bauer and her colleagues found that job-relatedness, among other things, would likely be related to perceptions of the overall fairness of an employer's selection procedures). And in a study of court cases involving employment interviews, Williamson, Campion, Malos, Roehling, and Campion (1997) found that elements of interview structure such as job-relatedness, standardization, and other subdimensions of procedural fairness figured significantly in judicial opinions sustaining the selection practices of employers against both disparate treatment and adverse impact claims, although to differing extents.

Similarly in the performance appraisal context, Werner and Bolino (1997) found significant effects for elements of procedural fairness, due process, and accuracy in federal appellate cases decided for the employer, even though formal mention of validation processes seldom arose. In addition to this empirical study, a number of sources already mentioned (for example, Landy & Conte, 2004; Malos, 1998; Martin et al., 2000; Williams et al., 2003) have also cited procedural justice as likely to increase perceptions of accuracy and fairness, thus decreasing the likelihood of discrimination litigation involving an employer's personnel practices.

Other more integrative models have been proposed that link various justice-based concepts with desirable organizational outcomes: for example, increased perceived fairness, increased employee desire to improve performance, and decreased incidence of discrimination claims (Flint, 1999; Goldman, 2001). These models seem conceptually sound as far as they go, and offer promising guidance for improving personnel practice effectiveness and legal defensibility, but as yet have received only preliminary empirical support. In addition these models do little to balance the already heavy focus on appraisal procedures, which are probably more amenable to direct employee scrutiny or input than are job analysis or validation processes. Further development and extension of such models will thus be needed before they are likely to prove useful in driving advances in professional standards and practices for job analysis, validation, and performance appraisal, as well as in encouraging judicial acceptance of these standards and practices in court.

Conclusion

It remains true according to the Guidelines and other professional standards, and according to the appellate decisions involving them, that "under no circumstances will the general reputation of a test . . . its author . . . or [unsubstantiated] reports of its validity be accepted in lieu of evidence of validity" as an adequate defense of challenged personnel practices (*Williams et al. v. Ford Motor Co.*, at 540–541). Indeed, the case law involving job analysis and validity, and to a certain extent that dealing with performance appraisal, does appear to support a trend toward explicit judicial consideration of the work of industrial-organizational psychologists and human resource professionals in determining the appropriate legal standards in this regard.

For example, with respect to job analysis and validity, the cases summarized in Table 12.1 reflect substantial appellate court reliance on expert testimony for evidence regarding accepted methods of developing and validating various selection devices in accordance with applicable professional standards. That said, in resolving the often epic battles of the experts that have led to find-ings for the defendant of late, even in the absence of technical or formal validation, some judges appear to have reached a point where they simply cannot bring themselves to burden the em-ployer any further in trying to ensure that tests adequately screen prospective hires based on predicted performance rather than impermissible demographic factors. To the extent that this may reflect something of a human, if not legal, presumption in favor of employers who have undertaken reasonably professional vali-dation efforts, plaintiffs in these cases should realize that they increasingly have their work cut out for them in practical terms.

With respect to performance appraisal, professionally devel-oped and job-related criteria, as well as various aspects of due process and procedural justice (for example, notice of performance deficiencies, opportunities to correct those deficiencies, and re-viewability of adverse decisions), have also figured prominently in at least some of these cases (see, for example, *Cerutti et al.* v. *BASF et al.* and other cases summarized in Table 12.2). If these examples represent a trend, then it is probable that litigants who pay more attention to such matters will be better able to identify and adopt effective strategies for persuading the courts to find in their favor.

In any event the interplay of professional and judicial consid-eration of these issues will most likely continue, and we can hope that it will lead to more widespread adoption of valid, job-related selection procedures and performance appraisal processes. Such developments would serve to enhance both organizational effec-tiveness and employee development while also providing more reli-able guidance in the context of litigation when the inevitable lawsuits do in fact occur. To this end the ongoing evolution of legal and practical analysis will be most welcome.

References

Books and Articles

Barrett, G. V., & Kernan, M. C. (1987). Performance appraisal and ter-minations: A review of court decisions since *Brito v. Zia* with impli-cations for personnel practices. *Personnel Psychology, 40,* 489–503.

Bauer, T. N., Truxillo, D. M., Sanchez, R. J., Craig, J. M., Ferrara, P., & Campion, M. A. (2001). Applicant reactions to selection: Development of the selection procedural justice scale (SPJS). *Personnel Psychology, 54*, 389–419.

Cathcart, D. A. (1996). Employment termination litigation: Collateral tort theories and the multimillion dollar verdict: A 1994 update. In American Law Institute's *Employment Discrimination and Civil Rights Actions in Federal and State Courts* (pp. 675–779). Philadelphia: Author.

Civil Service Regulations, 5 C.F.R. § 5.1 *et seq.* (2004).

Employment Practices: Basic Requirements, 5 C.F.R. § 300.103 (2004).

Flint, D. H. (1999). The role of organizational justice in multi-source performance appraisal: Theory-based applications and directions for research. *Human Resource Management Review, 9*, 1–20.

Goldman, B. M. (2001). Toward an understanding of employment discrimination claiming: An integration of organizational justice and social information processing theories. *Personnel Psychology, 54*, 361–386.

Harvey, R. J. (1991). Job analysis. In M. D. Dunnette & L. M. Hough (Eds.), *Handbook of industrial and organizational psychology* (Vol. 2, pp. 71–163). Palo Alto, CA: Consulting Psychologists Press.

Klieman, A. F., & Durham, L. (1981). Performance appraisal, promotion and the courts: A critical review. *Personnel Psychology, 34*, 103–120.

Landy, F. J., & Conte, J. M. (2004). *Work in the 21st century: An introduction to industrial and organizational psychology.* New York: McGraw-Hill.

Lubben, G. L., Thompson, D. E., & Klasson, C. R. (1980, May–June). Performance appraisal: The legal implications of Title VII. *Personnel,* pp. 11–21.

Malos, S. B. (1998). Current legal issues in performance appraisal. In J. W. Smither (Ed.), *Performance appraisal: State of the art in practice* (pp. 49–94). San Francisco: Jossey-Bass.

Martin, D. C., Bartol, K. M., & Kehoe, P. E. (2000). The legal ramifications of performance appraisal: The growing significance. *Public Personnel Management, 29*, 379–405.

Posthuma, R. A. (2003). Procedural due process and procedural justice in the workplace: A comparison and analysis. *Public Personnel Management, 32*, 181–195.

Roehling, M. V. (1993). "Extracting" policy from judicial opinions: The dangers of policy capturing in a field setting. *Personnel Psychology, 46*, 477–502.

Schwartz, M., & Moayed, T. (2001). Minimizing the likelihood of employment litigation. *Employee Rights Quarterly, 1*, 53–57.

Selmi, M. (2003). The price of discrimination: The nature of class action employment discrimination litigation and its effects. *Texas Law Review, 81*, 1249–1335.

Thompson, D. E., & Thompson, T. A. (1982). Court standards for job analysis in test validation. *Personnel Psychology, 35,* 865–874.

Thrasher, K. (2003). A direct defense: Using an employment practices compliance approach to avoid employee lawsuits. *Employee Relations Law Journal, 29,* 25–37.

Uniform Guidelines on Employee Selection Procedures, 29 C.F.R. § 1607 *et seq.* (1978).

Weisenfeld, D. B. (2003). The year employment law dominated the docket: How the Supreme Court's 2001–02 term affects employees. *Employee Rights Quarterly, 3,* 1–7.

Werner, J. M., & Bolino, M. C. (1997). Explaining U.S. courts of appeals decisions involving performance appraisal: Accuracy, fairness, and validation. *Personnel Psychology, 50,* 1–24.

Williams, S. D., Slonaker, W. M., & Wendt, A. C. (2003, Winter). An analysis of employment discrimination claims associated with layoffs. *SAM Advanced Management Journal,* pp. 49–55.

Williamson, L. G., Campion, J. E., Malos, S. B., Roehling, M. V., & Campion, M. A. (1997). Employment interview on trial: Linking interview structure with litigation outcomes. *Journal of Applied Psychology, 82,* 900–912.

Cases

Albemarle Paper Co. v. Moody, 422 U.S. 405 (1975).

Allen et al. v. City of Chicago, 351 F.3d 306 (7th Cir. 2003).

Association of Mexican-American Educators et al. v. State of California, 231 F.3d 572 (9th Cir. 2000).

Bryant v. City of Chicago, 200 F.3d 1092 (7th Cir. 2000).

Cardenas v. Massey et al., 269 F.3d 251 (3d Cir. 2001).

Cerutti et al. v. BASF et al., 349 F.3d 1055 (7th Cir. 2003).

Clady v. County of Los Angeles, 770 F.2d 1421 (9th Cir. 1985).

Cotter et al. v. City of Boston et al., 323 F.3d 160 (1st Cir. 2003).

Craig v. County of Los Angeles, 626 F.2d 659 (9th Cir. 1980).

Cullom v. Brown, 209 F.3d 1035 (7th Cir. 2000).

Dorsey v. Pinnacle Automation Co., 278 F.3d 830, 837 (8th Cir. 2002).

Espinoza v. Farah Mfg. Co., 414 U.S. 86 (1973).

Fine v. Ryan International Airlines, 305 F.3d 746 (7th Cir. 2002).

Griggs v. Duke Power Co., 401 U.S. 424 (1971).

Gulino et al. v. Board of Education, 236 F. Supp.2d 314 (S.D. N.Y. 2002).

Gulino et al. v. Board of Education, 2003 U.S. Dist. LEXIS 56 (S.D. N.Y. 2003).

Hawkins v. Pepsico, 203 F.3d 247 (4th Cir. 2000).

Haywood v. Lucent Technologies, 323 F.3d 524 (7th Cir. 2003).

Johnson v. Kroger, 319 F.3d 858 (6th Cir. 2003).

Lanning et al. v. Southeastern Pennsylvania Transportation Authority, 181 F.3d 478 (3d Cir. 1999).

Lanning et al. v. Southeastern Pennsylvania Transportation Authority, 308 F.3d 286 (3d Cir. 2002).

Liu v. Amway Corp., 347 F.3d 1125 (9th Cir. 2003).

Mayer v. Nextel, 318 F.3d 803 (8th Cir. 2003).

McDonnell Douglas Corp. v. Green, 411 U.S. 792 (1973).

Meeker et al. v. Merit Systems Protection Board, 319 F.3d 1368 (Fed. Cir. 2003).

O'Neal v. Ferguson Construction Co., 237 F.3d 1248 (10th Cir. 2001).

Peele v. County Mutual Insurance Co., 288 F.3d 319 (7th Cir. 2002).

Petit et al. v. City of Chicago, 2003 U.S. App. LEXIS 25221.

Pryor v. Seyfarth, Shaw, Fairweather & Geraldson, 212 F.3d 976 (7th Cir. 2000).

Reynolds et al. v. Alabama Department of Transportation, 338 F.3d 1221 (11th Cir. 2003).

Russell v. Principi, 257 F.3d 815 (D.C. Cir. 2001).

Sauzek and Koski v. Exxon Coal USA, 202 F.3d 913 (7th Cir. 2000).

Scott v. Parkview Memorial Hospital, 175 F.3d 523, 525 (7th Cir., 1999).

Shackelford v. Deloitte & Touche, LLP, 190 F.3d 398 (5th Cir. 1999).

Shannon v. Bell South Telecommunications, Inc., 292 F.3d 712 (11th Cir. 2002).

Spears v. Department of Corrections, 210 F.3d 850 (8th Cir. 2000).

Stout et al. v. Potter, 276 F.3d 1118 (9th Cir. 2002).

Thomas v. Eastman Kodak Co., 183 F.3d 38, 51 (1st Cir. 1999).

Thorn and Curran v. Sunderstrand Aerospace Corp., 207 F.3d 383, 389 (7th Cir. 2000).

Tyler et al. v. Union Oil Co., 304 F.3d 379, 396–397 (5th Cir. 2002).

Vaughn v. Edel, 918 F.2d 517 (5th Cir. 1990).

Watson v. Fort Worth Bank & Trust, 487 U.S. 977 (1988).

Williams et al. v. Ford Motor Co., 187 F.3d 533 (6th Cir. 1999).

Winarto v. Toshiba American Electronics Components, 274 F.3d 1276 (9th Cir. 2001).

Yates v. Rexton, Inc., 267 F.3d 793 (8th Cir. 2001).

CHAPTER 13

Cut Scores and Employment Discrimination Litigation

Jerard F. Kehoe
Angela Olson

This chapter describes the treatment of cut scores in employment litigation and compares these legal considerations to features of the most common methods for setting cut scores. We begin with a brief review of the laws and regulatory guidelines that govern employment discrimination litigation relating to cut scores and of the professional standards that guide the development of cut scores and courts' decisions about cut scores. Following those summaries, we review court decisions that have established the legal considerations on which discrimination charges involving cut scores have been decided and then review the implications of these decisions for specific methods for setting cut scores.

Laws and Regulatory Guidelines

Statutory Law: Title VII

Title VII of the 1964 Civil Rights Act, as amended by the Civil Rights Act of 1991, is by far the most common statutory basis for employment discrimination challenges involving cut scores. (A thorough treatment of Title VII is provided in Chapter Two of this volume.) Title VII prohibits employment practices that cause adverse impact . . . if "the respondent fails to demonstrate that the challenged practice is job related for the position in question and consistent with business . . . necessity" (§ 2000e-2.k). It also establishes "that it shall be unlawful . . . to adjust the scores of, use different cutoff scores for, or otherwise alter the results of, employment related tests on the basis of race, color, religion, sex, or national origin" (§ 2000e-2.k).

As of early 2004 the Supreme Court has not ruled on the meaning of either "job related for the position in question" or "consistent with business necessity." However, lower courts have addressed cut scores used for employment purposes in a number of cases with a number of general perspectives emerging from those rulings.

The Uniform Guidelines

The *Uniform Guidelines on Employee Selection Procedures* (1978) (*Guidelines*) are the joint governmental agency guidelines that guide the enforcement of Title VII (and are described in detail in Chapter Three of this volume). Part 1607, Section 5H, of the *Guidelines* addresses cut scores and makes two points. First, the *Guidelines* describes its fundamental perspective about cut scores: "Where cutoff scores are used, they should be normally set so as to be reasonable and consistent with normal expectations of acceptable proficiency within the workforce." Although this guideline is open to considerable interpretation, it clearly establishes the expectation that the defense of challenged cut scores will be grounded in the relationship of the cut score to work proficiency. It is very different from the guidelines offered by professional standards for establishing cut scores (discussed later in this chapter), which allow any number of factors, not just work proficiency, to influence the choice of a cut score. Furthermore, not only does this guideline emphasize the importance of work proficiency but it also appears to focus on proficiency in the "acceptable" range, however that might be defined. It is noteworthy that the *Guidelines* does not establish a *minimum qualifications* standard for the defense of cut scores.

In general the *Guidelines'* brief treatment of cut scores places them in the narrow context of work proficiency rather than the broader context of business value. In this regard the federal government's *Guidelines* is quite different from professional standards for setting cut scores. The *Guidelines'* perspective is that the defense of cut scores rests on some demonstration of their relationship to work proficiency that does not include other organizational values such as the speed or cost of employment.

Constitutional Law and Administrative Law

Whereas Title VII is statutory law, the due process and equal protection clauses of the Fourteenth Amendment, under which some employment discrimination charges have been tried, are constitutional law. Although the courts have still to clarify important terms in Title VII law, the Supreme Court has established generally clear standards regarding the meaning of Fourteenth Amendment protection in charges of employment discrimination. Essentially, the Court has ruled, in *Washington* v. *Davis* (1976) and in *Schware* v. *Board of Bar Examiners of the State of New Mexico* (1957), that in order for a governmental organization to be found to discriminate under the equal protection clause a plaintiff bears the burden of proving intent to discriminate. Further, in *Washington* v. *Davis* the Court ruled that discriminatory intent cannot be implied from the fact that the decision maker knows that the selection procedure or cut score will lead to adverse impact. As Cascio, Alexander, and Barrett (1988) note, "the courts now point out routinely that the Constitution only forbids purposeful discrimination . . . (*Personnel Administrator of Massachusetts* v. *Feeney,* 1979)" (p. 3).

Similarly, administrative regulations having the force of law hold administrative agencies to a standard different from that imposed by Title VII. Cascio et al. (1988) describe the general principle this way: "the administrative body has been given the legal authority to give tests and to set passing scores, and it is not the function of the courts to second-guess that body unless there is some compelling reason to do so" (p. 3). The Supreme Court in *Guardians Association* v. *Civil Service Commission of the City of New York* (1983) held that a compelling reason would arise when administrative regulations were "arbitrary, capricious, or an abuse of discretion." In the context of cut scores, Carson (2001) argues that the courts use the term *arbitrary* to refer not to subjective judgment-based standards but to "unreasonable and capricious decision making." Like constitutional law, administrative regulations generally are interpreted as imposing a significantly lighter standard on administrative agencies than Title VII imposes on employers. For this reason our discussion of the implications of court decisions for cut score–setting methods will focus on Title VII cases.

Professional Guidelines

Two documents provide the primary sources of professional guidance for choosing and using cut scores for employment decisions. The *Standards for Educational and Psychological Testing* (American Educational Research Association, American Psychological Association, & National Council on Measurement in Education, 1999) (*Standards*) provides largely technical standards for test development and use in a wide range of educational and psychological applications, including those appropriate to employment and to credentialing and licensing. The recently revised *Principles for the Validation and Use of Personnel Selection Procedures* (Society for Industrial and Organizational Psychology, 2003) (*Principles*) provides largely technical guidance that is more narrowly focused on selection procedures used for employment decision making. In general both sets of professional guidance acknowledge that the determination of employment cut scores may be influenced not only by considerations of the work outcomes the tests were intended to predict but also by separate organizational considerations such as costs and employment process management. The *Standards, Principles,* and *Guidelines* are rarely cited by the courts in Title VII employment litigation, with the *Guidelines* being cited most often (see Chapter Three in this volume).

The Standards

Two types of guidance are provided by the *Standards*. Specific standards describe detailed methods or practices, and the commentary surrounding the specific standards provides background, context, and assumptions to improve understanding of the specific standards. Standards and commentary relating to cut scores are located in a variety of chapters. The perspective of the *Standards* can be captured by citing the following points and comments in the text surrounding the specific standards:

- "There can be no single method for determining cut scores for all tests or for all purposes, nor can there be any single set of procedures for establishing their defensibility" (AERA, APA, & NCME, 1999, p. 53).
- "Assuming that the employment test is valid for its intended use . . . the designation of the particular value for the cut score may be largely determined by the number of persons to be hired or promoted" (p. 53).
- "In employment settings, although it is important to establish that test scores are related to job performance, the precise relationship of test and criterion may have little bearing on the choice of a cut score" (p. 60).
- "Professional judgment is required to determine an appropriate standard-setting approach . . . in any given situation" (p. 60).
- And perhaps most significantly: "Cut scores embody value judgments as well as technical and empirical considerations" (p. 54).

The *Standards* recognizes that determining and using employment cut scores relies on more than a consideration of the relationship between scores on the employment test and desired work outcomes. The *Standards* acknowledges that value judgments as well as pragmatic considerations appropriately influence an organization's choice of cut score. At the same time, however, the *Standards* also enumerates technical methods or practices in a number of specific standards relating to employment cut scores. These standards are summarized here:

- Standard 4.19. The cut score rationale and procedures should be documented.
- Standards 4.20, 4.4, and 6.12. Cut scores used to distinguish different substantive interpretations of scores above and below the cut score(s) should be established "on the basis of sound empirical data concerning the relation of the test performance to relevant criteria" and their interpretations should be described and justified. However, the *Standards* also acknowledges that employment cut scores may not distinguish different substantive interpretations.

- Standard 4.21. The process of using expert judges should be designed so these experts "can bring their knowledge and experience to bear in a reasonable way."
- Standard 2.14. Standard errors of measurement should be reported in the vicinity of the cut score.
- Standard 2.15. The unreliability of the test should be described by providing estimates of the percentage of candidates who would be classified in the same way on two applications of the selection procedure.

In addition to these specific standards, the *Standards* makes the assumption that selection procedures used to make employment decisions will be valid for that purpose. This means that the many standards about the validity of employment selection procedures are directly relevant to the premise underlying cut scores that the assessment instrument is valid for the use for which the cut score is being established.

The *Standards* acknowledges that cut scores for employment decisions depend on values and pragmatic considerations, such as pass rates, that are beyond the scope of science-based principles of professional practice. However, the *Standards* adopts a very different view of cut scores used for credentialing purposes. Standard 14.17 states: "The level of performance required for passing a credentialing test should depend on the knowledge and skills necessary for acceptable performance in the occupation or profession and should not be adjusted to regulate the number or proportion of persons passing the test."

Clearly, the *Standards* endorses the widely accepted public policy about credentialing exams that holds that their purpose is to protect the public against the harm of poor performance. The *Standards* embraces the view that cut scores for credentialing tests should be based only on the requirements for a level of performance that avoids harm to the public. As we will discuss later, this policy of setting credentialing cut scores to avoid harm appears to correspond to a minimum qualifications standard.

The Principles

The recently revised *Principles* shares the *Standards'* view that cut scores for employment decisions should be based on valid measures:

"There is no single method for establishing cutoff scores. If based on valid predictors demonstrating linearity or monotonicity throughout the range of prediction, cutoff scores may be set as high or as low as needed to meet the requirements of the organization" (SIOP, 2003, p. 46).

The *Principles* also shares the *Standards'* view that cut scores may be influenced by considerations in addition to the work performance against which the selection procedure was likely validated: "Professional judgment is necessary in setting any cutoff score, and typically is based on a rationale that may include such factors as estimated cost-benefit ratio, number of vacancies and selection ratio, expectancy of success versus failure, performance and diversity goals of the organization, or judgment as to the knowledge, skill, ability, or other characteristics required by the work" (p. 47).

Indeed, the *Principles* goes even further and expresses the view that professionals who recommend cut scores *should* consider factors that take into account organizational values and interests beyond the work performance predicted by the selection procedure: "When researchers make recommendations concerning the use of a rank ordering method or a cutoff score, the recommendation should take into account the labor market, the consequences of errors in prediction, the utility of the selection procedure, resources needed to monitor and maintain a list of qualified candidates, and other relevant factors. The goals of the organization may favor a particular alternative" (p. 47).

In short, the *Principles* uses even stronger language than the *Standards* to express the view that cut scores are organizational decisions that appropriately balance a variety of potentially competing interests and values.

Title VII Case Law Relating to Cut Scores

A Framework for Relating Title VII Cases to Cut Score Methods

In this section we provide a framework that summarizes the major considerations in setting cut scores. The purpose of this framework is to organize the description of court cases around the key elements of cut score–setting methods in order to clarify the implications of these cases for the practice of establishing cut scores.

The framework consists of five sets of considerations, arranged in a typically occurring sequence, that arise in a typical process of setting cut scores for employment purposes:

1. Establish the *purpose* of the selection decision.
2. Determine the *relevance* of the selection procedure to the desired work outcomes.
3. Determine the *threshold* level of desired work behavior and the test score corresponding to that threshold.
4. Choose the desired level of *certainty* associated with the selection decisions.
5. Adjust the cut score to reflect *trade-offs* between the level of expected work behavior and other organization interests.

The threshold, certainty, and trade-off considerations (framework items 3, 4, and 5) are the steps most directly related to the choice of the cut score itself. Purpose and relevance (items 1 and 2) generally relate to decisions about the selection procedure itself: for example, What is the intended purpose of the selection strategy? What applicant attributes should be assessed? Which instruments should be used? What validation evidence should be gathered? However, in some cases the purpose of the employment decisions may have direct implications for the target threshold of work behavior. For example, in teacher licensure cases the widely accepted purpose of avoiding harm guides the threshold decision. These considerations generally take place before the process for establishing a cut score. For this reason, this description of court cases related to cut scores will be organized around the threshold, certainty, and trade-off considerations. Although courts' views about the purpose and relevance of the selection procedure in question are certainly central to case outcome, they are generally not specifically directed to the choice of a particular cut score. Figure 13.1 shows the key elements of this framework for setting cut scores and reviewing court cases.

**Figure 13.1. A General Framework
for the Process of Establishing Cut Scores.**

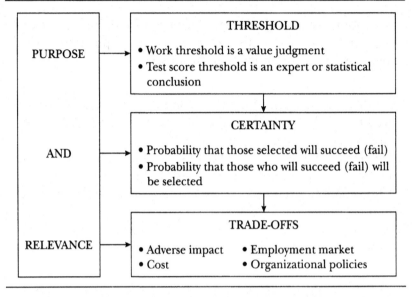

The threshold step includes two decisions. The first decision is about the threshold of work behavior (for example, task proficiency, helping behavior, retention, tardiness, workplace theft, and so forth) that the organization intends to target as the level of behavior desired of new hires. Unlike the determination of job relevance, which is a scientific conclusion, the determination of a work threshold is ultimately a value judgment, typically made by the employer. In some cases the employer's value judgment will be informed by other key stakeholders. For example, organizations that provide safety services or licensed services to the public will consider public policy relating to acceptable levels of risk to the public. No amount of scientific investigation of work tasks, outputs, consequences, or context can lead to an unambiguous conclusion about the "right" work threshold. Even if the work threshold judgment is made on behalf of the organization by some other agent, such as a court or an independent job expert, it remains fundamentally a value judgment. Even where the level of acceptable risk is precisely quantified—such as the standard for nuclear plant operators that the probability of a radioactive release should be no greater than 10^{-7} (F. Landy, personal communication, 2004)—the work threshold remains a value judgment. The second decision in the threshold step is the identification of a specific selection procedure score that is associated by some rationale with the desired work threshold. This process of linking the score threshold to the work threshold is a conclusion based on scientific or expert analysis. It is not a value judgment.

The certainty step addresses the organization's interest in effectively and efficiently hiring employees who will succeed. There are two types of certainty of interest to the employer. The first is the certainty that those selected will succeed. This certainty relates to the employer's interest in effective selection. The second is the certainty that candidates who would succeed will be selected. This certainty relates to the employer's interest in efficient selection, because a high level of this certainty will reflect a selection process that does not miss many good candidates. This certainty that candidates who would succeed are chosen also relates to considerations of fairness. One view of selection fairness is that all candidates who would succeed if hired should have the same probability of being selected. This view of fairness, however, has been persuasively criticized on technical grounds (Peterson & Novick, 1976) and is excluded from the *Guidelines'* and *Principles'* descriptions of bias in employment decisions. In general the desired levels of these certainties are value judgments or, at the least, are based on value judgments that inform the analysis leading to the target certainty levels. Frequently, this certainty consideration is expressed in terms of true and false negatives and positives.

The final choice in setting a cut score often involves trade-offs between work outcomes and other interests that are independent of work outcomes. Perhaps the most common trade-off involves employment process cost and the degree of impact on protected groups. Desired trade-offs are a composite of value judgments and scientific and expert analysis.

It is important to note that these three key elements of the cut score–setting process may or may not be part of any particular method. However, we include them in this framework because, whether or not they are part of a particular employer's cut score-setting process, courts may evaluate every cut score with respect to the work threshold, the certainty of the selection decisions, and the trade-offs it represents.

Business Necessity as It Relates to Cut Scores

This review will describe court decisions that interpret the meaning of business necessity as it applies to cut scores. This discussion is at root a discussion about the threshold question. In addition we will review cases that have addressed issues specifically relating to thresholds, certainty, and trade-offs in choosing cut scores.

Perhaps the most compelling current legal issue regarding the establishment of cut scores is the meaning of the term *business necessity*. This is at issue primarily because the Supreme Court has not interpreted this term (or "job related for the position in question," for that matter), and lower courts have offered differing interpretations. Two perspectives have emerged—a *minimum qualifications* interpretation and a *business relevance* interpretation. The minimum qualifications perspective has its roots in language used in three Supreme Court cases, *Griggs v. Duke Power* (1971), *Albemarle Paper v. Moody* (1975), and *Dothard v. Rawlinson* (1977). In *Griggs* the Court interpreted Title VII as requiring ". . . the removal of artificial, arbitrary, and *unnecessary* [emphasis added] barriers to employment." In *Albemarle* the Court considered a validation study that included only high-performing incumbents. The Court ruled that such a validation study does not necessarily validate a cut score for the "minimum qualifications" to perform the job at an entry level. In *Dothard* the Court concluded that a discriminatory cut score "must be shown to be *necessary* [emphasis added] to safe and efficient job performance." The common threads in these three interpretations are the terms *necessary* and *minimum qualifications*. This perspective has been most clearly articulated by the third circuit court, in *Lanning v. Southeastern Pennsylvania Transportation Authority (SEPTA)* (1999), when it said of the Title VII provision that employment practices should be "job related . . . and consistent with business necessity" that "[t]he business necessity prong must be read to demand an inquiry into whether the score reflects the minimum qualifications necessary to perform successfully the job in question." The court went on to add not only that a cut score should correspond to the "minimum qualifications necessary to perform successfully" but also that "a business necessity standard that wholly defers to an employer's judgment as to what is desirable in an employee . . . is completely inadequate." Since the *Lanning* ruling in 1999, however, no other federal appeals court has agreed with the third circuit. The seventh circuit reinforced the *Guidelines'* standard in *Bew* v. *City of Chicago* (2001) and the ninth circuit concluded in *Association of Mexican-American Educators* v. *State of California* (2000) that separate validation of cut scores is not required.

The business relevance interpretation has its roots in the language of Title VII itself, the *Guidelines, Griggs, New York City Transit Authority* v. *Beazer* (1979), *Washington* v. *Davis* (1976), and *Fitzpatrick* v. *City of Atlanta* (1993). As noted earlier, neither Title VII nor the *Guidelines* uses the term *minimum qualifications* when referring either to job relevance or business necessity. Indeed, the *Guidelines'* specific reference to cut scores only advises that they be . . ."reasonable and consistent with normal expectations of acceptable proficiency." Further, although in *Griggs* the Court refers to "unnecessary barriers," it also explains its reference to business necessity as the "touchstone" for a defense of a discriminatory employment practice, whereas "if an employment practice . . . cannot be shown to be related to job performance, the practice is prohibited." Although *Beazer* was not a case that hinged on cut scores, the Court's interpretation was that a discriminatory selection standard needed only to bear a "manifest relationship to the employment in question." In *Washington* v. *Davis,* although it was not a Title VII case, the Court referenced *Griggs* and *Albemarle* in dismissing challenges to the test and supporting evidence of the test's relationship to training success as consistent with the "job-relatedness requirement." Finally, the eleventh circuit interpreted business necessity in *Fitzpatrick* v. *City of Atlanta* as requiring only a showing by the employer "that the practice or action is necessary to meeting a goal that, as a matter of law, qualifies as an important business goal." The implication of the business relevance perspective is that a cut score may be defended by showing a reasonable rationale that relates the cut score to an important business interest, which for some jobs might include a public interest.

The ninth circuit court's decision in *Association of Mexican-American Educators* v. *State of California* (2000) is an example of how the business relevance perspective has been applied to cut scores. The court held that defendants are not required to "validate" cut scores and that when a test is valid, defendants may use professional estimates of the requisite ability levels to determine the appropriate cut score.

This distinction between minimum qualifications and business relevance is related to the issue of avoiding harm in licensure tests. In a recent teacher certification case tried under Title VII, *Gulino* v. *Board of Education* (2003), the district court ruled in favor of the defendants, who showed that the certification test "bears a manifest relationship to teaching." The cut score issue of interest in *Gulino* involves the distinction between the commonly accepted standard to be applied to cut scores on certification and licensure tests and business necessity. As in *Association of Mexican-American Educators*, the tests challenged in *Gulino* were certification tests that were part of a state teacher licensure process. The challenge to these tests was heard under Title VII because licensure directly affects employability and because of the close relationship between the licensing organization and the employer. Courts have generally been willing to try discrimination challenges to teacher licensing tests under Title VII. It is generally accepted (see Standard 14.17 of the *Standards*) that the cut score chosen for licensure tests will be one designed to protect the public from the harm of low performance. In effect it is generally accepted that a minimum qualifications standard is appropriately applied to cut scores on licensure tests. Although the court in *Gulino* did not specifically interpret the meaning of the term *minimum qualifications,* it did uphold the challenged tests where the cut scores recommended by experts were estimated to represent the "minimum level of knowledge and academic skills necessary for competent performance as a beginning teacher." In supporting this standard the court made no mention of business necessity as a separate consideration beyond the consideration of job-relatedness. Curiously, although the court also found that the "avoid harm" standard had not been supported by the defendants, it nevertheless accepted the "minimum level" language used by experts to define the target cut score. A possible implication is that Title VII challenges to licensure tests may routinely rely on a minimum qualifications standard, without any explicit or independent interpretation of whether this licensure principle is consistent with the intended meaning of business necessity. Interestingly, *Gulino* is typical of other teacher licensure Title VII cases in which experts estimate the test score expected of minimally qualified performers and then the test owner sets a substantially lower cut score to accommodate other considerations such as employment market conditions and the probability that a minimally qualified performer will pass.

Decisions Related to Thresholds

Other than the meaning of business necessity, the most commonly considered issue relating to thresholds is whether a cut score may be higher than scores achieved by some incumbents. In several cases subsequent to *Griggs*, the Supreme Court and lower courts have shown a willingness to uphold cut scores higher than the level of test performance demonstrated by some incumbents. In *Washington v. Davis* (1976) the Supreme Court held that government employers may seek to upgrade employees' skills by setting a cut score higher than the lowest score achieved by incumbents. Similarly, in *Rogers v. International Paper* (1975) the eighth circuit ruled that a cut score that would have excluded 40 percent of the incumbents would require a rationale but, on its face, should not be rejected merely because some incumbents fail to achieve it. In *Pegues v. Mississippi State Employment Service* (1980) the district court upheld a cut score that would exclude the bottom one-third of incumbents on the basis that only the top two-thirds were performing at a satisfactory level. In *Bew v. City of Chicago* (2001) the seventh circuit court stated that "[w]e do not hold cutoff scores to standards so strict that they must select all good performers and reject all bad." In *Thomas v. City of Evanston* (1985) the district court did not uphold a cut score that would exclude 16 percent of the incumbents, because the court found there was no evidence that 16 percent of the officers were performing at an unsatisfactory level. Although the *Thomas* decision contrasted with many others that upheld higher cut scores, the court noted the lack of a rationale and evidence supporting the claim that some incumbents were performing at unsatisfactory levels. In general courts have not required that cut scores be limited to the lowest scores exhibited by incumbents. Courts have been accepting of higher cut scores where a reasonable basis is established for choosing a score higher than the minimum incumbent score. Typically, that rationale is based on some demonstration or claim that the organization has a legitimate interest in a higher level of performance than exhibited by some incumbents. Those low-scoring incumbents may tend to be unsuccessful performers, or the organization may have an interest in raising the overall level of performance.

One implication of this review of courts' interpretations of business necessity and cut score thresholds is that the context of the job and setting appears to be an important consideration. In teacher licensing cases such as *Gulino*, courts seems to be willing to accept the minimum qualification standard implied by the avoid harm policy, although it is remarkable that the same courts are also willing to support substantial reductions in cut scores to accommodate other considerations where those reductions may themselves substantially increase the prospect of harm. In cases involving police, firefighter, nuclear power plant operator, and airline pilot jobs, the public's substantial interest in safety is given paramount consideration, which may or may not trigger a minimum qualification standard. In cases not involving public safety or harm the courts' focus appears to be primarily on considerations of job-relatedness rather than on some standard of performance suggested by any public interest.

Decisions Related to Certainty

Although a degree of certainty that new hires will succeed on the job is central to the organization's interest, few court decisions have addressed this particular issue as a condition for the successful defense of a cut score. However, in *Lanning* v. *SEPTA* (2002) the third circuit offered two perspectives about certainty that warrant careful attention because they may lead to conflicting standards for the defense of cut scores. In applying its minimum qualifications interpretation of business necessity, the court concluded that the appropriate cut score is one that distinguishes candidates who are "likely to be able to do the job" from those who are not. In the same decision, however, the court also concluded that the appropriate cut score should not exclude many candidates who would succeed on the job. These two considerations—the probability of job success given that one has passed the test, P(success|pass), and the probability of passing the test given that one will succeed on the job, P(pass|success)—are quite different standards likely to conflict with each other. All else being the same, choosing a cut score to increase the P(pass|success) will decrease the P(success|pass). The first standard, P(success|pass), relates to the organization's interest in selecting successful employees and, as the third circuit acknowledged, relates directly to the meaning of business necessity, which refers to the employers' need for successful employees. In fact the third circuit's acceptance of a cut score that distinguishes those who are "likely to be able to do the job" from those who are not is consistent with this first standard. The second standard, P(pass|success), is relevant to two considerations that generally conflict with the first standard. The first consideration is selection efficiency; the higher the P(pass|success), the greater the efficiency of the selection system. The second consideration is different and relates to a standard for fairness in selection. It seems likely that the third circuit's interest in P(pass|success) was based on concerns that were more about fairness than efficiency. Of course, P(pass|success) as a standard for fairness corresponds to the Cole definition of fairness that was discredited three decades ago (see Peterson & Novick, 1976) and is inconsistent with the currently accepted definition of selection fairness expressed in the *Uniform Guidelines* (§ 14B-8.a) and in the *Principles* (pp. 31–33). (Chapter Five in this volume discusses the implications of these competing standards in more technical detail.)

Decisions Related to Trade-Offs

Courts have frequently found in Title VII cases that many factors in addition to incumbents' performance on the selection procedure may appropriately influence the choice of a defensible cut score. In a teacher certification case, *National Education Association v. South Carolina* (1978), the Supreme Court upheld a cut score–setting process that considered not only the expected test performance of minimally competent teachers but also the agreement among experts, test reliability, local labor market conditions, and teaching workforce diversity. Biddle (1993) provides a detailed summary of this cut score–setting process, the modified Angoff process, which is discussed later. In *Black Shield Police Association* v. *City of Cleveland* (1986) the district court held that experts should set cut scores with the aid of a range of factors, including the validity, reliability, and utility of the selection procedure. Similarly, the district court in *Cuesta* v. *State of New York Office of Court Administration* (1987) upheld a complex cut score–setting process that included a consideration of the accuracy expert judges demonstrated in their judgment about the appropriate cut score.

In other cases, such as *Officers for Justice* v. *Civil Service Commission of the City and County of San Francisco* (1992) and *Chicago Firefighters Local 2* v. *City of Chicago* (2001), banding processes have been upheld that consider score reliability and applicant diversity and availability when using cut scores to define bands and employment decision rules. Although Title VII explicitly references job relevance and business necessity as the governing conditions for defense of employment practices, courts also accept that the decision to set a specific cut score may take into consideration factors unrelated to the organization's interest in work behavior.

Summary

These cases point to several principles and considerations relevant to cut scores that courts are likely to apply in Title VII cases:

1. A reasonable rationale will be necessary, showing the relevance of the cut score to some important business value, which may include an interest in improving performance.
2. In some cases—certainly in licensure cases—the reasonable rationale will need to show the relevance of the cut score to a minimum qualifications standard. At this point it is not clear whether the minimum qualifications standard will be more likely to apply in some jobs or in some courts.
3. It is important that job experts and other professionals have a significant role in establishing that professional standards have been followed and, where there is a public interest either in safety (as in police, firefighter, and nuclear plant jobs) or in consumer protection (as in teacher jobs), that there is a reasonable link between the cut score and the public's interest.

4. A cut score may be higher than scores achieved by some incumbents where there is a rationale showing that low-scoring incumbents perform below a reasonable standard of success.
5. An adjustment to a cut score is acceptable where it accommodates employer-relevant factors such as cost of employment, employment market considerations, P(success|pass), and P(pass|success). It appears to be important that such trade-off adjustments be informed by professional expertise.
6. A strategy of post hoc reductions of cut scores to very low levels solely for the purpose of avoiding adverse impact is not likely to be supported without a substantive rationale other than litigation avoidance.

Implications for Cut Score–Setting Methods

This section summarizes the implications of these court rulings for specific cut score–setting methods. To organize this summary, we introduce a general taxonomy, shown in Table 13.1, for classifying cut score–setting methods. The purpose of this simple taxonomy is to cluster cut score–setting methods so that court considerations have similar implications for all methods within a group.

Groups of Methods

The description of cut score–setting methods in this chapter employs a simple, general taxonomy of methods formed by two categorical dimensions: (1) *source of work information* about criteria of interest and (2) *source of test information*. The source of test information dimension is further divided into two subcategories—*expert* and *empirical*. *Expert test information* consists of the estimates and judgments provided by experts about the test performance of targeted groups of test takers. *Empirical test information* consists of observed test results for groups of test takers. The source of work information dimension is similarly divided into three subcategories—*none, expert,* and *empirical*. The none category is used to capture those cut score–setting methods that do not rely on any information about work outcomes. Work information includes outcomes of value to the organization, such as work performance,

Table 13.1. A Taxonomy of Cut Score–Setting Methods.

	Group 1	Group 2	Group 3	Group 4
Source of Work Information →	*Name*	*Empirical*	*Expert*	*Expert*
Source of Test Information →	*Empirical*	*Empirical*	*Empirical*	*Expert*

Methods	• Predictive yield
	• Adverse impact minimization
	• Test distribution based
	• SEdiff banding
		• Criterion banding
		• Regression
		   Forward
		   Reverse
		• Expectancy charts
		• Decision-theoretic
			• Contrasting groups
			• Bookmark
			• Borderline group
				• Angoff
				• Nedelsky
				• Ebel
				• Jaeger

Potential litigation strengths	• Direct control of selection rates • Relies on test experts	• Explicit consideration of work threshold • Rationale linking work threshold to test threshold • Relies on work experts and test experts	• Explicit consideration of work threshold • Rationale linking work threshold to test threshold • Relies on work experts and test experts	• Rationale linking work threshold to test threshold • Relies on work experts • Training of experts
Potential litigation weaknesses	• Obscures trade-offs with work outcomes • Does not consider desired work threshold • Does not rely on work experts	• Trade-offs considered outside the method, except decision-theoretic	• Trade-offs considered only outside the method	• Work experts may not be test experts • Does not specify likelihood of work success of those chosen • Trade-offs considered only outside the method

contextual performance, turnover, absence, workforce diversity, counterproductive behavior, and adverse impact. Work information also includes effects of worker behavior that have an impact on public interests such as safety and consumer protection. These are outcomes associated with the candidates who are selected. Work information excludes organizational outcomes that are not a function of who is chosen, such as the cost or time of the employment process. Table 13.1 shows this taxonomy and identifies specific methods associated with each combination of these dimensions. Two groupings of work information and test information are not shown (no work information combined with expert test information and empirical work information combined with expert test information) because there are no standard methods that fall into those two groups.

The entire process of setting a cut score may rely entirely on one of these methods or may incorporate more than one method. The methods are not necessarily mutually exclusive. Nor are they fixed. Each of these methods is likely to be adapted to the particular circumstances in each situation. It is also interesting to note that except for decision-theoretic methods, none of these standard methods adjusts cut scores for considerations that are external to the relationship between test results and work outcomes, such as cost of employment and employment market. These trade-offs routinely affect final cut scores, but the methods for choosing them are typically appended to the specific cut score–setting method used.

Group 1: No Work Information and Empirical Test Information

Cascio et al. (1988) provide an insightful discussion of this class of methods, calling them *norm-referenced* methods and noting that the primary reasons favoring these methods are purely administrative, such as cost control and process management. The three specific methods mentioned by Cascio et al.—Thorndike's method of predictive yield, adverse impact minimization, and test distribution considerations—share the essential feature of relying only on empirical test information. They do not take into account any criterion information, such as target work thresholds or work outcome variation among incumbents. To these three methods we have added SEdiff banding, which did not exist in 1988 but which is gaining popularity, particularly in public sector selection applications.

Shortly after Cascio et al.'s (1988) review of cut scores, Cascio, Outtz, Zedeck, and Goldstein (1991) introduced a selection strategy that relies on bands of test scores to govern the selection process. Although it is beyond the scope of this chapter to describe banding strategies in detail, banding is a cut score–based selection strategy in which multiple cut scores are established. Certainly the use of multiple cut scores is not an uncommon practice in employment. For example, commercial test publishers often describe empirically defined zones of test scores that differentiate levels of candidate attractiveness. In fact, any cut score–based strategy can also be described in terms of test score bands. For example, a test used with a single pass-fail cut score divides candidates into two bands—those with scores at or above the cut score and those with scores below the cut score. The Cascio et al. (1991) method, labeled *SEdiff banding* here, defines the bandwidths as a function of test reliability and does not use information about criteria of interest other than the fundamental assumption that the test is valid. Bandwidths are defined as approximately two times the standard error of the difference (SEdiff), which is a function of the test's reliability and standard deviation.

Courts have accepted SEdiff banding strategies as shown, for example, in *Officers for Justice* v. *Civil Service Commission* (1992) and *Chicago Firefighters Local 2* v. *City of Chicago* (2001). In particular the courts have accepted the statistical rationale underlying SEdiff banding that test scores differences within a band are completely unreliable. This is significant because this statistical rationale has been thoroughly debated in the scientific community without any acknowledged resolution (see Campion et al., 2001). Clearly, courts have found credible the claim that small test scores differences should not have large effects on employment decisions, and have attached little importance to the detailed statistical points underlying this debate.

A second point is worth noting about courts' support of SEdiff banding. The cases at issue were tried under Title VII as amended by the Civil Rights Act of 1991, which prohibits making adjustments to test scores based on group status (§ 106), a process also known as *race-norming,* and also prohibits the use of group status as a factor in making employment decisions (§ 107). Where SEdiff banding has been scrutinized by courts, one of its purposes has been to help reduce severe adverse impact. In *Officers for Justice,* the court considered only the Section 107 issue of whether banding, which was designed in part to mitigate large group differences in selection rates, was in effect a process for making race a factor in employment decisions. The ninth circuit held that banding did not violate the Section 107 prohibition. Separately, in *Chicago Fire-fighters,* the seventh circuit supported banding by finding no showing that banding was adopted to adjust the scores of minorities, which would appear to support banding under Section 106.

Group 2: Empirical Work Information and Empirical Test Information

This grouping makes use of four distinctively different methods but all share the feature of using both test and criterion data to determine the most appropriate cut score. Criterion banding methods use empirical information about the relationship between the criterion of interest and the test to derive test score bandwidths determined by criterion outcomes of interest to the organization. The two regression methods described here, forward regression and reverse regression, determine a test score that is statistically associated with the criterion score defining minimal competence. Expectancy chart methods represent a graphical version of one of the statistical regression methods. Decision-theoretic methods provide analytical procedures for simultaneously optimizing competing values.

Criterion Banding Methods

Criterion banding is not a single method but a class of closely related methods that define bandwidths based on information about criterion outcomes. To our knowledge, these methods have not yet been used. They were developed to address the SEdiff banding limitation of not taking criterion information into account. Kehoe and Tenopyr (1994) describe two methods, criterion consistency bands and criterion success bands, that take explicit account of organizational values for similar criterion outcomes and do not rely on the assumption that scores within a band are statistically indifferent. A criterion consistency band is defined as the range of test scores the employer is willing to treat alike because the candidates scoring lowest in the band have an acceptable probability of outperforming the highest scoring candidate. A criterion success band is defined as the range of test scores the employer is willing to treat alike because the highest- and lowest-scoring candidates within the band have reasonably similar probabilities of achieving or exceeding the target level of performance. An important feature of criterion bands is that in contrast to SEdiff bands, they define bandwidths in terms of ranges of practical indifference, not ranges of statistical indifference. They rely on the organization's judgment that it is indifferent to reliable but small differences in work outcomes, rather than small differences in test scores.

Aguinis, Cortina, and Goldberg (1998) describe a method, labeled criterion indifference banding here, that extends the rationale of SEdiff banding to statistical insignificance between criterion outcomes. They extend the SEdiff's assumption of statistical indifference between similar test scores to criterion outcomes. Criterion indifference banding is similar to criterion consistency and criterion success banding in that all three are methods for determining an organization's indifference, for selection purposes, toward candidates who are expected to perform similarly once hired.

Given that the courts have placed no importance on the technical criticisms of SEdiff banding, it is likely that the criterion banding methods would be well received by the courts for the same reasons that the courts support SEdiff banding. Also, because criterion banding methods make explicit use of information about differences in work outcomes, it is possible that the courts would prefer criterion banding to SEdiff banding in cases that hinge on questions of work performance.

Regression Methods

In cases where empirical data are available for both the test and the criterion, regression methods may be used to set a cut score. For example, Chuang, Chen, and Novick (1981) describe a method for establishing a cut score based on the *forward* regression of the criterion on the predictor, whereas Cascio et al. (1988, research suggestion no. 7) suggest that the method of regressing the test scores on the criterion scores, that is, *reverse* regression, could

CUT SCORES AND EMPLOYMENT DISCRIMINATION LITIGATION **433**

be investigated to learn its properties as a cut score–setting method. Recently, Jeanneret and Stelly (2003) compared reverse and forward regression methods and found reverse regression to produce cut scores that are closer to the test mean than those produced by forward regression, which can produce impractically extreme cut scores in many common situations. The consequences of both can be demonstrated by applying both forward and reverse regression in a set of hypothetical cases. Tables 13.2 and 13.3 show the cut scores that are produced by forward and reverse regression methods at each of six levels of work threshold for four different levels of validity. Test and criterion scores are expressed in z-score units in this demonstration. The use of z scores simplifies the regression weights in each case so that the intercept is 0 and the slope is equal to the validity coefficient. The six levels of work threshold on the criterion can be expressed as percentages of successful incumbents, 95 percent, 75 percent, 55 percent, 50 percent, 25 percent, and 5 percent, which correspond to criterion z scores of –1.65, –0.68, –0.13, 0.0, 0.68, and 1.65, respectively. The four levels of test validity are .10, .20, .40, and .60. As an example, in the case in which validity = .20 and the work threshold is set equal to a criterion z score of –0.13 (the 45th percentile of the criterion distribution):

Forward regression $\qquad -0.13 = 0 + .20 \times (\text{Cut score}),$

$\qquad\qquad$ therefore, Cut score $= -0.13/.20 = -0.65.$

Reverse regression $\qquad$ Cut score $= 0 + .20 \times (-.013) = -0.026.$

Table 13.2 shows the cut score values (in z-score units) and the resulting pass rates for both forward and reverse regression approaches for each combination of validity and work threshold level. Certain patterns stand out. The forward regression cut scores and pass rates tend to be extreme where the target threshold is either very low or very high. The higher the validity, the less extreme the forward regression cut scores are. Just the opposite occurs with reverse regression cut scores. The cut scores and pass rates tend to be homogeneous and near the mean of the test score distribution. The higher the validity, the more extreme the reverse regression cut scores are.

Table 13.2. Cut Scores and Pass Rates for Forward and Reverse Regression Methods.

Threshold Competence (job z score)	Base Rate of Job Success	Validity .10 Forward		.10 Reverse		.20 Forward		.20 Reverse		.40 Forward		.40 Reverse		.60 Forward		.60 Reverse	
		Cut Score	Pass Rate	Cut Score	Pass Rate	Cut Score	Pass Rate	Cut Score	Pass Rate	Cut Score	Pass Rate	Cut Score	Pass Rate	Cut Score	Pass Rate	Cut Score	Pass Rate
-1.65	95%	-16.5	100%	-0.16	56%	-8.25	100%	-0.33	63%	-4.12	100%	-0.66	75%	-2.76	100%	-0.99	84%
-0.68	75%	-6.80	100%	-0.07	53%	-3.40	100%	-0.14	56%	-1.70	96%	-0.27	61%	-1.14	87%	-0.41	66%
-0.13	55%	-1.30	90%	-0.01	51%	-0.65	74%	-0.03	51%	-0.32	63%	-0.05	52%	-0.22	59%	-0.08	53%
0.00	50%	0.00	50%	0.00	50%	0.00	50%	0.00	50%	0.00	50%	0.00	50%	0.00	50%	0.00	50%
0.68	25%	6.80	0%	0.07	47%	3.40	0%	0.14	44%	1.70	4%	0.27	39%	1.14	13%	0.41	34%
1.65	5%	16.5	0%	0.16	44%	8.25	0%	0.33	37%	4.12	0%	0.66	25%	2.76	0%	0.99	16%

Table 13.3. Job Success Rates for Candidates Scoring at Cut Scores Established by Forward Regression, Reverse Regression, and Angoff-Like Methods.

Threshold Competence (job z score)	Base Rate of Job Success	Validity							
		.10		.20		.40		.60	
		Forward Regression	Angoff & Reverse Regression	Forward Regression	Angoff & Reverse Regression	Forward Regression	Angoff & Reverse Regression	Forward Regression	Angoff & Reverse Regression
-1.65	95%	.50	.95	.50	.95	.50	.93	.50	.91
-1.04	85%	.50	.85	.50	.85	.50	.83	.50	.80
-0.68	75%	.50	.75	.50	.75	.50	.73	.50	.71
-0.39	65%	.50	.65	.50	.65	.50	.64	.50	.62
-0.13	55%	.50	.55	.50	.55	.50	.55	.50	.54
0.00	50%	.50	.50	.50	.50	.50	.50	.50	.50
0.13	45%	.50	.45	.50	.45	.50	.45	.50	.46
0.39	35%	.50	.35	.50	.35	.50	.36	.50	.38
0.68	25%	.50	.25	.50	.25	.50	.27	.50	.29
1.04	15%	.50	.15	.50	.15	.50	.17	.50	.20
1.65	5%	.50	.05	.50	.05	.50	.07	.50	.09

Note: Success rates for regression methods are estimates based on the assumptions of forward and reverse regression. For Angoff-like methods, the success rates should be interpreted as approximations based on the assumption that experts accurately judge the test score expected of incumbents performing at the threshold level.

Table 13.3, which is very similar to the well-known Taylor and Russell (1939) tables, shows the probability of job success for those candidates whose test scores are equal to the cut score in each combination of validity and work threshold level. These are the selected candidates who have the lowest probability of job success, because all other selected candidates achieve higher test scores and are expected to have higher probabilities of job success. With forward regression the job success rate is .50 in each case, by definition. With forward regression the cut score is the test score that predicts the critical criterion value corresponding to the target work threshold. As a result, when predicting criterion values from test scores, 50 percent of the candidates scoring at the particular test score (the cut score in this case) are expected to have a criterion score above the predicted criterion value and 50 percent are expected to have a criterion score below the predicted criterion value.

Just the opposite occurs with reverse regression. The cut score is the test score predicted by the criterion value representing the target threshold. If, in turn, this predicted test score is used to "predict" a level of work performance, in general it does *not* predict the criterion score representing the target threshold level. Rather, it predicts a level of performance that is substantially closer to the criterion mean than the criterion threshold value is. The Angoff-like methods suffer from exactly the same limitation. Angoff-like methods estimate (predict) the test score that would be achieved by incumbents who are performing at the criterion threshold value. However, this estimated test score, if used as a predictor in a forward regression, would not be expected to predict the criterion threshold value. In contrast, the cut score defined by forward regression is the observed test score for which the predicted (expected) criterion value corresponds to the target level of performance.

From Tables 13.2 and 13.3 it can be seen that sole reliance on either forward or reverse regression to choose a cut score is not likely to yield a meaningful or useful cut score, except in certain specific conditions. When reverse regression provides the cut scores, the probability of job success for candidates scoring at the cut score can vary considerably, mostly with the base rate of job success in the population. Although forward regression fixes the probability of job success for candidates scoring at the cut score to be .50, it will produce uselessly extreme cut scores where the target work threshold is extreme or validity is low.

Table 13.3 can be used to estimate the likelihood of job success for candidates who score at cut scores established by reverse regression. To estimate the probability of job success, the validity of the test and the base rate of job success must be estimated.

Courts' reaction to either regression method may depend on the issues salient in the case. In cases where the likelihood of success is an important consideration, as it was in *Lanning,* forward regression, which specifies this value, is likely to be preferred to reverse regression, which does not. However, if the court's focus is on moderate pass rates, for example to mitigate adverse impact or to maximize $P(\text{pass}|\text{success})$, then courts may well prefer reverse regression to forward regression.

Expectancy Chart Methods

When both criterion and predictor data are available, a useful method for describing the relationship between them is to create expectancy charts showing the level of criterion performance or outcome associated with each possible score or narrow range of scores on the predictor. Although there are limitless variations of such displays, the Taylor and Russell (1939) tables are perhaps the classic example, showing the expected impact of selection cut scores on job success rates given the level of validity, the selection ratio, and the base rate of job success. In addition to the clarity they usually offer, the primary advantage of using such charts to set cut scores is that the process is designed to select a cut score based on the expected criterion outcomes that would result from the chosen cut score. In this regard, expectancy charts are in effect graphical versions of the forward regression method for determining a cut score. There are no professional or technical standards for setting cut scores using expectancy charts. However, the basic rationale is straightforward; the user examines the expectancy chart to locate the test score associated with the level of job success desired by the organization.

Although the courts have shown considerable support for judgment-based methods—particularly variations of the Angoff method—they have also shown support for expectancy chart–like methods. The most notable recent case is *Lanning,* in which SEPTA chose the cut score based on a consideration of the empirical relationship between the aerobic capacity measure and various outcome measures, particularly those related to public safety.

Although SEPTA did not describe its method as an expectancy chart method, the method shared expectancy chart core features in that there was a demonstrated relationship between predictor levels and criterion outcomes and the choice of cut score was based on this representation of expected outcomes.

Decision-Theoretic Methods

A variety of cut score–setting methods have been designed to quantitatively optimize combinations of costs and benefits that are affected by cut score choice. Some, such as that described by Martin and Raju (1991), focus exclusively on the trade-off between cost of recruiting and employment processes and the benefit of selectivity. Others, such as that described by Cronbach (1976), attempt to incorporate other organizational values, such as diversity. In any case, decision-theoretic methods require that all values be quantified. A key feature of decision-theoretic methods is that they simultaneously optimize multiple inputs. In contrast, there may be considerable practical value in a sequence of steps through which a cut score is identified that directly corresponds to the desired threshold of job success and then subsequent adjustments are made, first to accommodate the organization's interest in more or less certainty of job success and then to accommodate other interests. When these trade-offs are managed in a sequence, the organization and the courts are likely to have a clearer understanding of the amount of expected job success that is sacrificed (or gained) to achieve other desired interests.

Group 3: Expert Work Information and Empirical Test Information

The methods in this group are used infrequently for employment decisions. In our review of Title VII employment discrimination court cases for this chapter, no cases were found that evaluated any of these methods. Furthermore, the employment selection literature generally does not address these methods except in broad-based reviews of cut score methods, such as that of Cascio et al. (1988). Well-known examples of these methods include the contrasting groups (Gulliksen, 1987) method, which requires experts to identify relatively high- and low-performing groups; the borderline group method (Livingston & Zieky, 1982), which requires experts to identify the performers at the borderline between success and failure; and the more recent bookmark method (Lewis, Mitzel, & Green, 1996), which orders test items from most to least difficult and requires experts to locate the point along this continuum where minimally competent performers would have a .67 probability of answering correctly.

The contrasting groups method, in particular, appears to have some of the features favored by courts that have an interest in expert methodology for choosing cut scores that best distinguish successful and unsuccessful performers. Because the courts generally favor an important role for experts in determining cut scores, it seems likely that this method would be well received by courts. Of course this method is subject to the same criticism as the reverse regression and Angoff-like methods in that it does not generate any estimate of the likelihood that selected candidates will perform successfully once chosen.

Group 4: Expert Work Information and Expert Test Information

This class of methods relies on job experts to make two judgments: (1) identify the incumbents (real or hypothetical) who perform at the target work threshold and (2) estimate the test scores they are expected to achieve. Generally, these methods require several job experts to estimate the test scores that incumbents performing at the criterion threshold are expected to achieve, and then to define the recommended cut score as some function, such as the average or the median, of these estimated scores. The four most commonly referenced methods in this category are the Angoff (1971) method, the Ebel (1972) method, the Nedelsky (1954) method, and the Jaeger (1982) method. Although there are many variations on each of these methods, a modified version of the Angoff method has become by far the most commonly used method in this group. The Angoff method generally has been well received by courts in employment discrimination cases (see, for example, *U.S. v. South Carolina; Gulino; Contreras v. City of Los Angeles*, 1981). In *Gulino*, even though the court found that the defendant did not support the avoid harm rationale for establishing a cut score, the court nevertheless supported the defendant's use of the Angoff method.

Biddle (1993) and Falcone and Raju (2003) have summarized the key steps of the generic Angoff method. Biddle's summary emphasizes the features that have been supported by the courts whereas Falcone and Raju's summary focuses on features associated with professional standards and principles for the use of subject matter experts. The key features of these steps are as follows: (1) choose a minimum number of experts, typically five to fifteen (courts have accepted as few as five, statistics argue for up to fifteen); (2) train the job experts thoroughly in the meaning the organization attaches to the target work threshold and in the test content; (3) produce final ratings from an iterative process of independent ratings and collective feedback, in which experts usually have access to empirical test data such as item difficulties and actual test scores; (4) aggregate the individual expert ratings into a single score, usually the mean or median, that represents the test score expected of incumbents performing at the threshold level; and (5) if necessary, adjust this score to account for other considerations.

It is generally understood that the job experts are not necessarily experts in test performance. This limitation was viewed as a critical flaw by the National Academy of Education (1993) in a report drafted by highly regarded measurement experts including Lorrie Shepard, Robert Linn, and Robert Glazer. In evaluating this method for establishing education test standards, the Academy concluded that such methods are fundamentally flawed. The Academy asserted that the cognitive task of estimating test performance of individuals at the boundary of a given achievement level is nearly impossible.

Whether or not this flaw is fatal, the training of experts should address the test behavior they are being asked to judge. Certainly, courts have not viewed the Angoff method as critically flawed and selection experts have not acknowledged this criticism even though it is compelling.

This group of methods, Angoff in particular, is generally well received by the courts, in part because of the procedural ease with which thresholds are handled. This class of methods is based on the assumption that there is a threshold of work behavior that the organization desires to achieve in choosing a cut score. The organization then trains job experts to have a common understanding of this threshold. The courts generally favor such training and accept the assumption, Shepard et al.'s cogent criticisms notwithstanding, that job experts are capable of estimating the test performance of a targeted group of performers.

A limitation of this group of methods is that they do not consider the organization's desired certainty that new hires will perform at the threshold level. The cut score can be interpreted only as the test score expected (in an expert judgment sense, not a statistical sense) of incumbents who perform at the work threshold level. The candidates who achieve this score may have a high or low probability of job success, depending on the validity of the test and the base rate of job success defined by the targeted work threshold. The traditional output of this group of methods provides no information to the employer or the court about the certainty with which candidates who score at the cut score will succeed on the job.

However, the likelihood that candidates who score at the cut score will meet or exceed the target work threshold can be approximated if the validity of the test and the base rate of job success can be estimated. (Job success refers to performance at or above the target work threshold.) With these two estimates, Table 13.3 can be used to determine the approximate success rate of candidates who score at the cut score. (This is the cut score produced by an Angoff-like method *before* any adjustments due to other considerations.) The basic observation from Table 13.3 is that for Angoff-like methods applied to tests with typical validities, candidates who score at the cut score are likely to have job success rates very similar to the overall base rate of job success. Such success rates may or may not satisfy the organization's interest in hiring people who are likely to succeed. It would also appear that in general, Angoff methods are unlikely to satisfy the third circuit's decision in *Lanning* that the cut score should distinguish those who "are likely to be able to do the job" from those who are not.

The problem that Angoff-like methods provide no information about the likely job success of selected candidates is further exacerbated by the generally accepted practice of adjusting the initially estimated cut score by lowering it by some amount (Biddle, 1993). A rule of thumb is to lower the initial cut score by one or two standard errors of measurement (of the test). But this will also decrease the still unknown $P(\text{success}|\text{pass})$ by a substantial amount in most cases.

In summary, among these methods the Angoff method has achieved considerable acceptance in the courts in spite of the substantial technical criticisms that can be levied against it that job experts are not expert estimators of test results and that the process of choosing the cut score does not control or estimate the likelihood that selected candidates will succeed on the job.

Can Cut Scores Be Validated?

It is not uncommon for courts and authors to refer to the *validity* of cut scores. In considering whether courts require cut scores to be validated, Cascio et al. (1988) concluded that courts have not imposed that requirement and, further, speculated that it may not even be possible to validate a single cut score because a cut score is a single point that cannot be correlated with any criterion variable. It is the question of whether cut scores can be validated that is briefly considered here.

In short, cut scores cannot be validated, with one exception, because validity is not relevant to the typical processes for setting cut scores.

As described in the *Principles*, the process of validation uses scientific procedures to confirm that evidence and theory support the specific interpretations of test scores entailed by the proposed uses of a test. Validity is a conclusion about the intended meaning (that is, interpretation) of a measure. Validity is not an opinion or decision about the costs of a measure or the optimality of a measure or the sociopolitical acceptability of a measure; it is a conclusion about the meaning of a measure.

Certainly, any single test score is a measurement, and it is meaningful to ask whether evidence and theory support a specific intended interpretation of that particular test score as a measure with an intended meaning. For example, if a particular score on a reading skill test is intended to represent the level of reading ability necessary to, say, successfully assemble a bicycle from a set of written instructions, then a validation study could be undertaken to confirm that intended interpretation. This validation could be accomplished by showing that persons with the target test score are able to assemble bicycles successfully, whereas persons with lower scores are not. However, if another score on the reading test was chosen to represent only, say, the 75th percentile on the distribution of reading scores, then the meaning of the score as a measure of reading skill is irrelevant to its use as an indictor of a particular point on the distribution of scores. Although evidence can be gathered to verify the correctness of the assertion that the score is in fact at the 75th percentile, such evidence is irrelevant to any interpretation of the score as a measure of reading skill. This is not validity evidence. Validity is irrelevant to this use of the test score that merely distinguishes the top 25 percent of test scores from the bottom 75 percent.

It is meaningful to refer to the validity of a cut score where the cut score is chosen solely for its interpretation as an indicator of the level of the attribute necessary to achieve the target threshold level of work behavior. In this case, validity evidence may be gathered to confirm this interpretation of the meaning of the specific test score. The validity evidence may involve evidence of the job performance of employees who achieve that score and of the performance of other employees who achieve other scores. The evidence may also be content-related, such as evidence that experts judge the specific knowledge or skill level represented by the specific test score to be necessary to achieve the target level of job performance. The fact that a cut score is a single score and not a distribution of scores does not prevent this interpretation of a cut score from being demonstrated. Of course the likely result of any such validation of a particular cut score is that the same evidence is very likely to show that other possible test scores in the region of the cut score may have virtually the same interpretation as the cut score. The validation of a particular cut score does not invalidate other nearby scores. The validation of a cut score does not imply that other possible cut scores are substantially less valid nor does the validation of a cut score imply that the score chosen as the cut score was the optimal score. Validation evidence supporting a cut score may not necessarily demonstrate that the chosen cut score was optimal.

In other cases the choice of cut score is influenced by factors independent of the meaning of the test score, such as cost of the employment process, the degree of adverse impact expected, the likelihood of job success among new hires, and so on. Here validity is no longer a relevant consideration because the cut score was chosen for reasons other than the meaning of the measured attribute at the level targeted by the work threshold. The specific meaning of the attribute at the cut score is no longer the intended interpretation of the cut score. In these cases cut scores cannot be validated because they are chosen for reasons other than the interpretation of their meaning as a measure. Like the reading score chosen because it marked the 75th percentile, cut scores chosen for reasons other than their meaning can be verified for correctness (for example did the actual cost of employment equal the targeted cost) but cannot be validated for any intended meaning of the underlying attribute at the level of the cut score because the cut score was not chosen to correspond to any particular meaning of the underlying attribute.

It is important to note that this perspective on the question of whether cut scores can be validated interprets *validate* as having the same meaning as expressed in the *Standards* and *Principles*. In those professional guidelines, validation is a process of drawing a conclusion about the intended meaning of a measure. This perspective does not apply to different, more colloquial meanings of *validate*. For example, sometimes the word *validate* is used simply to refer to credible assurance that the process as described was actually followed. Also, *validate* is sometimes used to refer to a process of persuasion that convinces a court that the choice of cut score was a reasonable one. Any cut score can be validated in all of these colloquial senses, but not in the sense of confirmation of the meaning intended by the measure.

Looking Ahead

Having reviewed the current state of legislation, litigation, guidelines, and methods relating to cut scores, we offer here a few forward-looking observations. These are part prediction and part persuasion.

The first and most fundamental need is that the meaning of *business necessity* be defined. There appears to be sufficient inconsistency now in the interpretation of business necessity that the need is great for the Supreme Court to clarify at least three dimensions of the term. The most frequently discussed dimension is whether business necessity requires a minimum threshold or allows other thresholds. Our own suggestion is that there may not be one answer. There may be circumstances under which a minimum threshold is appropriate or possibly even required, as is the currently accepted public policy that licensure cut scores should be set no higher than necessary to avoid harm to the public. There may be other circumstances where the social value of fair employment does not impose a minimum threshold on employers that they would otherwise not choose. Under what conditions might an employer's interest in "more is better" be the basis for a defensible cut score? Much as the Supreme Court has acknowledged the special nature of affirmative action in institutions of higher education, are there classes of jobs or circumstances in which different business necessity standards may or should be applied? Of course such distinctions will be important only where they influence the relative importance of valued outcomes.

A second dimension is the public's interest in the employment decision. It will be important to clarify whether the standards that should apply when the public has a strong interest in the level of performance driven by the choice of cut score are any different from the standards that should apply when the public does not have such a strong interest. The third dimension is the question of whose business necessity values matter. This is a subtle but important consideration. Certainly the term *business necessity* implies that the needs of the employer are at issue. But whose values define the needs of the employer? The third circuit was emphatic in *Lanning* in asserting that the employer should not be the sole determiner of the guiding value judgments. Is it the courts' role to make value decisions on behalf of an employer's own organizational interests? Is it the role of experts? If not the employer, who then? The concept that other stakeholders' values regarding an employer's business necessity may trump the employer's values brings into question the fundamental meaning of both job-related and business necessity.

Any clarification of business necessity should also address a related and growing concern among employers about the implications of Internet-based employment processes: Does the employer have an obligation to treat all people who submit resumes via the Internet as applicants? As this chapter was in its late stages of revision, proposed record-keeping guidelines that specifically address Internet sourcing were issued jointly by the Equal Employment Opportunity Commission, the Labor Department's Office of Federal Contract Compliance Programs, the Department of Justice's

Civil Rights Division, and the Office of Personnel Management ("Proposed Interagency Guidance on Applicant Definition . . . ," 2004). In short, the proposed new regulations would require that employers treat as applicants all individuals who have indicated an interest in a particular position and have followed the employer's standard procedures for submitting applications for positions the employer has acted to fill. The new guidance goes on to explain that all search criteria used by employers are subject to disparate impact analysis. The implication is that employers may need to defend automatic, high-volume resume search criteria based on considerations of business necessity. Although most search criteria are not managed as cut scores, some are. In any case it is now clear that employers need to know how the business necessity standard will apply to Internet search criteria.

If the 1990s were the decade of the banding debate, it seems quite possible that the first decade of the new millennium will be the decade of debate over reverse and forward regression as methods for setting cut scores. We encourage the I-O psychology community to evaluate these methods for setting cut scores before court cases involving such methods accumulate.

In addition to the issues relating to forward and reverse regression, other technical issues should be thoroughly investigated so that they are more clearly understood.

The role of adjustments made to cut scores in order to trade the work performance implications of a cut score off with other interests such as cost and scarcity should be the subject of considerable research to improve the understanding of the impact of these adjustments. For example, the apparently widely accepted rule of thumb in the modified Angoff method of reducing the cut score set by expert judgment by one or two standard errors of measurement will have very substantial effects on the likelihood that selected candidates will succeed on the job.

Further research should be conducted on the methods that target the $P(\text{pass}|\text{success})$, such as Angoff-like methods and reverse regression, to determine what the relationship is between the outputs of those methods and employers' predominant interest in $P(\text{success}|\text{pass})$. The distinct possibility is that by blindly relying on the reputation of such cut score–setting methods, employers may be hiring lower-performing people than they believe they are.

In sum, as it should be, the process of setting cut scores continues to be a brew of art and science, influenced by values and risk as well as conclusions of science. Nevertheless, courts expect compelling reasons for the choices employers make.

References

Books, Articles, and Government Documents

Aguinis, H., Cortina, J. M., & Goldberg, E. (1998). A new procedure for computing equivalence bands in personnel selection. *Human Performance, 11,* 351–365.

American Educational Research Association, American Psychological Association, & National Council on Measurement in Education. (1999). *Standards for educational and psychological testing.* Washington, DC: American Educational Research Association.

Angoff, W. H. (1971). Scales, norms, and equivalent scores. In R. L. Thorndike (Ed.), *Educational measurement* (2nd ed., pp. 508–600). Washington, DC: American Council on Education.

Biddle, R. E. (1993). How to set cutoff scores for knowledge tests used in promotion, training, certification, and licensing. *Public Personnel Management, 22*(1), 63–79.

Campion, M. A., Outtz, J. L., Zedeck, S., Schmidt, F. L., Kehoe, J. F., Murphy, K. R., & Guion, R. M. (2001). The controversy over score banding in personnel selection: Answers to 10 key questions. *Personnel Psychology, 54,* 149–183.

Carson, J. D. (2001). Legal issues in standard setting for licensure and certification. In C. J. Cizek (Ed.), *Setting performance standards: Concepts, methods and perspectives* (pp. 427–444). Mahwah, NJ: Erlbaum.

Cascio, W. F., Alexander, R. A., & Barrett, G. V. (1988). Setting cutoff scores: Legal, psychometric, and professional issues and guidelines. *Personnel Psychology, 41,* 1–24.

Cascio, W. F., Outtz, J. L., Zedeck, S., & Goldstein, I. L. (1991). Statistical implications of six methods of test score use in personnel selection. *Human Performance, 4,* 233–264.

Chuang, D. T., Chen, J. J., & Novick, M. R. (1981). Theory and practice for the use of cut-scores for personnel selection. *Journal of Educational Statistics, 6,* 129–152.

Civil Rights Act of 1964, 42 U.S.C.

Civil Rights Act of 1991, 42 U.S.C.

Cronbach, L. J. (1976). Equity in selection: Where psychometrics and political philosophy meet. *Journal of Educational Measurement, 13,* 31–41.

Ebel, R. L. (1972). *Essentials of educational measurement* (2nd ed.). Upper Saddle River, NJ: Prentice Hall.

Falcone, A. J., & Raju, N. S. (2003). Setting standards. In J. E. Edwards, J. C. Scott, & N. S. Raju (Eds.), *The human resources program evaluation handbook* (pp. 91–108). Thousand Oaks, CA: Sage.

Gulliksen, H. (1987). *Theory of mental tests.* Mahwah, NJ: Erlbaum. (Original work published 1950)

Jaeger, R. M. (1982). An iterative structured judgment process for establishing standards on competency tests: Theory and application. *Educational Evaluation and Policy Analysis, 4,* 461–475.

Jeanneret, P. R., & Stelly, D. J. (2003). *Setting cutting scores using regression: Would you do it backwards?* Master tutorial presented at the annual conference of the Society for Industrial and Organizational Psychology, Orlando, FL.

Kehoe, J. F., & Tenopyr, M. L. (1994). Adjustment in assessment scores and their usage: A taxonomy and evaluation methods. *Psychological Assessment, 6,* 291–303.

Lewis, D. M., Mitzel, H. C., & Green, D. R. (1996). *Standard setting: A bookmark approach.* Paper presented at the Council of Chief State School Officers National Conference on Large-Scale Assessment, Boulder, CO.

Livingston, S. A., & Zieky, M. J. (1982). *Passing scores: A manual for setting standards of performance on educational and occupational tests.* Princeton, NJ: Educational Testing Service.

Martin, S. L., & Raju, N. (1991). *Determining optimal cutoff scores in criterion-related validity studies.* Paper presented at the conference of the Society for Industrial and Organizational Psychology, St. Louis, MO.

National Academy of Education (1993). *Setting performance standards for student achievement.* Washington, DC: Author.

Nedelsky, L. (1954). Absolute grading standards for objective tests. *Educational and Psychological Measurement, 14,* 3–19.

Peterson, N. S., & Novick, M. R. (1976). An evaluation of some models of culture-fair selection. *Journal of Educational Measurement, 13,* 3–29.

Proposed Interagency Guidance on Applicant Definition Under Uniform Guidelines on Employee Selection Procedures, 43 Fed. Reg. 38295–38309 (2004).

Society for Industrial and Organizational Psychology. (2003). *Principles for the Validation and Use of Personnel Selection Procedures* (4th ed.). Bowling Green, OH: Author.

Taylor, H. C., & Russell, J. T. (1939). The relationship of validity coefficients to the practical effectiveness of tests in selection: Discussion and tables. *Journal of Applied Psychology, 23,* 565–578.

Uniform Guidelines on Employee Selection Procedures, 29 C.F.R. § 1607 *et seq.* (1978).

Cases

Albermarle Paper Co. v. Moody, 422 U.S. 405 (1975).

Association of Mexican-American Educators v. State of California, 231 F.3d 572 (9th Cir. 2000).

Bew v. City of Chicago, 252 F.3d 891 (7th Cir. 2001).

Black Shield Police Association v. City of Cleveland, 42 FEP Cases 270 (N.D. Ohio 1986).

Chicago Firefighters Local 2 v. City of Chicago, 249 F.3d 649 (7th Cir. 2001).

Contreras v. City of Los Angeles, 656 F. 2nd 1267 (9th Cir. 1981).

Cuesta v. State of New York Office of Court Administration, 42 EPD Section 36, 949 (S.D. N.Y. 1987).

Dothard v. Rawlinson, 433 U.S. 321 (1977).

Fitzpatrick v. City of Atlanta, 2 F.3d 1112 (11th Cir. 1993).

Griggs v. Duke Power Company, 401 U.S. 424 (1971).

Guardians Association v. Civil Service Commission of the City of New York, 463 U.S. 582 (1983).

Gulino v. Board of Education, 96 Civ. 8414 (S.D. N.Y., 2003).

Lanning v. Southeastern Pennsylvania Transportation Authority, 181 F.3d 478 (3d Cir. 1999).

Lanning v. Southeastern Pennsylvania Transportation Authority, 2002 U.S. App Lexis 21506 (2002).

National Education Association v. South Carolina, 434 U.S. 1026 (1978).

New York City Transit Authority v. Beazer, 440 U.S. 568 (1979).

Officers for Justice v. Civil Service Commission of the City and County of San Francisco, 979 F.2d 721 (9th Cir. 1992).

Pegues v. Mississippi State Employment Service, 488 F. Supp. 239 (E.D. Miss. 1980).

Personnel Administrator of Massachusetts v. Feeney, 442 U.S. 256 (1979).

Rogers v. International Paper Co., No 74–1086, 1087, 1101, & 1115 (8th Cir. 1975).

Schware v. Board of Bar Examiners of the State of New Mexico, 353 U.S. 232 (1957).

Thomas v. City of Evanston, 610 F. Supp. 422 (N.D. Ill. 1985).

United States v. State of South Carolina, 445 F. Supp. 1094 (D.S.C. 1977), aff'd. 434 U.S. 1026 (1978).

Wards Cove Packing Company v. Atonio, 490 U.S. 642 (1989).

Washington v. Davis, 426 U.S. 229 (1976).

CHAPTER 14

A Lawyer's View
Avoiding Junk Science
David Copus

As a veteran defense counsel in employment discrimination lawsuits, I regularly encounter psychologists (industrial and organizational psychologists as well as social psychologists) in the form of plaintiffs' expert witnesses. These psychologists often claim that gender stereotypes have permeated the defendant's workplace and are likely to have caused the widespread discrimination that the plaintiff seeks to eradicate. I believe that plaintiffs' experts have no reliable scientific basis for offering such opinions. In the jargon of my trade, I believe that such opinions constitute *junk science.*

Let us begin our examination of that issue by looking backward to the beginnings of stereotyping research. At first, major contributors to stereotype literature, such as Walter Lippman (1922), wrote thought-provoking essays that loosely defined stereotypes as inaccurate overgeneralizations about the characteristics of some racial or ethnic group. Those early contributions also offered opinions about the questionable purposes that stereotypes served. Later, *empirical* research began to examine the *content* of stereotypes. Work in that area continues, although at a greatly reduced pace.

Along the way, researchers on cognition (Tajfel, 1969; Hamilton, 1981) took center stage and defined stereotypes as *cognitive* structures (a kind of formalized and theory-based approach to Lippman's "little pictures in the head"). That empirical research shifted focus from the content of stereotypes and concentrated on how stereotypes affect the cognitive process of forming impressions of others. Just about the time that the cognitive framework came to dominate stereotype research, interest in *gender* stereotypes increased dramatically and came to be the focus of stereotype researchers (Deaux, 1985). Consistent with the original slant of the early thought-provoking essays, the empirical stereotype researchers generally agreed that gender stereotypes *negatively* affected the cognitive process, were themselves the product of errors in cognitive processing, and almost invariably led to errors in judgment when forming impressions of others. Many competing theories emerged on how and why the brain uses gender stereotypes when forming (generally erroneous) impressions of others (Fiske & Neuberg, 1990; Brewer, 1988; Kunda & Thagard, 1996).

Soon, researchers immersed themselves in laboratory explorations of the varied aspects of cognitive processing and the ways gender stereotypes might cloud that processing. Unfortunately, the tightly controlled features of their experimental models led them to ignore the major shortcomings of their research. In order to conduct experimental studies of the cognitive process itself, researchers had to structure their experiments very carefully so that research subjects would be given tiny microns of information under tightly controlled conditions while the researchers studied how the subjects processed that information. In the traditional language of research methodology, stereotype researchers used various items of information about the stimulus person as independent variables in their experiments and eliminated any possible impact of "extraneous" variables by carefully controlling the experimental conditions (Goldberg, 1968).

Doling out independent variable information one micron at a time while controlling all extraneous variables in order to see how that information was processed necessarily meant that researchers had to limit their research to classic laboratory experimental paradigms in which they could manipulate independent variables, whether those experiments were actually conducted in a formal laboratory or in a more "naturalistic," nonlaboratory setting. Researchers decided that they could not conduct experimental studies of cognitive processes in the real world because the real world was too "messy"—it was complicated with information and conditions that could not be controlled and might affect the research results (Harré & Secord, 1972). To ensure that such uncontrolled information and conditions did not affect the results, researchers designed experimental strategies in which the researchers themselves titrated the information to the research subjects under very carefully controlled situations designed to neutralize all extraneous variables.

Titrating the information given to subjects necessarily required that the target of impression formation (the stimulus person) be a *stranger*. After all, if the study participants had prior exposure to the stimulus person, the researchers lost all control over the information about the stimulus person that was potentially available for the subjects to process. Hence research on gender stereotypes not only used an experimental laboratory model but invariably used a laboratory model that focused exclusively on stranger-to-stranger impression formation.

The stranger-to-stranger experimental model has two plausible parallels in the real world: the typical process by which some corporations screen resumes and the process by which applicants are interviewed for hire off the street. The resume screening done in the real world (if done by a human as opposed to an electronic screening device using some natural language algorithm) does in fact closely resemble some aspects of the process followed in stereotype researchers' laboratory experiments. Oddly, however, employment discrimination lawsuits challenging alleged discrimination in the screening of resumes are exceptionally rare. Indeed, in my thirty-six years of litigation I have seen only one such lawsuit (and it involved an automated computerized screening of resumes). Hence, in this contribution, I am not addressing expert witness testimony in resume screening litigation.

In the real-world applicant interview process, employment decisions are ordinarily made after one or more stranger-to-stranger interactions (interviews). So at least the stranger-to-stranger mode of laboratory experiments has a parallel here as well. In the real world, however, the interview is a give-and-take affair in which the perceiver (company interviewer) is highly motivated to make an accurate decision and places a premium on gathering personal work-related information from the interviewee. These give-and-take and motivational conditions are rarely mimicked in laboratory studies. Nevertheless, one could possibly make a plausible argument that the results of laboratory experiments shed at least some light on real-world, new-hire interviews.

Odd as it may seem, however, very few employment discrimination lawsuits challenge hiring decisions. I estimate that upward of 90 percent or more of all employment discrimination lawsuits involve current or former employees, none of whom are strangers to company decision makers. Hence, again, in this contribution I am not addressing expert witness testimony in litigation challenging the interviewing of applicants off the street.

My concern is with social psychologists and industrial and organizational psychologists who seek to extrapolate from the sterile, stranger-to-stranger world of laboratory experiments to the real-world employment decisions affecting current or former employees—decisions on such matters as promotion, performance appraisal, merit pay increases, discipline, and discharge (for a review, see Bernardin, Hennessey, & Peyrefitte, 1995). In those real-world employment decisions the parties involved have had extensive personal contact over an extended period, a critical condition that few if any laboratory studies have even attempted to replicate. The decision makers have had extended opportunity to observe the employees and gather much information relevant to the decision at hand—diagnostic individuating information, in the jargon of psychologists (Tosi & Einbender, 1985).

Moreover, such decisions routinely occur under multiple conditions affecting the decision maker's motivation to make an accurate decision. For example, the decision maker typically anticipates having further interaction with the target employees. To the extent that the decision maker's own performance may be affected by that of the target employees, the decision maker has an economic self-interest in the employment decisions. Ordinarily, a decision maker's employment decisions are subject to review by his or her superiors as well as subject to internal and external challenge by the target employees. In addition most companies make extensive efforts to make equal opportunity and nondiscrimination a salient goal in all employment decisions. Each of these factors can motivate the decision maker to be accurate and to avoid reliance on stereotypes (Taylor, Peplau, & Sears, 2003; Fiske, Lin, & Neuberg,

1999; Kunda, Davies, Hoshino-Browne, and Jordan, 2003). As a practical matter, laboratory studies cannot simultaneously investigate all of these conditions while using an interactive process in which the perceiver gathers diagnostic information about the target over an extended time period.

Finally, because stereotype researchers were often academics and, as a result, because they often had college students taking psychology courses available as a captive audience for their experiments, more than 80 percent of all cognitive research on stereotypes has been done on the proverbial college sophomore (Schultz, 1969).

Because stereotype researchers were focused entirely on examining the cognitive *process* in a sterile and tightly controlled experimental environment, some researchers openly declared that the results of experimental laboratory research on impression formation could not be extrapolated to the real world—a world in which individuals ordinarily receive far more than micron bits of diagnostic individuating information, in which it is common for individuals to regularly interact with others with whom they have had substantial prior contact, and in which the frequent interaction occurs under a wide variety of work-relevant conditions that can affect the outcome of impression formation (Gorman, Clover, & Doherty, 1978, p. 191; Powell, 1987; Bretz, Milkovich, & Read, 1992; Osborn & Vicars, 1976; Jussim & Eccles, 1995; McCauley, Jussim, & Lee, 1995, p. 301; Dipboye, 1985; Wendelken & Inn, 1981, pp. 150–151; Katz & Proshansky, 1987). Critics also pointed to the almost exclusive use of college students, who were demonstrably not representative of the population of company decision makers in the real world (Sears, 1986).

In short, these critics concluded that experimental laboratory research on stereotyping had no *ecological validity*, a term popularized by Bronfenbrenner (1977, p. 516). This criticism held that the results of experimental laboratory research on impression formation (stereotyping) could not legitimately be extrapolated to the real world of decision making with respect to current and former employees, the very individuals who bring employment discrimination lawsuits. I believe that the critics are absolutely correct.

Faced with mounting criticism that their hygienic laboratory studies on university students lacked any semblance of ecological validity, stereotype researchers adopted various strategies in an effort to demonstrate the real-world importance of their work. These efforts have fallen far short.

For example, in an effort to shore up the ecological validity of their laboratory experiments, some researchers made the research task performed by the college student subjects as similar to real life as they could. Thus, instead of having subjects simply review paper resumes of fictitious people, some researchers hired actors to perform simulated tasks that a worker might perform; the researchers then asked the subjects to evaluate the performance. Still, the amount of information provided to the subjects was extremely limited (for example, a five-minute video), and the evaluation remained stranger-to-stranger under tightly controlled conditions that had no similarity to real life. And the participants in most of these laboratory studies were still college undergraduates.

One pair of researchers took a slight step toward more realism in a laboratory experiment with college students (Rudman & Borgida, 1995). In that study, male students watched a videotape of sexually enticing or sexually neutral commercials. The researchers then evaluated the students' behavior as the students interviewed a woman who they were told was a job applicant for an office manager position. The researchers sought to determine whether priming the students' stereotype of women as sexual objects would affect their behavior and judgments in the mock interview. Commendable as the researchers' efforts were to make the laboratory experiment realistic, the barren laboratory conditions meant, for example, that the college students had no training in how to conduct a job interview, had no experience in conducting job interviews, had no information about the content of the job other than the job title, and had no expectation that anyone would review their recommendations. Even apart from these major differences from the real world, how frequently in real life will decision makers interview female outside applicants within minutes of watching a sexually stimulating video? In any event the experiment failed to show any impact of negative gender stereotypes in the students' ratings of the female applicant. Indeed, on average, the students who saw the sexually stimulating videotape gave the applicant higher ratings and would have offered her a higher starting salary than would the students who saw the bland commercials. Furthermore, even this elaborate laboratory experiment still involved a stranger-to-stranger encounter, quite unlike the daily, repeated interactions that occur between employees and their supervisors and managers.

To avoid criticism that the research subjects were college undergraduate students, some researchers simply moved their experimental research out of the classroom and used adult subjects rather than college students (see, for example, Dipboye & Wiley, 1977). A nonclassroom experimental study might take, for example, a group of actual managers and ask them to evaluate the performance of actors who engaged in various work behaviors scripted to be as realistic as possible. Researchers labeled this type of study a *field study* and claimed that it overcame the shortcomings of traditional laboratory research using college sophomores. The label given to a study, however, cannot increase its ecological validity.

Thus stereotype researchers' experimental studies using lifelike simulations with non–college students or field studies with adults still did not have meaningful ecological validity because they suffered the major infirmities of all laboratory research on stereotypes—a limited amount of information and stranger-to-stranger evaluation with no interaction among the individuals in a sterile environment free of any other motivational variables that could affect the outcome.

When considered in relation to applicant interviewing in the real world, even experimental laboratory studies using actual working interviewers have questionable ecological validity because, as a practical matter, researchers could not incorporate the full range of motivational variables that could affect the outcome. A laboratory study that does not include those variables can tell us little if anything about what would happen if those variables were allowed to operate freely, as they would in real life.

At least two other factors significantly compounded the lack of ecological validity of stereotype researchers' experimental paradigms, whether in the classroom laboratory or in naturalistic conditions, whether the subjects were college students or working adults. First, most of the laboratory studies failed to yield the predicted results (Swim, Borgida, & Maruyama, 1989, pp. 409, 420; Tsui & Gutek, 1984; Harris, 1989). If tightly controlled experiments in a laboratory cannot regularly produce the predicted result, of what value are any of the studies in describing how information processing occurs in the world at large? Researchers continue to scramble to figure out why laboratory results are so inconsistent.

Second, in the clamor to explain the contradictory results of their studies, researchers have identified a host of *possible* causes for the inconsistency, such as the amount of information the subjects have about the targets and the relevance (diagnosticity) of that information to the decision that the subjects must make. Thus meta-analyses of laboratory research studies show that a modest amount of diagnostic individuating information generally neutralizes gender stereotypes, even in a stranger-to-stranger context (see, for example, Tosi & Einbender, 1985). Laboratory studies have also identified other real-world conditions that could affect impression formation, such as whether the subject expected to interact in the future with the subject (Taylor et al., 2003; Gilbert & Hixon, 1991), whether the subject's decision is subject to review by a third person (Fiske et al., 1999), and whether the stimulus person and subject need to work together toward a common goal (Fiske, 1998). In addition, other research has shown that individual differences among subjects, such as whether the perceiver is low- or high-prejudiced, has an important impact on whether stereotypes are used (Devine, 1989).

Although these further laboratory studies identified additional factors that might influence the outcome of impression formation (stereotyping), the very nature of empirical research of cognitive processing meant that laboratory studies could examine only one or two of those additional independent variables at a time. Thus, even though individual laboratory studies had identified multiple independent variables that could affect the result of impression formation, no laboratory research paradigm can effectively incorporate even a majority of those factors in a single study. Hence, stereotype researchers have no way to study the cumulative and simultaneous effect of all the factors that their own laboratory research indicates might be relevant. Meta-analysis does not solve this problem—meta-analysis can only consider moderator variables that are available for some substantial number of the studies reviewed. If these variables have not been incorporated into (or cannot be coded for) the studies that are used for the meta-analysis, they cannot be examined. So, as long as stereotype research uses stranger-to-stranger interactions in which subjects are given very limited information under conditions that tightly control extraneous independent variables, that stereotype research will have no ecological validity, even if lifelike simulations are used with non–college student participants.

In short, psychologists have never tested their hypothesis that social cognition behaves in the real world of decision making about real employees the same way it does in the laboratory. Although stereotype researchers may sometimes be able to demonstrate the "harmful" effects of stereotypes under the artificial constraints of their laboratory studies, they have not yet tested the hypothesis that those same effects *can* and *do* occur in the real world when managers and supervisors make decisions about their subordinates. Thus stereotyping research cannot be reliably applied to impression formation in those contexts. There is no reliable scientific basis on which any psychologist can offer an opinion about the operation of stereotypes in the formation of impressions in employment discrimination lawsuits challenging promotions, performance appraisals, merit pay increases, discipline, and discharges.

Finally, let me say a word about the efforts to justify the admissibility of testimony on stereotypes under the rubric of social framework analysis (Fiske & Borgida, 1999). In 1986, Monahan and Walker, two law professors, coined the term *social framework analysis* (originally called *social authority*) as a guide to understanding when the testimony of social scientists such as psychologists would aid the court or jury in its fact-finding mission and therefore should be admitted into evidence. Essentially, Monahan and Walker proposed that courts should admit social science testimony whenever the testimony might illuminate some issue in the case, without much regard to the scientific reliability of the testimony or its specific relationship to the facts of the particular lawsuit. That approach has not gained favor because the social framework analysis is inconsistent with a subsequent Supreme Court decision. In 1993, in *Daubert v. Merrell Dow Pharmaceuticals,* the Supreme Court definitively established the standards for the admissibility of expert witness testimony in federal court. According to that decision, the two most important factors governing the admissibility of expert testimony are (1) the scientific reliability of the expert's underlying opinions and (2) the scientific reliability of the expert's application of those opinions to the facts of the particular case. These standards, which the social framework analysis did not incorporate, are covered in considerable detail in Chapter Six of this volume. The purpose of these rigorous standards was to keep junk science out of the courtroom. In the last eleven years, that is, since the *Daubert* decision, only two federal courts case has even referred to social framework analysis as a possible standard against which to evaluate the admissibility of expert testimony. Ironically, those two federal trial court decisions were rendered in 2004, and both embraced the social framework analysis in the context of admitting the testimony of a stereotyping expert (*EEOC* v. *Morgan Stanley* and *Dukes* v. *Wal-Mart, Inc.*). The *Wal-Mart* court, however, expressly held that it was applying a "lower" standard than required by *Daubert* because of the procedural posture of the case. Thus, only one decision—*EEOC* v. *Morgan Stanley*—has embraced social framework analysis in the context of a *Daubert* analysis. I believe that the *Morgan Stanley* decision is erroneous; clearly one case does not establish a trend.

In any event, a psychologist seeking to offer testimony on the impact of gender stereotypes in a particular employment discrimination case has the burden of proving that his or her opinions are not junk science. Because I do not believe that a psychologist can satisfy that standard, industrial and organizational psychologists should think very carefully before agreeing to testify about the impact of gender stereotypes in federal court. Moreover, to the extent that testimony about race, age, or disability stereotypes depends on the same literature and experimental design, it is subject to the same criticism if the stereotype paradigm is being applied to current employees or is not a legitimate instance of a stranger-to-stranger interaction.

References

Allport, Gordon W. *The nature of prejudice.* Cambridge, MA: Addison-Wesley, 1954.

Bernardin, H. J., Hennessey, H. W., Jr., & Peyrefitte, J. (1995). Age, racial, and gender bias as a function of criterion specificity: A test of expert testimony. *Human Resource Management Review, 5,* 63–77.

Bretz, R. D., Jr., Milkovich, G. T., & Read, W. (1992). The current state of performance appraisal research and practice: Concerns, directions, and implications. *Journal of Management, 18,* 321–352.

Brewer, M. B. (1988). A dual process model of impression formation. In T. K. Srull & R. S. Wyer Jr. (Eds.), *Advances in social cognition: Vol. I. A dual process model of impression formation* (pp. 1–36). Hillsdale, NJ: Lawrence Erlbaum.

Bronfenbrenner, U. (1977). Toward an experimental ecology of human development. *American Psychologist, 32,* 513–531.

Daubert v. Merrell Dow Pharmaceuticals, Inc., 509 U.S. 579 (1993).

Deaux, K. (1985). Sex and gender. *Annual Review of Psychology, 36,* 49–81.

Devine, P. G. (1989). Stereotypes and prejudice: Their automatic and controlled components. *Journal of Personality and Social Psychology, 56,* 5–18.

Dipboye, R. L. (1985). Some neglected variables in research on discrimination in appraisals. *Academy of Management Review, 10,* 116–127.

Dipboye, R., & Wiley, J. W. (1977). Reactions of college recruiters to interviewee sex and self-presentation style. *Journal of Vocational Behavior, 10,* 1–12.

Dukes v. Wal-Mart, Inc., 222 F.R.D. 189 (N.D. Calif. 2004).

EEOC v. Morgan Stanley & Co., Inc., 2004 U.S. Dist. LEXIS 12673 (July 2, 2004, *aff'd in relevant part,* 2004 U.S. Dist.) LEXIS 12724 (July 8, 2004).

Fiske, S. T. (1998). Stereotyping, prejudice, and discrimination. In D. T. Gilbert, S. T. Fiske, & G. Lindzey (Eds.), *The handbook of social psychology* (4th ed., pp. 357–364). New York: McGraw-Hill.

Fiske, S. T., & Borgida, E. (1999). Social framework analysis as expert testimony in sexual harassment suits. In S. Estreicher (Ed.), *Sexual harassment in the workplace* (pp. 575–583). Boston: Kluwer Law International.

Fiske, S. T., Lin, M., & Neuberg, S. L. (1999). The continuum model ten years later. In S. Chaiken & Y. Trope (Eds.), *Dual-process theories in social psychology* (pp. 231–254). New York: Guilford Press.

Fiske, S. T., & Neuberg, S. L. (1990). A continuum of impression formation, from category-based to individuating processes: Influences of information and motivation on attention and interpretation. In M. P. Zanna (Ed.), *Advances in experimental and social psychology* (Vol. 23, pp. 1–74). Orlando, Fla.: Academic Press.

Gilbert, D. T., & Hixon, J. G. (1991). The trouble of thinking: Activation and application of stereotypic beliefs. *Journal of Personality and Social Psychology, 60,* 509–517.

Goldberg, P. (1968). Are women prejudiced against women? *Trans-Action, 5,* 28–30.

Gorman, C. D., Clover, W. H., & Doherty, M. E. (1978). Can we learn anything about interviewing real people from interview of paper people? Two studies of the external validity paradigm. *Organizational Behavior & Human Performance, 22,* 165–192.

Hamilton, D. L. (Ed.). (1981). *Cognitive process in stereotyping and intergroup behavior.* Mahwah, NJ: Erlbaum.

Harré, R., & Secord, P. F. (1972). *The explanation of social behavior.* Oxford, U.K.: Blackwell.

Harris, M. M. (1989). Reconsidering the employment interview: A review of recent literature and suggestions for future research. *Personnel Psychology, 42,* 691–726.

Jussim, L. J., & Eccles, J. (1995). Are teacher expectations biased by students' gender, social class, or ethnicity? In Y.-T. Lee, L. J. Jussim, & C. R. McCauley (Eds.), *Stereotype accuracy: Toward appreciating group differences* (pp. 245–271). Washington, DC: American Psychological Association.

Katz, I., & Proshansky, H. M. (1987). Rethinking affirmative action. *Journal of Social Issues, 43,* 99–104.

Kunda, Z., Davies, P. G., Hoshino-Browne, E., & Jordan, C. H. (2003). The impact of comprehension goals on the ebb and flow of stereotype activation during interaction. In S. J. Spencer, S. Fein, M. P. Zanna, & J. M. Olson (Eds.), *Motivated social perception: The Ontario symposium,* vol. 9 (pp. 1–20). Mahwah, NJ: Lawrence Erlbaum.

Kunda, Z., & Thagard, P. (1996). Forming impressions from stereotypes, traits and behaviors: A parallel-constraint-satisfaction theory. *Psychological Review, 103,* 284–308.

Lippman, W. (1922). *Public Opinion.* New York: Macmillan.

McCauley, C. R., Jussim, L. J., & Lee, Y.-T. (1995). Why study stereotype accuracy and inaccuracy? In Y.-T. Lee, L. J. Jussim, & C. R. McCauley (Eds.), *Stereotype accuracy: Toward appreciating group differences* (pp. 293–312). Washington, DC: American Psychological Association.

Monahan, J., & Walker, L. (1986). Social authority: Obtaining, evaluating, and establishing social science law. *University of Pennsylvania Law Review, 134,* 477–517.

Osborn, R. N., & Vicars, W. M. (1976). Sex stereotypes: An artifact in leader behavior and subordinate analysis? *Academy of Management Journal, 19,* 429–449.

Powell, G. N. (1987). The effects of sex and gender on recruitment. *Academy of Management Review, 12,* 731–743.

Rudman, L. A., & Borgida, E. (1995). The afterglow of construct accessibility: The cognitive and behavioral consequences of priming men to view women as sexual objects. *Journal of Experimental Social Psychology, 31,* 493–517.

Schultz, D. P. (1969). The human subject in psychological research. *Psychological Bulletin, 72,* 214–228.

Sears, D. O. (1986). College sophomores in the laboratory: Influences of a narrow data base on social psychology's view of human nature. *Journal of Personality and Social Psychology, 51,* 515–530.

Swim, J., Borgida, E., & Maruyama, G. (1989). Joan McKay versus John McKay: Do gender stereotypes bias evaluations? *Psychological Bulletin, 105,* 409–429.

Tajfel, H. (1969). Cognitive aspects of prejudice. *Journal of Social Issues, 25,* 79–97.

Taylor, S. E., Peplau, L. A., & Sears, D. O. (2003). *Social psychology* (11th ed.). Upper Saddle River, NJ: Prentice Hall.

Tosi, H. L., & Einbender, S. (1985). The effects of the type and amount of information in sex discrimination research: A meta-analysis. *Academy of Management Journal, 28,* 712–723.

Tsui, A. S., & Gutek, B. (1984). A role set analysis of gender differences in performance, affective relationships, and career success of industrial middle managers. *Academy of Management Journal, 27,* 619–635.

Wendelken, D. J., & Inn, A. (1981). Nonperformance influences on performance evaluations: A laboratory phenomenon? *Journal of Applied Psychology, 66,* 149–158.

I-O Psychology and the Department of Justice

Richard S. Ugelow

I joined the Employment Litigation Section (ELS), Civil Rights Division (CRD), U.S. Department of Justice (DOJ), in August 1973 as a trial attorney. In August 1989, I became a deputy section chief in the ELS and held that position until my departure in May 2002. One of my main duties was the investigation and the prosecution of allegations of patterns or practices of employment discrimination under Section 707 of Title VII of the Civil Rights Act of 1964, as amended. Pattern or practice matters were the bread and butter of the ELS litigation program because they had the potential to make systemic changes to employment practices and they served as a signal to other employers to take voluntary measures to bring their own practices into compliance with Title VII.

During my twenty-nine-year career at the ELS, I was a participant in every aspect of Title VII enforcement. I was a player in the development of Title VII enforcement strategies and efforts to make job opportunities available to minorities and women who had been denied employment for reasons related to their race or sex and not their ability to perform the job successfully. I have also seen how the priorities of different presidents and their attorneys general affected the enforcement of Title VII.

In the pages that follow I hope to provide the reader with an understanding of the what, the how, and the why of Title VII enforcement by the ELS from 1973 to the present. Although I have tried to be objective and factual, I must emphasize that I write from my perspective and I editorialize from time to time. I appreciate that others might disagree with some of what I have to say or come to different conclusions.

Griggs and the 1972 Amendments to Title VII

I was fortunate to join the ELS shortly after two seminal events in Title VII enforcement—the Supreme Court's decision in *Griggs* v. *Duke Power* (1971) and passage of the Equal Employment Opportunity Act of 1972 (1972 Amendments).

In *Griggs*, the Supreme Court held that Title VII was violated where an employment practice was fair in form but had a disparate impact upon a protected group and had not been demonstrated to be job related. *Griggs* gave legitimacy to the concept of disparate impact—a legal theory of proving a Title VII violation that had been evolving but had not previously been fully embraced by the courts.

The 1972 Amendments changed Title VII in several significant ways. From the ELS perspective, the 1972 Amendments extended Title VII's protections to applicants and employees of state and local government employers. Before 1972, the federal government was not permitted to sue state and local governments over their employment practices. Individuals could pursue such claims under the equal protection clause of the Fourteenth Amendment in actions brought pursuant to the Civil Rights Act of 1866 and the Civil Rights Act of 1871. But plaintiffs in such constitutional challenges had to demonstrate disparate treatment (intentional or purposeful discrimination) to prevail, as the disparate impact theory of *Griggs* was not available to them (see *Washington* v. *Davis*, 1976). Because it was difficult to convince a court that a facially neutral employment test intentionally discriminated against a protected group, constitutional lawsuits generally were not considered good vehicles with which to challenge the lawfulness of state and local government selection criteria.

The 1972 Amendments also authorized private lawsuits against state and local government employers (§ 2000e-5). Thus, the disparate impact theory was available to individuals who on behalf of themselves or a class challenged the lawfulness of a governmental employment practice. The ability of private plaintiffs to succeed in such challenges was therefore greatly improved.

The 1972 Amendments also gave the EEOC authority to judicially enforce Title VII against private employers. Up until then the EEOC had authority to investigate and to conciliate claims of private sector employment discrimination but lacked authority to initiate enforcement litigation. Also, before the amendments, the DOJ was the sole federal agency with authority to enforce Title VII through litigation, and that authority was restricted to private employers. The DOJ's enforcement was largely confined to disparate treatment cases and focused on eliminating stereotype-based employment practices that had the effect of artificially restricting employment opportunities to minorities. For example, lawsuits challenged hiring and assignment policies and transfer practices that had the purpose or effect of segregating employees by race in lower-paying and less desirable positions (see, for example, *United States* v. *U.S. Steel*, 1975; *United States* v. *Lee Way Motor Freight*, 1979).

The EEOC's increased authority extended to both individual claims of employment discrimination and pattern or practice claims. However, there was a two-year transition period beginning on March 24, 1972 (the effective date of the 1972 Amendments), during which the DOJ and the EEOC had concurrent authority to initiate pattern or practice suits against private employers. The 1972 Amendments (§ 2000e-6.c) also authorized President Nixon to transfer the EEOC's private sector pattern or practice authority to the DOJ by submitting a reorganization plan to Congress under the Reorganization Act. The DOJ had anticipated that the President would exercise this authority, but the Reorganization Act lapsed in 1973 and was not reauthorized. At the time, those of us in ELS speculated that the Watergate investigation might have played a role in this. It is likely that the Congress declined to extend reorganization authority because of its distrust of Nixon. For myself and the other attorneys in the ELS, it was disappointing to lose private sector pattern or practice authority, especially because that loss had been unexpected. We felt that the ELS's litigation program had been effective, that we were experienced litigators, and that "nobody could do it better."

Congress continued a pattern of bifurcation of enforcement authority between the EEOC and the DOJ in later enacted statutes prohibiting employment discrimination. The Disabilities Rights Section within the Civil Rights Division is responsible for enforcing Title I of the Americans with Disabilities Act of 1990 against state and local government employers. And the EEOC is responsible for enforcing Title I in the private sector, as well as enforcement in the public and private sectors of the Age Discrimination in Employment Act of 1967 and portions of other federal laws that prohibit discrimination in employment (see Equal Opportunity Commission, 1997).

The Targets of DOJ Title VII Enforcement

The 1972 Amendments created a new universe of potential defendants, and in *Griggs* the Supreme Court had provided a potent weapon. The DOJ used its newly acquired authority to challenge the lawfulness of long-standing employment practices that had resulted in the severe underrepresentation of minorities and women in state and local government employment. These lawsuits alleged that the employer was engaged in a pattern or practice of employment discrimination in violation of Title VII that had the purpose or effect of discriminating against minorities or women. By far, the favored targets of these lawsuits were state and local protective service agencies—police, fire, and sheriff's departments—that used selection procedures, particularly tests of cognitive ability that had an adverse impact on minority applicants. Often the lawsuits included a claim of gender discrimination either because employers had separate job categories for males and females or because employment opportunities were intentionally limited for women.

Between March 1972 and the end of 1979, for example, the DOJ filed fifty-three lawsuits under Section 707 of Title VII, forty-nine of which challenged the employment practices of police and fire departments. Generally, the targets of these lawsuits had relatively few minority or female uniformed police officers and firefighters when compared to the qualified and available labor pool. For example, among the first state and local cases filed by the DOJ were cases against the police or fire departments in Los Angeles; Montgomery, Alabama; Chicago; Buffalo; Boston; and the State of Maryland.

Police and fire departments were targeted for policy and practical reasons. When it considered the 1972 Amendments, Congress had before it a report that noted, "Barriers to equal employment are greater in police and fire departments than in any other area of State and local government" (U.S. Commission on Civil Rights, 1969, Finding No. 5). In addition, the Kerner Commission Report (prepared following the 1967 urban race riots) had identified the importance of having the workforces of police and fire departments better represent the demographics of the communities they serve.

A review of the demographics of state and local protective service agencies in 1972 confirmed the absence of significant numbers of minorities and women in uniformed police and firefighter positions. These factors, combined with the judgment of the ELS leadership that protective service positions were highly visible to the community, were prestigious and well paid, and offered significant opportunities for advancement, led to the decision to focus on integrating police and fire departments.

It was easy to identify the reason(s) for the insignificant numbers of minority and female police and fire officers. Assuming reasonable and fair recruitment efforts (often a problematic assumption), the opportunities for minorities were reduced by tests of cognitive ability. Women were excluded because protective service agencies did not permit females to be policemen or firemen (often the gender requirement and the title of the job) or because of unreasonable physical ability requirements (see, for example, *United States* v. *City of Philadelphia,* 1978). For example, it was not uncommon to require applicants to meet a minimum height requirement of five feet seven inches in order to apply for a protective service position—a standard that disproportionately excluded women, Hispanics, and Asians (see, for example, *Dothard* v. *Rawlinson,* 1977).

Identifying Targets for Pattern or Practice Investigations

There was no shortage of jurisdictions to investigate, as every state agency and virtually every local government was a potential target for a pattern or practice investigation. More than one target of an investigation suggested that its selection had been entirely arbitrary. In 1972, one could have thrown a dart at a map of the United

States and probably have been able to justify an investigation of the nearest large city because of its lack of uniformed minority or female officers. However, the ELS approach was much more sophisticated than that, as we were looking for political and practical impact in our investigations and cases.

The primary method of identifying targets was to compare incumbent workforce data (contained in the EEO-4 reports filed by state and local government employers) with relevant census data. The EEO-4 reports provided race, sex, and national origin statistics by job category and the census data furnished sufficient information about the potentially available qualified and interested labor force. A statistically significant difference between the incumbent workforce and the qualified and interested minority or female availability provided a basis for deeper inquiry into the jurisdiction's employment practices.

The key was what was meant by *qualified and interested*. And the answer was (and is), "it depends." It depended on the legitimate minimum qualifications that the employer required for a particular job. In *Griggs*, for example, it would have been lawful for the employer to maintain an age requirement, because that requirement did not have a racial impact, but not lawful to impose an education requirement (at least for the position at issue) that disproportionately excluded black applicants.

In its early investigations the DOJ asserted that *qualified and interested* was determined by the demographics of the general population: that is, the number of minorities in the relevant age group (see *Mackin v. City of Boston*, 1992). As the case law developed, the courts refined the definition of *qualified and interested* to cover those persons who meet all the lawful minimum qualifications for the position in question. For uniformed police and firefighter positions this may mean, for example, meeting minimum age, education, and background standards (see *Aiken v. City of Memphis*, 1994). Although the DOJ often believed that the courts went too far in approving minimum qualifications that would shrink the available minority applicant pool, there was no political will to push the issue.

Another basis for initiating an investigation was a review of Title VII charges of discrimination filed with the EEOC and referred to the DOJ that indicated a possible pattern or practice of employment discrimination. A pattern or practice suit alleging that the Newark, New Jersey, police department discriminated against black police officers was initiated owing to a referral by the EEOC to the DOJ of a charge of discrimination. Other reasons for conducting a pattern or practice investigation were complaints received directly from citizens or media reports. The DOJ sued the District of Columbia after the U.S. assistant attorney general read an article in the *Washington Post* that suggested the city's fire department was engaged in a practice that unlawfully benefited minorities. After reading the newspaper article, the assistant attorney general at the time was reported to have said something to the effect of, "We can't let racial preference hiring go on in our backyard."

In the 1980s, for enforcement and pedagogical reasons, the ELS also began to file suits based on referrals of individual charges of discrimination that had been filed with and investigated by the EEOC. Unlike pattern or practice cases, where the U.S. attorney general had self-starting (self-initiating) authority to commence an investigation, under Title VII (§ 2000e-5.f) the investigation and litigation of individual charges of discrimination could be based only on a referral of a charge of discrimination from the EEOC.

These cases often involved novel issues that would not otherwise have been pursued because the charging party would not have been able to afford or to find counsel willing to take the case. Many of these cases involved jurisdictions in smaller communities where there were few experienced Title VII attorneys. Moreover, the defendant in these cases was always the municipality, and it was not in the self-interest of local attorneys who wanted to have a viable legal career in the community to be the plaintiff's counsel in such suits. Another interesting aspect of these individual cases was the right to a jury trial created by the Civil Rights Act of 1991 in cases of intentional discrimination brought pursuant to section 706 of Title VII. Proponents of this change thought that a jury was more likely than a judge to find that a defendant had discriminated against the plaintiff and to award generous relief. It is my experience that it did not quite work out like that, at least in the cases brought by the ELS.

Before the 1991 Act, judges were the sole decision makers, and they determined whether a violation of Title VII had occurred. If a violation of Title VII was found, the judge also determined the nature of the relief, which was limited to *equitable* or *make-whole* relief. Equitable relief consisted of back pay, instatement or reinstatement in a job, and an injunction against future acts of discrimination. Following the 1991 Act, juries became the decision makers and had the authority to provide back pay, front pay, compensatory damages, and in the case of private employers, punitive damages. The ELS was uniformly unsuccessful in convincing a jury that a violation of Title VII had occurred in the very few cases it pursued that actually went to trial (most settled). I am not aware that the reasons for this outcome have been analyzed. My belief was that local juries, especially those in smaller communities, did not want to believe that their municipality was or could be guilty of treating someone unfairly or did not want to compensate a victim for damages because that might result in a tax increase.

Once a decision was made to conduct an investigation—whether a pattern or practice investigation or an investigation based on the EEOC's referral of an individual charge—the procedure was identical. The first step was to send a letter to the jurisdiction to set forth the general nature of the investigation. Thereafter the DOJ attorney(s) to whom the investigation had been assigned would contact the employer's counsel. Because the DOJ, unlike the EEOC, did not have authority to compel the production of records prior to commencing a lawsuit, the success of the investigation was dependent on the voluntary cooperation of the respondent. Invariably, perhaps because the employer wanted to be perceived as cooperating, the DOJ had little difficulty in obtaining access to relevant records, personnel, and evidence.

At the conclusion of the investigation, which could take as long as two years, respondents would be notified of the results by letter. If a suit were authorized, the letter would summarize the evidence and law and seek to engage the employer in discussions that it was hoped would lead to a settlement's being filed with the court simultaneously with the complaint.

Disparate Impact Investigations

The DOJ's pattern or practice disparate impact investigations begun following the 1972 Amendments focused on first-generation examinations that were either written or physical ability tests or both. The written tests were tests of general cognitive ability that had been adopted and used by employers without Title VII considerations in mind. They were commonly either homegrown tests that had been prepared by a local civil service commission or off-the-shelf tests purchased from commercial test developers and not tailored to the knowledge, skills, and abilities of the job in a particular jurisdiction.

Cognitive ability tests typically have a statistically significant adverse impact (two or three standard deviations) on minority test takers. Unless the pass point has been adjusted downward, minorities fail at disproportionately high rates and are thereby disqualified from the selection process (Rose, 1989, pp. 1121, 1177, nn. 277, 278). The disparity between minority and nonminority performance is further magnified when the test results are rank ordered, which was the norm in many jurisdictions (see *United States* v. *City of Garland*, 2004; *United States* v. *State of Delaware*, 2004).

The DOJ's Position on Job-Relatedness and Adverse Impact

I do not mean to downplay the importance of developing selection procedures that are job related and predictive of successful job performance. Clearly, it was then and is now important for employers to review their selection procedures to ensure that they identify qualified candidates for employment, and where appropriate, to develop innovative approaches. Nevertheless, history and experience show that the test development process is complex, expensive, and disruptive to the employer. And even when done in the most sophisticated way, it was not a process likely to produce a selection procedure (at least with respect to cognitive abilities) that reduced adverse impact in a meaningful way.

Procedures that resulted in minimum improvement in adverse impact were not likely to satisfy the ELS. The ELS's goal was to eliminate statistically significant adverse impact or at least to reduce adverse impact as much as possible. Thus procedures that had greater validity but did not improve the opportunities for minority or female hires were problematic in the ELS's view. To paraphrase a Clinton campaign slogan, "It's the adverse impact, stupid."

One potential way to reduce adverse impact was to encourage the use of a criterion-related test development methodology. The

ELS could have its statisticians review the supporting statistical data to determine if it were possible to reconstitute the test or its components in a way that improved or maintained test validity and reduced adverse impact. If that were possible, the revised test use could be proposed as an equally valid alternative use of the examination. The alternative test use could also be suggested to other jurisdictions, if supported by an appropriate transportability study (see *U.S. v. City of Garland*). Procedures developed using a content-related strategy, however, were not subject to the same type of statistical scrutiny, and there was no principled means for reviewing the test instrument to determine whether adverse impact could be reduced.

I do not recall a newly developed selection process for a protective service position that entirely excluded a cognitive component. The industrial organization psychology (I-O) profession and employers were wedded to cognitive tests, and for political and practical reasons the DOJ was as well. It simply did not resonate within the DOJ or among the public, employers (including the federal government), the I-O profession, or the courts to argue that having a certain level of cognitive ability was not necessary. Indeed, the federal government, as an employer of many thousands of protective service employees, historically had used cognitive tests as part of the selection process. It was inevitable that the position on job-relatedness and adverse impact advocated by the ELS would affect and perhaps call into question the practices of the federal government as an employer. This fact had to be considered by the ELS when it developed its legal strategies.

For all of these reasons the ELS policy was not to eliminate the cognitive component but to reduce its impact on the overall selection process. This was accomplished by recommending that cognitive components be used on a pass-fail basis and that their impact on the overall selection process be diluted by adding biographical data tests, psychological inventories (more commonly referred to as personality tests by I-O psychologists), oral interviews, and the like.

It was primarily because of the adverse impact of cognitive tests that the DOJ did not accept the concept of *validity generalization* (VG). Although VG was recognized in the *Principles for the Validation and Use of Personnel Selection Procedures* (Principles) of the Society for Industrial and Organizational Psychology (SIOP), neither the *Uniform Guidelines on Employee Selection Procedures* (1978) nor the DOJ's policy recognized it as an alternative to the development of tests tailored to the specific requirements of the job. To do so, the DOJ believed, would have encouraged the use of tests of general cognitive ability and discouraged the development and use of selection procedures that moved away from reliance on cognitive tests. Remember that the overarching goal for the DOJ was to reduce adverse impact, and one way to do that, we believed, was to minimize the use and effect of cognitive tests in the selection process. Perhaps, mistakenly, others and myself were under the impression that VG was not consistent with a reduction in adverse impact.

Similarly, first-generation physical ability tests, because they were based on male standards, had an adverse impact on female applicants—even if used on a pass-fail basis. The ELS, with mixed results, had litigated several cases involving the lawfulness of physical performance tests. The first-generation tests at issue typically were tests of raw power and speed. For example, the Cleveland Fire Department used a test that included a barbell exercise (*Zamlen and the United States v. City of Cleveland*, 1990). The ELS viewed such tests with great skepticism and as of dubious lawfulness. The thrust of the ELS's effort in the area of physically demanding jobs was a push for gender-normed tests of general physical fitness: for example, flexibility, aerobic capacity, abdominal strength and muscular endurance, and upper body strength. The theory was that employers should recruit and hire the most physically fit individuals and, in the case of police and fire departments, train them on the specific physical requirements of the job in a training academy program. A related reason was that it made sense to select individuals for physically demanding positions who demonstrated healthy lifestyles, the assumption being that such individuals would maintain that lifestyle on the job. Although the ELS had made some progress in promoting a physical fitness battery, it was opposed by a number of experts, police and fire departments, and unions representing public safety officers (see *Alspaugh v. Michigan Law Enforcement Officers Training Council*, 2001; *Lanning v. Southeastern Pennsylvania Transportation Authority (SEPTA)*, 1999; *Powell v. Reno*, 1997).

The Political Response to Disparate Impact Investigations and Suits

Employers and the general public often perceived investigations of facially neutral selection criteria as ill-conceived attacks on a fair, objective, and politically neutral civil service system that was working well. The suits were further portrayed as a veiled effort to require race- or gender-conscious employment decisions and the employment of less qualified minorities and women hired over more qualified nonminority males. Usually, the DOJ was accused of jeopardizing public safety by "dumbing down" long-standing employment standards that had generated a high-quality workforce.

In addition, in the 1970s, when many of the disparate impact investigations and suits were initiated, the dominant race in the civilian population of many defendant jurisdictions was Caucasian, and political control usually rested with the white establishment. Further, the police and fire departments and their collective bargaining representatives were also predominantly white and the DOJ's interference often upset the hiring expectations of white male applicants and the promotional expectations of the incumbent workforce. Collectively, these considerations created substantial political pressure to challenge the DOJ and reject overtures to enter into negotiated settlements. For these reasons many of the early disparate impact cases were heavily litigated, which meant extensive discovery, temporary restraining orders and preliminary injunction hearings, and motions. Nevertheless, many were resolved on the eve of trial through the entry of court-approved, negotiated consent decrees.

Disparate Impact Litigation

From a litigation standpoint, especially in the early years, the DOJ had the upper hand in terms of the law, legal expertise, litigation resources, and a favorable judiciary. Under the formulation established by *Griggs*, the plaintiff's initial burden was simply to show that the selection procedure used by the defendant had an adverse impact on a protected group. This meant that the facially neutral selection device selected minorities or women at a rate substantially lower than the rate for whites or for males. Once this showing was

made, usually through the testimony of a statistician, labor economist, or I-O psychologist, the burden shifted to the defendant to
demonstrate the instrument's validity. It was at this stage that the
fundamental issue of test validity and job-relatedness was joined,
and the battle between expert witnesses began. (See, for example,
U.S. v. *City of Garland,* 2004, where it is remarked: "This case involves
a substantial amount of highly technical documents and testimony,
and with eleven experts is really a battle between the heavyweights
on each side," Memorandum Opinion and Order, at 12.)

Even if a defendant carried its burden of proof at this second
stage and demonstrated the job-relatedness of the selection procedure, a plaintiff could still prevail if he or she showed that a less
discriminatory alternative existed that met the employer's legitimate needs. It is my experience, however, that litigants did not
have much success in convincing courts that reasonable alternatives were available, especially for police and fire department jobs,
where the courts were inclined to defer to the standards established by the employer (see *U.S.* v. *City of Garland,* 2004; *Lanning* v.
SEPTA, 2002).

In litigation filed in the 1970s and 1980s, many state and local
defendants relied on their in-house counsel for representation.
Typically, such counsel, though competent, were generalists and
often learned Title VII law on the fly. In litigation where the complexities of test validity were at issue, this was a daunting task. The
DOJ's Employment Litigation Section attorneys, however, could
expect to work on a testing case, and therefore efforts were made
to provide training opportunities and to expose them to testing
issues. Not only did the ELS conduct an in-house training program
for inexperienced attorneys but also new attorneys would learn
testing case skills as the second or a third chair on a disparate
impact investigation or case. Moreover, ELS attorneys had the benefit of learning from attorneys who had helped to develop much
of the Title VII law and theory.

The availability of financial and litigation resources also provided
DOJ with an advantage. The litigation of disparate impact testing
cases requires the use, among other things, of a computer support
system to process statistical data and of expert witnesses—typically
statisticians, labor economists, I-Os, and exercise physiologists—
all of whom were expensive to retain. Indeed, the Employment

EMPLOYMENT DISCRIMINATION LITIGATION

Litigation Section at various times had between one and three statisticians on its staff. State and local government defendants often did not have the same litigation or financial resources when defending a pattern or practice case.

On occasion, the DOJ joined forces with private litigants. This, however, was often a double-edged sword. Though it gave the DOJ access to the private plaintiffs and other supportive witnesses in the community as a resource, the objectives of the private litigants and the U.S. government did not always overlap, and conflicts would arise. For example, in *Zamlen*, counsel for the private plaintiffs challenged the job-relatedness of both the cognitive and physical performance entry-level tests, seeing both tests as being discriminatory to female firefighter applicants. The United States, in contrast, challenged only the physical performance test. The cases were consolidated for discovery and trial. Because the plaintiff parties had different objectives and needs, it was inevitable that conflicts would and did arise about witnesses and the type of evidence to present. At the heart of the problem was that the DOJ did not have a client per se (its client, as always, was the public interest). Counsel for private parties are bound by the rules of professional responsibility to zealously represent their client's interest, which may not be congruent with the *greater good*, at least as that term is interpreted by the DOJ.

In some instances, jurisdictions committed significant financial and other resources to oppose DOJ lawsuits. The City of Warren, Michigan, for example, spent more than $3 million in an unsuccessful effort to defend a pattern or practice case brought by the United States. Likewise, the City of Garland, Texas (successfully) and the State of Delaware (unsuccessfully) easily spent millions to defend the validity of their selection procedures for police officer and state police positions, respectively. It is likely that these defendants made a political calculation to defend their employment practices. It is also possible that they thought a Republican administration would be friendlier to them and not vigorously pursue the litigation. If that was their thinking, they were wrong.

Despite having the resources to pursue litigation, litigation was not the first choice of the ELS; we preferred to encourage voluntary change and compliance with professional standards for the development of lawful selection procedures.

DOJ Reliance on the Uniform Guidelines

The Uniform Guidelines have a long history in the Employment Litigation Section. Indeed, in ELS they were considered to be the Holy Grail. One of the primary drafters of the Uniform Guidelines was David L. Rose, the first and longtime chief of the section. Rose, who was chief from 1968 to 1986, was widely viewed as one of the foremost government authorities on the Uniform Guidelines and a proponent of their use. He set the tone for the ELS's adherence to the Uniform Guidelines' applicability and relevance to disparate impact investigations and cases.

There were important substantive reasons for ELS's continued adherence to the Uniform Guidelines. When they were promulgated, the Uniform Guidelines were considered to be consistent with the standards of the I-O profession, and, especially important, the courts gave them deference. The Uniform Guidelines also provided employers, the courts, and interested professionals with a relatively understandable set of standards for determining adverse impact and validity. My sense is that over time, the SIOP Principles went beyond the Uniform Guidelines by, for example, recognizing validity generalization. To that extent the Principles might make it somewhat easier for employers to demonstrate the job-relatedness of their selection devices and to meet their burden to demonstrate validity.

A related question was whether or not the Uniform Guidelines or the Principles applied or had relevance to physical ability tests. In my discussions with David Rose and others, I concluded that when the Uniform Guidelines were drafted their exclusive focus was on cognitive and written tests. As the ELS litigation program began to target physical ability tests in a serious way, the DOJ applied the standards of the Uniform Guidelines to them as well. This was almost like making the proverbial square peg fit into the round hole.

Exercise physiologists also have a concept of validity different from that of the I-O profession; their notion of validity is closer to the psychometric concept of reliability, or possibly accuracy. Generally, exercise physiologists are not familiar with the Uniform Guidelines or the Principles, and they are likely to use a test development approach that is like a content-validity model. Likewise, there was disagreement on the use of construct validity in determining the job-relatedness of a physical performance test.

Retention of I-O Psychologists and Other Experts

The most important expert witness in a testing case was the I-O psychologist. Despite the significant fees (at least by the standards of a government attorney), a relatively small group of I-Os worked with the DOJ at any given time. There was a core of four or five I-Os who were regularly (sometimes reluctantly) retained by the DOJ and perhaps another three or four experts who would be hired by the ELS at any given time.

My own view was that many I-Os simply did not want to get into the fray of litigation. They were wary of the litigation process and found it disruptive to their professional and personal lives, not sufficiently lucrative, or too adversarial. Many I-Os were academics, and litigation demands—travel, report preparation, deposition preparation, making depositions, trial preparation, and participating in the trial itself—wrought havoc with their schedules. In addition, there were bureaucratic procurement, payment, and travel rules that some experts found too vexing to warrant working with the DOJ.

The continued use of the core group of experts and the inability to expand the pool of I-Os was a matter of concern to myself and other DOJ attorneys and, to my mind, had not been adequately addressed. Continued use of the same experts tagged them as plaintiff's witnesses or defendant's witnesses or people beholden to the DOJ. This presented a potential credibility problem for the witnesses and the DOJ. Respondents and the courts always had an argument that the witness had never found a test he or she liked, was always critical and not constructive, and was a hired gun. Moreover, the failure to engage new experts meant that the DOJ was not being exposed to different points of view and fresh ideas in the I-O area.

As is true with any expert witness, it is not sufficient just to retain an I-O, it has to be the *right* I-O (or statistician or labor economist or exercise physiologist) for the circumstances. For example, if the test being challenged was a criterion-related test, the expert needed to be fully knowledgeable about criterion measures (usually job performance ratings). In the area of physical ability tests, it was desirable to retain an expert who was familiar with the physiological demands of protective service positions and was willing to acknowledge that at least some women possessed the necessary physical attributes to perform the job successfully.

The scope of the I-O's work needed to be clear from the very beginning of the project. Would the expert serve as a consultant without a testifying role or was the expert expected to testify? As part of the investigation, attorneys in the ELS might have retained an expert as a consultant to evaluate the employer's evidence of test validity and to provide advice. Thereafter it might not have been advantageous to use this consultant for purposes of litigation, because the consultant likely would have been required by the applicable discovery rules to reveal in a deposition otherwise privileged information and candid advice given to the attorney. Experts also had to be prepared to meet the requirements of the federal Rules of Civil Procedure, which, among other things, require the preparation and disclosure of a signed written report containing the expert's opinions and the reasons therefore, supporting exhibits, the expert's publications for the last ten years, the amount of the expert's compensation, and a list of the other cases in which the expert has testified over the last four years. In addition, the expert must submit to an exhaustive (and occasionally exhausting) deposition. As discovery deadlines drew near there was, to say the least, usually a high level of anxiety between the expert and counsel over the content of the report and preparation for the deposition. Unless both were on the same page, they had an unhealthy working relationship that could affect the outcome of the case.

Some I-Os were known to be sticklers on detail. They wanted every *i* dotted and *t* crossed, sometimes causing them to lose sight of the big picture. A detail person might be fine in some circumstances but not others. For example, I always preferred a detail person when the test at issue was developed using a content validation strategy. I wanted someone who was willing to spend the time to review the procedure used to develop the job analysis and its results in exhaustive detail. Other I-Os might look at the bigger picture and not concern themselves with technical deficiencies of the test development process. Some I-Os believed that a validity strategy must be clearly identified and supported, whereas others believed that validity could be determined from a variety of sources and strategies, which would be inconsistent with the DOJ's reliance on the *Uniform Guidelines on Employee Selection Procedures.*

Some I-Os were reluctant to involve themselves in physical ability testing cases. This presented a problem when retaining an I-O for cases or investigations that involved both cognitive and physical ability tests. Should there be one I-O for the cognitive component and one for the physical test or one I-O to handle both? There was of course no clear answer to this question as it depended on the circumstances of each case. For some litigants, cost was a consideration. However, a second expert might have been necessary where the scope of the investigation expanded to include a physical ability test and the original expert was not comfortable testifying about its job-relatedness.

Whenever possible, I felt it preferable not to have multiple I-Os on a case because it added an unnecessary level of complexity and confusion. Disparate impact cases regularly had several experts beyond the I-O—a statistician, a labor economist, or an exercise physiologist. It is difficult enough to coordinate the reports, testimony, personalities, philosophies, and schedules of experts in different domains without adding a second I-O to the mix. Moreover, use of multiple I-Os gave the opponent an opportunity to obtain possibly contradictory evidence from my own witnesses. Yet there may have been strategic reasons for retaining a second or third I-O—for instance, where several tests were at issue or the test development strategy was so complex that I-Os with different areas of specialization and viewpoints were warranted. It also might have been necessary to retain an additional expert to provide relevant testimony about an alternative selection device that he or she developed. The *Garland* and *State of Delaware* cases mentioned earlier are illustrative of the use and pitfalls of multiple I-Os.

Before retaining an I-O, or for that matter any expert witness, it was essential to know about the individual's professional writings and testimony and whether his or her works were consistent with the case theory, because all relevant writings and testimony needed to be provided to the opponent. Thus it was important to know whether the expert's prior work supported the case theory. However, an attorney considering the retention of a particular expert should not necessarily be put off because some past work and opinions may be inconsistent with the I-O's current opinion. I-O theory has evolved in light of experience and research, and showing that the I-O's current opinion has been influenced by experience and scholarly research can enhance the expert's credibility even when there are apparent inconsistencies.

It was important to educate the expert about the litigation process, particularly the area of attorney work product. Experts needed to be carefully counseled about the process of drafting reports, maintaining drafts and notes, and discussing the investigation or case with third parties, because the opponent was going to seek to discover all underlying documents and any contradictory statements of the I-O. I-O's statements about the case to third parties not associated with the litigation were particularly vulnerable to discovery because such statements were not likely to be protected from disclosure in the discovery process.

Although going to court had the aura of glamour, preparing for "your day in court" was hardly glamorous. Rather, it was tedious, deadline driven, frustrating at times, and nerve-racking. Experts did not always understand (or accept) all of the behind-the-scenes work that takes place before the trial date and that even after everyone's hard work there might be a settlement or a trial postponement. If experts do not understand what lies ahead, there will be a stressful relationship between them and counsel. Thus one of the most important assessments that had to be made was whether counsel and the expert could work well together, because the success or failure of disparate impact cases in large measure depended on the credibility and persuasiveness of expert testimony, as was made abundantly clear in the *Garland* and *State of Delaware* cases.

Notwithstanding the exercise of due diligence in retaining an expert, things had a way of not working out as planned. I retained an I-O for a case because he had successfully testified in another case that raised issues similar to mine and the court had relied on his testimony in reaching a very favorable decision. After meeting with the I-O and speaking with the attorneys in the other case, I was convinced that this was the right person. Indeed, during discovery everything went along as planned. The expert took his job seriously, he was readily available to counsel, he prepared his expert reports on time, he assisted with the deposition of the city's experts, he did well in his deposition, and generally did all that was asked of him. The problem arose while he was being prepared for trial. As the day of his testimony got closer, the I-O started doubting the credibility of his testimony. For instance, this testimony relied in part on statistical analyses prepared by the DOJ's expert statistician. I vividly recall the witness saying at 2:00 A.M. on the morning of his testimony (we were up most of that night cajoling him) that because he did not perform the analyses he could not rely on them. He questioned his ability to respond to our opponent's experts. Ultimately, he was convinced that his opinions were solid and well founded in law, fact, and the professional standards—and he presented brilliant testimony at 9:00 A.M. This anecdote points to the need for the attorney to be fully conversant in the expert's domain. It would not have been possible to convince the I-O that his testimony was credible and reliable without fully understanding his concerns and being able to respond to them.

Settlement of Disparate Impact Cases

The DOJ always engaged in settlement discussions before bringing a case. There were at least two reasons for this. First, the DOJ considered Section 706 of Title VII (giving the EEOC private sector litigation authority and allowing the referral of individual charges of discrimination against state and local government employers to the DOJ) to require a good faith effort at settlement before initiating any litigation, whether an individual or pattern or practice suit. Although Section 706 does not on its face apply to Section 707 pattern or practice suits brought by the DOJ, it is the DOJ's consistent long-standing practice to resolve allegations of employment discrimination voluntarily and before a trial.

This policy did not mean that there would be out-of-court settlements, with no judicial oversight. On the contrary, the DOJ insisted that pattern or practice cases be resolved through court-enforceable orders. However, it did not matter what the settlement document was titled—court order, consent decree, or settlement agreement—so long as a judge signed it and the court retained jurisdiction for enforcement purposes. Disparate impact settlements generally had several common features—they provided injunctions against the use of unlawful examinations; required back pay and job opportunities for victims of discrimination, development of lawful selection procedures, and submission of compliance reports; and gave victims the ability to seek enforcement from a court. In recent years, not only has the DOJ had a program that encourages voluntary resolutions of all litigation but also the courts almost always require that negotiations be held, accompanying this requirement with a prohibition on discovery until settlement efforts have failed. Individual judges have great influence over the settlement and negotiation process. Judges may make it known that a case should settle and may suggest to a party that it is in that party's best interest not to litigate a matter. In other words the court can essentially force a settlement—usually one that neither party likes.

The Evolution of DOJ Thinking on Litigation and Job-Relatedness

The DOJ Title VII litigation program in 1972 was purely a law enforcement program. There was no effort to help potential defendants address their shortcomings or to resolve cases without the filing of a court complaint and, ultimately, a court decree. The DOJ's litigation challenged the selection criteria used by state and local government employers as unlawful and did not offer alternatives or solutions. Thus the DOJ's I-Os pointed out the legal and professional deficiencies in tests but did not answer questions about, for example, what selection criteria should be used. Alternative selection devices and procedures were never proposed. Indeed, the DOJ's I-Os were not test developers. Thus, at least in the early years of litigation, the DOJ's experts were unable to answer affirmatively to a question along the lines of, "Have you ever developed a test with no adverse impact or one that is valid?" The response to these and similar questions was that the DOJ was a law enforcement agency and not in the business of developing or recommending selection procedures to employers. This response was by design. Quite simply, the DOJ's sole focus was to stop employers from using selection criteria, particularly written tests, that discriminated against minorities, and there was no desire to assist employers to develop alternative selection procedures.

This answer was acceptable in the 1970s and into the early 1980s. *Griggs* and its progeny were relatively recent decisions, the need for state and local government jurisdictions to integrate their workforces was largely acknowledged, the courts were more receptive to plaintiffs' Title VII suits, and particularly important, many examinations were patently inadequate. On more than one occasion the DOJ's I-O would be prepared by counsel to read a question from a written test to the judge and suggest that the judge try to answer it correctly. Invariably, the judge would fail to do so. Usually, that was the beginning and end of the argument. This strategy was effective because it illustrated for the court in an understandable way that the test was not predictive of successful job performance. Equally important, the example put into context the dry and rather boring statistical evidence and expert testimony presented about the Uniform Guidelines, the SIOP Principles, statistical significance, the .01 or .05 level of significance, one- or two-tailed tests, two to three standard deviations of adverse impact, outliers, confidence levels, content validity, criterion validity, and other technical matters.

The testimony in disparate impact cases was not the most scintillating, and the litigator needed to tell a story that supported his or her case theory. Reliance on expert testimony, without anecdotal testimony, rarely would be adequate for a plaintiff to prevail, especially in cases that challenged the selection procedures for protective service jobs. It is well documented that the federal judiciary has become philosophically more conservative. One of the consequences of a conservative bench, especially after the terrorist attacks of September 11, 2001, has been a greater reluctance to find unlawful standards in the selection of police officers and firefighters. In effect, the courts today will require plaintiffs to prove their case with evidence that is more convincing than a mere preponderance-of-the-evidence standard. There is evidence of this result in the ultimate *Lanning* v. *SEPTA* decision. First, the Court of Appeals for the Third Circuit, in a pre–September 11 decision, held that SEPTA had not carried its burden to demonstrate that the physical abilities test at issue was job-related and consistent with business necessity. Then, in a post–September 11 decision on substantially the same evidence, the court of appeals arrived at the opposite conclusion. The district court in the *State of Delaware* case, using the legal standard established in the first SEPTA decision (the second SEPTA decision held that the legal standard had been met), determined that the rank-ordered use of the cognitive test at issue was unlawful. The *Garland* district court, which was not bound by the *Lanning* legal standard, ruled that use of the same test as was used in Delaware to select state police officers *was* lawful!

These decisions cause me to wonder if there would have been a different result in the first SEPTA appeal if it had been rendered post–September 11.

The End of Race- and Gender-Conscious Hiring Decisions

The DOJ's first wave of Title VII litigation in the 1970s and 1980s resulted in decrees, either court ordered or by consent, that in part (1) forbade the continued use of the challenged selection procedures unless used in a way that eliminated adverse impact and (2) required the development of new procedures that met the requirements of the Uniform Guidelines and, until that was accomplished, race- and gender-conscious hiring. The reality was that many jurisdictions were quite content to make race- and gender-conscious employment decisions because they resulted in an integrated workforce and saved the expense and effort of developing new selection procedures (see, for example, *Petit* v. *City of Chicago*, 2003). This result also met the needs of the DOJ, which prior to the Reagan administration was primarily interested in seeing minorities and women hired and promoted and not interested in test development. Those decrees and orders would not go on forever, however, and the jurisdictions needed to adopt new selection procedures.

The Reagan administration was openly hostile to race- and gender-conscious selection methods and looked for opportunities to have the courts declare them unlawful. Further, perhaps emboldened by the rhetoric of officials in the Reagan administration, white males who had been denied positions as a result of the courts' race-conscious orders filed a number of "reverse" discrimination suits, with some success. In addition, Section 106 of the Civil Rights Act of 1991 (42 U.S.C. § 2000e-2) prohibited the use of race- or gender-normed *employment-related* examinations. In sum, the political and legal tide turned against the use of race- or gender-conscious measures to reduce adverse impact.

In the mid-1980s, the DOJ began an initiative to cooperate with protective service employers to develop job-related tests that eliminated or substantially reduced adverse impact. The foremost example was an agreement with the Nassau County, New York, police department. The goal was to look beyond traditional tests of cognitive ability and to incorporate the use of biographical data and personality instruments, which had been shown to reduce adverse impact and to predict successful job performance.

In San Francisco, the fire department and the union, as part of court settlement with the United States and private plaintiffs, undertook to develop new written and physical performance tests for entry-level positions, with the involvement of experts for all parties. A consortium of I-Os, including those retained by the city and those selected by the private plaintiffs (but paid for by the city), the United States, and the union, developed new written and physical performance tests under strict court supervision. Early in the process the lead I-O for the city determined that a content validity strategy would be used because, as I recall his words, "it would not be possible to obtain reliable criterion data"—that is, job performance data—due to the hostility to the litigation among the incumbent firefighters. In addition to the I-Os, the parties retained exercise physiologists to develop new physical performance standards. The tests that were ultimately developed, at a cost of many hundreds of thousands of dollars, seemed to me to be traditional cognitive and physical performance tests, which if they had been used in strict rank order would have had the typical levels of adverse impact. In order to address the issue of adverse impact, which was of great concern to the court and of course the plaintiffs, the test developers used a sliding band methodology to reach enough minorities and women (Campion et al., 2001).

An interesting footnote to this case is that the court did not believe that the United States was committed to enforcing Title VII, at least in a way that the court thought it should be enforced. This case was being litigated during the Reagan administration, which vocally opposed any type of affirmative relief. The private plaintiffs and San Francisco had negotiated a consent decree that called for the development of the new tests and affirmative relief for women and minorities. The decree was entered over the objections of the United States, which had argued that the affirmative relief was not lawful. As a result, the United States was viewed by the court as not supportive of enforcing the decree and after its entry, the court did not seek or consider U.S. views on its implementation. Indeed, I and other counsel for the United States were not allowed to participate in many of the conferences and hearings held by the court concerning compliance with the consent decree.

Even during the development of the Nassau County police test and its progeny and the San Francisco tests, the DOJ, internally at least, was less concerned with job-relatedness and more concerned with finding measures that would reduce adverse impact. Hence in Nassau County the goal was to minimize the adverse impact of the cognitive component, and in San Francisco it was the use of a sliding band that reduced adverse impact.

During the Clinton era an effort was made to reach out to constituencies that had an interest in the DOJ's Title VII enforcement function. For example, ELS personnel would speak at conferences of groups like SIOP, the International Personnel Management Association, national and local police and firefighter organizations, and meetings of union officials. A particular effort was made to work cooperatively with the International Association of Fire Fighters and the International Association of Fire Chiefs, who were jointly developing a physical abilities test for entry-level firefighters in conjunction with ten fire departments in the United States and Canada. These efforts were not a retreat from litigation. Rather, they were an alternative to litigation and were true to Title VII's objective to eliminate artificial barriers that served to restrict employment opportunities to all persons regardless of their race, sex, religion, or national origin. Indeed, where voluntary efforts failed, the DOJ did not hesitate to pursue litigation (see *U.S.* v. *City of Garland* [rank-ordered use of cognitive test held to be valid]; *U.S.* v. *State of Delaware* [rank-ordered use of cognitive test held *not* to be valid]; *Lanning* v. *SEPTA*, 2002 [validity of physical abilities test]).

The Future of DOJ Disparate Impact Litigation

The DOJ's Title VII enforcement has changed markedly during the current Bush administration. Most important, there has been a movement away from all types of litigation—pattern or practice cases, including disparate impact and treatment, and also individual disparate impact cases. In the three years of this administration, the ELS has filed a total of ten cases, including only two pattern or practice cases. One of the latter challenges on the disparate impact theory the lawfulness of a physical performance test used by the City of Erie, Pennsylvania. This investigation was begun during the Clinton administration and lingered for several years until the complaint was filed. The U.S. Attorney's Office for the Southern District of New York filed the other case, which alleges a pattern or practice of disparate treatment (in an investigation also begun during the Clinton administration). In contrast the ELS in past administrations averaged fourteen case filings a year, including several pattern or practice cases. In light of discussions with current members of the ELS and a review of the ELS Web page (http://www.usdoj.gov/crt/emp/papers.htm), it appears that this administration has a lack of will and desire to vigorously enforce Title VII. This is evidenced by a failure to bring litigation, to identify new enforcement initiatives, and to maintain the outreach efforts begun in the Clinton administration. In particular, it is highly unlikely that this administration has the will or desire to file disparate impact cases challenging cognitive tests.

Private litigants are not likely to fill the enforcement void. There are few nongovernmental organizations that have the financial and professional resources to pursue disparate impact cases. In evaluating the legal and judicial landscape, they are also likely to conclude that they are unlikely to prevail in litigation. This situation does not bode well for continued progress in employing women and minorities in representative numbers in state and local governments and particularly in police and fire departments. In theory and probably in fact the DOJ is the only organization that has the resources, will, and expertise to bring successfully disparate impact cases. Without that threat, it is likely (and I hope I am wrong) that there will be a reduction in the numbers of minorities and women employed by police and fire departments.

State and local governments need to have an incentive to spend their limited financial resources on revisions to their selection processes. In the absence of the threat of litigation or jawboning by the ELS, they may find little reason to devote money and personnel to test development and other measures to increase the representation of minorities and women in their workforce. The hope is that employers will recognize that it is good public policy and politics to take voluntary measures to maintain and improve minority and female employment. This is a serious issue that deserves serious consideration and involvement by the DOJ. All objective signs are that the U.S. Department of Justice is not giving enforcement of Title VII the attention it needs and deserves.

References

Articles and Government Documents

Age Discrimination in Employment Act of 1967, 29 U.S.C. §§ 621–633a (2000).

Americans with Disabilities Act of 1990, 42 U.S.C. § 12101 *et seq.* (2000).

Campion, M. A., Outtz, J. L., Zedeck, S., Schmidt, F. L., Kehoe, J. F., Murphy, K. R., & Guion, R. M. (2001). The controversy over score banding in personnel selection: Answers to 10 key questions. *Personnel Psychology, 54,* 149–183.

Civil Rights Act of 1866, 42 U.S.C. § 1981 (2000).

Civil Rights Act of 1871, 42 U.S.C. § 1983 (2000). Civil Rights Act of 1964, Title VII, 42 U.S.C. § 2000e *et seq.* (200).

Discrimination in Employment Act of 1967, 29 U.S.C. §§ 621–633a (2000).

Equal Employment Opportunity Commission. (1997, January). *Laws Enforced by the EEOC.* Retrieved from http://www.eeoc.gov/policy/laws.html.

Rose, D. L. (1989). Twenty-five years later: Where do we stand on equal employment opportunity law enforcement? *Vanderbilt Law Review, 42,* 1121–1182.

Uniform Guidelines on Employee Selection Procedures, 29 C.F.R. § 1607 *et seq.* (1978).

U.S. Commission on Civil Rights. (1969). *For all the people, by all the people: Report on equal opportunity in state and local government employment.* Washington, DC: Author.

Cases

Aiken v. City of Memphis, 37 F.3d 1155 (6th Cir. 1994).

Alspaugh v. Michigan Law Enforcement Officers Training Council, 634 N.W.2d 161 (Mich. App. 2001).

Dothard v. Rawlinson, 433 U.S. 321 (1977).

Griggs v. Duke Power Co., 401 U.S. 424 (1971).

Lanning v. Southeastern Pennsylvania Transportation Authority, 181 F.3d 478, 482–484 (3d Cir. 1999).

Lanning v. Southeastern Pennsylvania Transportation Authority, 308 F.3d 286 (3d Cir. 2002).

Mackin v. City of Boston, 969 F.2d 1273 (1st Cir. 1992).

Petit v. City of Chicago, 352 F.3d 1111 (7th Cir. 2003).

Powell v. Reno, No. 96-2743 (NHJ) (D. D.C. Jul. 24, 1997).

United States v. City of Garland, 2004 WL 741295 (N.D. Tex. Mar. 31, 2004).

United States v. City of Philadelphia, 573 F.2d 802 (3d Cir. 1978).

United States v. Lee Way Motor Freight Co., 625 F.2d 918 (10th Cir. 1979).

United States v. State of Delaware, 2004 U.S. it. LEXIS 4560 (D. Del. Mar. 22, 2004).

United States v. U.S. Steel Corp., 520 F.2d 1043 (5th Cir. 1975).

Washington v. Davis, 426 U.S. 229 (1976).

Zamlen and the United States v. City of Cleveland, 686 F. Supp. 631 (N. D. Ohio 1988), aff'd, 906 F.2d 209 (6th Cir. 1990).

Employment Discrimination Lawyers, the Doctor Will See You Now
Joshua Sohn

Lawyers are well schooled in the art of rhetoric. (I refer to rhetoric in the classical sense, that which Plato described as "the art of winning the soul by discourse," and Aristotle as "the faculty of discovering in any particular case all of the available means of persuasion.") Generally, the better the lawyer, the more effective is his or her rhetorical style. Rhetoric, however, gets a bad rap; the term has come to have pejorative connotations, suggesting that all things rhetorical—except perhaps for the rhetorical question—are dishonest. But the most effective rhetoric is more than simply unadorned "argument"—it is well-crafted argument with an impregnable foundation. That's where the expert-scientist enters the litigation arena.

Scientists generally, and I-O psychologists specifically, are expected to function somewhere in the ether—above rhetoric. They are expected to rely on data derived from a scientific method that requires forming hypotheses, testing those hypotheses, observing the results of those tests, and drawing conclusions or inferences based on those results. In so doing, the scientist provides the lawyer with data to support his rhetorical skills. The lawyer will often present his rhetoric in the form of "common sense" or elementary principles, and the psychologist provides the scientific foundation for that common sense or those basic principles. In contrast the lawyer's job, assisted by the psychologist, may sometimes be to debunk notions of common sense either presented by the opposing lawyer or held by the judge or the jurors. Thus, by combining their unique skills and training, the lawyer and the psychologist create a scientifically persuasive case.

Background

I am a commercial and securities litigator by trade and training. Most commonly, I litigate cases between corporate entities involving disputes over contracts, insurance, securities, fiduciary duties, and the like. Accordingly, in my day-to-day legal practice, my experience with experts has typically been in the areas of commercial and securities cases. In those cases I work with experts who in their previous or other professional lives are, among other things, economists, securities market professionals, and business school professors. Those experts opine on questions such as how much money a party lost or did not lose, how a piece of information affected stock market activity, how an event's occurrence or nonoccurrence influenced other events, or how entities may be properly valued. In these situations experts are typically required to quantify something (for example, the value of a business or a transaction) that laypeople (and in particular jurors) could not.

Until the fall of 2000, I had no experience with employment law, Title VII, or industrial and organizational (I-O) psychology. At that time I saw a description of a case that struck my interest in a listing distributed by a New York City pro bono case clearinghouse. The case involved a Title VII disparate impact challenge to two tests used as part of New York State's teacher certification requirements. *Gulino* v. *Board of Education* is an employment discrimination class action brought pursuant to Title VII on behalf of a class of African American and Latino teachers who were employed as teachers in New York City. I was a member of the team of lawyers who represented the plaintiffs in this case. Individually, we each brought different skills, perspectives, and experiences to our collective representation of the class.

The case alleges that two of the standardized tests required of New York's teachers had an impermissible discriminatory affect on the members of the plaintiff class. The teachers in the *Gulino* class suffered either of two consequences as a result of failing the tests. First, some members of the class had their city teaching licenses revoked based on their inability to pass either of the state-mandated tests. Second, other members of the class were prevented from ever receiving permanent teaching credentials because of their inability to pass the tests. In both instances the teachers remained employed as teachers in New York City's public schools—albeit at reduced pay and with reduced benefits—in most cases teaching the same classes as they had before they failed the tests.

Over the course of the next four years, I received a comprehensive education in employment tests, test development, test validation, Title VII, and disparate impact law. Included in that education was more than I had ever expected (and sometimes *wanted*) to know about I-O psychology. During that time the case progressed through the phases described in Chapter One of this volume, beginning with class certification, and it is currently in the appeal stage, with a four-month trial having occurred in between.

Welcome to the World of I-O Psychology

For the uninitiated (or at least for me before I was initiated), the term *industrial and organizational psychologist* conjures up images of people in white lab coats clutching clipboards behind one-way mirrors. I would have imagined them looking out over a warehouse stretching as far as the eye can see, advocating group calisthenics by employees sporting T-shirts bearing their employer's corporate logo, hypnotically chanting the corporate mantra, and drinking their sports drink from water bottles similarly emblazoned with that same logo. In other words I had no idea what I-O psychologists do. Fortunately for me, the actual work of I-O psychologists—examining the underlying principles of work behavior—was just what was needed to buttress my rhetoric.

What Do I-O Psychologists Actually Do?

As I subsequently learned, I-O psychologists are psychologists who specialize in the psychology related to work and work environments. Although it's hard for many lawyers to admit, there are myriad things we know nothing about. One of the things I did not know I did not know about, but now know I did not know much about, was I-O psychology. In retrospect, it is good that I now know what I did not know about, because the principles of I-O psychology and psychometrics were central to the case I had decided to take on. Most important for me, I-O psychology can help to operationalize the concept of *harm* as it is used in public policy discussions. The core of the defendant's case in *Gulino* was that the particular tests in question would protect the schoolchildren of the City of New York from harm done through ineffective teaching. It was through the unique contribution of I-O psychology that the question of harm could be framed in a way that could be understood by a non-psychologist and nonscientist (in this case, the judge hearing the case). (See Chapter Thirteen in this volume for a detailed discussion of harm and cut scores.)

Harm means different things to different people in different situations, but that's the point. In virtually every employment situation there is a possibility for harm to be present. The type and degree of harm falls along a continuum, its place depending on the employment at issue. It doesn't take an I-O psychologist to point out that the potential harm of an unqualified nuclear power plant operator is considerably greater than that of an unqualified dog groomer. In *Gulino* the issue was, what was the potential harm to students of an uncertified teacher, and how could that harm be predicted before it actually occurred? The defendants believed that palpable harm could be predicted through the use of a test that purported to measure a teacher candidate's *mastery* of the liberal arts and sciences, broadly construed. It was the position of the plaintiffs that it was the responsibility of the defendants to articulate more precisely what that harm might be, and, more important, the extent to which the test in question could actually predict that harm, once the harm was defined adequately. It was the role of the I-O psychologist to help articulate that harm and how the tests at issue in the case either did or did not effectively predict that harm.

Lawyers and Psychologists Use Different Languages

From the perspective of both a lawyer and a psychologist, an employment selection device is supposed to—pun intended—work. For the lawyer the device must not violate the law. For the psychologist the device must not violate psychometric principles, which means that it must accomplish what it was intended to do. At the end of the day, or the case, legal principles and psychometric principles should be coextensive, but because the final arbiter is typically a judge and not a psychologist, the decision will be framed in the lexicon of the lawyer, not the scientist. For example, *disparate impact* is a critically important phrase to an employment discrimination lawyer but is considerably less important to an I-O psychologist. *Disparate impact* is a legal and administrative term and not a psychological one. To the lawyer, this is the first threshold that must be satisfied for a disparate impact case. Title VII provides that an unlawful employment practice is established when a "complaining party demonstrates that a respondent uses a particular employment practice that causes a *disparate impact* . . . and the [employer] fails to demonstrate that the challenged practice is job-related for the position in question and consistent with business necessity" (Civil Rights Act of 1964, 2002, codifying the Supreme Court's holding in *Albemarle Paper* v. *Moody*, 1975). If the lawyer cannot establish a prima facie case of disparate impact, everyone goes home and the expertise of the I-O psychologist is irrelevant to the case. But regardless of disparate impact the I-O psychologist is interested in a particular selection device, and interested in concepts such as reliability, discriminability, fairness, and validity. It is precisely when the case moves forward, when the prima facie case of disparate impact has been made, that we enter into the arcane world of the I-O psychologist.

From the lawyer's perspective, validity is what a testing case is all about. You win or lose based on one seemingly simple question: Is the test valid? But from the psychologist's perspective you've only just begun. I can hear my inner-psychologist's voice in my head saying, "Valid for what?" And here's where it gets interesting. By asking this straightforward question, valid for what? the psychologist invites the lawyer into the psychologist's realm and necessarily strengthens the lawyer's case in the process.

As with any case the lawyer's ultimate success depends in large part on how well he not only knows but also (and more important) can articulate his case. Generally speaking, disparate impact cases are no different from other cases in this regard. As a practical matter, however, testing cases require extensive specific knowledge of psychometric principles and procedures. Here, the key to mastery of the subject matter is being able to speak technical jargon with your psychologist but not needing to use the jargon to explain the concepts to the court. This process is laborious and reminiscent of learning another language. In the beginning the words all sound familiar (*valid, reliable, fair,* and so forth) and suggest meanings that you think you know. How quickly you realize that lawyers and psychologists use the same words to mean very different things may determine how quickly you are able to prepare your case. When your domestic partner leaves the dinner table understanding the meaning of a term like *construct validity,* you can take some pleasure in your newfound mastery (although you may eat alone for awhile after that).

Lawyers are good at research. They can find cases, citations, precedents, and so forth. Whether the case is about employment discrimination, tortious interference with contract, or insider trading, this process is the same. There are certain seminal cases and lines of cases that set forth the general principles governing employment testing cases. These cases (for example, *Griggs, Albemarle,* and *Wards Cove*) are discussed in detail in other chapters of this volume. But beyond these seminal and well-known cases, there are myriad other cases, many dealing with the exact focus or issues of your case. But how would the lawyer know *which* of these cases is apposite? Is a *cut* score the same as a *critical* score? the same as a *pass* score? Is *generalizability* the same as *reliability*? the same as *consistency*? the same as *accuracy*? It is the I-O psychologist who leads the lawyer through the forest of technical terms so that the lawyer may collect, use, and truly understand the relevant case law.

Although there are some cases that describe with some detail the attributes of *valid* tests and what courts may look for, most Title VII cases do not describe in detail the psychometric analysis required for a court to proclaim whether a test is valid or violates Title VII. One must dig beneath the veneer of the opinion for those inferences, and this is when it is valuable to have the I-O psychologist digging along with the lawyer. I-O psychologists can easily parse terms such as *construct, content,* and *criterion-related validity.* Terms such as *norm-referenced* and *criterion-referenced exams* roll easily off their tongues. They understand, without detailed explanations in a written opinion, what these terms mean. It is this understanding that lightens the load of the lawyer. In addition to offering input in figuring out what legal standard may apply, the psychologist is equally valuable in deciphering what the *opposing* expert might be saying.

The Lawyer-Psychologist Relationship

By the end of a big case lawyer and psychologist may each feel confident that he or she could take over the role of the counterpart—the lawyer could be expert and the expert could be lawyer—but that is fantasy. It is enough that at the end of the case, each has gained greater insight into the world of the other, and along with that will come a commensurate amount of respect for the distinct roles that each plays in this process and the unique skills required by each.

Proper Care and Feeding of Lawyers

As a threshold matter, lawyers take their cases very personally. Although this may differ by degrees from lawyer to lawyer, every good lawyer invests blood, sweat, and tears into every case (especially those that take years to resolve). This is in part because the lawyer is responsible for preparing the entire case and presenting every aspect of the case to the court, not just the topics covered by the psychologist. The lawyer must concern himself with pleading requirements, court rules and schedules, conducting discovery, motion practice, and seemingly endless logistical issues. Accordingly, there are a few very basic and important ways in which the psychologist can best help the attorney prepare the case.

Think Big Picture and Issue Spot Early in the Process

In the context of an employment discrimination case, the psychologist's greatest attribute from the lawyer's perspective is simply that she is a psychologist. Lawyers are good at thinking like lawyers. They are terrible at thinking like psychologists. Accordingly, it is the psychologist's unique perspective and knowledge base that is invaluable to an attorney from the psychologist's first involvement in the case. Not only can the psychologist provide insight into what facts the lawyer should work to establish during discovery, but she can also help the attorney approach the case more effectively by discussing the issues in the case from the psychologist's unique angle. With the psychologist's insight from early in the case, the lawyer will be able to formulate a discovery plan that makes sense and is likely to uncover the facts necessary to win his case.

Listen and Ask Questions

It should go without saying that everyone is different. Although it might sound trite, it is critical to remember this as you navigate through the case. Just because the last lawyer the psychologist worked with wanted things done in a certain way does not mean that this lawyer wants things done in the same way. By their nature lawyers tend to be idiosyncratic and rather inflexible. As a result, they likely have ways in which they prefer to deal with experts, including such issues as whether communications should be written, whether drafts should be circulated, whether all work should be preapproved, and more. It is often counterproductive for the psychologist to lecture the lawyer about how another lawyer worked a case.

Many peculiarities of the lawyer are opaque to the expert. For example, due to issues of privilege or confidentiality, the lawyer may want to prevent the psychologist from creating discoverable documents reflecting certain speculative studies or theories. Thus the lawyer's lack of enthusiasm for a clever new analysis may actually have a strategic foundation. In addition, the lawyer might have a statistical expert examining particular data, obviating the need for the psychologist to do so. The best way to avoid tripping over any potential stumbling blocks, regardless of the reasons for them, is open communication between the lawyer and the psychologist. It may be incumbent on the psychologist to ask the lawyer whether certain documents should be reviewed, certain data should be analyzed, or certain observations should be included in a memo. By asking first the psychologist may run the risk of pestering the attorney, but she steers clear of the risk of damaging the relationship or, much worse, the case.

Check in Periodically

Odds are that the particular employment discrimination case is not the only professional endeavor being pursued by either the attorney or the psychologist. Accordingly, both are probably extremely busy and neither may be particularly focused on future deadlines or future tasks in the case. The best way to ensure that the lawyer keeps the psychologist apprised of case developments—even during the slow periods—is to maintain regular communication. Because the psychologist is likely being paid an hourly fee, there is always a risk of creating the impression of "running the meter" through frequent calls to the attorney asking what more work needs to be done. If, however, there is good communication between psychologist and lawyer, this is less likely to happen as a result of regular communication than it is through sporadic partial communication. Moreover, regular communication should prevent the overwhelming majority of crises, typically caused by previously unknown deadlines.

Not only should regular communication ensure against preventable crises but it should also help both psychologist and attorney do their jobs better. By having regular interdisciplinary conversations about the case, each by necessity will think about the case in a slightly different manner than if left to his or her own devices.

How Best to Use Your Psychologist

Unlike in many cases, in a discrimination case the psychologist can help the lawyer virtually from day one. In order to understand the elements that he must prove to carry his burden or, alternatively, that must be proven to establish a viable defense, the lawyer needs to understand the mechanics and principles of I-O psychology. Accordingly, if the lawyer uses his psychologist effectively, odds are that he will be better versed in the psychometric principles in the case than at least the fact witnesses.

Discovery

The psychologist can prove invaluable in formulating a discovery plan. She will know what sort of documentation should exist, what particular tasks should have been performed, and what potential holes are in your opponent's case. Similarly, there is no one better to help prepare for a deposition of an I-O psychologist than another I-O psychologist. Because I-O psychologists are typically academically trained and members of a rather small community, odds are that your expert has at least heard of the other side's expert and is familiar with his or her reputation and or work. As a result, your expert should be able to point you to treatises or leading articles in the field that will be fruitful ground for developing questions and theories for your depositions of the opposing side's experts. Moreover, the adage that "a little learning is a dangerous thing" is particularly apt in this context. It is appealing for a lawyer to think that by reading *Griggs* v. *Duke Power* and the 2003 SIOP Principles or the 1999 American Psychological Association (APA) Standards, he is ready to take a bulletproof deposition of the other side's expert, who happens to have twenty years of experience in psychology. It is also a recipe for near-certain disaster. To effectively examine any expert, a lawyer needs to understand that expert's unique language as much as possible, know when he doesn't, and really know where and how to score points and stick to those areas. Without your psychologist this is difficult if not impossible in an employment discrimination case.

Trial Preparation

Use your expert early and often. There is, however, an obvious problem with this approach. Money. Expert time is expensive and trial preparation is time intensive. So, absent unlimited money, what do you do? The simple answer is do your homework early in the case when time is plentiful. And depending on budgetary constraints, use your expert as often as makes sense.

Assuming your case goes to trial, there are, by definition, factual issues remaining. This of course presents the attorney with the challenge of assembling the facts into a digestible story, which the fact finder(s) can sink his, her, or their teeth into. To do this, however, requires a schizophrenic approach: how do you tell a story that a layperson can follow, understand, and empathize with while simultaneously establishing the technical and legal elements required to make your case?

The first part of this equation requires common sense and perspective, two traits not universally possessed by lawyers but invaluable in virtually all situations. The second piece—perspective—is where your expert earns a significant portion of his money. It is incumbent upon you to use your psychologist to make sure you understand the relevant professional standards so well that you will necessarily include the requisite elements in your case in chief.

Trial: The Big Dance (Rhetorically Speaking)

I recently heard that something like 1 percent of civil cases go to trial. From a statistical perspective this means that the overwhelming odds are that your employment discrimination case will not go to trial. Accordingly, you probably do not have to worry about trial preparation, unless of course you do. In which case, if you have not been preparing for this trial all along, you may find yourself in both an objectively and rhetorically bad way. If, however, you have worked with your psychologist throughout the development of the case, the hard part of the process is done. You have learned all that you can about the controlling law, as well as the controlling professional principles. You have also involved your psychologist in discovery so she is generally aware of the story of your case and she has probably helped you isolate the critical facts that your case depends on. All that remains is the trial itself. You need to prepare your psychologist to testify and you will need your psychologist to help prepare you to cross-examine your adversary's expert. Additionally, you might want to involve your psychologist in planning general trial strategy, planning particular direct examinations, planning particular cross-examinations, or providing general psychological services. This is the point in the process where the lawyer is in danger of thinking he knows more about psychology than the psychologist, and the psychologist that she knows more about law than the lawyer. There is, however, a reason that each has his or her particular vocation and it's best not to change those until after the trial.

Accordingly, at the end of the day, the trial is where the lawyer is called upon to marshal all evidence and rhetorical devices he can muster—psychologist included. This means that the enormously difficult decisions of which witnesses to call (and in what order), what facts to put into the trial record, what facts to ignore, and fundamentally what the theory of the case is, are difficult decisions for the attorney to make. This is where the attorney's rhetorical training and skills are put to the ultimate test, and the role of the psychologist becomes less important.

Assuming that the lawyer and psychologist have worked together effectively throughout the process, each will understand how the other approaches the crucial issues in the case, and they will have developed a common understanding of what they need to prove, both through the trial generally and through the psychologist's testimony specifically. When done right, the attorney's direct examination of the psychologist at trial should gracefully display the results of the (often years of) hard work that both have put into the case.

Conclusions

By the end of this process in the *Gulino* case, I felt equipped to edit a book on test development practices, complete with sections on score setting, job analyses, item tryouts, pilot tests, and validity studies. That being said, the critical question for this type of case is the same as the central question for all cases requiring specific, particularized knowledge, how much is too much? Because you can be relatively certain that your judge, her clerks, and the majority of the witnesses will have had no experience with tests other than having taken them over the course of their lives with varying degrees of success, this is the hardest part of the process.

Your psychologist can help you through some of the difficult decisions along the way, but at the end of the day—or the trial—the responsibility of presenting the best case possible falls on the shoulders of the lawyers alone. And because the decision will be made by nonpsychologists, legal rhetoric—not scientific analysis or hypotheses—inevitably must carry the day. Nevertheless, rhetoric without substance can be as damning as substance without rhetoric. The substance is the *necessary* condition and the rhetoric the *sufficient* condition in an effective argument in employment cases.

References
Albemarle Paper Co. v. Moody, 422 U.S. 405, 431 (1975).
Civil Rights Act of 1964, 42 U.S.C. § 2000e-2.k.1.A.i (2002).

CHAPTER 15

A Judge's View
Interviews with Federal Judges About Expert Witness Testimony
Frank J. Landy

Remember the old joke about the narcissist who says to the person he's talking to, "OK, enough about me. Let's talk about you. What do you think about me?" This chapter is a bit like that but perhaps more functional than narcissistic. In litigation both the credibility of a body of scientific knowledge and the credibility of an individual expert witness are often critical in determining which side prevails. Throughout this book you will find case citations that relate both directly and indirectly to the work of industrial and organizational psychologists. This means that at least *some* judges know who we are and what we do. Further, it means that at least *some* judges permit the expert testimony of I-O psychologists.

Chapter Six in this volume presents an excellent architecture for considering issues of scientific and individual credibility at a distance. This chapter takes a different approach. I contacted a number of federal district judges, federal magistrate judges, and federal court of appeals judges and asked if they would be willing to sit for an interview on topics related to Title VII and 1983 cases, as well as, more specifically, their views of expert witnesses. Six agreed—four trial court judges (Graham, Sifton, Baer, and Smith), one appeals court judge (Posner), and one federal magistrate judge (Grimm). The interviews ranged from forty-five minutes to three hours in length. The content varied somewhat from judge to judge, based on the experiences and interests of the particular judge. Each interview was recorded, transcribed, edited, and approved by the judge in question. The bulk of this chapter consists of those interviews. I summarize the major points in a concluding section.

A Previous Survey

I will begin this chapter by discussing a review done by the Federal Judicial Center (one of the research wings of the judicial branch of the federal government). This particular study (Krafka, Dunn, Johnson, Cecil, & Miletich, 2002) considers the views of federal judges and lawyers on expert testimony. Although the purpose of the study was to consider the influence of Daubert principles on expert testimony (see Chapter Six in this volume), there is considerable information that addresses ancillary issues related to expert testimony. For that reason, I will review the results of this study as a backdrop to a consideration of the opinions of the federal judges that will follow.

The Krafka et al. (2002) study was based on a series of surveys that were mailed to federal judges in 1991 (pre-Daubert) and 1998 (post-Daubert) and to attorneys in 1999. In both the 1991 and 1998 judge surveys, the response rate was over 300 (this represented, respectively, a 65 percent and 51 percent response rate). A total of 302 attorneys (66 percent) returned usable surveys. Thus, both on a relative and absolute basis, the response rate was sufficient to draw inferences. The following observations are based on the Krafka et al. study.

By far the single most common expert witness is the medical or mental health witness (40 percent of all experts) and the most common trial in which expert witnesses appear is one that concerns medical issues. In contrast, only 3 percent of the expert witnesses who appear in federal court can be considered "scientists." The next most common witness category to the "medical" expert is economists (12 percent), often for the purpose of estimating damages in a civil trial. I-O psychologists as witnesses are not sufficiently numerous to warrant a unique category and would most likely be placed in the categories of "other business/law/financial" (6.6 percent), "other scientific specialties" (3.2 percent), or "other specialty" (3 percent). No matter how you look at it, I-O expert witnesses are few and far between in the experience of most judges. Consider that their dockets may be populated by as many as six hundred cases in a given year (aggregating both criminal and civil actions). This means that they may see an I-O psychologist once every few years (assuming that they even *know* that the expert is an I-O psychologist as opposed to an HR specialist, statistician, or psychometrician). (See Chapter Six in this volume for an additional survey of judges and magistrates on this topic.) It may be tempting to dismiss this survey and the following interviews with judges as irrelevant because there is so little exposure to I-O expert testimony. This would be a mistake. Generic issues are raised that relate to all expert testimony, regardless of the area of expertise. These issues are relevant to I-O psychology as a discipline as well as to individual I-O psychologists as expert witnesses. Here are the most relevant of these issues and findings.

Exclusion of Testimony

It is very unlikely that a judge will exclude the testimony of an expert unless that expert or his or her testimony is disputed by one of the parties to the lawsuit. Only 3 percent of the judges surveyed had excluded an expert or expert testimony without a direct objection or challenge raised by one of the parties. Nevertheless, the rate of such objections is increasing. In 1991, expert testimony was disputed in 31 percent of the cases covered. By 1998, that percentage had risen to 46 percent. This is likely the result of the increased awareness of scientific testimony following the Daubert decision. A related finding is the increase in the percentage of excluded testimony when comparing 1991 with 1998. In 1991, 25 percent of experts or some portion of the expert's testimony was excluded by the judge. By 1998, that percentage had risen to 41 percent. The most common reasons for excluding testimony were

1. It was not relevant (47 percent).
2. The expert was not qualified to render an expert opinion on the topic (42 percent).
3. The testimony would not be likely to assist the judge or the jury understand the issues (40 percent).

4. The facts or data on which the expert based his or her opinion were unreliable (22 percent).
5. The testimony would have been too prejudicial to have been of ultimate value (21 percent).
6. The principles and methods underlying the expert's testimony were unreliable (18 percent).
7. The testimony would have been repetitious and wasteful of the court's time (10 percent).
8. The expert testimony was not reliably applied to the facts of the case (10 percent).

The Use of Experts by Judges

Judges have wide latitude with respect to the appointment of experts to assist the court in understanding complex matters. It is reasonable to ask how often they avail themselves of that latitude. The answer is not very often. For example, only 10 percent of the judges surveyed had ever appointed an expert on their own volition. Only 11 percent had ever asked one or both parties to provide expert education to the court on a topic. Less than 2 percent had ever appointed an "advisor" to help the court understand scientific or technical issues. Thus it appears that most often experts will testify only if one or the other side to a dispute introduces expert testimony.

Reported "Problems" with Expert Testimony

When judges and attorneys were asked to identify areas where they experienced discomfort with expert testimony, there was substantial agreement. Judges and lawyers identified the same issues. In descending order of magnitude, these problems areas were as follows:

1. Experts were not objective and acted as an advocate.
2. Experts were expensive.
3. Expert testimony was of questionable validity or reliability.
4. The disagreements between opposing experts defied reason.
5. There were often dramatic disparities in the level of competence of opposing experts.

6. The expert testimony was not comprehensible.
7. The expert testimony was comprehensible but useless.
8. Information about the expert was withheld by the party retaining the expert.

This is a daunting list. You will see that many of the points in this list are repeated in the interviews that follow, particularly points 1 and 3.

The Interviews

With the Krafka et al. (2002) results as a backdrop, we can now consider the judicial interviews.

In the interview transcripts that follow, my questions are identified by the initials FL. The judges' responses are identified by their initials. Each interview was conducted in the judge's chambers and tape recorded for eventual editing.

James L. Graham
Chief United States District Judge,
Southern District of Ohio
November 13, 2003

Judge Graham's clerk Karen Martin was also present during this interview. Her comments are identified by the initials JC (judge's clerk).

FL: I sent you some questions prior to my arrival. Were you familiar with the concepts and issues that were addressed by those questions?

JG: As I reviewed the materials I was struck with the fact that whenever we encounter cases like this we have to go through a learning curve and it's not unlike confronting issues of technology and patent cases. We . . . federal judges are generalists and we deal with all kinds of sophisticated and complicated issues and we have to learn many things all over again and it is certainly true in this area, and while we may be intensively involved in the kinds of matters that you deal with on a day-to-day basis and have for decades, for us it's an intensive learning experience, hopefully we learn everything we need to know and apply it and then move on to something else and promptly forget all about it. So I say this as an apology, I suppose, at the beginning of our conversation because you are going to find that I'll need to have my memory refreshed on many things. Your questions were very helpful in that regard. But a lot of the things that I knew a lot about have faded away because we have not had a case for several years involving these issues. To make matters worse, the last Title VII case I heard, two years ago, never really got into the merits phase. We had a hearing on class certification where we got into the merits peripherally, but it has been quite awhile since we have had a case in which we really dug into the merits and had to apply the kinds of principles that you live with and carry around in your head in a daily basis.

FL: Can you give me an idea of the frequency with which you encounter Title VII and 1983 cases in terms of your typical caseload?

JC: I pulled the Title VII and 1983 cases using our automated filing system. Here is a table that shows the frequency. In terms of our total cases it's not really too significant in terms of numbers.

FL: On the average, how many active cases of all kinds are on the judge's docket in a typical year?

JC: Six hundred and fifty cases a year are filed, and our normal docket is around 350 cases a year. This would include approximately 90 criminal cases.

FL: What has been your exposure to industrial and organizational psychology as a discipline and to industrial and organizational psychologists as expert witnesses?

JG: I'm pretty sure that my first exposure was in a trial in the late '80s involving police officers or firefighters—I had several cases involving both professions. I may have also encountered something like this perhaps in the area of products liability, human factors, human factors engineering. I can't remember a specific, but we may have encountered it in such a situation. I'm pretty sure that my first real exposure was probably in the Police Officers for Equal

Rights [POER] case. That would have been the first time that I heard of this special language in this science, the first time I heard of the SIOP principles, the first time I heard of chi-square in the field of statistics; it was all new, and it would be still all new because I would have to learn it all over again. That's not unusual; that's what judges do. That is one of the great things about this job as a matter of fact. Every day brings new cases and new issues.

FL: Generally, do you find yourself dealing with Daubert issues or the admissibility of scientific testimony often?

JG: Well, I can think of some so-called medical disciplines or theories that involved such issues. I remember there was a wave of quote "experts" that were testifying about thermography and how measuring subtle differences in the heat output of various parts of the body could be used to make medical diagnoses, which was all craziness. If the field itself were not a recognized field, then I think, yes, obviously a judge has to be concerned with that. Someone claims to be an expert and claims that there is a field of expertise—well, gee, really what is it, and what are its tenets? Does it measure up to the usual standards of scientific investigation?

FL: How would you investigate those issues, that is, does it measure up to the usual standards of scientific investigation? Would you do your investigation in the context of a hearing?

JG: We work in an adversarial context, and so we probably wouldn't begin to look into this issue unless somebody raised it as an issue. So when we are proposing to admit a new expert in this field we never heard of, we would expect that the other side might raise an issue about that and say there isn't any such field of expertise and this is all witchcraft, this is not science. And that would be raised by a motion of some kind, probably a motion *in limine* and that would then focus the court's inquiry, and it would also be at least the beginning point in obtaining information with which to evaluate the merits of this new science. And we would be looking to the parties initially, but you find out pretty quickly in this job that you can't rely on the parties exclusively. They will sometimes do a great job, and then other times they may overlook things. So, yes, I would ask someone like Karen Martin here to see what she could find out through her own independent research. And it's amazing sometimes—we'll find out things that the lawyers have completely overlooked. So if it is a significant issue and looks like it could be affecting the outcome of this case, then we are going to be looking for input from the lawyers and doing our own independent research. We might in some circumstance appoint a neutral, court-selected expert to assist us in this task—a lot of precedent for doing that. In general that is how we would approach it.

FL: Would you ever consult Lexis or Westlaw in this investigation?

JC: That is where I would start because it is amazing to me you could even plug in a particular expert's name. You can pull up whether he has been recognized as an expert before or whether his subject matter has been found to be relevant in other cases.

FL: Would it be a mistake to assume that a judge is familiar with industrial and organizational psychology as a legitimate science or area for scientific testimony?

JG: A big mistake, that would be a mistake. If both sides come in with people in this field then of course we are going to assume this must be in a recognized field, they both have experts in this field so you're going to take this for granted. Then you are going to be focusing on whether these experts are in fact qualified. In addition we would focus on whether testimony or theories in this particular case withstand analysis under the principles of science they are proposing and offering.

I recall a case in which there were recognized medical experts but they were talking about an issue that medical science really, in my opinion, doesn't really have the answer to, and this was a case of repetitive motion injury involving a carpal tunnel syndrome. It was railroad workers. At that time I asked and was informed that the only documented medical evidence that repetitive motion of a joint could result in this kind of disease was from industries where the repetitive motion was truly repetitive, constant chicken pluckers, people who worked in the factories where they dissect chickens. There were two other areas in which people, in which medical experts in general, would agree that, yes, the repetitive motions were causing this. But in this case these qualified physicians, otherwise qualified, were trying to interpolate, and then there were actually some standards out there established by the government. I forget which agency, but they again dealt with these three major industries. They were trying to interpolate that into the work of a railroad worker. This fellow was sometimes a brakeman, sometimes he had to throw brake switches, but he might do that for fifteen seconds several times per day, and they were trying to say, well, yes, he did it less frequently but it required more force, so they were trying to say, well, more force should equal more repetitions. It was all kind of guesswork in my opinion. So I suppose that is a good example of what we are talking about. You've got a qualified expert but the opinion is not based upon sufficient empirical data; it is more or less, well, it is just the expert's unfounded opinion. It is a possible speculation of the clever person who might very well get a research grant to study that, but it falls short of saying that I'm confident that A leads to B.

FL: Do you encounter the Uniform Guidelines in Title VII cases, and do you give them deference?

JG: We would have to go back to those, we wouldn't be carrying them around in our head, but we might be giving them significant deference on these issues. We would have to have some good reason to ignore them.

JC: But on the other hand it would be a question of whether the employer was cognizant of these standards, wouldn't it?

JG: Well, it wouldn't make a whole lot of difference if they knew about it or not; if they violated it they probably are in trouble. But another question would be if [the Uniform Guidelines] have the force of law. Probably not, but as a practical matter they are going to have a considerable weight in the court's decision as to whether or not a test is a proper test instrument or not. Because they are going to represent a formal embodiment, a stamp of government approval on certain testing principles. So I think they are going to have a lot of weight.

If they have been promulgated by the EEOC and they have been promulgated correctly—and this going to be an issue I expect a lawyer to raise, somebody on the one side saying these are the principles adopted by the EEOC and they apply to employment testing—they're going to have the force of law if they are promulgated pursuant to the authority granted by Congress. Now these agencies also do guidelines and manuals. They are not promulgated as a rule, so they don't have the force of law; they may have considerable persuasive value. But if they have been adopted pursuant to congressional grant of authority, then they are going to have the effect of law.

FL: The Uniform Guidelines were published in 1978. Suppose science and practice have changed since then. Do they remain as applicable as an authority as they may have been when they were published? And how would you balance the deference given to these guidelines versus the deference given to judicial opinions or "precedent"?

JG: Well, precedent has to be applied in the light of accumulating knowledge, and this may lead to the ability to distinguish the case at hand from the case involved in the precedent, because if the new knowledge was something that could not have been anticipated or was not considered in the case that resulted in the precedent then you have a basis for distinguishing this case from the precedent. So this is how the law grows. The issue of regulations in relation to precedence raises a separate question. Let's suppose we have a set of regulations that adopted in 1970 and then we have a series of Supreme Court decisions that are inconsistent with the regulations. The regulations are going to have to be interpreted now in light of this subsequent development of the law, and in fact some of them may no longer be applicable; they may no longer be valid as a matter of fact. The court may have to say, all right, this is what the EEOC said and this, but the Supreme Court said this, and you can't reconcile the two. And the decision of the

Supreme Court of course is the supreme law of the land. It takes the place of the regulation now or initiates the regulation.

FL: What about new developments in a scientific field, such as industrial psychology, which may have occurred since a set of guidelines were published?

JG: Well, if there were new developments in the science of industrial psychology, I think that when there are new developments and they have the weight of some consensus behind them, some consensus and science, then there is room for the court to say, well, we know more about this today than when this case was decided, we have new evidence, and therefore we are permitted to consider whether or not the precedent applies in view of this new evidence. So I suppose there is the possibility that you could end up with different results because of the advances in the science.

FL: By the time a case is actually heard before a judge, there have been reports filed, affidavits presented, conferences with the attorneys, and possibly motions to exclude issues and testimony. What, then, is the role of live testimony? Is there added value?

JG: The judge is the finder of fact. I'll assume that we are not talking about a jury trial, since the jury would not have known what came before. Yes, I'll tell you, at least from my standpoint, there is considerable added value. Simply receiving information directly from a person that you can see and you can watch and you can listen to carefully, and also a person that you can address questions to. I cannot conceive of a case where I would want to dispense with direct examination. Even though I have read the reports, I don't think there is any substitute for a live testimony. Maybe you could say you could judge credibility by cross-examination only; I don't know. But I generally think I need all the help I can get in understanding something, and I really want to be sure about it. I want to hear. I want to hear the expert on direct examination, I want to think about what the expert witness is saying as I listen. As I read the reports questions may have occurred to me. Many times this happens. I want to ask those questions myself.

And if all I've done is read a report, I don't have that kind of interchange.

Also, when I'm in the courtroom there are no distractions. I am not sitting at my desk reading a report where the phone may ring and, you know, when I start reading again I may skip a few sentences, my concentration has been interrupted, whatever, but when I am in that courtroom I am in there for only one reason and that is to hear and to understand and to be able to ask questions. So that is my framework for making decisions, and to me that really is an important part of the process, seeing the person, listening in this environment where that is all I have to do is very, very helpful. I know that I learn best from that context. Not to simply read off a page but to see and hear and to ask, that helps me to learn. And usually that is exactly what I am in there doing. I need to understand what are often very complicated concepts—the ones that you deal with every day—you know them because you deal with them every day. I don't. I need to understand them as well as you do, and I've only got a short period of time to reach that understanding so I need all the help I can get. And it is the best way for me to learn.

FL: What type of structure or format for expert testimony is most desirable, in your opinion?

JG: There has to be a logical progression in the questioning, there have to be specific questions or you will run into problems with the Rules of Evidence, unless the lawyer is following the traditional way of developing the expert's testimony. If you adopt a kind of conversational approach, I think the lawyer on the other side can interfere with that approach pretty easily. I don't think you can ever be concerned about starting from too simple or basic a beginning. You know the judge is always in a position to be able to say, all right, I understand this area; let's move on to something else. I will often do that. On the other hand I think that the lawyer would be making a mistake if he assumed that the judge knew anything to begin with, so I would tend to favor a detailed and exhaustive approach, keeping it simple, keeping it tutorial in nature. I think that the best attitude that an expert witness can take is one of a professor in class and the judge is the student, and then I think, if the judge is asking questions, you can pretty quickly discern how well or how ill informed the judge is and then gauge your own presentation accordingly. Your job as an expert is to teach this judge as much as possible about the concepts so that he will understand what you are saying in support of your position. So the learning analogy, the teaching analogy, I think, is a good one for me.

FL: Do you ever get bored with expert testimony?

JG: You get bored when it is not relevant. When you are talking about things that are just not germane. They may be things you are interested in or whatever. But if they are not really germane to the case, that is when I get bored, or when it is repetitive. If you are telling me the same thing over and over again. That's when I get bored. If you are telling me the same thing the last guy told me. This is the lawyer's job. There comes a certain point when, hey, I heard this already, I don't want to hear it anymore. I want to hear things that are relevant to this case, not extraneous things. Well-structured testimony is the joint responsibility of the lawyer and the expert witness. I mean, after all, your job is to provide the court with the information and to do it in such a way that it is understandable and it is concise and direct and informative and hopefully persuasive as well.

FL: What is your reaction to the use of terms of art or arcane language by experts?

JG: I think you've got to be very careful to avoid the use of arcane language. The judge may be embarrassed to ask what it means. If I ask what that term means, that's going to suggest I didn't read the report. Don't assume anything. It gets down to the principle of teaching: how do you teach students? Assume they don't know anything. You don't start teaching them by using sophisticated terminology that is a part of the jargon of the profession; you start out with simple terms. That's exactly what you want to do with the court; you define terms before you use them or when you use them.

FL: Would it be more acceptable for an expert to use technical language with a judge than with a jury?

JG: It might be presumptuous, and I think there would be a certain risk involved in making that assumption. If you are being too basic, I think the judge would let you know that pretty quickly. If I were going to make a mistake, it would be to err in the direction of being more basic. I think the safest assumption would be to treat the judge just like an average juror.

FL: When an expert begins his or her testimony, is it fair to assume that the judge has read and understood the expert reports that may have been filed?

JG: I think that is a mistake. I think you are giving us too much credit. . . . And everyone is different. It is a different discipline and today it may be . . . cutting-edge chemistry . . . patent case, countertops, oh, good grief. I mean, you may know it all for a week or two. I may know as much as you do because you taught it to me, but a year from now, after all this other stuff has intervened, it's all been forced out; it can't all stay in there, it won't. I think the safest thing you can do is just like writing on a blank sheet every time. Oh, you tried this case before Judge Graham in 1983 and he knew all this stuff? You cannot just take it for granted that he still knows it. You are going to find judges who are going to want to show off and show you that they know all this stuff, and that is good; then you can assume that they do and then move on and be more sophisticated in your approach. But I'm just saying the safest thing is to start off assuming the judge is not going to know anything. Nine times out of ten you are going to be right.

FL: Do you ever independently step back from a case and consider the issues in light of a simple doctrine of *fairness*?

JG: Well, I find it hard to apply such a general concept as fairness, and when I try to think of cases in which I've concluded that something was unfair, it is generally based upon some standard and not some general concept of fairness. There are some discrete facts that add up to a conclusion of unfairness. In the employment context those are generally discrete facts. Things like was there a legitimate level of performance expected by the employer? Did the employee meet that legitimate expected level of performance or not? Was it an expected level for the job in question? And if it wasn't, then maybe the application was unfair. Did the employee meet certain standards of attendance, let's say, or timeliness? And so I have a real difficulty with such a nebulous concept as fairness. Well, OK, here you have a person who needs the job, yes, and the impact of losing the job is very severe, and you can have the human emotion of regret and sorrow for the consequence, but that doesn't mean that it was unfair.

FL: How about an individual who has worked for an employer for forty years and has always been a good employee and who was led to believe that he or she would have a job until a retirement decision had been made?

JG: Well, the hypothetical case that you just described lends itself to some legal arguments. And the legal doctrine is the doctrine of promissory estoppel—I'm sure you are familiar with it—and the judge may very well be called upon to decide whether or not those facts invoke the rule of promissory estoppel or whether they don't or whether or not they are sufficiently close, but the jury should decide whether or not there was a binding promise made and, if there was, consideration was given by the employee by continuing to work. If the facts fit the doctrine of promissory estoppel, then the case would be decided by a legal rule; it wouldn't be decided on the basis of fairness or unfairness. You might say that the legal rule was formulated by the courts to avoid the unfairness of the situation that you described so, but you wouldn't find a judge saying, "I'm making this decision because it's the fair one." The judge would say, "I'm applying this rule of law to reach this result." You might find a juror in the jury room saying this is not fair, and they may use it to arrive at their decision and they may or may not follow the rule of law. The judge has the duty to give them that rule and to explain when it applies and when it doesn't. When they get back there in the jury room they are pretty much on their own, and they can stray from the court's instruction either knowingly or unknowingly, I suppose, and they have the power to decide a case on such general principles as fairness because we don't know what they ultimately decided the case on, whether they really followed the judge's instructions or not.

I think fairness in a bench trial context is based upon application of the law. It is the rules of law that have been developed to reach a fair result, and I would in making the decision in bench trial be looking for the facts and deciding the facts that lead to that conclusion.

To return to your hypothetical case, I think the average person would say it is unfair for someone to have worked for a corporation for forty years, to have done their very best, and then have their job eliminated in a downsizing. That is unfair, but it is not unfair in the legal sense unless there was a binding contract which called for the payment of compensation or continued employment and that very rarely is the case.

FL: Do various characteristics of an expert witness matter to you once you have decided to admit his or her testimony? Do you care if the expert comes from inside or outside of the defendant organization? Do you care if the expert has many or few scientific publications? Do you care if the expert works exclusively for defendants or exclusively for plaintiffs?

JG: Sure could, it could matter a lot in a given case. Let's go back and talk about some of the specific issues that you mentioned. One is whether or not the expert always testifies for one side or the other; yes, that could be a consideration.

JC: It certainly reflects a difference in philosophy, the manner of approach to things.

JG: Well, is this person just saying what they are paid to say? They have identified with one side, this is what they are always going to say, so you are going to listen to that expert's testimony with a bit of suspicion. But that not may be it. You may listen to the testimony and say, well, it all makes sense; it doesn't make any difference whether they testify for one side or the other. I would say as a general matter it would be awfully nice if you were presenting an expert, as a lawyer, to be able to have them say, "No, I testify for both sides." That would give that expert more credibility, and we do hear that occasionally. Then you say, well, this expert's not a hired gun, that's good.

Now, inside expert versus outside expert, big credibility problem with the inside expert. I mean, his paycheck comes from the party he's testifying for in this case. That person's testimony may be discounted, maybe even be totally disregarded. That may be a real impediment, and that is not a very effective expert to use. Now, there may be some things that person has to say that are significant and important, the person may have played some, that person knows how this company operates; but "my opinion is thus and so," that's not going to carry a lot of weight.

With respect to an expert who has lots of publications versus one who has practical experience, I think that the person with practical experience has an edge. I think, at least from my standpoint, the person who has practical knowledge, who has actually used these principles in a real-world environment, is going to have more credibility. As a general rule I think that would probably be the case.

FL: Not many cases actually go to trial. Why is that?

JG: The good ones settle, and the bad ones go out on summary judgment.

FL: There seem to be fewer and fewer Title VII cases involving basic entry-level tests. Do you have an opinion about why that might be the case?

JG: Well, I assume part of it is industry has learned how to prepare nondiscriminatory tests, tests that are job related, and they understand, yes, our tests have to be job related. This was something maybe not much attention was given to: well, here we got a test and it will screen out applicants, but no one stopped to think whether it was really related to the job. They have to now.

FL: Would you expect a written opinion from a judge to include the complete foundation for the ultimate decision?

JG: It should, and I think that would be the intent of every judge in writing an opinion. To the extent that it doesn't simply represents a failure to accomplish that goal. It's interesting: why do we write opinions? I sometimes think maybe the best reason for writing an opinion is to make sure we've got it right in the first place. Sometimes you think you have decided, you think you have reached the right result, you sit down and write it, and it won't write. It just won't hang together, and this is what I thought the right result was, but I can't justify it when I sit down to write it. I was wrong, so it keeps me honest intellectually. I am writing it so the parties will understand the result, that's important. I'm writing it so the reviewing court will understand how I arrived at this result, that's very important. I'm writing so the public will understand why this result was reached in this case.

FL: If an issue were too complex technically, would you either leave it out or gloss over it in a written opinion?

JG: If it is a controlling issue, there is no way to avoid analyzing it. In my opinion the right way to do it is you summarize the testimony you have heard from both sides on this issue, and then you give your decision, and you are going to have to recite it in a logical and coherent fashion. That is one of the reasons why writing opinions is difficult. And that is one of the reasons why we do note taking and sometimes after the hearing studying the transcript. You may not even be able to rely on your notes or your recollection, and that is why sometimes decisions are delayed. If you want to get it right, you may need to get that transcript out and study it very carefully. That way you understand it and you are able to put it down in black and white. If it is not a controlling point then why go to the trouble? If it is just an incidental thing, if it doesn't bear on the final decision of the case, then you are just simply spinning wheels and wasting your time. It may have been an interesting element of the case to you but from a professional standpoint—and you had a disagreement with your counterpart on the other side—but it may not have been a deciding factor in the case and the judge may ignore it for that reason. And it takes a lot of time to sort it out, but it's not worth the work because it is not controlling. If the issue of the case is going to be decided on the issue of poor job analysis, then why in the world spend the time working on this coefficient of validity of this test? Wouldn't do it.

FL: Have the Daubert standards resulted in a greater or lesser likelihood that purportedly scientific testimony would be admitted?

JG: I think if you looked at the decisions since Daubert there has been a tightening up of the requirements for expert testimony, which is a paradoxical result of the decision because the decision was supposed to liberalize the admissibility of expert testimony, and I think it has had exactly the opposite result. It has increased the focus on critically examining the grounds for expert testimony, and this has probably resulted in more exclusionary decisions than it has in decisions admitting testimony.

On the other hand, you know this came at really a kind of a crescendo, if you will, of the criticism of junk science in the courtroom, and it came at a point in time when it was literally possible to hire an expert to say anything about anything, whereas fifty years ago when the Fry Rule was formulated that wasn't the case. This whole industry of experts arose, and so more need for the gatekeeper function, so I guess I'm tempering my response a little bit it by saying it probably wasn't Daubert itself, it was this excess of experts that probably resulted in the fact there were more decisions excluded because there are more experts advancing theories that need to be controlled.

FL: What about the difference between a bench trial and a jury trial?

JG: Look, if you are the trier of fact why not let it all in, because otherwise it is presumed on appeal that you only considered the good evidence. If you are ruling in a jury case, however, this is critically important, because you are either right or wrong in your ruling, and if you are wrong then the presumption is that you influenced the jury. If I'm the trier of fact I'm probably going to be much more lenient and rely on my own ability to sort out the wheat from the chaff and the junk science from the real science, and I'll simply express it in terms of the credibility of the experts, and I don't really have to pass necessarily on the whether this is an established theory, whether all the rules of Daubert have been applied or satisfied, but I can just simply say that I didn't believe it.

If it is a jury trial you have to make a decision, and I'm going to make the best decision that I can applying these Daubert principles, and I've been reversed on one, but I think most of the time, even if they are exclusionary, if you follow the rules and explain your reasoning there is a deferential standard of review, and so I'm going to make a critical analysis and I'm going to make a decision and I'm not going to worry about whether it's an exclusionary decision and I'm going to make the best call that I can. I don't make that decision looking over my shoulder for a possible reversal or remand. I am going to call the shot the best way, and I guess I've been known to say I'd rather be right than affirmed.

FL: Written opinions will often include comments about an expert's opinion not being *credible* or not being *reliable*. What do those terms mean when they appear in a judicial opinion?

JG: In common parlance that would seem to mean that the person's veracity is being doubted, that the expert is being called a liar. But in judicial opinions, it is a term of art. It simply means that the testimony was not persuasive. It does not mean this expert got on the witness stand and perjured himself, not at all. When I say that testimony is not credible, I am not reflecting upon the truthfulness of the witness but upon the persuasiveness of the testimony the witness presented, and that is what judges mean when they use that word. The reason that judges use that word is because they, as the trier of fact, have the discretion to decide issues of credibility. And so they use the word *credible* that tells the court of appeals, "I made this decision as the finder of the fact, that's my job; you stay out of it."

JC: And it is very difficult to get reversed on that basis. Or it could mean that the expert is an expert in general in the field but in a particular area you find out that he has not had a whole lot of experience in that particular area, and so you decide he hasn't persuaded me because he is not really an expert in that little particular area.

JG: Now in a criminal case if I say he is not credible, it probably means he's lying.

Charles Sifton
Senior Judge, United State District Court,
Eastern District of New York
December 10, 2003

FL: Do you handle many employment cases?

CS: I do handle a lot of employment discrimination cases. The majority are 1983 cases. Usually somebody has either not bothered or, out of ignorance, has failed to exhaust remedies under Title VII. The cases that I've had recently involve individuals who are disgruntled by employment decisions who may not have an effective union or grievance or personnel procedure on the job and so they go to a lawyer who turns an ordinary dispute over employment, which may or may not have racial overtones, into a 1983 case. Nineteen eighty-three has expanded to cover all sorts of ordinary job-related grievances by converting them into discrimination lawsuits.

FL: You presided over one of the early and extensive cases involving physical abilities and gender discrimination. How did you approach that case? It was highly technical and relatively unique at the time. It was the Berkman case brought against the New York City Fire Department.

CS: This was all brand-new to me. At the time I was totally uninterested in exercise or physical abilities. I decided to familiarize myself with the issues by going to where the test was being administered. I recall the test was being given in an armory out here in Brooklyn. I drove out there on my own. I got there early. There was somebody from the fire department, my own age, which must have been in the late forties or early fifties. He was a senior fire department officer who was administering the test. He met me and said, "Why don't I just familiarize you with the test by walking through it." So he walked through the test, and I walked along beside him. He did all of the routines (I didn't), and then the people who were going to demonstrate the test by taking it the way candidates would take it came in. These younger and stronger and more athletic candidates were going to be rated on their time to completion. In the end this guy who led me through the test, introduced me to it, said, "Let's compare my time to the time of the guys who didn't walk through the test but tried to make the best time." And of course their times were remarkably close. This helped me understand that the question of what physical abilities were required to do the job of firefighting was a lot more complicated than it appeared. It wasn't just a matter of strength or anaerobic energy. There was also a question of stamina.

FL: Are you generally familiar with the field called industrial and organizational psychology?

CS: I can't say that I can recall any expert from that field announcing that this was his area of expertise.

FL: Is that because the experts are typically qualified as experts in testing or experts in statistics rather than their discipline?

CS: Maybe they realized that forensically it's not a good idea to announce that you're a specialist in matters having to do with industry. One of the problems with a title like industrial psychology is that it already begins to raise issues of bias, which are always there lurking in litigation. I can imagine a juror saying, "This guy isn't your usual psychologist; this is a psychologist who has some take on industry or management," and it doesn't help.

At the same time my views about the discrimination, which I prefer to call prejudice, lead me to welcome psychologists. In my view what we are dealing with when we confront prejudice is the fact that many people don't recognize their biases, so that it is extremely useful to get someone in there who can talk in a sensible way about aspects of human behavior that are dictated by things of which one may be unaware. I believe that's true not only of the litigants but it's also true of the jury, the experts, and the judges, that you're dealing with this unconscious level of decision making. A very good way to deal with this is to get someone in there to focus everybody's attention on the fact that you are dealing with the unconscious. I've come to feel that the division of discrimination cases into explicit racial hatred on the one hand and another type of discrimination that is only disclosed by adverse impact analysis is rather artificial. In almost all of these cases what we are dealing with basically is something that people will not acknowledge.

FL: Are you saying that they may not be aware of their prejudices?

CS: Yes. It would be a very helpful thing to diffuse all the emotions that are generated by calling someone a racist or saying you've discriminated against someone. If we could get someone in here to say to the ordinary laypeople on the jury and in the courtroom that what we're dealing with here is not immoral behavior. We're dealing with an aspect of human behavior that scientists recognize that may well be dictated by mechanisms of which you may be unaware.

FL: So what do you think the role of the expert should be in a bench or jury trial?

CS: Over the years I have come to charge juries on the subject of experts in a way that tries to play up the role of experts in assisting the jury in dealing with the evidence and approaching it in a way that they can think about it and understand it.

FL: Can you give me an example of a case where you used such a charge?

CS: Sure. I recall a case in which I appointed the expert in computer technology. Neither side was going to present an expert on computers even though the case involved the ownership of new software which either had or hadn't exploited old software belonging to one of the litigants. So I asked somebody at Columbia who was in the field to come down to create a glossary of terminology so that the jury could understand the witnesses and the lawyers as they talked about it. And I said, I do not want the expert to be prepared by either side or asked any questions about his opinions or conclusions about how the issues in this case should be resolved. This was going to be a court-appointed expert whose sole task would be to help the jurors understand the evidence in the case. As a result of this quite successful experiment I began to see a connection between what lawyers do in a trial and what experts do. After all, lawyers are experts. They go to a specialized school. They become familiar with typical fact patterns from case books and from their experience in trying other cases. On the basis of that training, study, and experience they become adept in recognizing the logical commonsense questions that ought to be asked in all sorts of situations that typically arise in lawsuits, and as a result, I tell the jurors, they speed up the process of thinking about the case, remembering the key pieces of evidence, and understanding the arguments that can be made about a particular set of facts. In the end the lawyers and the other experts in the case are doing what you'll have to do as a finder of fact— whether you are a judge or a jury—which is apply reason and common sense to determine what the facts are, who's telling the truth, and what conclusions should be drawn. And it's pretty much the same with experts. You say about the experts as you say about the lawyers, that in the end it depends on whether they make sense: their opinions aren't binding on you, they are doing more or less the same thing that you're doing, but they have the advantage of having gone to school and seen this kind of situation before, so they can speed up the process of thinking about the facts and suggest to you commonsense considerations that it would otherwise have taken your jurors a long time to come up with.

FL: Is the issue of expert credentials or degrees important to you?

CS: As far as I am concerned, your credentials are less important than your ability to give the jurors reasons that are suggested to you by your training and experience that the jurors can understand and accept or reject.

FL: Do you think that the Daubert analyses of expert testimony have been a help or a hindrance to the litigation process?

CS: I happen to think Daubert is pretty jejune, in the sense of being pretty thin and lacking in substance. It hasn't gotten us very far in thinking about expert testimony. If we are really going to address this problem, we have got to deal with ethics. Just as a lawyer cannot vouch for the truth of a witness's testimony, I think we ought to have a rule that an expert cannot say I personally believe in this conclusion and I have these credentials and that's all I have to tell you. An expert, by definition in the law, doesn't know the "right" conclusion or result. He's not a fact witness. All he can do is reach conclusions using reason and common sense, just like jurors, and his conclusions may turn out to be wrong for a whole variety of reasons. Even in expressing his or her opinions, an expert should have to make clear that it's only an opinion that's being expressed. I could easily accept a process in which witnesses, expert witnesses, are unsworn and get to address the jury the way lawyers do at the end of a case.

FL: What are your thoughts about various authorities that often are introduced in employment cases, authorities such as the Uniform Guidelines as well as guidelines suggested by professional and scientific societies?

CS: What if the people who draft the guidelines are themselves prejudiced or do not realize the unconscious motivations that were used to create the tests that they were developing? There ought to be an avenue in the courts to say, wait, Judge, you can't just move the question one step back from a human resources officer to the authorities that human resources officer relied on. The guidelines or authorities may excuse this particular individual from the consequences of doing whatever he or she did, but we've got to confront the possibility that there remain large societal problems that ought to be addressed. So you need to put authorities into perspective.

FL: In the ramp-up to a trial, there are motions filed, reports submitted, and depositions taken. Why do you then need any live trial testimony? Can expert documents serve as well as expert testimony?

CS: The decision-making process takes time and you forget a lot of things. You can be involved in some early stage of the proceeding and get to the trial two years later. What you've learned or the opinions you've formed two years before, with all the other things you've been doing in the interim, trying other cases, is not very likely to have stuck there. To me, it's extraordinarily useful to have the whole thing come together at an event called the trial. I get the information I need at the trial. I sometimes eliminate opening statements, particularly in nonjury trials, by asking for a trial brief. I hold a pretrial conference a week or two before the trial starts, and then we just go right through to the end. I try cases, once I get started, from day to day until it's over.

FL: Judges often use the words *credibility* and *reliability* in describing the testimony of experts. What do those words mean to you?

CS: I don't use the term *credible* to describe expert testimony if I can help it. Remember, if I had it my way, experts wouldn't even be sworn. In my ideal world, I would have a canon of ethics for experts, telling them that there are some things you cannot say as an expert. You cannot say, "I know this is the case." That kind of language, which vouches for the result that an expert is arguing for, seems to me ought to be unethical simply because an expert expressing a conclusion should not pretend to a juror that he knows his conclusion is correct as a matter of fact. He's not a fact witness, and he shouldn't attempt to deceive the jury into thinking that he is one.

FL: So what would you consider to be appropriate expert testimony? Do you care if the expert has actually used a test or a practice him- or herself in other circumstances?

CS: Well, I go back to a school that used to insist that experts first express their opinion by stating that they hold that opinion to a reasonable degree of certainty and then explain to the jury the assumptions and reasonable, common-sense process by which they have arrived at that conclusion. I don't care, really, if the expert has done the same thing him- or herself one hundred times. When an expert says I have done this one hundred times, he is really saying I've done this before and I know what's right and you've got to take it from me. It's like a lawyer saying I've tried hundreds of cases, and take it from me, this man is innocent (or guilty). That kind of conduct, I think, we really have to develop a means of sitting on.

FL: You have suggested several times that in your ideal world you would not have expert witnesses sworn in trial. Why do you feel this way?

CS: I don't swear the lawyers in. For similar reasons I don't see why we swear the experts in. I say to jurors, "These people are offering you their commonsense take on this same body of information that you are being shown as the jury. They are presenting to you opinions, conclusions that may not have occurred to you unless you studied and thought about this and argued about it in deliberations for months. They are jump-starting your thinking by bringing to bear their training as a doctor or whatever to have you look at the right issues and understand how a doctor would think about this injury. This is a complex medical case. You are going to have to look at an operation on a man's head and decide whether it was done competently or incompetently. You may well say, 'How am I possibly going to do that?' Well, we are going to have a doctor come in here and educate you about medicine to the limited extent that you have to know about medicine so that you can think like a doctor and arrive at a commonsense evaluation of a complex medical situation. This is not something you usually do, but think of the situation in which you yourself have to decide whether to accept the doctor's recommendation that you have a surgical procedure. It is possible, with a doctor who takes the time to sit down with you and explain to you the pros and cons of how your brain works or how your heart works, for you to make a reasonable decision whether or not to do it." And if a judge puts the expert in that sort of context, it elevates the expert; it makes the expert in a sense someone that people listen to more closely than they would if one just said the plaintiff has his experts, the defendant's got her experts, and they are just going to take potshots at each other.

FL: What about when scientific evidence is just emerging, when an opinion might be "speculative"?

CS: I am amazed that more experts don't say more often, "No, I don't have an opinion to a reasonable degree about this, because at this stage any opinion would be speculative." I give a charge about speculation and about using reason and common sense to develop a unanimous verdict. I say on the one hand that the only way we can get to unanimous verdicts is by applying what we have in common, mainly logic and common sense, to the evidence we now all have in common. I say don't be emotional or nonrational on the one hand, because you'll never get to a unanimous verdict. And I also say don't speculate, don't guess, don't be hypothetical. I tell the jury that speculation, guesswork, hypothetical thinking may be perfectly all right in some areas, such as on the frontiers of science where there isn't enough information to reach any conclusion one way or the other. But that's not what we're doing here. In a trial there must be evidence sufficient to permit you to draw reasonable conclusions as to whether the case has been proved or not. That kind of charge makes it easy to exclude experts who present speculative conclusions. And it bolsters the expert who refuses to engage in speculative thinking, an expert that comes in and says, "Look—there are a lot of hypotheses here as to how this cancer came about, but there is just not enough information to say to a reasonable degree of certainty that it was one as opposed to another."

FL: Let's change topics again. As you know, many Title VII cases devolve into arguments about "alternatives." If the plaintiff meets the burden of demonstrating adverse impact and the defendant presents reasonable evidence of job relatedness, then the plaintiff may argue that there was an alternative procedure or assessment device that was equally job related but had lesser adverse impact and should have been used by the employer. Suppose that the plaintiff has no direct evidence that such an alternative has ever been used but simply speculates that such an alternative *could have* been used. How do you weigh such testimony?

CS: Calling it speculation may be an improper use of the term. A reasonably available alternative with less adverse impact must refer to something that would have occurred to a reasonable employer as an alternative based on the information available at the time. The fact that the alternative has never been used in actual practice tends to undercut an argument that a reasonable person would have thought of it. On the other hand there has to be a first time for every new practice. So the fact that a particular technique hasn't been used before doesn't mean that by definition it is speculative. Speculation exists where there is no evidence whatsoever that something will work, and you simply guess or speculate that it will. Not having a prior instance of using a particular technique means that you lack evidence from practice that it will work. But if common sense makes obvious that the technique would work, then the fact that it hasn't been used before shouldn't in and of itself rule the idea out as a solution to an adverse impact situation.

FL: What about credentials? Do you care if the expert is on the faculty of Queens College or Harvard?

CS: I think credentials ought to play a less important role than they do at present. I think it is an unfortunate practice to try to overwhelm either the adversary or the juries with credentials. We tell lawyers, don't put before the jury the fact that you're from Legal Aid. We say to plaintiff's lawyers, don't keep emphasizing the fact that the defendant is represented by a prestigious law firm. Don't get into your personal character, who you are. Don't make the lawsuit turn on whether we like you or don't like you. I think a witness's credentials are addressed first of all to the judge to determine whether to qualify the witness, whether to permit the witness to come before the jury and express his opinion. Once you have gotten through the qualification process, the witnesses' credentials really ought to play a lesser role in the jury's or the fact finder's evaluation.

FL: So you are saying, in your experience, you first decide to qualify an expert, then you really pay very little attention to what led to that decision and you listen to the substance of his or her testimony. Is that right?

CS: I look for a witness who makes sense. I don't care where he or she is employed.

FL: What about educational credentials versus practical experience? Does one count more than the other for you or for a jury?

CS: If you can get it down to a particular reasoning process in which the academic witness is more likely to miss the commonsense argument as to why this test is valid or invalid, then the practitioner prevails. But there are other instances in which the more theoretical argument makes more sense. But that ought to be shown in the reasoning process, not by name-calling about who went to the better school or has more years on the job. I have never heard anyone even propose to put before the jury the fact that their lawyer went to Harvard and was on Law Review. The same should be true with experts. I think you might say to an expert, bring your credentials down to where it matters and let the jury decide about the arguments you are presenting here, and then we can go into it. Don't tell me about who is your employer. Let's not hear about it.

FL: What about statistics? Statistical testimony, particularly about adverse impact, can be very sophisticated and complex. Does it help or hinder the finder of fact?

CS: I value statistics for illuminating situations of unintended consequences or unconscious discrimination that nobody knew they were engaging in. Statistics, if used properly and honestly and in a straightforward way, can reveal situations in which someone is being hurt that nobody knew was being hurt, detecting situations of discrimination that nobody recognizes or if they recognize they wouldn't admit to. I think that most discrimination is unconscious. It is not intentional. It's not even necessarily a result of negligence. It's just an injury that somebody commits against another person or group inadvertently, and it has to be corrected by litigation, usually involving damages of one sort or another.

FL: Many employment litigation complaints revolve around arguments about *fairness* or *justice*. Are those concepts important in how you decide a case?

CS: There are an awful lot of complaints about unfairness in the world that are getting into the funnel of discrimination litigation. They don't all belong there. Fairness is not really a legal issue. It is an issue best worked out between an employer and an employee, or a union and an employer. The courts are often involved as a substitute for genuine discussion.

FL: So if complaints about fairness appear with some regularity, and there is no clear Title VII foundation for the claim, will the judiciary ignore the complaints or will they open an avenue for these complaints to be heard?

CS: Well, I can tell you one thing that is developing in the law is equal protection litigation.

FL: Do you mean Fourteenth Amendment claims?

CS: Right. If the courts don't come up with some relief for all of these unfair injuries which are not traceable precisely to age or traceable precisely to race, that are staring everybody in the face, it is inevitable that someone's going to devise a remedy or cause of action which will begin to address the rage that people feel about being treated terribly. The unions don't come in to help. The union often gets joined as a defendant for failing to deal with it. I think it may well end up being the responsibility of the courts, by default, to devise new claims or causes of action. Simply because Congress and the administrative agencies are doing nothing does not mean that the judiciary will not enter the fray.

FL: The concept of justice is becoming more salient to I-O psychologists in describing the "experience" of work. Is justice in the workplace salient to judges?

CS: I used to have on my desk a clipping from a New York paper about an employee who went up into IBM headquarters upstate and blew away all of his superiors over some job dispute. I used the clipping at the time to get my law clerks to stop using the phrase "frivolous lawsuit" because these lawsuits are not frivolous to the complainants. To call them frivolous simply exacerbates the rage of a person who is already feeling aggrieved.

FL: Assessment experts often point to test score results as a fair way of deciding who gets a job offer. Sometimes, there are only 1- or 2-point differences between those who get offers and those who do not. What do you think about that?

CS: Well, my reaction is to take that question back to your profession and say I seriously doubt that the equipment that you have to identify the best and the brightest is as reliable as you think it is. You really have to recognize that you can only go so far in identifying who is the best employee and that after that you ought to go into some other alternate means of selecting people that promotes diversity or promotes overall fairness. You can, in other words, establish to a reasonable degree of certainty that a particular test is job related. I don't think that is the same thing as saying you can pick "the best" applicant.

FL: Well, let's get more directly to the issue of diversity in a workforce. Do you value diversity or is it irrelevant in your opinion?

CS: I am in favor of diversity. I think it is beneficial to everyone involved. Diversity brings to bear different perspectives on things that may not occur to people in a homogeneous society. I remember thinking at the end of the women firefighters' litigation that the examination of the job of firefighting from the perspective of the so-called weaker sex exposed aspects of firefighting that could be improved to everyone's benefit. Lightening the Scott airpack made the job easier for both men and women; made it possible for men who might have failed the physical test even though they passed the mental test with flying colors to pass both parts of the test and qualify for a job that otherwise they might have lost. Fire is a force that can overwhelm the strongest as well as the weaker, as the World Trade Center has taught us. Having the women firefighters force all of us to focus on the real physical requirements of the job and on alternatives with less adverse impact was a wonderful thing. This is just an illustration of the myriad of insights we get when we add new perspectives in the workplace. And one way to get new perspectives is to invite in people from different backgrounds.

Harold Baer Jr.
United States District Court Judge,
Southern District of New York
December 12, 2003

FL: Do you have any experience in hearing testimony from industrial and organizational psychologists in Title VII cases?

HB: I don't; that doesn't mean that there aren't other judges who do; I don't remember using an expert in a Title VII case. I may be wrong but not by much, and in terms of the sort of psychologist-type witnesses or testimony, I have no recollection of ever having used any of them. And further, just so you understand how it works at least in this district, I have probably as many of these cases as any of my fellow judges, but I have probably settled or mediated and resolved 80 percent of them. So in terms of trial, I've probably had an average of three a year, and that may be high.

FL: When you think back over your Title VII and 1983 cases, what are the issues that you recall as significant?

HB: With respect to the discrimination cases, I suppose my first focus is an effort to determine if the plaintiff has met the prima facie case requirements. If those requirements are met, I then concentrate on the proof that the defendant provides or goes forward with as to a legitimate excuse for the apparent discrimination. A common overlay is always whether there is any discriminatory animus, because frequently there are people that are clearly hurt by activities but there is almost always an excuse, and very often the excuse is simply that the budget didn't allow us to keep this person and she was one of twenty-five we let go, and so finding any discrimination is the focus of my attention. I do not equate discrimination with the fact that an individual may experience a negative experience with an employer.

FL: In many Title VII cases, one or both sides will introduce various authorities to structure their case. One common authority is represented by the Uniform Guidelines promulgated by the federal government. Other authorities are promulgated by professional or scientific societies. Do such authorities play an important role in your consideration of the complaint?

HB: Well, generally, I guess, I pay attention to anything lawyers provide me that's helpful. If there are guidelines, I would look at them if they were provided, but frankly I don't find a lot of lawyers providing me with any of that kind of help. Basically, I prefer to cut to the chase. Lawyers pretty much do the same kind of analyses I mentioned earlier—the prima facie case and the explanations for any actions that were taken. The defendant will usually agree to most of the facts being true. At the same time, the defendant might argue over qualifications of a job, but very rarely do they spend a great deal of time arguing the basic facts. Instead they will attempt to show that there was a legitimate reason for why this employee was discharged. The plaintiff comes back and tries to say that is a lot of baloney, and generally I suppose that's the way I look at it. It is mostly facts and logic. Was the reason provided by the defendant for the discharge a legitimate one or a pretext for discrimination?— That's the basic question.

FL: In the cases you have been alluding to up until now, I think you have been thinking of single plaintiff or individual plaintiff actions. Have you had much experience in class action suits?

HB: Anytime I avoid a class action of any sort, I feel fortunate. I have not had many. Usually, they get resolved before trial.

FL: Many, if not most, civil cases never get to trial. They are either settled through a mediation process, often involving the judge, or dismissed on summary judgment. In your experience, why is it that some cases do not settle and proceed to trial?

HB: Well, most commonly, a senior person for the defendant firm will say that is ridiculous; we didn't do anything wrong here and we are going to trial. Often in a Title VII case, there is a significant corporate defendant who is concerned about whether this will set some kind of precedential value and bring on lots more lawsuits by other people, other employees, who either believed [they were] or actually were discriminated against on the same basis.

FL: What about the public versus private status of a defendant? If the defendant is a publicly held company, do you think there is any additional pressure on them to settle from shareholders or stock analysts?

HB: I'd have to think about that. My gut feeling is that publicly held corporations have a significant number of additional regulations and people looking over their shoulder and stockholders too and might have the feeling that they really ought to try this case where they think they are right. I have also found that where there are large financial gains and losses for both defendant and plaintiff, a trial is more likely. For example, where a vice president making five hundred thousand dollars a year thinks she was not promoted because she was a female, so the amount of money involved is substantial, I think [that] makes a significant difference in whether the case can be settled or not. If we are talking about a lower-level employee, I usually am able to mediate those cases. It is easier for the parties to see how much money would be spent on litigation that could have been used for settlement. Sometimes plaintiffs cannot even afford a lawyer. Happily, we have a program that we just initiated a couple of years ago in which we supply lawyers for mediation where there is a plaintiff who is representing him- or herself in an employment discrimination case.

FL: What about public versus private sector employers? Do you think public sector employers are less likely to settle because of the possible political fallout from not fighting a charge of discrimination? Do you think that it may be more politically expedient to have a judge make the decision rather than a public official?

HB: No, I don't see those pressures. If we take New York City as an example, it is often the city controller who must make the decision on whether or not to settle, not an agency head or a manager. In addition, assistant corporation counsel are paid monthly. They don't get five hundred dollars per hour, so the city has already accepted the cost of the legal staff. There are no additional monies involved in the legal costs. These people are going to be there, they are going to get their money anyway, and so the city sometimes figures why don't we roll the dice and see what happens; it's not going to be a major extra expenditure unless there is a big verdict and we don't think there will be.

FL: Judicial opinions will often use the word *credible*, or *not credible*, to characterize expert witness testimony. Do you often use that word? And if so, what meaning do you intend?

HB: Well, I would say I use the word *credible* more than I do *incredible* or *not credible*. When I use the term *not credible* or *incredible*, I often mean to connote that I do not believe the person. I must admit that on the infrequent occasions when I do use the term *incredible*, I am seeing a certain willfulness on the part of the expert. Now, I don't mean to say that the expert is actually trying to deceive me or to lie, but I am not sure the testimony actually tracks or follows from the facts of the case. And of course I must admit that the term *credible* is used for several other reasons as well. First, it has always been used in opinions, it is almost a term of art, so sometimes it is used because it is a throwaway phrase. And it also signals to the circuit court of appeals that you did listen to the testimony. But if you characterize it as either credible or not credible, it would be very difficult for the circuit to remand a case on appeal, at least based on some argument based on what the expert said.

FL: By the time you actually come into the courtroom to hear a case, there have been many motions filed, status conferences, etc. You have before you 95 percent of what might be said in trial. Why bother with live testimony from experts?

HB: Well, the jury has heard or seen none of that.

FL: Of course you're right about a jury, but what about a bench trial?

HB: I am hard put to remember the last bench trial I had, if I ever had one. Since I have been in this building, I think that almost every Title VII or 1983 case has involved a jury.

FL: And there have not been many of those cases either, have there been? It appears that most of the cases either settle or are dismissed on a motion.

HB: Yes, that's true. I hear very few. Usually, I take care of most of the cases right here at the table where we are now sitting. I bring the parties in and try to help them see the value of a settlement rather than the time and expense of a trial. I sat across the street for ten years (in the Supreme Court) and here for nine years, so I have had a lot of practice in mediating.

FL: In what way do you consider the credentials of an expert, from either a qualifying or a Daubert perspective?

HB: I try to prevent the lawyers from going into a long description of the credentials of an expert. They can submit the
CV and I will probably admit the expert. I set the bar fairly
low. The jury may receive the CV as well, but I doubt that
they ever look at it. The lawyers may bring credentials
up again in a number of subtle ways, and I can see what
they're trying to do, but I go ahead and let them. I think
it's a waste of time and it doesn't influence me much, but
I don't stop it. The only important thing to me with the
expert is whether he or she can actually explain complex
issues in a way that I (and the jury) can understand. I don't
care if they come from Harvard or Brooklyn College. Once
I have admitted them as experts, the only thing I care about
is what they have to say.

Fern M. Smith
United States District Judge,
Northern District of California
February 2, 2004

FL: Has it been your experience that you deal with more individual employment actions than class actions?

FS: Yes, pretty much, and nobody gets fired for cause anymore;
everybody gets fired for some discriminatory reason.

FL: Does it appear that the courts are becoming an avenue of
last resort for unhappy employees?

FS: Well, I think the courts are being suffocated. I mean,
frankly, one of the complaints that I hear right now is that
the percentage in a normal docket that is now employment
discrimination continues to grow and grow and grow. I
think there is a feeling that a lot of the employment discrimination cases are weak or may even be without merit.
More and more plaintiffs are now representing themselves,
without legal counsel. The reason for that may very well
be that many lawyers see these cases as without merit and
won't take them. Of course many cases—even when the
plaintiff represents him- or herself—do have merit, but losing a job is such a traumatic event that I think individuals

are sometimes driven by emotion to file a case. And because it is such an emotional issue, they don't represent themselves as well as they might have been represented by a lawyer. Some circuits, the ninth circuit as an example, bend over backwards to permit individuals to represent themselves. So we, the judges, are often caught in the middle when the individual represents him- or herself. It's not our role to be an advocate, especially if it's a jury trial where if it might appear that we are siding with the plaintiff. On the other hand, if you want the case to end, you have got to do something to help it along.

FL: To put it most simply, do you think that everyone is entitled to their day in court?

FS: Yes, a day. But not a week or a month.

FL: How do you decide which cases arrive in the courtroom to have "their day"?

FS: By granting summary judgment motions on issues that are clear. We have some relatively clear guidelines in the circuit regarding what issues can be decided on summary judgment. This helps clear the calendar of many cases. We can also urge the parties to settle rather than going to trial. Sometimes a trial is almost a last resort in some of these cases.

FL: How do you use your magistrate judges?

FS: Our magistrate judges do a tremendous amount of settlement conferences as well as handling their own dockets. We have additional mechanisms of alternative dispute resolution, such as the courts of arbitration, mediation. In addition there are lawyers who donate a certain amount of their services and time to acting as mediators.

FL: Have you ever dealt with an expert witness in statistics or human resources in an employment case?

FS: No, because they really were cases where I have felt either I or a jury could determine who was telling the truth or what really happened in a he said–she said type case. More to the point the lawyers in those cases did not introduce expert testimony of statisticians or human resource experts, and I saw no need to bring one in on my request. Most of my cases have been disparate treatment claims, not disparate impact claims.

FL: Have you ever heard of the discipline of industrial and organizational psychology?

FS: Oh sure. I have some acquaintances who I would consider industrial psychologists, who come in and help companies come up with better relations and better performance criteria. Actually, I am not sure they are psychologists. They may be management consultants. But I should say that even though an industrial psychologist has never testified before me, I would have no hesitancy in using an industrial psychologist if someone told me that it would be helpful to have someone testify in this regard. I am not hesitant about using experts when I think I can learn something. In some cases, technical ones such as patent cases, I am sometimes lost in the complexities of the technology. When that happens, I'll have technical people come in: for example, scientists to explain how genetic splicing works or how semiconductor processing works or that kind of thing. The purpose of introducing such an expert would be to help me understand the background of what went on and so that I can make intelligent decisions rather than to say one side should win and the other should lose.

FL: You have addressed a scenario where you, the judge, bring in an expert. What about when experts are introduced by the parties who do offer opinions regarding which side is "right"? What are your reactions to that type of situation?

FS: I have a healthy skepticism because I think experts are not impervious to becoming advocates, and I think in most cases they do become advocates. It's very easy to get caught up in advocacy. It's a sexy kind of a business, and it's a contest, and the lawyers use their experts in that way. There was a project done by the Federal Judicial Center that addressed exactly this issue [Krafka et al., 2002]. The biggest criticism that federal judges have about experts is that they are not neutral. They become caught up in the game as it were. So, unless it is someone in whom I have a great deal of faith for a variety of reasons—either I've read

stuff by this person or I know this person by reputation—
I don't give a lot of weight to experts. I had a very big intellectual property case, and it involved several pioneer
patents and potentially hundreds of million of dollars in
royalties. Each side put on a PhD with sterling credentials,
qualifications, etc. And one basically said black and one
said white—well, how am I supposed to judge this? You
know, is Yale better than Harvard, is anybody better than
Stanford, my alma mater? Do I look at the cut of their suit?
Is their grammar better than the other's? That's a really
tough choice to ask a judge to make when you've got people with incredibly good credentials who have looked at
the same documents and the same facts and who are up
to date in the same science and opine in completely different ways.

FL: Do you ever use the term *credible* when referring to the
testimony of experts? And if you do, what do you mean by
that term?

FS: I do use the term, and I can mean a couple of different
things. Sometimes I mean that he is just a liar. That's the
worst. Sometimes what it means is that the expert has made
too big a jump from the analysis that was done to the opinion and there is a gap. I would be likely to say that this type
of leap is not credible. I don't know how you got from A
to D. You have left out B and C. A third application of the
term *credible* is that the expert may not have done his or her
analysis in a respectable way.

Another instance of credibility is when an expert testifies well beyond his or her area of expertise. You might have
a perfectly respectable obstetrician who may be board certified, who starts opining on what silicone does in the breast.
Well, it's a different field. You are very qualified here, but
your qualifications aren't strong enough to get you over
there. I may believe anything you'd say about difficult pregnancies and uterine pregnancies or whatever, but what you
have to say about silicone in the breast just doesn't ring true.

FL: Do you think a role for an expert witness is to help jurors
understand why a particular behavior may have occurred?

FS: No, in fact I think you have to be careful about it because then you get off and it's really collateral. It doesn't matter why; it just matters that it is.

FL: Do you, as a trial judge, have discretion in considering and applying precedents to a case at hand?

FS: At an evidentiary level we have tremendous discretion, and so if you can explain yourself well enough on the record as a trial judge, you can do a tremendous amount—I mean unless there is a bright-line precedent out there on evidence. For example, an expert may not testify as to the state of mind of the criminal defendant. That's just a given. That's not going to change. But scientific knowledge does change. One of the real problems that judges have is the fact that science keeps [moving] faster and faster and so it's hard for us to keep up with it. On one day there may not be general acceptance that this theory that you've proposed makes any sense whatsoever. Six months from that day, when that case hits the ninth circuit or the third circuit, maybe there is some viable evidence. At trial there may have been too big an analytical leap between the method the expert used and the conclusion he reached. It is conceivable that by the time that case gets up to the circuit, this gap has narrowed.

FL: How do you go about resolving or dealing with Daubert challenges?

FS: I think the best way is to have the opposing experts in the courtroom out of the presence of a jury and just go at them and see if you can try and figure it out. In intellectual property and patent cases I often conduct a special hearing. I call it a *tutorial*. I allow each side to bring in one expert of their choice. I close the courtroom. The only ones permitted into the courtroom are the lawyers, the experts, my clerks, and me. There is no record—no court reporter. Nothing that is said in that hearing can be used against any party as an admission or anything else. Nobody is put under oath, and I give each side some period of time for the expert to basically tell me what his or her theory is, his or her understanding of the science, and then the experts may ask each other questions. The lawyers may cross-examine the opposing expert. This has become quite popular among judges in this courthouse and circuit.

FL: Have you ever instructed lawyers to simply submit their experts' reports as the direct testimony and moved immediately to cross-examination without oral testimony on direct?

FS: I have done that. I don't do it in jury trials, but I've done it in bench trials. I don't see any substantial value in expert direct testimony in a bench trial as long as there is live cross-examination. On the other hand, direct testimony permits [people] to use visual aids in a way that is more effective than simply the written word.

FL: What are the characteristics or behaviors of expert witnesses that impress you favorably?

FS: I guess I tend to be most impressed when there is a witness who is willing to, number one, answer the tough questions, not answer the question the witness wants to answer but answer the question I ask or that the lawyer asks, and number two, is willing to admit the weakness in his or her theory or the party's case but then goes on to explain reasonably why that weakness is not material in this particular case. Once a judge has had to direct the expert witness several times to answer the question that has been posed, the judge becomes suspicious of that witness.

If a witness starts by answering yes or no and says, "Yes, generally, but, Your Honor, this question really needs some further explanation. May I explain further?" I would typically say yes. And then if in fact the witness really goes on to be helpful in expanding on the answer, then, you see, he has won some credibility with me. If on the other hand he says, "I really need to explain," and then just dances around and tries to weasel out, then the next time he says, "May I explain?" I'll just say no.

FL: Are you influenced by the credentials of an expert? Where they received their training or the institution with which they are affiliated?

FS: I probably would consider that as a factor at least, but not the most important factor or the only factor. Yes, I am probably more influenced by someone who comes out of

Harvard Medical School or Stanford Medical School than I am by someone who comes out of Western Illinois Medical College. That doesn't mean the person from Western Illinois can't overcome that, but all things being equal, if there is a major difference in credentials, the person with the better blue ribbon may have a slight edge.

To some extent the same principle holds for jurors in considering dueling experts. Jurors don't really sit and watch these people day in and day out, so the topics being addressed by the experts are foreign to the jurors. The jurors are trying to do the best they can, and credentials can seem very objective to the jurors. They can understand credentials. Everyone has heard of Yale and everyone has heard of Harvard and everyone has heard of Princeton, and at least in San Francisco, everyone has heard of Stanford, and so credentials do often make a difference to jurors.

FL: How about an expert from within the defendant organization as opposed to an outside expert? Does that make a difference to you?

FS: Well, I think that there is an assumption that in most cases an inside expert is not going to dump on the corporation. But then again, I think most of us now assume that a paid, retained expert isn't going to dump on the party who hired him either. I would say that I think most judges are skeptical about people whose primary source of income is from expert testifying. I don't often see people who are professionally or scientifically active as well as full-time expert witnesses. I basically see the professional hired gun who now has his own consulting company. There are some exceptions, but they are few and far between. What you often run into are people who had a good reputation either as a practitioner or as an academic and then were retained as an expert and suddenly realized that this is a whole new world. Then three years later, they're not teaching anymore, maybe they are an adjunct professor but they are not writing or publishing or they're not really running a practice, and they are making several hundred thousand dollars a year just testifying. Am I skeptical, more skeptical of those people? Yes.

Richard A. Posner
Circuit Judge,
U.S. Court of Appeals for the Seventh Circuit
Senior Lecturer, University of Chicago Law School
April 1, 2004

FL: If you consider the three arenas of science, practice, and the law, how might they be temporally arranged? Does science develop too fast or too slow for the law?

RP: The law is going to lag practice and science, but the order of practice and science is not rigid; there are practices that are the result of scientific research. Many products, services, and activities that are products of scientific or other academic thinking find their way into practice.

FL: What are your thoughts on Type I and Type II errors in trials? Orthodox science commonly concentrates on minimizing Type I errors. Do the courts behave similarly?

RP: It depends on the situation. We worry a lot about Type I errors in criminal cases because acquitting a certain number of guilty people is not regarded as equal in harm to convicting the innocent. Even in civil cases the plaintiff has a burden of proof, so that may be weighting Type I error slightly more heavily than Type II.

FL: How about in employment discrimination cases. Is the relative importance of Type I versus Type II error related at all to the type of job in question? Is the risk of harm in hiring a less-than-effective police officer or airline pilot considered greater than hiring a less effective retail store cashier?

RP: Not really. On one hand, if the firm is falsely found to be engaged in discrimination, that's a cost to the firm, but if the individual is mistakenly denied relief, that's an equivalent injury. As I said earlier, the plaintiff has the burden of proof and that implicitly weights the Type I errors a little more heavily, but I don't think it is a big factor.

FL: In an opinion, you wrote, "the courtroom is not the place for scientific guesswork no matter how inspired." What is your objection to inspired scientific guesswork?

RP: Because it can't be tested. It might be an inspired scientific guess, but the courts don't have the resources to do the actual testing. This becomes even more problematic when there are opposing experts engaging in inspired scientific guesswork. How can the court decide which "inspiration" is more compelling without testing or data related to the two positions?

FL: But in many areas of science, speculation is often valued highly. As an example, many of the sciences publish what is known as an *annual review*. In this publication expert scientists are asked to review the past research on a topic and draw conclusions that may not have been drawn before and to speculate with respect to trend lines that emerge from the review.

RP: If all an annual review does is summarize what has been published in the previous year, that's unexceptionable. If instead it is speculative—glancing ahead—the problem for the judge is, how am I supposed to evaluate that? And of course I would wonder if this "speculation" was fueled by the retainer fee from the side for which he was testifying.

FL: What about simply using a court-appointed expert to sort it all out? Wouldn't such an expert be considered neutral?

RP: Sometimes there are no genuine neutrals, or the genuine neutrals aren't real experts; and if the neutral gets into an argument with the party experts, and he's speculating, and they're questioning his speculations, that's going to be a problem for the judge.

FL: How are you using the word *neutral*? Does that mean that he or she has no opinion on the matter at hand?

RP: When I use the term *neutral,* I mean the expert is neutral in a sense that he is not beholden to either party.

FL: But he may very well be aligned with either of those parties, not because he is being paid but because the research he has done convinces him that one or the other party is correct in their assertions.

RP: That can be minimized with a simple procedure—simply have the parties' experts agree on a third expert. Neither party is going to agree to someone who is aligned with the other party.

FL: Are you implying that using such a procedure, you would find someone whose position actually fell midway between the two experts?

RP: No, I wouldn't put it that way, because it might well be that one of the extreme positions was clearly wrong and the other clearly right. The point is rather that if you can find a neutral in the sense of someone who doesn't have a stake in the case, then that's the person you can trust, at least to be unbiased by any connection to one side or the other. That neutral might say that A is right or B is right. And actually, if the neutral takes an intermediate position, he doesn't really help the judge very much.

FL: Would you ever consider appointing several neutral experts who represent various points on a continuum stretching from the plaintiff's expert to the defendant's expert?

RP: Well, how is the judge going to arbitrate the disagreements among the neutrals? I am back where I started, with disagreements between the retained experts. I've done a couple of patent cases recently with very distinguished experts who had very different views on the same question. It is difficult for a judge to figure out which is telling the truth. You look for signals—which one is better prepared, did one of them make a mistake, does one of them seem less informed than the other, did either arrive at his conclusions in a seemingly careless fashion. That is about all you can do. Now these were not neutral experts. At least with a neutral, the element of being beholden to the person who hired you falls out of the picture.

FL: Let me ask you to consider an area in our field, industrial and organizational psychology, in which extrapolation is done. There is a model or doctrine known as *validity generalization*. This model, based on thousands of studies of thousands of occupations over a period of fifty years, holds that virtually any job that exists requires some nontrivial amount of general mental ability to be completed successfully. Suppose that an employer wanted to hire workers for a job that was not part of the original database, for example the job of a cell phone repair technician.

RP: Let me ask a preliminary question before you continue. What do you mean by *nontrivial*?

FL: Correlations ranging in the vicinity of +.30 between general mental ability and job performance.

RP: That's a modest amount. But regardless of its value, there must be some jobs like cell phone repair technician in the database.

FL: You used the word *like* in your response.

RP: Is that a hard question? It doesn't sound like a hard question. What is the difference between repairing a cell phone and repairing a telephone? There must be telephone repairmen in the database.

FL: For the sake of discussion, let's say there are telephone repair technicians in the database, but these jobs were analyzed in 1960 and 1970. If the defendant were to attempt to extrapolate from that earlier database, would you permit such extrapolation as expert testimony?

RP: Well, you would certainly allow the testimony in. Then the plaintiff would have the right to argue, perhaps, that cell phones are simpler to repair than telephones. I don't see that as a problem.

FL: But let me take this a step further. Suppose the expert for the defendant said that he or she had never actually analyzed the job of cell phone repair technician and based his or her opinion on the doctrine of validity generalization as I described earlier.

RP: I would think it would be appropriate for him to present the data for telephone repair and then someone else can testify about the differences between cell phones and telephones. In fact that is a better way to do it, because the psychologist doesn't know anything about the difference between cell phones and telephones. That is an engineering question, not an IQ question.

FL: So our hypothetical expert would simply testify that the test in question was a reasonable example of a test of general mental ability, as those types of tests existed in the validity generalization database, and a second expert would testify about the differences and similarities between traditional telephone repair and cell phone repair.

RP: Right, sure.

FL: I will change directions here a bit. The Federal Judicial Center published a report in 2002 that described the discomfort of judges with expert testimony. One of these discomforts was related to a possible mismatch between the competencies of the opposing experts. Do you agree that this is a problem?

RP: It certainly is a problem, especially in a jury case. The jurors will have difficulty understanding the issues, and so they will be grasping for signals, and often they will find these signals in very superficial characteristics of the witnesses. But even in a nonjury trial, if there is a real difference in competence, rather than just in ability to articulate a position, the judge will find it hard to make an adjustment for that difference.

FL: If it were clear to you that one expert was considerably less competent than another and this one side was not being well represented in the expert phase of the case, would you consider a court-appointed expert?

RP: No, I don't think so, because the long-run effects of that would be bad. You would have a situation in which one person goes out and hires the best expert, and the other person says, well, I'm not going to spend a lot of money on an expert; I'll hire someone more within my budget, and look to the judge to appoint the expert.

FL: Could you ever imagine jurors being permitted to directly question an expert?

RP: Oh sure.

FL: Have you ever done that?

RP: Yes.

FL: You let them ask questions directly or through the court?

RP: I permit them to ask question with one constraint. I instruct them and the witness that the witness is not to answer immediately, in order to give the lawyers an opportunity to object. But with the exception of that one constraint, it is fine for the jurors to ask questions. They tend not to, but they like knowing that they can ask the question. It makes them feel they are being treated as more active participants in the trial process.

FL: I know that you accept John Dewey's philosophical notion of distributed intelligence. Is the willingness to allow jurors to question witnesses an endorsement of that principle of distributed intelligence?

RP: Yes, but largely with respect only to matters that are part of their experience. If the case is about biochemistry or about statistics or something equally beyond the ordinary experience of jurors, then unless you have very unusual jurors you are not going to have anyone who will bring relevant knowledge to the table.

FL: Would you permit experts to question each other directly without having to go through lawyers?

RP: I think that would be fine. In nonjury cases I ask the experts a lot of questions, so I get a pretty good idea of their different views, but I imagine it would also be useful if they could talk directly to each other in the judge's presence. It wouldn't work in a jury case, but in a bench trial it would.

FL: In several instances, both in scholarly writing and in judicial opinions, you seem to take a dim view of academics who offer expert testimony. The impression I get is that you feel that there are few checks and balances to keep the academic from testifying irresponsibly. Could you further elaborate on that position?

RP: There's no accountability, because whatever stupid thing or exaggeration they say in the courtroom is not going to reflect on their academic standing. There is no real feedback from their litigation forays into their academic careers, so they don't have real discipline. And on the other hand they are going to know what the score is in the court, because the lawyer who hired them is going to explain exactly what they have to do to be an effective witness, and they'll be well paid, and the lawyers will work hard to make them feel part of the "team." Cross-examination amplifies that effect. In cross-examination you are being needled by the opponent, and it makes you state your opinion more strongly. Psychologically, cross-examination makes you want to identify more strongly with the person who hired you, who has become your friend—and now an enemy is taking potshots at you. I believe that this type of academic expert witness knows exactly what he or she is doing in the courtroom—but it is not academic work. Unlike the academic arena, the witness will have been instructed by his lawyer not to qualify his opinions, to take strong positions, to simplify, etc. They would not do these things in their normal academic work.

FL: Have you ever heard an expert say, "I don't know"?

RP: In an adversarial situation there are checks, and an expert witness can sometimes be forced into making certain concessions, but he will be reluctant to do so. In most cases his lawyer will tell him, "Whatever you do, don't make concessions that could be used against us." So the expert learns to testify in a different way, not the way an academic would speak in an academic setting. It's a different forum, with different rules, different expectations, and if academics are effective witnesses it is because they have made this transition from the academic world and understand the courtroom is a different world.

FL: I know you are concerned with the credibility of expert witnesses. Doesn't the publication record of an individual, what he or she has said in print, act as a safeguard against distorted or exaggerated testimony?

RP: Yes, to some extent, their paper record can act as a check against noncredible testimony. But of course, when a lawyer is shopping for an expert witness, he looks at the prospective witness's paper record. You are not going to hire someone who would be easily demolished on cross-examination by being confronted with his previous publications.

FL: In scholarly publications you have described the expert shopping exercise as an example of Type I error, implying that it is difficult to consider the person who actually appears to testify as representative of a domain of knowledge. Can you elaborate?

RP: Sure. They may have to go through twenty resumes before they find someone whom they can ask. That equates to the five times out of one hundred that you observe a phenomenon as a result of chance alone.

FL: In scholarly publications and in at least one judicial opinion, you have suggested that scientific and professional organizations publish the names of their members who have testified as experts, as well as the substance of that testimony. Can you elaborate on that a bit? What purpose would that serve?

RP: What I envisioned was the professional organization posting on its Web site the list of the consulting and testimonial activities of its members in the last year, with a link to the actual testimony, since more and more evidence is online or could be placed online. The professional or scientific organization could obtain public copies of documents so there would be some kind of archive, either electronic or paper, in which anyone who was interested could track the expert witness activities of these people year after year.

FL: To what end?

RP: One purpose would simply be to see to what extent a person's focus of activity had shifted from academic work to expert witness work.

FL: Why would that be important?

RP: Because the more a person is engaged in the practice world as opposed to the academic world, the less he is going to be held in check by considerations of academic reputation, because he is shifting into another sphere of activity; there will be less of an academic publication record to compare his testimonial positions with. He is also likely not to be as productive and not to keep up as much in his field if he is spending a lot of time as a consultant. In addition, if the person's testimony is readily available to his colleagues, other interested persons, and lawyers, he is more likely to be honest in his testimony. It will be easy to compare his testimony with his earlier testimony and his academic work in search of possible inconsistencies.

FL: But lawyers could do that through discovery whether such a Web page existed or not.

RP: I don't see the lawyers as the primary consumers. I see university officials and colleagues as the target audience.

FL: And would you expect those university officials and colleagues and members of professional organizations then to take some kind of action to address this issue of accountability?

RP: Well, I see an immediate implication for those experts who are employed full time by a university—and I am thinking more about the very fact of testifying than about the substance of the testimony. Many universities have a limit on outside activities of their professors, such as one day a week. It may be that the sheer volume of outside testifying might call for an investigation. But the more important point would simply be that the university and colleagues could keep track. They could, if they wanted to, ask questions about the testimony: is it scientifically responsible, is it consistent with the genuine scientific commitments of the expert, has this person become an advocate and a lawyer rather than a scientist? It is a sunshine sort of thing. I am not suggesting sanctions or punishments. Simply having the testimony readily available to anyone interested will have the effect of inhibiting dishonest testimony. If experts know that this aspect of their lives is public, they'll be more careful both in what they do and how much time they allot to expert witness activities.

FL: But wouldn't such activity by professional and scientific organizations open them up to becoming experts themselves? Can you imagine an official of the professional or scientific body being called as a witness and asked about the particular individual's methods, whether the individual has maintained professional standards and the scientific standards of that society?

RP: No I don't think so, because whoever is running the organization is not going to have detailed knowledge of all of the subfields in which people do their work and testify.

FL: But you would think that the major advantage of this is what you call the sunshine advantage, simply making it open, and that the very fact of making it open makes it less likely that someone would testify in a disingenuous way.

RP: I am not limiting my concerns to simply the substance of an expert's testimony. There is a lot of controversy now about the fact that so many biochemists have financial stakes in pharmaceutical companies. That is something that should be public knowledge. These are human beings; they are likely to be influenced by the financial implications of their research. I think academics are excessively secretive about their outside activities.

FL: Why do you suppose that is?

RP: Everybody wants to conceal much of what he does.

FL: Why do you say that?

RP: If someone is making five million dollars a year and is supposed to be a professor, do you think that person would like that fact to be known? Let's use a law professor as an example. The reason he doesn't want it known is that people might say you are obviously getting clients in part because of your reputation as a professor, but what kind of professor are you, because in order to make five million dollars a year in the practice of law requires you to be practicing full time, so as a professor you can't be doing much for your salary. Some scientists have outright conflicts of interest. They have contracts with private firms that influence their research, or they may hesitate to engage in certain types of research that might raise questions about the quality or therapeutic properties of the drugs of the companies in which they are invested. And universities are complicit in these conflicts. Universities are now business firms. And so the leaders of universities often applaud these faculty activities. That's why I think it is best to turn to the professional and scientific organizations to supply the sunshine.

FL: In a scholarly publication you made the point that when an academic testifies, he or she may be incurring a cost that is passed on to society—the cost of not doing scholarly work but instead moonlighting to make some extra money. Can you accept the possibility that the academic, as expert, might actually contribute to society through his or her role in changing a policy?

RP: Yes, I might, in principle. You could have an expert witness who made some significant contribution to a trial and explained things well. The overall impact on society is hard to evaluate. You want trials to be based on good expert testimony; that's a benefit. It also makes these fields more lucrative, so you can attract better people. But there is a distortion here, because expert witness opportunities are very unevenly distributed across fields. If you are in economics there are a lot of opportunities, but if you are in history you wouldn't have any opportunities; so maybe you would get too many economists and too few historians. So it is complicated; I wouldn't put too much weight on loss of overall social value. Nevertheless, I do think there is value in knowing what these people are doing so that a professional community can make a judgment. Maybe the professional society will say that all these economists testifying as experts are actually doing more good in testifying than they are doing in their academic work. But conversely, the judgment might be that these people are able economists who are seduced by the lure of consulting and that they are simply hired guns and they are not doing anything for society.

FL: What about authors of leading textbooks in economics or physics who are academics? Aren't they engaged in the same conflict—using their reputations to make outside income?

RP: Sure. The only difference is that their writing activities will be very well known. But how much time an academic is spending in litigation activities nobody will know, unless they look. And it is not that easy actually; it is not that easy to track down someone and discover all his litigation activities. I grant you that universities like having celebrities on the faculty. It's part of the business orientation of universities. They are managed in a much more professional way than they used to be, and one dimension of professionalism is to exploit all the financial opportunities you have. So if you have a celebrity professor, even if he is not making any academic contribution, you can see him as a source of alumni donations and of publicity that will attract students.

FL: Do you have any objection to the practice of using consulting or nontestifying experts in litigation?

RP: I certainly think there is a role for nontestifying consultants, that they can be very helpful to lawyers, but there is a problem. The problem is a kind of shell game in which the work is done by the consulting economists, and the one who testifies is relying on this work, and maybe what the underlying people who are not being produced as experts did was where the crucial judgments were made. In a case I had involving groundwater contamination, an expert testified about groundwater flow as estimated from a computer model, but he hadn't been involved in the development of the model. The people who did the actual modeling should have been produced as experts, but weren't. A related problem is that if you have twenty different experts do twenty different studies and nineteen are busts, the author of the one "good" study will be the only one to testify.

FL: As an economist and a judge, what are your thoughts on the concept of *statistical significance* in litigation?

RP: The 5 percent and 1 percent and 10 percent significance levels were not designed with litigation in mind. They were designed partly to ration space in journals. So statistical evidence that doesn't meet professional standards for publication might still be as reliable as eyewitness evidence and the other forms of nonstatistical evidence that courts accept unhesitatingly. The problem is that exceedingly weak statistical evidence may take up a disproportionate amount of court time. When you get evidence that has really low significance levels, you begin to wonder whether it has any significance at all. What troubles me is that in employment cases a court will sometimes state, as a matter of law, if it's not 5 percent it's inadmissible. That could be too wooden; maybe there are a whole bunch of studies and they are all 6 percent. And that has meaning. So I am uncomfortable with a rigid rule stating that anything other than the 5 percent level is unacceptable.

FL: In your experience, do cases with weaker rather than stronger statistics end up in trial?

RP: Yes. That is the essential problem with litigation in general. The one-sided cases—the cases where you could be really confident—don't get tried. So there is a disproportionate number of indeterminate cases, and that means cases on the frontier of science where you are not going to have a scientific consensus and the judge will be faced with equally confident and articulate experts who disagree profoundly and there is no time to perform an empirical test.

Paul Grimm
United States Magistrate Judge,
District of Maryland
April 6, 2004

FL: Would you describe the role of the federal magistrate judge?

PG: If you go to the local rules of our district court and you examine the section on magistrate judges, it delineates the potential duties of the magistrate judge. These duties start off at subparagraph a and go through subparagraph qq. Magistrate judges were introduced to help facilitate the workload in the federal courts. The position can be traced back to the earliest days of our republic, where there were judicial officers called *commissioners*. Their duties were exclusively dealing with criminal cases, and their compensation was a percentage of the fines they collected! In the late 1970s, it became clear that the federal judicial workload had increased appreciably, but there was no commensurate increase in district judges. At that point, commissioners were integrated into the system and called *magistrates.* Approximately thirteen years ago, as part of a judicial improvement initiative, they became known as *magistrate judges,* so therefore their title is *judge.* Magistrate judges are not Article III judges, because they are not confirmed by the Senate or appointed by the president. They are selected by statute as a result of a merit selection panel which recommends names to the district judges. The district judges on the bench then appoint them; they serve for eight-year terms and may be reappointed. Although some magistrate judges are involved in criminal cases, most of what we do, at least in this district, is civil, and so 40 percent of our civil jury trials are tried by magistrate judges, although there has to be consent by both parties. So we try an awful lot of jury trials here in the civil arena. I've tried medical malpractice cases, employment discrimination cases, business commercial disputes, civil rights cases, and anything else district judges would handle. But you also need to keep in mind that not many cases actually go to trial. Take last year as an example. The *New York Times* published the annual survey for the percentage of cases that go to trial, and about 1.8 percent of all civil cases filed go to trial. This is largely because of court-supervised settlements. In my district we believe it is our duty to help in the resolution of disputes, in ways other than simply having trials. Certainly, the parties could go out and pay three hundred dollars an hour to an external arbitrator or retired judge to help them resolve the dispute, but if this court can make those services available, we are pleased to. I believe we are successful because in my district, in the District of Maryland, at least [according to] the court statistics that were gathered last year, my fellow magistrate judges and I do the largest number of judicial settlement conferences in the fourth circuit—we have about six hundred a year. And in many respects, settlement conferences are more in the spirit of the notion of one's "day in court," much more so than a summary judgment. In the settlement scenario you can spend as much time as necessary to resolve the issues. I spent five years mediating the resolution of the Maryland State Police profiling case. Can you imagine a five-year trial?

FL: So in this district, all settlements are presided over by magistrate judges?

PG: Exactly.

FL: Do the district judges preside over any settlements at all?

PG: Very few. Although they have continued to retain the authority to handle settlements, they have delegated that to the magistrate judges. I need to remind you, however, that every single district court has the flexibility to tailor what their magistrate judges do. In our district, we inform parties that their case will be assigned to a magistrate judge and ask for their consent. The only thing that magistrate judges cannot do in our district is handle felony criminal cases.

FL: Do magistrate judges handle class action cases?

PG: I am not absolutely certain of this, but there may be some restriction on the ability of the magistrate judge to handle class action cases because of the difficulty of consent. Whose consent do you need—the lawyers representing the class or actual putative class members?

FL: Would a magistrate judge be involved in any motions related to class certification?

PG: Yes. Most directly, it might be at the request of a district judge for a magistrate judge to review briefs and supporting materials and make a recommendation to the district judge. Of course the parties would be permitted to file objections to that recommendation. The theme in our work is efficiency. If a district judge is tied up in a lengthy case, say a death penalty case, it makes sense for the magistrate judge to do the analysis and make the recommendation so that the civil case does not stall. But there is no value in having the magistrate judge simply duplicate what the district judge may have to do. It's a judgment call.

FL: Do magistrate judges handle Daubert or other *in limine* motions?

PG: Yes. I have done a number of Daubert hearings in connection with my own cases as well as for cases being handled by a district judge, at the request of that judge.

FL: As you know, the Daubert standards are largely based on the precepts of science. They ask the trial judge to consider issues of general acceptability, error rate, peer review, falsifiability, etc. Nevertheless, many, if not most, Daubert exclusions seemed to be based on more pragmatic issues: for example, will the testimony assist the finder of fact? Will the testimony be "relevant"? Some have speculated that Daubert is seldom "correctly" applied because many judges are not schooled in the traditional scientific method. What are your thoughts on that?

PG: Evidentiary relevance is defined by Evidence Rule 401 as follows: evidence is relevant if it has any tendency to make a fact that is of consequence to the litigation either more probable or less probable than it otherwise would be. As an example, the elements "of consequence to litigation" in a Title VII case involving a hostile work environment would be different than the elements you would have in an ADA claim involving someone who was not given reasonable access as a result of a problem that they had going up and down stairs. The elements tell you what is important in the case, and then the evidence is relevant if it has any tendency to make it more powerful or less powerful. The problem is that you could easily spend a lot of time with marginally relevant information that would just confuse or overwhelm or be prejudicial. Where it marries up with experts is under Evidence Rule 702, which says that in three specific spheres—scientific, technical, and specialized—if information will assist, it should be admitted. I don't think the issue is so much that the judges are poor scientists. It is just that we tend to use more basic language to explain our exclusion. We may very well know that there is no known error rate for a particular test or methodology, or we may know that a theory is not "generally accepted," but we are more likely to simply say that this proposed testimony will not be relevant or helpful to the finder of fact. It is much cleaner that way. I could certainly dig down into the arguments and look at the error rate as a basis for exclusion, but even that is relative. Let me give you an example. If I give you a test and you get a 98 percent, you would be pleased because you had only 2 percent errors. But suppose I hand you a jar of jelly beans and say there are two poison jelly beans and ninety-eight good jelly beans, shake it up, and ask you if you want a jelly bean—you're not going to eat a jelly bean. The acceptable error rate in those two situations is totally different.

I also think that traditional science looks at things somewhat differently than does the law. As I understand it, and I admit I am viewing science as a nonscientist, science takes the position that nothing can ever be proven, and since a theory cannot be *dis*proved, it is worth looking at over a long period of time. Law doesn't have that luxury. We have a limited question, a limited amount of time, limited resources; we've got to do the best we can to find out what happened. So we sometimes become impatient with the traditional scientific posture.

FL: What is your feeling about the use of court-appointed experts?

PG: I am a bit skeptical. First of all, how would you go about selecting such an expert?

FL: Well, you might have each side submit a list of possible experts who might be acceptable to them and hope for a match, or they might be permitted to strike some number from the list of their opponent and the judge could choose one from those remaining.

PG: In theory that sounds interesting, but it may simply be another layer in the process and make that process less efficient.

FL: Would you ever use a court-appointed expert?

PG: Very infrequently because it adds additional time to the process. You have to let everybody weigh in, you have to let everybody come in and have their piece. If the expert comes in, it takes time. You have to first let the adversaries' experts weigh in, do their discovery, say what it is. This then has to be shipped to the court-appointed expert. They have to review it; they may have questions because they are coming at it from a different perspective; now you have to go back and do it again. It adds time to the things. We have to resolve disputes quickly enough to keep cases moving so that the docket system doesn't clog down. Another issue is who would pay for that expert, because the court does not have a fund for such purposes. One way or another the parties would have to pay for the cost of the court-appointed expert, and that becomes a sort of tax on them.

FL: If you were to appoint an expert for the court, how would you assess the costs of that expert?

PG: You can do it a number of ways. You can assess it to the party that loses, or you can split the cost down the middle.

FL: Are there any circumstances in which the court could pay for the expert itself?

PG: Under Rule 706(b) there are certain types of things where there may be money available. Sometimes in criminal cases money may be statutorily made available. This may also be the case for certain types of civil actions or eminent domain. But that same rule says that in other civil actions, the compensation to court-appointed experts shall be paid by the parties in such proportion and in such time as the court directs. So they're paying for their experts as well as the court expert.

FL: In your experience, is there a growing tendency for judges to grant motions for summary judgment?

PG: Yes, I think there is that growing tendency. We sometimes expect the courts, which are the least democratic branch of our government, to resolve through an individual case issues that are at the vanguard of societal problems that haven't been resolved yet, where there is no consensus. Take a look at the Massachusetts Supreme Court on gay marriage. Are you for it or against it? Is it good, is it bad? There is no one view. There are strong views, there are polar views, but there is no one view. Take a look at issues involving the right to work of people who claim disabilities or claim that they are victims of age discrimination or gender discrimination. The caseload is enormous, and somehow we have to whittle it down. Summary judgment is one of the ways to whittle.

One of the reasons for the enormous caseload in employment litigation might also be the role of work in how we view ourselves. We spend much more time at work than we do with our families. We are in a culture where work defines how we view ourselves. Think of the exacerbating effect of downsizing, mergers, and acquisitions. You don't stay with the same organization for thirty years any longer. Your job is outsourced. There is an enormous collective angst within our country associated with what you are doing vocationally and where you are going in terms of your career. People invest a lot of themselves in work, so when things go bad, they want someone to answer for that. Too often, they use the courts to get that answer.

FL: But what about the complaint that if a summary judgment motion is granted, someone is denied their "day in court"?

PG: They can have their day in court if they can demonstrate that there is a triable fact that is in dispute for the jury to consider. But there are so many cases that no one would be entitled to their day in court if everyone were, because you just can't do it. Otherwise it would be judge for a day. You wouldn't just get jury duty, there would be judge duty too, and we would all be taking turns trying cases. The point is you just have to deal with the fact that there are limited resources, and you have to do the best that you can with the challenges that you have. And it is often obvious from *in limine* challenges that the expert testimony falls well below any acceptable standard, so you don't want that expert in front of a jury. You know the old jokes about expert witnesses: the expert is the guy who wasn't there when it happened, but he will, for a fee, tell you how it did. Often the exclusion of an expert is tantamount to granting a motion for summary judgment, because without the expert that party does not have a prayer of prevailing. So exclusion of expert testimony may very well make the settlement discussions more serious.

FL: Some judges have suggested that experts might adhere to higher standards in their testimony if that testimony were made available through their professional societies for any of their colleagues to examine. What are your thoughts on that?

PG: I would endorse anything that serves as a check and balance for experts who try to fly below the radar screen of their professional colleagues. It should not be possible for the same expert to be absolutely in favor of this particular thing in one case and be dead set against it in the next case. This might help prevent that.

FL: One of the judges I interviewed suggested that experts not be sworn since one cannot swear to the truth of an opinion. What are your thoughts about that?

PG: I think that might miss the point. The purpose for swearing the expert is so that he or she will swear to answer truthfully.

FL: Do you believe that a more persuasive expert with a weaker scientific argument can prevail over a less persuasive expert with a good scientific argument?

PG: Sure. I don't think that can be denied. I think that there are many times where the more surely righteous, if you would pardon that phrase, expert may be the one who will be more cryptic and see questions or limitations of his facts or his analysis or something of that nature, whereas the advocate will gloss over, smooth over, and try heavy fog or whatever else, and so you might pay less attention to the one who is actually the better at the science end of the thing or the technology end of the thing and who is more likely to admit his own limitations and therefore by comparison appear to be less certain or equivocal than the advocate. It is sad but true.

FL: And would that be equally true of a judge or a jury? Would both be similarly influenced?

PG: It is not exactly the same. If an expert were to admit that he or she was uncertain about something or did not have an answer to a question, a judge might think that the credibility of the witness has been enhanced by his or her candor. That does not mean that the testimony would be compelling, simply that the credibility would generally be enhanced. A jury might not be similarly inclined. Juries are tough to figure out. They seem to have a healthy disregard for everything the judges and lawyers are telling them they should look at during the course of the process. They have the good grace to pretend as though they are going to follow all these instructions, but when they get back in the jury room, they apply a lot of factors—both cognitive and emotional—to make their decision, and then they try to figure out how to justify that decision. Unfortunately, they don't have to come in and explain how they got there. I think the clever expert, the slippery expert, might be able to pull one over. The jury might say that the slippery expert stuck to his guns and that the more credible expert waffled.

FL: Are you more conscious of your language, including body language, in a jury trial than in a bench trial?

PG: Certainly. Not only is the jury watching but so are the lawyers. There is a lawyer's joke about judges asking questions during a trial that goes like this: Judge, if you are going to try my case for me, please don't lose it. Most of us exercise a great deal more self-restraint when we open our mouths in a jury trial than we do in a bench trial.

FL: Would you agree with the proposition that when issues are very complex or technical, the finder of fact may place greater emphasis on the credentials of the opposing experts?

PG: Yes, I would agree. Imagine yourself as a finder of fact: I don't understand this. This guy just explained to me how you calculate present value, and I'm clueless. He said the answer is X; now this other person over here has just explained the same calculation and come to a different

conclusion, and I can't understand what he is saying either.
I don't have the choice to say I can't figure it out. I mean
we can hang of course, but juries don't like to do that, they
have spent so much time and money, they want to get an
answer and go on and do something else. So who do I
believe? They look for reasons to figure out how they can
align themselves with one or the other expert.

I go back and talk to the juries after every single jury
trial: What did you think? I always ask questions about the
experts, things that they say, things that they don't say.
"Well, the one expert was very experienced in this, that,
and the other thing, but he offered a whole bunch of opinions that were pretty distant from his experience so even
though we liked him and he was a great person but he
stretched too far so we placed less emphasis on his testimony." Or, "I couldn't understand what he said." I have
never heard a jury say, "Well, that guy has better credentials
than the other." Well, maybe they don't want to say that
and they think there is some kind of lack of appreciation or
depth on their own part. But I think that if everything else
is equal and you don't have anything else to go by to send
you from one side to the other, you go back and you have
to make a decision, and you don't want to say I can't decide,
because you put a lot of time and energy into it. What do
you look at to try and go back and do it? The guy that went
to a more prestigious place and had more credentials may
be better.

FL: In your interviews with juries after a decision, have they
identified other aspects of expert testimony that have influenced their decision?

PG: They tell me that when two explanations both appear to
account for the same phenomenon, the simple one is usually better. They like the simple even if the more complex
explanation is the more accurate one. Juries, like judges,
tend to like someone who gives the appearance of not being an advocate. They want a little subtlety. They absolutely
resent being talked down to. Any hint of arrogance or supe-
riority or being condescending resonates wrong with them.
They tend to not like people who are slaves to jargon, who

can't or won't translate testimony into concepts they can understand. Now, none of those things necessarily have a darn thing to do with the underlying science, not at all. But the jurors are looking for a series of cues that they can identify with and combine with an explanation that seems to be consistent with the facts they have heard. They are also looking for any clue that the expert is trying to fool them somehow. They tend to be skeptical of expert testimony generally.

On the other hand looks can be deceiving. I had a case involving some medical testimony. The expert came in and was very cocky, easy to dislike on a lot of different scales: young guy, obviously financially secure, without hesitation talked about how he made nine hundred thousand dollars last year doing expert witness things on top of a million dollars in salary. He had shoulder-length Prince Valiant hair and was wearing silver-toed cowboy boots. Every reason in the world not to like him, but he sat up on the stand with literally two banker's boxes of stuff, and every question that he was asked by either side, it was bam, bam, and he just nailed it; he had it. After trial I had jurors say to me, what was that guy's name? They wanted to know who that guy was because if they had a problem they wanted him. Now that's counterintuitive: he wasn't warm and fuzzy; he wasn't in a safe blue suit, white shirt, and red tie; he didn't pander to them. Basically came out and broke all the rules and knocked them dead.

It's just tough sometimes to figure out what information jurors are using to make a decision. Have you ever seen that cartoon about what the man says and what the dog hears? We tend to think of a trial as consisting of what the judge and the lawyers and the witnesses say, but that may not be exactly what the jury sees and hears. They have their own way of processing information. The truth is we don't have the slightest clue in how jurors think or what they find important.

FL: When lawyers cross-examine an expert, they will often try to goad the expert into being more extreme, more emotional, and to appear to become an advocate for the party who retained him or her. Does this have an influence on the jury in your experience?

PG: I believe it does. Often a strategy on the part of a lawyer will be to ask a hopelessly muddled series of questions on cross-examination so that the expert becomes frustrated because he cannot answer the question as it was asked. In fact what the lawyer is trying to do is to get the jury so confused that they can no longer remember which end is up. He may also be trying to needle the witness or get the witness to equivocate. At some point then, the lawyer may ask a question that the witness can agree with, and say, "Finally, we can get you to admit to something"—to leave the impression that the witness has been refusing to answer completely or honestly. As far as the lawyer is concerned, when you are strong in the facts and weak in the law, you pound on the facts; when you are strong on the law and weak in the facts, you pound on the law; and when you are not strong on either the law or the facts, you pound on the table. There is some of that stuff going on in terms of what the lawyers are doing.

FL: Do you agree that when the statistics in a Title VII case are weak for either side, you will more likely end up in trial than when the statistics are strong for either side?

PG: I think that is absolutely true.

FL: And would you also agree that when the case is a weak one for either side, you are more likely to have the testimony of one or more expert witnesses?

PG: Let me qualify that a bit. You will be more likely to see experts clustered around the weak aspect of the case. Often, fact witnesses can bear the burden in the strong part of the case. Let me put it another way. I sometimes refer to the expert as the "flea collar" for the weak parts of the case. The expert comes in and testifies about methodology and statistics and lots of things that are really unimportant. But he has the effect of diverting attention from the stronger part of the opposing case. That's why I call him the flea collar.

If you have a person who is a young professional who is making a hundred thousand dollars a year and just got a fellowship and had all the problems in the world solved and he is killed, you don't need an economist to talk about what he was going to make. On the other hand, if the decedent wanted to be a veterinarian but had never worked full time, worked odd jobs, had an English degree, and had worked as a receptionist at the veterinarian's office, it might be different. In this case an economist might very well assume a four-year vet degree and assume that he would have a lucrative veterinary practice right after graduation. This is in spite of the fact that it is harder to get into veterinary school than it is to get into medical school! I have had cases just like that. To some extent I am almost amused by testimony like that. When the lawyer has nothing, he has to try and create something. An expert is oftentimes the vehicle you try to do that. The expert was injected into the process because there was no work history at all. Worked odd jobs here, odd jobs there.

FL: I represent a scientific-professional organization known as SIOP—the Society for Industrial and Organizational Psychology. Have you ever heard of that society?

PG: I am not certain that I have.

FL: How about the discipline of industrial and organizational psychology?

PG: Well, I am more likely to think in terms of more specific areas of expertise, like testing or human factors, or reliability of a field sobriety test. So if industrial and organizational psychologists would testify about those types of topics, then I guess I would be familiar with them, just not by that name. In Title VII cases, if I were to learn that a "psychologist" was going to be offered as an expert witness, I would imagine that the topic for testimony would be emotional injury. I have encountered expert witnesses who testified about [whether] the notes of interviewers contained any hint of discrimination. Would that have been an industrial or organizational psychologist?

FL: It would not have necessarily been an industrial or organizational psychologist, but that is a topic on which we might testify.

Of all the experts who appear before a judge in federal court, fewer than 10 percent are scientists or offering scientific testimony. As far as judges are concerned, are all experts put into the same basket? An expert is an expert is an expert. Or are scientific experts considered using different standards?

PG: Well, I think after the Daubert decision, we certainly started noticing what might be called *novel science*. Novel science was not an obvious issue before Daubert.

When Daubert came out, in the context of medical epidemiological studies, the initial reaction was to compartmentalize testimony and consider very narrow scientific fields in order to determine if the testimony represented novel science. It required you to at least consider the four Daubert factors. But later rulings have required us to ask the same type of questions about nonscientific expert testimony as well—even a garage mechanic. Take a case that involves whether or not a mechanic tuned a car correctly. By rule, I have to consider whether there is a sufficient factual basis, whether the methods and principles are reliable. "Well now, Mr. Mechanic, what were the methods that you used to tune that car?" They look at you like you are an idiot. But now I have to look at those kinds of things in a way that I have never done before. Most experts are testifying from experience, not from a scientific method. In those cases Daubert seems a little beside the point. You don't ever ask a doctor when they hit you with that rubber hammer what the error rate of that is; the idea is to be a test of reflexes. That's ridiculous; it's based upon judgment and a sort of experience.

Daubert challenges require us to ask a series of questions that don't always fit the model of what most experts are doing. You get a human relations expert who says, "I know what a good employee handbook should say. I can tell you what the design of an effective reporting and investigation system is for a business to respond to harassment in the workplace, and the current handbook and reporting procedures are a recipe for disaster." Well, that's not going to get into testability, error rates, general acceptance, and peer review.

FL: Have you had the experience of being confronted with diametrically opposed expert testimony based on the same underlying scientific research?

PG: Yes. But the issue is not usually the same underlying scientific research. It is more likely that I will have one expert who insists despite all evidence to the contrary that his opinion is reasonable. In those cases I am likely to limit or exclude the testimony of that expert. A somewhat different problem is one of jargon. This is particularly true in computers and complex electronic systems. The experts in those fields talk in a language which is just absolutely indecipherable—I think even among themselves. Often they "talk" without even using words—they're talking letters and acronyms, and it is totally opaque, and everything you read to try to discuss it is even more opaque. That's the worst case for me. Far more than statistics—which is opaque enough—or anything else. This represents a serious challenge to the finder of fact. You are listening to testimony on a topic and there is not even a common framework, and yet one says this is the thing, absolutely clear—no question— and the other one says absolutely not, and they both appear credentialed in ways that you have never encountered but seem to be recognized by others in that field.

FL: When you characterize the testimony of an expert as *credible* or *not credible,* what do you mean?

PG: It's a multifaceted word. In its pure sense *credible* means believable or not. It can be just a polite way of calling the witness a liar. If I say that you are not credible it is a nice way of saying you are incompetent or lying or, more charitably, misinformed. But it has a different significance as well. Appellate courts will always be more deferential to trial courts in matters of credibility determination because the trial judge saw the witness testify face to face, under oath, particularly under cross-examination. A trial judge is more likely to get a deferential review if he or she actually considered the testimony and found it credible or not credible. If the judge shows that she considered the testimony, it is less likely that her decision will be remanded or reversed, since it will be tough to show that she abused her discretion as the trial judge. There is one final use I might make of the term *credible* and it has a less sharp edge. I might simply mean *persuasive.* I might find you to be a credible person, but the other expert may be a little bit more credible than you. In other words, I am more persuaded by the other expert than I am by you, so I say he is credible. I might stop short of saying that I find you *not* credible, but that is the context in which I am using the term. I mean persuasive. The fact is that most experts have opinions about the issues that are in their domain of expertise. I tell my students that opinions are like feet, everybody's got them and lots of them stink. What distinguishes the stinky ones from the others are the foundations for them. That's what the finder of fact needs to focus on—the foundations for opinions, not just the opinions themselves.

Reference

Krafka, C., Dunn, M. A., Johnson, M. T., Cecil, J. S., & Miletich, D. (2002). Judge and attorney experiences, practices, and concerns regarding expert testimony in federal civil trials. *Psychology, Public Policy, and Law, 8,* 251–308.

PART 4

Conclusions

CHAPTER 16

Concluding Thoughts

James L. Outtz
Frank J. Landy

The chapter authors have done a wonderful job of laying out issues, describing the state of the art in their respective areas, and pointing to emerging trends. In this chapter we briefly elaborate on several issues that we see as particularly salient for employment litigation in the next decade. We arrange our comments around three conceptual anchors: technical issues, societal issues, and procedural issues.

Technical Issues

Status of the Authorities

Richard Jeanneret (Chapter Three) describes three authoritative sources of information and guidance that can be relied on in employment selection litigation:

1. *Standards for Educational and Psychological Testing* (1999) (Standards)
2. *Principles for the Validation and Use of Personnel Selection Procedures* (2003) (Principles)
3. *Uniform Guidelines on Employee Selection Procedures* (1978) (Guidelines)

All three authoritative sources help define sound professional practices in the area of employment selection.

The Standards (1999) and the Principles (2003) are recent revisions of earlier editions of each document. The intent of the revisions is to bring the documents up to date with current scientific findings and accepted professional practice. The Standards address testing and assessment generally, with some guidance on employment selection. The Principles focus primarily on employment selection. Jeanneret points out that the Standards and the Principles are quite compatible.

The Uniform Guidelines were published in 1978 and have not undergone revision. This has created significant problems with the utility of each document in providing substantive guidance to practitioners involved in employment issues. In many instances the Guidelines are not consistent with either the Principles or Standards. In some instances the Guidelines fail to address issues that are addressed by the Standards and Principles. The lack of consistency between the Guidelines and the other authoritative sources is problematic because the Guidelines were intended to be consistent with accepted professional practice. This incompatibility is not surprising, however, because, as mentioned, the Guidelines have never undergone any revision.

Unfortunately, none of the authoritative sources is cited much by the courts in deciding employment discrimination cases. Nevertheless, the Uniform Guidelines—the least current source—are cited more than the Standards or the Principles. Because the three documents are not compatible in many important respects (for example, in their definitions of *validity* and the meanings they give to *fairness*), the courts must resolve inconsistencies between them in making a decision. In the future, industrial and organizational psychologists and other professionals will have to do a better job of familiarizing judges with the Standards and the Principles to ensure that decisions in discrimination cases are based on current scientific knowledge and accepted professional practices. This could be difficult in light of the fact that judges may be reluctant to accept the advice of industrial and organizational psychologists as to which document to rely on for any specific issue.

For example, Frank J. Landy (Chapter Fifteen) asked chief judge James L. Graham about the significance of new developments in a scientific field such as industrial psychology, developments that might have occurred since the Guidelines were published. Judge Graham's response indicated that advances in science might possibly have an effect on the court's decisions. It appears however that decisions at the appellate level and Supreme Court decisions will be the determining factors.

The Changing Role of Job Analysis and Validation

Stan Malos (Chapter Twelve) suggests that the courts may be shifting away from a technical view of job analysis and validation to a more relaxed consideration. He suggests that trial courts appear more likely to apply a reasonable-effort-by-the-employer standard than a checklist of required activities derived from the Uniform Guidelines, APA Standards, or SIOP Principles. There is good reason to believe this may be true. It is quite clear from the interviews with judges (Chapter Fifteen) as well as the empirical research on the judge as scientist reported by George C. Thornton III and Peter H. Wingate (Chapter Six) that the average judge knows little about job analysis or test validation. Further, the review conducted by Jeanneret of citations in written judicial opinions (of the federal judiciary) to what I-O psychologists might call "authorities" (that is, the Guidelines, Principles, and Standards) shows quite clearly that written opinions pay scant attention to what those authorities would seem to require for an adequate job analysis or validity study.

Plaintiffs' experts often take a reductionist view of job analysis or test validation, raising arcane questions about the characteristics of subject matter experts (SMEs), the wording of anchors in a rating scale, or whether a link had been shown between a specific task and a specific test question. Defendant's experts answer (rebut) in kind with detailed analyses of data collected to demonstrate the adequacy of the SMEs, the meaning of anchors, or the multiple linkages between similar test items and similar tasks or task groups. Judges seldom ask questions about these issues, nor do they craft their opinions around these arcane points. Juries are even less interested in technical issues. Instead, these fact finders appear to use much lower levels of magnification and to consider issues more broadly, using a criterion of *rationality* or even fairness rather than one of *technicality*. They appear to evaluate whether the employer has made a reasonable effort to identify successful applicants. Fact finders do not seem to require perfection, just a reasonable and well-intentioned effort. It would be wise for I-O psychologists involved in employment litigation to step back and ask the broader questions related to rationality and reasonableness on the part of a defendant employer. This is not to say that technical issues are not important. But it is to say that the prudent plaintiff expert will not rely *solely* on technical issues but will instead show how the technical issues relate to the practical outcome. Judges are very good at masking their emotions, particularly when a jury is present. They may appear interested in the partial correlation between two items with the effect of a third item removed—but they probably aren't—and it is likely that days of technical testimony may go unheeded by both the judge and the jury.

There are two areas where orthodox job analysis, in particular, will remain important and possibly even grow in importance—litigation based on the Americans with Disabilities Act (ADA) and litigation based on the Fair Labor Standards Act (FLSA). Both types of litigation revolve around the identification of *essential* tasks. As Cristina Banks and Lisa Cohen (Chapter Eleven) illustrate, FLSA cases are won and lost on a very specific determination of how much time is spent in management compared to nonmanagement tasks. It seems clear that in FLSA venues, cognitive task analysis should become more commonplace. In ADA litigation, job analysis is likely to continue to play a central role, particularly techniques that will distinguish between essential and nonessential tasks. But in more traditional Title VII litigation involving hiring, promotion, or termination decisions, the more technical issues may play a lesser role in ultimate decisions.

Less Discriminatory Alternatives

James L. Outtz (Chapter Seven) points out that under the *Uniform Guidelines on Employee Selection Procedures,* even if an employer can demonstrate that its selection procedures are valid, plaintiffs can still prevail if it can be shown that (1) there is an alternative selection procedure that is substantially equal in validity and has less adverse impact or (2) there is an alternative method of using the employer's selection procedure that is substantially equal in validity and has less adverse impact. Both of these conditions have proven extremely difficult for plaintiffs to demonstrate. There are few if any cases in which a court has ruled that a plaintiff has met the burden of demonstrating an equally valid alternative that has less adverse impact. A major problem with the search-for-alternatives argument is the definition of *equally valid*. One might argue that to be equally valid an alternative must predict the same criterion. If, for example, an employer's selection procedure predicts task performance, should an alternative procedure that predicts contextual performance be considered equally valid? A more fruitful approach for plaintiffs may be to demonstrate an equally valid method of use. This approach may garner increasing interest in the future. The current debate over banding versus strict rank order selection as a method of score interpretation is an example of the method-of-use debate (see Jerard F. Kehoe and Angela Olson's discussion in Chapter Thirteen).

Recent scientific research dealing with the possibility that different predictor combinations will have varying degrees of adverse impact is also pertinent (Sackett & Ellingson, 1997). Rather than identifying a totally different alternative test or procedure, it may be more feasible for plaintiffs to show that adjusting the method of use for the employer's procedure (for example, using a compensatory rather than multiple hurdles model, giving greater weight to the predictors in a predictor battery that have lesser adverse impact, without diminishing validity) or establishing score bands and using low adverse impact assessment devices such as personality tests or interviews to select applicants from within a band are viable alternatives.

One of the difficulties plaintiffs have in attempting to demonstrate an equally valid alternative is the assumption that the alternative must first be applied to the employer's situation and actually be demonstrated to be successful. This may not be the case. The comments of senior judge Charles Sifton on this issue are quite interesting (see Chapter Fifteen). Judge Sifton indicated that the fact that a proposed alternative has never been used in actual practice does not, in and of itself, render the proposed alternative "speculative." He offered the eminently sensible notion that if it is obvious that a proposed alternative would work then it may be a viable alternative even if it has not actually been used.

Identifying alternative ways that an employer could use its selection procedure to produce equal validity and less adverse impact seems too inviting from a feasibility standpoint to be overlooked by plaintiffs in future. It seems quite likely that employers will have to explain why they had to use a selection procedure in a particular manner rather than having to simply explain the business necessity for using it at all.

Cut Scores

No fewer than four of the preceding chapters (Chapters Three, Five, Twelve, Thirteen) have addressed issues related to setting a cut score. The preferred method for setting cut scores will remain a contentious issue in future litigation because it is likely that employers will continue to adjust test scores upward as a strategy for increasing the effectiveness of their workforces and remaining competitive. There will be resistance to these upward adjustments from those who will claim there is no rational or empirical justification for the chosen cut score. The employer will then be expected to demonstrate that the score is linked in some logical or empirical manner to anticipated increases in workforce effectiveness. The debate is far from over.

At present there is disagreement among the circuits on "the law" regarding cut scores, at least at the trial court level. Because several of the cut score cases are still being prepared for appeal or considered by the appeals courts, there may soon be a need for the Supreme Court to consider the issue and add clarity, at least from the legal perspective. Although such an opinion might well resolve any legal uncertainty, it will not resolve the psychometric or public policy disputes. If an employer is permitted to set a score based on expectations of normal proficiency (including the circumstance where the employer anticipates a requisite increase in normal proficiency levels to remain competitive), that score is likely to be higher than it would be if the employer were required to show that the cut score is a *true minimum* score, a score below which all or almost all of the applicants would be expected to fail at the job. In the case of tests of cognitive ability, higher cut scores will almost certainly lead to greater adverse impact for minority applicants than lower scores would. This effect is exaggerated when a hurdle system is used, when the first hurdle is a cognitive test, and when an applicant is not permitted to advance in the hiring process unless he or she is able to obtain a score equal to or greater than the cut score that has been identified.

Licensure or certification represents a special instance of the cut score debate. The employer (or more often a licensing or certifying body) will often claim that some palpable form of *harm* will result unless a cut score determined to be necessary for licensure or certification is met or exceeded. This argument is applied to teacher certification and public safety positions, for example. But the claim of harm is often vague and abstract, eventually reducing to the traditional "more is better" logic. When a cut score is anchored in the concept of harm, it would seem logical to identify that harm with some specificity and to show through logical or statistical means that there is some reasonable selection point that distinguishes between the likelihood of harm and no harm. That point would be identified as the cut score.

Ultimately, the argument will devolve into a discussion of the cost of a Type I versus the cost of a Type II error. Is it more costly for some known constituency (the public, an employer, a student, or the like) to reject an applicant who might very well succeed in the job or to accept an applicant who will eventually fail in some (possibly catastrophic) manner? This raises a final point: when considering cut scores and how they are set, it would be best if the *criterion* were parsed more finely than is usually the case at the present. For example, a cut score predicated on "overall performance" seems less logical than a cut score predicated on a particular and central criterion dimension (such as production errors or customer satisfaction) or even a composite weighted by the importance of several criterion dimensions. Additionally, as was suggested earlier, if harm is the criterion, one would expect harm to be operationally defined.

Societal Issues

The Changing Landscape of Employment Charges

There have been quantitative changes in the types of discrimination charges filed over the past ten years. Donald L. Zink and Arthur Gutman (Chapter Four) present data that show, for example, that retaliation charges have doubled as a percentage of the total charges under Title VII since fiscal year (FY) 1992. Zink and

Gutman's data also show that for all statutes enforced by the Equal Employment Opportunity Commission (EEOC), the number of retaliation charges has increased from approximately 11,000 in FY 1992 to over 22,000 in FY 2003. Malos (Chapter Twelve) suggests that the trend toward more retaliation charges may be due to a desire on the part of plaintiffs to increase the likelihood of obtaining higher damage rewards. Outtz (Chapter Seven) suggests that the increase in retaliation cases may be due to the fact that the retaliation provisions of Title VII provide broad protection for persons who file charges with the EEOC, and the EEOC typically expedites investigations of retaliation charges and seeks injunctive relief. Whatever the reason, it would appear that retaliation will be one of the common themes in discrimination charges in the years ahead, particularly charges filed under Title VII.

Although some forms of discrimination claims, such as retaliation, are on the rise, others are on the decline. Outtz (Chapter Seven) points to a decline in challenges to entry-level selection procedures in recent years. This decline is particularly noticeable for private sector employers. Whether this trend will continue remains to be seen. Given that the overall number of discrimination charges has remained relatively consistent over the past decade (see Chapter Four) the decline in entry-level cases may simply indicate that plaintiffs are shifting their focus.

One trend that certainly warrants mention is the increasing variety of charges in race cases noted by Outtz, (Chapter Seven). The spectrum of charges in race cases ranges from failure to properly recruit to failure to mentor. The decrease in entry-level cases together with an increase in the variety of claims by employees may indicate that racial minorities are having less difficulty getting hired but are more likely to perceive their treatment after hiring as unfair. It may also signal an increase in sophistication in understanding the mechanisms of discrimination.

The Sociopolitical Context of Discrimination Charges

It is clear from the statistical trends presented by Zink and Gutman (Chapter Four) and the views of the attorneys proffered in Chapter Fourteen that employment discrimination charges occur in the

context of a sociopolitical environment. Zink and Gutman, for example, suggest that the increase in age discrimination cases that occurred in FY 2002 and FY 2003 relative to the preceding seven-year period may have been related to a deep recession in the U.S. economy in which there was considerable loss of jobs. Zink and Gutman also point out that this rise in age discrimination charges coincided with charges made by Arab and Muslim groups after the incidents of September 11, 2001. Given the events that have occurred since 9/11 (for example, the wars in Afghanistan and Iraq) it is likely that the trend toward an increase in charges based on religion and national origin will continue. The monetary benefits derived from resolutions of cases under each Act are also likely to affect future trends in the types of charges that are filed. The data presented by Zink and Gutman indicate, for example, that Title VII accounted for four times as many claims as the Age Discrimination in Employment Act (ADEA) or the ADA, yet the ADEA resulted in the greatest monetary benefits, particularly in recent years. Given that the U.S. workforce is aging rapidly and that age discrimination cases produce significantly greater monetary benefits, it is reasonable to assume that the number of ADEA cases will increase relative to cases brought under other Acts.

In presenting the lawyer's view (Chapter Fourteen) Richard Ugelow offers fascinating insights into the political, social, and practical considerations that influenced the enforcement strategies at the Department of Justice prior to and during his tenure with that agency. Early on (between 1972 and 1979 or so) the Department of Justice focused its enforcement efforts primarily on the public safety hiring practices of local jurisdictions. Ugelow explains that the rationale for this strategy was both political and practical. On the one hand, when Congress considered the 1972 Amendments to Title VII (amendments authorizing private lawsuits against state and private employers), it took account of a report that indicated the greatest barriers to equal employment in state and local employment were in police and fire departments. In addition, social science reports following the urban race riots of the 1960s pointed to the importance of having police and fire departments that represented the demographics of the communities they served. After examining statistical data showing that racial minorities and women were in fact

severely underrepresented in uniformed police and fire positions (positions that were considered highly visible in the community, well paid, and offering significant opportunities for advancement), the Justice Department decided to focus its enforcement efforts on police and fire departments. Had the political and social winds blown in a different direction, enforcement efforts no doubt would have taken a different course. Obviously, this raises the question of the direction the political and social winds will blow in the future. With a burgeoning Hispanic and Latino immigrant population gaining greater and greater political influence in U.S. society, will these groups be the next recipients of heightened enforcement protection under Title VII? There is also the possibility that religious cases brought on behalf of Islamic citizens (Muslims) will increase if the religious backlash that occurred after September 11, 2001, does not subside.

It should be noted that the nature, direction, and focus of discrimination charges is an evolving process. Ugelow describes the enforcement strategy of the U.S. Justice Department as evolving from one of forcing employers to eliminate adverse impact to working cooperatively with employers to find equally valid alternatives with less adverse impact. As new racial, ethnic, or religious subgroups make their presence felt, novel issues involving civil rights and equal protection under the law no doubt will surface. Consider the issue raised by Ellis (2003) of genetic testing as a new form of discrimination that will have to be addressed. What if genetic testing indicates that certain racial groups are predisposed to particular debilitating illnesses? As an example, it has been shown that African Americans are genetically predisposed to sickle-cell disease (Voet, Voet, & Pratt, 2002). This genetic predisposition has evolved because the sickle-cell gene increases resistance to malaria, the most lethal infectious disease that presently affects humans. The regions of Africa where malaria is most prevalent coincide with those regions where the sickle-cell gene is also most prevalent. African Americans have a greater incidence of sickle-cell disease because they inherited the sickle-cell gene. Would use of genetic testing information by employers and insurance companies constitute racial discrimination against African Americans?

The Connection Between Perceptions
of Justice and the Likelihood of Litigation

A number of researchers have proposed that employees feel anger, outrage, and resentment when they perceive organizational practices and management decisions as unfair (Folger, 1987; Greenberg, 1990; Sheppard, Lewicki, & Minton, 1992). The principal foundation for this research is organizational justice theory (Thibaut & Walker, 1975). According to organizational justice theory, individual employees define fairness in terms of the outcomes they receive and in terms of the procedures used to determine those outcomes. A number of researchers have investigated the relationship between perceived organizational justice and subsequent employee behavior. Skarlicki and Folger (1997), for example, found a relationship between distributive justice and retaliation against the organization when procedural justice was low. Organizational justice research predicts a relationship between perceptions of justice by minority applicants and employees and the subsequent actions these individuals choose to take, including litigation. The broad spectrum of discrimination charges filed by minority group members as described in this volume shows that they watch employers very closely for indications of differential treatment. The results of this continuous scanning of the work environment may very well determine whether the employer will be the target of a discrimination claim.

An excellent example of the effect of perceptions on the likelihood of litigation is provided by Harvey L. Sterns, Dennis Doverspike, and Greta A. Lax (Chapter Nine). They describe a performance appraisal process that is typically perceived by employees as grossly unfair. This process is called the *forced ranking* method or the *rank and yank* method by some critics. Under the forced ranking method only a specific number of employees can receive certain performance ratings. For example, the system may be designed so that only 5 percent of employees can be given the highest appraisal ratings and 10 percent must be given the lowest. Employees who remain in the lowest rating category for more than two rating periods face termination. Forced ranking systems such as this are likely to be perceived by employees as grossly unfair, as was the case at

Ford Motor Company in a case that eventually settled (see Chapter Nine). Virtually every employee group that could filed suit against Ford. The Ford case clearly demonstrates the link between employee perceptions and litigation.

Procedural Issues

Challenges to the Testimony of I-O Psychologists

As we have seen in Chapters Six, Fourteen, and Fifteen, it is becoming more common to challenge the testimony of expert witnesses. This is just as true (and possibly more true) of testimony related to the behavioral sciences as of testimony related to medicine or the physical sciences. I-O psychologists who serve as expert witnesses should anticipate increased challenges to their testimony in the form of *in limine* motions prior to trial. Most likely, these challenges will conform to the *Daubert* principles and will include questions regarding methodology, general acceptance, peer review, and the extent to which any explanatory "theory" has a known error rate associated with it.

But it appears that judges, although aware of the *Daubert* principles, use a more primitive set of decision rules. These decision rules include a consideration of whether the testimony will actually assist the finder of fact (the judge or the jury) in rendering an ultimate decision. For example, in a case involving gender discrimination a trial judge accepted psychological testimony on stereotypes about women. The court of appeals, however, overruled the trial judge, reasoning that "[i]nformation about and commentary on gender issues is so abundant in our society that it has become a common stereotype that women receive disparate and often unfairly discriminatory treatment in the workplace. . . . Gender stereotypes are the stuff of countless television situation comedies and are the focus of numerous media treatments on a nearly daily basis. . . . [This type] of testimony is hardly the type of evidence without which laypersons are incapable of forming a correct judgment. . . . [Thus] the expert's testimony [does not] qualify for admission as expert testimony" (*Ray* v. *Miller Meester*, 2003, at 7). Thus in this case the appeals court ruled that jury members knew enough about stereotypes and needed no additional expert

testimony to make a judgment. It is possible that similar arguments might be made to exclude testimony about performance appraisal, job requirements, or even business relatedness. It is the responsibility of the I-O expert to provide testimony that is *not* part of a domain of common experience. For example, in a case alleging age discrimination a juror might believe that physical strength will *inevitably* decline as a function of age or that there is a *universal* difference between the strength of men and women. The I-O psychologist expert could provide testimony that runs counter to these beliefs. This would be an instance of assisting the finder of fact through expert testimony. This "assistance" standard should be part of the preparation of an I-O psychologist for testimony—how does what the expert witness says *help* the finder of fact?

A second general principle applied by judges in determining the admissibility of expert testimony is relevance. Although an expert may present masterful testimony about a particular concept—say, the contribution of grade point average (GPA) to a hiring decision—if there is no evidence suggesting that GPA was used or considered in the hiring decision, the testimony is simply not relevant. The expert might argue that because the GPA was available on an application form, it *could have been used,* but without any fact evidence to suggest it *was* considered, the expert testimony is irrelevant.

Recently, social scientists and lawyers have suggested that social fact may play a role in expert testimony. This has been labeled *social framework analysis* (see treatments of this approach in Chapters Eight and Fourteen; also see Monahan & Walker, 1998). Social framework analysis holds that there are generally accepted bodies of knowledge that speak to an issue in litigation at a broad level. These generally accepted research results are called *social fact.* In criminal cases, social fact may include conclusions about eyewitness testimony or rates of recidivism among those who have battered their wives or engaged in pedophilia. In employment discrimination, social fact might be involved in proposed testimony regarding stereotypes (as discussed earlier) or the role of general mental ability in job performance (that is, validity generalization) or even subjectivity in performance evaluation. Social framework analysis will remain controversial for several reasons. Most important, the general nature of social fact (that is, research results and conclusions) might argue against specific relevance to the case at hand. The social fact must be linked directly to the case in question. In addition experts for the parties are bound to debate the nature of that social fact. Is it "generally accepted"? Is there rebuttal social fact evidence? Thus social framework analysis becomes no different from any other form of expert testimony and would be treated accordingly (that is, subject to exclusion on a pretrial motion or rebuttal through cross-examination and opposing expert testimony).

In summary, an expert who expects to testify simply on the strength of his or her credentials ("trust me, I'm an expert") is likely to be disappointed. Instead the expert should be prepared at all stages of litigation to justify his or her role in the litigation in terms of both the relevance of the testimony to the particular case and the helpfulness of that testimony in assisting the judge or jury member in rendering a decision.

What Judges Know About I-O Psychology

Very little. In spite of a substantial caseload it is clear (see Chapter Fifteen) that judges handle very few employment discrimination cases in the course of a year (or even a career). Many of the cases are resolved prior to trial through mediated settlements or the granting of summary judgment motions. In the few cases that do go to trial, the judge may qualify an expert in a specific area, such as testing or statistics or performance assessment, rather than a broad area such as I-O psychology. Judges are not at all clear about the difference between a psychologist and a sociologist or human resource expert. Even considering just the area of psychology, judges are most familiar with clinical psychologists, who might testify with respect to psychological "damages" for purposes of estimating compensatory awards.

The lesson to be learned from the fact that judges and juries are unfamiliar with I-O psychology is that they must be educated with respect to what I-O psychologists do and how their field differs from other professions or specialty areas. There is a tendency to think of judges as omniscient, but they are like the rest of us in many respects—overworked and underinformed. This means that the introductory sections to reports or testimony should be very carefully crafted to inform judges and juries about what we do. It is generally acknowledged that this education is an important part of a jury trial. It is less well known that it should be an equally important part of a bench trial, and is essential to do this when responding to motions for exclusion of I-O testimony, either in written form or in hearings. Experts should not assume that judges know what I-O psychology is.

How Judges View Experts

The interviews with judges that appear in Chapter Fifteen, as well as the results of surveys of judges reported in Chapters Six and Fifteen, should be cause for concern for expert witnesses. Judges distrust expert witnesses for several reasons. The most extreme examples of this can be found in the interview with Judge Posner, but his skepticism is widely shared by his colleagues. The belief is that an expert is often tempted to become an advocate for the attorney who retained the expert. In essence, the concern is that there is (or can be) a conflict for the expert between testifying objectively and pleasing the party that pays the invoices. An expert witness must be aware of this presumption of advocacy and guard against it. The techniques for avoiding the appearance of advocacy are relatively simple: present all relevant research findings (not simply the ones that support your position), do not appear to instruct the judge or jury with respect to what they *must* conclude based on your testimony, don't appear unwilling to answer uncomfortable questions or concede points even if your position is weakened, and stay within your area of expertise. Judges often observe that an expert has provided opinions that could not be supported either by the research reported or the experience of the witness. Strange as it may sound, an expert should be prepared to answer, "I don't know," or, "I have no opinion on that issue."

There is another, more existential reality to the role of an expert witness in the employment litigation context. Many judges are uncomfortable with the shift in power—sometimes slight and sometimes dramatic—from the bench to the witness chair that occurs when an expert testifies. If an expert's testimony has been admitted by the judge, then the judge must attend to that testimony. If it is apparent that the judge has not even considered expert testimony, that can be grounds for a successful appeal of a verdict or opinion. Nevertheless, the judge or jury (not the expert) remains the finder of fact. But knowledge is power, and the expert may very well exert an influence on the outcome of the trial. The judge would prefer that this influence be realized through knowledge, but the judge is often at a loss to determine whether the expert testimony represents good science. Certainly, the process of cross-examination and rebuttal can help distinguish between good and bad science, but the effectiveness of that check and balance is determined by things other than simply the knowledge base. The competence of an opposing expert and the competence of the trial attorneys will also enter into the equation.

The point to take away from this discussion of how judges view experts is that the expert does not enjoy the mantle of helpfulness and objectivity that he or she might presume. Credibility is more often something to be *earned* in litigation than something to be *lost*.

References

Ellis, A. (2003). Genetic justice: Discrimination by employers and insurance companies based on predictive genetic information. *Texas Tech Law Review, 34,* 1071–1099.

Folger, R. (1987). Reformulating the preconditions of resentment: A referent cognitions model. In J. C. Masters & W. P. Smith (Eds.), *Social comparison, and relative deprivation: Theoretical, empirical, and policy perspectives* (pp. 183–215). Mahwah, NJ: Erlbaum.

Greenberg, J. (1990). Organizational justice: Yesterday, today, tomorrow. *Journal of Management, 16,* 399–432.

Monahan, J., & Walker, L. (1998). *Social science in law.* Westbury, NY: Foundation Press.

Ray v. Miller Meester, C3-02-1605, LEXSEE 2003 Minn. App. LEXIS 773 (2003).

Sackett, P., & Ellingson, J. (1997). The effects of forming multi-predictor composites on group differences and adverse impact. *Personnel Psychology, 50*(3), 707–721.

Sheppard, B., Lewicki, R., & Minton, J. (1992). *Organizational justice: The search for fairness in the workplace.* San Francisco: New Lexington Press.

Skarlicki, D., & Folger, R. Retaliation in the workplace: The roles of distributive, procedural, and interactional justice. *Journal of Applied Psychology, 82*(3) 434–443.

Thibaut, J., & Walker, L. (1975). *Procedural justice: A psychological analysis.* Mahwah, NJ: Erlbaum.

Voet, D., Voet, G., & Pratt, C. (2002). *Fundamentals of biochemistry.* New York: Wiley.

Name Index

Subject Index

610 Subject Index

420, 421
Douglas v. Anderson, 263, 291
Downbidding, 267
Driving, 31
Dual tasking, 349
Duke Power Company, Griggs v. *See*
Griggs v. Duke Power Company
Dukes v. Wal-Mart, Inc., 459, 460
Duties test, 346
Dvorak v. Mostardi Platt Associates,
Inc., 323, 334
Dyslexia, 21

E

Eastman Kodak Co., Thomas v., 397,
403, 409
Echazabal, Chevron U.S.A., Inc. v.,
310, 311–312, 313, 334
Ecological validity, 454–456
Economic downturn, 104, 110
Economists, as expert witnesses,
16–17
Edel, Vaughn v., 393, 409
80 percent rule. *See* Four-fifths rule
Elected officials exemption, 259–260
Eleventh Amendment, 103, 296
Ellerth, Burlington Industries, Inc.
v., 118, 129, 131, 236–237, 246,
255
Ellison v. Brady, 238, 255
Emotional distress damages, 7
Employee performance evaluation,
183, 184, 186, 356–360. *See also*
Performance appraisal and man-
agement systems
Employee Retirement Income and
Security Act (ERISA), 278, 287
Employer defense strategies. *See* Defense strategies
Employment discrimination cases:
cut scores and, 410–449; of De-
partment of Justice, 474–476;
filed by EEOC, 119–121; importance of valid selection and performance appraisal in, 373–409;

job analysis and validation in,
role of, 374–388, 405–406; performance appraisal in, role of,
388–403, 406; phases in litigation
of, 3–19, 187–189; procedural
justice and due process in, 404–
405, 585–586; societal trends
and, 581–586; statistical issues
related to, 132–165; statistical
trends in, 101–131, 581–582
"Employment Practices: Basic Requirements," 386, 407
En banc hearing, 18
Entergy Operations, Oubre v., 278,
293
Enterprise Rent-A-Car, Fernandez &
Scanlon v., 342, 344, 370
Equal Employment Opportunity
Act of 1972 (EEO-72), 78, 101,
464–466, 467, 470, 583
Equal Employment Opportunity
Commission (EEOC), 4, 5, 6, 28,
35, 45, 131, 468, 469, 470, 482,
489, 512, 582; age discrimination
and, 257, 258, 259, 264, 266, 267,
268, 272, 278, 287, 288; alternative dispute resolution (ADR)
plan of, 127–130; Americans
with Disabilities Act and, 294,
296–298, 300, 302–304, 307, 310,
312–314, 316–318, 320–321, 323,
325–329, 332; *Annual Report FY
2002*, 119, 123, 125; Compliance
Manual of, 313; creation of, 101;
Department of Justice and, 465–
466; enforcement action by, significance of, 29–30; enforcement
coverage and duties of, 101–103,
465–466; Internet sourcing, 445–
446; lawsuits filed with, 119–121;
litigation statistics of, 118–125;
1972 Amendments and, 465; performance appraisal and, 397;
public relations goal of, 128–130;
race discrimination cases and,
202, 203, 204, 207, 208, 217, 226;

ence," 450–462; lawyers' perspectives on, 450–502; methods of, 183–185; social science research of, on sexual harassment, 250–253; societal issues and, 581–586

Inexorable zero, 25–26

Infinity Broadcasting, DeLoach v., 262, 291

Information technology jobs, older workers and, 285

Injunctive relief, in race discrimination cases, 203

Institutionalized discrimination, 201

Internal structure, 56, 87, 95

Internal validity, of evidence, 169, 176–177

International Association of Fire Chiefs, 487

International Association of Fire Fighters, 487

International Brotherhood of Teamsters v. United States, 25–26, 34, 35, 36, 39, 45

International Paper Co., Rogers v., 423, 449

International Personnel Management Association, 487

International Task Force on Assessment Center Guidelines, 184, 197

Internet recruiting: cutoff scores and, 445–446; older workers and, 285; race discrimination cases and, 206, 207–208

"Interpretations," 346, 370

Interrogatories, 9

Interstate, Gilmer v., 130, 131

Interview, job: age discrimination in, 281; experimental research on, 452–453; race discrimination in, 210

Inverse estimation or regression, 154–155

Investigation phase, 3–5

Item sensitivity analysis, 75

J

Jackson, Smith v., 283, 293

Jackson v. Sears, Roebuck, 276, 292

Jacksonville Shipyards, Robinson v., 245, 255

James v. Stockham Valves, 192, 198

Job Accommodation Network (JAN), 327, 328, 332

Job analysis: analysis of work *versus*, 70–71; case law on, 377–386; changing role of, 577–578; for content validity, 70–71, 94–95; for disability discrimination, 326, 327, 578; in employment discrimination litigation, importance of, 374–388, 405–406; for former employees, 364–366; in I-O psychology, 183, 184; *Principles for the Validation and Use of Personnel Selection Procedures* on, 70–71; for race discrimination cases, 221; recall problem in, 364–366; test construction and, 40–41; *Uniform Guidelines* on, 84, 85, 376–377; validity and, 373–388, 405–406, 577–578; for wage and hour cases and compliance, 343–344, 353–354, 360–368, 578. See also Analysis of work

Job descriptions: for disability discrimination, 327; for race discrimination cases, 221, 225; for wage and hour compliance and cases, 354–355

Job design and redesign, for exempt status, 366–368

Job evaluation, 183, 184

Job performance appraisals, 47

Job-relatedness, 15; Civil Rights Act of 1991 on, 37–38; court interpretations of, 21, 27, 42–43; Department of Justice position on, 471–473, 483–485; in disability discrimination cases, 323; job analysis and, 375–388; pattern or practice and, 25; in race

Williams, Toyota Motor Manufacturing, Kentucky, Inc. v., 131, 310–311, 316, 317, 325, 331, 335
Williams et al. v. Ford Motor Co., 380–382, 387, 409
Williams v. Vukovich, 40, 46
Williamson v. Owens-Illinois, Inc., 263, 293
Wilson v. Sealtest Foods, 277, 293
Winarto v. Toshiba American Electronics Components, 398, 403, 409
Wisconsin Department of Health and Social Servs., Torres v., 231, 255
Wisconsin Department of Transportation, Vollmert v., 322, 335
Withdrawals with benefits: defined, 112; statistics on, 113–114, 116–118
Within-subject effects, modeling of, 146–147
Witnesses: nonexpert, in class certification phase, 8; types of, 16–17. *See also* Expert witnesses
Women: adverse impact heavy and, 31; glass walls for, 215; height and weight requirements and, 22, 23; as prison guards, 26; "reason-

able," 237–238, 251. *See also* Gender stereotypes; Sex discrimination; Sexual harassment
Woodfield v. Heckler, 275, 276, 293
Work directly and closely related, 351
Work expectations: job exempt status and, 359–360, 367; organizational communication of, 354–355
Worker attributes taxonomies, 185–186
Worker performance taxonomies, 185–186
Wright v. Universal Maritime Service Corporation, 305, 335
Written opinions, 519–521, 522

Y
Yates' correction factor, 138
Yates v. Rexton, Inc., 395, 409
Yeshiva, Sobel v., 135, 166
Yosemite Water Co., Ramirez v., 348, 349, 370

Z
Z tests, 271
Zagel, Popkins v., 266, 293
Zamlen and the United States v. City of Cleveland, 473, 476, 490
Zero tolerance policies, 246–247